THE BATTLEFIELDS OF THE FIRST WORLD WAR

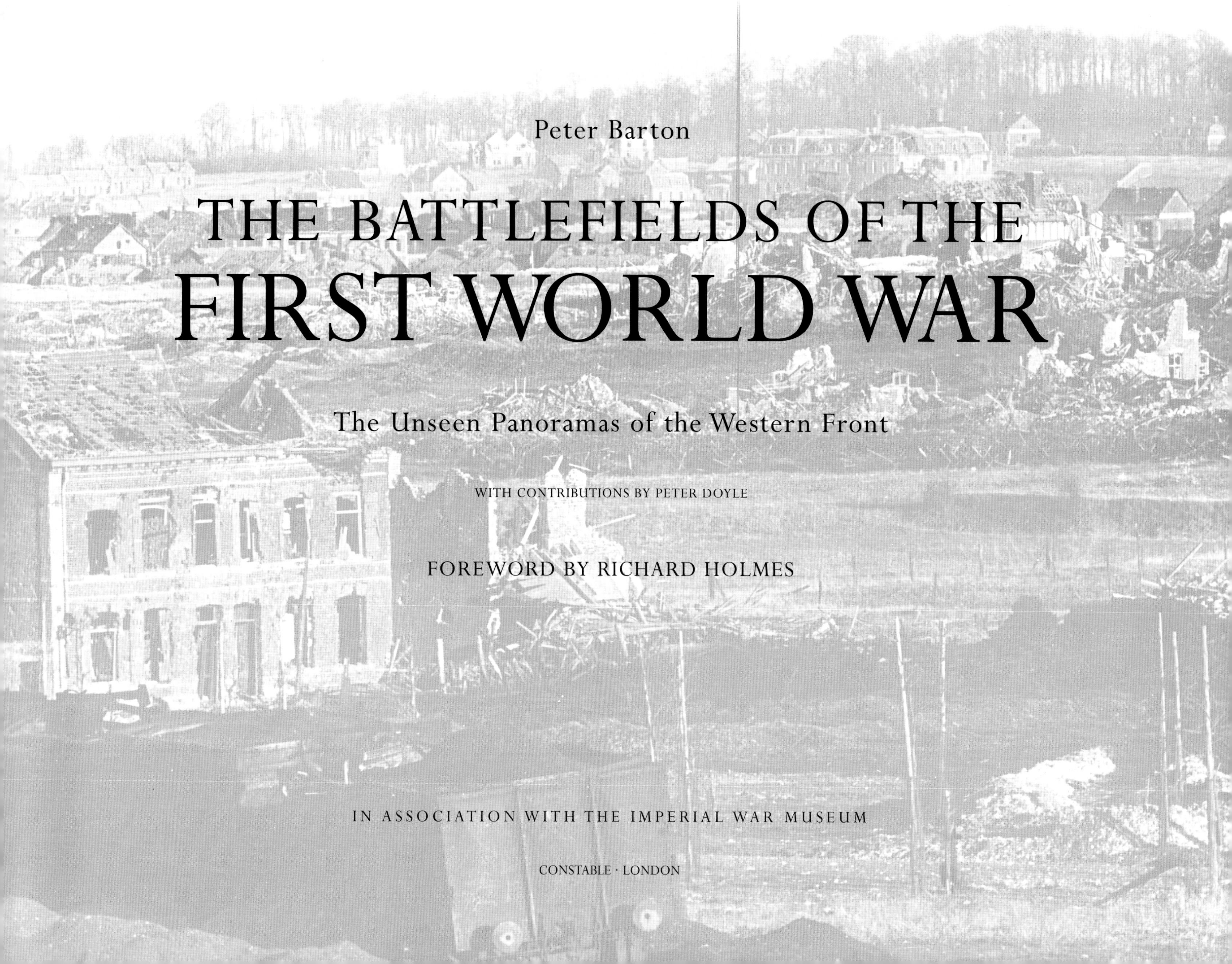

Peter Barton

THE BATTLEFIELDS OF THE FIRST WORLD WAR

The Unseen Panoramas of the Western Front

WITH CONTRIBUTIONS BY PETER DOYLE

FOREWORD BY RICHARD HOLMES

IN ASSOCIATION WITH THE IMPERIAL WAR MUSEUM

CONSTABLE · LONDON

Constable & Robinson Ltd
3 The Lanchesters
162 Fulham Palace Road
London W6 9ER
www.constablerobinson.com

First published in the UK in 2005 by Constable,
an imprint of Constable & Robinson Ltd

Distributed in Canada by Vanwell Publishing

A copy of the British Library Cataloguing in
Publication data is available from the British Library

ISBN 1-84119-745-9

Designed by Les Dominey
Cartography by William Smuts
Printed and bound in Singapore

Title page
A segment of First Army Panorama 120: the industrial battleground of the Calonne sector near Lens in the spring of 1917.

Opposite
Observation in action: An Officer of the King's Own Royal Lancaster Regiment using one of the first trench periscopes, probably made in the Royal Engineer 'factory' at Armentières.

Page 6
Segment of a panorama over Arras cemetery taken during the winter of 1916-17.

Pages 12–13
Canadian troops entering a burning Cambrai during the advance to victory, September 1918.

Pages 14–15
Third Battle of Ypres. The squalor of the Salient in late 1917.

Pages 18–19
A Group Panorama. British, French and American troops gathered to celebrate the fourth anniversary of the outbreak of hostilities.
4 August 1918.

FOR M.L.R.

CONTENTS

Foreword 8
Preface 16

PROLOGUE: THE CAMERA GOES TO WAR – 1914–18 19
The First World War on the Western Front 20
Life in the Trenches 32
Photography and Warfare 46
The Panorama Goes to War 52

CHAPTER ONE: THE WAR BEGINS – EARLY BATTLES AND THE BELGIAN COAST 61
The Marne and the Aisne 62
The Race to the Sea 68

CHAPTER TWO: THE SALIENT – FIRST AND SECOND YPRES AND MESSINES RIDGE 83
The Canal Bank to the Railway 90
Hooge 108
Hill 60 and the Caterpillar 122
The Bluff 132
St Eloi 140
Messines Ridge 144
The Salient's Southern Hinge 152

CHAPTER THREE: THIRD YPRES 163

CHAPTER FOUR: THE FORGOTTEN FRONT – ARMENTIÈRES TO GIVENCHY-LES-LA BASSÉE 191
Armentières 194
Aubers, Neuve Chapelle and Fromelles 210

CHAPTER FIVE: COALFIELDS AND CRASSIERS – THE GOHELLE BATTLEFIELDS 229
Cuinchy and Cambrin 238
Hohenzollern, the Quarries and Hulluch 244
The Dumps and Crassiers 252

CHAPTER SIX: VIMY RIDGE AND ARRAS 265

CHAPTER SEVEN: THE SOMME 287
Gommecourt and Serre 302
Redan Ridge and Beaumont Hamel 308
The Ancre to Leipzig 314
Across the Roman Road 320
Fricourt and Mametz 326
Carnoy and Montauban 332

CHAPTER EIGHT: ARMOUR AND ARMISTICE – CAMBRAI AND 1918 341
Cambrai 342
1918 350

Epilogue 360
Timeline of the First World War 362
Bibliography and Further Reading 364
Acknowledgments and Picture Credits 368
Index 372

FOREWORD

The Western Front has become part of my life. When I first visited it, and stood in awe under the Menin Gate at Ypres as the bugles sounded the Last Post, the fighting in the Salient was then closer in time than D-Day is to me now. What seemed to be very old gentlemen standing to attention as the echoes died away under the great arched roof were not much older than I am now. When I first began to study First Ypres and Loos, the Somme and Cambrai, Messines Ridge and Passchendaele, there were plenty of surviving veterans to whom I might have spoken had I had the wit to do so: indeed, General Sir Hubert Gough, youngest of Haig's army commanders, died only two years before I went to university. Now the last outposts of this huge, enduring army have all but faded away. As I write there are just over thirty British veterans still alive, and there will probably be fewer when this book appears in print.

During my lifetime the debate over the conduct of the war on the Western Front has ebbed and flowed. I do not propose to plumb its swirls and eddies here, but I take some comfort from the fact that many of the simplistic views of the 1960s have been replaced by an altogether more balanced approach, with scholars like John Bourne, Robin Prior, Gary Sheffield, Hew Strachan, Trevor Wilson and Tim Travers analysing primary sources to illuminate this appalling conflict which had such a profound and lasting effect on Britain. It would be rash to suggest that we have a consensus view on the war: the sheer scale of suffering it engendered means that, on the one hand, even the most accomplished historian can easily have the objective assessments of his head jolted by the urgings of his heart, while, on the other, youthful historical passions can be cooled by the calmer reflections of middle age.

But although we are now able to look at the Western Front in a broader way than before – there are good specialist studies of, for example, logistics, tactical development, capitals courts martial and the war underground, as well as a whole raft of books using unpublished personal accounts, with Malcolm Brown's marvellous study of 1914 as the latest of the genre – there is still a depressing tendency for the debate to swing back, as if tugged by some malign lodestone, onto the generals, for and against. I remain surprised that the politicians who, after all, took Britain into the war, played a crucial role in the formulation of its strategy, and were largely responsible for the fact that the fruits of victory were allowed to rot, successfully managed to off-load as much of the blame onto the generals. Both David Lloyd George and Winston Churchill (the latter something of a personal hero and the former quite the reverse) consciously twisted history when they wrote about the Western Front. The generals of 1914–1918 certainly have a case to answer, but they should not stand in the dock alone.

There is, or rather was, for this book goes far towards filling it, a major gap in the historiography of the war. The term Western Front is, after all, a geographical expression. For much of the war the front line ran more or less south from the coast near Dunkirk, to the little town of Noyon, where it swung away eastwards towards the Vosges, finally dipping off to the southeast and the Swiss border. It was some 724 km – 450 miles – long in mid-1916, and rather less after the Germans shortened their line in early 1917 by pulling back onto the Hindenburg Line from the nose of the huge salient that had bulged out towards Paris. The British share grew progressively bigger as voluntary recruiting and then conscription turned the tiny army of 1914 into a mass continental army for the first time in its history. It took over more and more of the front from the French, able to garrison first the Ypres Salient and Flanders, and then to push down into Artois and across Picardy, extending its right wing beyond the Somme in the last winter of the war.

A variety of factors conspired to make this northern sector of the front its most operationally significant. It covered one of the most promising German approaches to Paris. It protected the Channel ports and the main British line of communication running down to their major logistic bases and their chief port of entry, Le Havre. Just behind it lay the German-held ports of Ostend and Zeebrugge, seen by the British Admiralty as a source of major submarine threat, and the important rail junction of Roulers. An Allied advance of 32 km – 20 miles – in this part of the front might have decisive consequences: on many other parts of the line there were no useful objectives, for either side, within even distant reach.

There were geopolitical implications too. Ypres was the only Belgian town of any significance still unoccupied by the Germans. The front line ran right through those tough little towns of coal and sweat in the Lens-Loos-Douai plain, so well described in Emile Zola's darker novels, leaving the mighty city of Lille in German hands. At the tip of the great Ypres Salient the Germans were as close to Paris as Canterbury is to London, and, indeed, they were able to shell the French capital with long-range guns sited on the limestone uplands above the River Aisne. Whatever the tactical attractions of giving up territory in the northern sector (the abandonment of the Salient's overlooked ground made good sense in purely tactical terms), there was a general strategic presumption in favour of attacking to get the Germans off French soil.

Allied generals did not always attack because they had a poor appreciation of the effectiveness of modern weapons or a high regard for the offensive spirit (although they were sometimes guilty on both these counts), but because the war's opening moves had left the Germans in possession of most of Belgium and huge tracts of France: the status quo represented a German victory on points. In one sense victory would go to the side which so combined doctrine, technique and technology as to make the offensive, generally the weaker form of war on the Western Front from October 1914 to the spring of 1918, its stronger form; to weld disparate arms together to fight a combined-arms battle; and to develop techniques of command and control that could cope with mobile operations on a wide front. It was a measure of the British Army's success that it achieved all this triumphantly by the summer of 1918, although it is partly because of the army's pragmatic, doctrine-resistant character that the process of evolution can be charted by a learning-curve marked with too many crosses.

The British Army's relatively slow adaptation also reflects its rapid growth. There were around a quarter of a million regulars, and roughly as many part-time Territorials, in August 1914: by the war's end the army had put the best part of six million men through its ranks. It did so without any plans for such large-scale expansion, and so the British Army, uniquely among European combatants, faced the task of evolving to meet the changing demands of a vicious war while at the same time growing from the tiny acorn of 1914 to the spreading oak of 1918. It was this growth, as I have already observed, that enabled the British to play an increasingly important role on the Western Front. We should never forget that this was, start to finish, a coalition war, and that the term 'British Army' describes a force from the whole of the British Isles and from Britain's overseas dominions too. It is always worth remembering that in the last desperate three months of the war the British Army captured roughly twice as many Germans as the French and the

Americans. And, on the Western Front, for the only time in its history, it confronted the main land strength of a major adversary, and – in concert with its Allies – won.

So much for both the strategic importance and the sheer extent of the Western Front. But there is a good deal more to it than that, and this book shows us exactly why. For soldiers, terrain has a particular reality: it is their home and workplace, and its minutiae are a matter of life and death. The terrain of the Western Front varied enormously. At its extreme northern end, dunes ran from the sea's edge onto flat, low-lying land laced by canals and drainage ditches, turned, by a mixture of inundations and field defences, into an area where military movement was extraordinarily difficult. The fact that this sector was thus frozen off added to the importance of the Ypres Salient, much of it also low-lying, but dominated by low ridges (they would scarcely merit the word ridge almost anywhere else in the world) that remained in German hands for much of the war. Tiny features, some of them man-made by-products of canal-digging or railway construction, assumed an immense importance because of the observation they afforded: the south-central part of the Salient saw repeated fighting for Hill 60, the Bluff and the mound at St Eloi. It was here that mining was both critically important and, because of the layer of pressurized 'running sands' that expanded when penetrated, extremely difficult.

The Messines–Wytschaete Ridge, on the southern end of the Salient, is the most serious natural feature so far crossed by the front on its journey from the sea, with well-sited German positions glaring out over the valley of the little Douve. The ridge was the target of the most successful mining operation of the war, when sappers of General Sir Herbert Plumer's Second Army broke the back of the defence, paving the way for a well-planned set-piece attack (it was there that the future Field Marshal Montgomery saw how the careful 'Daddy' Plumer handled his citizen soldiers) in June 1917. The Ploegsteert sector, inevitably Plugstreet to the British, at the southern foot of Messines Ridge, was dominated, then as now, by the dark mass of Plugstreet Wood: Lieutenant-Colonel Winston Churchill commanded his Royal Scots Fusilier battalion just outside its southern edge in 1916. The little town of Armentières lies just on the French side of the border, just south of Plugstreet, and to its south the front line ran below Aubers Ridge, scene of futile British offensives in 1915 and 1916. One of the most poignant parts of the front for me is the La Bombe crossroads, on the edge of the village of Neuve Chapelle. There, the Indian Memorial to the Missing, strikingly designed in 'indo-saracenic' style, and a Portuguese cemetery just along the road, both provide mute testimony to the breadth of the Allied coalition.

Between the La Bassée canal, which marks the southern edge of the Armentières sector, and the great escarpment of Vimy ridge, which divides the chalk uplands of Artois from the clay of Flanders, lies the Gohelle, in 1914-1918 an industrial area strewn with pitheads, slag-heaps and miners' cottages. In the late nineteenth century the mining industry had sucked in labour from as far afield as Poland: now the mines are closed and the area has a run-down, forsaken look. In September 1915 the British attacked between Loos and the La Bassée canal as part of a bigger French attack in Artois. The battle saw the first British use of chlorine gas, and was eerily both ancient and modern: two Scots divisions were amongst those attacking, with their pipes shrieking out through the drizzle and the poison gas.

From the slag-heaps around Loos, most of them now truncated or grassed over, but still there, the ground rises sharply onto Vimy Ridge: the slope is much gentler on its southern side. The ridge is now crowned by a dazzling white memorial to the Canadians who took it in April 1917, in a feat of arms every bit as significant for Canada as Gallipoli in 1915 had been for the Australians and New Zealanders. The French had struggled manfully, since late 1914, to wrench a handhold on it, and their sacrifice is enshrined in the huge cemetery and memorial on the nearby hill of Notre Dame de Lorette. The attractive town of Arras, whose sensitive restoration gives little clue to the dreadful damage it suffered, lies just south of the ridge. It had once been the scene of fighting between the French and the Spaniards, when the whole of this area formed part of the Spanish Netherlands: both the future King James II of England and Rostand's hero Cyrano de Bergerac (the former in fact and the latter in fiction) served there. The tunnels, known locally as boves, that open out below the Town Hall once gave access to the front line, which ran just east of Arras for much of the war: they are another good illustration of the impact of geology on the conflict.

Most soldiers preferred the southern part of the British front to the northern, and on leaving Arras and heading south we can see why. The chalk landscape is broad, benign and confident, with dense, broad-leafed woodlands, tightly-nucleated villages, and big farms: their house and outbuildings usually forming three sides of a square. The next major break in the landscape comes with the River Somme, which does not so much flow as meander, with reedy ox-bows set in its gentle valley. Henry V's army passed this way on its route to Agincourt in 1415, tramping over this downland with, no doubt, the same sort of ribaldry that characterized the men of the New Armies, moving up for the Somme offensive in 1916. South of the Somme lies the Santerre plateau, its southern edge effectively marking the boundary of the British Expeditionary Force (BEF). There were though, British soldiers deployed even further south. In 1918 a corps, already hard hit by a German offensive in March and April, was sent to the Chemin des Dames, the ridge running along the northern edge of the River Aisne between Soissons and the start of the great, open wine-growing landscape of Champagne. By sheer bad luck the British found themselves squarely in the path of the German offensive launched in May. The distinctive cap-badges of the old county regiments are carved on headstones in cemeteries along the little Aisne. Some of the soldiers buried here died when the BEF was on the river in 1914: other graves mark what one veteran called 'the last of the ebb'.

It has taken me the better part of a lifetime to get this under my skin, to sense the rise and fall of the ground, to feel its changes and mood-swings, to have my morale raised by a spring morning on the Somme and cast down by autumn rain on Passchendaele Ridge. How much easier my task would have been had this book been at hand when I started. It is wonderful to see these panoramas, unexploited for so long, in print. They provide a strong fulcrum for our understanding of the war, for they enable us to link personal accounts and official records to the all-important ground on which battles were fought. And, at a human level, they put us eye-deep in hell, looking out across a landscape so familiar to that generation whose endurance and achievement – as I concluded in *Tommy*, my own attempt to give the war's real heroes the credit they deserve – lift my spirits and break my heart.

Richard Holmes

PREFACE

Photography has become a household word and a household want; is used alike by art and science, by love, business, and justice; is found in the most sumptuous salon, and in the dingiest attic – in the solitude of the Highland cottage, and in the glare of the London gin-palace, in the pocket of the detective, in the cell of the convict, in the folio of the painter and architect, among the papers and patterns of the millowner and manufacturer, and on the cold grey breast of the battlefield.

LADY EASTLAKE, 'PHOTOGRAPHY', *Quarterly Review*, 1857

Despite the capture of tens of millions of images, the First World War and its photographers feature surprisingly little in photographic history. The focus has settled on a relatively small band of world-renowned practitioners such as Roger Fenton, Matthew Brady, Felice Beato, Margaret Bourke-White, Robert Capa and Bert Hardy, who together with others helped shape the iconography of warfare in the nineteenth and twentieth centuries. The First World War was overlooked. Yet it too had its distinguished practitioners, and their often unattributed images are reproduced year on year as the flow of books on this compelling conflict continues unabated. Today, more than eight decades later, the work of the 'official photographer' immeasurably helps to mould our impressions of 'life in the trenches'. Amongst the most anonymous photographers of all are those whose sole mission was to provide visual military intelligence and reconnaissance. Their photographs, underused and underappreciated, are some of the most outstanding to emerge from the war. This book is an exploration, for the first time, of the remarkable images captured by these men.

The jigsaw puzzle of facts and figures which inform our modern perception of the First World War is a complex one. The pieces which make up the puzzle are abundant and varied, comprising official documents, private diaries and letters, photographs, film dramas and documentaries, books and memoirs, art and poetry, maps and plans, a variety of memorials, and of course human testimony: the words of the men, women and children who played a part. Each separate category is integral to the whole, yet the jigsaw has an infinite number of solutions: it is constructed by each individual according to information gleaned from education, research and received wisdom derived from family history, friends and legend. It is therefore highly personal. One thing, however, remains constant: the photograph plays a major role in the development and establishment of each of our private perceptions.

When we look at 1914–1918 archive photographs we are confident in believing what we see. Because the cameras of the early twentieth century are generally supposed not to 'lie', as they can be made to do so easily today, pictures do more than simply provide an instant and accessible communication with a difficult subject. For the most part this is actually a fallacy: both film and still photographs were often posed and/or indeed faked for propaganda purposes. Nevertheless, it is through them that we construe the ambience and character of the physical environment of the First World War – the battlegrounds.

In fact, pictures are really the only rigid context we have. Take, for example, the landscape of the battle during the 1917 offensive in the Ypres Salient – now known as Passchendaele: no printed word could make such a tortured region imaginable to one who was not present at the time. We need the photographs of Frank Hurley, William Rider-Rider, Ernest Brooks or John Warwick-Brooke simply to embark upon the process of comprehension and empathy – and to make any sense of what we read about the battle. This applies equally to the whole of the war: without pictures we are without context. Even the greatest poetry and prose engender a vastly different sensation to viewing images of the events which the author is attempting to describe. Images are the sole foundation upon which our imaginations are able to build perceptions.

It does not require a complete photographic collection to achieve this: the ravages of war, the destruction, the migration of peoples, the heroic defences, gallant retreats and glorious victories of armies; and terror, sadness, joy and relief of soldier and civilian alike can each be embodied within a single powerful shot. Indeed, picture editors have summed up whole conflicts with little more than a handful of carefully selected images. With such iconic photographs we feel we do not have to imagine history, we can see it for ourselves – or at least a part of it, in a vivid and hopefully authentic moment. Photographs, therefore, are as much a part of the social biography of the war as the writings of the great authors and poets; they anchor us to the 'truth' by an apparent realism that is beguiling, and without them as a guide we would be unable to make decisions about what is significant or relevant within the context of our own knowledge and experience.

Amalgamating all the photographic and document-based material from archives around the world relating to the First World War would produce an immeasurably vast collection. The interlocking jigsaw of historical material available to researchers might therefore appear to be as complete as one could possibly need to build an accurate picture. However, wide, fundamental – and bluntly obvious – gaps in the puzzle have existed for over eighty years, and until recently there seemed to be no pieces left to fill them. Apart from aerial photographs – an unearthly view – there were no representations of the *full* landscape of the various battlefields, ones to which we as latter-day observers might easily relate. Without these final pieces, our perceptions would always remain flawed and imperfect. The re-exposure of an extensive archive of panoramic photographs at the Imperial War Museum in London has now provided those critical pieces, and in these breathtaking pictures we are at last presented with the ultimate view of the battlefields. It is a 'lost world' of immense historic and symbolic importance – and a world entirely unseen for over eighty-five years.

Panoramic photographs were used by all the combatant nations throughout the war, predominantly for reconnaissance and intelligence purposes. For the British, it was the Royal Engineers who shouldered the burden of production. Taken in a systematic manner, and covering all the sectors held by the Imperial forces, the panoramas today provide an unique resource: an entirely unbiased, propaganda-free representation of the contested landscape of battle – predominantly from trench level, and on the grandest of scales. In effect, we are presented with the soldier's eye view of every battlefield on the British Western Front.

Within each lies a throng of detail that exists in no other photograph, indeed, in no other medium. They present a powerful tool that empowers the modern observer to view the battlefields as they actually were, rather than as the authorities wished the public to see them. Indeed, in not pandering to nostalgia or propaganda they place all other archives of the First World War into temporal, topographical and geographical contexts, revealing more about the nature of the battlefields than any other kind of archival record. If the maxim 'the camera does not lie' can be applied to any First World War images without fear of contradiction or argument, these are they. There can be no doubt that absolute reality is depicted – for that was the sole purpose of panoramic photography. Ironically, their historical importance today probably transcends the original military application.

It will be noticed that much of the personal testimony quoted in this book derives from Royal Engineers. This is deliberate: because the Sappers were largely responsible for the physical character of the Western Front – the design of the interlaced web of trenches, battery positions, roads, drains, signals et al. – they tended to appreciate and record their feelings and experiences through a different lens than the men of other corps. The detail in the panoramas shows off their often disregarded work. With digital technology we are now able to view these extraordinary photographs in an accessible form. I hope this book will reveal a new vision of the symbolic landscapes upon, above and beneath which millions of men lived, toiled, fought and died on the Western Front.

Peter Barton, 2005

PROLOGUE

THE CAMERA GOES TO WAR, 1914–18

The First World War on the Western Front

I left Wareham on the 21st November 1915 to sail from Folkestone for France. It was a cold bleak, wintry day and a pitiless easterly wind was blowing that cut like a knife. But in spite of the weather I was in great spirits. I was going on Active Service. The dull, depressing routine of training was being left behind and I was hurrying forward to experiences such as I had never dreamed of 16 months before, and such as perhaps only the young men of this generation will be privileged to see. If I live through the next 12 months I shall have lived a lifetime. I do not dread the hardships and dangers ahead of me, rather do I look forward to them with a sort of pleasurable anticipation. The danger I do not attempt to minimize, I am fully conscious of the risks I shall have to run, yet I would not have it otherwise. I hope to win through unscathed, but if the fates decree that a soldier's death be mine, I shall at least have done a soldier's duty and I shall have fallen in a good cause. My one regret is for the dear folks at home. They will suffer, are suffering even now, far more than I shall ever be called upon to endure.

LIEUTENANT MATTHEW ROACH, 184 TUNNELLING COMPANY RE

The origins of the First World War – the Great War to many – were the source of discussion and dissent even before the conflict came to an end in 1918, and have remained controversial ever since. Another rendering is neither desired nor required here, and readers are left to draw their own conclusions from the myriad publications available on the subject. Whatever its genesis, the war that seethed for four years across three continents was to have grim personal and international consequences. The empires of Germany, Russia and Austria-Hungary fell, the British Empire began its inexorable decline, and tweny-one million people died. This was a war which was industrial in scale and outlook, a war in which great advances were made in the technology of killing, a war waged on land, across the oceans, beneath the ground and, for the first time, in the air; it was the source of revolutions: scientific, political, medical, industrial, and civil – and twenty years later it was to spawn a second yet more devastating global conflict.

Cock of the north. A proud and keen Private Wilf Wallworth of the South Lancashire Regiment.

Perceptions of its 'horror' and 'futility' – both much overused terms – have arguably been shaped by the tremendous legacy of literature, war art, photographs and film. This legacy so often portrays devastated landscape stretching from horizon to horizon, a perpetually shattered scene where men, animals and machines are swallowed up in vast swamps of glutinous mud which cover entire countries. Ask a schoolchild to describe the battlefields of the First World War and they offer this vision; ask then how long they envisage the battlefields to have existed in such a state, and invariably the reply is from day one in August 1914, until the Armistice on 11 November 1918 – the perception is of a permanent wasteland spreading across whole countries, with troops constantly enveloped in rain. Nonsense, perhaps, but a myth which some historians and educationalists are content to perpetuate, if unknowingly. And the perception is not restricted to children. Scholars have been struggling for decades to make sense of the meaning of the landscape of the Western Front both in terms of the combatants of the day and in the 'collective memory' of modern researchers and readers. The panoramas are the only photographs capable of telling the true story – and they portray scenes that are more often than not brutally counter-intuitive to our received perceptions of the Western Front.

The formation of the Western Front

The First World War was fought and won principally on the battlefields of northern Europe. Reams of paper have been expended in books about the costly 'sideshows' – Gallipoli, Salonika, Mesopotamia (Iraq), Palestine, and East Africa for example – but in reality the war was conducted in just two theatres of consequence, fronts which had been pre-determined by the German High Command during the decade prior to 1914. The Schlieffen Plan, a great scheme for European domination named after Count Alfred von Schlieffen, Chief of the German General Staff, had been visualized in 1905 when the Central Powers of Germany and Austria-Hungary settled upon the creation of twin battlefronts to achieve their territorial goals: Russia in the East, and France in the West.

The difficulties of waging a two-front war had long exercised the minds of German military strategists. Von Schlieffen approached the problem through the delivery of a massive and rapid knockout blow in the West via Belgium and northern France, using the speedy movement of troops along the well-developed European road and rail system. Belgium, a country created in the 1830s specifically as a neutral buffer state between Germany and France, was given little choice in the matter: if she failed to allow German troops free movement, her neutrality was simply to be ignored. In this way France would be dispatched in the opening weeks of war, leaving time for Germany to deal with the perceived greater might of Russia (the 'Russian steamroller') in the East. The plan was a failure for a variety of reasons, mostly concerning tactical provision and disposition of troops, but it could easily have worked – after all, in 1940 France fell in six weeks. To the surprise of the French, who believed that the United Kingdom would procrastinate as an ally despite the diplomatic Entente Cordiale, the British Expeditionary Force (BEF) joined the fray on 7 August 1914. On the surface the reason for this lay in the British adherence to the Treaty of London which guaranteed the neutrality of Belgium;. however, unbeknown even to some members of the British Government, during the months preceding August behind the scenes agreements had been made with the French Army as to precisely where British forces would position themselves should conflict erupt. In the event the plan was followed to the letter. Germany's strategy was not to occupy France as she did in the Second World War but to politically subjugate her people by seizing the great prize – Paris. By the end of 1914 however, after just under five months of fighting, the scheme had failed and the mobile conflict in the western theatre already degenerated into stasis. What was about to materialize was the most colossal conflict in history, and to the surprise of everyone drawn to its embrace, every nation would employ tactics used not only in the previous century but millennia before. When the more volatile Eastern Front finally crumbled with the Russian armistice of 1917, the West became the primary and decisive battleground. For the nations of the British Empire the war was to be won or lost on the fields of Flanders, Artois and Picardy.

The birth of trench warfare

The Commander in Chief wishes the line now held by the Army to be strongly entrenched, and it is his intention to resume a general offensive at the first opportunity.

OPERATION ORDER NO 26, GHQ [BEF], 15 SEPTEMBER 1914

The issue of this order by Field-Marshal Sir John French helped to guarantee a static struggle on the Western Front, and indeed form the character of the whole war. Although French makes it clear that entrenchment was intended as a temporary measure, he and millions of others were to be disillusioned. A ribbon of ground stretching right across Europe was soon to be more than just 'strongly entrenched':

August 1914 – the German Army I Corps march to war.

it was to be made into an impenetrable bastion. As similar instructions repeatedly emanated from General Headquarters (GHQ) during the next three months, the conflict was doomed to deadlock. With the approach of Christmas 1914 most of the lines which the General Staff had directed to be held and fortified would remain in place and practically immobile for almost four years.

As a result of the increased application of the scientific elements of modern warfare, military machinery, largely in the form of artillery and machine guns, came to far outweigh the offensive power of both infantry and cavalry, nullifying assault after assault with disturbingly growing ease. After the Battle of the Aisne in September 1914, the importance and numbers of these weapons increased with each passing day, and by mid-1915 commanders had discovered to their exasperation that a battlefield might easily be flooded with attacking troops, but it was a relatively straightforward task for the enemy to swathe that same battlefield with an impenetrable hailstorm of bullets and shrapnel. There was nothing wrong with the fighting spirit of the troops – they were simply beaten by the application of military science. As time passed, field defences on both sides of no man's land became ever more difficult to assault, and the perceived importance of making them entirely impregnable increased. The result was stalemate.

In this new static war, trenches became fortresses, and siege warfare – with some tactics echoing the most ancient of conflicts – was resurrected: sapping and mining for example made a decisive comeback. Developing siege practices on a battleground the size of the Western Front – 640 km (400 miles) long – meant minutely appraising and appreciating the landscape of battle in each individual sector, as a detailed knowledge of the character of the now strictly limited area of 'fighting ground' – no man's land and the enemy's advanced positions – became increasingly critical for both attack and defence. Each side therefore developed a highly sophisticated survey system, mapping out not only qualities in the natural landscape such as hills, valleys, woods, marshes, streams etc., but also the features of opposing fieldwork constructions within that landscape – the enemy trenches and their affiliated man-made defences. This elaborate survey emphasized a long accepted fact in warfare: that control of high ground was of paramount importance. Occupying an elevated position, albeit only marginal, allowed improved observation, clearer fields of fire, straightforward artillery ranging, easier drainage of trench lines, and the all-important psychological advantage of looking down upon one's enemy. On the 'British' component of the Western Front these benefits lay largely but not entirely with the Germans. The specific geological make up of the ground naturally influenced and often controlled the effectiveness of trench positioning, design and construction, but it also determined the very nature of trench life itself, as well as the ability for troops, animals and transport to manoeuvre. Taken together, the study of terrain was one of the most important factors in the waging of the Great European

2nd Battalion Scots Guards digging in near Ghent on 9 October 1914.

War, and it was the desire to gather the maximum volume of this kind of data that encouraged the use of panoramic photography.

With few exceptions, localities defended during centuries of conflicts prior to 1900 were limited in size. Whether the objective was a fortified city, a town, or a village, an attacker needed to capture or destroy the position in order to move on to the next target or perhaps win the war outright: at the same time the defending garrison was determined to stall an assault until the arrival of reinforcements, or simply to live to fight another day. However, unlike the attack, which was often improvised according to local conditions, the defence of fortified places was more often than not meticulously pre-designed. And so it was to be on the Western Front. The one critical difference here lay in the fact that both sides were besieging each other.

The introduction of gunpowder for mines and guns in the fourteenth and fifteenth centuries had forced new and more complex modes of defence to be devised, and throughout subsequent centuries more and more elaborate fortresses were built, usually to protect centres of population. The most noteworthy constructions sprang from the imaginations of the great siege-masters such as Vauban and Coutele. As an island race, however, the British had no need for such intricacies; the sea was their defence, so all the great fortress cities were to be found on the continent of Europe. By the end of the eighteenth century fortresses were no longer the tall and proud castles of the Middle Ages, which were easy targets for gunpowder artillery. Instead they had become bastions, low, strong structures built in stone or brick, sited within great systems of ditches, ramparts and glacis, complete with carefully coordinated defensive firepower, and often a fully developed permanent scheme of underground countermining galleries to guard against the oldest and most dangerous enemy, the military miner.

Then, in the mid-nineteenth century, the rifled gun barrel emerged, a revolutionary development that in the case of artillery allowed an explosive shell to be accurately fired from a position out of sight and often out of range of defenders. As for the individual soldier, light, rifled carbines allowed men to be shot down at far greater ranges, and far more rapidly, than before. Simply by rifling the barrel, destructive power was multiplied tenfold. By 1880 the new generations of artillery were exalted as the most important advance in military science for centuries; even Vauban's great bastioned fortresses were at risk. It was largely this single innovation which persuaded military commanders that the days and tactics of old-fashioned siege warfare were swiftly drawing to a close.

For almost four decades following the Franco-Prussian War of 1870–71, the last time major sieges had taken place, the perception amongst military strategists was that defence against the ever escalating power of artillery lay in increasing the material protection of existing fortresses, i.e. making a position stronger and better able to withstand attack from shelling. Thus, the fabric of huge numbers of long established European fortifications was gradually augmented by the new medium of steel-reinforced concrete. At the same time defensive weaponry, also rifled, lay better protected within the fortress by being semi-interred or housed beneath steel cupolas. Three continental forces soon to be involved on the Western Front, France, Germany and Belgium, each favoured this approach, remodelling the most strategically important fortresses and their 'outworks', the rings of smaller detached defensive installations. This work, it was hoped, would create the barrier upon which an attacking force might blunt their swords.

The presence of the fortresses had an important effect on the early stages of the First World War. Worries over the potential delay which those located on France's eastern border might cause forced the Germans to adapt the original Schlieffen Plan. The solution was plain: these forts would simply be avoided, with more power being added to the advance through northern France and Belgium. In the earliest moves of the war, cities like Namur, Liege and Antwerp, whose defences had been modified and strengthened at huge expense by the Belgians, were simply to crumble beneath the might of Germany's 21, 28 and 42 cm howitzers. In following the northern route to reach the Channel ports and Paris, the Germans had no choice but to reduce these positions, but even the frighteningly short period required to do so – a matter of weeks – bought the Allies at least a little valuable time to regroup and despatch support. Only one fortress in France was attacked at the beginning of the war, that at isolated Maubeuge on the northern frontier. As one of the few towns not to have enjoyed any modernization, it capitulated after a ten-day mauling (Verdun, a fully modernized fortress which the Germans refrained from attacking until 1916, would 'survive'). Observing the demise of the Belgian forts the French quickly dismantled many pre-war outworks, utilizing their armaments within a new fully connected trench system dug several kilometres in advance of the old permanent defences. Indeed, this was precisely how the infamous Verdun salient was formed; a salient which was to develop as great a symbolic resonance for the French nation as did Ypres for the British.

But there was little in the pre-war military manuals to inform the British forces flowing and ebbing through France and Belgium in the autumn of 1914 about how to deal with the conflict that was developing around them. For the British Army, the Boer War of 1899–1902, the most recent conflict in which the nation had been involved, was a useful precursor to some aspects of battle on the Western Front, but it had been a minor expedition compared to the great drama which was about to unfold in Europe.

The widening front

The First World War began under conditions of open warfare, with mobile infantry engagements, the reduction of the fortress cities, and fiery skirmishes between mounted troops: Uhlans, Hussars, Cuirassiers, Dragoons, and Lancers. After a few short months all this had ceased. As action in sector after sector stalled during the autumn of 1914, the Germans, in search of a vulnerable flank to exploit, pushed ever further northwards until they reached the sandy beaches of the Belgian coast. Here, with no further room for manoeuvre, attacks were violent and prolonged – but still unsuccessful. They were then driven back inland by the inundation of thousands of hectares of land between Nieuport and Dixmude – and beyond towards Ypres. After failing to break through in October and November 1914 during the First Battle of Ypres – by now the only field of battle available – both sides lay exhausted. In a few weeks they were held in the grip of a bitter Flemish winter.

During the early months of 1915, assisted by Germany's strategic imperative to pursue her eastern campaign against Russia, the early trench lines on the Western Front began a relentless expansion. It was this twin-front strategy that forced Germany into a defensive stance on the battlegrounds of France and Belgium. Forming and holding a firm line in the West was a sound military decision, for after the debilitating battles of the previous autumn the German General Staff knew that neither they, the British nor the French were capable of launching a major assault until the spring.

During this first winter of war a very limited degree of localized fluidity was still detectable here and there, but by the end of May 1915 all movement had ceased. What followed was the ultimate in siege warfare, with two vast but impermanent linear fortresses facing each other across a band of unclaimed ground – no man's land. For the next three years neither side was able to break the deadlock. The tactical

October 1914. Civilians watch and wait for the war to arrive from the ramparts of Ypres.

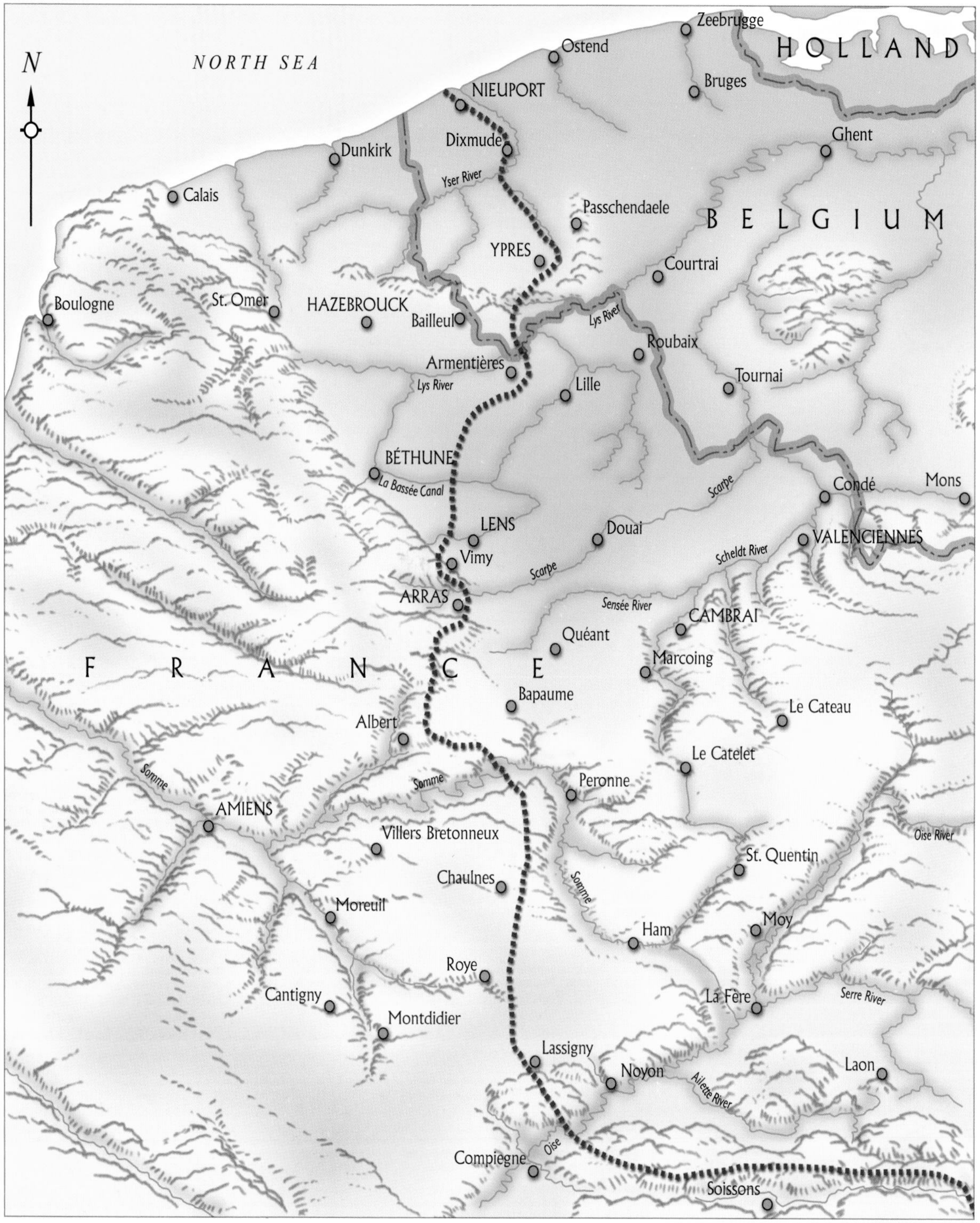

bankruptcy of the High Commands on both sides led to the death of hundreds of thousands of men for little or no territorial gain. Tens of millions served the process behind the lines, in industry at home, and from outposts of empire around the world. At the front the clear differentiation between attack and defence, which for many thousands of years had been so markedly defined in warfare, became blurred before disappearing altogether. By the summer of 1915 with the siege decidedly fixed and decidedly mutual, both sides were already unwilling to give up a metre of field position, and along the length of the Western Front defence had established total superiority over attack.

13 June 1915

I went on, by bye-roads again, St Omer to see Faber and the BM, GHQ, also Wace who is supposed to run the organization of us Tunnelling Companies. He was out but I saw the others, also the ADC to General Robertson the Chief of the Staff. I rather gathered that this distinguished officer expected the Germans to hold on to their present line almost to the very last. It is probably as good a 'Line' as any before the Rhine, with good railways behind, and has the great advantages from Fritz's point of view of being in the Enemy's country and sufficiently far from home to prevent accurate news of defeats etc. leaking back once they begin to happen. Seems quite a sound idea, though not very comforting. I wonder when, if ever, the end will come, and where Peace will be signed, and what the new map of the World will look like.

MAJOR S. H. COWAN, OC 175 TUNNELLING COMPANY RE

In 1916, as a direct response to the complete dominance of barbed wire and bullets over massed frontal infantry attacks, the tank made its first appearance on the field of battle. In suitable conditions tanks proved eminently capable of forcing a passage through enemy wire and trench lines, but more often than not insufficient numbers of machines, mechanical unreliability, and the limitations of a shell-blasted or waterlogged landscape proved prejudicial. As with the development of camouflage against aerial and ground observation and attack, so special obstacles and weapons were devised to combat the menace of mechanized assault, with anti-tank ditches and anti-tank guns being swiftly designed and deployed. The tank, however, could be said to be the only weapon of the war which went at least a part of the way to solving the problem of deadlock. In 1918, it was to both prove its true worth – and signal the future of land warfare.

Another endeavour, asphyxiating gas, was also ultimately a failure. 'Adequate' protective measures against gas were swiftly, indeed instantly, developed. Within a week of its first employment on the Western Front in April 1915 60,000 rudimentary masks had been manufactured and issued by the British. Its first employment could have delivered far greater success, but failed precisely because it was a first employment: both the planners and the troops were unacquainted with the potential effects. Subsequently gas came to be used mainly as a method of lowering morale, of harassment, of disrupting supply behind a selected localized area of line rather than a weapon to facilitate breakthrough on a grand scale. As time passed, the pendulum of the gas war swung in the opposite direction: towards defence. The application of mustard gas in shells was found to be equally effective for defence by making large areas of ground uninhabitable for days and even weeks. An attacker using such a weapon as an adjunct to an assault would therefore need to use gas with great prudence to make sure that captured territory would be fit for his own troops to occupy. And no one could fight wearing a gas mask for any length of time. Ultimately, it was only surprise that could help an offensive gas attack, and due to the extreme vigilance and rapid counter-measures practised by both sides, by the end of 1915 the possibility of gaining such an advantage had already practically disappeared. The development and continued prosecution of gas warfare throughout the conflict epitomizes the overwhelming psychological imprint of the First World War – that of attrition.

Aircraft were used for the first time for military purposes. Like gas, the benefits of aerial warfare affected both attack and defence without conferring especial advantage on either: the opportunity to locate gun batteries behind ridges and bomb military targets, railways, dumps of stores, towns and cities far behind the front lines became entirely mutual. Likewise, both sides soon found that the critical points in their ever more complex defensive dispositions in the field such as machine-gun and mortar emplacements were, without careful construction methods, easily identifiable and plotted from the air; this encouraged swift and ingenious advances in the art of camouflage, and also the science of anti-aircraft defence.

With movement stalled, harassment in the form of sniping and trench raiding became universally commonplace. Protection from indiscriminate but persistent minor attack was vital, so the desire to defend one's field fortifications assumed a higher profile than in any previous war. In South Africa the Boers had excelled in making their positions practically 'stormproof' – and this came to be the keyword in trench warfare. Post-Boer War British military manuals such as *Military Engineering, Part II, Attack and Defence of Fortresses, 1910* define 'stormproof' as a position so designed that, 'given a complete and efficient garrison, attacking infantry can be destroyed as fast as they can approach, no matter how great their dash and determination'. From the summer of 1915, this description could comfortably have been applied to virtually any trench on the Western Front – on both sides of no man's land – and the scenario would persist for practically the entire duration of the war. Ultimately, the trench lines were a combination of the three traditional fortification categories recognized by all armies: they were neither temporary, semi-permanent, nor permanent, but a curious conglomerate based on an overall policy of passive but massive defence.

Positions were therefore developed for supreme security, and constructed in the knowledge that any sector might be chosen as the platform for a major attack. At British GHQ perverse tactical thinking encouraged some to equate trench warfare with ancient military models: the trench was the shield, whilst the infantry (armed with bayonets) were the 'pike-men' of old. Time after time these pike-men were charged with the task of creating the conditions for mounted troops (cavalry) to restore the all-important key to victory – mobility. But cavalry were no more bullet-proof than infantry, and until the arrival of the tank, all mobile forces would remain entirely unprotected once they left the security of a trench. The bullet, be it delivered by rifle, machine gun or shrapnel shell, reigned supreme over no man's land.

The continuing stasis after the debilitating and unresolved battles of spring 1915 conferred substantial benefits upon those choosing to adopt a defensive stance – which was of course both sides. It was seen and acknowledged that the new generations of artillery bestowed the greater advantage not upon the attack, as had been anticipated and indeed witnessed at the beginning of the war, but in conjunction with automatic weapons, upon defence. Both sides therefore pursued similar defensive tactics, continually extending and strengthening protective fieldwork systems. The strategic environment was ideal because there was no longer any question of having to cope with the difficulties of supplying an advancing force. With a static front the furnishing of tools, raw materials, weapons, ordnance and rations became relatively simple. Stores could be drawn from dumps close to where materiel was required, and civilian labour safely employed on a myriad

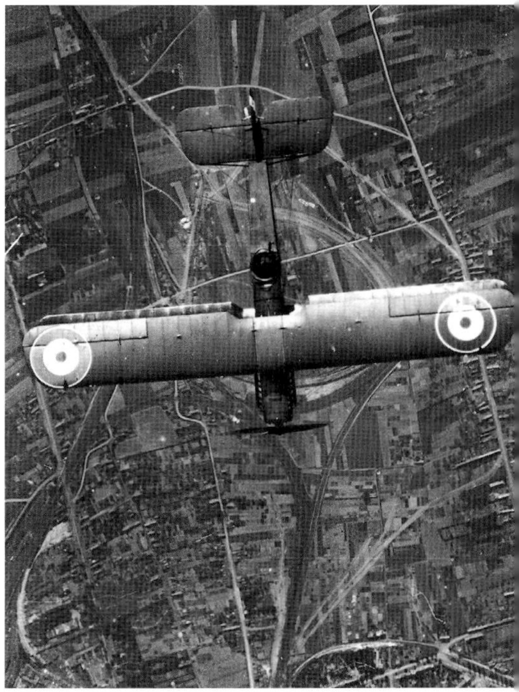

Aerial photography, a critical part of military reconnaissance, was developed to a high degree during the First World War. The observer in this aircraft had just been killed by fire from the ground.

military projects in rear areas, sometimes even in the front lines themselves. Furthermore, with the lines eventually stretching unbroken from the North Sea to Switzerland, there were no vulnerable flanks to worry about. Any and every attack *had* to be frontal. Above all these considerations, warfare on the scale of the Western Front meant that fighting was restricted by season – it needed reliable weather. Outside the 'campaigning season' therefore, weeks and months could be spent adding to the strength and durability of defences.

Although the military engineers of all sides were to play a colossal role in creating the physical manifestation of the Western Front, it was ironically civil engineering that made the fields of Flanders, Artois and Picardy viable as battlegrounds. Without the existing interconnected network of docks, railways, canals, metalled roads, electricity grids and telegraphic communication systems, the millions of men facing each other across no man's land could not possibly have been supplied with the wherewithal necessary to fight such a vast war. The ultimate irony, however, was that in employing and continually enhancing an overwhemingly defensive stance, an ever more resilient 'prison' was being created, a prison where the effort required to break out (or break in, there was no difference) was equal on both sides of no man's land.

There was also a shift in mental attitude. Supremely defensive postures went entirely against the time-honoured British doctrine that the offensive was the soul of the defence. The long and uncomfortable first winter of war had initiated in the British the first fading of the hope of a swift and decisive conclusion: her regular army had been decimated in the autumn of 1914, and continuing deadlock following the fruitless battles of spring 1915 practically snuffed out the flame of aggression demanded by GHQ. Despite the best efforts of commanders to preserve the spirit of the offensive, in the line troops gradually ceased to look upon the trenches as merely temporary; on the contrary, they became potentially eternal, and this attitude was only to intensify as weeks turned to months, and months to years. The offensive spirit waned, and fresh defensive doctrines waxed. So stubborn, costly and symbolic had been the initial defiant preservation of territory that many officers came to believe that every bit of the line was as essential a point as any other. There was a growing fascination with security, resistance and protection, which led many to regard defensive systems as a means to an end. Being fully aware that GHQ abhorred any notion of relinquishing *any* ground *anywhere*, the detail of trench warfare started to become mesmerising to commanders in the line. Those staff officers who believed that bending the line or pulling back to better positions – quite different to giving way – was a judicious move, were seldom bold enough to brave the wrath of GHQ by declaring it. Had line officers' countless requests to withdraw from some truly execrable field positions in late 1914 and early 1915 been acceded to, the nature of the First World War may well have been very different.

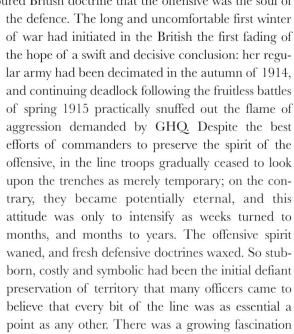

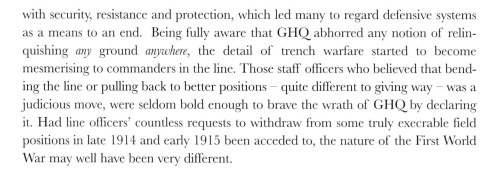

French civilians under RE supervision digging cable trenches in the rear areas.

Our policy on the Western Front was never to give up an inch of ground unless forced by the enemy to do so, and in this latter contingency we often counter-attacked to recover ground of no tactical value. Hence our defensive line seldom lay on ground of our own choosing but was placed haphazard in any location where the Germans had held up our last offensive. These positions were therefore often sited on ground unsuitable for defence, devoid of observation, commanded by the enemy, waterlogged, insanitary, and difficult to place in a state of defence. The Ypres Salient and Lys valley are well-known examples.

THE KIRKE REPORT ON THE LESSONS OF THE GREAT WAR, 1932

Digging in

The British military engineering effort on the Western Front began in haste. In the earliest months whilst combat was still mobile, elementary rifle pits and disconnected trenches were hurriedly dug to secure occupied ground. As fighting lulled, a little added spadework provided a position shielded from enemy fire and view until the next orders arrived – orders which were likely to be of the offensive variety. This apparently simple sentence sums up the principle that lay behind all field fortification during the First World War. Whether it was a simple pit, a breastwork, or a massive and complex fortified system such as the Hindenburg Line, all were clearly built to allow troops to use their various weapons – especially the rifle and machine gun – to greatest advantage. However, above all they were meant for *temporary* occupation. Ostensibly, trenches existed solely as platforms for attack.

The evolution of these fieldworks corresponded directly with the evolution in offensive tactics. During the closing months of 1914 Germany launched assault after assault against severely limited numbers of regular Belgian, British and French troops – and failed catastrophically. The failure proved that even an apparently overwhelming force was incapable of penetrating the most rudimentary of positions when defended by expert riflemen alone, never mind machine guns. With each subsequent assault battle tactics were scrutinized and adjusted, and as all persistently fell far short of success, artillery came to be perceived as the key to the deadlock: if sufficient guns could be deployed, they could simply obliterate the target and its garrison before it was attacked. In 1914 with strictly limited numbers of artillery pieces, the effect of shellfire on fieldworks was minimal, and it was thought that simple rigid trench lines could comfortably withstand the limited bombardments of the day. At this time surprise infantry attacks were possible. In 1915 the picture began to change. Barbed wire was arriving in quantities sufficient for distribution in more substantial belts, and the trench lines, although still rigid, had elongated, connected and multiplied. At the beginning of the year the pre-attack artillery barrage was not yet an established tactic; six months later this had changed radically: the barrage had become obligatory, and with it the element of surprise began to vanish. 1916 dawned with greatly increased numbers of guns, howitzers, mortars and ordnance, allowing concentrated, prolonged and devastating fire. But a barrage of a week's duration was an all too obvious sign of impending heavy attack. Excepting nocturnal (and very occasional diurnal) trench raids, almost all hope of surprise had entirely disappeared from the battlefield. Artillery and the bullet now shared the throne of no man's land. As a result, troops began to go deeper underground to escape shelling, whilst on the surface broad and dense entanglements of wire were commonplace. In turn, an attacking force was compelled to expend huge amounts of ammunition in cutting a way through these thorny defences, as well as pummelling the opposing trenches – an action which required more guns. On all parts of the front meticulous protection and concealment of defensive weaponry had become obligatory: machine guns, also proliferating ceaselessly, were safely stored – with their operators – below ground during bombardments. Meanwhile areas of defence had also broadened, covering an average depth of around a kilometre from front line to reserve positions.

The following year, 1917, saw further vast increases in the numbers and employment of artillery. In many sectors troop accommodation now had to be deep underground, or housed beneath several feet of ferro-concrete. British trench lines were changing to a more flexible defence-in-depth system, mirroring tactics successfully employed much earlier by the Germans whereby field defences within deep zones of territory were deliberately designed to be 'elastic', allowing a hostile force to make costly headway over front and support positions before being driven out by counter-attack. It was agreed that a breakthrough might be effected if enough troops could be assembled to attack not on a front of 16, 32, or 48 km (10, 20 or 30 miles) but of 160 km (100 miles), thereby drawing in almost the entire establishment of enemy reserves. The prospect was of course out of the question, and traditional frontal attacks continued, with similarly limited and costly results as the previous year. On both the Somme and at Passchendaele, the rate of advance was so slow that it was possible for new defensive lines to be installed *during* the offensive! The final year of the war, 1918, confirmed that the ultimate defence of a position was based upon its ability to withstand shellfire, on extensive provision of deep protective dugouts, concealed and numerous machine guns, and on the defender's aptitude to counter-attack. More flexible trench systems combined with the use of shock troops (by the Germans) and massed forces of tanks (by the Allies) finally led to the return of mobile warfare.

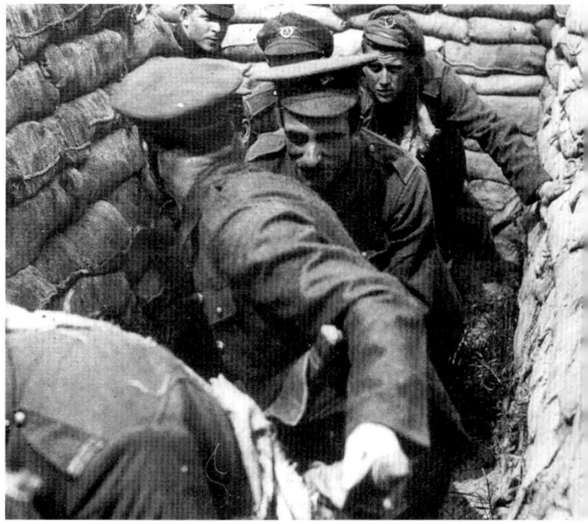

Canadian troops carrying out a bombing exercise.

The landscape of battle

The fieldworks revolution of the First World War was driven by a variety of circumstances: the basic need to escape the ravages of the bullet and shrapnel shell, to stop the invader, or, in the case of Germany, to define the boundaries of a new empire. In this static war military engineers possessed defensive opportunities denied to their historical antecedents, and were able to exploit the tactical advantages which nature provided, and to improve them. Theoretically, by the end of 1915 a determined soldier could walk, with head carefully tucked below the parapet, all the way from the beaches of Belgium to the Swiss border, passing en route comrades of many nationalities and seeing and feeling many changes in the ground beneath his feet. This was the landscape of the greatest siege the world would ever know, and it was controlled by the basic geological foundations of continental Europe.

Flanders and the coast

The area of Europe known as Flanders links northern France to Belgium. It comprises an extensive flat plain across which numerous rivers run, stretching from the North Sea to the foot of Vimy Ridge. The rivers are fed by streams that flow down from the slight topographic highs that break up an otherwise monotonous landscape. But the plain has many subtle localized variations. On the Belgian coast, the sea is prevented from inland incursion by an impressive kilometre-wide belt of sand dunes, some of which rise to a height of 50 m (164 ft). The dunes act as both a barrier against the sea and a dry highway along the coast. In Victorian times the wide sandy beaches and bracing air helped create the seaside resorts of La Panne and Dunkerque, and also Nieuport-Bains (now Nieuwpoort-Bad), the little holiday town where the trenches of the Western Front came to an end – at Barrel Post on its old promenade. In 1940 these same beaches were the scene of Operation Dynamo – the seaborne evacuation of the second British Expeditionary Force to serve in France and Belgium in under thirty years.

The dunes protect a vast area of flat, rich farmland known as the Polder Plain. Stretching northwards from France, crossing Belgian territory and continuing into

Plan of a part of the Polder region of Flanders showing the density and complexity of drainage channels.

the Netherlands, the Polders are farmed by a hardy people who over countless centuries have teased, coaxed and engineered the land into one of the most productive agricultural areas of Europe. Lying at and occasionally just below sea level, periodic inundation by the sea in times past added valuable nutrients to the soils. But the Polders have always been wet, very wet, when left unmanaged. Underlain by clays, silts and peats, the terrain was developed and improved through painstaking drainage by generations of Flemish farmers. Their work left the area criss-crossed by tens of thousands of waterways of all sizes, from ship canals to tiny leets, with multitudes of locks, sluices, culverts, ditches and weirs, all interconnected and carefully controlled to maintain the optimum water level for each season and each crop. The Polders were an ideal location for army manoeuvres; but only when dry. In October 1914 the German invader, sweeping all before him, advanced from Antwerp to Ostend and on across the Polders towards Nieuport, determined to cut off the Channel Ports and advance on Paris. He was stopped by both a supremely resolute defence and a brilliant manipulation of the water system, a manipulation which flooded the German line of advance and created the 'inundations', a vast, waist-deep, man-made sea stretching from Nieuport via Dixmude, almost to the ramparts of Ypres itself, almost 30 km (19 miles) inland. The barrier brought the advance to a standstill, and its careful management throughout the war prevented all further offensive action on the Polders.

At Dixmude, 14 km (9 miles) from the sea, the West Flemish landscape subtly begins to alter. Canals, sluices and drainage ditches are still present, but now many fields are distinctly above sea level, situated firmly on a clay plain that almost imperceptibly swells from the Polders. Here, heavier, stickier soils created by the underlying Argiles de Flandres (Flanders or Ypres Clay) are more obvious underfoot. The Ypres Clay, identical in type and age to that found beneath London, the remnant of a seaway present some 90 million years before the First World War. Unlike the lighter sandy Polder ground, the heavy soils of the Flanders plain are difficult to cut with the plough, and the increased clay content makes the earth more impervious: water does not percolate readily, and rainfall tends to sit stubbornly on the surface. This geology was to play a major role in the life and death of hundreds of thousands of men.

Three critical topographical features disrupt the regularity of the Belgian Flanders plain: the lazy flow of rivers and streams which meander sluggishly across the land, the canals and smaller waterways connecting all the major towns, and, of prime importance, the rather ambitiously entitled Alpes de Flandres, a chain of low-lying hills which together form a semi-circular ridge system of spurs and valleys. These latter are collectively known as the Passchendaele Ridge, and within their embrace nestles the medieval city of Ypres.

Sitting proud of the plain, the Passchendaele Ridge is formed from alternating layers of sands, silts and clays. Shaped over millennia by the actions of streams flowing down to the rivers Lys and Yser, it is not a uniform feature. A complex system of spurs reach out finger-like from the main north-south oriented arc, many of which were to become well known between 1914 and 1918 as the ridges of Pilckem, Frezenberg, Broodseinde, Menin, St Eloi and Messines, the sites of bitter fighting on more than one occasion.. At a height of 58 m (196 ft), the most impressive topographical feature in Belgian Flanders is Mont Kemmel, but this too is an integral part of the Passchendaele system. Although less imposing, several man-made features played roles just as critical as the ridges: for example, the spoil heaps resulting

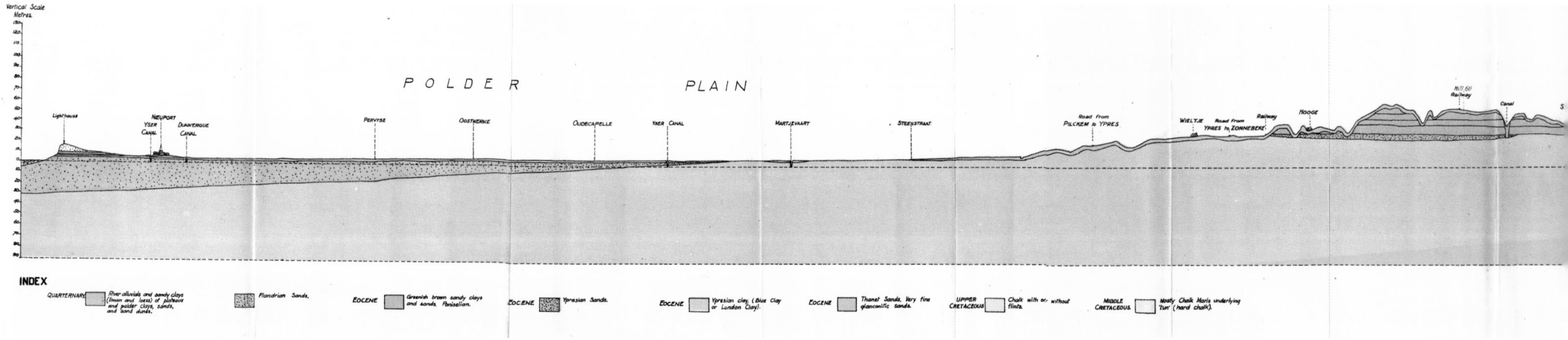

from the cutting of rail and canal links during the nineteenth and early twentieth century were to become major topographic and tactical military positions: Hill 60, the Bluff, the Canal Bank, the Caterpillar, all were to play key parts in the First World War. And most curious and telling of all, even tiny prehistoric tumuli such as The Mound at St Eloi would affect the fate of hundreds, indeed thousands, of men.

Travelling further inland from Ypres, beyond the village of Messines at the southern tip of the Passchendaele Ridge system, the landscape drops gently down to a continuation of the clay-based plain, this time lying within French Flanders. Beyond the billiard table flatness of the Armentières sector, another low ridge, Aubers, runs south towards Givenchy and the La Bassée canal. Although appearing far less of a barrier than the Passchendaele system, this gentle swelling conferred a majestic advantage upon those in control – the Germans. Several Allied assaults, all abortive and costly, took place in 1915 and 1916, and by 1917 the trenches and villages which hugged its slope had become veritable fortresses.

Beyond La Bassée, the terrain – and the nature of the front – alters again. Now the Flanders clay, having turned from a vivid blue to yellow, begins to taper away altogether near Neuve Chapelle, to be replaced by a fresh geology. Between Annequin and Vimy Ridge a thick blanket of chalk-based strata covers deep and rich coal beds, remnants of a prehistoric world folded and distorted tens of millions of years ago by the same forces that created the Ardennes mountain range. By 1914, a century of mining had made much of the area in and around the main city of Lens into an industrial landscape. Small villages and settlements such as Loos, Auchy, Wingles, Vermelles, and Hulluch are clustered nearby, each founded and dependent upon the coal industry. Close to every pithead or *puits*, lay the ubiquitous slag heaps of waste mine material known as *crassiers*. Varying in shape from low flat-topped dumps to linear fingers, both were to be critically important forms of artificial topography, offering valuable vantage points for military observation over the almost smooth battlefields of the plain. Complementing their usefulness were the skeletal iron and steel winding mechansisms of dozens of pitheads, and a multitude of railway embankments joining shaft to shaft and dump to dump.

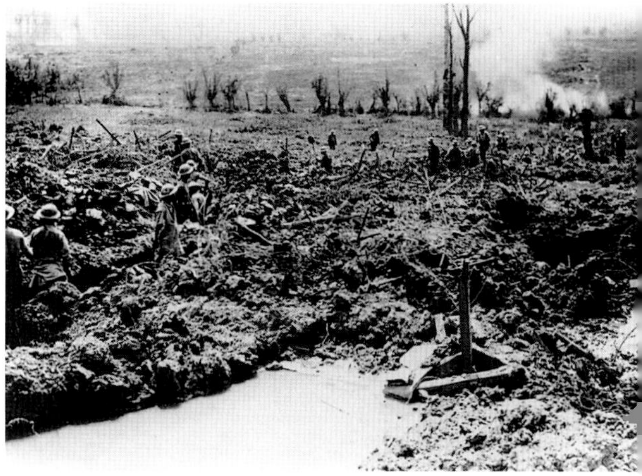

Standing water on the Messines battlefield, high summer 1917.

Artois and Picardy – the Somme region

The plain comes to an abrupt end at Vimy Ridge, a steep scarp slope that also sharply defines the boundary between two great geological battlegrounds. The geology and landscape of Artois, and to its south, Picardy, is completely different to that of French Flanders. Southwards from Vimy, a thick layer of chalk reaches close to the surface. Both regions also sit topographically higher than Flanders, on a plateau again formed by geological movement, this time the massive tectonic shifts and consequent surface upheavals which shaped the Alps. The pure chalk bedrock was sculpted into the present landscape during the last Ice Age, when warmer periods created melt water streams and rivers which, surging over the still-frozen surface, carved out wide valleys leaving a realm of rolling hills identical to the downland of south-east England. After the final thaw waterflows decreased, and the rivers could no longer run over the porous and soluble surface. The remaining water drained down to form caverns and underground streams, a common phenomenon in limestone geology the world over. Only the major watercourses now flowed, and many valleys, some almost gorge-like, fell dry and silent. Thus, the population came to face the precise hydrological opposite of their northern neighbours: whereby in Flanders people struggled to rid themselves of water; in Artois

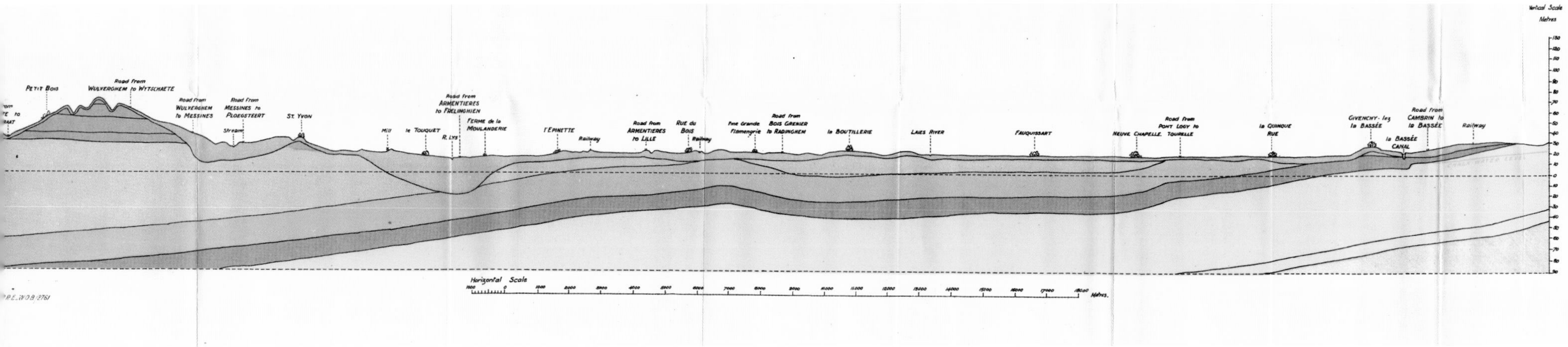

Trenches in chalk near Loos. Note the excavation depth, the nature of the geology, and the lack of timber revetment to support the trench walls.

and Picardy it became a scarce and valuable commodity.

In places, the chalk is covered by layers of sediments, also formed during the latter stage of the Ice Age. This topsoil is a mixture of clays, loams and a fine dusty wind-blown silt known as loess – equivalent to the valuable brick earth of Kent. The mixture is known as the *limons de plateaux*, and its behaviour is complex, loess being porous, but the loam, with a higher percentage of clay, much less so. This means that in places, particularly where a cap of clay sits on the chalk, the ground can be sticky and muddy, especially in winter. In areas where the chalk is capped by this clay-enriched geology, water is retained leaving a heavy soil which is often left uncultivated, except for forestry. Many of the symbolic woods of the Somme – hard fought over during the battle – exist purely because of the presence of a localized clay cap. In summer, the dry and dusty *limons* have been worn away over the centuries by the passage of men and animals; these ancient roads and paths, became the sunken lanes so characteristic of the Somme battlefields. Thus, both living and fighting conditions were strongly affected by localized geology.

The British battlegrounds

It was upon this multifaceted landscape that the battlegrounds now so much a component of world history came into being. Every sector and sub-sector upon the ribbon of contested ground which snaked across Europe is writ large in our shared understanding of the war, and each is deeply engraved in the collective awareness of dozens of nations around the world.

The bastion of the Ypres Salient remains prominent, partly because of the several great and costly battles fought in defence of the ancient city, but also because the arena was so terribly limited in size, and fighting of one kind or another so apparently unremitting. To many, the nature of warfare in the Salient epitomizes the First World War. The British occupied the trenches from the early days of war until the Armistice; as a result millions of men developed an intimate acquaintance with every inch of the landscape and trench network. With battles great and small punctuating four years of constant tension, by the end of the war the ground had become cherished, hallowed even, as a part of Belgium forever sacred to the peoples of Britain and her Commonwealth. Around a third of a million soldiers of all nationalities still lie undiscovered beneath the pastures of Belgian Flanders. Although the ridges were almost universally German held, both sides made supreme efforts to create stormproof positions: to the British the trenches were the front lines of Empire, whilst on the other side of no man's land lay the new borders of Germany. And neither side considered yielding for a moment.

By comparison to Ypres (and the Somme), the battlefields of French Flanders and Artois lying between Armentières and Vimy Ridge have been relatively unstudied. Yet in 1915 the battles fought here were profoundly influential, setting the philosophical and tactical profile for much of the later actions. This was the birthplace of attrition, the stratagem that relied on artillery to demoralize and subjugate before the infantry occupied. The battles of this seminal year were beset with difficulties, from shell shortages, poor planning, and under-resourcing, to seriously deficient communications both before and during battle. All were disappointing and costly failures, yet from an historical perspective they remain some of the most fascinating, incorporating neglected sectors such as Fromelles, Loos, the Cuinchy Brickstacks, and the 'nursery' sectors where little of strategic consequence took place throughout the war. The panoramas therefore show rural vistas, market towns and picturesque villages, and near Lens and Loos, industrial landscapes, some of which are almost identical to the scenery of today. The Arras sector too is also often overlooked, except in relation to the long-awaited triumphant assault on Vimy Ridge in 1917. Yet here,

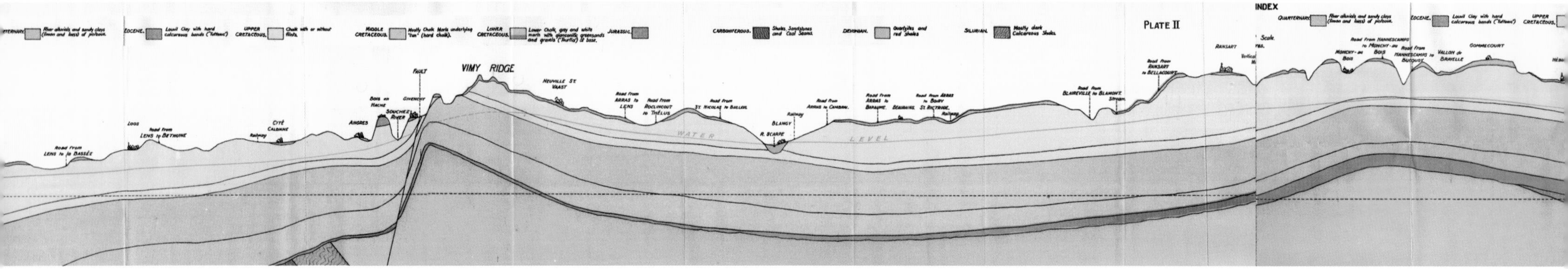

The Ypres Salient, early June 1915. Lieutenant Robin Skeggs, 3rd Battalion, Rifle Brigade, shelters in the simplest of dugouts at La Brique.

where the front lines closely skirted the town's perimeter, the most costly battles of the war took place. Arras was to become as 'Anglicized' as Ypres, and still shows countless signs of British occupation today. The ancient and beautiful town was severely punished for its trouble.

The Battle of the Somme in 1916 is thought by many to be the most damaging and costly British offensive of the war. Psychologically this was perhaps true: the battle did indeed mark a turning point for the Imperial Forces, sociologically and tactically. Taking over the rolling pastoral chalk downland from the French in the summer of 1915, the beauty – and indeed peace – of the setting must have been striking to the fresh British incumbents arriving from Flanders, for a 'live and let live' approach had long been practised. Within twelve months the Somme would be twinned with Verdun as two of the most significant battles in military history – the first of pure attrition. Panoramas taken in preparation for battle, during the fighting, and in its aftermath are an important component of this book, and tender some of the most unexpected views of all. Cambrai meanwhile offers us vistas of a grand battlefront – the scene of the first major tank battles in 1917.

Above all, the panoramas depict the trenches in which the life of the infantryman, from protracted periods of tedium to fleeting moments of terror, was played out. This was their world, and is captured without manipulation just as they saw it. The web of fieldworks from the North Sea to the Somme river – seen here in their remarkable entirety for the first time – were not simply sites of victory or defeat, and life or death; more often than not they were simply 'home' to millions of men for four long years. As we shall see in the next section.

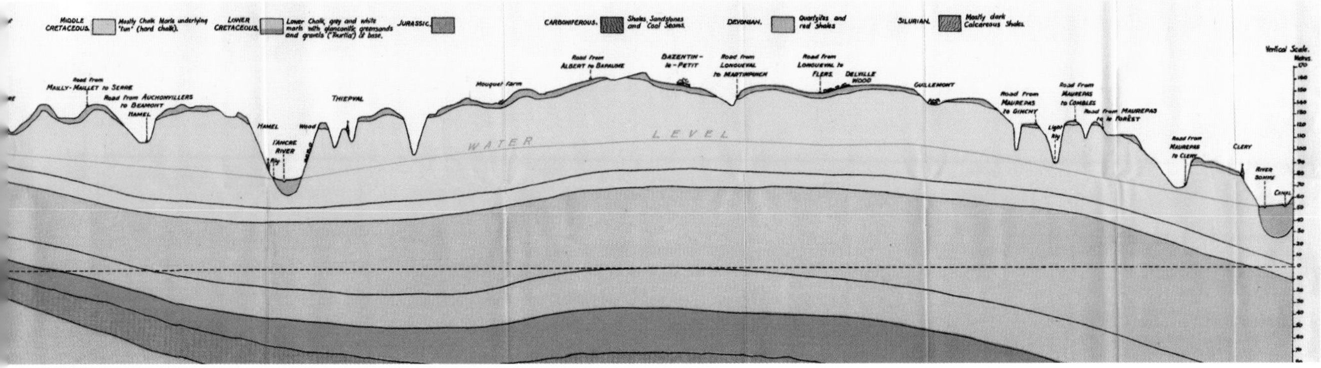

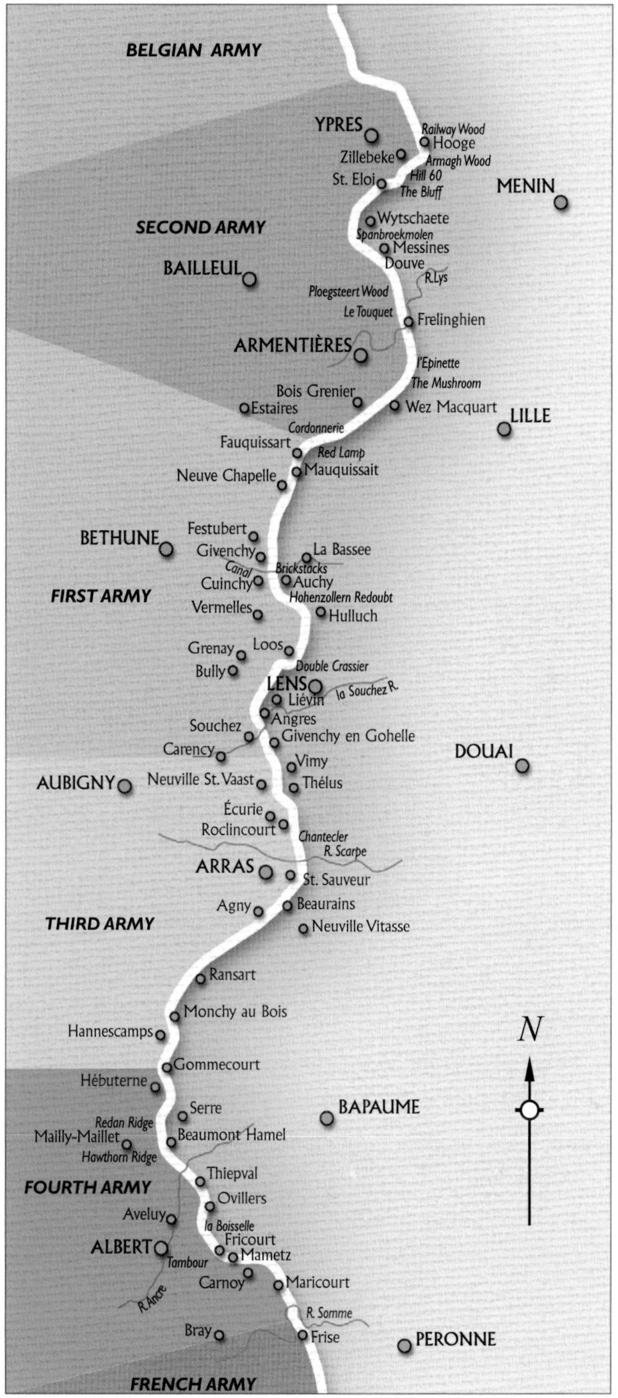

A generalized division of the British armies in France and Belgium during the period of stasis from May 1915 until July 1917. A 'Reserve Army' came into action during the summer of 1916. It later became Fifth Army.

Life in the Trenches

The most recurrent image of the First World War is the trench; the prerequisite of positional warfare and the foundation of the linear fortress of the Western Front. The imagery triggered by the simple phrase 'the trenches' is so strong that it has become a part of everyday parlance the world over. It is sensible to keep one's head below the parapet, rather than have it shot off by the sniping of one's senior colleagues, and we still have the opportunity to 'go over the top', but with different results. Dugouts too have remained – this time in the sporting arena – and the language of politics is coloured by the language of the war: politicians become entrenched, and the polarization of political ideals is often expressed by reference to irreconcilable distances across no man's land. Here is ample evidence that popular cultures remain steeped in the terminology of a war fought almost a century ago. In these and many other ways the still-shocking troglodytic imagery of 'the trenches' lives on.

The reasons are plain. The First World War brought about a wave of exemplary national pride and commitment. It was the first war to be fought both at home and abroad at the same time: civilians were critical to the struggle whether in uniform as volunteers or conscripts, or in boiler suits in factories. It was the first conflict in which the mainland Britain came under concentrated enemy fire, and the first to be comprehensively reported in words and pictures. With the combatants themselves being largely hastily-trained civilians, and no longer the ill-educated and often illiterate troopers of earlier conflicts, a far more intimate connection was possible between home and front line. Some were scholars, many could read and write to some degree, and did so, whilst others had letters written for them. News from the trenches – censored of course – came daily via millions of letters. Whilst on leave soldiers told stories of an environment, events, and a comradeship to which none at home could relate. In the post-war years, the inheritance of men shattered in body and mind, all of whom had to be cared for, was simply immense; if a man was lucky enough to survive the 'ten per cent terror, ninety per cent boredom' experienced by most front-line troops, and the ruthless pandemic of Spanish influenza in 1918–19, the war often tainted and steered the rest of life. The experience of the post-war world would prove a trial in itself for many former soldiers. Although loss and grief were ubiquitously experienced from Land's End to John O'Groats, London to Sydney, Capetown, Wellington or Ottawa, 'heroes' were not to return to a land or a society designed to assist and care for them and their families. If the breadth of this influence was not great enough, as the seed for the Second World War, the First World War was also to prove the seminal catastrophe of the twentieth century. Put simply, the legacy of 1914–18 was to leave deeper and more abundant scars than any other conflict in history.

Many soldiers on rest behind the lines struck up close friendships with local families. These three Highlanders (two Camerons and an Argyll and Sutherland) are in Poperinghe, near Ypres.

The concept of living in the open for extended periods is entirely alien to the overwhelming majority of Western society today, so alien in fact that in 2002 the BBC commissioned a 'reality' television series which placed young twenty-first-century men in reconstructed early twentieth-century trenches. Kitted out with authentic equipment, they were deposited at 'the front' and marched into the 'line'. Here, fed on 'authentic' food, and adhering to authentic orders (barked out by somewhat less authentic officers and NCOs), they lived the life of the 'Tommy'. Spectacular pyrotechnics simulated hostile artillery, and parties went out 'on patrol' into a no man's land protected by plastic barbed wire and devoid of both enemy and risk. Alarm was fabricated by unexpected noisy but harmless explosions, or surprise visitations by low-flying aircraft. The 'trench' itself could not be installed at an accurate depth because of BBC Health and Safety regulations. Ultimately, the only authentic aspect of the programme was the weather and the testimony of veterans interviewed; nevertheless, it was a strangely fascinating exercise, although quite what was learned is still nebulous. The purpose of the project appeared to be to make the volunteers as miserable as possible whilst portraying all the many cliches which have come to

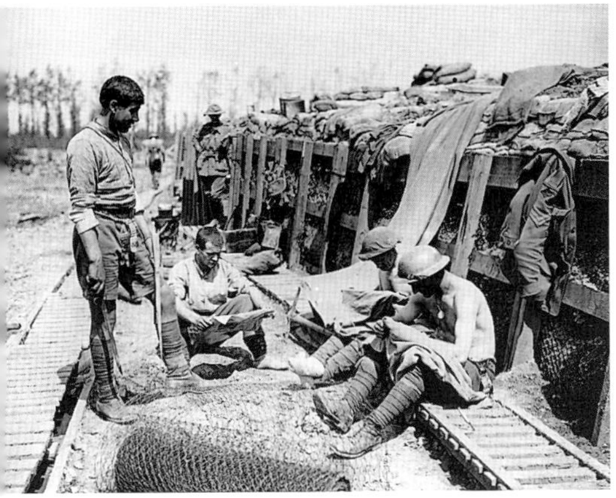

Australian troops on a louse-hunt in a support line near Armentières, May 1916.

characterize the Great War during the eight decades since it came to an end.

So what is real? A predominating iconic image of the First World War is mud. In fact, devotees debate which mud, whether that of Flanders, Artois or Picardy, was the worst. They argue long and hard over causes, leading to statements that are often unsupported by the stark geographical facts, particularly with regard to Flanders.

The battlefield, it was said, was 'a reclaimed swamp', which was only prevented returning to its original condition of a soggy morass by an elaborate system of drainage. A glance at [the] map will show that…it has never been a morass, except, perhaps, in Mesozoic times, and was drained by its natural slope and a number of small streams.
Brigadier-General RE Edmonds *Official History*, 1917, Vol. 2, 1948, p.vi

At some point in history the Flanders plain lay under the sea. It is reclaimed bogland, which it was only possible to inhabit and cultivate by constructing a complicated network of drainage ditches … Beneath its covering of meadows and hopfields Flanders is a natural bog.
Lyn Macdonald, *They Called it Passchendaele*, 1978, p.11

In fact, muddy conditions are a combination of many factors, meteorological, geographical, geological; and anthropogenic – shelling and traffic. Waders, duckboards, plank roads, drainage, breastworks, all these and more were tried to combat the periodic menace and lessen its impact. While it certainly was not muddy all the time, the imagery of the First World War appears to suggest that it was, at least in the compressed collective memory. The predominantly black-and-white photography of the time portrays a uniformly grey landscape and climate, yet both minor and major offensives were strictly restricted by season, and the opening of many battles occurred in brilliant sunshine and summer heat; perhaps the sight of flowers on the battlefields and men in shorts confuses decades of received wisdom. In this respect the panoramas, often showing a pastoral landscape at relative peace, strongly challenge us to engage more fully in the true nature of the war.

Flanders mud has always been the bugbear of advancing armies, not only for centuries, but millennia. The Romans were halted by it, while Phillip Augustus, King of France, became stuck fast near Ypres in 1197. Conditions had not improved centuries later when in 1735 a defensive study stated that the highways around Armentières and Cassel were impassable almost all year round.

Before the days of paved or metalled roads many towns both in Belgium and France were often cut off due to the terrible state of the highways. In Bailleul during the winter of 1635 the population almost reached the point of starvation; disaster was only averted when supplies were brought in by small boat on the Becque du Mont Noir. In other places only pedestrians could negotiate highways, and then only by leaping across specially placed *pierres de marchepied* (stepping stones) armed with a long balancing pole. To fall off into the waist deep mud was said to be tantamount to suicide.

Trenches and mud probably remain highest in the iconographic visual hierarchy of the First World War, and are an important component of the panorama collection. The architecture, life and landscape of trench warfare must therefore be explained in order to interpret the nature of the photographs themselves.

Trenches and terrain

In the British Army's pre-war organization, all field fortification was the domain of the Royal Engineers (RE) – the sappers. Soon after the outbreak of hostilities, but long before the onset of positional warfare, the dearth of trained engineer troops became manifest. When fighting came to a standstill for the winter of 1914/15 and trenches began to multiply and connect, it left military engineers farcically overstretched – a situation which was actually to persist for the whole of the war. There was one fundamental problem during the early period – the majority of the work

A tractor of the Agricultural Directorate ploughing right up to the wire defending positions in the rear areas; Foye, 9 March 1918.

required to establish positional warfare consisted of entrenchment – a great deal of entrenchment.

It may be thought that anyone could pick up a spade and dig a trench, and this was true up to a point as so many men in uniform came from civilian backgrounds rooted in manual labour. But the regular infantry of the British Army – those who shouldered the burden in the formative months of 1914 – had not 'enjoyed' such benefits, and soon discovered that this new warfare required more than rough-hewn slit trenches or rifle pits. Before the war no provision at all had been made for infantry entrenchment training on anything more than a small and temporary scale. Indeed, more digging may have been done by cadets of university Officer Training Corps than by the lower ranks of the Regular Army. When spadework was required in peace-time manoeuvres, the regulations decreed that the infantry were to backfill their trenches at close of play – a task even more boring than digging them in the first place. In typical fashion, entrenchment was therefore simply avoided whenever possible. The tradition was long standing.

As the men paid for their own uniforms, all field training was looked upon as a punishment, and even though, in 1898–99, a few officers recognized that there would be grovelling on the ground in war, grovelling in peace time was avoided – in fact grovelling became a lost art. So the result was, that in ninety-nine out of every hundred parades and field operations, the soldier preserved an erect attitude, and in the hundredth he gingerly knelt down after having carefully selected the right spot. The duration of field training was governed by the dinner hour. The spade was never used or suggested because it might give the soldier "a dangerous facility for going to ground", and in some battalions, not mine, skirmishers were not allowed to kneel. "That will never do," said an officer. "If you let them kneel down before the enemy, they won't get up again and go on." – True, they would have been shot kneeling.

Brigadier-General J. F. C. Fuller, 1935

The Boer War, where the British were made to dig, and despite doing so were shot down in droves, still changed little in the minds of British military tacticians: the conflict was looked upon as an aberration, the winning side learned least, and the General Staff decided there was no need to change anything. So the professional soldiers of the BEF arrived in France and Belgium supremely well trained in drill and musketry, but not in how to dig in a systematic and effective manner. Within weeks of the outbreak of war, however, reality intervened, and 'grovelling' to produce amateurish trenches became the norm. The engineers stepped in with established fieldwork designs as soon as they could, but it would take time to pass on the far from mundane basic skills to the tens of thousands of troops who would flood into the budding war zones in the coming months and years.

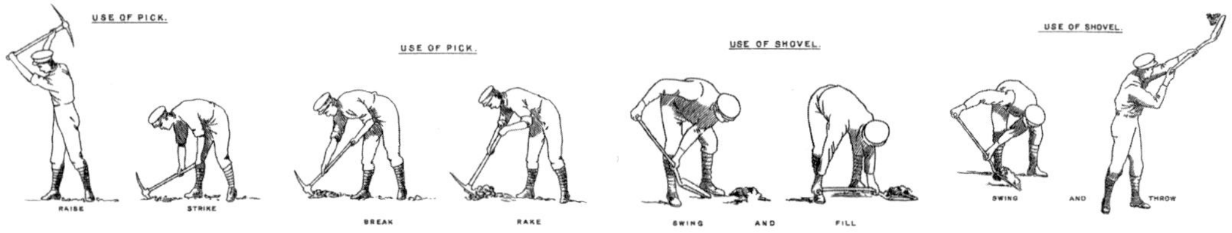

How to dig: from the Army's *Manual of Field Works*.

The humble spade was to remain the key tool in trench warfare, but its use was not quite so mundane as one might think. Just like the rifle, a spade required diligent care if maximum utility was to be extracted. In pre-war civilian work such as railways and canals, an experienced man could move up to 18 cubic metres (23 cubic yards) of earth per day – a huge volume – if, and only if, his implements were in good order. Navvies' spades were kept permanently clean, honed to a fine sharpness (each man had a sharpening stone), and polished and oiled each night. In warfare this kind of discipline was generally lacking outside the ranks of the RE probably because, unlike the rifle, the troops did not 'own' the kit they were using, and of course they were hardly on a productivity bonus.

In France, it was pitiful to see hundreds of men trying to dig with tools with an edge an eighth of an inch thick, with the blades rusty, and caked and made heavy with a pound or two of Flanders mud.

Field Company Commander Major W. L. Wood

Tools of all kinds were also often drawn in large numbers from dumps only to be discarded willy-nilly and unused on the battlefields. For this very reason there were sometimes acute shortages of picks and spades at places where they were needed most – on newly captured ground which required urgent defensive 'remodelling'. Throughout the war a constant battle was fought to instil in the minds of all troops how the spade was capable of saving not only enormous personal effort if properly used and looked after, but also human life.

The conditions of trench life, and therefore the efforts necessary to improve them, were dictated partly by enemy action, partly by the weather, partly by supply of clothing and food, partly by the personal habits of the individual, but especially by the terrain. How 'comfortable' trench life would be lay in the individual geology of the locale: it was conflict with soils and subsoils that created most of the headaches, toil and discomfort for the ordinary soldier at the front. For the most part British trenches in Belgian and French Flanders were situated on the lower contours of hills and ridges or in valleys. In a land underlain by impervious clay, water was held close to the surface – particularly during the winter, the wettest months of the year. This inevitably created problems the moment troops broke ground to take up residence, and early trenches were often little more than 'ditches'. On the lowest valley-bottom contours 'digging a trench' was a misnomer, as no trench at all could be dug. Here, protection invariably involved the erection of breastworks – a sheltered

Water – the perpetual bane of the trench-dweller, especially low-lying areas such as here at Ploegsteert.

'corridor' constructed partly or entirely above the natural ground level – and the digging of 'borrow-pits' to the front and rear of the site to win enough earth to create parapet and parados – the protective front and rear walls. Trenches had to be dug according to the prevailing water table, so depths varied, and in many places half-trench, half-breastwork affairs were common. Finding timber for revetments, the essential skeletal stabilizing framework for the walls of both breastworks and trenches, was always trying, particularly early in the war. During the first winter thousands of buildings, which often appear to have been ravaged by shellfire, were actually deliberately demolished (often by explosives) simply to procure wood for trench work and fuel, and bricks for horse standings and other purposes.

Water, water everywhere

The most demanding and frustrating challenge of all for the British was land drainage – an aspect of engineering unambiguously influenced by geology, and probably the most critical and permanent feature of positional warfare. Indeed, in their post-war histories the RE state that far more trenches were destroyed by neglect of drainage than by enemy shellfire. The problem was that in saturated terrain one could not simply shift unwanted water by pumping it elsewhere, firstly because the ground itself was often as flat as a pancake, and secondly because the clay-based soils grimly resisted drainage by percolation. To effect any degree of cure the whole of an area of countryside had to be 'bled', constantly and permanently, to keep the general water table at a manageable level. Some remarkable schemes were completed in Flanders, one of which in the Armentières sector involved the permanent drainage an area of just under 30 sq km (12 square miles).

Especially problematic were the sectors from Boesinge at the northern tip of the Ypres Salient down past Messines, and into French Flanders as far as La Bassée, all low-lying sectors with a substantial clay element in the surface soils. Between La Bassée and Vimy Ridge conditions improved as the proportion of clay diminishes, and chalk subsoils draw closer to the surface. Any admixture of chalk (or sand) assisted percolation, and as British forces took over more southerly sectors from the French, firstly around Arras and then north of the River Somme, the problem was further ameliorated as the plains of Flanders fully gave way to the rolling hills and free-draining chalks of the Artois and Picardy uplands. The effect of this geological variation on fieldworks and trench life is distinct in the panoramas which show the radical alteration in trench depth and design as the lines pass from one geological area into another.

Contrary to popular perception weather patterns were no different during the First World War than before or after. It did not rain every day, the troops were not permanently wet and cold, and mud was often entirely absent. But many authors dwell upon mud, mud and more mud, and endless rainfall. Despite their assertions warm and dry periods – droughts even – were entirely normal. At such times the ground, particularly in clay-rich areas, baked, becoming so hard that digging was only possible with immense effort. Flies and mosquitoes bred at an alarming rate as surface water stagnated, while the heat brought other unavoidable effects: in keeping rifle mechanisms clean, dust was as much of a problem as mud, and a brisk wind over fine topsoil guaranteed clouds of it. In conditions such as these an increased supply of clean drinking (and washing) water was required, as the soldier in the trenches, devoid of any hope of a cooling breeze, simply sat and sweltered beneath his tin hat.

In the sand dunes of the Belgian coast the troops actually prayed for rain, even a light shower was welcome, as it stopped dry sand blowing into everything, food, drink, eyes, rifles, machinery. Here, reaction to sandfly bites created daily queues for medical officers, and hundreds of horses died from the inclusion of sand in their feed; on post-mortem, one poor beast was found to have 50 Kg (110 pounds) of sand in its stomach.

During wet times the nature of the geology made little difference – life was

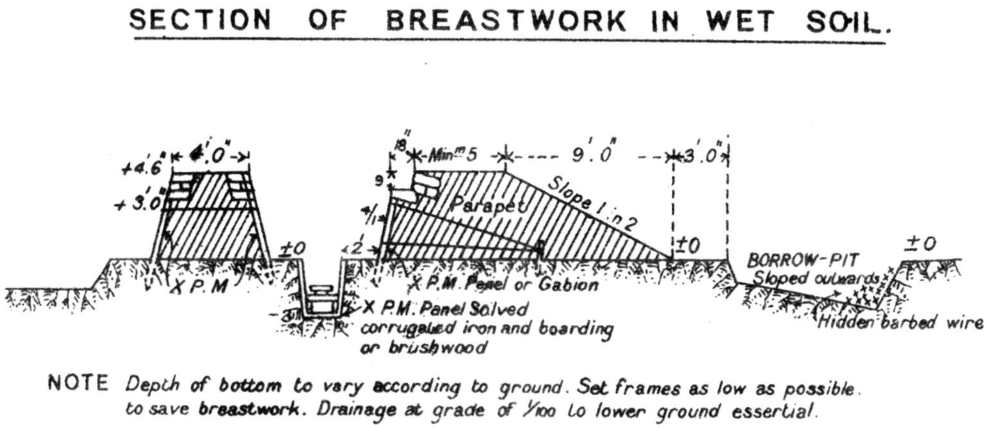

A section through a typical breastwork showing the construction method. The depth of the trench component varied, controlled solely by the prevailing water table.

uncomfortable, movement awkward, and upkeep of trenches wearing. In all but the pure chalk areas where the firmer ground allowed trenches to be more 'self-supporting', digging new works during rainy periods was often entirely unprofitable, as the sides of an unrevetted excavation would constantly slip, simply making the work wider rather than longer or deeper, and creating a filthy morass of the site. The Army found that it proved possible to dig hundreds, indeed thousands of kilometres of trenches during periods of good weather, but come winter it was soon seen that maintenance, an unending task regardless of season, required far more manpower and effort than establishing the original construction. In the forward areas there was therefore a limit to what could be usefully created and garrisoned.

DIY

Throughout the first twelve months of war the engineers made an effort to persuade the infantry to make their own part of the line as strong and dry as possible for their own safety and comfort. They were encouraged to dig trenches and install revetments according to serviceable patterns, under some form of RE control whenever possible. This semi-do-it-yourself activity was known as 'RE fatigues'. A sapper officer or NCO would mark out a task and expect it to be done, remaining on site as overseer. But the practice was disliked by the infantry, and it was easy to understand why. Much forward work took place at night and was frequently carried out by men extracted from comfortable billets behind the lines, on rest from front-line duty. Parties were often required to work in sub-sectors which their own unit were not holding; thus, they might arrive in strange surroundings, in a bad mood, with a tiring night ahead of them, and the possibility of facing sporadic harassing shell, rifle and machine-gun fire. It was also an inefficient process. Because of the lack of training, work followed the pace of the most inexpert men in the party. To cap it all, the infantry officers or NCOs in charge often knew as little of what was required to be achieved as those under their control, their main concern being to return the men to billets with as few

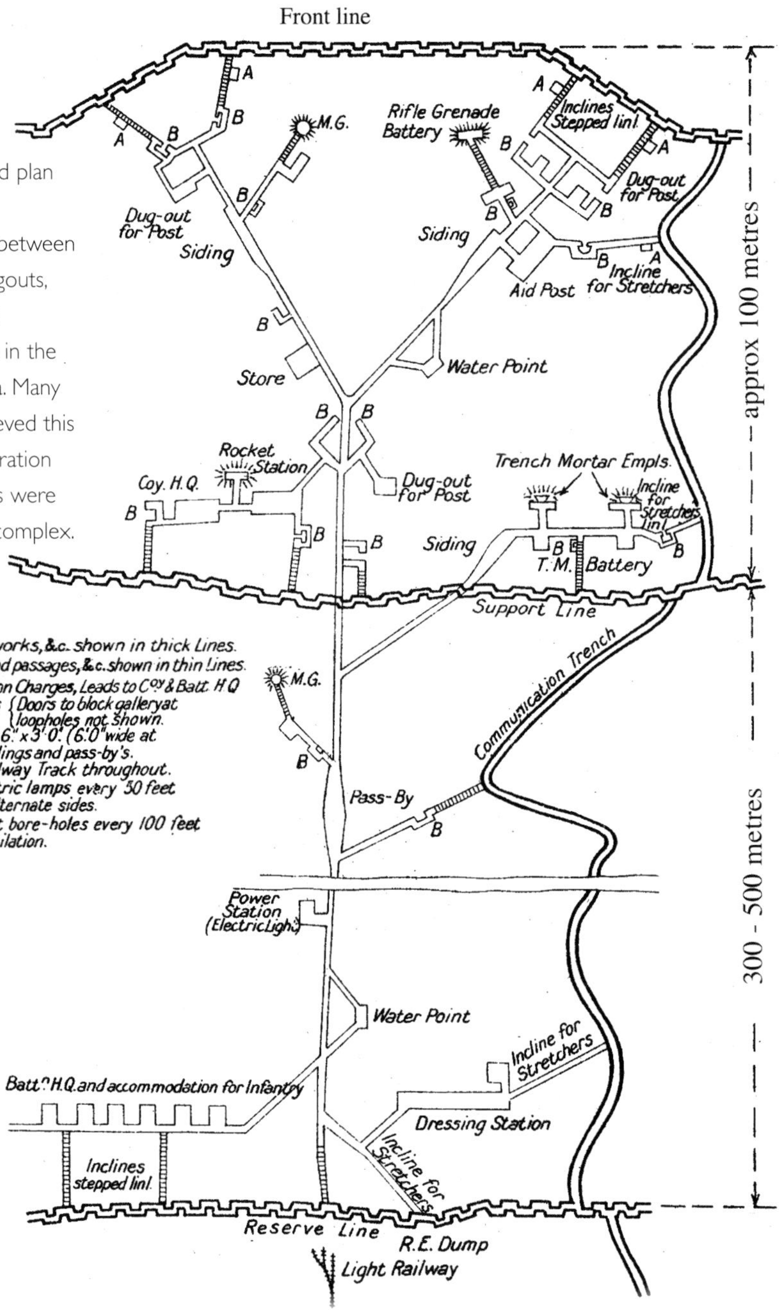

A generalized plan showing the relationship between trenches, dugouts, subways and strongpoints in the forward area. Many sectors achieved this ideal configuration whilst others were even more complex.

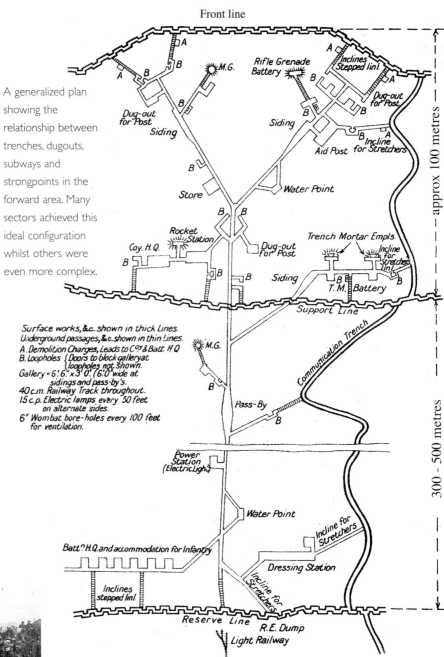

Far left

Water supply, always a problem, could be as difficult during cold periods as in droughts.

Left

Mud on the Somme battlefield in autumn 1916. Conditions were made worse by endless traffic to and fro along the major routes.

casualties as possible. It would not be an exaggeration to say that working parties were detested by the infantry, and indeed not over-loved by the sappers.

After the Flanders battles of spring 1915 engineering personnel were augmented with the attachment of a battalion of pioneers to each division. Although not fully trained sappers they were especially welcome, and eased the fieldwork burden considerably. As infantrymen with basic training in field fortification, Pioneer Battalion troops worked well under engineer supervision, especially when given substantial schemes to realize such as long lengths of communication trench, a major wiring plan, a trench tramway scheme, or the construction of a redoubt or strongpoint. Indeed, continuity was the best recipe for good engineering work: if a company could be kept together from the start of a job to its completion, the quicker the task was finished, the better the result, and the more fulfilled the men felt. But the appetite of the Western Front for fieldworks was unappeasable, and continuity was unfortunately an aspiration that was seldom achieved. As the conflict intensified in the spring of 1915 with the battles of Neuve Chapelle, Aubers and Givenchy, the message that everyone had to be capable of creating protective fieldworks got through to all units, and many infantry officers recognized the need for a more 'do-it-yourself' approach.

Nuts and bolts of trench warfare

The world wasn't made in a day
And Eve didn't ride on a bus
But most of the world's in a sandbag
And the rest of it's plastered on us

The Wipers Times, c. 1916

An immaculately constructed communication trench in front of Messines. This one, the Medicine Hat trail, is boarded and revetted with expanded metal fixed to timber frames and, for extra strength in the shifting clay geology, the extended 'A-frames' are 'strutted' overhead.

The walls of trenches, except in very firm ground, were loath to 'stand up' on their own. Weather, human traffic and hostile shelling and mortaring so eroded and shook the ground that supporting revetments were obligatory. Taking the form of hurdles, timber planks or sheets, corrugated iron, frames with attached wire or expanded metal, sandbags or gabions – even packing cases, boxes or suitcases filled with earth – all demanded prodigious quantities of raw materials. The staple of trench warfare, however, was the humble sandbag.

Between 1914 and 1918 around 1,300,000,000 sandbags were used by the British alone. On the outbreak of war, all stocks in Britain were immediately bought up by the War Office, but the quantities obtained still fell far short of requirements. Whilst arrangements were made for the construction of dedicated manufacturing plants in India, whence most of the raw material, jute, originated, millions of bags were shipped from North America. To further enhance supply convicts were put to work producing the standard item, plus a curious miniature example which, filled with sand and a tiny charge of explosive, was used for hand-grenade training. Varieties made of paper, canvas, even vegetable fibre, were tested for suitability, and special coloured examples produced to suit certain geologies: white bags for chalk country, yellow for the clays of northern France, and so on. Some curious shapes, sizes and patterns can be seen in the panoramas.

A communication trench revetted in corrugated iron sheeting, with expanded metal gabions filled with earth.

Sandbags, being supplied empty of course, were not as awkward or burdensome to carry as other trench materials, even in very large quantities: a bale of 250, for example, weighed 43 kg (95 lbs). But light as they were empty, they had to be filled. A large (but seldom willing) labour force was always available for this dull and endless task. As it was not easy to count the finished article in situ, fatigue parties were usually given a certain number of bags to be filled within an allotted time, with the work overseen by an NCO who would check that no empties were left. The greatest problem he faced was in spotting troops filling sandbags with sandbags.

The erection of a sandbag structure simply required adherence to a set of basic rules to assure the edifice was stable. The filling, the nature of which of course varied according to prevailing geology, was required to be as densely packed as possible, and when well-constructed, results could be surprisingly strong and resilient. Employing the 'loose-built' but bonded form stipulated in the manuals – a little like a brick wall without mortar – provided a potentially life-saving measure of energy absorption from shell burst. A double thickness of well-filled bags offered adequate protection against a bullet, shell fragments and shrapnel, whilst dense, well-made parapets and parados were often capable of withstanding the shock of larger calibre shells and even heavy trench mortar fire. Should damage be sustained, repairing and maintaining sandbag structures was relatively simple and swift, as old material could simply be reused in new bags.

For overhead shelter from the elements, shrapnel and shell splinters, the traditional systems of cover laid down in Victorian and Edwardian military engineering manuals continued to be employed, and were found to be adequate for a while. By the end of 1915, however, as a direct result of the galloping proliferation in artillery, shallow refuges were being supplanted by specially designed and more substantial steel shelters and dugouts mined deep in the solid earth, often capable of housing huge quantities of men and materiel.

The trench system, which all additional fieldworks served, was not only built for defence, but for living in: it had to be looked after in the same way as a house. As a consequence day-to-day life was one of intense tedium. To keep the semi-military mind of a volunteer and, later, a conscript army from dwelling on all-too-potential dangers, officers and NCOs demanded that, just as in camp, cleanliness and hygiene regulations were fiercely observed in the trenches. It created inter-unit and indeed international rivalry, such that many accounts bemoan the state of lines taken over from other units. British regulations were rigid: troops were charged to leave a position in the condition they would wish to find it. Photographs reveal that although the general battlefield was full of clutter, trenches were indeed tidy and highly organized places, seldom showing signs of poor upkeep. Latrines were numerous, well signposted, and positioned 'conveniently' in the lines, whilst the structures themselves were often surprisingly well designed for comfort. All were subject to regular inspections by an orderly sergeant or officer, and locations were frequently changed. Quicklime was available to cast on to each 'deposit'. General refuse in the form of toilet paper etc., was required to be put in sandbags or tins and buried at night by 'sanitary men' (not a permanent position, but a fatigue duty) in 'safe' places which were clearly marked – for the benefit of those extending or improving the trenches. Other wastes, tin cans and the like, were often disposed of in front of the trenches in the early part of the war, an act seemingly at odds with the military mind – but actually serving an important purpose in providing a potentially audible indication of the presence of the enemy, inadvertently rattling tin cans as he approached the parapet. Subsequently the practice was banned for hygiene reasons. Rats were a perennial problem and needed no extra encouragement to scavenge – so empty bully-beef and Maconochie tins were buried. It should also be remembered that plastics had not yet been invented, and 'packaging' was universally recyclable or bio-degradeable. Fresh food, bread and cheese for instance, were delivered in the handiest fashion – in sandbags – whilst water arrived in petrol tins and earthenware jars.

As all trench systems became labyrinthine in scope, vast in scale and disturbingly similar in appearance, a means of identification was necessary to allow the troops to both know and report their position and successfully navigate to, from and within the lines. The christening of fieldwork features began during the winter of 1914–15; ultimately every trench on the Western Front received its own individual identity. Names were at first devised to relate to existing features in a locality, or (very commonly) were a bastardization based upon British pronunciation of foreign words. In new trench work, name boards were erected almost as soon as the lines were laid out. Likewise, latrines, bomb stores, dugouts, gas alarms, emergency flare positions and strongpoints were clearly marked. Ultimately, as the surveyors mapped every inch of France and Belgium, many trench names became alphabetical, corresponding with the letter of the trench map square inside which the positions lay. A change in name might be expected at a point where the line was intersected by a communication trench. The locations of centres, intersections or changes in map square on the ground were particularly clearly indicated with large notice-boards visible well to the rear – a custom revealed in many panoramas. Front, support and reserve lines – those which ran parallel to the front, received the title of 'trench', whilst communication routes, running perpendicular, were known as avenues, parades, lanes, alleys or ways.

The main British communication cable system between Ypres, Zonnebeke and Broodseinde. Uncovered during roadworks near Railway Wood in 1995.

During an advance, rapid signage of captured ground was critical, especially during the great offensives of 1916 and 1917 when parts of the landscape became so bludgeoned by shelling that few if any visible reference points remained by which infantry might report position and progress. In an empty landscape it was far too easy (and dangerous) to lose one's sense of direction completely, so the first teams to enter captured territory were often engineers, whose immediate duty was to erect boards confirming the map reference of particular locations. Signage indicating previously hostile trenches, pillboxes (which were both named and numbered) etc., was installed once the ground had been fully secured. Later, the positions of buried cables and water pipes were also marked, and forward tracks, used only after dark, named throughout their length, with directional signs indicating origin and destination. To facilitate movement at night all routes were regularly dotted with metal pickets painted (on the side not facing the enemy) with white or luminous paint. Consequently, panoramas of captured ground exhibit hundreds of signposts in the landscape of battle.

Life in the trenches

Engineering and comfort in the lines were inextricably intertwined. If trenches had been carefully dug with the correct gradient for drainage, and properly revetted, it was then possible with regular, indeed incessant, 'housekeeping', to be able to stay

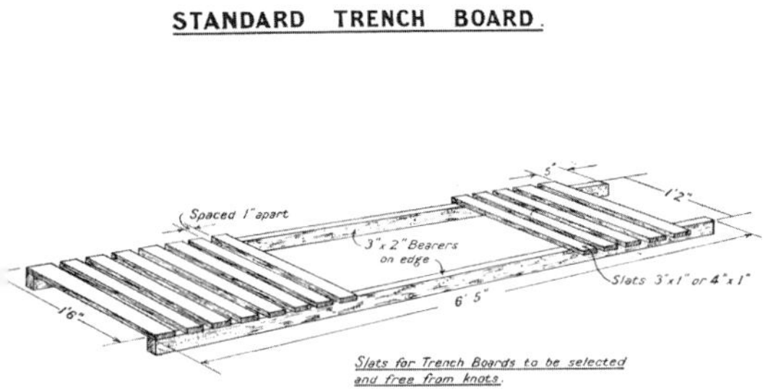

The duckboard: far from being mundane, this was a carefully designed piece of military equipment. Different patterns were produced for different climates and geologies.

relatively clean and dry – an important aspect of life in the line. Once the initial construction had been completed, the entire responsibility for upkeep devolved upon the residents, the infantry. They would carry out basic repairs and renewals, and the quality of their workmanship controlled living conditions. The degree of cleanliness, and therefore comfort, depended upon how assiduous the trench officer was in having his men service their lines. Sandbags soon wore out with constant traffic and had to be replaced; duckboards needed lifting to clear drainage channels of mud from soldiers' boots; sumps (the regularly spaced pits into which water was drained and collected) had to be kept free and unobstructed; tens of thousands of pumps had to be maintained in serviceable condition, and manned whenever necessary to keep water levels down; timber, the universal structural element of trench warfare, rotted sooner or later and had to be replaced.

Surprisingly, much of the materiel used in trench construction (and indeed warfare) emanated not from sources in Britain, but workshops in Belgium and France. The provision of duckboards (sometimes known as trench-mats) was of enormous significance. Being suspended above the trench bottom, they not only allowed men to keep their feet dry and move freely, but to actually reach the forward trenches. Long before Christmas 1914, RE field companies began to open their own 'factories' to manufacture and supply duckboards and the other indispensible article of trench warfare, the 'A-frame', the simple but ingenious device which carried the duckboard whilst at the same time acting as an important structural element. A-frames were individually designed to suit specific local geological and hydrological conditions, and several 'new and improved' patterns regularly appeared during the war. Both boards and frames were produced in prodigious quantities. In the month of August 1917 alone, by which time trench materiel was being sourced and manufactured from raw materials gathered from around the world, 375,000 duckboards were delivered, sufficient to build 640 km (400 miles) of track. The RE factories also produced revetment frames, hurdles and gabions, and trench tramways with light timber rails for easy transportation of stores to forward areas. In addition, thanks to the almost complete absence of suitable weaponry during the first year of trench warfare, the manufacture of homemade grenades and mortars, all from locally sourced materials, was initiated in earnest. By spring 1915 these factories were churning out trench pumps, mud scoops, snipers' plates, grenade carriers, Bangalore torpedoes (for the destruction of barbed wire entanglements), petrol bombs, water carts and fixed rifle rests. With at least one factory behind every army front, they developed a reputation as a sort of trench warfare supermarket. They were 'open to all comers, and few visitors went away empty-handed: even if they could not get what they came for it was seldom that they did not find something to take away with them'.

Dugout frames being manufactured at an RE yard: the first designed and manufactured form of weatherproof shelter used by the British Army on the Western Front.

Reliefs, the regular handing over of a trench sector from one infantry unit to another, took place at regular intervals, and invariably occurred at night. To sidestep unwelcome hostile enemy attention the hour of changeover varied, but the manoeuvre was nevertheless tricky as darkness and trenches made awkward bedfellows. Troops were frequently led into the line by a guide to avoid parties becoming strung out or indeed hopelessly lost in the maze of interlaced workings, which in most sectors came to constitute the forward zone. Incoming troops habitually brought with them 'iron' rations sufficient for forty-eight hours, plus 150 rounds of small arms ammunition, and also conveyed quantities of other items collectively known as 'trench stores'. These might included picks and shovels, sandbags (forty per man), revetment materials in timber or steel, rolls of barbed wire and cable, screw pickets, braziers, disinfectant, and fuel in the form of coal, wood or charcoal for cooking and heating. Iron rations consisted of bully-beef (corned beef in tins), hard army biscuits, tea, sugar, jam, and cheese.

Upon relief, the senior officer of the outgoing unit vacated his HQ dugout, handing over paperwork, trench maps, aerial photographs and panoramas; if the

Chinese Labour Corps personnel unloading new duckboards at a railhead. From here, the boards then had to be transported by truck, mule and human muscle-power to their final destination.

After stand-down in the breastworks near Bois Grenier: the pleasure of breakfast after a long night of trench duties is evident. One can almost smell the bacon.

incoming unit was unfamiliar with the sector, a 'guided tour' was proffered, carried out by individual platoon commanders for the benefit of their fresh counterpart. Sentry arrangements were explained, and the locations of posts, gas alarms, magazines, water points and latrines made clear. All the materiel of trench warfare – the trench stores – belonged to the sector, not the occupying troops, so tools, RE stores and ammunition, including grenades, were left in situ, replenished in agreed quantities for the use of successive reliefs.

Officers and NCOs needed to know the varying widths of no man's land in their subsector, how patrols had been organized, the quantity of trench repair or expansion work in hand, the location of any weak or hazardous points, how satisfactory the wire was, plus details of enemy activity and the prevalence of sniping and sapping. Whilst this exchange of information took place the new men had taken up sentry positions on the firestep, awaiting further orders. Within twenty-four hours the monotonous cadence of trench life was re-established.

Night and day in the trenches were delineated by two important and potentially perilous interludes, one at dawn, the other at dusk. Each was known as 'stand-to', and both were followed by 'stand-down', which was called after daybreak and nightfall. At stand-to every man was required to be armed, alert and ready on the firestep, for dawn and dusk were customarily the periods when enemy trench raids or larger attacks were most likely to occur. Invariably, nothing hostile materialized, although in some sectors morning stand-to also formed the temporal stage for a bizarre but usually bloodless ritual called 'morning hate' when both sides habitually blasted away with machine guns, small arms, and occasionally artillery, in a ten- to fifteen-minute gesture of mutual belligerence. Although 'unofficial' the act probably served to release tensions and maintain at least a little of the aggressive spirit so desired by GHQ.

The greater part of general trench activity at the front took place beneath the security blanket of darkness. After nightfall at least half the garrison would be put to work in the forward trenches, on sentry duty in the front line, or out in no man's land, listening, patrolling, wiring or perhaps, and very occasionally, raiding. A certain number of men were also required to fetch and carry essential provisions, and carry out trench extension, improvement or repair work. The remainder stood on sentry duty. A sentry group might consist of six men in pairs under the command of an NCO. Each pair took their turn on the firestep, two hours on and four off, peering into the darkness, reporting any movement and challenging suspicious figures. An officer was also on duty all night, visiting sentries, organizing ration, store and water-carrying parties, checking sentry and listening posts, and generally 'being seen'.

Stand-down in the morning was followed by the highly important breakfast. Although sentries were always on duty, daytime was a period of relative safety, and troops busied themselves with trench maintenance if required, but mainly used the time to catch up on sleep, letter-writing, washing and other activities of everyday life. It was also an officer's duty to check the cleanliness of rifles, and his men – especially their feet. Trench foot, and other afflictions peculiar to the semi-troglodytic nature of warfare on the Western Front, could be a major cause of absenteeism if regular and careful inspection was ignored. As omnipresent as they were unpleasant, with some men, a severe lice infestation could result in a debilitating sickness known as 'trench fever' which might take a man out of the line for several weeks. Scabies, a severe and easily transmitted rash caused by microscopic mites, was also a far from uncommon source of illness, whilst trench foot, literally a softening and rotting of the flesh due to feet being permanently damp, might remove a soldier from the ranks altogether if left untreated. Indeed, in serious cases death from gangrene poisoning was possible. Precautions against all these afflictions were as strict as an officer chose to make them. In an army of several million men, the risk of sickness was permanent and ubiquitous, and during the war an extraordinary 34,000,000 doses of vaccine, and 1,088,000,000 'cure-all' tablets were dispensed.

Foot inspection was carried out no matter what the circumstances. Here Australian troops in action at Third Ypres are being examined by an officer.

The likelihood of death or injury resulting from enemy action was by no means uniform along the Western Front, but varied enormously from sector to sector. The wide view offered by panoramic photography clearly reveals the

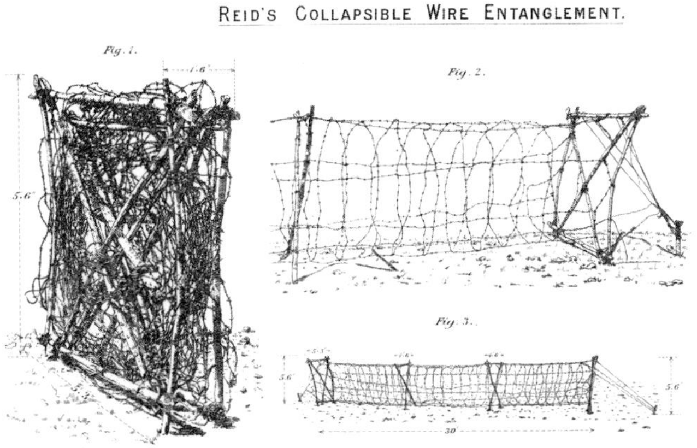

The RE produced and tested hundreds of designs of wire entanglements. This one could be carried out and sited by just two men.

'hotspots' where regular shelling, the major cause of casualties, took place. Some sub-sectors, even in the very early period of war, are seen to be severely pummelled by shellfire, whilst an area immediately adjacent remains practically or entirely unmolested. There were two main reasons for increased activity at one place in preference to another, both of which were often related: the observational qualities of the position, and underground warfare – tunnelling. Wherever these two aspects coincide one unfailingly sees evidence of greatly increased artillery attention as both sides seek to capture the heights and/or hinder each other's mining efforts by destroying shafts and entrances, upsetting work patterns by shell and mortar fire. Day-to-day casualties sustained in simply holding the line were known by the rather distasteful term 'natural wastage'.

No man's land

No man's land, that contested region separating the opposing front lines, was a permanent feature of trench warfare, and in many sectors fluctuated but little in size during the years of conflict. Its breadth averaged around 250 m (273 yds), but varied from a few metres to almost a kilometre. The panoramas clearly show this irregularity, and how a substantial disparity was possible even within a trench sub-sector only a few hundred metres in length. Dependent upon the intensity and duration of fighting, the landscape character of no man's land also altered from sector to sector, with some areas staying almost untouched throughout the war, whilst others were almost obliterated within the first few months of conflict. Every feature in no man's land was significant. Buildings stranded between the lines were demolished to eliminate their use as observation positions, initially by reducing them to ruins by shelling, then reducing the ruins to rubble with portable explosive charges.

One of many vast stockpiles of barbed wire. One billion two hundred and forty-five million yards were supplied by the British alone.

Before the advent of massed barbed wire entanglements, the ground between the opposing lines was kept clear of long grasses and undergrowth, characteristics which might veil enemy movement. It was not uncommon for small teams armed with scythes or sickles to emerge under cover of darkness (the period of the majority of activity in no man's land) and open up fields of fire and observation. As wire defences expanded however, many sectors became so overgrown with wild flowers and grasses during spring and summer as to practically mask the existence of the trenches themselves – an ironic contrast of the relentless rebirth of nature with war's relentless destruction. Indeed, nature proved time and again that the only things that were truly fragile on the battlefields were the lives of the soldier and his trusted companions the horse and mule.

Above all, no man's land was a killing ground – for both sides. All man-made features within the trenches were carefully designed, constructed and placed to inflict the greatest toll on human life; configurations of barbed-wire entanglements were purposely planned to 'herd' and hold up an assaulting force in places where they could most easily be cut down with small arms and machine guns, and by shrapnel, another supremely efficient tool against men in the open. No man's land clearly had to be crossed in any kind of attack, and it was this problem of how to eliminate the machine gun and rifle – in effect, eliminate the bullet – and negotiate the contested ground to reach the enemy which predominantly exercised the minds of the military tacticians. As attritional warfare took an obstinate hold no man's land came to develop a dual personality: for those defending, its breadth was measured in metres – how far away the enemy danger lay; but in attack it was time that mattered – how long it might take to cross the killing ground.

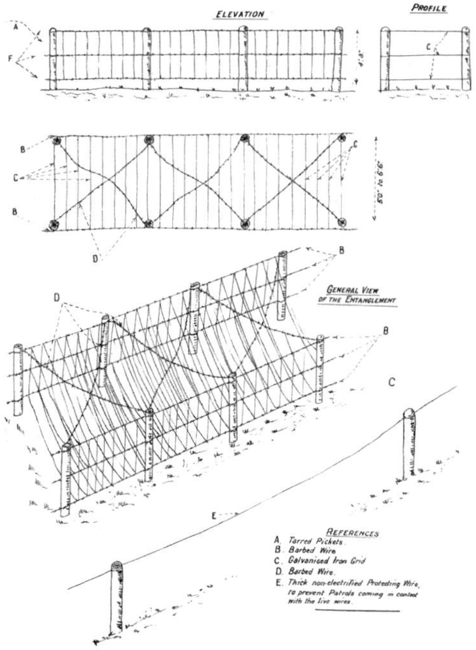

An electrified barbed-wire system erected by the Germans on the Vosges front.

As both sides wished to govern

activity between the lines, the more one knew of what was going on beyond the wire, the more prepared one might be for offensive or defensive action. Being able to hear (and occasionally see) what the enemy was up to was clearly of great significance. Sapping therefore became an important pursuit. Saps were narrow trenches driven from the front line beneath the barbed wire and out into no man's land. A party of men would occupy the furthest extremity – the sap-head – and by diligent watching and listening hope to glean information about enemy troop concentrations and reliefs, patrols, and even underground activity. Both sides were devotees of the sap, and most aerial photographs will reveal an array of short, blind trenches, some with a T-shaped head, protruding into no man's land. So widespread did the practice become that it was not unknown for friendly and hostile saps to approach within chatting distance, and even actually abut.

The technique of sapping was also used in two of its most ancient applications. Firstly to advance one's front line position by driving several saps forward, connecting the ends laterally, and wiring the position in – effectively creating a more advanced front line. This was a common practice especially in 1915. One such feature, some 1,500 m (1,640 yds) long, was constructed in preparation for the Loos battle in September of that year. The second method was to sap forward to mine craters in no man's land in the hope of occupying their raised 'lips', thus gaining both territory and a little extra height. Both procedures were slow, backbreaking and highly dangerous; they inevitably drew hostile fire and offered meagre results at the best of times. Several examples can be seen in the panoramas.

A British dugout gallery built entirely from steel I-Beams (girders) to counteract the immense pressure of the clay in which the gallery was driven. It is more than 10 m (32 ft) underground. Such an extraordinary state of preservation is not uncommon in Flanders.

Underground warfare

It was naturally in the narrower sectors of no man's land that military mining was most likely to emerge and proliferate. Alongside the suitability of the geology and the necessity for targets to remain immobile long enough to be undermined, the close proximity of enemy positions was of critical importance to mining schemes. A great many sectors of the Western Front supplied all three of these requirements in abundance, and tunnelling – the most ancient application of military engineering – was employed on a scale never before seen. The First World War was the quintessential era of the tunneller, and the unprecedented extent and almost primeval nature of their endeavours has long been unappreciated.

Summer 1917. An entrance to an Australian-built tunnel in the sand dunes of the Belgian coast. Tunnellers encountered different challenges within each geological variation on the Western Front.

By the close of 1915 mine warfare was more or less continuous wherever trench lines lay within striking distance – up to perhaps 200 m (218 yds), but latterly much firther. Indeed, when viewing the panoramas it is worthwhile encouraging one's imagination to dwell on what was taking place *beneath* the apparently calm surface of many pictures. The panoramic prospect was of course not a view a military miner would normally ever see, except perhaps after a successful offensive when the results of his complementary subterranean handiwork could be safely examined. Without horizons, dawns or sunsets, his struggle was the most bizarre conflict of the First World War.

By mid-1916 the British had around 25,000 trained tunnellers employed underground. Almost twice that number of 'attached infantry' worked alongside them, acting as beasts of burden, fetching and carrying the various elements of mining paraphernalia, and removing spoil – the waste earth produced in digging the tunnels. Those not directly involved in tunnelling (including attached infantry) were allowed to know little of the methods or aims of the tunnellers, for the simple reason that the gestation of mining schemes could be so long – well over a year for the Messines offensive of 7 June 1917 – and so arduous, that any leakage of information might lead not only to the ruin of the scheme, but the loss of many lives in the most hideous of circumstances: entombment, gassing or obliteration in cramped and

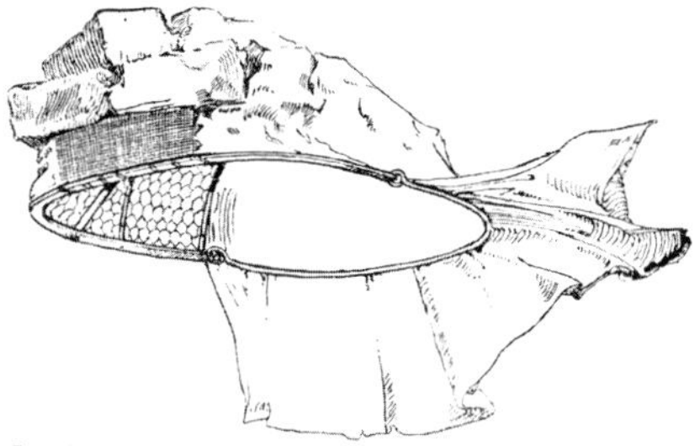

Portable Beehive O.P. unarmoured (weight about 10 lb.). Showing "brick" camouflage. Any surroundings can be similarly imitated.

The 'Beehive' observation post was fixed in position on the parapet and simply required the observer to put his head inside.

Portable Beehive O.P. in use.

claustrophobic galleries beneath no man's land.

During 1916 1,500 mines and thousands of smaller charges were blown on the British front. The smaller charges, known as *camouflets*, were controlled, localized underground blasts designed not to break the surface and form craters, but to destroy a limited area of underground territory – and its occupants. Indeed, *camouflet* fighting was the predominant occupation of the tunnellers on both sides, and only a very small percentage of mines were blown as part of a combined surface assault.

Observation

In being almost universally devoid of visible humanity, the panoramas perfectly illustrate how in trench warfare one seldom caught a glimpse of one's enemy. It was simply too dangerous to take the chance of peering over the parapet. Snipers were both the reason for the rule – and the exception to it. Operating from carefully selected and concealed posts or loopholes (camouflaged protective steel shields) a sniper either worked alone or as part of a team. The team consisted of an observer (with a periscope, telescope or binoculars) and marksman armed with a standard issue Lee Enfield .303 rifle, often fitted with telescopic sights.

They were a permanent thorn in the side of the garrisons on both sides of no man's land, as even in the quietest sectors the practice was commonplace – the unwary or careless were most likely to meet their end with a bullet through the head. So serious did losses to sniping become that devices were quickly designed to pinpoint the source of the trouble and deal with it, either by employing one's own marksmen – or by the more heavy-handed means of trench mortars and artillery. Due to the snipers' talents, safe daytime observation of enemy lines even through tiny apertures in the trench parapet was hazardous, yet it was absolutely essential to keep an eye on changes in the enemy front lines – and as far beyond as possible. Several effective designs for concealed trench observation posts (OPs) were fashioned, and a few drawings are reproduced here. The effectiveness of enemy sharpshooting was a serious concern, especially in 1915 and 1916. By 1917 the problem had been ameliorated by careful anti-sniping measures. Various techniques were employed, the most effective of which was the use of a dummy head to pinpoint the origins of a bullet. With well-trained personnel it was possible to rapidly locate offenders and permanently suspend their activities.

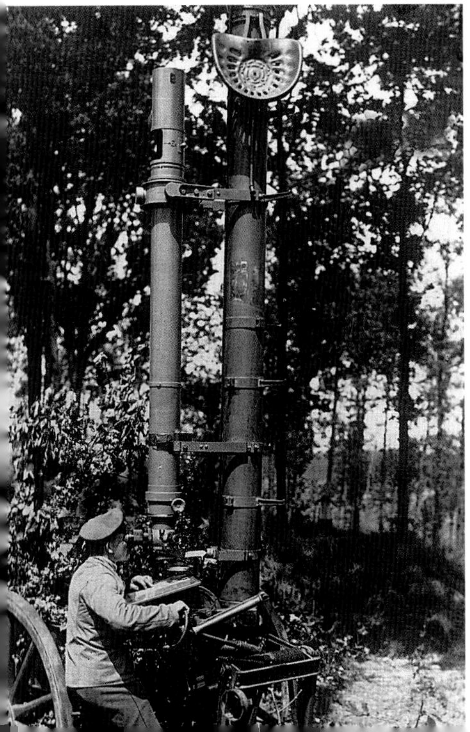

A German telescopic periscope in use. Later in the war when sitting on the surface became less wise, such equipment was also installed in forward dugouts.

Papier-mache heads made by the RE for use as targets to deliberately draw the fire of enemy snipers.

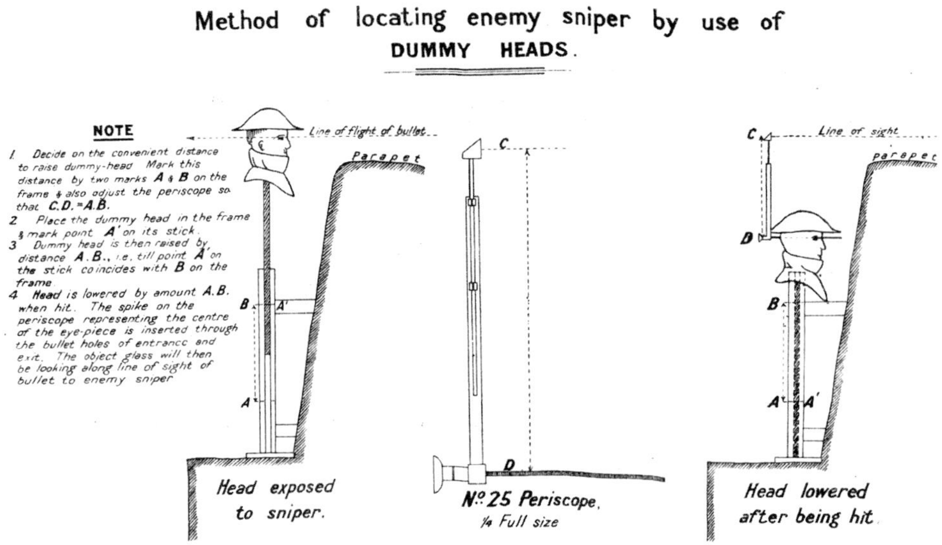

Method of locating enemy sniper by use of
DUMMY HEADS.
NOTE
1. Decide on the convenient distance to raise dummy-head Mark this distance by two marks A & B on the frame & also adjust the periscope so that C.D.=A.B.
2 Place the dummy head in the frame & mark point A' on its stick.
3 Dummy head is then raised by distance A.B., i.e. till point A' on the stick coincides with B on the frame.
4 Head is lowered by amount A.B. when hit. The spike on the periscope representing the centre of the eye-piece is inserted through the bullet holes of entrance and exit. The object glass will then be looking along line of sight of bullet to enemy sniper
Line of flight of bullet
Parapet
Line of sight
Parapet
A
B
A'
C
D
Head exposed to sniper.
No. 25 Periscope, 1/4 Full size
Head lowered after being hit

Dummy heads in use. The precise location of enemy snipers could be discovered by lining up the periscope with the bullet trajectory through the 'skull'.

A two-man sniping team in action behind the front line breastworks in the Fleurbaix sector, June 1916.

Observation from trench level was therefore a critical and permanent necessity. Everyone could catch a limited and narrow glimpse of the enemy line and no man's land through carefully camouflaged apertures in the parapet or via the numerous forms of periscopes, but for the wider view required by personnel of the Field Survey companies everything from simple mirrors to complex optical devices was produced commercially.

A bright thought on the part of "I" [Intelligence] was to install such a powerful telescope near the line that hostile shoulder-straps might be read, and identification obtained without the blood and disturbance of a raid. A 15-foot telescope was installed in an abandoned trench north of the Corons de Maroc. Pivoted at the muzzle end, the eyepiece ran on a small rail and was supported on an eccentrically-pivoted grooved wheel, so that it could be set to fine angles of elevation. The observer, seated on a species of sliding seat, shoved himself about with his feet, so that he felt thoroughly at home.
MAJOR R.L. BOND, D.SO., M.C., R.E.

This ingenious periscope was devised purely to gain something that the British sorely lacked in the majority of sectors on the Western Front: topographic elevation. With such poor field position, the problems faced by the British not only in panorama reconnaissance but observation in general were manifold. From their predominantly ridge-top strongholds (there were few sectors where the opposing lines were on the same level) the Germans enjoyed round-the-clock opportunities to both see and hear what was going on behind British lines – without periscopes. A height advantage of just a few metres was often quite sufficient to reveal a wide range of information about communication, fieldworks, transport, troop movements and concentration etc., by contrast, without the use of balloons or aircraft (both entirely dependent upon the weather for success), in many sectors the examination of German defences could sometimes not be made from anywhere but over or through the front-line parapet, from whence results were often unedifying. Observation from trench level dramatically foreshortened the view, so extra height was keenly sought wherever possible. This might take the shape of a house, a factory chimney, a tree, a church tower, or even a haystack. The Germans were well aware of British shortcomings in this respect, and ruthlessly shelled any feature that might cloak an (anxious) observer armed with binoculars, sketch pad or camera.

An early British observation balloon masquerading as a haystack to confuse enemy aerial observers.

Throughout 1915 and for the first half of 1916 the installation and especially the concealment of OPs was at the top of the RE work list. The reasoning behind the priority was simple: unless the infantry and artillery could be made aware of the exact positions of hostile machine-gun and trench mortar positions, barbed-wire entanglements, pillboxes, gun batteries, supportive fieldworks, and of course natural obstacles in no man's land like streams and embankments, no assault could be launched with any degree of confidence. One had to know the terrain, its condition, and precisely where the enemy and his weapons were located. This could be achieved partly through aerial photography, an innovative form of survey that was to become highly developed during the war, partly through meticulous mapping, but also through panoramic pictures.

It was also largely in the pursuit of enhanced surveillance that the art of

French camouflage work on a railway line under enemy observation.

A most unusual private photograph of a British truck fitted with an artillery piece; it has been painted (on one side only) to resemble brickwork. Near St Eloi, Ypres Salient.

camouflage came into its own. If suitable elevated sites were unavailable, something had to be created – in the most effective possible location. Some of the most imaginative devices of the war were designed and produced for the sole purpose of improved observation. Camouflage, in the form of canvas, hessian, calico or fishing net screens had been employed to hide movement since early 1915, and these can be seen in use in many panoramas. Several examples from the Third Battle of Ypres era show rows of screens stretching across the complete battlefield.

The concept behind British camouflage work was to create effective observation positions whilst preserving an unaltered appearance to the searching eyes of the enemy. This either entailed replacing an existing feature with an identical fake one, or making the OP aperture so well camouflaged as to blend into the landscape around it. The former technique, for instance, included counterfeit trees and telegraph poles concealing periscopes. In these cases the feature to be simulated was first drawn in situ by a camouflage officer, then modelled and painted as a plaster miniature, before being handed over to the RE workshops for full-scale production. Once complete, Camouflage Company personnel removed the 'old' feature and erected the new during the hours of darkness, if necessary having already excavated a dugout for an operator beneath the chosen spot. More 'mature' observation trees were stout enough to conceal human observers within the structure. They were usually clad in natural materials (the first was covered with bark from a willow in the King's Park at Windsor), whilst those with periscopes were made from canvas stretched over a metal framework. The larger manned variety was bullet-proof – to the front at least. Forty-five counterfeit trees were erected in total, with only about half-a-dozen being destroyed by enemy action.

In the absence of decent field position, it was equally important for the British to confuse enemy observers, consequently the importance of concealment was paramount for their own defensive purposes. A camouflaged machine gun, for instance, was likely to be many times more effective if the enemy were surprised when it opened fire. If the position was obvious – perhaps heavily protected by concrete – it became not only a target for hostile shell and mortar fire, but also a place to avoid in an attack. Likewise, well-camouflaged troop shelters could simply and effectively cloak a garrison's true strength. The Germans enjoyed considerable success during the Third Battle of Ypres by covertly building and camouflaging large numbers of concrete emplacements which, being invisible from both surface and air, remained unknown to the British. When battle was joined far more enemy troops and weapons were encountered than had been detected or envisaged. Some positions were so well camouflaged that their presence was only discovered after capture. Here, the Germans had succeeded in putting into practice the RE axiom on the ultimate aim of camouflage: to conceal the fact that you are concealing anything. A dedicated school was formed for the purpose of devising new schemes.

I also spent a day at the Special Works Park near Wimereux, on the coast. This was the place where the art of camouflage was being worked out. There were two of us and we were not really welcomed, for sufficient reasons. One was that they didn't want to be bothered showing us around, and secondly they didn't know we were coming. So we did the best we could 'on our own'. I started off by falling into a camouflaged gun-pit. This taught us a lesson, so we proceeded warily, as undoubtedly things were not what they seemed. At this time camouflage was in its experimental stage. The well-known artist Solomon J. Solomon was working there. I saw armoured cars painted in various ways in order to find out the best method of deluding the enemy. It was explained that the object of camouflage was not necessarily to conceal, but to destroy identity. We saw parapets of sandbags painted on canvas. Steel trees indistinguishable even at close quarters from real ones. Models of heads mounted on poles from private's to staff officer's. There were 'lifelike' imitation corpses, and dummy guns. Nothing was real. All was trickery, fraud and delusion. A world of sham and make-believe.
LIEUTENANT F.G. HOWKINS RE

The wider authentic landscape of battle incorporating all these aspects of trench warfare is seen in unparalleled detail in the panoramas; the landscape and its meticulous study is the subject of the next two sections.

A fake corpse (German) made by the RE. The 'body' was located in no man's land. Approaching via a sap, the observer lay ensconced in a pit below, with his head inside the dummy, where he could examine the enemy lines through a section of painted gauze. Fake horses were used in the same way.

Photography and Warfare

Photography is one of the most important tools of warfare. Since the Vietnam War, conflicts have increasingly been exposed on our television screens until today we can expect to watch events in 'real time' as they unfold. However, what we see is rarely ever the whole truth. After the initial flurry of live telecasts, the editor steps in. Typifying the modern desire for a sentence or image which 'says it all', we are eventually presented with a set of selected 'bites' to suit this or that event. Thus, conflicts both past and present have been reduced by the media to a handful of 'representative images', judiciously chosen to evoke episode, time and place. The results almost transcend their role as photographs and become firmly fixed in our collective memory as symbolic icons. This is not a new phenomenon; its history reaches back to the beginning of the modern age, and almost to the birth of photography itself.

The photographic tradition and the British Army

The Crimean War (1854–56) was the first British conflict to be photographed. Three hundred and sixty photographs by a civilian practitioner, Roger Fenton, the acknowledged British pioneer of war photography and the first Secretary of the Royal Photographic Society, captured the most notable, celebrated and memorable images of the campaign. Fenton had been sent on a deliberate propaganda exercise to counteract the disturbing reports of military disorganization and ineptitude appearing daily in British newspapers. He was engaged to illustrate the well-being of the troops in a conflict which had become noted for dreadful conditions, disease, and a general lack of concern for the lot of the ordinary soldier. As a civilian Fenton gained access to his subjects by carefully observing the boundaries of his brief. As a result his pictures do not shock; indeed, many were landscapes that include no human life at all. Restricted by a fastest exposure time of around three seconds, the possibility of 'action' shots was entirely ruled out, and the photographs are simple and stark, displaying a carefully 'selected' reality.

The Redan at Sebastopol by James Robertson, 1855

He was followed by another civilian, James Robertson, an engraver from the Royal Mint, who produced a collection of about sixty images, many of which illustrate the legacy of destruction. The experiences and experiments of Fenton and Robertson were to influence the photographers of the first industrial conflict – the American Civil War of 1861–65.

However, before these two men became active in the Crimea, the War Office, in conjunction with the nascent Corps of Royal Engineers, also began to experiment with the new medium. Three men were dispatched to the Crimea: Richard Nicklin, an experienced commercial photographer under military command, and two fully trained sapper assistants, Corporal John Pendered and Lance-Corporal John Hammond. Landing at Balaklava in July 1854, the party pre-dated Fenton's arrival by eight months. But it was to be an ill-fated trip: their ship, *Rip Van Winkle*, carrying both the group and their equipment, foundered in the great storm of 14 November 1854, just before setting sail for the return voyage to England. All three men – and their photographs – perished. Two replacements, Ensigns Brandon and Dawson, were sent out to continue the work, arriving in spring 1855. They too took photographs, but preservation techniques so poorly observed that the results were useless. The negatives were subsequently destroyed, and no written records were retained. It is also worth mentioning that the War Office posted another photographer to the Crimea, a Major Halkett of the 4th Light Dragoons. A clue to the fate of the gallant major lies in the name of his regiment: Halkett lost his life in the Charge of the Light Brigade into the 'Valley of Death' on 25 October 1854. None of his work survives.

It has never been established exactly how many photographs were taken by Nicklin, Pendered and Hammond during their five months in the Crimea, but it is

An RE photograph of Balaklava Harbour, 1856. It was here that the Royal Engineer photographers went down with the *Rip Van Winkle* in the great storm of November 1854.

probable that the images would have been very different to those of Fenton or Robertson. But just how different might their photographs have been? Above all else, as serving soldiers they would have had more access to the battlefield at a time when the fighting was at its height, and the results would would have been for military not public consumption. What is certain, however, is that despite the tragic end to the expedition, it had initiated the beginning of a great tradition of photography in the British Army, with the RE as its main practitioners.

After the critical success of photography in the Crimea (subsequent exhibitions stunned the general public) it was inevitable that other conflicts would be recorded. The American Civil War, covered by Matthew Brady, Timothy O'Sullivan, Alexander Gardner and others, is a prime example. Here, Brady and his contemporaries were allowed access to generals, soldiers and the fields of battle. They recorded the results of Antietam in 1862 and Gettysburg in 1863 in such detail that images of bloated dead brought home the grim authentic nature of modern conflict, and as a result changed public perception of warfare for ever. However, as is so often the case, public interest in the war quickly waned when peace was restored, and the pictures began to lose their marketability; indeed, the complete photographic record could well have been lost at this time. The extraordinary American Civil War collections only survive today because Brady himself paid $25,000 in 1872 to save the archive from destruction.

Engineer photographers

Immediately after the Crimean War the British Army began the serious study of photography and its related sciences. From 1856 it was already a recognized part of the syllabus for selected officers, NCOs and other ranks of the RE at the School of Military Engineering. Founded by Colonel Henry Schaw in 1858, the RE 'Special Schools' included the disciplines of photography and electrical telegraphy. Great developments were quickly made in the former, especially from the year 1871 when Lieutenant (later Captain Sir) William Abney assumed command of the photographic department. Abney was to push back the boundaries of photography, publishing many books and scientific papers, and inventing new processes for reproduction and printing.

An outstanding body of photographic work was completed by the Engineers in the years following the Crimean War, firmly establishing the Corps' high position in the new science, both from a military and an aesthetic viewpoint. As early as the 1860s RE officers were lecturing on the application of photography for military purposes, including the use of photographic survey. A combination of an inquisitiveness for the still nascent technology, and the fact that the sites of many engineering tasks being undertaken around the globe, in both peace and war, were either inaccessible or prohibited to civilian photographers, ensured that the RE had few peers. In the five years following the Crimean War sapper photographers accompanied expeditions to Russia, Turkey, Singapore, Abyssinia (Ethiopia), China, India and Canada. There they experimented with the broad military applications of photography, including multiple reproduction of plans, the provision of illustrations for reports on terrain, the creation of time-lapse images showing the progress of large-scale building and bridging works, and, of course, practical military survey.

Today, the RE archives at Chatham still contain

One of the first photographs ever taken in Tibet. This shows a section of the road cut by Royal Engineers in 1856 joining China and India for the first time.

Taku Fort, one of the great Chinese emplacements captured in during 1860/Second Opium War. Note the forests of sharpened bamboo stakes guarding each parallel moat. Photographed by Lt J. A. Papillon RE.

both 'active service' photographs and those taken in times of peace when the Corps was occupied in some of the most notable and impressive engineering schemes in history. There are records of expeditions such as the surveys of Palestine, India, Ireland, North China and Somaliland, as well as dozens of Boundary Commissions, including the 49th Parallel expedition to define the border between Canada and the United States. There are also pictorial records of the building and repair (by the RE themselves) of cathedrals, dams, harbours, theatres, prisons, museums, canals and bridges across the world. The Engineers were also singled out

Crimean wounded in Fort Pitt Hospital, Chatham, 1855. Private William Young (left) lost his legs to shellfire. The limbs of Privates Richard Burland (left) and John Connery were victims of frostbite. The men have just been presented with artificial limbs by Queen Victoria.

to make photographic facsimiles of the Domesday Book, and a huge range of specially selected rare documents and maps from the National Records of England and Scotland. Strangely, despite the extraordinary quality, diversity and scale of the RE collections, they still remain largely unknown.

By the end of the nineteenth century technology had moved photography onto a different plane. Cameras had shrunk in size and weight and exposure times decreased, first from minutes to seconds, then to fractions of a second. Processing had been simplified by the replacement in around 1880 of the wet collodion-based system by the dry gelatin-coated photographic plate. This method was practically instantaneous, which meant that the coveted action shot was obtainable at last. Not only did the advance allow military photographers to work far more easily on the ground, it also gave them the ability to exploit the new dimension of free and captive balloons. The results were similar to the aerial 'obliques' of the First World War, themselves a kind of panorama.

The first active use of photographic ground reconnaissance was made by the REs in South Africa during the Boer War, 1899–1902:

A man-carrying kite. Originally the idea of the American Colonel William Cody (Buffalo Bill), this unusual method of observation was the subject of many tests by REs.

An example from the earliest known collection of forensic photographs, taken by the RE in 1855.

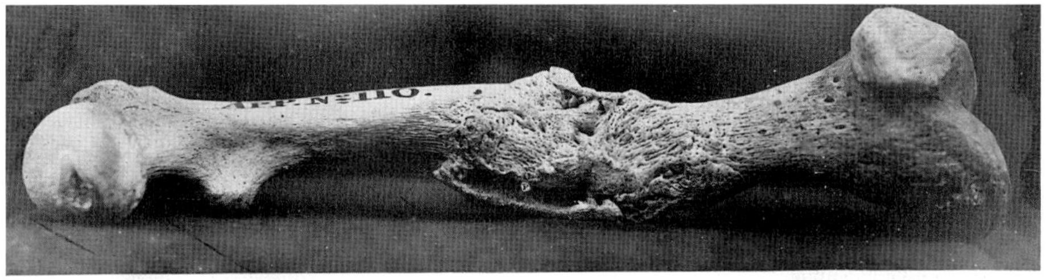

For the first time in history the telephotographer is about to play his part – it may be a very important part – in warfare. 2nd Corpl. Ford, of the Royal Engineers, Chatham, has been detailed as telephotographer to the army in South Africa, and has sailed from Southampton with his cycle and apparatus. Corpl. Ford's camera, which is fitted with "telephoto" lenses, is a wonderful machine, which will take a clear photograph of a man, or battery, or entrenchments at any distance up to two miles. So that beyond the range of the enemy's rifles Corpl. Ford will be able to get photographs of their positions, which should prove of great value.
Daily Mail, 5 DECEMBER 1900

The 'telephotographic' unit consisted of two men and a bicycle (in case of rough ground the bicycle could be replaced by a pony), with panniers for the camera and developing equipment, and a tent which doubled as a dark room. The *Daily Mail*, which was also able to publish a photograph of both man and kit thanks to the invention of another significant advance, the 'half-tone' printing process, went on to provide details of the equipment.

This special apparatus was devised by Lt. Foulkes RE and made up by the London Stereoscopic Company. It is fixed to Corporal Ford's bicycle in such small compass as to be hardly noticeable, and the whole thing is painted the familiar khaki colour.
Daily Mail, 5 DECEMBER 1900

Writing in 1957 as a retired major-general, Foulkes (who in 1916 had been Director of Gas Services – the RE 'Special Companies') outlined a typical mission.

Lance-Corporal Ford and his pony, fitted with panniers for carrying camera equipment over rough ground; the bicycle was employed over smoother terrain.

Commissioning photograph of C. H. Foulkes, 1898.

I then took a panoramic photograph of Taiboschlaagte and noted where the sangars were visible on the skyline etc., and was preparing to fit in the telephoto lens to record a 'nek' in which a field gun was supposed to be mounted when a small party of Boers began to gallop in my direction; so I had to pack up hastily and ride back under cover of rifle fire from the Inniskillings. Boer marksmanship was, I think, greatly exaggerated, and at long range it was very poor.
MAJOR-GENERAL FOULKES, *Royal Engineers Journal*, 1957

Fifteen years after the Boer War military photography – the strategic photography of landscape – was commonplace. The foundations for its use in the looming global conflict had been laid. When war came in August 1914, the General Staff knew they need turn to only one corps for photographic reconnaissance: the Royal Engineers.

Photographing the First World War

Photographic technology advanced in leaps during the final few decades of the nineteenth century. Cameras became smaller and lighter, and by 1910 several models were simple and portable enough to be used by the untrained amateur, most now employing roll film as opposed to glass plates. Taking pictures had become cheap, fashionable and popular. By 1914, many future British soldiers, particularly of the 'officer class', were either already adept at photography or had purchased cameras on mobilization to record their part in what was expected to be a war of short but glorious duration. As a result, the first year of the First World War was prolifically recorded by amateur photographers.

It has been estimated that one in five British officers carried a VPK – Vest Pocket Kodak – or a similar compact camera during the first seven or so months of the war. These men captured some of the most memorable images at a time when the 'over by Christmas' spirit, be it 1914 or 1915, still persisted. Their

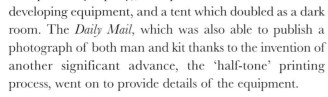

An early telescopic observation tower. RE HQ, Chatham, 1856.

Another RE pioneering photograph: an early example of aerial photography. Taken from a balloon above the Citadel of Halifax, Nova Scotia, 1883.

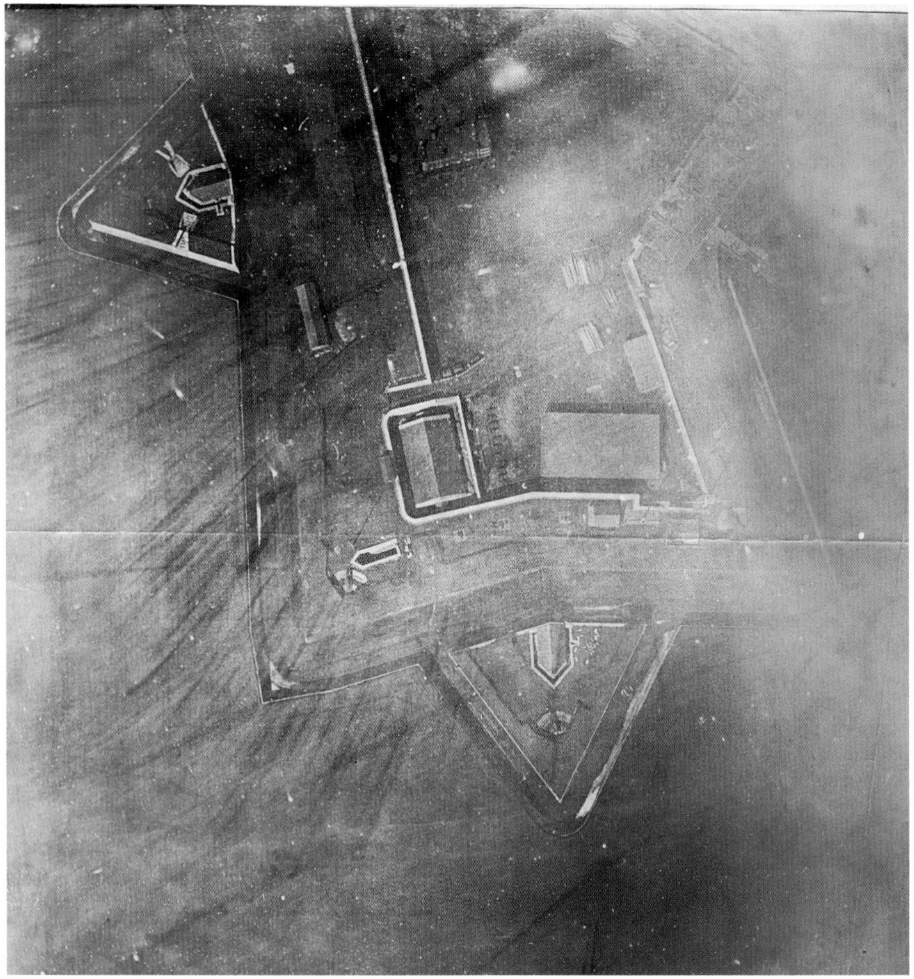

pictures were the first uncensored record, not only of the activities, appearance and attitude of the troops, but also the landscape of the early Western Front, and many a periodical bought in both pictures and story for publication, usually attributed to 'an officer at the front'. The era of intense military suspicion and censorship had not yet dawned.

Gentlemen of the press accompanied the soldiers of the BEF when they arrived in France in 1914. From the first day, 4 August, photography had been recognized as a potent journalistic weapon that could be wielded for propaganda and counter-propaganda purposes. Many periodicals, such as *War Illustrated*, *War Budget* and *Illustrated War News*, were launched specifically to recount the story – with photographs. These and many other established papers clamoured for images, even 'toothless' photographs which told the viewer little about the nature of the war soon supplanted the traditional preference for *Illustrated London News* style presentation featuring artistic impressions supported by the written word. By the end of the war almost every publication had converted to photographs.

Whilst the press in Britain were stifled by censorship, they also maintained a certain code of conduct regarding the 'suitability' of pictorial content, even during the first year of war when private photographs were still available. Images of casualties, those of the enemy included, were uncommon. Whereas lightly wounded (and cheery) men were considered suitable subjects, mangled corpses certainly were not, but this was a result of simple consideration for relatives combined with a sense of good taste, rather than deliberate suppression by the authorities. Pictures of casualties were certainly published, particularly in the early months, but they were carefully selected to illustrate an apparently swift, clean and 'serene' demise – the composure of the British soldier even in death. Day after day pictorial papers such as the *Daily Mail*, *Daily Mirror* and *Daily Sketch* showed images of confident troops, and activities in rear areas such as the loading of ships and vehicles, and horses and men supplying the guns. Photographs taken behind the lines were staged to illustrate combat: manning machine guns, rifle pits and the like; their jaunty peaked service dress caps so different from the sinister spiked *pickelhaube* helmets of the enemy. Ex-press photographers in uniform rarely had the opportunity to take snaps under combat conditions; the very few exceptions, at Ypres and later in the Dardanelles, provided a tremendous (and genuine) sense of battlefield tension.

Things began to change in June 1915 when a modification to British policy on photography at the front was made:

We hear that we are to be restricted to one camera in each battalion. I suppose I shall have to rely upon Trotter for pictures to send to you from now on, as he has been awarded the dubious honour.
LIEUTENANT R. O. SKEGGS, 3RD BATTALION, RIFLE BRIGADE.

This War Office intervention, voluntary at first, brought a sharp decrease in the number of cameras at the front, and it was at this time that the 'official' photographer began to come into his own. Eventually sixteen men, mostly professionals with a journalistic background, were employed as official photographers on the Western Front. The static nature of trench warfare presented conditions that eminently favoured their work, and each found an endless supply of subject matter in the huge diversity of everyday activities among the multi-cultural, multi-national and multi-talented units of the British Empire. As time passed, and the siege-like conditions expanded both on the ground and in the minds of the military, the authorities became ever more concerned about careless broadcasting of information; by the

The Ministry of Information shop where civilians could buy battlefield images passed by the censor.

end of 1915 concern had been superceded by paranoia, and having a camera on active service had was a court-martial offence.

From 1916 onwards, British official photography became highly structured and regulated, and was steered by a policy of 'propaganda of the facts'. This showed the British people the truth, albeit in a carefully sanitized fashion. Engaged directly by the War Office, official photographers were enlisted to tell the story that the authorities wished the people to see. Although many pictures are quite clearly posed, the pictures were usually taken at the front (or near it) or in training, so there was no 'real' fakery involved. They concentrated mainly on the 'ordinary', focusing, like Fenton in the Crimea, on groups or individuals who represented the fit and happy spirit of the wider collective. The identities of individuals, unless decorated or of high rank, were seldom recorded, and the ordinary British soldier seems to have been left deliberately anonymous. This strategy suggests the deliberate portrayal of a generic 'Tommy Atkins', a man representing the whole of the British Army – cheery and stoic, and unbending in devotion to duty. 'Tommy' is contextualized in pictures of battalions of smiling and cheering men marching to the front, and tired but eternally confident men on their way out of action.

A typically grisly example of German postcard propaganda from the Ypres battlefield.

The infrastructure and technology of trench warfare, new to a public hungry for details of what it was really like to be 'at the front', was well covered by the official photographers. Again forming a context for Tommy Atkins, soldiers are shown feeding the guns, feeding themselves, feeding their prisoners (humanely), and writing, reading, raising a glass in an estaminet, and most often of all simply transporting the paraphernalia of this most engineered of all wars.

What of the enemy? The German attitude to photography was quite unlike that of the British. By promoting a curious form of voluntary propaganda, they supplemented the 'message' contained within official photographs: from the outset German soldiers of all ranks were actively encouraged to 'snap' their comrades in the line to illustrate the spirit, confidence and welfare of the troops. The results were often printed as postcards to be sent home to families and friends. At the same time they were equally encouraged to photograph enemy dead – in all states, the more grisly the better – as proof of the futility of attempting to penetrate German lines. A great many examples of truly macabre picture postcards of this kind have survived, although their historical significance has perhaps also yet to be fully recognized.

The photographs required by the Army, however, were entirely different to those craved by the general public. Here, no message was required – reconnaissance was the sole objective. Only three categories existed: aerial pictures from aeroplanes, aerial obliques taken from balloons – and the military panorama. The stage was set for the first widespread use of all three in global warfare.

After the Second Battle of Ypres. A German postcard of an English trench and dead at S'Gravenstafel.

The Panorama Goes to War

The word panorama has Greek roots: *pan*, meaning all, and *horama*, view. It was no coincidence that its English coinage appeared in the final decades of the eighteenth century at the same time as a new type of painting. In a 360-degree depiction of the city of Edinburgh, the Irish artist Robert Barker (1739–1806) attempted to create a picture in which the viewer was 'immersed' and 'all seeing'. In 1796 a patent was granted for his system of representing a 'surround-landscape'. The panorama was destined to become one of the great mass-medium successes of the century, and was soon applied to images of the natural world, foreign cities, and historical events. Ultimately, buildings were to be specially designed to house the great paintings of those following Barker's lead.

Painted panoramas differ from other 'long views' such as the Bayeux Tapestry, which was effectively a chronological device to describe the development and outcome of an historical event. Instead they convey the character of a place or incident at any one given moment, and are therefore 'snapshots' frozen in time. The panorama was born at a time when it was not routinely possible for people, particularly the middle and lower social classes, to obtain a view of the world 'without boundaries'. Today, towers, skyscrapers and air travel fulfil our desires to see to the very edges of the horizon, an almost maritime tradition, but in the eighteenth and nineteenth centuries achieving this, particularly from within the confines of a city or restricted lowland countryside, was almost impossible. Unsurprisingly, consequent upon and contemporary with the growth of interest in panoramas of all types, came the development of towers and tall buildings, such as the Eiffel Tower in Paris.

Soon after the invention of photography in 1839 the same desire to capture and exhibit huge images prompted early practitioners to produce photographic panoramas. The nineteenth-century public were equally spellbound by the diversity and scale of this novel work as their antecedents had been by painted images. The earliest photographic panorama, produced in the 1840s, employed a set of separate Daguerrotype pictures arranged in overlapping sequence. Daguerrotypes, the first commercially available prints, were a revelation, but by 1885 advances in cameras and developing technology allowed much finer quality examples to be made. A huge public appetite grew for expansive urban and rural views, industry, interiors, and of course group portraits. Soon, galleries were exhibiting works showing strange and foreign lands with amazing countryside and cityscapes. To further increase the fascination, panoramas were often complemented by stills of (to Western eyes) bizarre societies, rituals and characters, and equally extraordinary flora and fauna – views that just a handful of people might experience first hand.

A 'home front' panorama taken from a tower on what is today the Royal Engineer Museum building in Chatham. The picture, from 1917, shows part of an area known as 'The Lines' arranged for trench warfare practice. The fenced-off zone contains dugouts and tunnels.

The replacement of painted panoramas by photographs began during the years of the Crimean War. French photographers had also been working in the region after the fall of Sebastopol, and Colonel Charles Langlois, an artist who had already exhibited painted panoramas, chose to use photography as the basis for his next great canvas. A series of pictures taken from the heights of the Malakoff fortress by professional photographer Léon Méhedin were used as the foundation for Langlois' celebrated panoramic painting 'The Taking of Sebastopol', exhibited in Paris in 1860 to massive public acclaim. The photo-based picture triggered an interest within both the military and the public. By the end of the nineteenth century the invention of relatively cheap hand-held cameras had taken this presentational style one step further: it allowed an amateur photographer to produce his own personal panoramas.

The panorama and the First World War

By September 1914 military photographers were already being asked for quality images of the landscape, and several panoramic views of the Aisne Valley battlefront were produced. Compared to later examples they show little – trenches can barely be seen in the far distance – but as a record of a pastoral landscape the pictures did what all later panoramas were able to do: instruct a remote viewer in the nature of a battlefield.

The earliest use of panoramic photography in the First World War, although using different photographic techniques – roll film as opposed to glass plates – was in capturing images of soldier groups, up to multi-battalion strength, for regimental records. However, it was in portraying the scene beyond the parapet, a view highly dangerous under normal conditions, that the panorama came into its own. The static Western Front was to be a surveyor's and reconnaissance expert's paradise.

Military panoramas: type and requirement

Panoramas became an integral part of the routine of trench warfare. Their value was determined by the nature of the conflict, but their purpose, in the simplest of terms,

Aerial photographs used to survey changes in enemy wire defences were particularly successful after snowfall. This is a vertical example.

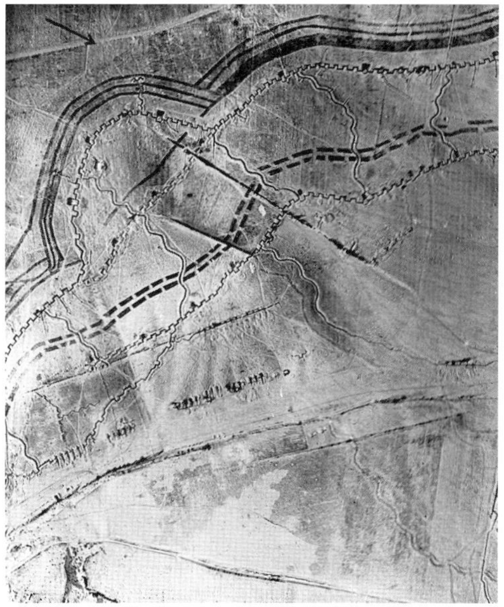

was to allow a company commander in charge of a section of line to examine an area he was unable to inspect personally except at the risk of a sniper's bullet.

Trench warfare proscribed that the time available for relatively safe investigation of no man's land and enemy defences was restricted to the hours of darkness, a situation that clearly had its drawbacks in gathering data for maps and plans that demanded the finest detail: information such as grass length, depths of depressions, and width of streams. The ubiquitous trench periscopes and loopholes, although widely used for observation, were less than satisfactory for photo-topographical work.

Aerial photography was undoubtedly the most valuable reconnaissance tool available to the Army during the war, indeed it was indispensable in helping to precisely

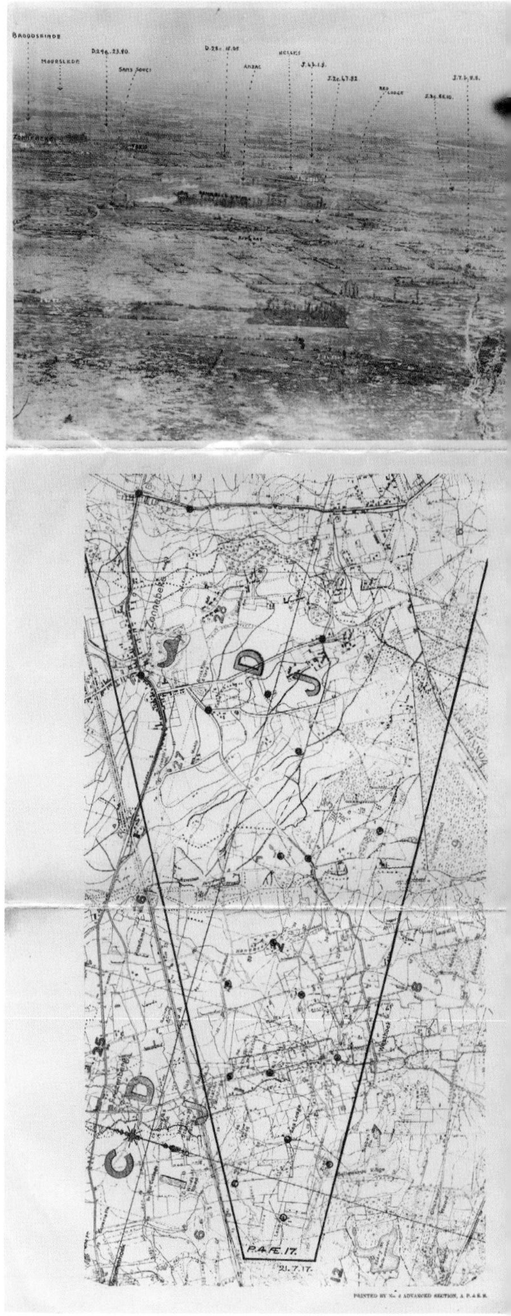

An aerial reconnaissance 'oblique', showing the Zonnebeke sector on 21 July 1917.

plot new features on trench maps, and spot fresh developments in defensive schemes. Aerials were particularly valuable when planning a raid or more substantial attack that required the temporary capture of enemy support or reserve positions – positions that were easily distinguished from the air. However, on a battlefield where the slightest fold in the ground could mean the difference between life and death for scores of men, a photograph taken from an aircraft high above the trenches offered inadequate local detail, and was subsequently of limited use. A further aspect was required, one with a wide field of view and maximum definition of features, taken from a location close to the front lines – in short, a panorama.

But what kind? Until the Boer War most had been hand-drawn. Following Foulkes' work there was a choice to be made. The RE considered that military panoramas fell into three classes:

1. Rapid sketches to be used in mobile warfare, for reports on positions, etc. Prior to 1914 the skills necessary to produce drawn panoramic sketches were an integral part of a RE surveyor's training. However, during the First World War drawn panoramas were almost completely superseded by photographs.
2. Panoramas intended to give a clear general idea of the landscape and nature of the country and tactical features for the use of commanders.
3. Panoramas for the exact identification of the position of targets or points of military importance.

It may come as a surprise to many, but the question as to which kind of panorama, drawn or photographed, was best fitted to trench warfare was never really resolved. Each was better suited to certain conditions. The ideal situation would have been to have an example of both formats every time a panorama was requested, but this was an unreasonable expectation.

On a battleground the size of the Western Front it was inevitable that photographic panoramas replaced, to a great extent, the drawn, for the simple reason that photographers were almost always available whereas trained and skilled panoramic draughtsmen were not. There was also a more practical explanation: a surveyor making a long and comprehensive sketch would potentially be in enemy view for a dangerously extended period. By necessity of course, the photographer also had to conceal or camouflage himself to carry out his hazardous task, but he was not as constantly exposed as the draughtsman. Fields of view are often seen to be interrupted by roof timbers, battle debris, trees and undergrowth or sandbags – even grave markers in one instance – but once the camera had been set up and levelled, the only exposure to enemy view came when plates were changed and the camera rotated. The rest of the time a photographer could keep his head down.

What infantry commanders would have liked to do during the long period of static warfare. An observer follows enemy movements during the advance to victory in 1918.

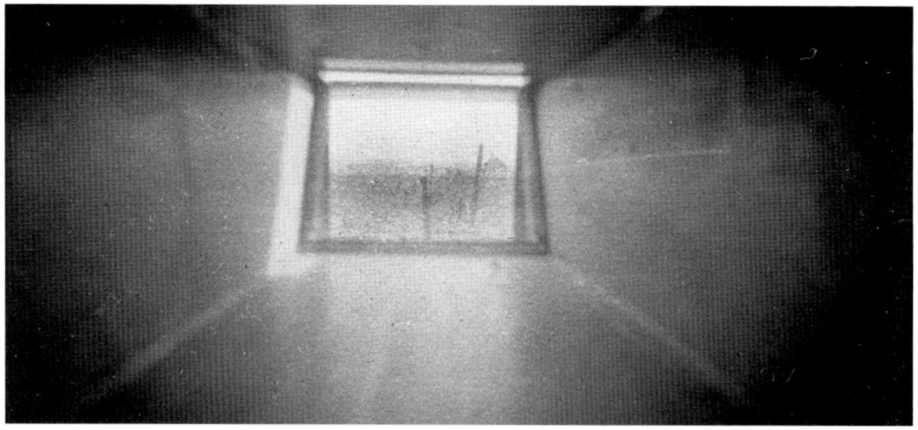

A view through a trench periscope on the Wez Macquart front. The limitations for photographic observation are obvious.

The main drawback to the photograph compared to the sketch was that unwanted detail could not be omitted, and in certain examples this made examination of content extremely awkward – there was too much extraneous and worthless visual information. On the other hand the drawn panorama, despite having the advantage of content selection, always relied upon a representation of the landscape as seen through the eyes of another person, rather than the absolute reality. Ultimately, neither was perfect.

The manuals stated that panoramas, drawn or otherwise, were required to possess certain essential characteristics:

1. They should eliminate all artistic and atmospheric effect; accuracy and freedom from ambiguity being the chief requirements.
2. They should be clearer than the original landscape, and as a rule accentuate features of military importance.
3. They should omit unnecessary detail, especially in the foreground.
4. They should represent the facts, not the author's interpretation of them.

If all these demands were met, a panorama when used in conjunction with aerial photographs and trench maps gave the commander in the field the most concise picture of his sector – short of climbing from the trench and examining the terrain at his leisure.

Panoramas and photographers at the front

Of the many photographs used by the British during the war, panoramas remained the most secret. They obviously had to be taken from various positions behind or within the front lines, so clear and uninterrupted views into the rear of British lines were unavoidable. They consequently provided a great deal of detailed information of precisely the type the enemy aspired to possess, and were thus rigorously guarded.

With this in mind every panoramic photograph was printed with the following cautionary rubric:

1. Panoramas are taken solely for military purposes.
2. The publication of them in the press will neccessarily give valuable information to the enemy.
3. This panorama is to be kept with as much security as is compatible with full advantage of it being taken by our own troops.
4. When troops are relieved this panorama should be handed over to the relieving troops.

These instructions further illustrate the differences between official stills and panoramas. They were not for public consumption and were never made available to the press. It is ironic that the Army took so much care to prohibit private photography, censor letters and control reporting, yet inadvertently produced an almost perfect historical record of the appearance of the First World War battlefields for posterity. However, the photographer himself had perhaps little knowledge or indeed concern that his work would ultimately form such a significant archive.

The most popular camera for panorama work was the 5x4 inch Panros manufactured by Ross and Co. at the Optical Works, Clapham Common, London. Early in the war a Ross had been tested in the field by the Headquarters of the Royal Engineers Printing Company, and later each topographical section was supplied with one. Variations and improvements in equipment were proposed and tested by the RE throughout the war, but the Panros remained the favoured kit. Fitted with a telephoto lens with three focal lengths of 76, 45 and 30 cm (30, 18 and 12 in), altered according to the quality of the light, the camera, which used glass plates rather than roll film, was mounted on a special tripod that had been manufactured with graduated arcs and pointers to assist the photographer in aligning each separate photograph with its neighbour.

Lieutenant OGS Crawford's Panros camera after treatment by a German sniper.

With snipers being the major threat for anyone operating above or through the parapet, the need for compact equipment was paramount. It might often take an hour to capture the many images (up to thirty) needed to construct the required wide field of view, and the task was neither simple nor safe. Having selected the site, made use of whatever camouflage was locally available and set up the tripod, the delicate process of photography began.

My duties involved the taking of panorama photographs from observation posts and from the front line, and I made quite a hobby of it, covering the front from Gommecourt to the Somme, and then later from Gommecourt to Vimy Ridge. The distance was about 40 miles and I took exactly one hundred photographs. I had to find my own viewpoints and got to know the country intimately. I had several narrow shaves. On one occasion I was taking a panorama from the front line south of Fricourt. It was a lengthy business, involving anything up to a dozen or more exposures of several seconds each, between which the plate had to be changed. The camera revolved on a graded tripod and to get the best view and the camera level one had to expose one's self. On this occasion, instead of exposing myself as usual, I was using a little periscope received only the day before as a gift from

Crawford and his assistant prepare to take a panorama from a front line trench in the Arras sector. The dangerous nature of the operation is evident in the body language.

Wellcome. A sniper had seen me and he aimed a shot which hit the corner of the camera, just missing the periscope. It was another lucky escape, for if I had not been using the periscope I might well have been hit in the head … which was a bigger target.
O. G. S. CRAWFORD

Whether positioned in the front line, in a church tower, or halfway up a factory chimney, like all other panoramic photographers at the front Crawford was forced to become a part of the landscape in order to carry out his work. The following episode relates to Somme panorama number 304.

We had the Field Survey unit that I had joined. I was the map officer for it. I was with the Fifth Army in front of Bapaume [on the Somme]. We were attacking on either side but more particularly on the south side of the Ancre Valley, and I remember being sent to take a panorama. In early October 1916 we had captured a place called Stuff Redoubt, and from Stuff Redoubt you got a very good view up the Ancre Valley, and they wanted me to take a panorama of this. I remember putting my little tripod, I don't know if it was exactly on the parapet of the trench but it was in that sort of position. And then the camera swivelled round and you had marks to show you how much to twist the camera. And of course the camera was a plate camera requiring a long exposure, and you'd take the cap off and count seconds, and put the cap on again, then turn the thing a little bit, pass the plate down to the photographer and he would hand up the next one and I'd put that in position. It seemed to take an eternity going slowly round the arc.

I don't know if it was that occasion or some other panorama I took, but I remember coming to number thirteen, and I said to my photographer "I'm not going to expose this one, hand up the next one!" The only time I've ever given in to that superstition.

I handed in the panorama to the staff when it was stuck together and somebody else added in all the things you could see. Somebody who knew something of what the country looked like. This was done by the printing and stationery section at the base.
LIEUTENANT TRESSILIAN C. NICHOLAS

After developing, the 5x4 prints were enlarged to 10x8 inches, printed on paper, and 'stitched together' (overlapped and glued) to create a complete image; when rolled up they were an easy item to carry, use and store. The finished article would include details of the photographer's location, giving map reference and name of observation post if applicable, the date and occasionally the time of production, the total field of view in degrees, plus an indication of its orientation on the compass face; often a scale (one degree equals X inches on the panorama) was noted. In some armies the relevant portion of a 1:10,000 scale trench map was attached to the finished print, upon which the camera location and angle of view were clearly marked.

The many well-annotated examples are especially useful from an historical perspective, but there are a surprising number of completely unmarked, and indeed unidentified, panoramas. These require a detailed knowledge of the landscape of the Western Front and a close familiarity with the rest of the collection to place th eimage topographically. However, after years of cataloguing and study one finds oneself doing precisely that which the interpreters of 1914–18 did: spotting differences in the shape of hills and ridges, the detail of buildings, profiles of church spires, peculiarly formed (or rather deformed) trees, the appearance of trench sections, the trace of a footpath, or the grouping of pillboxes.

Panoramas and the Royal Engineers

Particularly unfortunate for posterity is the loss of the original war diaries (and their duplicates) of the three RE Field Survey Companies (FSC) employed on panoramic work. We know little of who the photographers were, how many worked in each sector, or what their fate was. O. G. S. Crawford's autobiography supports the assumption that one panorama unit was allocated to each army in the BEF, but overlapping of territories and exchange of personnel clearly occurred, as during his service Crawford himself worked on two different army fronts.

For the British Army, the task of taking panoramas for reconnaissance was to

Panorama S-83 of March 1918 showing part of the Salonika theatre – the dramatic terrain around Lake Doiran.

be largely the responsibility of the FSC map or printing officer, although occasionally an NCO or even an ordinary sapper might be offered the job if sufficiently qualified and experienced. As a rule only one officer and an assistant were necessary for each army. The results of their labours were developed, printed, stitched and annotated in France by the Army Printing and Stationery Service (AP&SS). For some reason best known to the Army, drawn panoramas, which were produced in lesser numbers than photographs, were reproduced in Southampton.

Throughout the war the RE sought improvement and greater efficiency in all their duties. Photography did not escape attention. Some of the foremost creative initiatives came from Captain Bernard Wilbraham RE during his period as OC Printing Company. Early in the war Wilbraham continued the engineer tradition of experimentation: he tested stereoscopic cameras, and in 1916 designed his own Periscopic Field Camera. It was intended both to capture stills for single images and multiple shots for composite panoramas. Both systems were based upon Ross equipment, and were largely successful. Stereoscopic pictures were soon considered to have a limited application however, and dropped, but several Survey Companies continued to be supplied with various adaptations of his periscope apparatus. Wilbraham rose to command 1st Field Survey Battalion RE, and ended the war as a lieutenant-colonel with a DSO.

Annotation – the handwritten or printed identification of important points within an image – was and remains enormously important in assisting the viewer in orientation and recognition. The author, who has struggled with many unannotated examples, can vouch for the fact that this process must have taken time, particularly with an extensive panorama built up of a large number of composite images. If the picture had been produced especially for the use of artillery, it invariably carried much more information than those supplied to infantry units, naming potential targets as well as the usual topographical highlights, and providing a carefully estimated distance in yards to each one. In some examples the whole image was provided with a grid to further assist the gunlayers.

An observation balloon being prepared for ascent with the assistance of Australian troops. Unlike aeroplane pilots, the crew were issued with parachutes.

A typical trench map (here seen folded). Almost 40 million examples of varying scales were printed during the war.

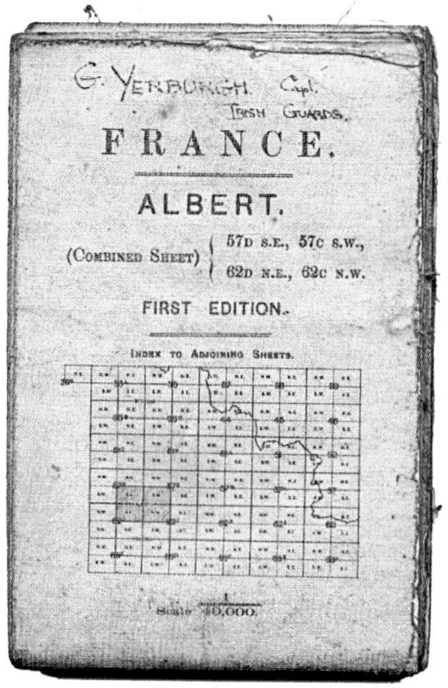

The Imperial War Museum panoramas cover all the British sectors of the Western Front, and others besides: a smaller series on the Salonika and Italian theatres uniquely depict the dramatic terrain of the battlefields. The whole collection consists of more than a thousand separate panoramas, each being constructed from three to thirty single stills. The shortest image is approximately 0.3 m (1 ft) in length, and the longest almost 4 m (13 ft). Chronologically, they span almost the entire duration of the war, from a view of the Aisne Valley on 15 September 1914, to the Dickebusch sector of the Ypres Salient in September 1918, just before the advance to victory. Although taken on different dates throughout the war, careful selection and sequencing could produce a complete and unbroken overlapping image of the entire landscape of battle between Boesinge, north of Ypres, to the River Somme. By far the most awkward examples to identify are those which are not only unnanotated but have been printed back to front, so that the entire 'stitched' image is reversed. They are surprisingly common. On digitizing and horizontally 'flipping' the image however, the scene is often (but not always) instantly recognizable.

The panoramic perspective

Whilst not detracting from the value of both official stills and official movies of the First World War, the immense historical merits of the panoramas, particularly when appearing so long after the event, are immediately apparent. An instant impression is the panorama's illustration in many cases of the dominance of the higher German positions. Beyond this well-documented aspect it is the sheer scale of the image that predominates. In no other photograph is the observer able to examine the whole of a battlefield from a viewpoint that does not confuse the eye. Aerial photographs of the Western Front require practice and experience to be used effectively, and to most people carry an 'other-worldy' feel, rather like looking at the surface of the moon. It takes practice to generate the required familiarity for swift comprehension, whereas panoramas, reproducing the view of the relaxed observer, demand only a trench map and the knowledge of how to plot a map reference.

In trench warfare both still and movie format photography laboured under major restrictions which limited their ability to adequately record the terrain for detailed tactical assessment. Still photographs are arguably the most critical resource for understanding the First World War today, but few provide genuinely useful views of the fields of battle. In a trench the photographer is habitually below ground level and the field of view narrow; this confinement means that only very localized detail can be included, offering little or no clue as to the ground being held, defended or attacked. Moving images predominantly provide views of the rear areas, with many sequences purporting to be taken at and near the front being either posed, faked or lacking sufficient clarity for close study. No such restrictions applied to panoramas.

Typically, fields of view ranged from 30 degrees to an extraordinary 165 degrees. As a general rule the narrower the field of view, the closer to the front line the photographer's location. Indeed, many panoramas were taken within fifty metres of the German trenches. In examples with a wide field, particularly if the observation position was elevated (which was always desirable and always attempted) many dozens of square kilometres of battlefield can be examined. Furthermore, the static nature of trench warfare allowed the same photographic location to be used on several separate occasions, often over a period of many months. This process produces a fascinating 'time lapse' effect which in certain sectors reveals the growth of trench systems, alterations and additions to defences, the changing nature of the battlefield long before battle was joined, and ultimately, when it did begin, the efficacy of the artillery and the gradual devastation of the landscape.

At the same time as showing some areas remaining almost undamaged throughout the war, the painfully slow rate of advance of the major offensives is also clearly illustrated, as is the extreme narrowness of the area of destruction caused by creeping barrages and day-to-day artillery fire. The latter is strongly marked in panoramas taken from high ground behind the lines in the Ypres Salient: for three years only a very narrow ribbon of damage is seen snaking along the slopes of the ridges; in most places it is only in 1918 that it substantially expands beyond the immediate front line area The pictures also illustrate the concentration and surprising accuracy of artillery during offensives. For example, the ruins of the same church may be visible in a similar location in a sequence of panoramas taken at different times during a battle. The ruins remain as the recognizable point of reference, but in each subsequent panorama the destruction, particularly in the foreground and middle distance, can be seen to increase until it even impedes the viewer's ability to discern the season. However, a glance just beyond the battle zone, beyond the middle distance, often reveals relatively undamaged houses, church spires, hedgerows and trees – and the season immediately becomes evident once more. This effect is seldom reproduced in aerial pictures as the photographers concentrated vertical shots of strictly limited zones. The panoramas also take the action one stage further by illustrating the immediate repair of the landscape and the installation of communications infrastructure as soon as ground is secured.

An iconic First World War photograph: Chateau Wood, 1917, by Official Australian Photographer Frank Hurley whose diary reveals that shortly before this episode he had been complaining about dust!

Possibly the most reproduced photograph of the war: William Rider-Rider's image of Canadian machinegunners near Passchendaele in autumn 1917.

In official stills the wider landscape is sometimes camouflaged in favour of atmosphere and message, and the viewer's eye is guided to what the photographer wants us to see and feel. Two of the most famous First World War photographs are illustrative: William Rider-Rider's Canadian machine gunners on the Passchendaele Ridge and Frank Hurley's Australian artillerymen in Chateau Wood. In these images the soldiers clearly know the camera is present. Equally clearly one may see that they have been asked to respond by either remaining stationary, looking into the lens, or both. Producing both these photographs therefore required a degree of direction, compositional deliberation, and framing; the desired atmosphere and message was thus formed. The following passage from Guy Chapman's *A Passionate Prodigality* is illustrative. The men he describes are worn out and traumatized following their ordeal at La Boisselle on 1 July 1916, the first day of the Battle of the Somme.

They lay stretched on the hillside, their uniforms daubed with chalk, their faces and hands brown with mud, their hair tangled and their unshaven cheeks bloodless, the colour of dirty parchment, just as they had fallen in attitudes of complete exhaustion. Every now and then a figure moaned or beat the air with his hand. I found Cuthbertson engaged in an elaborate toilet. Even he who was ever the mirror of fashion was unkempt. 'We went up that night,' he said, 'and got orders to attack at half past eight in the morning, to the right of and above La Boisselle' ... While he talked there was a sudden stir. A few men rose, others woke and joined them, collecting in a mob round a khaki figure with a camera. Pickelhaubes, German helmets, Teutonic forage caps, leaf-shaped bayonets, automatics, were produced from haversacks. The faces which ten minutes earlier had seemed those of dying men were now alight with excited amusement. 'Come on, come on an' have your picture took,' echoed from man to man: and amid much cheering, the official press was obliged with a sitting.

In panoramas the care taken in concealment of the photographer and camera, and the lack of interest in the surrounding troop activities meant that soldiers more often than not had no idea they were a part of the scene – indeed, they continued to be a part of the landscape.

Relatively few panoramas contain figures, and only a handful include visible casualties. A large proportion show pastoral scenes that seems incongruous to the modern observer imbued with 'classic' iconic images and writings of the First World War – rain, mud, death, destruction. An illustration of this is provided by a random event during the cataloguing of these photographs. On a table in the Imperial War Museum reading room lay an open panorama of the St Julien area of the Ypres Salient. The immediate response of another researcher – an historian of note and certainly an 'informed' viewer – was to question why such pictures were taken after the war. It later became apparent that, for this observer, the assumption that the photo was post-war was based on two things only: the lack of troops – and the absence of mud! His subsequent surprise when the date was uncovered – September 1917 – illustrates why the panoramas may have such an influence on First World War studies. Although highly experienced, his knowledge that the survival philosophy of the average soldier during daylight was to make himself as invisible as possible was clouded by the scale, content and detail of the image, and an unfamiliarity with the panoramic format. Although the photograph irrefutably revealed the true nature of the landscape at that location and at that particular point in time, over many years he had already formed his own mental image through the influence of figure-based stills, aerials, the printed word, trench maps and regular trips to the battlefields. If this was the Third Battle of Ypres, then there must be total devastation, oceans of mud, thousands of weary troops, and wall-to-wall corpses of man and beast.

The soldiers he thought to see were indeed there, but they had simply become a part of the landscape in order to survive – if this observer could not see them nor could the enemy! In fact every panorama seethes with invisible humanity, it is just that our willing acceptance of received wisdom seems to lead to a cheating of the imagination. This aspect gives the panoramas a unique sense of mystery. What we see is very often not what we have been led to believe. The inclusion of any humanity in an image, just a single soldier, is relatively rare, even with very widest fields of view. And when troops are evident it is clear that they are entirely incidental; indeed, the RE considered them to be a form of unwanted 'adventitious detail' – a distraction. It was solely the landscape that mattered.

In the light of earlier observations it is also important to illustrate the scale of the panorama collection. The total number of stills taken by official photographers is estimated to be around 30,000; if the composite panoramas are broken down into single stills they would number approximately 12,000 images. If emphasis were needed to illustrate the importance of the collection, it might be done with this statistic alone. However, the collection can never stand alone as a separate archive. In combining the photographic forms of amateur 'snaps', official stills and tactical panoramas, we are able for the first time since 1918 to visually remove the First World War soldier from a localized and restricted environment, the composition of which may be loaded with symbolism, and confidently place him in the true and unbiased milieu in which he lived, fought and died.

Having made the case for the importance of the panorama collection, it now must be said that their application was severely limited; on a mobile front they were quite useless, except perhaps as a record; for instance, none exist in the IWM collection which were taken during the advance to victory in 1918. One of the problems the Army had to face was the desire on the part of officers to preserve meaningful mementoes for themselves, and also to show the 'folks at home' where they had served. Stills could do this to a certain extent, but panoramas made by far the most splendid 'souvenirs'.

Until the advance to victory in September 1918 panoramas continued to play a very secret and important though underrated part in proceedings; ironically, as the church bells rang out at 11 a.m., 11 November 1918, the combined tactical value of every panorama taken during the war instantly vanished.

The splendid photograph which relates directly to Guy Chapman's quote.

CHAPTER ONE:

THE WAR BEGINS

EARLY BATTLES AND THE BELGIAN COAST

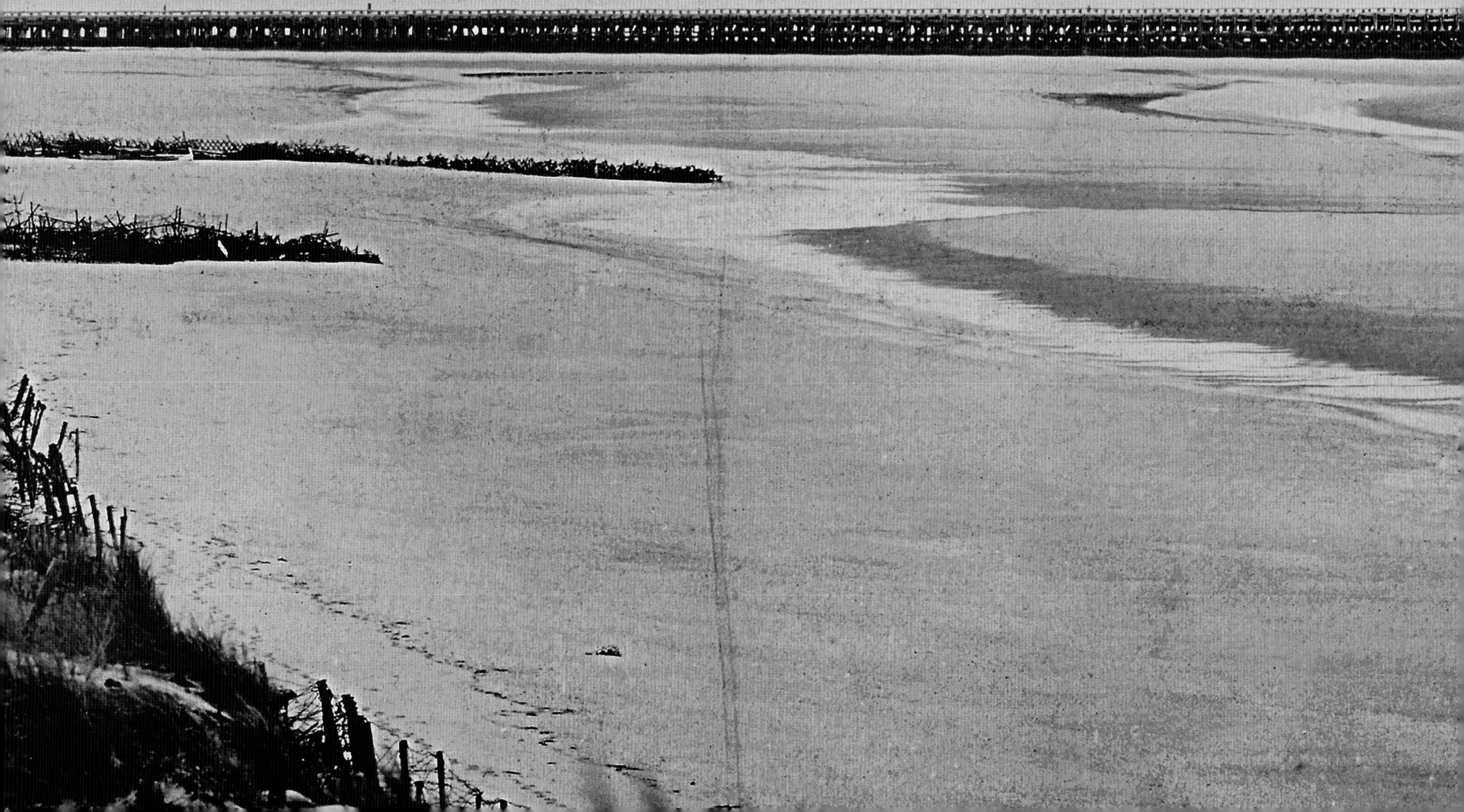

The Marne and the Aisne

The early history of the Western Front was one of movement, a movement controlled by the titanic ambition of the Schlieffen Plan; the great German scheme to sweep through Belgium and defeat France – fast.

The Allied armies of three nations, France, Britain and Belgium, met the initial German thrust head on. The opening days (14–25 August) saw the Battle of the Frontiers; four separate but related clashes along the borders extending from Metz in France to Mons in Belgium. The British entered the war on the extreme left of the Allied line. Four divisions of the BEF took up positions along the Mons Canal on 23 August, facing the German First Army under von Kluck. Although more than twice the size, the Germans were held partially in check by skilled professional troops, especially accurate and rapid rifle fire. However, the British soon found themselves outflanked by the forced withdrawal of the French at Charleroi. II Corps under Sir Horace Smith-Dorrien were then required to fight a rearguard action at Le Cateau, before joining a general Allied withdrawal towards Paris. The relentless German war machine rolled forward. The BEF, arguably the best-trained small army in the world, at first produced an orderly fighting retirement, stalling the German advance at every opportunity.

To many though, the onslaught appeared unstoppable. In just three weeks after war erupted on 4 August, Brussels, Lille, Laon and Namur had fallen, the Germans were driving hard against the Allies on several fronts, and for more than just the ordinary soldier the 'fog of war' was fast becoming opaque. The diary of a young regular officer, 2nd Lieutenant B. G. 'Biffko' Marden of the 9th Lancers, illustrates the confused nature of this period, and stands in sharp contrast with the conflict that was to emerge later.

21 August, 1914

Trek northwards to Harmignies. Hear of the fall of Brussels and of the presence of a very large German force north of Mons. The General [De Lisle] promises the DSO or DCM to the first officer or NCO who 'sticks' an opposing patrol leader. Sleep on a table.

22 August

Reveille 2 a.m. to move at 4 a.m. – but hang about until 11.30 a.m. – we then move 250 yards. We are cheered up by seeing numerous batches of prisoners. The 4 DG's [4th Dragoon Guards] draw first blood – chasing and scuppering an Uhlan patrol. At 9 p.m. we trek to Thulin, where we arrive at 2 a.m.

Pages 60–61
German 1916 Panorama G-1 on the Belgian coast, showing the northernmost point of the Western Front.

Left
Refugees leaving their homes in advance of a German onslaught.

Above
Haystack HQ. Private photograph of 21st Infantry Brigade (7th Division) headquarters.

From 24 August the British were in full retreat. The weary troops covered many a laborious mile on Belgian and French *pavé*, believing that the enemy were on their heels, or indeed behind them. Major (later Brigadier-General) G. Walker DSO, commanding 59 Field Company RE, calculated that during the withdrawal his men trudged wearily rearwards at an average of 27 km (16.9 miles) per day, with the greatest distance covered being 52 km (33 miles) in 17 hours! Fighting was continuous all the way. This was the era of the skirmish: man to man, hedge to hedge, and especially between mounted troops.

24 August – Shrapnel Monday

In the early morning we are attacked by apparently several divisions and we get N[orth]. Wortham wounded in the chest. Retire to railway in rear and hold embankment – shelled – aeroplanes directing. Mark wounded – shrapnel – thigh – flesh only. Fire at German planes. No success. Retire to south of Audregnies – await move in a field, then round a corner into a wire enclosure, behind a house. I wasn't behind the house! Then we come under a terrific infantry fire – Micheleau, French interpreter, fairly grovels. Suddenly see squadron (we are in squadron column) moving out at a gallop – have a good start of me – what the hell are they doing? We go through a hail of bullets and shrapnel – must be charging – find my sword and draw it – cannot see any Germans. We then right wheel and come into fire-action – more or less – my troop is on the Mound and rather well-collected – a few silly fire orders – nothing to shoot at. Then the Colonel disappears – for three days – says he's going to find the General. Then Lucas [Captain D. K. Lucas-Tooth, killed in action on 13 September] leads us back to the Quarry under a heavy shrapnel fire. Our "feet" [the infantry] get away and so we follow in single file at a gallop to behind a railway embankment. Hear of Francis' rescuing of guns [Captain Francis Octavius Grenfell was awarded the war's first VC for this action. He was killed on 24 May 1915 at Hooge in the Ypres Salient]. Then a wild gallop back in column of troops in open order under an appalling shrapnel fire. Lucas takes us back to Ruesnes, where we arrive at 12 p.m. – about one third strong.

From day to day the Germans grasped more and more of the initiative. Few Allied officers had any idea of what was happening, nor even which map sheet they were marching across.

25 August

Leave Ruesnes at 1 a.m. (no sleep), retiring slowly, holding positions: bring down an aeroplane – 2 officers in it escape. Do some looting and cook 2 eggs for 6 officers! Arrive in pouring rain on hill N.W. of Vertain – rendezvous with Cav. Div. Am sent off to find 18th Horse who are lost for the third time today! Cannot find them. Roger on the same job does not return for three days! Retire under high-explosive fire on Le Cateau. See infantry holding Le Cateau ridge – pass thro' them to Catillon – hear that we have taken knock badly. Confusion in Le Cateau is extraordinary – rumours that our right has been hopelessly turned – situation desperate.

27 August – Death and Glory Sunday

After outpost duty, we leave at 4 a.m. and wander about in circles without watering – I get my troop watered privately in buckets by inhabitants. We finally arrive at Forget N.E. of St Quentin. The General says good-bye to us officers, saying that we are to sacrifice ourselves to save a defeated English Army – oh! low – we are already surrounded – the French at Charleroi were hopelessly smashed – also in Alsace. They are no good and run like hares. Ian v. depressed – but cannot say I am cheerful myself. It turns out, however, that what the

Right
A Troop of British cavalry goes out on patrol during the period prior to the onset of trench warfare. Autumn 1914.

General thought were Germans, were really French. We see a few Germans and billet at Savy – at a stud farm – excellent place for horses and men – we have a wonderful dinner!

The entire British force was in a similar state of confusion. One of the most trying problems was procuring hot food. There was no shortage of dumps on the line of retreat, but no one was able to linger long enough to produce any meals at all, never mind a cooked one. Many men took advantage of the apple trees on roadsides; as they were not eating but cooking varieties the consequences were often unpleasant. By the time the withdrawal came suddenly and unexpectedly to an end, the infantry faced shortages of everything, especially energy. Then came more bad news: Lille and Mezières were in enemy hands.

The retreat may have been hasty and chaotic – but although stretched to its limit, the line did not break; the French held, and with them an emaciated BEF. The German advance was finally checked on the Marne during the battle of 5–9 September, where Allied elasticity was truly tested.

3 September

Leave at 4 a.m. – am advanced troop till I find 4th Cav. Bde. In front of us on the same road – what wonderful staff-work! Arrive Gournay-sur-Marne at 10 a.m. Hush! We are to trek 20 miles to take part in a wild and woolly counter-attack to fill in a gap between the French and English Armies. We must lighten baggage so we hurl away with great enthusiasm all the necessities of life (including the men's greatcoats). Then we hear the attack is off! Well, I'm damned! Hear of imminent victory by the French – about time too!

The German armies in the southern sectors had moved rapidly, neatly adhering to the Schlieffen Plan; it was the decision by von Kluck, commanding the First Army, to swing east of Paris thereby exposing his flank that was to prove fatal.

6 September

Leave at 5 a.m. to fill a gap between English Army whose right is at Chapelle, and French Cavalry Corps at Curtacon. There are two French cavalry Brigades at Etang-les-Parts, 5th English Cavalry Brigade on our left – 1st under Briggs on our right. This must be the promised counter-strike – hurrah! We try to push north but come under heavy shrapnel fire, 'C' Squadron take up position in wood but get shelled out of it. To Beaulieu Wood at 11.30 a.m. where Private Cousins is shot by Corporal Perry – defective safety catch. Loot a poultry yard – no good – as the 'relentless pursuit' starts! Hear of victory of the Marne to our left – dash off in pursuit. I hear the enemy's transport escaping to the north – why not hurry on?

The invasion had been stalled, then stopped. Instant French counter-attacks along the line of the River Ourcq forced a shocked German Army into their own fighting retreat to the Aisne. The deceleration and subsequent reversal created a hiatus that allowed the Allies to catch their breath, regroup – and attack.

13 September

Reveille 3 a.m. Saddle up. Counter-order arrives. Saddle down. Ordered to move at 6.45. 6.25 new order to move at once. Off in confusion at 6.35. Good work by regimental staff! We then attack

Below

Panorama 15: one of the earliest examples of the war, showing (on the far bank of the river) the Aisne battlefield in September 1914.

Above
20 October 1914: Scots Guards gingerly approach Gheluvelt in the Ypres Salient. The enemy's precise whereabouts at this time were unknown.

Bourg and the crossings of the Aisne and parallel canal – the further bridge of the two having been blown up. We go to the right and cross by sixes in a ferry under an irritating sniper's fire from a church tower – gave the ferry boy a franc for courage. De Lisle orders the 4 DG's to gallop the bridge – they gallop into a barricade and come under hot fire. Fitzgerald and three men killed. We come into action from the right and the 4 DG's cross directly. We then climb up a hill and form up in mass behind a battery in action – our usual unusual procedure: naturally we receive several hostile overshoots aimed at the battery. We retire in open order at a walk for 300 yards. Six horses in my troop wounded, Lucas killed, two men wounded. The General thinks it a brave thing to do, to sit down behind a battery in action in close formation. Anyhow, he has thrown away his best Squadron Leader – feel v. depressed as I was fond of Lucas.

14 September

At 3.25 a.m. when just about to enjoy a breakfast of hot rabbit stew and mashed potatoes, order comes to move at once. A map is shoved into my hand and I find myself advanced troop to the brigade – not at all ready – no breakfast, and pitch dark. Also, as there is a shortage of maps, this is the first occasion I've had to study this sheet! I move off a fast trot – messages arriving from the rear to hurry on! Having lent my electric torch to Lenny (as he went off to patrol Chemin des Dames ridge) I endeavour to strike matches to see the map with – but each time I stop to strike one I get a fluent message from the rear. Thoroughly exasperated, I go on without being able to use the map, through our own infantry in Troyon and then up a ridge valley past rows of Germans asleep in trenches. Ably supported by the squadron we retire in a hurry, as they wake up when we get to the far end! A regular steeplechase back over sunken roads and wire fences. Luckily it is too dark for accurate shooting and bullets only begin to get near as we near home.

We and Briggs' Brigade move off to help Guards Brigade. 'A' Squadron move west to be on outpost duty. A fool Queen's Bay sentry shoots Pte. Gardner in the thigh…and might have hit me. 'Halt! Who goes there?' BANG! All in one breath. I put on a tourniquet and leave Taylor with him in an old woman's cottage – she is v. frightened! Later he takes it off and bleeds to death. I think I put it on right. We move on to an outpost line east of Chavonne. An hour and a half of broken sleep.

The following day, 15 September, is an important date in the Great War calendar for it marks the day when the northward extension of the Western Front began. During the previous fortnight, the momentum of the German advance had been decisively arrested by the French; now the opportunity for a general Allied advance suddenly presented itself. The Germans had shot their bolt and the Schlieffen Plan lay in ruins.

Panoramas on the Aisne

The earliest panoramas in this book were taken during September 1914 whilst the Battle of the Aisne was in progress. Although it is difficult to glean any inkling of conflict in the landscape, it was on the far banks and slopes of these deep river valleys that the great outflanking manoeuvres of the opposing sides began.

After the dispiriting trek back from Mons, news of an advance put a spring in everybody's step. Most of the fighting units of the BEF were on the north bank of the

Aisne by 14 September, struggling to drive back an enemy who were strongly dug in. Having spent the last six weeks destroying bridges, it was now up to the hard-pressed engineers to repair old crossings and erect as many new ones as possible to keep the forward flow of troops constant. Wire was stripped from field boundaries and strung up in single strands as a stop-gap defensive measure; simple dugouts were excavated for cover against shell splinters and shrapnel (the steel helmet was not issued for another 18 months); and battery positions installed. As the Allied foothold on the northern bank was far from stable, reserve lines were dug in case a further withdrawal became necessary. Rumours abounded. It was at this time that certain facets of the conflict begin to shift towards a form more readily associated with the Great War.

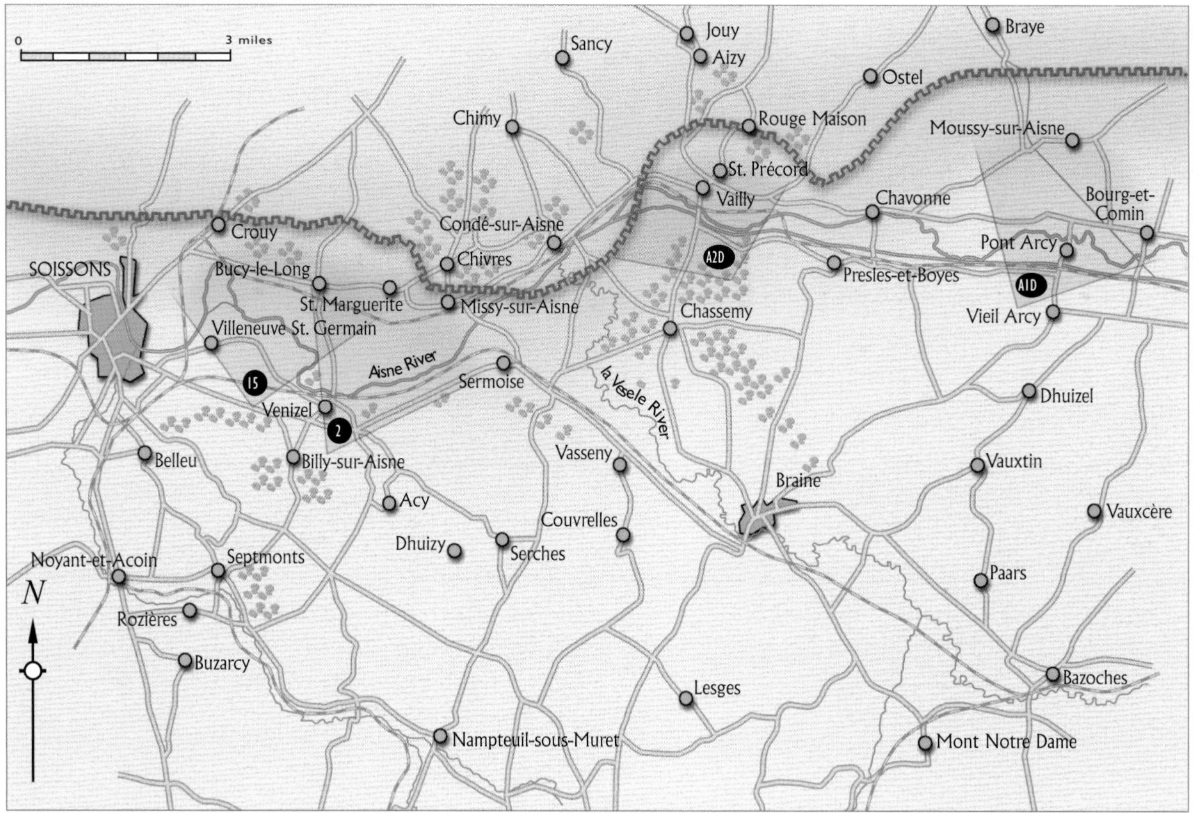

15 September

Sleep at [Calmette's] Chateau all day – bathe in fountain – better than nothing. Box of acid drops arrives from Aunt Agatha – we all gorge. A few high explosives drop during the day – one kills 7 men and 8 horses of a horse battery with us. See a Daily Mail. Ludicrous account of our charge – what on earth is a press-censor for? Hear that the Guards Brigade, tho' facing 9 to 12 hostile battalions and masses of guns, is advancing. Bravo! World's best "feet". Official news read out that 80,000 Russians were at Mons yesterday. Good! That explains everything. What a clever scheme!

Left
The skirmishing period: soldiers moving from hedge to hedge and house to house, seeking out enemy troops.

On 16 September the French commander General Joffre, the architect of German reversals on the Marne, began to abandon his tactics of frontal assault in favour of turning the enemy right flank; the fighting was thus extended northwards along the Aisne river valley, with intermingled French and British troops fighting almost as one. Indicative of so many future actions, the battle began to run out of steam. It was all over by 18 September, and in its place, that 'temporary' phase: trench warfare on a grand scale.

20 September, 1914

Turn out at 4.30 and rush off to Paissy to help the "feet". Move round skyline to draw gun-fire away from Turco's [French-Algerian troops] who are about to bolt – good mark to the General – rather skilfully done. Only one horse hit. Carry a wounded Zouave down the hill to our trench, tie him up and try my morphia on him! He sleeps – later I tell his friends where he is. I have left one man (a fool) Pte Cotton with Col. T. : later, he tears down in a great hurry to say that the XY's [the French] have bolted and that the Germans are on the ridge – see the Zouaves to our right bolting too. This is cheerful – I may be captured. Run up hill and see no Germans – but the XY's have left their wounded behind and bolted – even the reserves! Get my horse and head them off down valley and try to stop them. Up comes old De Lisle. "Take them up to the firing line; shoot anyone who won't go." Blow! Over the ridge we go, back to the forward trenches. The Deutschers are trying to get there first. We win, however! The run forwards was a most dangerous show as everyone fired as they ran, in any direction. Once there I fired at a few easy "masses", until a silly fool hit me in the head. I tied it up with a Tommy's handkerchief. There was a wounded German who had been left near our trenches in the race. He kept pointing to his leg and shouting "Gewundert": we couldn't restrain the men however, and they finished him off.

At intervals all afternoon we had sentences such as these passed up and down the line to cheer us up: "Can you see anyone on your right?" … "No, only some dead French." … "Be careful to watch your right flank" … "We think we see some Germans there, Sir." As we knew that the Turco's had bolted, the prospect was cheerful. There are no supports or reserves of "feet" within miles. I spend my time sitting on a corpse, then report to General. He says "well done etc" – he has some souse! Have my head dressed. This hurts. Get food 11.30 p.m. The Times of 15th says that there is no foundation for the "Russians in Belgium" story. I wonder! I've to go to Paris and have my head healed. Wonder how long I'll be? Doctor says more than a fortnight. It will be a short rest anyhow – and the fight seems stationary. And there will be plenty more!!

By 24 September a relative stalemate had been reached, and in the days leading up to the 28th, only localized skirmishes occurred. The first trench-based battle on the Western Front was over. As the first October of war began the Germans mirrored the French outflanking tactics but on a massively increased scale, striking hard and fast far to the north: Antwerp fell, Ostend followed, Lens, Comines and even Ypres and Poperinghe were occupied. An identical Allied response meant that the period known as 'The Race to the Sea' was underway. As a result of the strategy, between 3 and 12 October the BEF transferred entirely from France northwards into Belgian Flanders.

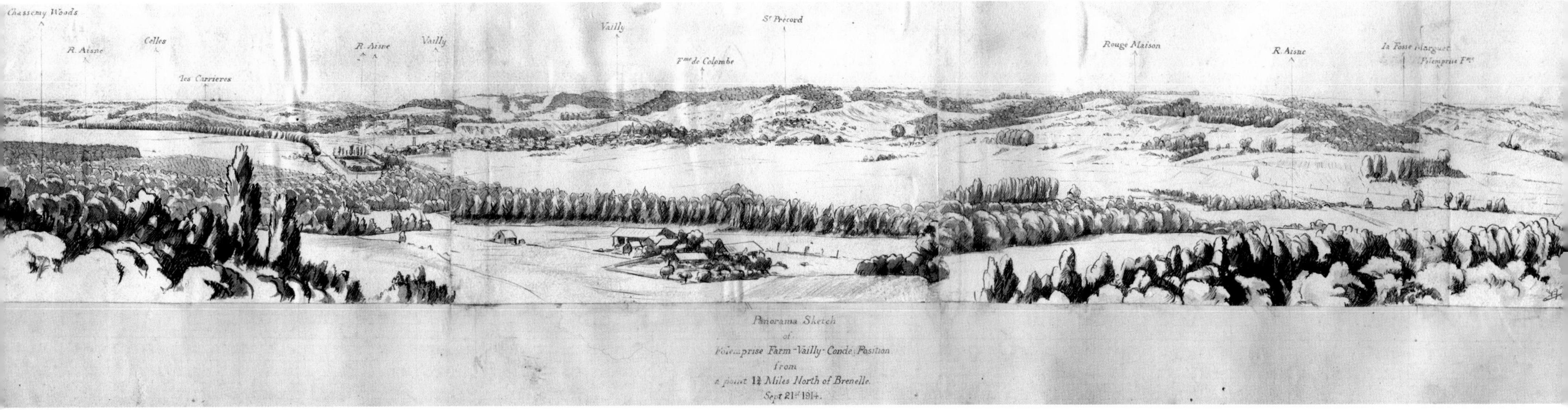

Below

A drawn panorama of the Aisne battleground by Captain J. G. Gandy RE, 21 September 1914.

The Race to the Sea

Right

Map recording the extent of ground covered by the inundations. The majority of territory between Nieuport and Ypres was rendered impassable.

Below left

Belgian military engineers pile-driving to strengthen one of the many dams at Nieuport. This single structure consumed 900,000 sandbags in its construction.

By October 1914 most of Belgium was already in the hands of the invader. By 14 October a wizened Belgian Army had been forced to retreat to the banks of the last natural barrier on Flemish soil, the River Yser, which cuts across the Polder plains through Dixmude and Nieuport before flowing into the North Sea at Nieuport-Bains.

The Yser had been canalized many years before and the last 65 km (40 miles) to Nieuport was 'embanked'. It was hoped that these earthworks could be made into adequate positions to hold back the invasion and preserve the last tiny corner of West Flanders. But the Belgians would need all the help they could get. The British could spare no troops from positions guarding Ypres, and the French had their hands full elsewhere; if anything was to assist the Belgians it was going to have to be brought about by their own efforts. There was a hope, but it was slim.

After the evacuation of Brussels and Antwerp, Ostend and Zeebrugge, and with no Allied support immediately to hand, it seemed almost inevitable that the Germans would achieve their goal of French subjugation before Christmas – just as the Kaiser had stridently pronounced to his subjects. The axis of their advance, which in late September and October of 1914 shifted ever more northwards into French and then Belgian Flanders, was halted by two things: six weeks of dogged fighting by an exhausted Belgian Army (with assistance from a few French troops), and the application of one of the most ancient of military stratagems: inundation – defence by flooding.

At the heart of the coastal sector lay the old fortified town of Nieuport. Here, just a kilometre from the open sea, the tides which surged twice daily into the mouth of the River Lys were (and still are) controlled by a complex cluster of locks and sluices that keep water levels in the five major radiating canals, and many other smaller inland waterways, at the optimum height for navigation, irrigation

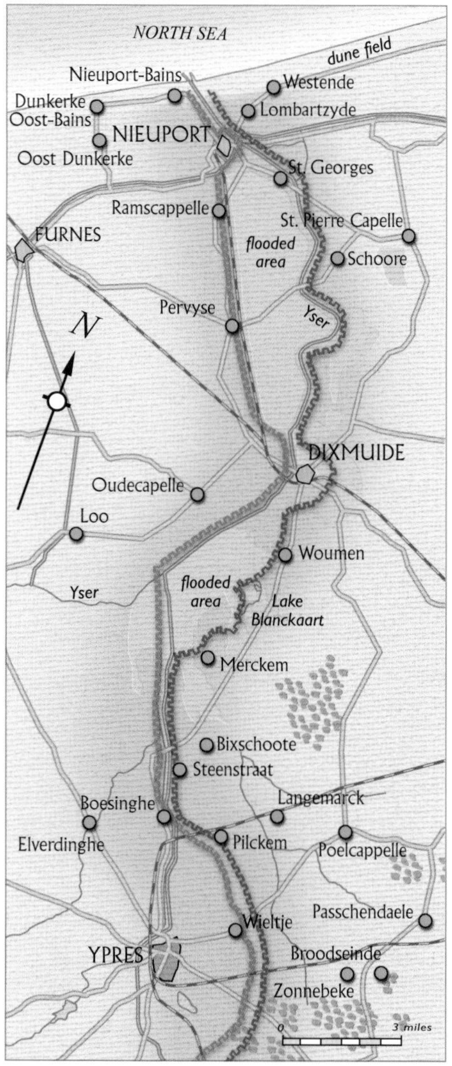

Above
An early panorama from 18 February 1915 – No 39 – taken by the RE on behalf of the Belgian Army showing the mouth of the River Yser and Nieuport-Bains station. Two years later 7 Australian tunnellers began a project to undermine the Grand Dune, but the scheme was truncated by the German July 1917 attack in which they captured all the Allied positions in the dunes on the north bank.

Right
Barge-mounted 4.7-inch naval gun in action on a canal near Nieuport. The sector developed a grim reputation for artillery battles during 1917.

Far right
Nieuport lock-keeper Henri Geeraerts (left) with his mother and father.

Below
Panorama 38: the view inland over the rooftops of Nieuport on 18 February 1915, with the inundations to the north and east.

and – most important of all – drainage of the Polder Plain.

It was common historical knowledge that since its foundation in the twelfth century the town of Nieuport, sitting astride the tidal section of the Yser about a kilometre from the sea, had several times relied upon the ancient practice of inundation for its defence. Lieutenant-Colonel Nuyten of the Belgian HQ staff investigated the tactic as a possible way of stemming the impending German advance in the coastal sector. On 17 October the weary Belgians were positioned along the Yser, with forward outposts to the east. The following day the Germans attacked the outposts and shelled Nieuport heavily; attacks continued for the next two days, and as the Belgians grew ever weaker the order was given to flood as much ground as possible. After a disturbing delay in finding a civilian who was sufficiently well acquainted with the system of waterways, Henri Geerearts, an old waterman told Nuyten which weir sluice to open, and which siphon to close to prevent the flooding of the Belgians' own positions. This was done, but it was found that only 4 sq km (1.5 sq miles) was inundated: an area entirely insufficient to have even a moderate effect. During the next few days the Germans pushed on again, taking the riverbank positions and pushing the Belgians from the Yser back to another embankment – that of the Nieuport–Dixmude railway. The situation was now more than serious: this was the final defensible position on Belgian soil. It had to be held at all costs.

As a result of his earlier investigations and discussions with Geerearts, Nuyten was struck by the possibility of using the railway embankment itself as an aid to further

flooding. He enquired with the engineers, but their knowledge of the complex tidal locks at Nieuport and the intricate chequerboard drainage system of the Polders was more than just deficient, it was non-existent. By another stroke of luck, an old lock-keeper named Cogge was traced and asked for assistance. He had had many years' experience of the Polders and suggested that it may indeed be possible to flood a much larger area of ground to the east if one of Nieuport's sluices was opened at high tide and closed during the ebb. The water could be carried around the back of the town along the long disused Canal de Furnes, through a siphon which passed under the present Canal de Furnes, and beyond onto the Polders. However, for the plan to work it would also be essential to block twenty-two culverts under the railway, build a dam at the point where the railway and canal met, close certain other sluices, and make sure that other key water-control points were maintained.

At 4 p.m. on 25 October Belgian engineers began the task of damming and sealing. Before the final few culverts had been blocked the situation had become desperate: the Germans were only about 350 m (382 yds) away and the Belgian artillery had exhausted their ammunition. It was decided that the locks must be opened before the blocking work was complete. Having been closed for 35 years the gates stubbornly refused to budge; only the integral sluices could be freed – and they released only a little water. On the night of 27–28 October the gates at last creaked apart and water gushed through. The result was not at all as successful as had been hoped: dry ground soaked up the flood, and bridges and other bottlenecks arrested its flow.

By now the Belgians had been fighting non-stop for four days and four nights, hoping all the time that the waters might be their salvation. Cogge then informed Captain Robert Thys of the Belgian military engineers, that if the sluices in the great weir of the Noordvaart Canal could be opened with the rising tide and closed as it fell, the results might be satisfactory. However, there was a major problem: the weir was now behind German lines. But the Belgians were left with little choice. The situation called for desperate measures: they would raid the Noordvaart weir.

On the night of 29 October at 7.30 p.m. a small party crept out into the darkness. Reaching the weir they found to their astonishment and relief that the positions were unoccupied by the enemy. The handles of the system, which had been hidden in a bush, were found, and the sluices opened. During high tide the waters surged through, and at midnight as the flow was ebbing, the sluices were closed.

Above
Belgian troops negotiating a flooded road near Ramscappelle, 26 November 1914.

Right
German photograph of support line trenches and a telephone dugout in the dunes near Lombartzyde-Bains north of Nieuport.

Above
Panorama 72 shows the inundations to the east of Nieuport, and how decisively the German attack route was closed off.

Right
A farmstead isolated by the rising waters. Several positions like this were connected to the lines by duckboard tracks suspended above the water, and used as forward observation posts.

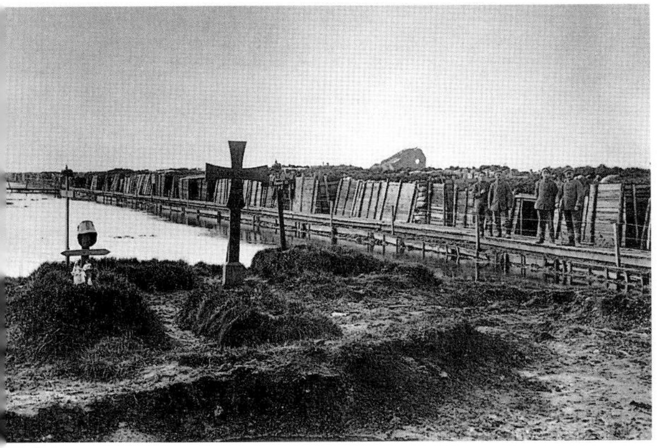

The next day the Germans launched a huge general attack on the northern front, advancing along the entire line between Nieuport and Lille, taking parts of the railway and threatening to overrun the whole of the coastal sector. Sixteen hours after opening the sluices however, the water had already advanced almost 5 km (3 miles) across the Polder Plain. On 30 October, tides were not only higher, but augmented by onshore winds. The sluices were opened and closed again, and once more tens of millions of litres of seawater streamed inland. The Polder Plain sank beneath the flood; the next day the lost positions on the railway line were recovered and the Germans forced to pull back behind the advancing flood. For the next four years the great man-made sea, 13 km long and 6 wide (8 miles long and 3 wide), was kept in place, and never again were the Germans to set foot west of the railway.

Railway to Dixmude

The inundations

The Belgian coast presents a wholly different historic environment to other battlefields of the First World War. Often ignored almost entirely by historians, the sector played a fundamental role in the establishment of positional warfare, and indeed of the Western Front itself. If, following the Battle of the Aisne in September, German forces had broken through at this most northerly extension of the European theatre, the Channel ports and Paris would have been exposed – and Britain would have been left open to invasion. Strategically, therefore, the inundations were of paramount importance.

The waist-deep inland sea was a barrier that was impossible for troops or animals to cross on foot. Later, further smaller-scale inundations of suitable depressions in the Flanders plain between Dixmude and Ypres sealed off more potential battlegrounds. Panorama 72 (5 June 1915), photographed from Nieuport Tower, perfectly illustrates the role the railway played in containing the waters to its northern side – this great inundation was known as the *Inondation du Chemin de Fer*. The dam built in late October 1914 can also be seen in the angle between the railway and the Furnes canal. Note the long narrow footbridges connecting the railway with forward 'island' posts, usually farm buildings on slightly raised ground. Note also the barbed-wire entanglements in the water.

The Belgian defensive positions can be seen dug into the rear of the bank. Panorama 38 (18 February 1915) gives an earlier view over Nieuport rooftops towards enemy positions in the coastal dunes and skirting the open ground in front of the town. On the right of the image is the Templar's Tower, , which still exists today but is now known as the Devil's Tower. Just to its left the River Yser can be seen, here at low tide. No 63 (20 May 1915) presents another view of the railway inundations from a chimney in Ramscappelle, a small village behind Allied lines inland of Nieuport which had been occupied by the Germans just before the inundations took hold. No 94 (22 October 1917) shows the positions defending the town on the north side of the River Yser, including the two small yet equally important floods, the Geleide and Pont de Pierre inundations, and the rickety and often-shelled bridges which were the only connection between the arrowhead of front lines north of the Yser and Nieuport town.

It had been the fierce German Fourth Army assault on Dixmude that had encouraged the opening of the locks on 27–28 October. The attack was initially contained by the Belgian Army and a battalion of French marines, but the position had been too precarious and defences too frail to hold out for long. It took three days for the waters to fully saturate the plains. This historic action, which became known as the Battle of the Yser, was overlapped by the next German foray further inland. As the inundations rose and then stabilized, the last dry corridor open for major offensive action was at the point where the Flanders Plain gently swelled from the table-like flatness of the Polders–Ypres. On 2 November German forces previously fighting on the Yser front were withdrawn to concentrate on breaking through via the ancient medieval market town. It was the Kaiser's last – and very late – chance for

Pages 72-3

Panorama 72 taken on 20 May 1915, from Ramscappelle. It shows the Nieuport–Dixmude railway embankment holding the inundations to its north side.

Far right

The railway from Dixmude at the point where it entered Nieuport. Note the Belgian shelters installed in the lee of the embankment. These can still be visited today. The railway bridge here has been transformed into a dam, the water on the near side being pumped over in dry periods to augment the inundations.

Below

Segment of Panorama 63, 5 June 1915, showing a part of the great inundations to the east of the town of Nieuport.

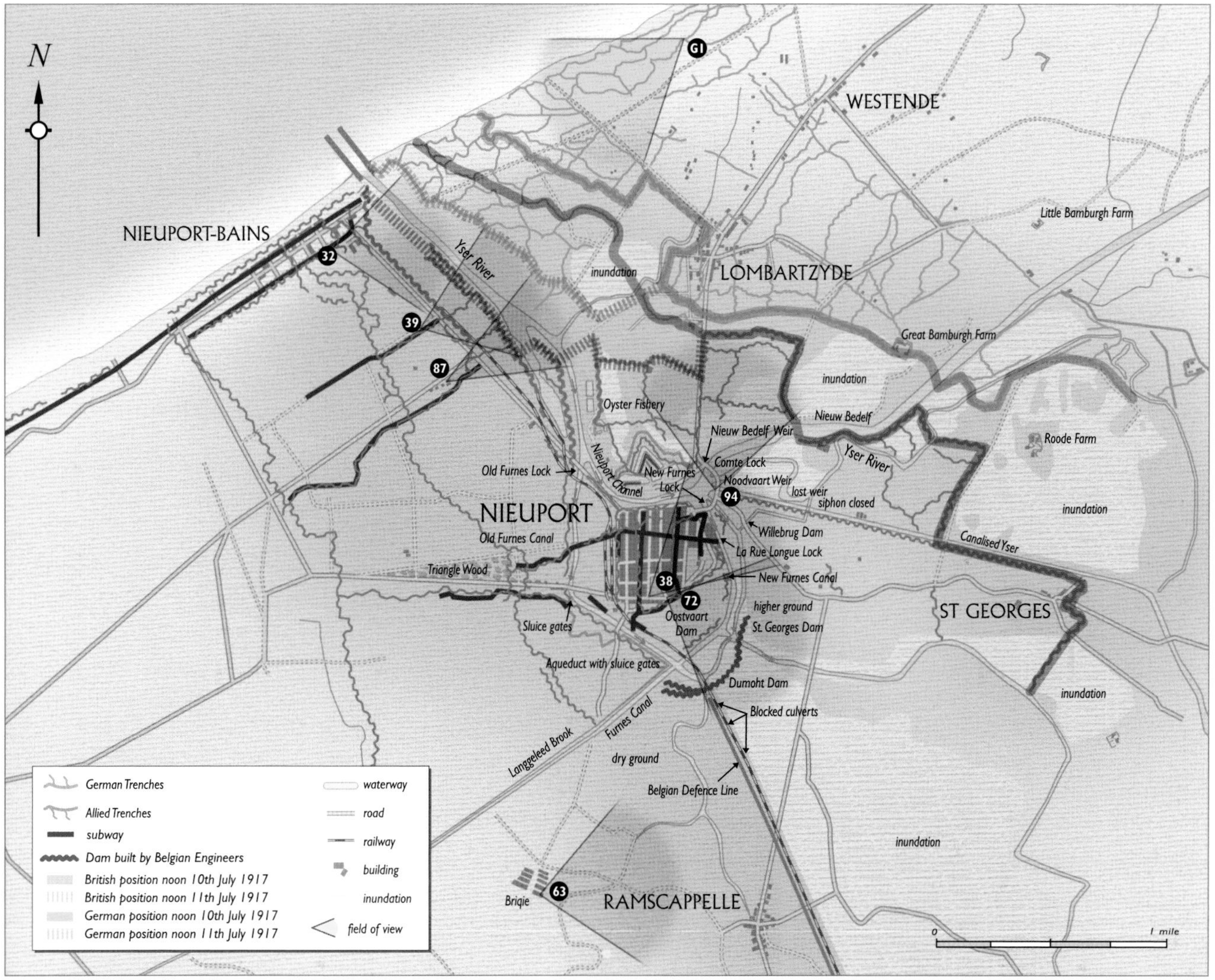

victory before winter rain and frost brought the campaigning season to an end.

After the floods had reached maximum distribution it was of course critical to maintain them in place. In the warm summer months this duty fell to the British RE, who installed vast barge-borne pumps to transfer 4.5 million litres (one million gallons) of water per hour from canals behind the lines to the inundations combatting drainage and evaporation. When winter set in it was the turn of Belgian artillery: this time, cold was the enemy. A brief chill was not a problem, but a prolonged period of frost certainly was, as it was feared the Germans might attack across the ice sheet. A light daily shelling made certain that open water continued to divide friend from foe.

1915 and beyond

Sharp fighting continued intermittently at Nieuport and Dixmude into 1915, but with attacks being staved off each time antagonism soon dwindled and a mutual live-and-let-live attitude arose. Ultimately, in the knowledge that neither side could exploit the flooded territory for attack,

M.16d. 98.37.
Lombartzyde
Plasschendaele Canal
Westende
Nasal Support
Nasal Trench
Concrete Dugout
M.17.D.32.75.
Carmen House.M.II.d.
Westende Bains
Pala
URTH ARMY.
Panorama No. 94 made on 22-9-17 from M 24c. 20-90.
uding a field of view of 85° from about N.W. & N.E.
(Approximate Scale of Degrees (1 degree equals 1'07 inches).
1 2 3 4 5 6
1. Panoramas are taken solely for military purposes.
2. The publication of them in the press will necessarily give valuable information to the enemy.
3. This Panorama is to be kept with as much security as is compatible with full advantage of it being taken by our own troops.
4. When troops are relieved this panorama should be handed over to the relieving troops.

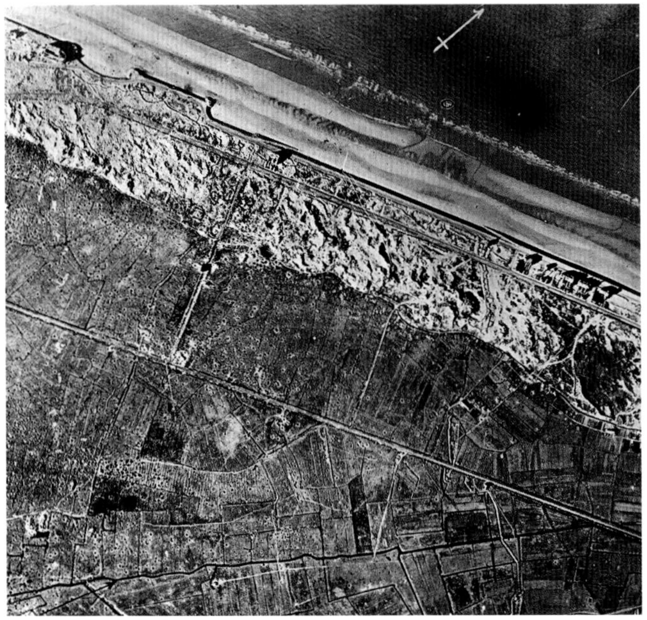

the Germans were content to leave the inundations precisely where the Allies had placed them. They concentrated their wrath (in the form of artillery) on the town of Nieuport and occasionally its adjacent coastal dunes – now the only dry and viable potential bridgeheads for an offensive between Ypres and the sea.

Tactically, the coastal sector was a curious one. There were four fronts to protect. There was a tiny landward one, made up entirely of breastworks, facing the Germans in the partly-flooded sub-sector in front of Nieuport – aptly named the 'Nose Trench' system, the wettest sector of the Western Front. The second front was where, after the German attack of July 1917, the lines were divided solely by the River Yser. This was only a few hundred metres from Nose Trench but was situated entirely in the dunes, and was therefore the driest sector of the Western Front. Panorama 94 (22 September 1917) shows the Nose Trench system and the shabby state of the battlefront after more than two years of action. Both British and German lines are seen; both are predominantly breastwork constructions as the water table was practically at ground level. Shielded walkway approaches feed the riverbank line and rickety bridges lead to the forward trenches north of the river and canals. It was critical to fiercely defend this zone; should it fall Nieuport would have been undefended, and the inundated lands left open to drainage.

Then there was the inundated front held by the Belgians on the Polders along the railway inland of Nieuport; and finally the front facing the North Sea. This latter was intriguing. Having traced a line right across Europe from the Swiss border, at the point where the trench lines hit the beaches, they did not end or track out onto the sand, but turned at right angles to continue along the coast, with German trenches heading north, and the Allies' south. Protected by swathes of barbed wire in the same way as conventional positions (the entanglements on

Above
Panorama 94 taken on 22 September 1917 showing the battered British positions guarding Nieuport – the Nose Trench system.

Left
Aerial view of the dune field and seashore north of Nieuport-Bains – the proposed landing-place for the aborted amphibious assault of summer 1917.

Below
The ruined Casino on the promenade at Nieuport-Bains. Note the density of the wire entanglements above the high-tide mark, placed to deter seaborne enemy attacks.

Above

German positions in the dunes. See also the view in Panorama G-1.

Right

Barrel Post on the beach at Nieuport-Bains. Although snipers occasionally plied their trade from the piers, this was the last manned British position on the left flank of the Western Front.

the German side were electrified), these seaward defences were never tested.

Panorama G-1 shows the very end of the Western Front from the German side of the line. Footprints – made at night-time of course – can be seen in the sand. This picture answers one of the most frequently posed questions of students of the war: what happened when the lines reached the sea? The closest Allied equivalent is No *32* (10 February 1915) which, of course, looks in the opposite direction. Note the train still standing in a practically undamaged Nieuport-Bains railway station to the right of the frame. The picture also includes the dune lines on the north bank of the river which were lost in July 1917. Ancillary German defences were as robust on the coast as anywhere, with massive concrete-protected guns pointing seaward to fend off seaborne attack, and line after line of pillboxes in the dunes stretching back to Ostend.

Astonishing to relate, in this bizarre war old tactics died hard, and here on the coast there existed an aquatic version of the night-time trench patrol. Small groups of swimmers were sent out after dark from Nieuport-Bains, an erstwhile genteel holiday village sitting directly on the beach, to quarter that portion of the North Sea which one might describe as 'no man's water' – the imagined continuation of trench lines into the sea. The swimmers were armed – with a revolver strapped to the top of the head. Presumably, in order to engage the

enemy a man would have to: a) tread water; b) unstrap his weapon; and c) attempt to aim whilst bobbing about. No meetings with enemy swimmers are recorded, and the bizarre practice was stopped during the summer of 1917.

A comparative pair of Nieuport-Bains panoramas, No 39 (18 February 1915), and No 87 (22 July 1917) are taken from elevated positions in the village. Both show the mouth of the River Yser, jetties, and also the railway station in contrasting degrees of destruction. No 87 was taken twelve days after the Germans had captured Allied trenches and tunnels (the 2nd Australian Tunnelling Company were undermining the Grand Dune) on the far bank of the river. This was a critical and severely damaging action for the British. Note the 'old' left and right Brigade HQ annotations. Panorama *32* (10 February 1915) also shows these positions crossing the Geleide Creek, skirting the inundation and connecting with the Nose Trench system inland of the dune field.

The Dunes

For more than two years following the inundations the dune sector was held by Belgian engineers and French infantry. Nieuport itself was subjected to regular bombardments, but the rest of the area became peaceful and was appreciated by all, Germans included, as a quiet front. Soon, units were being sent 'to the seaside' for rest and recuperation after actions elsewhere. However, from 11 June 1917 three British divisions, the 1st, 32nd and later the 66th appeared, entirely relieving the French garrison. Unsurprisingly, they found flimsy defences – there had been no need for anything substantial. Immediately upon arrival the British began training for Sir Douglas Haig's huge summer offensive in Flanders: an offensive which had been given a flying start four days earlier on 7 June by Sir Herbert Plumer's superlative Second Army assault on the Messines Ridge – the first stage of Haig's great scheme. Part two involved the definitive and long-hoped-for rupture of the Ypres Salient via the Passchendaele Ridge, and the subsequent capture of the German railheads and transport network at Roulers. The platform selected for part three of the offensive was the Belgian coast. With Ostend and Zeebrugge as the primary targets, the 32nd and 66th Divisions were to launch a conventional infantry assault along the narrow dune belt, crossing the Yser via pontoon bridges and boats. The attack plan for the 1st Division however, was to be one of the most ambitious and inventive of the war.

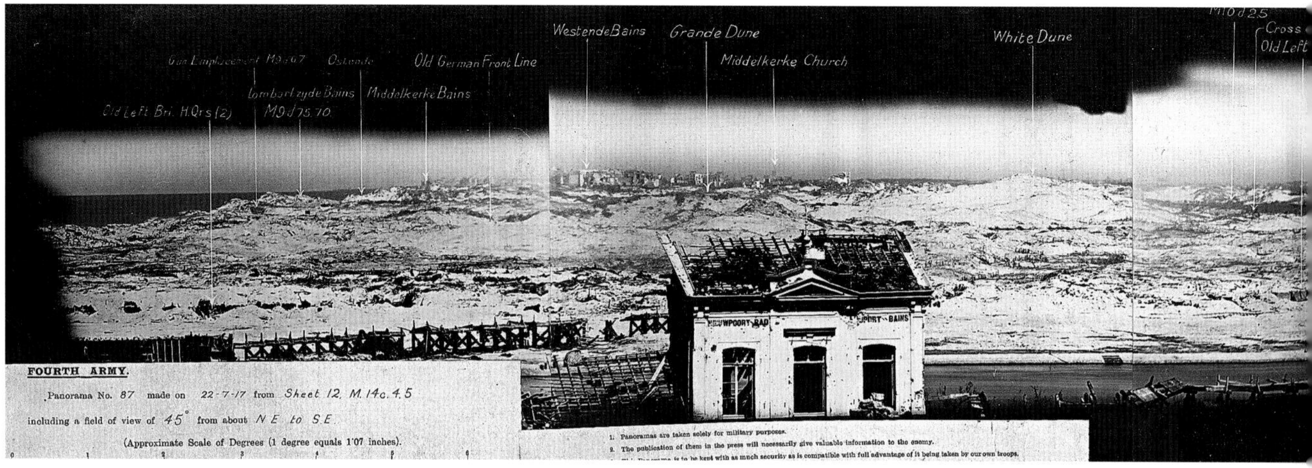

Below

How the great pontoons were to be loaded. Two monitors were to drive them ashore and offer covering fire alongside other Royal Navy vessels.

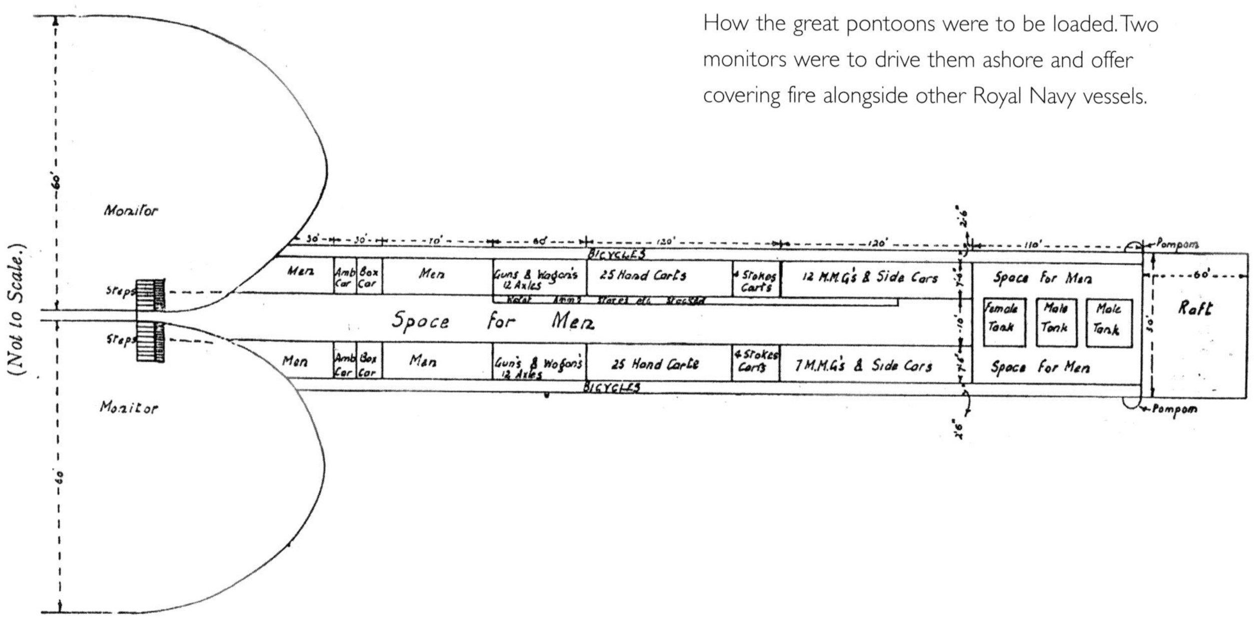

Below

Panorama G-1: the dune lines as seen from the German side.

Above
View from Nieuport-Bains in mid-summer 1917. The annotation indicated that the old British trenches on the far bank of the River Yser are now occupied by German troops. Fourth Army Panorama 87, 22 July 1917.

Below
A section of 2nd Australian Tunnelling Company sappers rest outside their subway entrance in the dunes behind Nieuport-Bains.

Arriving at Le Clipon on the French coast we were told a little, but very little, and started to work very hard getting something "concrete" ready: opinion varied between a heavy gun platform to an experimental seaplane launching way. It was only when the bullnose was shaped out that many realized that it was a replica of a sea wall, none of us knew where, and why was food for further rumours. The sea wall in hand, all preparations were made to convert a waste of sand dunes into a training camp for a Division; wells were sunk and water pipes laid, light railways constructed and camps and huts laid out, obstacle courses designed. These preparations over, the Scheme was gradually unfolded to us and we had a fortnight's intensive training previous to a landing on the coast. Inside that fence we lived our own self-contained lives training, bathing and basking in the sun in a delightful seaside camp.

Then rumours floated in that that the attacks at Ypres were not progressing and our Show was postponed and again postponed, and finally abandoned, but not before all had got thoroughly fit to enjoy a Sports Day before breaking up.

409 Lowland Field Company RE, Belgian Coast, June/July/August 1917

The aborted assault would have been the first mechanized amphibious landing in history. Leaving Dunkerque under cover of darkness, six monitor ships would push three huge pontoons loaded with trucks, motorized machine guns, field guns and howitzers, medical personnel with ambulances, three tanks, a whole division of infantry plus field company engineers, and deposit them (with the help of smoke screens) at dawn on the beaches of Middelkerke and Westende, just north of Nieuport. With the help of special wedges the tanks would climb the sea wall, and the entire force would surge inland behind the German lines, and northwards up the coast.

It is debatable what the assault might have achieved had it taken place. Although the 1st Division were sanguine about success, the enemy-held coastline between Nieuport and Ostend bristled with heavy machine guns and huge numbers of well-protected artillery of various calibres. Panorama 3 (undated) shows the huge emplacements of twin British 9.2-inch naval guns in the dunes. This is Carnac battery, sited just inland from Dunkerque-Bains, the next village south of Nieuport-Bains. The guns were rolled out on rails to fire their salvos, then rolled back under cover again. If these guns and other Allied land-based artillery had failed to put German artillery out of action in advance of the landings, the slow-moving monitors and pontoons may have been reduced to matchwood long before they reached the beaches. The chance of victory would have massively depended upon surprise.

The arrival of the British on the coast radically changed the complexion of conflict in the sector. Although they did not know of the amphibious assault plans, German intelligence was well aware of the reasons why the French had been relieved: security had been so poor that details of the land attack along the dunes had leaked out. Their response was painfully simple and effective: on 10 July 1917 they launched their own surprise assault on the short but crucial stretch of British lines in the dune sub-sector on the north bank of the Yser. Of the two battalions in residence only around 100 men managed to escape. By this single action the projected land-based attack had been severely complicated: the only bridgehead connecting British positions north and south of the river had been severed (see No 87). Then began a colossal artillery battle which continued throughout the summer and autumn until early November (No 3). In anticipation of the great attacks the British had even built prisoner cages in the dunes behind the lines (No 538). They never housed a single German soldier.

As Nieuport, already pummelled by earlier actions, was battered into a state of ruination perhaps even greater than Ypres, the coastal assault suffered a series of postponements before being abandoned altogether as Haig's Flanders offensive foundered at Ypres. Those units earmarked for the coastal attack were gradually siphoned away from the dunes to take part in the latter stages of fighting in the Salient.

Life in the dunes, even during the period of concord, was not all fresh air and afternoon tea. The unique geological nature of the sector can be appreciated in the German panorama that shows the scale of the dune field. Blown sand found its way into everything, food, tea, eyes, weapons and machinery. As if these problems and those of enemy artillery activity were not enough, the Germans had also chosen the coast to test their new varieties of poison gas. It

was here in the dunes that mustard gas was first encountered. The official War Diaries of the Assistant Director of Medical Services illustrate British puzzlement and concern over the symptoms of each new manifestation.

With tens of thousands of troops in the area awaiting orders to attack, all of which were in danger from shells and gas, the answer for the British was to employ their established protective tactic of going underground. Between June and November 1917 sufficient deep dugout accommodation was provided in the dunes to house over 25,000 men. In addition, dozens of kilometres of underground communication tunnels were installed, many connecting with dune-top observation and machine-gun posts (see Quinton Dune in G-1). Several panoramas were taken from these posts. The extraordinary underground endeavours of British and Australian tunnellers has created a serious legacy for today's inhabitants: many sections of the old timber and steel workings are decaying and collapsing, causing a serious threat to surface structures. A large system of underground communication tunnels (including HQs and an underground hospital) was installed beneath

Above
A British support line in the dunes. In times of high winds the trenches quickly began to fill with blown sand.

Below
Panorama 538: prisoner cage constructed in the rear dune areas. It never accommodated any German residents.

Above
Panorama 3: the Carnac battery – British naval heavy artillery emplacements in the *pannes* behind the front lines. The big guns, on railway tracks, were rolled from their shelters to fire a few rounds and rolled back in again before the inevitable German counter-battery fire ensued.

Right
One of the subways constructed by British and Australian tunnellers. This example is only half-buried – hence the daylight – but most undermined the streets and buildings of both Nieuport and its coastal satellite.

Below
It has never been acknowledged that Nieuport was even more severely battered by shelling than Ypres. Returning civilians state that it was possible to stand on a chair and have an uninterrupted view clear across the town.

Nieuport town to allow troops to reach the river, its bridges and the front lines beyond without risking the shell-blasted streets of the town. The French christened the system 'Le Metro' on their return to Nieuport in mid-November 1917. The sector then once more slipped into inertia.

In the spring of 1918, during the Kaiserschlacht (Kaiser's Battle) offensive inundations were once more employed. During the long years of stasis military and civilian engineers and geologists had pinpointed many other places on the Western Front where flooding might prove advantageous in an emergency. Partial inundation tests were carried out to reveal weak points, and by mid-1917 a huge amount of work had been done behind the lines in building embankments, adjusting locks, creating barriers and raising roads to encourage maximum water surface area whilst still preserving lines of communication. Early in 1918 concern over a potentially significant German breakthrough encouraged the British to obtain Marshal Foch's permission to flood the area between St Omer and Furnes (now Veurne) to protect the port of Dunkerque. It remained submerged between 14 April and 17 August. Similar schemes had also been produced to shield Gravelines and Calais; in the event neither were necessary.

Inundation, therefore, proved to be the key to the coastal sector. By a combination of this most ancient of strategies, local knowledge, and tenacious defence early in the war, the Germans had been forced to shift their attentions inland – to the dry plains and ridges of French and Belgian Flanders. And ultimately to Ypres. In a way, it was the Nieuport inundations which created the Western Front.

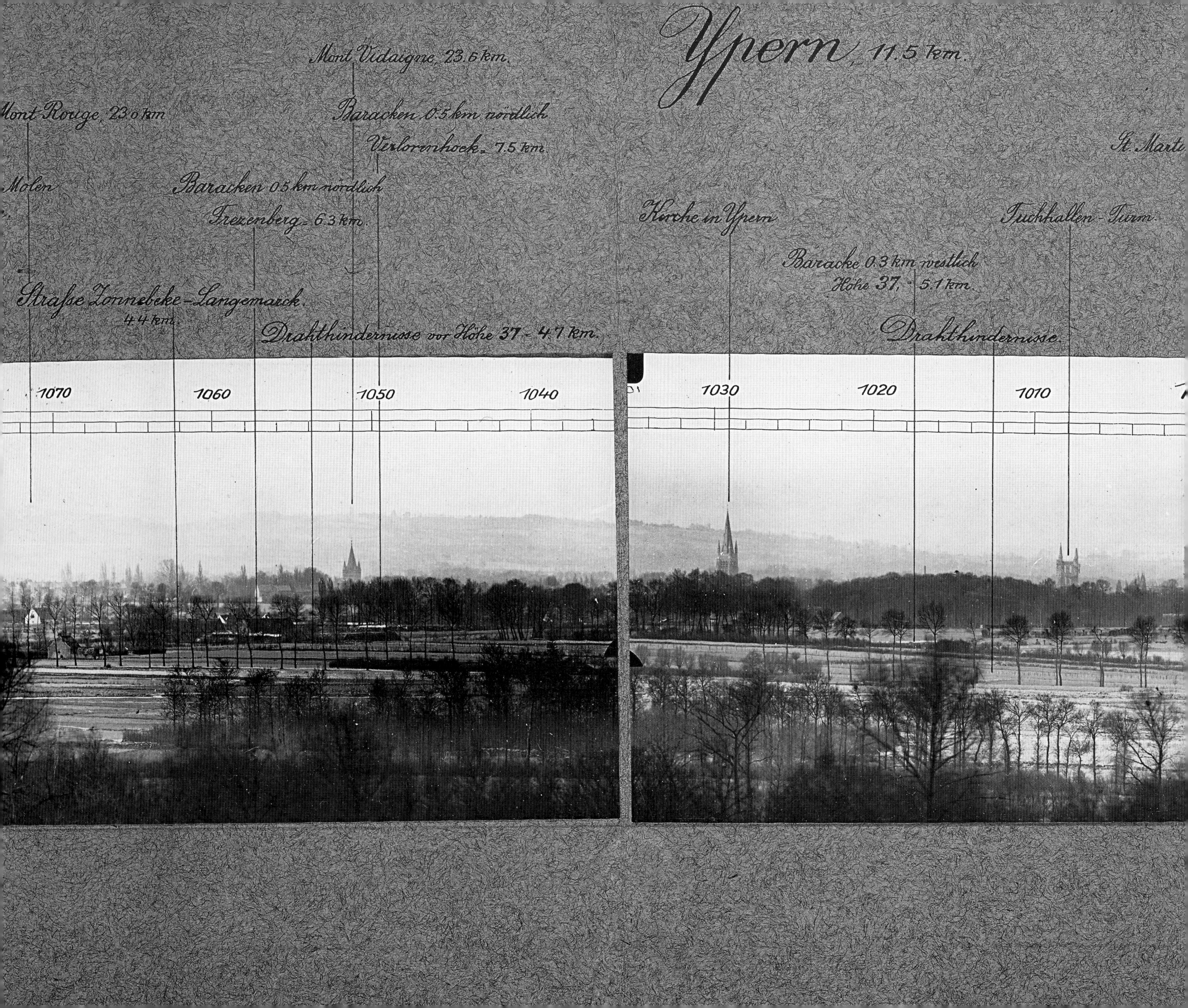

Ypern, 11.5 km.
Mont Vidaigne, 23.6 km.
Mont Rouge, 23.0 km
Baracken 0.5 km nördlich
Verlorenhoek, 7.5 km
Molen
Baracken 0.5 km nördlich
Frezenberg, 6.3 km
Kirche in Ypern
Tuchhallen-Turm.
Baracke 0.3 km westlich
Höhe 37, 5.1 km.
Straße Zonnebeke-Langemarck.
4.4 km.
Drahthindernisse vor Höhe 37, 4.7 km.
Drahthindernisse.
1070
1060
1050
1040
1030
1020
1010

CHAPTER TWO:

THE SALIENT

FIRST AND SECOND YPRES

AND MESSINES RIDGE

Just as the inundations forced the Germans inland from the coast, so actions further south had also created stasis on the Somme, at Arras and northwards to the small French town of La Bassée, not far from the Belgian border. In these sectors defences were already firm and becoming daily more established. The fluid battlefront had rapidly elongated towards the sea as each side tried to outflank the other, but it was now about to congeal. In mid-October 1914 its boundaries lay at Nieuport in the north and Arras in the south, an area incorporating the plains of French Flanders. However, it was especially the ridges of Belgian Flanders, where for millennia army after army had met an unhappy end, that the most shocking events were to take place: not for nothing was the region known as the 'cockpit of Europe'. But there was to be no other available battleground for the Germans to pursue their supreme ambition of taking the Channel ports and utilizing the excellent French transport network to sweep around and down upon Paris. And pursue it they must. A victory was essential, if only for the reason that the Kaiser had been promised conquest as a Christmas gift.

If a great push in French and Belgian Flanders could be made before winter the breakthrough could well be achieved; if not, however, the attack might also force the French and British to bring supporting troops from southern sectors, weakening their line and opening up other routes of attack elsewhere. A success on the left could expose an enemy flank on the Somme, on the right it may lead to a piercing of the Yser defences. Confidence was still high. The German public were told not to worry about the retirement forced by the inundations: it was only a localized setback, and should by no means be construed as a defeat.

Fighting at Ypres

During the summer of 1914 fear of war had escalated in Flanders, and when the first Belgian troops were mobilized on 31 July 1914, the first exodus of frightened civilians began. On 3 August the Belgian Government refused permission for Germany to use her territory as an invasion route into France; the following day German forces simply ignored Belgium's neutrality, crossed the border and marched on; Britain and Belgium both then declared war.

By the end of August a daily stream of refugees was moving from towns and villages across Belgium into France and Holland. Both Liège and the capital Brussels had fallen, and during the third week of August the first German scouts were reported to be drawing close to the Westhoek – the Ypres area.

On 24 August the BEF had already begun its long retreat from Mons; on the same day the first Uhlan cavalry were observed on the road between Poelcappelle and Westroosebeke: the peoples of West Flanders began to pack their belongings. On 11 September fighting between German troops and Belgian volunteers resulted in the first casualties on the Menin Road at Hooge – the first of many thousands at this place, just 4 km (2.5 miles) from the market place in the centre of Ypres. As more Uhlan cavalry arrived and skirmishes became increasingly likely,

Above
German telephoto photograph looking down the Menin Road from Hooge towards Hellfire Corner and Ypres.

Page 82 and below
German Panorama G-2 (this is only a quarter of the full image) taken from Passchendaele in April 1915. The Zeiss lenses used produce a superb quality print.

Above
Some of the earliest German trenches in the Salient located in the north-west corner of Polygon Wood; one of the many *dreves* can be seen disappearing into the trees in the background.

the tide of refugees swelled. Further clashes between German and Belgian forces followed, in Passchendaele, Becelaere and Zwarteleen.

On 3 October three German cavalry divisions entered Ypres, the nearby village of Voormezeele, and Wytschaete on the Messines Ridge. In Ypres they looted food, money, clothing and jewellery, stole thousands of Belgian francs from the civil coffers – but fortunately stayed just the one night. The following day the 8,000-strong force headed south towards the French border. En route they were greeted with the news that Sir Douglas Haig's I Corps was sprinting northwards to reinforce the British 7th Division which, having landed at Zeebrugge on 6 October had been forced to evacuate and move inland. Each was ordered to Ypres, joining with the Cavalry Corps and the whole of IV Corps on the 15th. The Germans had drawn back to suitable topographical locations in preparation for both assault and potential defence.

Both British and French troops then took up positions in and around Ypres and its satellite villages, and awaited orders. It was a powerful force. Plans were confidently made for an advance by the 7th Division. In conjunction with French and Belgian cavalry they were to capture the towns of Menin and Roulers to the east and north of the Passchendaele Ridge.

On 18 October Roulers fell swiftly to French cavalry, and Menin was expected to follow suit. At this perilous time every road in West Flanders was choked with refugees moving south towards the Franco-Belgian border. Whilst British and French commanders cursed the bottlenecks (having previously encouraged the populace to move out) the alarming cause of the problem was soon revealed. Air reconnaissance spotted a huge enemy force, no less than two armies, advancing towards Ypres.

Roulers was instantly reoccupied by the Germans; Menin was never even reached by the British – the town would not to be liberated until September 1918. This was the opening day of the First Battle of Ypres. Even though the whole of Belgium was now under German rule apart from a tiny corner of Western Flanders, and despite the very real and clearly imminent danger of serious large-scale conflict, many locals still chose to remain, guarding homes and farms, possessions, businesses and livestock, and hoping against hope that the period of peril would be temporary.

But the events of 19 October changed the ambience and outlook completely. Known as 'Black Monday', on this day in Roulers a German unit was ambushed by a section of French troops who having killed a number of soldiers managed to slip away unseen. Suspecting the attack to have been the action of Belgian civilians, the German authorities responded by burning houses and summarily executing local people. The news reached the Ypres area and encouraged a further flood of terrified refugees. Battle was joined amongst chaotic scenes.

The more optimistic souls who left Ypres when the first shells began to fall did not go far, and indeed many returned during the quiet period around Christmas 1914;

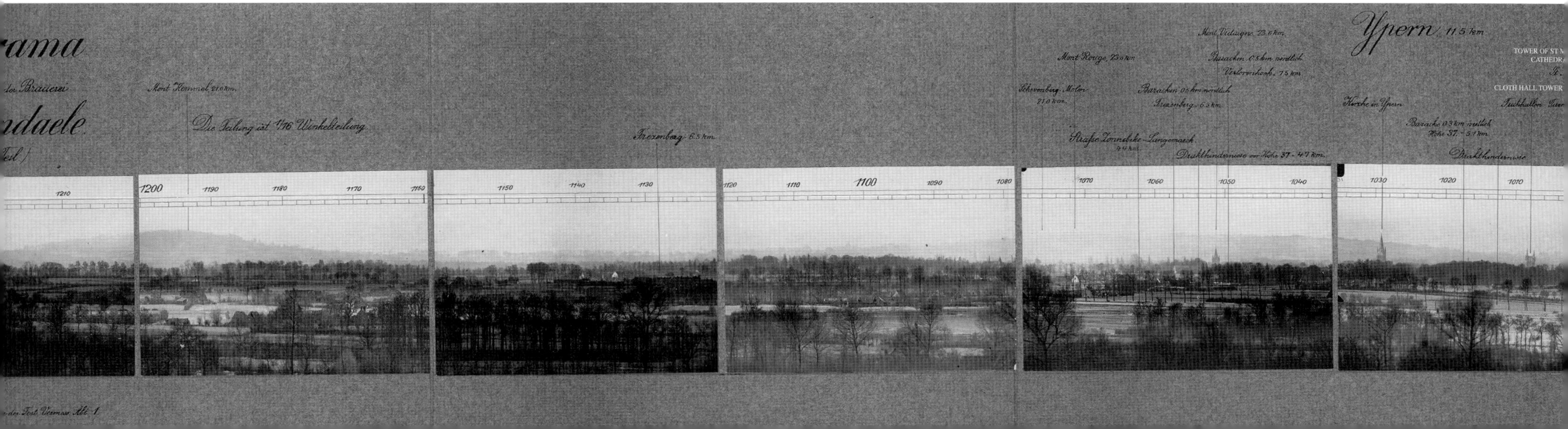

but Ypres soon became the object of wrath for frustrated German gunners – her many spires and towers presented fine targets – and by the end of March 1915 just a handful of civilians remained.

As critical as any of encounter of the war the First Battle of Ypres ended on 22 November in a 'defensive victory' for the Allies, but with debilitating losses for both sides. Within this grim struggle, the first of four battles to which the town would lend its name, the mould for the character of the First World War was cast. Although the term 'attrition' had not yet been coined, it was precisely what those serving in the European theatre now faced.

The Second Battle of Ypres, fought in April and May 1915 over practically the same territory as its predecessor, had a similar outcome. After this action the mildly fluid lines of the 1914–15 winter were solidly set in timber, steel and concrete for more than two years. The effect of this battle was to contract and stabilize the lines around Ypres into a constrained salient. When fighting ceased on 25 May 1915 the ten-month gestation of the Western Front was complete.

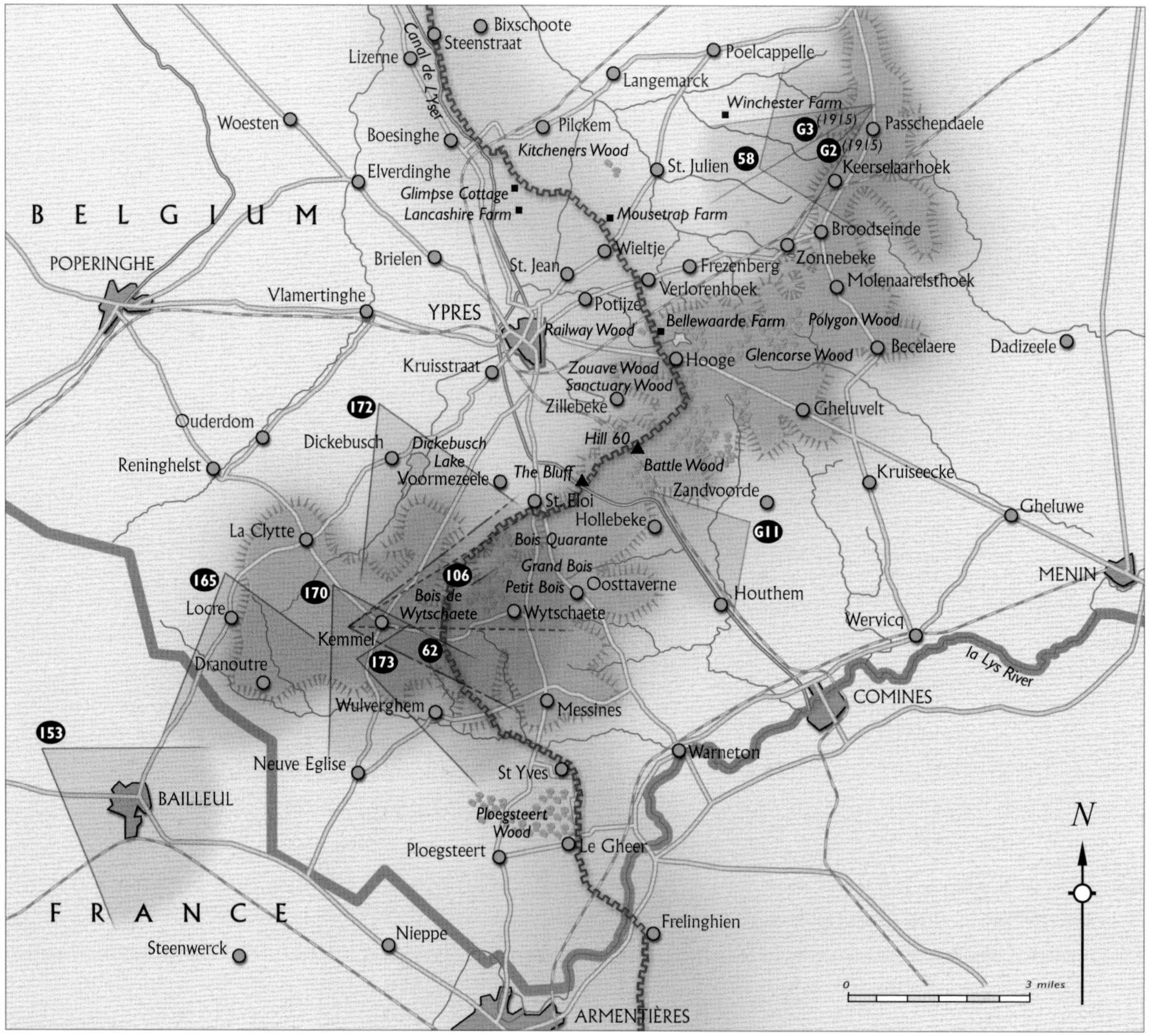

The First Battle of Ypres

The countryside around Ypres was low lying, generally wet, and, sat as it was on the unrelenting clay soils of the Flanders Plain, quite unlike the terrain experienced by British troops on the Marne and Aisne. Arriving in Flanders they were almost immediately faced by a great enemy offensive, involving furious attacks against the

Above
The remnants of the London Scottish, a Territorial battalion who, having been hustled to the sector in London buses, suffered 345 casualties in trying to hold the ridge on 31 October 1914. Only five of these men survived the war. 1 November 1914.

Belgians at Dixmude, on the Passchendaele and Messines Ridges, at Langemarck and Pilckem, and in France against the Armentières, La Bassée and Aubers Ridge sectors.

By 30 October the thigh-deep inundations had successfully done their work to the north, forcing the Germans to evacuate the area between Dixmude and Nieuport. At Dixmude itself, now the last major bridgehead on the River Yser, the Belgians were to endure continual attack well into the winter. Losses on both sides would escalate, but the German breakthrough on the Yser remained elusive. This was the first phase of battle.

Phase two involved the expected redeployment of troops from the inundated regions for a convergent attack upon the Ypres sector. On 31 October seven fresh German divisions pitched into battle between Gheluvelt and Armentières, taking the Wytschaete–Messines ridge and beginning a period of ferocious aggression against British, Indian (the Lahore Division arrived direct from the subcontinent on 22 October) and French troops in the woods and villages in front of Ypres.

On 11 November 1914 the third phase opened. This was to be the Germans' final desperate attempt to gain the Channel ports before Allied reinforcements arrived – and before winter set in. The fresh assaults followed the axis of the now infamous Menin Road, driving through Gheluvelt, Nonne Boschen and Polygon Wood and coming within a whisker of total success before being held, partly by valiant defence and partly by luck and confusion, at Hooge, just 3 km (2 miles) outside Ypres.

The British and French regiments who had defended Ypres for the last month were dramatically enfeebled. On 15 November fresh French troops took over the whole of the theatre – a theatre which had now become known as the Ypres Salient. With Christmas only weeks away the first of the heavy winter rains began to fall, turning primitive trenches and rifle pits into mires of sticky mud: for the infantry, staying dry and warm now became the priority. The rifle was substituted for the spade, and on the evening of 22 November a line was drawn in the annals of the Flanders campaigns for 1914: the First Battle of Ypres was over. The final action of 1914 came in mid-December when a half-hearted British attempt to recapture the Messines Ridge failed. In the Salient, proceedings were far from finished however: during the battles of spring 1915 the name of the ancient Flemish capital would assume a symbolism far exceeding even the heroic deeds of the warriors who defended it, to spread clear across the English-speaking world for ever.

Second Ypres

In early February 1915 British forces returned to the Salient. At first they took over 8 km (5 miles) of front from the outskirts of Poelcappelle past Zonnebeke to the Menin Road, renewing an affiliation which would soon embrace not only the regiments of Britain and India, but forces from all over the Empire.

By April, two-thirds of the territory was devolved to their care, and from 7 April the Indians were joined by a second overseas force, the Canadians. During the winter the front lines had remained relatively static, and although

Below
Panorama 19: the earliest Salient panorama, giving a view of Messines village on 13 December 1914. The ridge had fallen to German forces on 1 November.

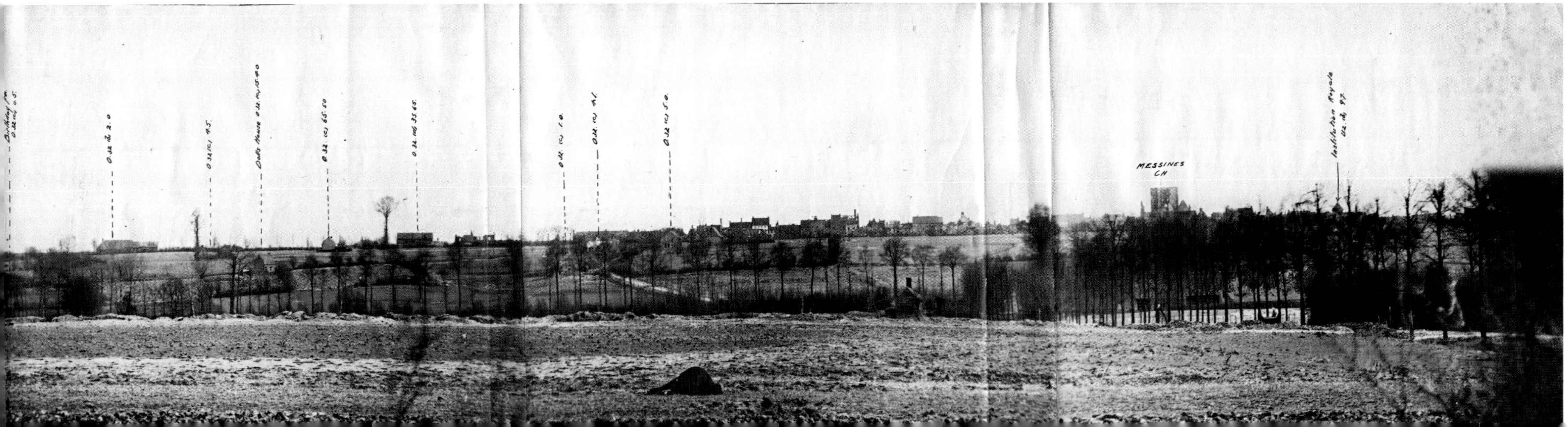

not yet fully connected to form the continuous belt of trenches which was later to characterize the Western Front, certain sectors such the Bluff, Hill 60 and Hooge were already well developed for defensive action. Patrols and trench raids had become frequent during the winter months, and mine warfare, albeit on a limited scale, had commenced.

Then came the sequence of gas attacks beginning on 22 April, followed by the gradual and relentless squeezing of Allied lines, and a series of forced withdrawals. On 25 May a noticeable quiet came over the battlefields. As guns cooled and troops held their breath in appreciation of the respite and in gratitude for salvation, Allied commanders surveyed the Salient. The arc of trenches was now nowhere much more than 3 km (2 miles) from the shell-ravaged ramparts of Ypres. To the south the German forces on the forward slopes of the Messines–Wytschaete ridge could almost gaze into the rear of the British lines, and it was a similar story in the north where the Germans had pushed all the way to the Yperlee canal. Ypres was now partially enveloped on three sides, and by day nothing could move without being spotted by hostile eyes.

After Second Ypres

Within days of the end of Second Ypres new, smaller scale, but equally bitter localized battles sprung up, mostly focused on sub-sectors along the ridges. For the Germans, already holding the most profitable elevated topography around Ypres, it was now essential to capitalize on their advantage and annexe the few remaining Allied positions of authority: Hooge, Sanctuary Wood, Observatory Ridge, Hill 60, St Eloi, and the Bluff. Apart from these few sub-sectors, the vast majority of Allied positions lay entirely within the low bowl in front of Ypres. This had not been a matter of luck, but sharp planning. Within this bowl northwards and eastwards radiated a parallel series of minor ridges created by ancient streams flowing westwards towards Ypres. Some were little more than gentle rises, but the tactical and psychological advantages of just a few extra metres of height were immense. The British were left in the uncomfortable position of looking up towards their enemy almost everywhere in the Salient.

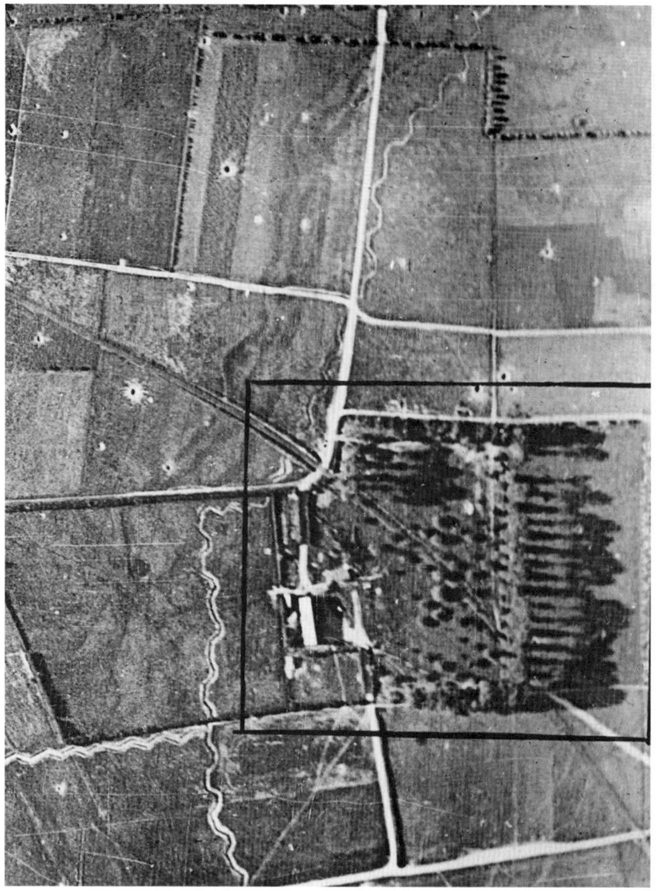

Now the war of the guns was about to begin. Concentrating upon localized areas of operation – often the target was not much bigger than a football field – enemy positions would be 'softened up' by artillery before an assault was launched. It was an old tactic of course, but in a battlefield like the Salient where the slightest swelling in the ground conferred such significant advantage, it was bound to lead to retaliation. This took the form of counter-battery fire, gun against gun rather than gun against fieldwork, and a vicious circle came into being. By this simple act the growth in the power of artillery on both sides was guaranteed.

On the ground the early unconnected, shallow and short trenches retained from the previous year's fighting were joined up and deepened where possible. Accommodation was provided in the form of simple surface shelters (even then called dugouts) for two, three or four men. Only support and reserve lines were added, and the whole system was linked perpendicularly by numerous communication trenches.

Left
Troops of the Honourable Artillery Company outside flimsy shelters in the leafy glades of Sanctuary Wood, June 1915.

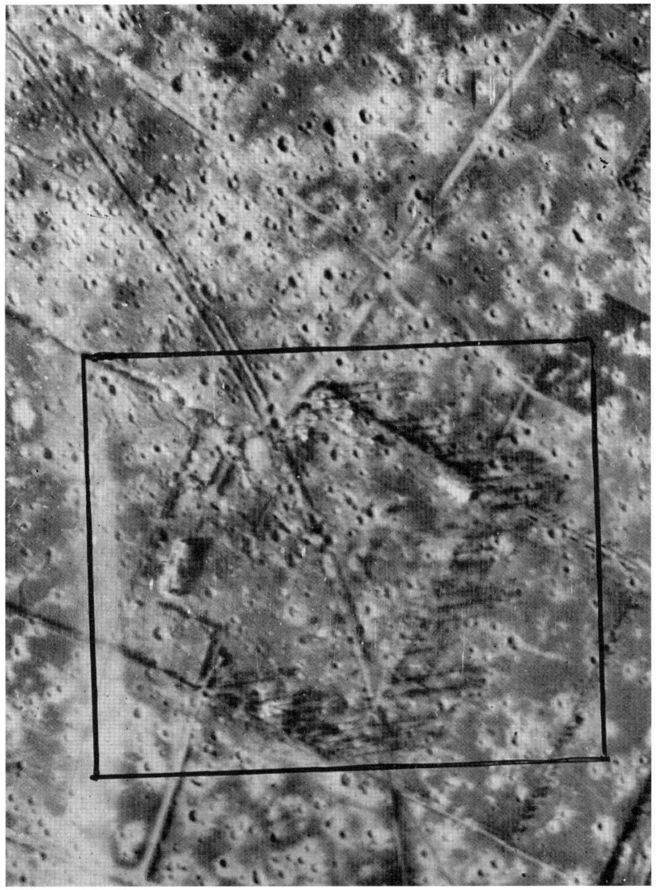

Above left and above
Aerial photographs showing the results of concentrated counter-battery fire.

Above right
Deep, dry and comfortable German trenches dug into the ridge slope north and east of Ypres. Small concrete shelters have been installed beneath the parapet.

Further lines were dug in rear areas so that in the event of an emergency troops might always have defensible positions to fall back on. Eventually, similar entrenchments would be installed at intervals all the way back to the Channel ports, and indeed on the British mainland!

After Second Ypres the wisest plan appeared to be to increase the strength and quantity of fieldworks against the ever-increasing power of artillery. As the RE later observed, both armies were able to equip themselves with new weapons far quicker than fortifications could be built or repaired. In choosing to employ huge numbers of steel-reinforced concrete blockhouses in many sectors of the Western Front, especially in front of Ypres, the Germans partly slipped back into the old nineteenth-century strategy of permanent fortification; strengthening the new 'Flemish frontier of the fatherland' with a multitudinous rash of small strongpoints rather than the traditional great fortress. From the ridges they could afford to feel confident, but the tactic spoke clearly of patience, and a deliberate and definitive long-term strategy.

The British looked at the war from a different angle: they were not going to expend energy on such enduring works because their whole military psychology leaned towards offensive thrusting action – launched at the earliest opportunity. In no way did they intend to be trapped in the cul-de-sac of the Salient, being bombarded from three sides, for longer than was absolutely necessary. The fieldworks die was cast in the summer of 1915, and from then on the prosecution of war would become more complex and demanding by the day.

The Canal Bank to the Railway

Above
April 1915. A captured British trench on the heights of Broodseinde Ridge. It would be October 1917 before an Allied boot once again made an imprint upon the ridge.

The convex curve of the Ypres Salient is bisected by the Ypres–Roulers railway. A single track line ran from Ypres station near the Lille Gate through Hellfire Corner and on to Zonnebeke, by-passing Passchendaele village via the infamous cutting south of Tyne Cot cemetery, and continuing north-east over the crest of the ridge and beyond another 8 km (5 miles) to Roulers.

The left sector incorporates the battlegrounds north of the railway including Boesinghe, the Kaaie Salient, Mauser, Pilckem and Mousetrap ridges, the villages of Wieltje, St Jean and St Julien, Frezenberg and Verlorenhoek. Each of the four battles of Ypres between 1914 and 1918 was partly fought over these pastures, and the contemporary landscape of all the actions are captured in the panoramas.

First Ypres (30 October to November 1914)

On 20 October 1914, whilst heavy fighting was in progress between Armentières and La Bassée, British cavalry and infantry of Sir Henry Rawlinson's 7th Division skirmished along the ridges near Passchendaele and around Zonnebeke (Panorama 58, although taken the following spring, illustrates the 'feel' of this early landscape of battle). It was also on this day that the name of General Sir Douglas Haig might first have been heard amongst the nervous populace of Ypres. Haig's command, I Corps, had just arrived from fighting on the Aisne, to be thrown straight into a fresh furnace: Germany's robust attempt to reach the Channel ports and Paris via Ypres before Christmas. Haig received immediate and urgent orders from Sir John French Commander-in-Chief of the BEF: the British and French were outnumbered several to one, the Germans had five times as many guns, and some heavy ones too, so it was imperative that Haig's men entrench for all they were worth on the lines they now held. The Germans must not be allowed to break through. But it was also the day that the French Cavalry Corps in Houthulst Forest, on the left of the British 3rd Cavalry Division, were forced to retire. Massed ranks of German troops swarmed towards Bixschoote, Langemarck, the Pilckem Ridge, and the Ypres–Dixmude canal.

Below
Panorama 58 shows the positions held by the British immediately before the Second Battle of Ypres. The trenches on the Passchendaele Ridge are all German. 17 April 1915.

Above

Segment of German Panorama G-2 taken from Passchendaele brewery. April 1917.

Below

German *Pionieres* adjusting equipment in preparation for a cloud gas attack. The hoses lead out into no man's land.

Below right

British message dogs with a concerned-looking handler. The dogs' feet are bound with bandages to protect them from the burning effect of mustard gas, which often clung to the ground before vaporizing.

There were precious few Allied reserves, so unless halted, the enemy could go as far beyond as they wished. The C-in-C's next order was for Haig to bowl men into the breach and block the line of advance. Although outnumbered, the regular British infantry and gunners had seen plenty of action since Le Cateau and Mons; their sappers too were experienced, having left a fine system of trenches behind for French use on the Aisne. By contrast, the German troops approaching British muzzles, although not the band of young, singing students with flowers in their caps as the myth perpetuates, were certainly predominantly 'unblooded' reservists with minimal training and no experience of battle whatsoever. On 23 October 1914 they were practically annihilated in the fields in front of Langemarck and Bixschoote by Haig's cool and skilled fifteen-rounds-a-minute professionals. This was the First Battle of Langemarck, 21–23 October 1914.

Almost 1,500 men died. Such a loss in so brief a period halted the advance in its tracks. Later, more attacks were launched against the Belgians and French at Steenstraate and Bixschoote, but the lines continued to hold. The effects of the attack and the French withdrawal forced a British reorganization in front of Ypres, resulting in the line pulling back in the northern half of the Salient. The Germans soon held all the outer crests and spurs of the main arc of the ridge, all excellent defensive positions, southwards from Passchendaele to the village of Becelaere.

Panorama 58 (17 April 1915), taken from a building on the S'Gravenstafel crossroads is the earliest example from this sector and shows German positions on the forward ridge of slopes and spurs beneath Passchendaele village, with primitive British lines on the lower contours below. These positions were to remain stable during the winter of 1914–15. The landscape is relatively undamaged and offers a reasonable impression of the 1914 conditions. Several of the 1917 panoramas also incorporate relevant landscapes of the 1914 battles, but they are hardly recognizable as such. If taken in 1914, No 102 (Third Ypres) for instance, would have revealed within the frame a wooded landscape, a chateau with sweeping formal gardens, gatehouses, stables and outbuildings. The only recognizable item in the 1917 picture however, is a foundered tank. Panorama 130 from the Broodseinde Ridge (undated but probably taken in March 1918 at the same time as 131 from Primus) shows distant untouched fields and church spires, whilst the tortured foreground landscape was actually that which witnessed some of the first engagements of the war, fought between horsemen armed with lances! However, it is G-2 and G-3, two connecting German panoramas taken from Passchendaele Brewery in April 1915, which remain particularly useful for gleaning an idea of the 'pre-war' landscape of almost the entire Salient.

Second Ypres (22 April to 25 May 1915)

It was against the sector from Wieltje to Boesinghe and the adjacent Belgian-held positions at Steenstraate that the first German cloud-gas attacks were launched on 22 April 1915, just a few days after Panoramas 58, G-2 and G-3 were taken. A distinction has deliberately been made between shell- and grenade-deployed gas, as it was in fact the French

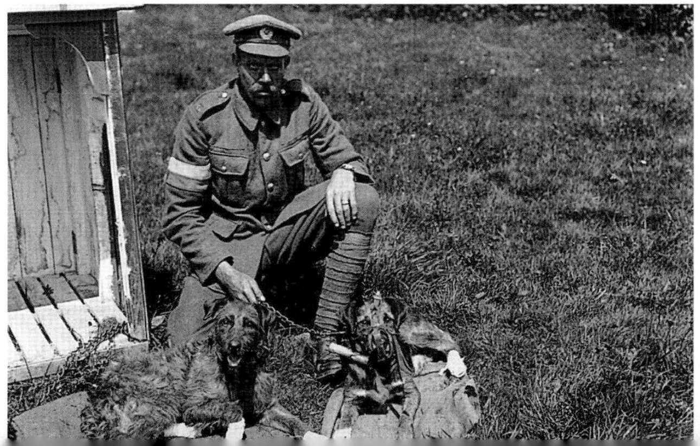

Left
Improvised gas gong made from a brass 18-pounder shellcase. Rattles and horns were also employed.

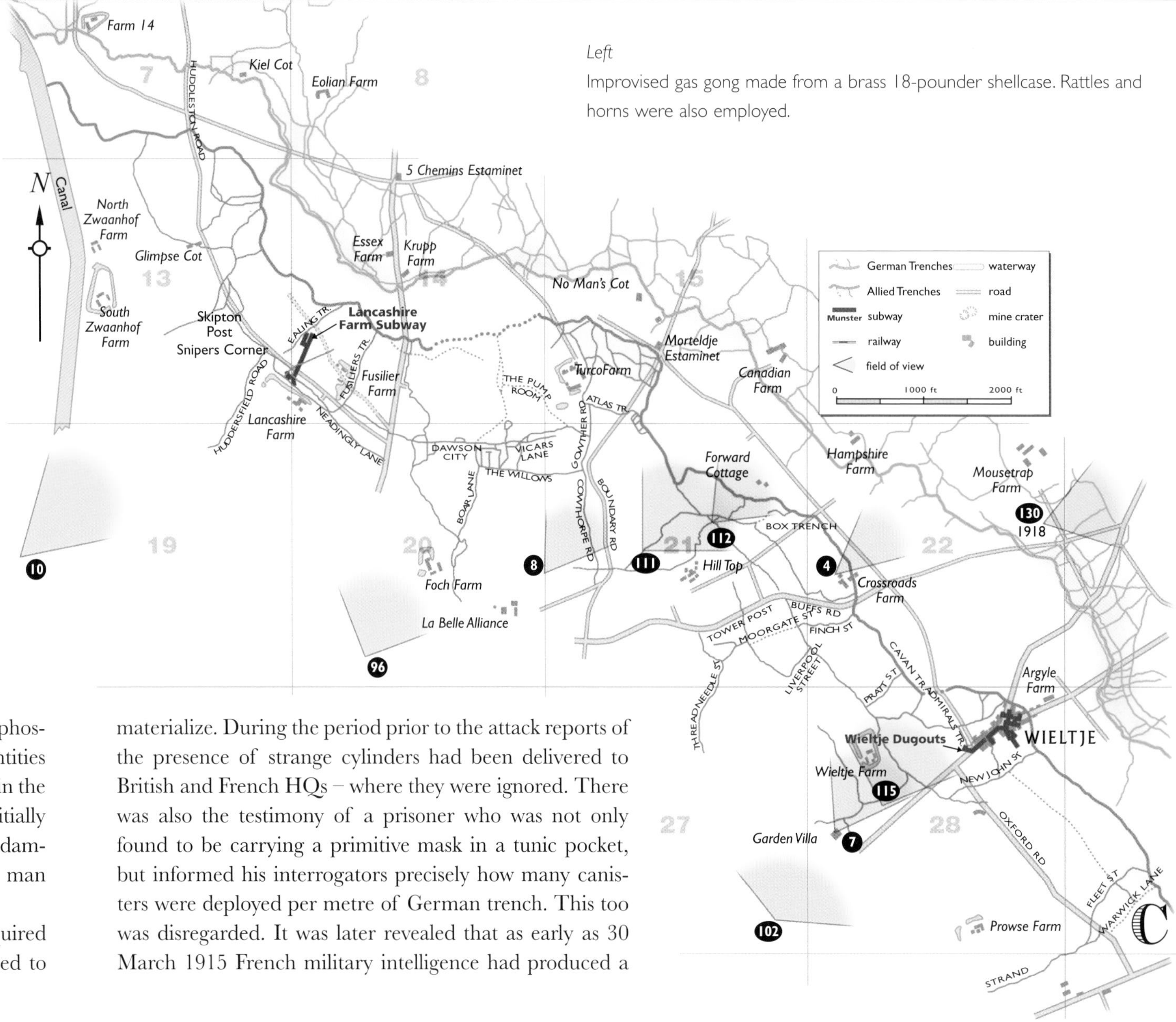

who first used these weapons in August 1914. At Ypres the product was chlorine, released from cylinders via hoses. Although a much less devilish weapon than successorssuch as mustard and phosgene, chlorine was nevertheless lethal if sufficient quantities were inhaled; a light dose induced a tickling sensation in the eyes, nose and throat, whilst a strong concentration initially caused choking, but was soon followed by irreparable damage to the respiratory system: in this latter case a man literally drowned in his own mucus.

A northerly breeze was what the Germans required for a successful release, and for several days it refused to materialize. During the period prior to the attack reports of the presence of strange cylinders had been delivered to British and French HQs – where they were ignored. There was also the testimony of a prisoner who was not only found to be carrying a primitive mask in a tunic pocket, but informed his interrogators precisely how many canisters were deployed per metre of German trench. This too was disregarded. It was later revealed that as early as 30 March 1915 French military intelligence had produced a

Above
Second Army Panorama 10 taken from the banks of the canal in July 1915 showing the part of the northern salient where the German gas attack of 22 April caused a serious breach in the Allied line.

detailed communiqué entitled the 'Employment of Asphyxiating gases by the Germans'. The information had not reached British eyes.

On the afternoon of 22 April a worthy wind blew across the Langemarck sector. Since mid-February thousands of gas cylinders had been installed beneath trench parapets between Bixschoote and Poelcappelle, the German XV Corps front. The attack itself was announced by an intense shelling of Ypres, to which French field guns answered mildly. Upon release at 5 p.m. the yellowish mist spread to cover a front of approximately 6 km (3.5 miles). Its pungent odour was later detectable by puzzled observers as far away as 10 km (6 miles) from the source. Panoramas 10 (29 July 1915) and *96* (9 November 1916) show a considerable part the ground over which the gas advanced, and French Algerian troops withdrew. Although the two views are separated by sixteen months they appear almost identical. But appearance deceives: a careful examination of the later picture reveals that the entire British defensive trench system has now been put in place and multiple wire entanglements have been constructed. The trench running across the foreground is a reserve position, with the front line situated on the slopes of the ridges beyond. So hazardous was this sector that at Lancashire Farm a steel shaft 15 m (49 ft) deep was later sunk and a tunnelled subway installed which connected to the forward positions. The tunnel, which also incorporated dugouts and a dressing station, allowed reliefs to take place without troops setting foot on the surface. A camouflaged and partly covered trench tramway was used to remove spoil during the digging, and was subsequently employed to transport everyday supplies in and wounded out. It linked the canal bridges (just behind the photographer) to the shaft head. Several

Below
Panorama 4 from Crossroads Farm, taken at the time when Skeggs and his battalion were in residence.

tunnels were also driven beneath the canal for the transfer of men and materials.

The effect upon the French 87th Territorial and 45th Algerian divisions occupying the windward axis of the gas cloud was catastrophic. If not killed or disabled, many men understandably bolted in dread, leaving a gap in the line some 7 km (4 miles) wide. With only disconnected support and reserve trenches in place, and little in the way of wire (as Panorama 10 illustrates), there were no field obstacles to arrest the German stride – and no opposing troops. A broad and ample route to Ypres lay wide open. As soon as the cloud had travelled sufficiently far across enemy territory, ostensibly fifteen minutes after initial discharge, German infantry wearing primitive but evidently effective protection followed behind. At first they faced no resistance, but moving ever nearer the Mauser Ridge and the Canal, it became clear that the moment the attack had been launched one or two quick-thinking onlookers, especially Brigadier-General R. E. W. Turner of 3rd Canadian Brigade, had acted instantly. At the same time as calling for support, he began pushing his own men and elements of the Buffs (Royal East Kent Regiment) into the gap. The artillery provided what meagre backing they could. On the left flank of the gas attack General De Ceuninck's 6th Belgian Division took similar action. In stark contrast to this swift work, it took an extraordinary hour and forty-five minutes for news of the action even to reach British Second Army HQ.

It was the rapid response of the Canadians and Belgians that ultimately saved the day. The axis of attack had been from the north; by pushing men into the void created between Wieltje and Steenstraate, the hostile momentum was arrested. These actions were also assisted by the hour: as the wind had only become favourable at 5 p.m., night was beginning to fall as the assault gathered pace – just at the time when the Germans needed all the daylight they could get. They paused – some troops as early as 7.30 – and began to dig in.

As the news of the discontinuation broke, elsewhere in the Salient commanders called up every available reserve and adjusted their lines to allow Canadian-commanded troops to bolster the affected zone – and to counter-attack. At 10 p.m. however, the position was still worrisome and still critical. Would the Germans move again? What was their ultimate intention? How many reserves had they available? How long could the Belgians hold? How soon could Allied support be brought up from the rear? And was there more gas to come?

The battle flared again as the Germans made further attempts to cross the canal, with attacks on the Belgian right flank and artillery bombardments over those areas where Allied reserves were known to be rushing forward to assist. At midnight the Canadians counter-attacked Kitchener's Wood (Panorama 4, from Crossroads Farm) under bright moonlight, but were forced to retire by heavy gunfire, pulling back almost to Mousetrap Farm (also No 4), at this time still unpopularly known as Shelltrap Farm but already a famous name on the map.

Below

Removing an identity tag and other belongings from a casualty. Personal items were sent back to the family. Because the original locations of so many casualties were lost in subsequent upheavals, the majority of those discovered on the battlefields today remain unidentifiable.

Above
A segment of Second Army Panorama 8 showing the Mauser and Pilckem Ridges with the German strongpoint called High Command Redoubt in the centre. The Turco Farm position later sheltered a large, deep British HQ dugout system beneath its farmhouse and outbuildings.

On 23 April, the Allied lines were reinforced. Thus far the German attacks had punched a deep fist-shaped indentation into the northern flank of the Salient. It left the Allies holding a peculiarly elongated pocket jutting eastwards from Ypres – an entirely unsuitable zone for even short-term defence.

Within twelve hours the Allies had improvised a continuous line across the breach created by the gas the previous evening. Extra artillery support was arriving all the time, and more was on its way from the First Army south of the Salient. But the new positions lying along the upper contours of Mauser and Pilckem Ridges (Panoramas 8, 10 and *96*) could be only thinly held, and were practically devoid of defensive fieldworks. A further Allied attack based upon a French plan (of General Joffre's) was agreed to further secure the breach and drive the enemy away from the sensitive canal sector. It achieved the former, but failed entirely in the latter.

During 24 May fresh gas and infantry attacks took place around the entire northern arc of the Salient, affecting all regions from the Canal to the Menin Road and slightly beyond (many of these sectors can be seen in the next section). Allied artillery, already reduced to a pathetic three rounds per gun per day, could offer only derisory assistance. St Julien was lost, Keerselaere followed, and pressure further mounted upon the drained and weakened defenders.

The pocket was growing narrower. Overwhelmed by the concentration and persistence of the German attacks, evacuation of casualties was desperately slow, and the front lines became congested with gassed and wounded men. Battalions were unsure which units lay to their left or right, and often of their own location on the map: most had little or no idea of where the enemy lay, or their strength.

One of the most tragic actions of this period was the attack of the Lahore Division against Mauser Ridge and Kitchener's Wood. On 26 April in conjunction with a 149th Northumberland Brigade assault on St Julien from Wieltje, both units barely advanced beyond their own front line. Losses were dreadful, almost two-thirds of the unit strength becoming casualties. Many Lahore Division troops were cut down by shrapnel on Hilltop Ridge whilst still moving towards their jumping-off position beyond Turco Farm. The fields in which the tragedy occurred can be seen in Panoramas 7 from Wieltje Farm (June 1915); 8, near La Belle Alliance (13 July 1915); 102A from Hasler House, St Jean, (1 March 1917); and in the right-hand half of *96* Zouave Villa, (9 November 1916). The village of Wieltje (visible in Nos 7 and 102) was later undermined by a deep and large British dressing station dugout. It was here on 31 July that double VC and MC winner Noel Chavasse was treated for an ultimately fatal head wound. He is buried in New Military Cemetery at Brandhoek. Chavasse won his MC in June 1915 in the Hooge sector, also covered in the next section.

The situation had become more than unfavourable, but Sir John French still hoped to evade a general withdrawal by re-expanding the Salient through offensive means. He had already been advised by his senior commander in the field Sir Horace Smith-Dorrien, that a retirement would be necessary. On 27 April Smith-Dorrien was replaced by General Sir Herbert Plumer; the following day Plumer was somewhat curiously informed by none other than Sir John French himself that a retirement was planned. The French High Command abhorred any notion of withdrawal, and beseeched the British to wait until a fresh French assault in the canal sector had been pressed the following day (Boesinghe, Panorama 100, 23 January 1917). Sir John French acceded. The attacks failed utterly in the face of pre-prepared German defence and intense artillery fire.

The withdrawal would therefore go ahead. The plan was to contract the dangerous elongated pocket by pulling in its eastern tip and constructing a new front line on the forward slopes of the gentle and relatively dry ridge spurs in the northern and central salient, much nearer to Ypres. Positions to the south at Hill 60, the Bluff, St Eloi, Wytschaete, Messines etc., were to remain in place. Number 58 is the only known British example which shows the Passchendaele sector immediately before the Second Battle of Ypres. The lines were occupied at this time by the 11th Brigade which managed to hold on for nine days following the gas attacks. A comparison with the two German panoramas G-2 and G-3 illustrate the immense benefit of holding higher ground – and also the quality of German cameras and lenses. French battery positions have been located several kilometres from the photographer.

The retirement was postponed several times, partly due to further requests from the French, but also by the RE, charged with preparing the new positions: where the ground was good, digging was easy and swift, so trenches of decent safe depth were possible; elsewhere it was a question of rifle pits and short breastwork emplacements. If a little extra time could be bought however, the new line might be made considerably more defensible. Although hostile shelling continued practically uninterrupted, the Germans did not renew infantry attacks on 27, 28 or 29 April. This was more than fortuitous for the Allies, but nerves became very frayed when at the last moment withdrawal was postponed yet again, once more in deference to another French venture in front of Boesinghe. It too failed utterly.

Between 1 and 3 May 1915 the long-awaited retirement was dexterously carried out, with British and Canadian troops abandoning over 4 km (2.5 miles) of territory with only minor complications. The area of the Salient was thus reduced by a third. But the contraction was not quite over yet. Beginning on 8 May, despite Plumer's orders to hold the line at all costs, German attacks against the Frezenberg Ridge and its northward extension in front of Wieltje and Mousetrap Ridge pushed the British off the slopes – out of their freshly-made positions. There was again no enemy breakthrough, but a 'rolling up' of the line began which drove the British back a further kilometre in the area between the Ypres–Roulers railway and Wieltje. On 24 May another gas attack, greater yet than others to date, was launched on a wide front stretching from Turco Farm (Panorama 8 and others) to Hooge on the Menin Road – almost 7 km (4 miles).

During this action Mousetrap Farm fell at last. Bludgeoned by shot and shell for weeks the ancient moated homestead lay entirely ruined as early as June 1915. So complete was its obliteration that the site, although appearing on several panoramas, shows only as a jumbled heap of brick. All the Allied positions were now put under such pressure that further withdrawal became unavoidable. At the end of the day, the British and Canadians had been ousted from all the high ground everywhere north of the railway.

Their new positions are illustrated in Panoramas 6 (10 July 1915) , *37* and 38 (both 11 November 1915) and 102 (1 March 1917). The German view appears in G-4, taken from a German artillery observation post 800 m (875 yds)

Above
An Australian soldier with an aeroplane wind vane. The device was pivoted and swung according to the direction of the breeze, giving warning of potentially dangerous conditions for enemy cloud gas attacks. Soon after the first gas attack, scores of these wind vanes sprung up along many front line parapets; see the right-hand frame of Panorama 7 from Garden Villa. Flags were also employed (see Panorama *42*, chapter two).

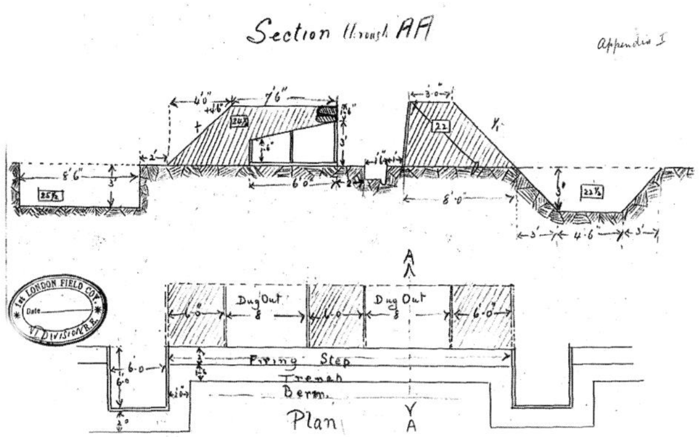

Above left
The first primitive gas masks: a simple impregnated gauze pad fixed in place with tapes. These men are also wearing goggles to counter the lachrymatory effects of chlorine.

Above and below
RE dugout frame design. These were the earliest form of shelter and were installed within the parapet structure. They are occupied here (*below*) by Australian troops.

south of Frezenberg village in June 1915, just as the Salient was settling into two years of stasis. The Ypres–Roulers railway runs along the lower edge of the photo; the point where it meets 'Strasse Ypern' – Menin is Hellfire Corner. 'Hallenturm in Ypern' is the Cloth Hall, with St Martin's Cathedral to the right, and the churches of St Peter and St Jakob to the left. The Menin Road runs through the first five frames. British field positions are being frantically connected and developed at this time. The position marked as 'Kit and Kat' on Panorama 101 (27 January 1917) is roughly where G-4 was taken. The same location can also be seen on the ridge behind the trees to the right of the railway line in No 70 (1 June 1915). Potijze Chateau was an important dressing station during the war. Known as White Chateau, it should not be confused with the other feature of the same name at The Bluff.

As a result of the loss of the ridge-tops it was agreed that the wedge-shaped piece of British-held territory between Mousetrap and Turco Farms should also be evacuated, and a new connecting defensive line dug which would sweep in a convex curve from Wieltje village, through Crossroads Farm, past Morteldje Estaminet to Turco. In this move the British gave up all their newly dug positions on the Frezenberg, Mousetrap and Mauser Ridges, and once more dropped back onto the lower contours.

The 25 May passed almost peacefully: no attacks materialized and shelling was almost desultory. On this day the Second Battle of Ypres drew to a close with a whimper. The lines now etched upon the fields of Belgian Flanders were to remain fixed for more than two years – but they would be extended, remodelled, refurbished and renewed until many hundreds of kilometres of fieldworks criss-crossed the Salient. It later transpired that the Germans had never intended to take Ypres at all by employing gas on 22 April, but simply capture the high ground either side of Pilckem. This, they believed, would make the town indefensible, thereby forcing an Allied retirement.

Some of the primitive trenches that appeared during the long and bitter first winter at Ypres, especially those in the sectors south of the railway, lie upon or close to the positions they would occupy after the Allied retirements and reconsolidations of May 1915. In the northern sector however, a certain realignment was needed as soon as the Second Battle was over. Here, the assaults of First and Second Ypres had come from the north; following the double contraction of the lines, and in particular the German capture of the ridges, the axis of threat was altered, and was now from the east. In places trenches were re-orientated a full 90 degrees to face an equally static enemy.

It was at this time that the development of the great web of supporting earthworks across the entire Ypres battlefield began. Between Wieltje and the canal the British, Canadians and French (soon to entirely leave the area until the summer of 1917) found themselves on ground of variable contour and consequently varied geological nature. The trenches which for approximately a kilometre ran roughly parallel to the canal from the extreme northern hinge of the Ypres Salient at Boesinghe benefited from two 'made ground' embankments, one on each side of the canal; these were useful both for cover and for shielding activity from enemy sight. In the same way that over 900 dugouts were installed inside the Ypres ramparts, within the canal embankments a great linear system of dugouts was later built, housing every kind of HQ, plus dressing stations, storage and billets.

The well-known 'John McCrae' dressing station adjacent to Essex Farm Cemetery is a part of this system. Cuts were made through the embankment to serve as many as twenty RE, Pioneer, and Army Troop-built bridges, while on the Kaaie Salient (as this section of front came to be known) these narrow little footways became both critical arteries for supply and relief, and vital escape routes. They received constant attention from German gunners.

The highest ground in the sector: the arc of Mauser, Pilckem, Mousetrap and Frezenberg ridges, was now entirely in enemy possession, with the Allied front lines lying at the foot or on the lower slopes of each. These were damp positions. Even in the summertime, trenches could only be dug to about a metre depth before the water table was reached. Consequently they were developed as part-trench, part-breastworks.

A subaltern's diary

The letters of Robin Skeggs, 3rd Battalion, Rifle Brigade, are some of the most revealing documents relating to the period immediately following the Second Battle of Ypres. The true era of industrialized trench warfare was just beginning, and those involved knew only that some form of order had to be put in place. By reason of enjoying similar geology, most of the working practices in the sub-sectors between the canal and the railway followed comparable practices, although localized trench design was often a matter for the officers in charge at the time.

An unsurpassed example of battlefield archaeology which revealed the formation, establishment, design and development of a British Great War front-line system was recently carried out in Flanders. The positions, part of the La Brique sub-sector, can be seen in Panoramas 4, 7, 8, 102 and 115 (Third Ypres chapter). These were the very trenches where Robin Skeggs first came into the Salient in June 1915.

Prior to moving north to Ypres Skeggs was serving at Wez Macquart near Armentières – a sector where breastworks were obligatory. A few days before transferring north to Ypres, grim rumours about the Salient were circulating:

29th May 1915 – Trenches, France

My dear Father, I am writing to try and give you a sort of notion where we are going during the course of the next few days. We are going, as the censor well knows, to XXXX [Ypres]. We have had a fellow here to tell us what it is like. He reports it not bad at all, and nothing near so black as it is painted. They really acted most promptly when the Boche began to use chlorine at Hill 60. They served out respirators to us the day after, and bicarbonate of soda the day following that. We saturate the pads in a solution of the soda. We have to wear the pads tied around our necks so that we are always ready for them. Apparently, as long as fellows don't lie at the bottom of the trench they are fairly safe with these respirators on. I should think our people will use chlorine after the vile action of the Germans. In a way I shall be glad of the change of scene and experience – and glad if we get a chance to really see what we can do. The trenches here are simply plastered with model aeroplanes now [to test wind direction since the gas attack]. Since the weather improved the men have had time to devote to frivolity, and they have evolved some marvellous things about two feet long, made of wood and tin and wire, with beautifully carved propellers. The propellers buzz furiously when there is any wind and they turn faithfully to meet the wind like a windmill. The planes are fixed on a stick and pivoted. Thank you so much for the parcel. Its contents were:

1 tin cocoa, 1 tin milk, 1 tin sugar – brown, 1 tin oxtail soup, 1 tin oatmeal biscuits, 1 tin loganberries, 1 tin spaghetti, 1 tin cherries, 1 tin damsons, 1 tin mock turtle soup, 1 box of dates, 1 packet, luminous paint and base, 1 pair boot laces, 2 packets Mexican chocolate, 1 packet muscatel raisins, 1 packet almonds, 1 packet tomato soup, 1 packet scotch broth, 1 vigoral chicken broth, Writing paper and envelopes, 1 respirator from Aunt Ruby, Toilet paper, 1 copy of Sphere, 1 packet pipe cleaners, 1 tin Vaseline, 2 brushes for paint.

Could you without much trouble get some water sterilising tablets for me please? Boots would have them I should think. I believe at this new place it is very difficult to get wood and other material up to the trenches as the roads have been so churned up by shellfire that carts cannot get along. Whether that is really so is open to doubt, but

Above
Segment of Panorama 7 showing the sub-sector taken over by 3rd Battalion, Rifle Brigade in June 1915.

Below
2nd Lieutenant Robin Oliver Skeggs, 3rd Battalion, Rifle Brigade.

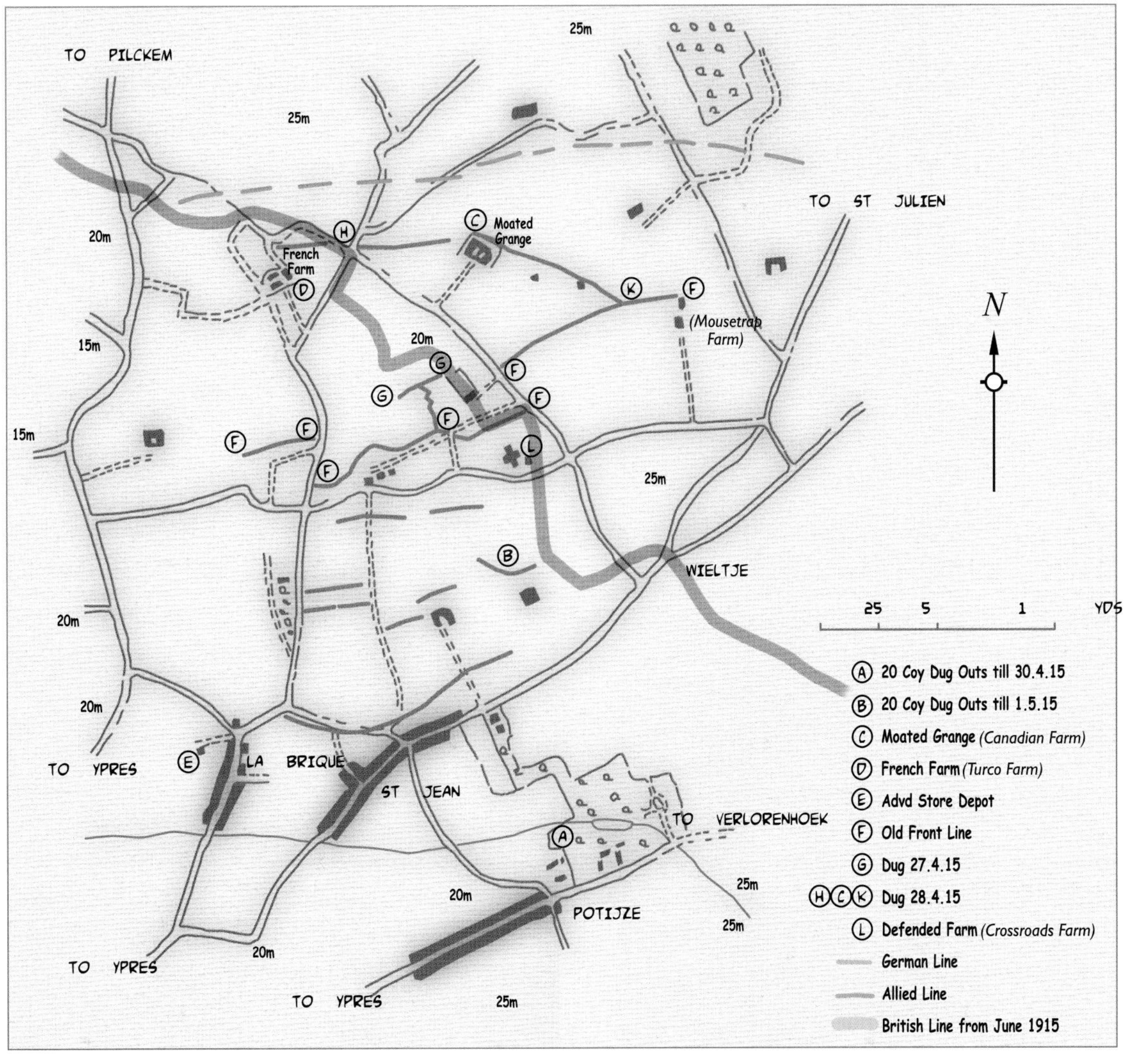

someone said so. Apparently it is a spot where there used to be much battling, but now it is much quieter. They think the Boche has so often failed there that he is at last tired of wasting his energy on it.
2ND LIEUTENANT ROBIN SKEGGS, 3RD BATTALION, RIFLE BRIGADE

Skeggs and his comrades were only sketchily aware of the nature of the Second Battle of Ypres. Arriving near Crossroads Farm just to the left of Wieltje village, the primitive state of the newly static line is evident from his next letter.

Left
Early hand-drawn map showing northerly trench orientation.

Above
The short unconnected rifle pits correspond to the line F-F running alongside the track on the map. The east-facing trenches, revetted in corrugated iron, are at the bottom of the frame.

8th June 1915 – Trenches

My very dear Father, Just a few more lines in answer to your two very welcome letters. I am indeed most grateful to you for all the manifold things you are getting for me. It must absorb an immense amount of time seeing to it, and I do appreciate your good work very much. These trenches are very practical as far as resisting shellfire and so on, but they are NOT comfortable. We exist in extreme muddle and have no dugouts. I should therefore be very glad of the usual sort of weekly parcel after all, in spite of what I said. The fruit is most comforting when it is blazing hot, as it has been, preferably the cherries and fruit salad, which are most thirst quenching. Could you please send a packet of lime juice or lemonade crystals – some with not much sugar in please. And just now (each officer has to dwell and feed by himself just yet) I should be very glad of something in the meat line which is not salted – if such a thing could be got. Some tinned thing. If possible small tins just enough for one meal (or two) in each tin.

The Boche has been shelling us a good deal today. He is a nuisance. Thank goodness no casualties in my company tho' the shells came very close. Of course we expected that kind of thing when we came here.

We are advanced company now – honoured post – we are all connected up, but just a bit in front, about 300 yards from the German front line. He has another line about 1,000 yards away. I took a patrol out last night and we succeeded in getting into the German trenches. It was great fun. We brought back several souvenirs – a cap, some grenades, ammunition and so on. I will try to send you one of the grenades when I have had it made safe. I laid two bombs to act as mines in the bottom of their trench. We hope to hear them go up tonight. We had a fearful long crawl to do it. We were out about three hours.

Trench raids on a more organized and greater scale than this were to become a common feature. The enforced stasis troubled the 'thrusters' at GHQ, and as early as February 1915 Chief of the General Staff Lieutenant-General W. R. Robertson had sent out a memorandum ordering localized small-scale attacks with a view to gaining ground and taking advantage of 'any tactical or numerical inferiority on the part of the enemy'. Robertson considered raids to be, 'highly valuable…since they relieve monotony and improve the morale of our own troops, while they have a corresponding detrimental effect on the morale of the enemy's troops and tend in a variety of ways to their exhaustion and general disquiet'. The order was issued to all units along the entire British front. The application of the tactic was confirmed in Skeggs' inimitable style.

11th June 1915 – Trenches

My dear Father, I have just had a whole bevy of absolutely spiffing parcels from you. It was like getting a week's leave, or anyhow having a birthday. I get a parcel from you practically every day now. You are doing me well! Now in detail:

Above
Panorama 4 from Crossroads Farm, taken at the time when Robin Skeggs and his battalion were in residence.

Below
Skeggs' first primitive trench in the Forward Cottage area.

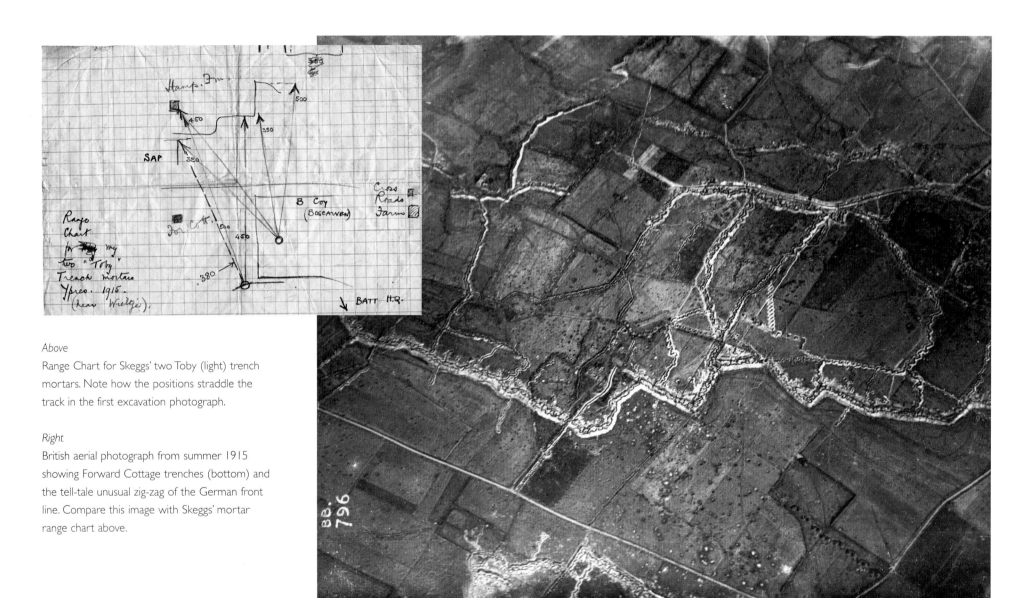

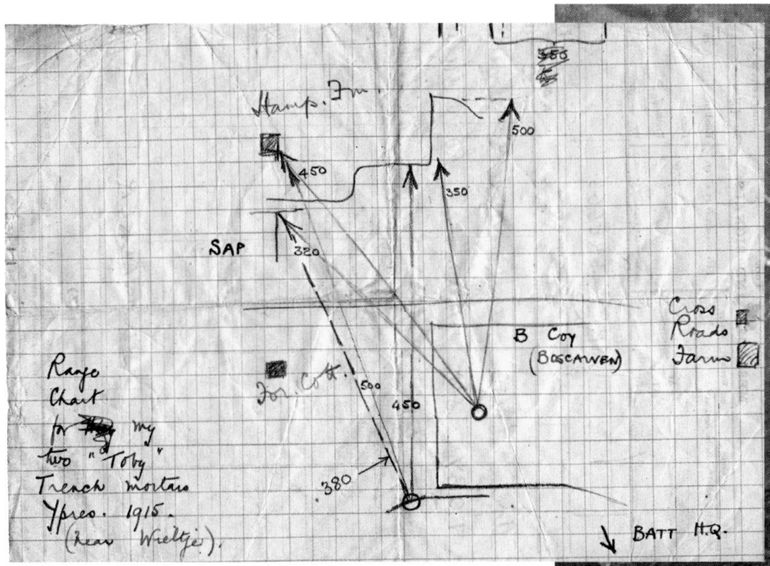

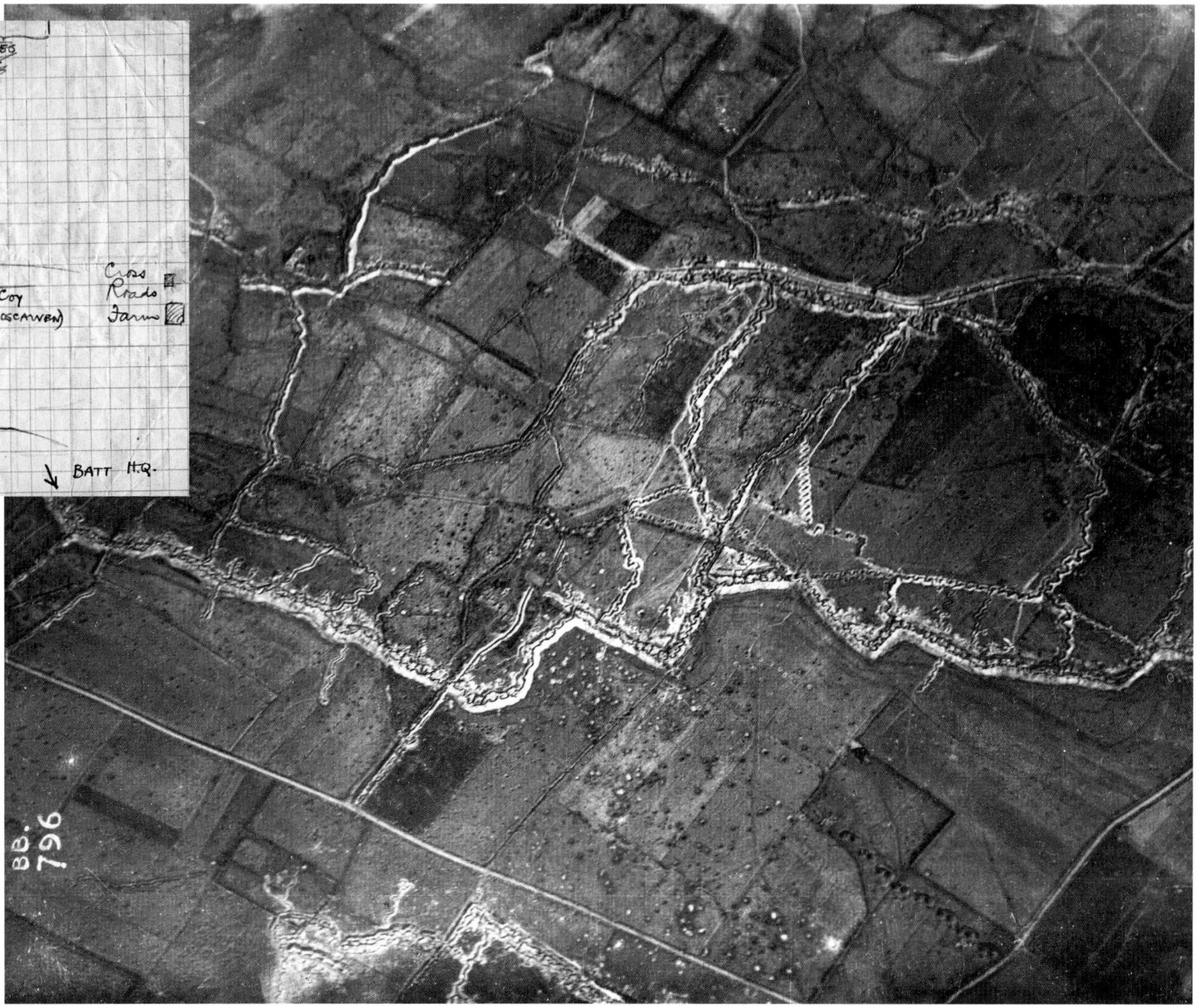

Above
Range Chart for Skeggs' two Toby (light) trench mortars. Note how the positions straddle the track in the first excavation photograph.

Right
British aerial photograph from summer 1915 showing Forward Cottage trenches (bottom) and the tell-tale unusual zig-zag of the German front line. Compare this image with Skeggs' mortar range chart above.

The coat is splendid. Every detail attended to. The collar arrangements are most effective – pockets and everything absolutely correct. The waist that Minks, tailor-like, was so nervous about, couldn't be better. It allows ample room for amplification and consolidation, and for vigorous movement. One loses one's taste for a waist in this show, somehow. The sleeves are comfortably loose too. Thank you ever so much for fixing it all up. The puttees too are beyond my expectations in excellence and practical utility. They must have been an expensive luxury, but I hope they will outlast the two ordinary pairs – then we can patent 'Skeggs' Special Puttees'.

I think you must be inspired to send these parcels on the right day. They always arrive at such opportune moments, containing the right thing for the right day. Witness the water sterilising tablets, the trench heater and the radium lamp, and now today, the coat, puttees, together with the shoes, have been invaluable as I got absolutely soaked from head to foot last night, and had nothing to change into. It was on this wise:

The General was apparently interested but not quite convinced about my patrol's discoveries the other night – so I was asked to go out again last night. I took 5 gallant braves with me and we strode forth into the night. It had been very wet all day, and just as we left it began to drizzle. A patrol of this sort simply has to crawl, and so we got wetter and wetter. Then, just as we got to a ditch by the road, the rain suddenly came on in a perfect deluge, and we crawled into the ditch and on again in this. So as we were out nearly three hours in rain the whole time, you may guess we came back a wee bit moist. I always stop when I reach a certain point to listen for Germans round the corner. It was as well that I did. This night I heard clanking and grunts – quite near – and approaching. I just had time to leap on to the top of the ditch and lie flat on my tummy, watching them with my nose just at the edge of the ditch. My companion had followed suit and lay behind me, trained to silence. I had been there about ten seconds when the first German appeared in the moonlight, marching steadily up my ditch. He was followed immediately by fourteen other large Huns, all carrying a rifle, bayonet, and a scythe. They had evidently become jumpy about my patrolling, and had come out to cut the long grass in No Man's land [for better observation and clearer fields of fire – the British did the same], thinking to make our work more difficult. It was one of the nearest squeaks I had. The Huns were within three feet of me – I could have stroked their cheeks as they walked past me.

I again got into the Boche trench, and found it unoccupied just at that spot, though we went along to hear our old friend Fritz chatting away to his pal a little further down the trench, just as he was the other night. I had a lot of bombs ready with me, but I didn't disturb him, as I found out what I wanted without asking him, and I thought he might not be in a good humour for a talk as it was so damp. We had a good rummage around the trench again, but couldn't find any more souvenirs, and then – then we nearly caught it. I was just about to go down to try to have a closer look at Fritz, quiet like, when in the far distance, from beyond the British lines, I heard a familiar boom – then swish, swish, and by gad I realised that one of our own lyddites was slowly but very deliberately wobbling its way to the exact spot where I lay. It was an awful moment – just the thing to put in a penny magazine story. I let discretion to the winds and, I confess, fled headlong! I just got away by about 15 seconds, but it did put the wind up me! To be done in by one of your own shells when out spying on patrol – really too much!

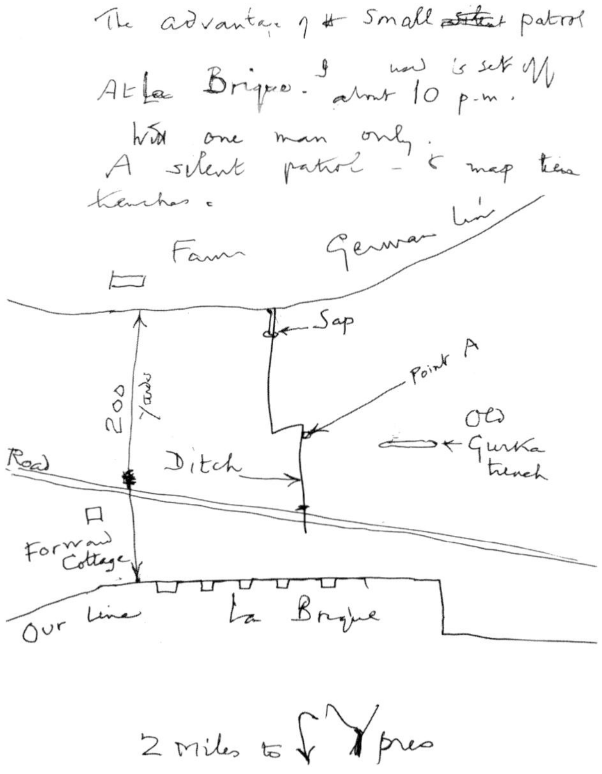

It was an awful crasher too – I got back to my patrol and gave the word to run for it – which we did, especially as we heard another just coming. One splinter even then only just missed us. We got back to our pals in the tranchee panting and cursing everything on earth – especially our own gunners. However, we found out what was wanted about saps and things.

So here we are again all merry and bright. I hope they will be satisfied now, and not want any more patrols for a bit. Patrols amuse me up to a certain point, quite well, but under such conditions they are not pleasant.

I must finish now, much love to you all my dears, ever your loving son, Robin.

Despite his regular patrol work Skeggs was in a similar position to most of the troops in the northern sector. Whilst both sides were busy consolidating, La Brique had become a fairly quiet front compared to certain other subsectors in the Salient, such as Hooge, Hill 60, the Bluff and St Eloi. Having been at Wez Macquart, one of the quietest

Above
Skeggs' first primitive dugout in the Forward Cottage trenches.

Left
The route followed by Robin Skeggs for his second foray into enemy trenches. Point A marks the place where the German patrol was encountered.

Below
Well-preserved duckboards in the British front line near Crossroads Farm. The high water table and the nature of the geology here imparts a permanent wetness below half a metre.

Right
Men of Skeggs' company in the front line. The trenches are narrow, shallow, and at this stage, unrevetted.

Far right
Front line trench intersection. The right-hand branch leads to Crossroads Farm.

Below left
Skeggs' men having breakfast in a revetted trench.

Below right
Corrugated iron revetment in the front line trench.

Below
The Military Cross awarded to Robin Skeggs for the patrols mentioned in his letters.

parts of the entire Western Front, and where the Christmas Truce lasted for many days, Skeggs' sense of delight in his new life of adventure is palpable.

19th June 1915 – Usual trenches

My dear Father, I can't let the day pass without writing to tell you how different this period in trenches is compared with the last, by reason of your ample provision for me. I have been enjoying some of the tongue, jam, St Ivel cheese (tophole) and strawberries in tins. Lilliot is just having a go at making cocoa with the 'Bivouac Mixture' and trench cooker, as it is cool this evening. I am glad of the cocoa now, as it is much cooler this week. Still, I appreciated 2 fizzlets in the drinking water today. I am not in exactly the same trench as before. I'm up in front alongside Boscy now, and I am absolutely designing the new trench line myself. Hopwood approves of my arrangement for all sorts of deadly flanking fire! I was working like mad from 8pm last night till 3 am this morning – planning, marking out, cursing digging parties, and digging myself another dugout. I'm very snug in this one provided it doesn't rain. I sleep on a stretcher and a found blanket – the stretcher idea is a very old game, and most comfortable. I have my tins of good things arranged on a little mud shelf – and there you are! It has been a very quiet day – only a few shrapnel over a few minutes ago, and two machine guns which seem to be aiming 300 yards short. I must give you the benefit of one or two letter extracts: one old wangler writes to his wife "I don't remember if I did receive that cake from Jim and Lizzie, but they can send another to make sure"! Don't you think the soldier's term for jam is good? POZZY! And a bloke wot's fond of pozzy is a pozzywollah!

I have sent the German hand grenade that I filched from the Boche trench. I have taken out the detonator and explosive, you can

therefore pull everything to bits safely. Also a German rifle grenade or what's left of it, also a German fuse for I think about a four-incher. And German buttons – which should be disinfected! I must prepare for tonights work. We have scores of men up from reserve to help us dig, All's going very well and cheery-like. Ever your loving son…

The trench lines mentioned here are exactly those pictured. Some are probably the very trenches designed by Skeggs himself and from which he wrote these letters home. They are also the trenches used by Edmund Blunden on 31 July 1917 when attacking with the Royal Sussex Regiment (he had spent the previous night in a deep dugout behind Crossroads Farm). The battlefield grave of three Lewis gunners of Blunden's own battalion were found during the excavations.

Skeggs' next missive betrays sensations which most men were feeling by this stage of the war: fatalism, boredom and acceptance of their lot. Patrolling no man's land is clearly a regular activity, as is housekeeping in the trenches. Falling foul of hostile shot or shell, at La Brique at least, had become more a matter of luck than evil design – it depended upon whether one's 'name was on it'. The monotonous cycle of trench life was becoming firmly established.

21st June 1915 – Usual front trenches

I am fourth senior subaltern of the battalion now! There are three of us up in the advance line now. I had another letter from you last night, as welcome as ever they always are. I had it to cheer me on my way when I came in from patrol. I took off my wet things, just tumbled into a roll of canvas in my dugout, and, between sips of a cup of cocoa, I read your dear letter. They say comparisons are odious – but contrasts are not always by any means. The pleasant contrast of coming in from the sweat of a patrol crawl to the joy of a letter from home, read by the soft light of a candle in a cosy little hut – it sounds worth it, and it is worth it. We get a daily shower, and heavy clouds, so I am writing this in my dugout, clad in a shirt and my new breeches. The new breeches I have just manufactured out of 3 sandbags – very effective – the usual breeches got wet through last night, as usual on patrol, and while they are drying I wear these. They shelled my farm [Crossroads Farm] this evening and some came unpleasantly close to the trench. No one was hit however. We get so used to shelling now though. I simply carried on washing, and trimming my nails. It was the first wash and shave I had had for five days, so I couldn't possibly forego it just because the blooming Boche happened to decide on wasting a few shells here.

Above

Letter from Robin Skeggs, written from the very trenches excavated by Belgian archaeologists in 2003. The annotation is by his father, who notes when the letter was read – and the receipt of souvenir German hand-grenades!

Left

Hasler House observation post: a British concrete emplacement built inside a building, the external shell of which was later destroyed leaving the position somewhat exposed. The panorama below was taken from this location.

Above
Second Army Panorama 101, 27 January 1917. A winter view of the Frezenberg Ridge from a position near Hellfire Corner. Part of the famous China Wall communication trench can be seen in the foreground.

I have existed on practically nothing but your parcels. We can't get the fresh fruit and things up here, and the rations just now are particularly dull. Ten months of the same rations must have nearly turned the men ill I should think. They simply won't eat the bully – one can't face it. They won't carry it from the ration carts up here. It is beastly stuff – why they make it so salty, divvil knows. It wouldn't be so bad if it had less salt.

The post corporal is waiting. All's well. Lovely weather – just right for the fruit salad! Don't send any more sterilising tablets please. I'm disappointed to say the doctor tells me I must boil the water even if I do use sterilising tablets. Very much love dears, I'm feeling absolutely in the pink, ever your loving son…

On the day the war was exactly one year old, life had become a uniform round of daily and nightly duties. But Robin Skeggs had just enjoyed a break to the monotony: his first leave since arriving overseas the previous October. Upon return to the trenches a week later, he – and others – were aware of a change in atmosphere.

4th August 1915 – Trenches, Belgium

My dear Father, the reaction of melancholy after leave is not pleasant, and I take comfort in writing to you. We had quite a good crossing, and no-one was indisposed. I have just been opening the parcel which was sent last week. I know now more than ever what pains you take to give me pleasure, and it makes me appreciate it so much more. I picture you debating what to send, then carefully weighing and fitting it all in, and finally making up the outer casing, which I'm sure must be a laborious process. I have tried the insect cream (in tube) for the flies, and it seems to act well. The parkin and things were extra good. It is the best lot of parkin Mrs Crookes has ever sent. I am sorry to tell you the greengages and cherries were rather badly bruised by the journey. What a disappointment it must be to you after all your trouble, to learn that they are partly wasted. Anyway, those which were alright were really delicious and I can assure you I made the most of them. But don't send more – it is such a wicked waste. I have been particularly thankful to have the socks as the trenches are already 3 to 4 inches deep in mud and water, and I have been very wet. It seems to me we are going to see some proper war hereabouts before long. It is time we did something after all – there has been heavy hammering on our right these many days, and nights, and we look on and wonder. We saw them use burning liquid the other night. It was a weird and awe inspiring sight. It made a huge quivering red flash and glow in the sky – lasting about 3 or 4 minutes. They say that it caused practically no casualties, I'm glad to say. It seems to have merely a moral effect, which is apt to make people run away. Talbot's brother was killed a day or two ago in an attack they made. I must finish here. I'm feeling quite fit and full of beans. Boscawen's gramophone has come, and is most cheering! Very much love to you all dear folks…

The Talbot referred to was Rifle Brigade padre, Neville Talbot. The famous 'Everyman's Club', Talbot House – Toc H – in Poperinghe was named after his brother Gilbert, killed in an abortive counter-attack following the liquid-fire assault (against Hooge) on 30 July 1915. This area can be seen within Panoramas 5, 87, *G-5* and *G-6* in the next section.

Skeggs' discomfort in the now wet La Brique trenches is plain. The ground behind his front lines however, was much more accommodating. Gently swelling hills, each

Below
Second Army Panorama 102, 1 March 1917. The sweeping view from Hasler House in the village of St Jean.

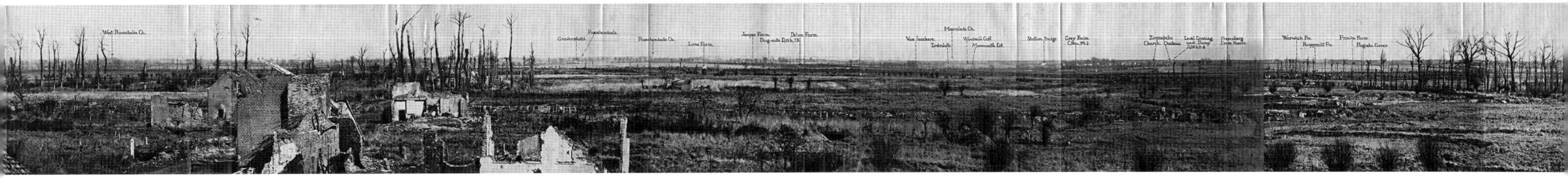

crowned by farmsteads such as La Belle Alliance, Turco, View, Hilltop, Wilson and Wieltje farms, offered higher and relatively dry ground for support and reserve positions, and after 1915 for many deep dugout systems. Here, the surface earth was light and easy to dig, so trenches could be constructed in a far shorter time than in the more difficult clay-enriched ground of the valleys and other sectors. Again, it would have been simple for GHQ to allow the forward British positions to be established on these slopes: the troops could then have shared roughly the same contour as their enemy, thus avoiding the uncomfortable sensation of being under permanent hostile gaze; the only tactical and practical difference would have been that the average width of no man's land would be increased by around 200 m (218 yds). But it was not to be, the disadvantages were dismissed and whenever it rained, snowed or froze from April 1915 until August 1917 the British Tommies grovelled about in mud.

During this time, harassing shellfire in certain sub-sectors grew day by day; occasionally, even a single figure seen within range of the guns would receive unwelcome attention. Defensive work in front of the trenches was permanently intense throughout the entire Ypres sector, and inter-unit synchronization of field work became highly organized.

April 18, 1916

Went to Canal Bank and round with Gardiner to take over. Only 2 jobs: barbed wire entanglement from St Jean to La Brique and tunnelling out a Battalion headquarters in Potijze Wood.

April 19

Numbers 1, 3 and 4 sections march up to the forward billets and take over. We were stopped on Brielen Road as the Artillery had the SOS signal, there being a German attack on the Wieltje Salient. This salient was shelled to pieces.

April 20

Wiring the Wieltje Salient across to Pratt Street. We had a machine-gun turned on us and Parsons got one bullet through his rifle but we had no one hit. We created a new record in wiring, erecting 1,060 yards with half a Company in one night.

April 21

Made a reconnaissance of drains and site for a new trench running from the Wieltje Salient to Pratt Street. We roughly pegged this line out on a pitch dark night and raining hard the whole time. 6 Division made an attack on our left and the bursting shells afforded us considerable light to see the pegs by.

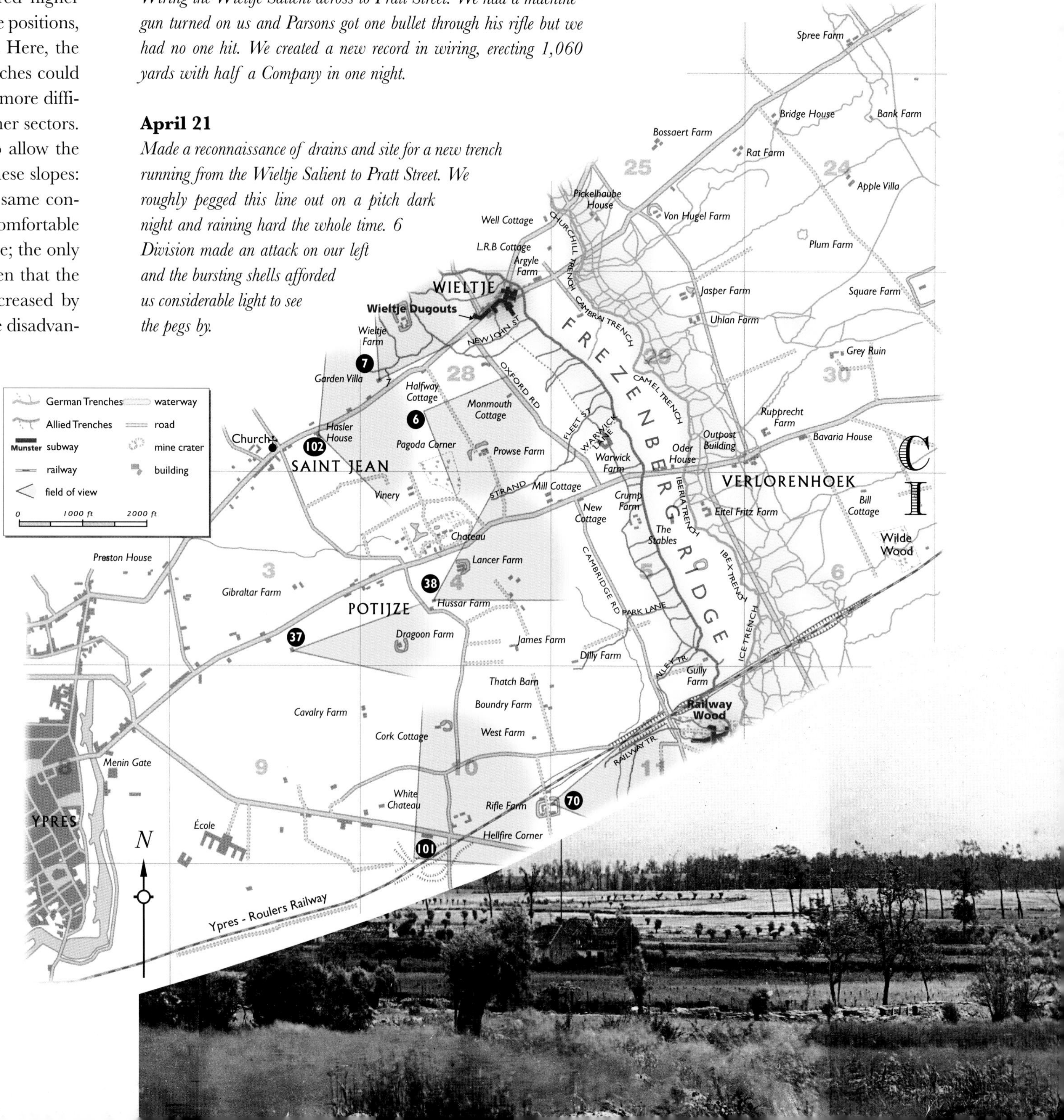

Above
The successful result of a German rat hunt

Right
British machine gunner sweeping no man's land at night, hoping to catch an enemy patrol or working party.

April 22
Took Pioneer officers round to see the new trench and pegged all the traverses out for them.

April 23
Dug new trench, readjusted the wire erected April 20 to suit the direction of new trench, made a bridge across the ditch which now acts as main drain and cleaned the drain out.
LIEUTENANT HAROLD RIDSDALE, 76 FIELD COMPANY RE

Ridsdale's company's work lies around Wieltje within the field of view of Panorama 102. This kind of intensity of effort was typical for every unit in the Salient. In the next two weeks 76 FC RE moved on to make tunnelled dugouts in the Ypres ramparts, install concrete emplacements for machine guns and underground shelters on the canal bank, repair and renew bridges over the canal, demolish the Ypres water tower (only recently rebuilt), gas-proof many dugout doors, fit ventilators, and strengthen cellars throughout Ypres. One particular Ridsdale entry perfectly illustrates the nature of life and work in the Salient between Second and Third Ypres.

8 July – [Canal Bank] Again we had to cease work on the new bridge owing to MG [machine gun] fire. We attempted to blow a tree down behind the front line. We were going to drill auger holes but firstly the auger wouldn't face the wood, and secondly there were too many bullets in the tree. We successfully demolished the tree with 6 slabs of gun cotton [a form of compressed gunpowder].

Part of the sector as it was in 1918 can be seen in No 130A in the Third Ypres section. These panoramas take us up to the Ypres–Roulers railway, which forms the division between the left and right sectors of the Salient.

Below
The Pagoda, a folly which marked one of the corners of the Potijze Chateau estate, was a well-known landmark until its obliteration by a single shell in November 1915.

Hooge

Right
Second Army Panorama 1, taken from the north-east corner of Railway Wood on 2 July 1915.

The tiny hamlet of Hooge lies about 3 km (2 miles) from Ypres on top of the nearest ripple of minor undulations that radiate down from the main Passchendaele Ridge. The village straddled the main route from Ypres to the industrial town of Menin – the infamous Menin Road. In 1914 its most notable feature was the splendid estate owned by the De Vinck family. The centre-piece, Hooge Chateau, was a large and comfortable country house nestling in landscaped gardens, with an ornamental lake, stables, estate worker's cottages and an annexe. Behind, sheltering everything from the chill north and east winds, lay Chateau and Bellewaerde woods. Sitting high on the shouder of the ridge, views of Ypres, its spires, and every inch of ground in front of the town was superb, and as a result Hooge became a key tactical position, to be fiercely fought over for almost two years. After the battles of April and May 1915, it had the misfortune of being at the apex of the newly contracted salient – and a reputation as one of the most odious and dangerous places north of the River Somme.

The sector was not large, stretching roughly from the Ypres–Roulers railway to the Menin Road, a distance of about 1,000 m (1,100 yds). To both sides of the village the trench lines curved southwards, semi-encapsulating beleaguered Ypres. In late spring 1915, the German lines meandered across the spurs and crests of the Bellewaerde Ridge, cutting through the centre of the Hooge estate and running beyond through Sanctuary Wood to Observatory Ridge and onwards to Hill 60 which has been incorporated into the panoramas for this area.

By the close of 1914 the De Vinck estate had already

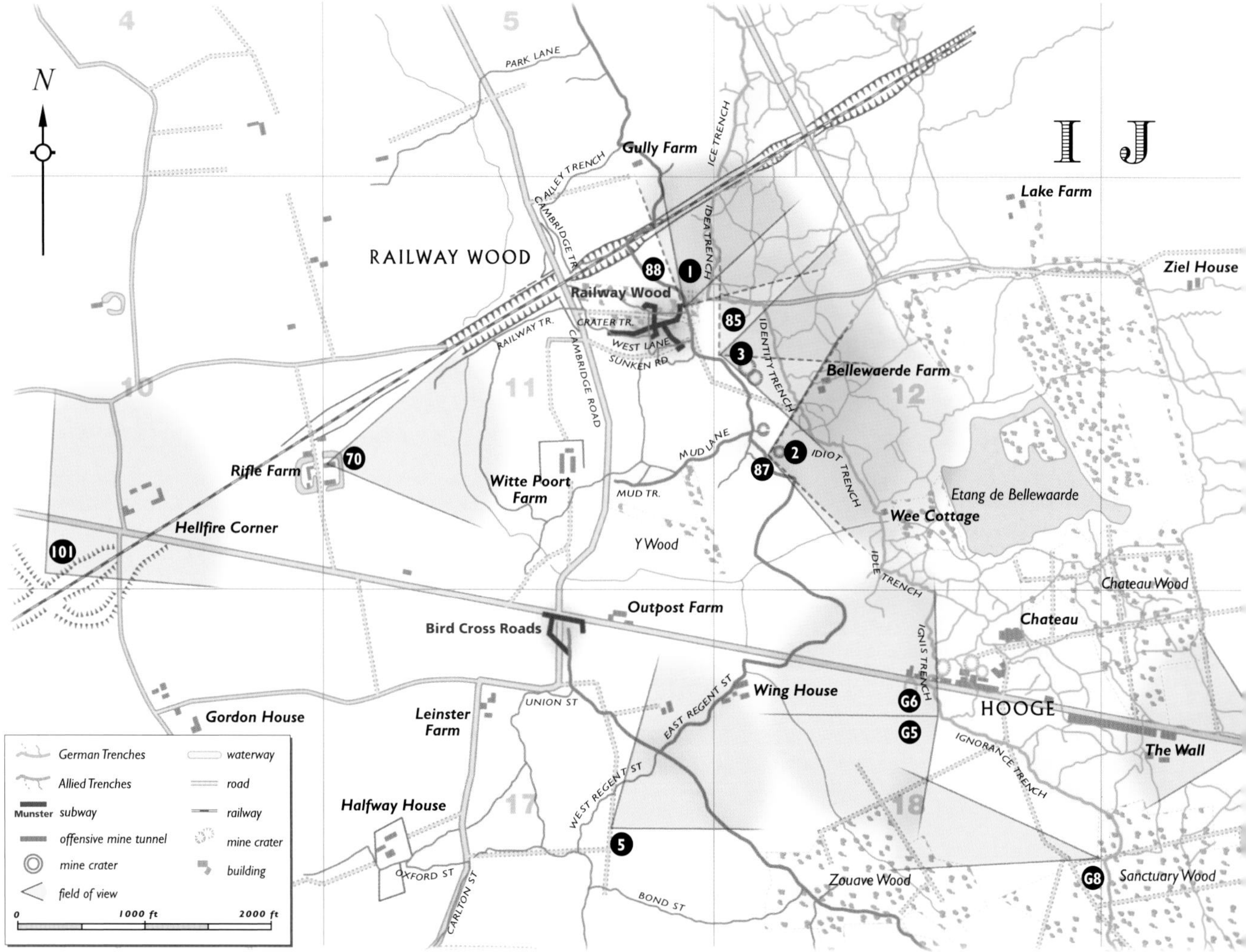

Below

Captain Julian Grenfell DSO of the Royal Dragoons, who operated from these trenches at the time the panoramas were taken.

Right

Trench map belonging to Grenfell, stained with his blood.

been battered but was not totally irreparable. Six months later the contrast was stark. The Menin Road was one of the main axes of German attack during Second Ypres, and the battle raged from the north-east, closer and closer to Ypres on either side of the ancient highway. British forces, comprising mainly regular troops, were pushed further and further back for six weeks; amongst them was a Canadian unit, the Princess Patricia's Canadian Light Infantry – the PPCLI or Princess Pat's. They were to play a leading role in stalling the German advance.

During an orderly fighting withdrawal from the Polygon Wood sector, the Princess Pat's brought repeated attacks to a standstill, and although defences broke and considerable gaps appeared in the British lines, the Germans had apparently become so pre-occupied with the Canadians' destruction that they failed to take advantage. The remaining four officers and 150 men were too weak to stop the enemy from occupying the Bellewaerde Ridge, but they arrested the charge down the Menin Road.

When the fighting died down, Hooge village was shared, with in places only a house separating the trenches. It was a similar situation on the Bellewaerde Ridge where the front lines were so close in places that it was difficult to tell whose barbed wire belonged to whom; on still nights one could clearly hear the enemy talking. Panoramas 1 and 3, both taken from the north-east corner of Railway Wood, illustrate the proximity of the lines. These are the very trenches where Captain Julian Grenfell DSO of the Royal Dragoons was mortally wounded on the afternoon of 13 May 1915. Sustaining serious head wounds from shell splinters he was taken to Boulogne, and died with his family around him on 25 May. Grenfell was the author of 'Into Battle', one of the most anthologized poems in the English language. It was published in *The Times* in the same edition that his death was announced.

Running diagonally across the picture in these two panoramas is the Ypres–Roulers railway, our dividing line for the Salient and today the main road from Hellfire Corner to Zonnebeke. In both images a trench signboard can clearly be seen; it is perhaps 10 m (11 yds) away on the German parapet. From 16 June 1915 until the first day of the Third Battle of Ypres, these lines remained immobile. See No *88* for a later example from the same location. At 3.50 a.m. on 31 July 1917 troops of the West Yorkshire and Devonshire Regiments (23rd Brigade, 8th Division)

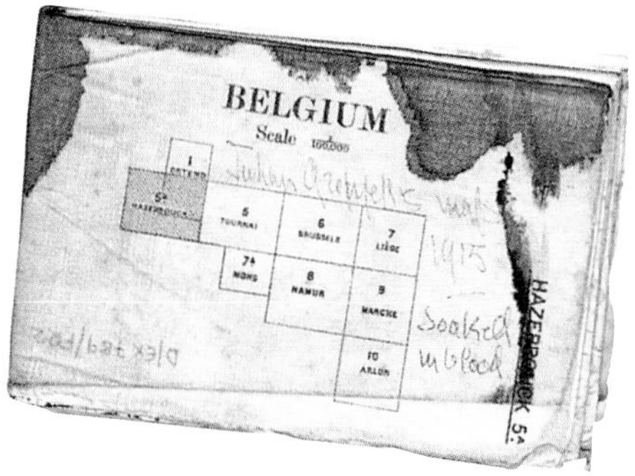

climbed from this trench and advanced northwards towards the Westhoek. At the same time Hooge village and the Bellewaerde Ridge fell at last to the Worcesters and Northants.

There are no known panoramas from 1914, but again, G-2 and G-3 offer a good indication of the nature of the landscape. Number 70 was taken within a week of the close of Second Ypres, between 1 and 3 June 1915. The camera location is Rifle Farm near Hellfire Corner. The picture shows the woods of the Hooge estate to be still dense and verdant with some estate buildings standing, retaining their roofs and offering good cover. The white crosses of the graves of earlier British casualties can be seen behind a hedge next to the Menin Road on the extreme right of the photograph. It seems a peaceful enough scene, but over the three-day period that this photograph was taken fierce fighting was going on in Hooge, with very heavy casualties being sustained by British troops. By 3 June the Germans had occupied the chateau and were stabilizing and extending the lines visible in No 5 (6 July 1915) across the Menin Road and into Sanctuary Wood to the south-east. Except for the chateau and stables every building in the village of Hooge is visible. The long face of masonry (actually terraced cottages) near the top of the hill beyond the village was known as 'The Wall'. Practically all would cease to exist within the next few weeks of fighting. The Culvert was an important tunnel driven under the Menin Road to connect trench systems on either side.

The first British attacks here after Second Ypres took place on Tuesday, 16 June 1915. They had limited aims, the targets being the German front, support and reserve trenches in the area between the railway and the Menin Road – precisely the territory encapsulated by Panorama 70. The purpose was to eliminate the troublesome salient pushing into British lines in front of Bellewaerde Farm and lake, which had been created by the German attacks of April and May, and in so doing regain the high ground.

The 9th Brigade of the 10th Division, a territorial unit, was to mount the attack. Moving up from Ypres to the jumping-off trenches the night before, the troops were in good spirits although there was an uncomfortable suspicion that the enemy were fully aware of the impending battle. The Royal Fusiliers, the Royals Scots Fusiliers and

Above
Communication centre for German artillery which dominated proceedings from the ridge tops around Ypres.

Left
Hooge Chateau in early 1915 before it was reduced to dust during Second Ypres and subsequent actions.

Top

Second Army Panorama 70, taken from Rifle Farm near Hellfire Corner on 1 June 1915, spans the territory between the Ypres–Roulers railway and the Menin Road (far right). This would have been Grenfell's view on his approach to the trenches. Photographed a few days after his death.

Above

German troops at Bellewaerde Farm in early 1915. The position held off several fierce British attacks in 1915, and only fell on 31 July 1917.

the Northumberland Fusiliers were to take the enemy front line, with the Lincolns and the Liverpool Scottish following through to secure the support trenches. The final objectives, the enemy reserve trench and Bellewaerde Farm, were then to be captured and held by men from the first three units in a 'leap-frogging' action. It had been arranged that each of the enemy trenches would be shelled in sequence before the infantry were required to take them.

Amongst those who marched forward on the night of 14 June was Noel Godfrey Chavasse VC and Bar, MC, a medical officer with the 10th Battalion King's Liverpool Regiment – the Liverpool Scottish – a territorial battalion of kilted Merseysiders with Scottish connections. The following day he would win a Military Cross scouring the fields on the ridge slope for wounded. On this night a frustrated Chavasse had been ordered to remain a kilometre back on the Menin Road whilst the fighting troops moved up to the line. Curiosity got the better of him and he made his way forward to survey the ground. At 2 a.m. the preliminary bombardment began and by 5 a.m. German defensive shelling meant that the first wounded began to appear. Chavasse mentions leaving his stretcher-bearers 'in some dugouts behind a little ridge'; the line of small shelters buried in the embankment stretching across the central section of Panorama 70 may be those positions. This view is practically identical today.

The Liverpool Scottish went into battle with 23 officers and 519 other ranks; after the action the statistics would read 2 and 130. Chavasse's letter home recounting the attack was copied and circulated privately by his family. He described the battle as a great initial success, with all the enemy trenches being taken in little more than a quarter of an hour. But as was to be so often the case in later years, communication during action broke down:, the British artillery correctly carried out their orders, but remained unaware that they were shelling their own troops, who had advanced much more freely than anticipated. Although within sight of artillery observers, the smoke and dust from barrage and counter-barrage had obscured the flags by which the infantry marked their position. When messages at last reached the British gunners and firing ceased, German shelling then prevented support troops from consolidating the captured ground. Eventually the right flank of the attack broke and retired. With the left flank already 'in the air', the most forward troops, those who had done so well to achieve their objectives, were left exposed. They had no choice but to retire to the first line, and many were captured in the process. The entire battle took place within the central section of Panorama 70. A memorial to the Liverpool Scottish has been placed on the crest of the ridge on the site of the German front line.

A more cynical view of the action survives from

another future VC winner present at the time of the attack, Rifle Brigade staff officer Major William Congreve (Brigade Major, 76th Brigade). In his diary for 9 June, a week before the attack, Congreve suggested that the scheme was being drawn up by a general who expected it to fail, that insufficient time had been devoted to planning, that ammunition supply for artillery support was too limited, and that if it did go well the credit would be due to the troops rather than those who had organized the affair. The most famous 'action' photographs of the war were taken here during the battle for Bellewaerde.

As fighting abated the British had clearly failed to gain the ridge, but the German line had been straightened a little and a few metres of much more commanding and useful terrain were held. The view from one of the captured positions can be seen in Second Army Panorama 2 (2 July 1915), taken from Listening Post D6, King's Royal Rifle Corps Trench. The final objective of the attack, Bellewaerde Farm, is seen tantalizingly close on the left of frame. Observation towards the farm is still uphill and awkward, but panning right the value of the new position becomes clearer. From here the British were at least able to look down upon German defences in Hooge itself. In the centre, also invisible before the attack, is Bellewaerde Lake, with the Eclusette (known to the British as Wee Cottage), the former estate caretaker's house, sitting almost on top of the German support line which runs past the front door. Hooge village is still shared.

A smaller assault with the same aims was launched from these trenches on 22 June. It failed completely. Whilst all these surface activities were being pursued a far more ancient form of warfare was already underway. Lieutenant G. R. Cassels of 175 Tunnelling Company RE was in charge:

> *My next assignment was at Hooge. Major S. Hunter-Cowan OC 175 Tunnelling Company took me to a convent used as a staff office and HQ. Here we met a General who gave us a plain lunch but who regaled us with apricot brandy found in the cellars. He told us of a plan to tunnel under the German trenches at Hooge and blow up a chateau there. As Hooge was at the apex of the Ypres Salient it was considered a most dangerous job and whoever undertook the work was to be a volunteer. The apricot brandy was extremely potent and its effect such that I would have accepted an assignment in Hell; as it turned out, in volunteering, I had indeed accepted such an assignation.*
>
> LIEUTENANT G. R. CASSELS, 175 TUNNELLING COMPANY RE

Without a single day off Cassels and his men completed their tunnel in six weeks, and on 19 July the mine was charged, primed, tamped and ready to blow. They had begun the work from the cellar of a small house on the Menin Road named Bull Farm. This building can be seen on the far right of Panorama 2, and also in 5. Cassels and his men were working underground as these pictures were taken. The original target for the mine, Hooge Chateau, had been changed in favour of a new concrete redoubt being constructed in a more forward position near the German front line. Cassels described the tunnellers' moment of glory:

Above
Photograph taken during the 16 June 1915 attack at Bellewaerde. British troops shelter in the lee of the German front-line trench. The flag denotes that the positions had been captured, signalling the guns to attack the next target. The photographer, Private F. A. Fyfe of the Liverpool Scottish, is himself wounded.

Left
Lieutenant G. R. Cassels, the officer of 175 Tunnelling Company charged with planting the Hooge mine of 19 July 1915.

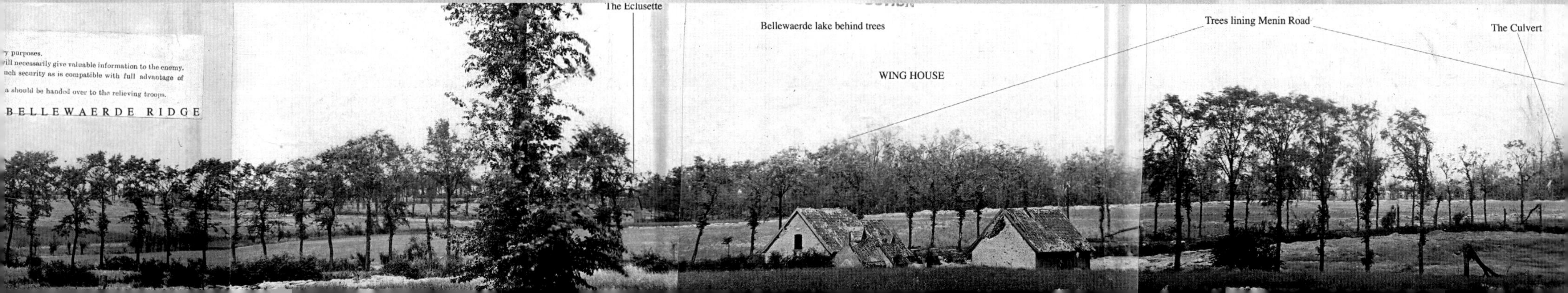

ry purposes.
vill necessarily give valuable information to the enemy.
uch security as is compatible with full advantage of
a should be handed over to the relieving troops.
BELLEWAERDE RIDGE
The Eclusette
Bellewaerde lake behind trees
WING HOUSE
Trees lining Menin Road
The Culvert

Right
Hooge crater as seen and photographed by Robin Skeggs in August 1915. The bottom of the crater was regularly and liberally strewn with lime to encourage the swift decomposition of the many bodies that lay there.

Below
German *Pioniere* miners at the head of a shaft at Hooge in 1916, a year of intense and bloody underground activity in the sector.

Bottom
A view of Hooge and Sanctuary Wood from a position south of the Menin Road. Second Army Panorama 5, 6 July 1915.

It was a beautiful evening, sun about to set, and everything at that moment quiet and peaceful. Some birds were singing and a little black cat which earlier had been sitting on my knee rubbed itself against my boots. [Curiously, Billy Congreve VC also mentions seeing a black cat in the trenches at Hooge in his diary for 9 September, and wondering how it had survived the shelling] *I and another tunnelling officer were standing in the trench outside the dugout and at exactly 7.00 p.m. by our synchronized watches, we simultaneously pressed our exploders. The whole ground beneath and around us sank and then rose again two or three times, and then it shuddered and swayed from side to side like a ship in a rough sea. Away in front the earth opened up with a huge woof and a roar like a miniature volcano. Concrete, bricks, earth, sand, timber and other debris, with volumes of smoke, soared high into the sky, and amidst it we could detect whole trees and bodies and limbs of German soldiers ascending and falling. But we did not wait for it all to come down, we ran for cover as the German guns opened up with heavy barrages. One wondered how anything could survive and we began to think that we not only had buried the Germans but our own troops as well, for we could see none of them.*
LIEUTENANT G. R. CASSELS, 175 TUNNELLING COMPANY RE

The Hooge mine was a typical First World War 'success': it delivered minimal territorial gains (the village was still shared after the explosion), a see-saw of occupation, and disproportionate loss of life. Having been blown and occupied on 19 July the crater was lost to the Germans on 30th; it was retaken on 9 August, and lost and recaptured again twenty days later. This was typical of crater fighting in mining areas. As soon as a mine was blown it was considered essential for the attackers to occupy the furthest lip – and equally essential for defenders to deny it, whilst they themselves strove to the take 'their' opposite lip.. When one side gained the advantage and managed to drive the

enemy out, usually after a grenade battle, every gun, mortar and machine gun was turned on the crater in retaliation. Very often mine craters became little more than mass graves. Hooge was no exception. Later, Congreve witnessed the carnage and commented in his typical phlegmatic style.

The crater is being made into a happy home! The 6th Division started good dugouts and we are making more. The bottom of the crater contains now at least 250 dead Boches and a good many of our own fellows.
MAJOR WILLIAM CONGREVE

However, in destroying the redoubt the mine had shown that tunnelling was a valuable adjunct to trench warfare. Despite the minimal territorial gains, it lifted British morale no end. There were logical repercussions however: if one side was mining, the other clearly had no choice but to retaliate, and so began the spiralling escalation of an extraordinary private underground conflict which ultimately encompassed, on several levels, much of the Hooge, Bellewaerde and Railway Wood sub-sectors, and indeed a

large part of the Western Front. At around 2,400 kg (4,500 lbs) of explosive Cassels' mine was by far the biggest mine yet blown in the Salient. But mining was already well underway in other places, and it was early days. Eventually the entire sub-sector from beyond the railway to Bellewaerde Lake became a mass of tunnels on four levels.

Since February 1915 mining had been a pet project of a man who did more to get the British tunnelling effort off the ground than anyone else: John Norton-Griffiths. He was not of military stock, but a self-made, wealthy engineering entrepreneur, and also MP for Wednesbury. It was Norton-Griffiths who had the notion of employing a digging technique used by his own civilian workers in a contract to renew and extend sewers beneath Manchester. It was known as clay-kicking and involved the use of a special implement called a grafting tool. This razor-sharp, spade-like device was worked mainly through the power of the leg muscles from a semi-horizontal sitting position. It was a swift method of digging, and especially functional if the tunnel in question was small – precisely what military mines had demanded for millennia.

When war broke out Norton-Griffiths appreciated that Manchester happened to have very similar geology to parts of both Belgian and French Flanders. After several false starts when he was unable to inspire first the War Office then GHQ with his clay-kicking idea, the go-ahead to form units of what he called 'Moles' was eventually given in mid-February 1915, largely as a result of worries over rapidly intensifying German mining activities. Now a temporary major, Norton-Griffiths instantly mustered six tunnelling companies from his own (entirely untrained) men, and within a week had them digging Flemish rather than Mancunian clay. Eventually over thirty companies were formed.

There were two overriding advantages to kicking: firstly, as the tool was pushed (it was not 'kicked' in the literal sense) into the tunnel face with the feet, then a 'spit' of clay was levered out, the digging process could, with skill and care, be almost silent. Secondly, and equally importantly, the Germans did not use this method themselves, either in military or civil mining: they employed mattocks, small short-handled picks with wide blades. A

Above

A German flame attack. This was a terrorizing weapon which was also subsequently used by the British.

mattock was wielded by hand and required considerable physical effort. With it one had to strike the clay – hard – to make any progress. This act of striking rather than pushing was a noisy one – and noise was of course the key to underground fighting. Put simply, the British method was far less easy to detect, far quicker, and far less tiring. The German 'Pioniere' never discovered it was being employed.

On 29–30 July 1915 the Germans successfully used a new and horrific weapon at the crater at Hooge – liquid fire: flamethrowers. At 3.15 a.m. Lieutenant G. V. Carey witnessed what followed.

There was a sudden hissing sound and a bright crimson glare over the crater turned the whole scene red. As I looked I saw three or four distinct jets of flame, like a line of powerful firehoses spraying fire instead of water, shoot across my fire trench. How long this lasted it is impossible to say, probably not more than a minute, but the effect was so stupefying that I was utterly unable for some moments to think correctly…Those who faced the flame attack were never seen again.
LIEUTENANT. G. V. CAREY

The attack drove the British from the village causing casualties of 31 officers and 751 other ranks amongst the 7th King's Royal Rifle Corps and 8th Rifle Brigade, who had come into the line only the night before. One of their officers, 2nd Lieutenant Sidney Clayton Woodroffe, led a counter-attack in which he was killed. Woodroffe was awarded the VC, but his body was never recovered. On 7 August a further German attack was launched, this time with the help of asphyxiating gas, and the British were pushed back further still. On 9 August two brigades of the British 6th Division recaptured all the lost trenches and made small extra gains north and west of the village. The shuttlecock war continued. The Hooge sector was now known as one of the most dangerous places on earth. On 14 August Lieutenant Robin Skeggs, late of the La Brique trenches, arrived at Hooge.

My Dear Father, we are in the place in the line now – where they shell 20 hours out of every 24 – and where our gunners actually shell as much as the Boche do! We are carrying out a proper campaign of hate here, in order to try to wear down Fritz and absolutely feed him up –

Below
Two panoramas taken from the same position but separated by two months. The difference in the landscape around Hooge is stark. Top: Panorama 2, 2 July 1915, and, below: Panorama 87, 11 September 1915.

thus causing him to stop crumping us, if possible. The ground is absolutely churned up by HE shell so that it is almost impossible to dig trenches – the ground is so loose and disturbed. Old equipment, old bombs, old rifles, and their late owners lie about all over the place. This is all in a comparatively small area, and within 400 yards the trenches pass through a most delightful wood, which is a most comfortable place. We are enfiladed – and not only enfiladed, but taken in rear by all manner of projectiles. However, it is quite an interesting place, and I appreciate such advantages as it offers.

I have had to do a lot of exploring – not patrol work – but merely skirmishing about the captured trenches. There are rifles, bombs and things by the hundred lying about – and the smell is too horrible to think about. I have been commissioned to select a new headquarters some long way off, and had an interesting afternoon looking round for it. The wood here is absolutely devoid of green. The branches have been annihilated by shrapnel, and I think possibly by the liquid fire. We expect to get a decent long spell in billets after we have done our whack here – and during that spell I trust I shall get some leave. Things are not so awfully miserable here – indeed far from it. The CO and doctor and Adjutant are at the present moment all busy making up souvenir walking sticks which they have cut from the wood here [Sanctuary Wood].

LIEUTENANT ROBIN SKEGGS, 3RD RIFLE BRIGADE

The 'delightful wood' is Sanctuary Wood, a place where 'rifle shots echoed in a most curious way.' Skeggs' words are beautifully illustrated by a comparison of panoramas 2 (2 July 1915) and 87 (11 September 1915), both taken from exactly the same location (I 12 c 3.6 near Leinster Farm). By September parts of the Hooge sector have been devastated by the constant shellfire; Bellewaerde Farm, a target for all the British attacks, on the far left immediately behind the German front-line trenches, has been reduced to ruins. The buildings in Hooge village (far right) are mere brick heaps and the protective screen of trees in Chateau Wood splintered and torn; yet to left, right and rear undamaged woodland is plainly evident, and not far behind the German lines houses and cottages can still be seen, illustrating how the artillery of both sides accurately targeted the limited areas deemed most critical – the crater, Bellewaerde Farm and the village. Even no man's land, in the foreground immediately beyond the sandbags and wire in the British front line, is relatively untouched. The crater blown by Cassels' mine (today backfilled and lost from the landscape. The craters purporting to be the Hooge crater were blown by the Germans in 1916) is on the far right, bludgeoned by shelling and mortaring of the August actions. Skeggs also comments upon one of these attacks, the first he had witnessed at Hooge. His tone has altered a little from earlier letters.

Our guns gave our division a splendid start. It was the finest bombardment I've yet heard – lasting half an hour. We had 3 or 4 of our biggest guns blasting away, firing a round every 2 or 3 minutes. Then

Left
British dead on the lip of a German mine crater: a result of the blows of June 1916.

Below left
Segment of Panorama 85 of 10 September 1915, taken from the British front line very close to where the Royal Engineer Grave now stands. A photograph taken a year later from the same spot would have revealed no more than a vast crater field. The RE Grave commemorates tunnellers who were killed underground but whose bodies were never recovered.

Below
The mass of craters between Railway Wood and Hooge shows the intensity of underground fighting in the sector. September 1918. The railway crosses the top right corner

the smaller guns were absolutely tumbling over each other in their eagerness to loose off. There must have been some French 75's helping. Of course, with a start like that the infantry can simply run across without being molested – and those are the fellows who get the honour and glory. We advanced some 600 or 700 yards on about a 700 yard frontage – that is we have retaken all the ground which was lost some week or more ago, and we have avenged the blood of our poor old 7th and 8th Battalions which suffered very heavily then. They were simply hurled into a counter-attack without any artillery preparation, without bombs, or anything, by order of the Corps commander, and they were absolutely wiped out in consequence. It was a criminal act and a wicked waste of one of our best Divisions to order them in like that. But it is the same as ever – bad staff work. About 90% of the staff ought to be shot as murderers – they may say what they like. Thank goodness the attack last night was a success – but it ought to be when they expend ammunition absolutely anyhow. It always seems to me that either 1. They use no guns at all, or 2. They waste all their shells on the attack, using far more than necessary, and then have none left to repel the inevitable counter-attack. We are still in doubt as to whether we will have to consolidate the regained trenches, or whether we shall simply go back to our old trenches at 25. The fighting has been at 27 of course. I must close now as the post is going. All's well and I'm enjoying the bomb work.
LIEUTENANT ROBIN SKEGGS, 3RD RIFLE BRIGADE

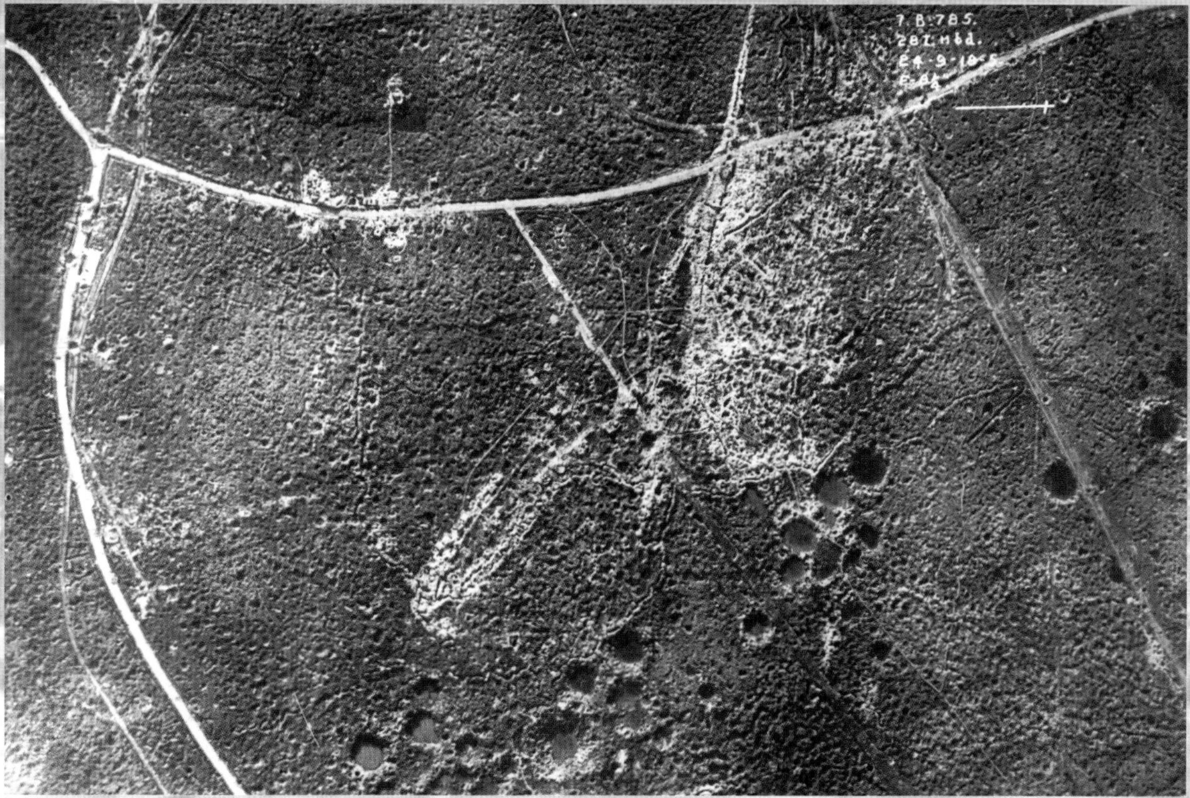

The appalling casualties of the summer fighting could not be sustained, and after minimal gains at Loos in September 1915 both sides dug in for the long winter ahead and began the construction of seriously complex defensive earthworks. The British expected a retaliatory German offensive during the spring of 1916, and on 2 June the blow fell at Hooge. The Germans blew three mines (these craters still exist) and advanced along a 4-km (2-mile) front – once more against the Canadians who held almost all the sector being attacked. After two days their casualties exceeded 7,000. Observatory Ridge (see Panoramas 15 and *82*), the only piece of high ground in British possession within the whole of the Ypres Salient, had been captured. Hooge was lost too. During the next two weeks the Canadians mounted counter-attack after counter-attack and clawed back almost every square metre of ground on Observatory Ridge. But not at Hooge.

A stalemate then settled into place, a stalemate that neither side were ready to attempt to break, and for the next 12 months action became highly localized. Artillery obliged with daily and nightly shelling, and infantry action was restricted to carefully planned trench raids to collect intelligence, destroy dugouts and mine shafts, and capture prisoners. The real war in the Hooge sector was now taking place deep beneath Railway and Bellewaerde woods in the dark and damp galleries scraped out by the British tunnellers and their German counterparts, the 'Mineures'.

One of the most remarkable features of Panorama 70 is that it shows the lines that were formed at the very beginning of static trench warfare in this sector in the spring of 1915. Precisely the same trenches from which the British attacked over two years later on the first day of the Third Battle of Ypres, 31 July 1917. On the left of the picture Passchendaele church is seen – the ultimate Allied position when the campaign was finally called to a halt on 10 November 1917. The distance between the camera (at Rifle

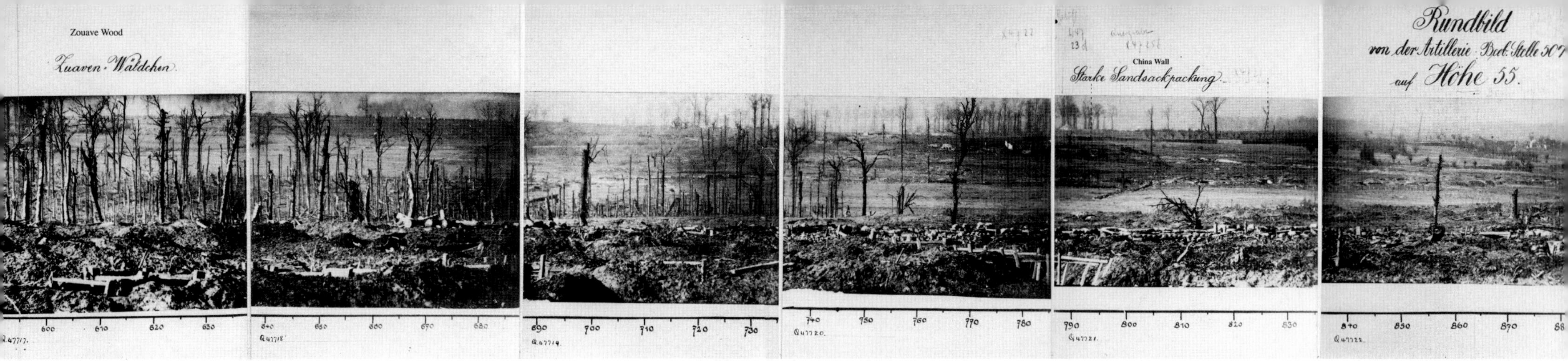

Farm near Hellfire Corner) and the church is approximately 5 km (3 miles) – the casualties sustained by both sides during the capture of this territory exceeded 500,000.

G-4 shows the tremendous advantage enjoyed by those holding higher ground. This is a German panorama of June 1915 taken near Frezenberg. Any movement in and behind the British lines could easily be spotted, and from this position and so many others like it artillery observers were able to range their guns by daylight on any number of targets such as the crossroads at Hellfire Corner, the town of Ypres, or individual trenches, gun positions, houses or churches. When night fell and the countryside became alive with the sounds of troops moving in and out of the line and transport bringing up supplies, German gunners could be confident that every shell fired was likely to cause damage.

German panoramas *G-5* and *G-6* (these two connect), *G-7* and G-8, are taken from newly-captured positions near Hooge village just 200 m (218 yds) from the crater, but on the south side of the Menin Road. Despite being midsummer – June 1916 – the landscape has a wintry feel with only distant trees being in full leaf, the others being shell-swept

Above
Segment of German Panorama G-8, early spring, 1916. Taken from the high ground (Hill 55) south of the Menin Road, it epitomizes the overwhelming advantage of holding the ridges.

Left
A view inside British tunnels beneath Mount Sorrel (Observatory Ridge sector) taken during a 1997 excavation of this highly dangerous system driven through sandy ridge-top geology.

Below
Panorama 44: a prospect from the edge of Sanctuary Wood looking towards the Menin Road in early March 1915. The building in the trees is the chateau at Stirling Castle. Note the evidence of mining.

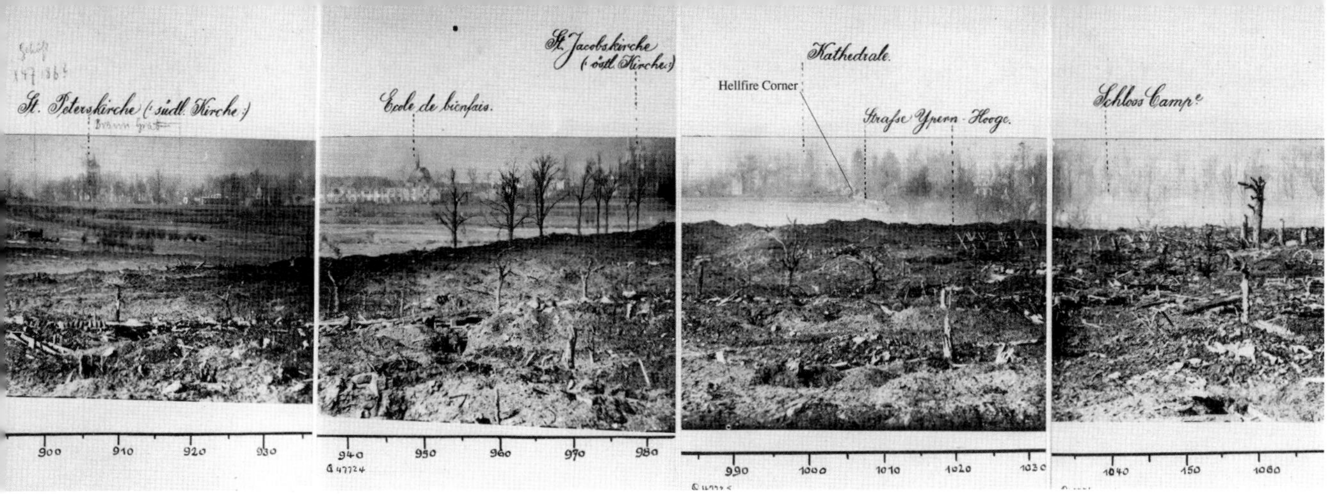

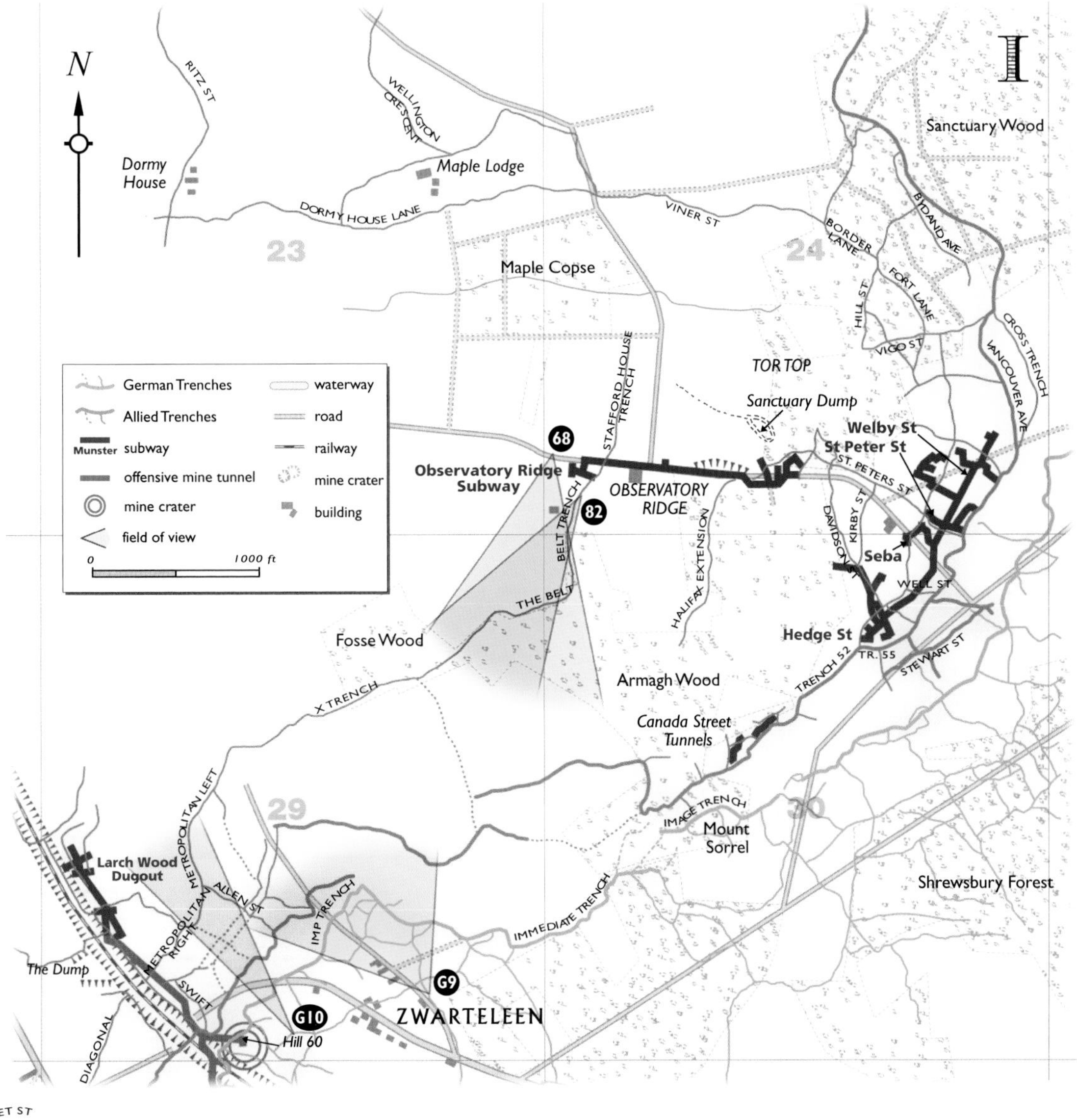

and struggling to sprout greenery following the devastating barrages used to drive the Canadians from the Observatory Ridge and Sanctuary Wood sectors. The panorama illustrates how the British arteries of supply, particularly the Menin Road, were so visible and vulnerable. One mat also see a clear evolution in defences. The barbed-wire entanglements are far more dense than the previous year, and now supported by metal screw pickets instead of knife-rests and wooden posts. In G-8 a famous British fieldwork is visible – the China Wall, a massive and immensely valuable breastwork communication trench connecting Hellfire Corner and Halfway House. The feature was such an obvious target it received special attention from enemy guns, and was permanently under repair.

Panorama 44 reveals the condition of the British front line trenches in the Sanctuary Wood sector. Apart from the ubiquitous Bully Beef, Maconochie tins and rum jars strewn about, the picture shows sections of armoured rubber hose, a sign of mining, which was fierce in this sector during 1915, 1916 and 1917. Unlike other areas, tunnellers here did not sink shafts into the clay but remained in the sandy ridge top layers. The fact that both sides were able to dig almost silently though the sand meant that no one enjoyed particular advantage; the result was highly intense camouflet fighting with several breakthroughs into opposing systems. When the German trenches were captured in August 1917, the enemy system was connected to the British tunnels, enlarged and made into accommodation for forward troops.

The building glimpsed through the trees to the left of frame is Stirling Castle Chateau. The chateau, where fighting in late 1914 was almost room to room, lies on the right-hand side of the Menin Road half a kilometre beyond Hooge.

Overleaf

A sniper of the Honourable Artillery Company in his lair in the wheat fields in front of Hooge. The left picture shows him at work, using two rifles. One (or perhaps both) is fitted with a telescopic sight. In the right photo the day's tally is marked in spent cartridges and chargers. It reads *III Huns* – three, not one hundred and eleven. 3 June 1915.

HUN
JUNE 3

Hill 60 and the Caterpillar

The sector that lies directly south-east of Ypres was dominated by a series of important localized hotspots. Like Hooge they developed their grim reputations due to local topographical elevation, a close proximity with the opposing trenches, and the consequent emergence of military mining: they are Hill 60 and the Caterpillar (sometimes called Hill 59), the Bluff, and St Eloi. All are unusual in that the most critical topographical features – that tiny patch of Flanders over which the most bitter fighting occurred – is man-made in each case.

As the Passchendaele Ridge sweeps around the lower arc of the Ypres Salient through Klein Zillebeke, Zwarteleen and on towards Wytschaete, its contours are etched in two places by remnants of the industrial revolution. The first, at Hill 60 (Zwarteleen), is the Ypres–Comines railway cutting, at The Bluff (Palingbeek) the feature is the Ypres–Comines Canal, but the third site has a much more ancient pedigree: at St Eloi the famous Mound (the Mound of Death) was a prehistoric tumulus.

The most northerly name on the list, Hill 60, along with its neighbour the Caterpillar, swiftly grew to be among the most hated and feared sectors on the Western Front for the British. As the ground sloped away on both sides of the ridge, excellent views in both directions were the prize for whomsoever held the tenancy. But the natural contours of the ridge had been further enhanced by the addition of man-made heaps of sandy spoil, products of the railway cutting driven late in the previous century. During this process the earth which came to constitute Hill 60 (the number denotes metres above sea level) was dumped to form a rough cone on the north side of the cutting, whilst that of the Caterpillar was deposited in a sinuous elongated 'S'

Above

German officers scrutinize British positions from the safety of one of many concrete emplacements near Hill 60.

Below

A segment of German Panorama G-9 taken from a position 300 m (328 yds) north-east of Hill 60 in July 1915. The trenches in the foreground are the German front-line positions.

Right
Attached map corresponding to Panoramma G-9 below. The main German artillery targets have been marked; each represents a building used by the British for observation.

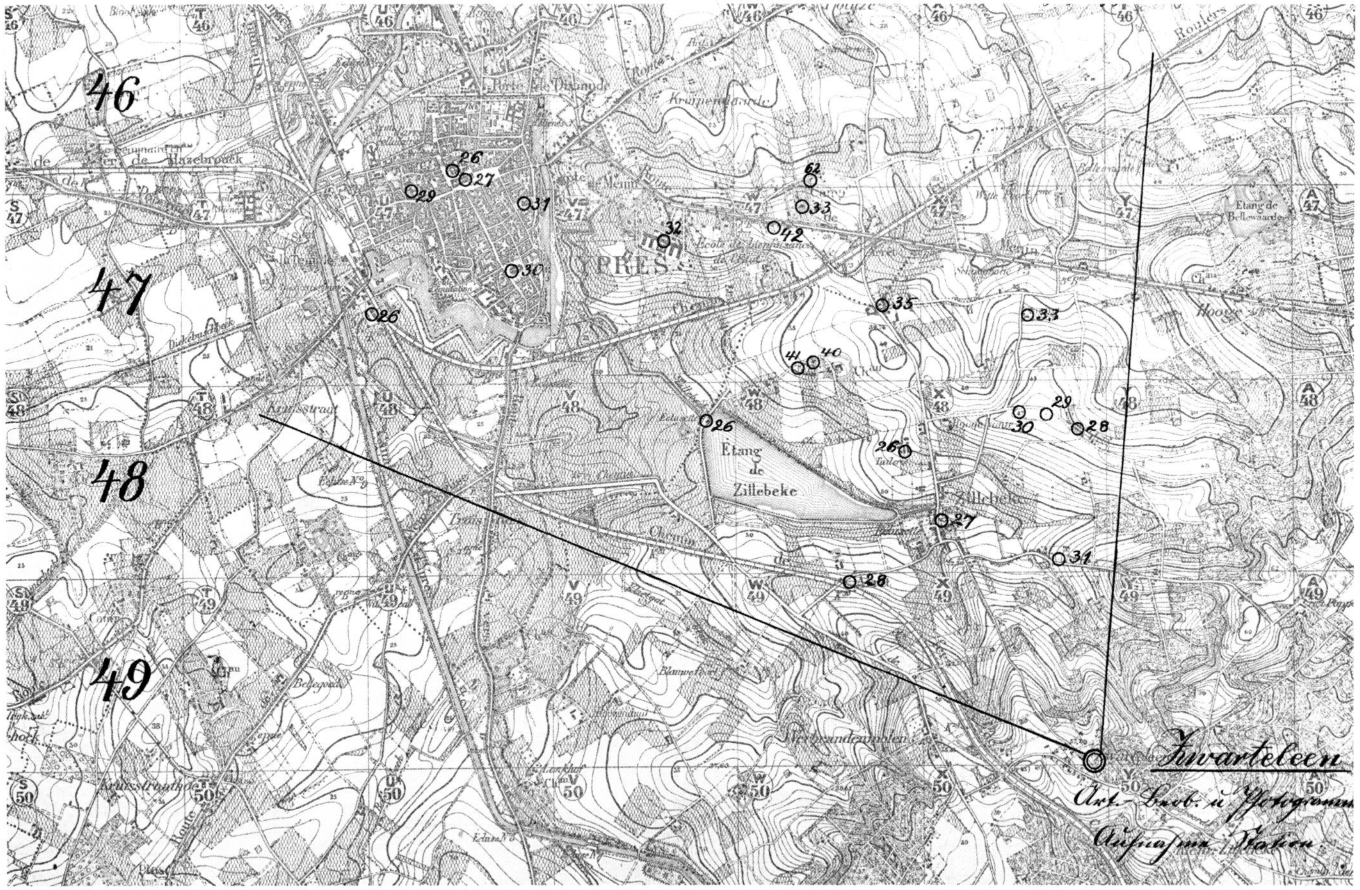

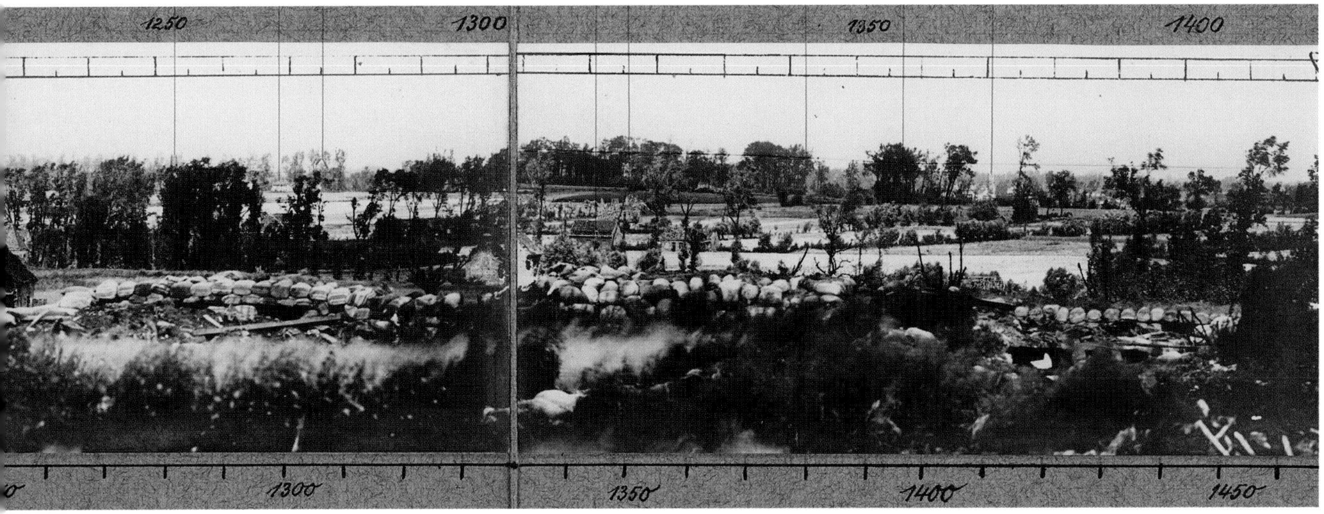

shape – hence the name – south of the tracks.

In early December 1914 both hills were wrested from the French during the actions which also secured the whole of neighbouring Messines Ridge for the Germans. The British took over the sector on 10 December, and brigade miners of the Monmouthshire's (this was eight weeks before the establishment of dedicated mining units, the Royal Engineer Tunnelling Companies) continued the primitive shallow work started by their French allies. The opposing trenches were almost farcically close on the western slopes of the hill, and this is illustrated in Panoramas 55 and *55a* (both April 1915) and G-9 (August 1915): the sandbags in the foreground of the latter are those of the British front line – within spitting distance. By the mid-summer of 1915 both sides had lost many lives in bitter fighting over

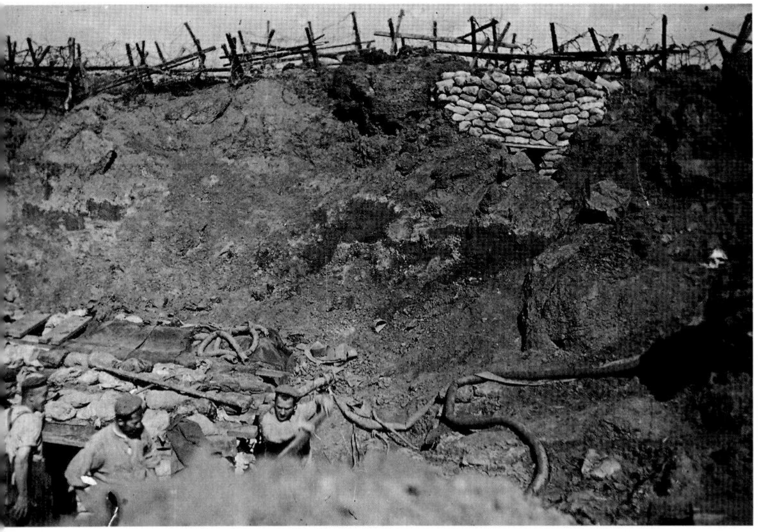

Left
German troops in a consolidated captured mine crater on the forward (north-western) face of Hill 60. New tunnels are being driven from the shelter of the crater.

supremacy of the crest. In addition to infantry assaults, and mines, asphyxiating gas had also been employed, and the sector was regarded alongside Hooge as a most undesirable locality. On 17 April 1915 the first British mines in the salient, six of them, were blown under Hill 60, and in subsequent assaults by the 5th Division four VCs were won. The Germans were driven from the summit twice in the next 48 hours, but British residence was to be brief and horribly costly.

18 April 1915
When we got to the cutting we found it full of the most awful fumes from the bursting shells which made our eyes water and smart and which were most unpleasant. As we were going up the cutting, which is about 20 yards broad with a single line, the Germans began putting great big crumps into the bank almost abreast of us. We waited in some dugouts for about a quarter of an hour being nearly blinded besides deafened and suffocated. We eventually made our way via 39 Trench through a communication trench to Hill 60 where the scene was too awful for words. There were hundreds of our dead lying thickly all over the place and in every conceivable attitude. Among them were also many wounded and two old craters about 40 feet across [these are the existing craters on the forward slope of the hill today] were packed with dead and wounded. They moaned and cried out to us all the time for help, few of the officers or men having even a first field dressing on their wounds. The stretcher-bearers were being ordered up but it appeared impossible for them to be able to deal with such numbers, and there was no doctor to help them.
DIARY, LIEUTENANT J. A. C. PENNYCUICK DSO, 59 FIELD COMPANY RE

Trench 39 was one of the major arterial routes to the Hill during the abortive attacks of 17 April 1915, and it can be seen in the earliest British panoramas of the sector, Nos 55 and *55a*, taken on 10 April 1915 just a few days before the mines were blown. The camera location for both images, The Dump, was another spoil heap 100 m (110 yds) or so behind the British line and the pictures show that, even at this very early stage of stasis, Hill 60 and the Caterpillar have suffered severely at the hands of artillery and trench mortars; they are already almost bare of vegetation, prematurely resembling parts of the Ypres Salient during the

Below
Panorama 68, May 1915 looking across towards Hill 60 and the Caterpillar from Observatory Ridge. The forward areas are stripped of greenery.

Above

A neat, strong and beautifully constructed German trench at Hill 60.

HILL 60

1917 battles. The ruins of Zwarteleen village are visible to the left of the hill. Lover's Lane, one of the main communication trenches feeding the sector, runs along the shoulder of the railway cutting. Behind the Caterpillar lies Battle Wood.

As Second Ypres began with the chlorine attacks of 22 April, the British still clung to the hill, but on 5 May the gas valves were also opened here at Zwarteleen. The vapour stole into trenches and dugouts, disabling and suffocating almost the entire garrison. That evening the British reassembled in the lines they had held on 17 April. By mid-summer all the forward positions from Sanctuary Wood to beyond Hill 60 were beaten into a similar state. Panoramas 68 (mid-May 1915) and *82* (14 August 1915), both taken from Observatory Ridge, show the denudation of the front line landscape across this area.

G-10 (taken with a telephoto lens in July 1915) again illustrates the splendid views enjoyed by the Germans from the crest of 'Hohe 60' – and how it was only the hill itself which was seriously battered; much of the ground between it and Ypres remains relatively unscathed and leafy in the summer heat. The spires of Ypres stand out in the bright summer sunlight; the village in the foreground is Zillebeke, later entirely obliterated, and the Ypres–Comines railway line is also visible to the left of frame, emerging from the cutting and curving around past the Zillebeke 'Arret' railway crossing. The scene appears to be – and was – relatively peaceful at this time. Desultory shelling and relentless sniping were the main threats. Following the April battles, a curious form of order was re-imposed upon the hill.

3 August 1915

Then we went along the line to Hill 60 correcting a sketch map as we went. Maps are all important and I never lose an opportunity of making my officers survey as much of our line as we can. Our line on 60 is very broken indeed. It used to be fairly straight but after they gassed us out, our line is now two ends with a sort of semi-circle backwards connecting the two ends. And Fritz is in the middle of our old front line. There are several old Comm. T. [communication trenches] which both of us hold with from 10 to 30 yards of No Man's land in between. And no one seems to know which trench is whose. The state of uncertainty is awkward. We were standing up having a good look around from one salient corner where the trench just in front was said to be ours. After about 90 seconds smack came a bullet just 6 inches too low, and threw the mud all over us. Then we left in haste with bended back. But fancy – what shooting – missed at about 80 yards. However thank goodness he did miss. It was the closest shave I've had or ever hope to have either.

DIARY, MAJOR S. H. COWAN, 175 TUNNELLING COMPANY RE

Hill 60 was permanently too 'hot' to clear the ground of the many casualties of the spring battles. A few weeks later

Top

Panorama 55: Hill 60 and the Caterpillar on 10 April 1915. Taken from The Dump.

Above

Positions on the British side of the Hill 60 railway bridge were invisible from the German lines. Some early mine schemes began here; entrances can be seen in the embankment close to the bridge.

Cowan's subordinate and planter of the Hooge mine, Lieutenant G. R. Cassels, visited the hill with a view to starting a fresh tunnelling scheme.

Below
The German front-line trench crossing the railway line and extending up the slope of Hill 60. It is strongly buttressed against shellfire and, on the hill, strutted for extra strength.

October 1915

My next assignment after Hooge was Hill 60. I had heard a great deal about it and I was anxious to inspect the effects of the six mines which of course were small compared with Hooge. The front line trench was deeper than that at Hooge but a poor place at that. Behind us was an abandoned trench full of dead and rotting French complete with uniforms, killed in previous actions. Behind that the support trenches where we had our dugouts [see 55 and 55a*]. The whole place was fly and rat-ridden, the rats as big as cats, and it stank to high heaven. The water in the shell holes was a stagnant green. In spite of rats running over one as one slept, and the usual tension, the personal atmosphere of the place was excellent, everyone friendly and willing to help. In front of the parapet complete with firestep – an amenity hardly known at Hooge – was no man's land with the two sets of barbed wire, ours and the German's, and between these the now nearly filled in remains of the small craters, hardly discernible as such. The whole of no man's land was criss-crossed with small trenches, saps, leading out of one or other of the front lines. These approached each other so closely in places that, looking over one it was possible to see into the other, and periscopes were used for the purpose, but only for seconds at a time as they always attracted a bullet.*

The main German trenches were evidently over the brow of the hill just out of sight, but there was a front line, lightly manned, on this side of it. On the eastern side, that is the right hand, of the hill, ran a deep railway cutting at right angles to the trenches. The railway cutting curved on our side before it reached the Germans, and here we were out of sight of the enemy. The bottom of the cutting at this point was marked by a circular board with 30 painted on it in red indicating that it was 30 metres above sea level. The top of the hill was 60 metres above sea level.

LIEUTENANT G. R. CASSELS, 175 TUNNELLING COMPANY RE

One of the tunnel entrances (adits) which Cassels would have seen on his visit to '60' lies immediately to the left of the bridge in *55a* and 55, covered by a blanket. This is No 10 adit. It is protected by a robust sandbag revetment, immediately above which the entrance to Trench 38 is visible. Sign boards for this and other workings can be clearly seen in Panorama 55. The section of communication trench leading to the front line used by RE officer Pennycuick and his colleagues is also marked; in *55A* the forwardmost British position is marked by dotted lines. Crossing the road towards the hill, Trench 38 passes directly beneath today's visitor car park. Mine craters are evident on the slope in front of the German line, which runs just below the crest, and the precariousness of the British positions is plain to see. A close look at the British front line in number 55 reveals rows of fixed bayonets glinting in the sun.

These are two rare panoramas where figures are visible. British greatcoat-clad troops can be seen standing to the immediate right of the bridge, and outside the shallow dugouts along Lovers Lane. These men may well have taken part in the assaults on the hill a week later.

Surface action calmed during 1916, but underground

it was an altogether different story – activity in the tunnels was constant day and night, and all-year-round. A labyrinth of shallow workings down to around 10 m (32 ft) depth grew organically during the first year of war. In the sandy ground of the Passchendaele Ridge system galleries could be cut quietly and quickly with bayonets and sharpened entrenching tools. Neither British nor German were able to gain any particular advantage and the fighting was supremely attritional – 'if you blow me, I'll blow you'. The 'blowing' was done by small controlled underground explosions known as *camouflets*, designed to kill or entomb the enemy. This strange, primitive form of warfare was based upon sound alone: as the enemy could not be seen, special listening devices were designed to detect movement. If thought to be within range of the listener (there were dozens of listening posts under this and all other hills – see plan) a charge was either placed in a gallery, or in a cylindrical hole quietly drilled towards the enemy with a special earth auger. A ready-charged and primed 'torpedo' was slid in and connected to an exploder. If one's enemy could be heard tunnelling, it meant that they were not planting mines of their own, and therefore posed no risk; it was when noise ceased that heartbeats quickened, as this might signify serious and imminent hostile intent. In this case an immediate destructive response was obligatory. Tunnellers did not care how their enemy died, be it obliteration, gassing or entombment, as long as they were the first to blow. Both sides worked in the same manner, and gave no quarter: it was kill or be killed.

Occasionally an explosion would crater the surface. This was often because perilous signals had been heard, a response was deemed urgent, but the enemy were a little too far away to use a *camouflet*. In these cases a heavier charge that would shatter all tunnels (including one's own) in a wider 'sphere of destruction' was used. Several of the lhe larger hollows evident on the forward slopes of the hill today are caused by 1915 and early 1916 blows of this kind rather than shellfire.

The nature of this private and secret hidden war was entirely dictated by geology, and in the Ypres Salient it was a critical discipline to master both in trench and tunnel work. Beneath the sandy surface layers of all the Flemish ridges lies a seam of saturated sands, known to the Germans as *Schwimmsande*, to the British as running sands. Trapped between the surface stratum and deeper beds of blue Flanders clay, the layer was not only waterlogged but under great pressure. The impervious clay beneath precluded any downward percolation so the only escape route for water was laterally from the ridge slopes as spring lines (in Hill 60's case mainly into the railway cutting). However, this was such a slow process that the wet layer remained permanently in place all year round regardless of weather conditions.

The *Schwimmsande* was a formidable barrier to miners. Sinking a shaft through dry ground was straightforward enough, but if the soil first erupted when the layer was pierced, and then acted like sloppy porridge, it was an almost impossible task. In the spring of 1915 at Cuinchy (covered in a later chapter), however, the British found a way of solving the problem by using sectional steel instead of traditional timber shafts. Strong, watertight and safe these

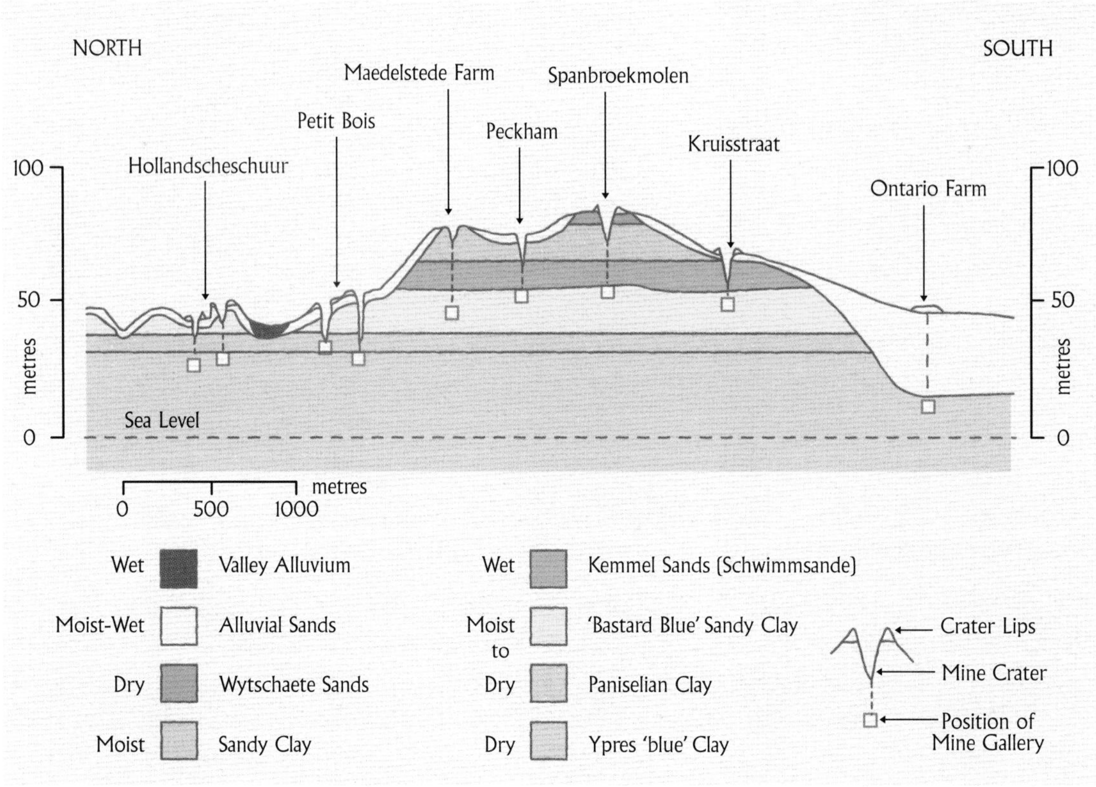

Left
Officers of 1st Australian Tunnelling Company who were present at the blowing of the Hill 60 and Caterpillar mines on 7 June 1917.

cylindrical 'tubbed shafts' were installed under strictest secrecy on many parts of the Allied mining front in Flanders in 1915, 1916 and early 1917. Meanwhile, the Germans continued to believe that if *they* were unable to overcome the *Schwimmsande* and reach the dry blue clay beneath, the British must be in the same invidious position. As a result their *Mineure* did not make serious attempts to solve the problem until it was too late: when the British blew their first deep mines in the clay beneath St Eloi in March 1916 (see Panoramas *48* and 94). By this time they were already too far behind to retaliate effectively.

The Hill 60 sector played a key role in the Battle of Messines Ridge in June 1917. It lay next to the extreme northern hinge of the battlefront of Mount Sorrel (68 and *82*). Employing a steel shaft, a pair of huge mines had been placed beneath Hill 60 and the Caterpillar – 24,000 kg and 31,700 kg (53,000 lbs and 70,000 lbs) respectively – and under seventeen other German strongpoints along the length of the ridge down to Ploegsteert Wood. The topography of the Messines Ridge is illustrated in Panoramas *56*, 62, 107 and173 which offer wide and elevated views.

Most of the British mine systems along the Ridge managed to negotiate a variety of thorny localized geological problems, including the running sand. The failure in conquering the *Schwimmsande* was thus fatal for the Germans. By the time they had incontrovertible evidence that their enemy had gone deep it was already too late to counter the massive offensive scheme which British, Canadian and Australian tunnellers were putting in place: a scheme which on 7 June 1917 was to result in the greatest mine attack in history.

Right
A German view along the cutting of the shell-peppered railway bridge at Hill 60. The British occupy the far side.

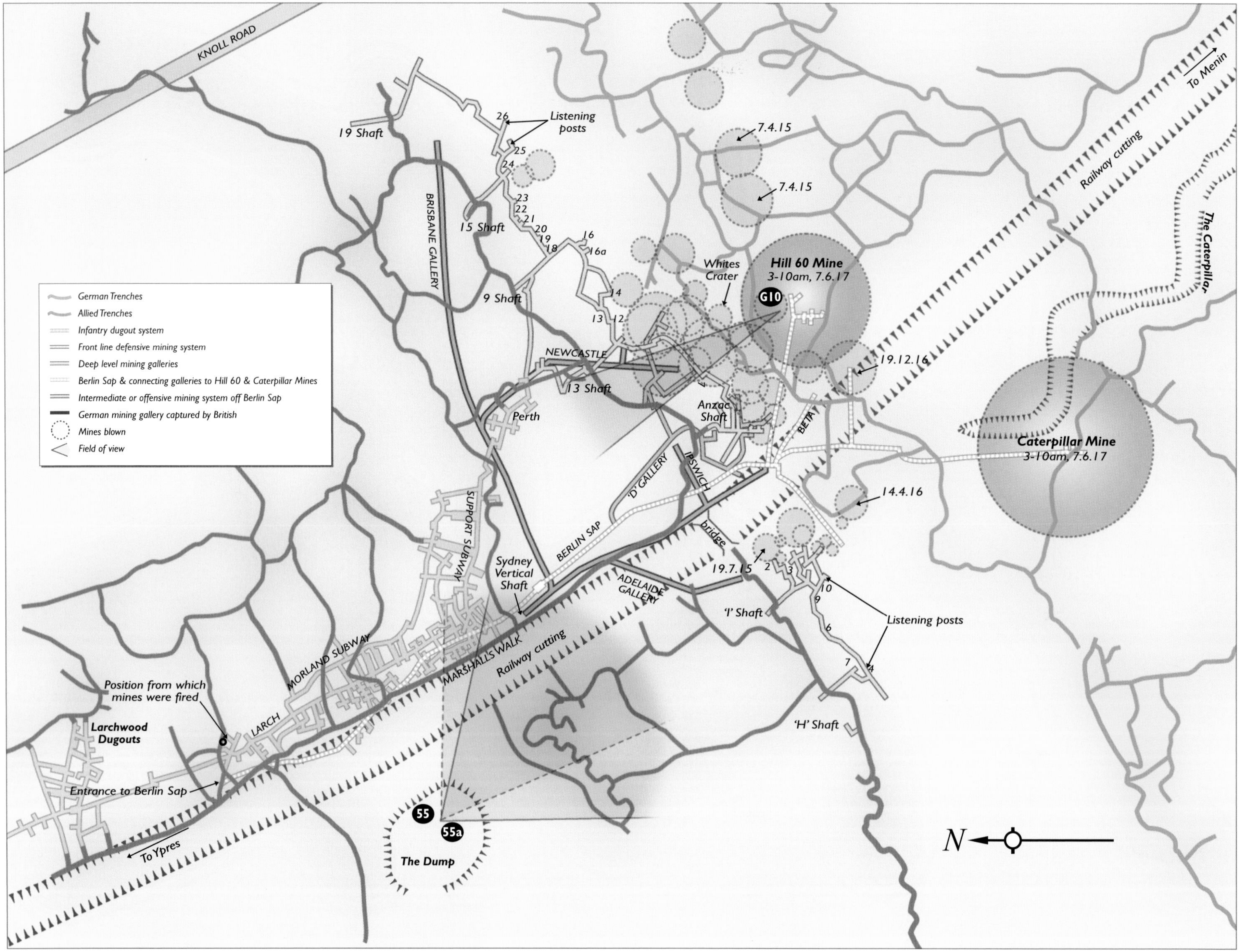
KNOLL ROAD
19 Shaft
Listening posts
26
25
24
23
22
21
20
19
18
16
16a
14
13
12
15 Shaft
9 Shaft
BRISBANE GALLERY
NEWCASTLE
13 Shaft
Perth
7.4.15
7.4.15
Whites Crater
Hill 60 Mine
3-10am, 7.6.17
G10
19.12.16
Anzac Shaft
BETA
'D' GALLERY
IPSWICH
BERLIN SAP
bridge
Caterpillar Mine
3-10am, 7.6.17
14.4.16
19.7.15
2
3
10
9
6
7
4
Listening posts
'I' Shaft
'H' Shaft
ADELAIDE GALLERY
Sydney Vertical Shaft
SUPPORT SUBWAY
MORLAND SUBWAY
MARSHALL'S WALK
Railway cutting
Railway cutting
To Menin
The Caterpillar
Position from which mines were fired
Larchwood Dugouts
LARCH
Entrance to Berlin Sap
To Ypres
55
55a
The Dump
N
German Trenches
Allied Trenches
Infantry dugout system
Front line defensive mining system
Deep level mining galleries
Berlin Sap & connecting galleries to Hill 60 & Caterpillar Mines
Intermediate or offensive mining system off Berlin Sap
German mining gallery captured by British
Mines blown
Field of view

Left

Hill 60

Plan of the Hill 60 and Caterpillar mine workings and associated dugouts. Three levels of tunnels are shown, including the deep level galleries serving the two vast mines blown on 7 June 1917. Neither German workings nor many earlier British and Canadian workings are included. Note the lines of listening posts defending front line positions. Larch Wood dugouts were connected to the mine system, and incorporated all the necessary services including a hospital. The dugouts could accommodate 3000 men.

Right

The Bluff

Tunnels and craters at the Bluff showing the German galleries annexed by the British in December 1916. The two largest craters are those blown beneath British positions in January and July 1916. In the same way as both Railway Wood and Hill 60, the mines at the Bluff were connected to large dugout systems. The entire area is now a heavily-wooded nature reserve.

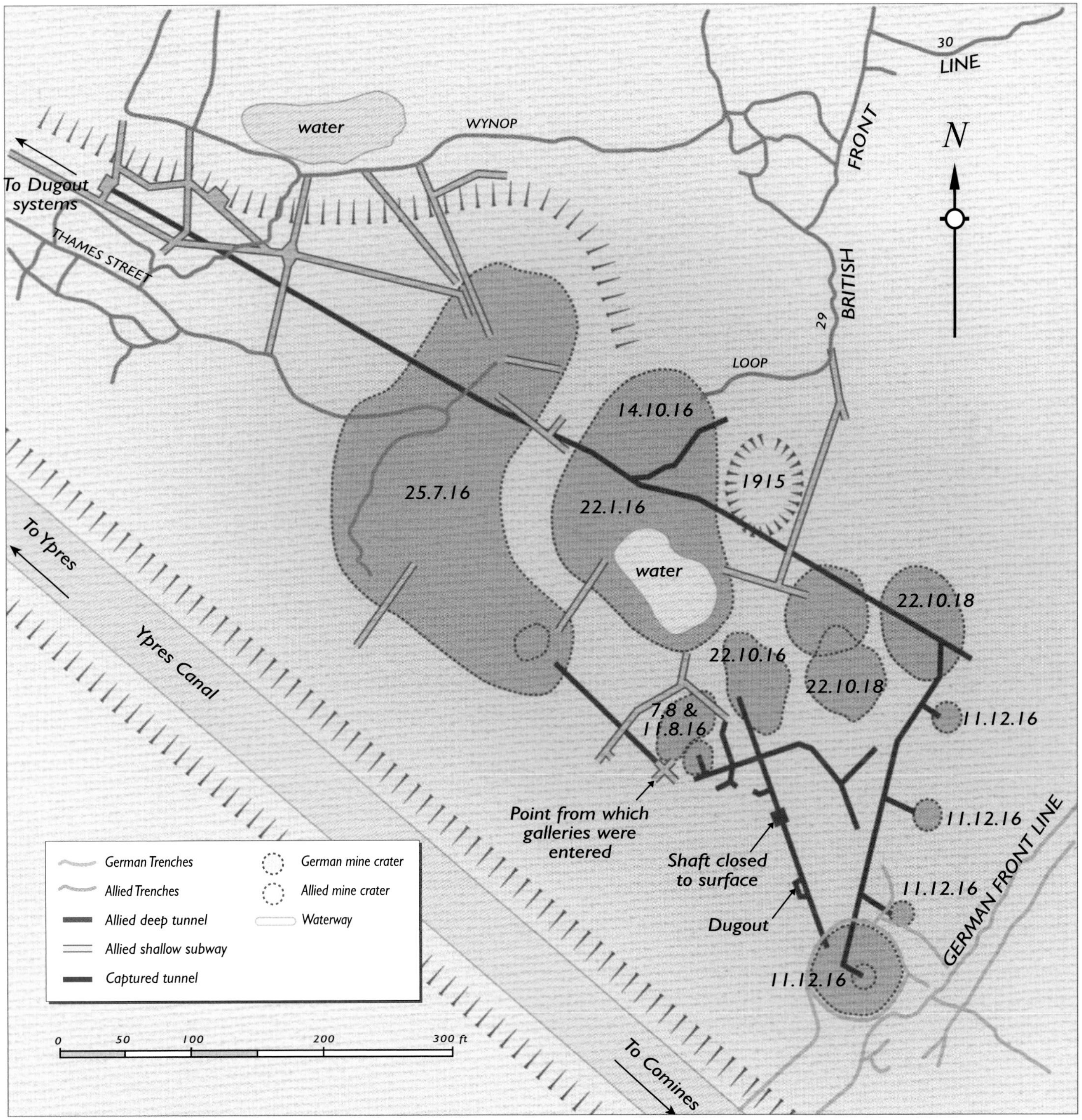

The Bluff

Known to the Germans as 'Die Grosse Bastion', the Bluff, just 2 km (1.25 miles) south of Hill 60, was also a major tunnelling sector, although destined not to be part of the mine attack on 7 June. Here, Canadian engineers had attempted to employ a machine to drive a deep gallery in the clay, with four branches leading to large chambers around the heavily fortified Eikhof Farm and Dammstrasse sunken road beneath the Oosthoek Ridge. The heavy, swelling clay subsoils beat the machine, a Whittaker, at every turn and the scheme was abandoned.

The Bluff was a fiery spot from the earliest period and had formed a part of the main German thrust upon Ypres in late 1914. The man-made geology over which the two sides fought here was created by the digging in 1880 of the Ypres–Comines canal. Like Hill 60 the work again demanded cutting through the ridge, but this time the spoil was arranged in elongated mounds on either side of the canal. The highest mound on the north bank ended abruptly and precipitously: this was the Bluff. Discounting the consequences of the First World War the whole canal project appeared to be doomed from the start: it was halted in 1870 until the outcome of the Franco-Prussian War had become clear, taken over by the Belgian state in 1885, then forcibly stopped again by serious geological problems. Only in June 1913 was the waterway at last completed. However, the bridge (see Panorama 69, 26 May 1915) which spanned the canal in front of Voormezeele Chateau (known as White Chateau during the war) elected to collapse a few weeks later. Whilst engineers cursed and scratched their heads, the war broke out. To this day the canal has never been open to traffic.

When First Ypres burst upon the fields of Flanders the Allied line was several kilometres forward of the Bluff at Zandvoorde (see German Panorama *G-11* taken later in the war when these were immensely strong German reserve positions which remained unbroken throughout the Messines and Third Ypres battles). On 11 November 1914 the great thrust pushed French and Indian forces in this region back, first to Hollebeke where the canal turns at right angles towards Comines, and then to the Bluff, where the advance was at last arrested – and where the lines would stay for over two and half years. The British 28th

Above

A spick-and-span captain of the Hampshire Regiment reconnoitring for a projected attack with a trench periscope.

Below

Panorama 69, 26 May 1915. This segment shows the collapsed bridge over the canal, and buildings of the White Chateau estate.

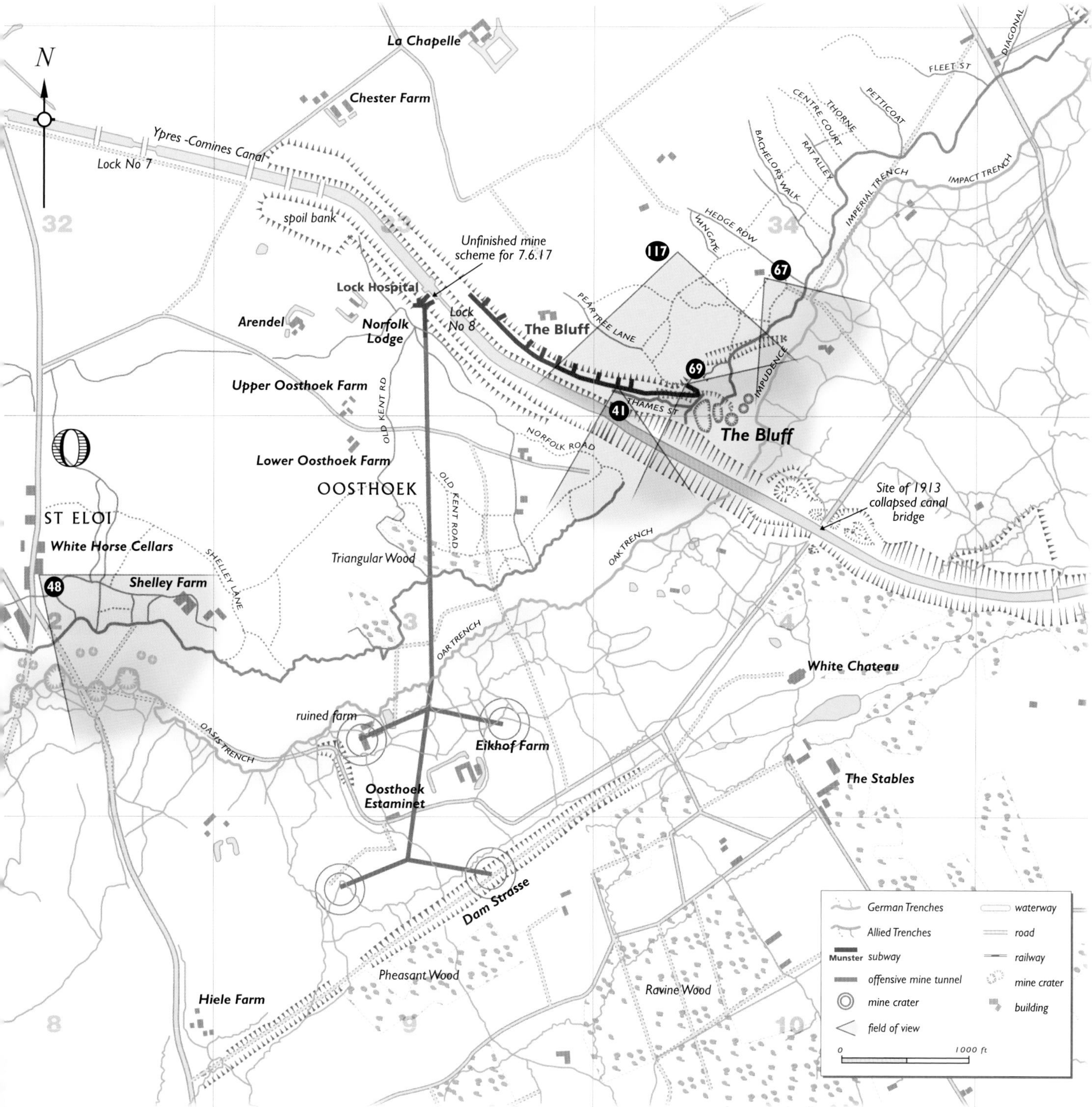

Division took over the sector on 1 February 1915.

As a defensive position the Bluff was both admirable and valuable. The 9 m (30 ft) high bank of made ground made it the highest position held by the British in the area, presenting panoramic views over enemy lines towards Hill 60, the Ravine sub-sector to the left and St Eloi to the right. They were determined not to let it go the way of other vantage points in the Salient. Protected frontally by a steep escarpment, and to the right by the abrupt banks of the cutting and deep water of the canal, the main route of hostile attack had to be from the north-east – the Hill 60 direction. Here, the front line was a boggy and filthy earthwork called International Trench, a position which was once occupied by both sides (hence the name). Number *67* is taken from a point in the nearby Hedge Row CT which fed this sub-sector. The camera is just behind the British front line (during a dry period) and shows no man's land and the proximity of the enemy. The face of the Bluff is just visible on the extreme right of frame. On the Bluff itself the British front line ran around the base of the escarpment. Panoramas 41 and 69 were taken from support positions on the apex of the bluff itself in February and May 1915. Hardly a crater mars no man's land at this time, but by May the imposing chateau, still partially standing in February, has been crushed beneath the tree line. Wire defences appear flimsy compared to later years, the same knife-rests can be seen protecting the German front line in both panoramas. The enemy lines south of the canal can be seen to be as well positioned as any in the Salient, sitting astride the Oosthoek Ridge with the fortified Eikhof Farm position at their heart. Panorama 41 reveals around twenty sad bundles lying in no man's land, the remains of a raid (possibly French).

With no man's land around 200 m (220 yds) wide at the foot of its forward face, enemy artillery

gave the Bluff constant therapy, with regular and multiple daily 'strafes' – accurate ones too, judging by the panoramas. A dangerous game of shuttlecock was played to grasp and hold control of the lines here. As frontal attacks failed, so the Germans charged their *Pioniere-Mineure* to undermine the hill and blow the British from its slopes. With the help of three mines, small by later standards but highly effective nonetheless, the Germans took the position for the first time on the evening of 14 February 1916. Despite counter-attacks it was not until 2 March that a surprise attack by 76th Brigade regained the trenches.

Tunnelling had also begun in the 1.5 km (1,600 yd) Ravine and Verbrandenmolen section between Hill 60 and the canal in the spring of 1915, but it was fighting at The Bluff which became the most highly concentrated in the area. A web of shallow defensive workings had been developed by the end of May. 172 Tunnelling Company RE were charged with defensive mining: stopping the enemy getting under the hill. Due to geology and contour, the workings were very wet, but fortunately several tunnels could be drained into the canal. Unlike Hill 60 the Germans grasped the underground initiative and for over a year the British were on the back foot. Practically all their hostile endeavours were foiled and on 21 January 1916 many tunnellers were killed when the Germans exploded a much larger than normal mine at the base of the escarpment. Almost 100 infantrymen were also buried by the fallout. There followed a heavy localized assault that captured 600 m (656 yds) of British front line. It had to be retaken.

In the German offensive of 14th February 1916 the whole of the 172 Company mining system was captured on the Bluff itself and the tunnels in front of Christmas Day trench, and all the sappers on shift at the time were killed or captured. The remaining 172 officers and men under Captain Brisco had reached the limit of exhaustion and it was essential to relieve them as quickly as possible.

Above

Panorama 128: the vast craters formed by heavy German mines blown beneath British trenches at the Bluff in 1916. The lips have been fortified with a 'crater-trench'.

Right
A German *Pioniere* on guard in the Bluff tunnel system.

I shall never forget my experience of that week on the Bluff. The initial counter-attack had been made and the old German front line recaptured on the 2nd March when our section was sent up. We left our company HQ at La Clytte and went by lorry as far as possible where we were met by a guide from 172 about 6 p.m. in a blinding snow storm. Holmes led the section in single column with the guide, and I followed up the rear to keep them together and try to prevent them from discarding their loads which consisted of full equipment, blankets and a week's rations. Also to rescue the men that had fallen into shell holes and were so heavily laden that they could not get out.

The going was at a snail's pace as thousands of infantry were being sent up to relieve the troops that had made the original attack, and it was not long before I realised that our guide did not know the way, and after wandering about for hours, Holmes found out that he came from another section and Brisco was so short of men he could not spare anyone who really knew the location of his section HQ. Holmes then took over and with the use of his map reference got us there eventually at 2 a.m. all soaked to the skin and chattering with cold. Late as we were Brisco had a hot meal ready for us and enough rum to swim in. It was wonderful to get into a warm dugout and thaw out after eight hours of blinding snow storm.

The next morning Brisco took me round the old German front line and we explored the German defensive mine system which he had been competing against for many months. As no communication trench had yet been dug, in order to get into our new front line we had to cross what had been no man's land only a few hours before. Here we found a company of one of our best infantry regiments in a state of fatigue and bewilderment, as they had relieved the men who had captured the

trench in the darkness more than 48 hours previously and had no idea where the German front line was as the trench faced the wrong way and they were being shelled by the Germans from both sides. We were just in time to stop one of their sergeants from going down the communication trench leading to the German front line in the hope of making contact with their regiment and getting rations for his men as they had had nothing to eat for two days.

CAPTAIN H. TATHAM, 250 TUNNELLING COMPANY RE

On 21 July another even bigger German mine blew a huge gash in the embankment – the large craters can still be seen today. But this time the blow was only half-heartedly followed up by German infantry. This was a critical day for British surface and sub-surface fortunes at the Bluff, for their tunnellers took the opportunity (and the risk) of finding a way into the previously undetected German mine system by immediately entering the new crater and digging down to find the hostile approach tunnel – which had to be done before the enemy could recover it for further use themselves. Ultimately, half of the complete German mine system was purloined by the British, halting any further enemy offensive ambitions at the Bluff. If the Germans wished to attack again a new system would have to be driven – in the sure knowledge that the British were listening everywhere.

As 1916 progressed Allied underground superiority was firmly imposed at the Bluff, and every German attempt to undermine the hill was nullified. To make absolutely certain that no skulduggery was possible, on 11 December 1916 a 5-tonne (5-ton) mine was blown deep amongst the German tunnels. Almost the whole of the remaining enemy mine system was then captured – and held. It was partly due to constant protective work such as this that a deep scheme to complement the other Messines mines was never put into action on the north bank of the canal.

As a result of military mining engendering such great danger and anxiety in the trenches, surface action was just as intense at the Bluff as at Hill 60 and Hooge, especially in the form of trench raids and mortar attacks. Whereas artillery was a somewhat inexact tool for destroying hostile shafts and dugouts, mortars were much more accurate, with the heavier variety being immensely destructive. A well-placed shot could entirely wreck many months of patient work. They were the bane of soldiers' and tunnellers' lives.

There was a little tramway up the back of the bank leading up to the Bluff trenches. You couldn't be seen by the Germans there, but they had it taped. For a while it was my job to take up ammunition, water, supplies, food and that, to a place just behind the trenches where it would be unloaded. This was at night of course. For the

Above
The tortured Bluff battlefield as seen from Beef Street trench in the British support line. Segment of Panorama 114, 25 January 1917.

Left
Aerial view of the Bluff showing the footprint of craters, the canal, and the shell-pocked landscape. The German front line is deeply inscribed to the left of the group of three small craters.

Right
Typical winter conditions at the Bluff. *Pioniere* Dohl negotiates the German front line after a heavy British strafe.

return trip they put bodies on the trolley – men who had gone west that day I suppose. I hated the homeward journey. I don't know why because I must have seen thousands of dead men, dead horses, mules, by then, and I was properly hardened to it. But pushing the tram back...well, I wasn't comfortable. You had shells and mortars and starshells going off regular, and in the flashes, especially the starshells which burned for a bit, I couldn't stop myself looking at my load. I didn't want to, but I was drawn to it. The track was uneven and wobbly, and it looked like they were moving, coming back to life. It made my skin creep, but I just couldn't keep my eyes of them when the lights went up. Everything in that war was down to luck. Although Minnies landed pretty close a few times – a hell of a crash, they made – and shook us about a bit, they never got me, and I never had anyone [a body] tumble off; I think I would have left him there for someone else if I did. I had been told of other blokes and their load just disappearing; just a smoking hole there in the morning. Funny what your mind does. If I hadn't been alone it wouldn't have been so bad, I suppose. It probably sounds ridiculous [to you], but my obsession with looking at those lads – who couldn't do me no harm, could they – took away the fear of the shelling.
PRIVATE WILF WALLWORTH, SOUTH LANCASHIRE REGIMENT

Panorama 114 shows the situation at the beginning of 1917. This is probably a little more like the Great War landscape that many people imagine to have been a permanent feature of the Western Front. However, the destruction is very localized: no man's land remains almost as clearly defined as in early 1915 panoramas, and even at this stage of the war it is still relatively unscarred – testimony to the accuracy of artillery and mortar teams of both sides. The White Chateau has of course been reduced to a heap of rubble. Above all, the Bluff itself has been completely pulverized by persistent mine, shell and mortar fire. Part of the canal escarpment can be seen to the left of the

Above and right
Second Army Panorama 41, 23 February 1915, showing on the far bank of the canal the sad remains of a raid.

Bluff, whilst to the right, on the far bank, lie the German front lines on the crest and forward slopes of the Oosthoek Ridge. The Dammstrasse, a sunken road and originally the driveway to the White Chateau, was developed into a powerful linear strongpoint. It was full of concrete emplacements and fiercely fought over during the first day of the Battle of Messines, 7 June 1917. Indeed, due to the failure to plant any mines in this supremely well-defended sector, the 47th London Division suffered greater casualties here than any other unit that took part in the battle.

7 June 1917

As we went over we passed through only a moderate barrage and met with no casualties, although the dead bodies that were scattered about shewed that other parties had not been so fortunate. When we reached the Dammstrasse however we were fairly in amongst the shells, for this was now our front line and Fritz was concentrating all his efforts in the attempt to prevent us getting any further. Also many of our own guns were firing short, and spiteful 18-pounder shrapnel was bursting all around us. The western bank of the Dammstrasse was lined with dugouts, now in a various stages of demolition. The one chosen for our signal office was fairly sound. One of our 18-pounder shrapnels burst about 6 yards above our heads and bits came hissing down viciously. I wasn't touched but Dagnell got it in both knees and Coltherd in the left knee. I used my own field service dressing on Dagnell and subsequently got into trouble for being in action without one in my possession. We carried them across the road to the dugout.

A shell burst right on top of the Signal Office and we went over expecting to find the place blown in, but it was quite unharmed inside – evidence that Fritz knows how to build dugouts. The Signal office was small and with two wounded men in it and one end under water, there was only room for one operator at a time, so I took a buzzer outside and rigged it up on a mound where the trench had been blown in. The dirt gradually wore away and disclosed the buttocks of a dead man, so I moved into the Dammstrasse where the only comparatively dry spot was alongside a dead German, but he was not badly mutilated. An infantryman close by me was hit in the face by a quantity of shrapnel dust, and his eyes trickled down his cheeks. He cried out 'Oh my eyes, my eyes – my God – I'm blind.' The sudden realisation of his blindness seemed a greater agony than the pain of his wounds. I shall never forget that terrible cry of anguish.
SAPPER ALBERT MARTIN RE , 41ST DIVISION SIGNALS

Ultimately, opposition at the White Chateau and Dammstrasse crumbled and the British advanced along the axis of the canal to where it links with the Ypres–Comines railway at Hollebeke. The lines reached and held by the Allies after these actions can be seen in Panoramas *115* (14 June 1917), *117* (11 July 1917), *120* (17 July 1917), and *121* from Wytschaete (17 July 1917).

Like most other sectors in the region, in 1918 the Bluff changed hands twice; first when the Germans advanced in April, and again in September when they were pushed into final retreat. Today, although wooded,

the embankments and locks along the canal retain many scars of 1914–18 actions, and a walk through the Palingbeek Domain is profitable. The large mine craters on the Bluff itself are especially impressive. A café now sits on what was once no man's land. South of the canal, the ground where the 47th London Division suffered so badly is today a beautifully manicured golf course, with the attractive clubhouse sitting close to the site of the original White Chateau (Panoramas 41, 69, 114). Each hole is named after a wartime feature. Sadly, whether winter or summer, densely wooded canal banks determinedly thwart those hoping to recreate these panoramic Great War vistas. However, a stable footbridge has replaced the ill-fated 1913 canal crossing.

The Bluff and St Eloi sectors are linked by Panorama *48* (11 March 1915) taken from White Horse Cellars, a position in the village of St Eloi itself, just behind the British front line. Both sectors are represented on the opposing ends of the photograph. The Oosthoek Ridge is visible through the trees to the left of frame, whilst the breastworks of the St Eloi trenches appear on rising ground to the far right. Their trace can be followed curving away left towards the ridge. The curious timber structures are tobacco drying racks. The important raised ground of the miniscule St Eloi salient is very clear from this photograph. This was part of the 47th London's battlefield on 7 June 1917.

St Eloi

Above
The dreaded 'Mound of Death' at St Eloi. Photographs of this feature are extremely rare, as it was suicidal to show one's head above the parapet in this sector.

The little village of St Eloi lies on the same ridge system as Hill 60 and the Bluff, but sits on a slightly lower contour, a fact which did not diminish but increase its significance Also taken over from the French in February 1915 it was to become a continually active mining sector, with many a grisly crater fight. The Germans blew the first mine here in April 1915 and from then on escalation of underground warfare was rapid. St Eloi was in fact to witness the most significant breakthrough in tunnelling in the Ypres Salient.

10 August 1915

It was quite a misty day so we took a short cut to Voormezele and of course the sun came out, but for once Fritz was asleep. Thence we walked up to St Eloi by a very long trench and had a look at things and said the usual communication service over the 'Mound', which heap of earth we once used to own. Now it is the local bugbear for the ground is fairly level but for its ugly head full of periscopes and snipers.

Major S. H. Cowan,
OC 175 Tunnelling Company RE

The village itself, more a hamlet really, lay within the British front line, and many trenches ran through and under buildings. Here, the local 'excrescence' was the Mound (of Death) mentioned by Major Cowan and indeed many other chroniclers of the war. The Mound the observational capabilities of the occupants by several vital metres. It can be seen on the left of Panorama 51 and right of *42*. During First Ypres ownership of the village and the Mound shifted back and forth; when calm fell upon St Eloi at last the British, as per usual, inhabited the lower ground. Although perching on a slight rise, conditions at St Eloi were as bad as anywhere in the Salient – even a year later.

2 November 1915

At the barrier at St Eloi we got into the front line. And branched off to the left. We discovered that the line was equally as bad as the CT [communication trench]. It was water-logged, and the inky darkness of the night added to our difficulties. This sector of the line was held by the North Staffords, and the fire bays were fully occupied. Gradually the line became worse, and when we got to our company flank we found practically no trench at all. We seemed to have been in

Below
Panorama 51 of 20 March 1915 shows a distant view of the St Eloi landscape. The Mound is just visible to the left-hand edge.

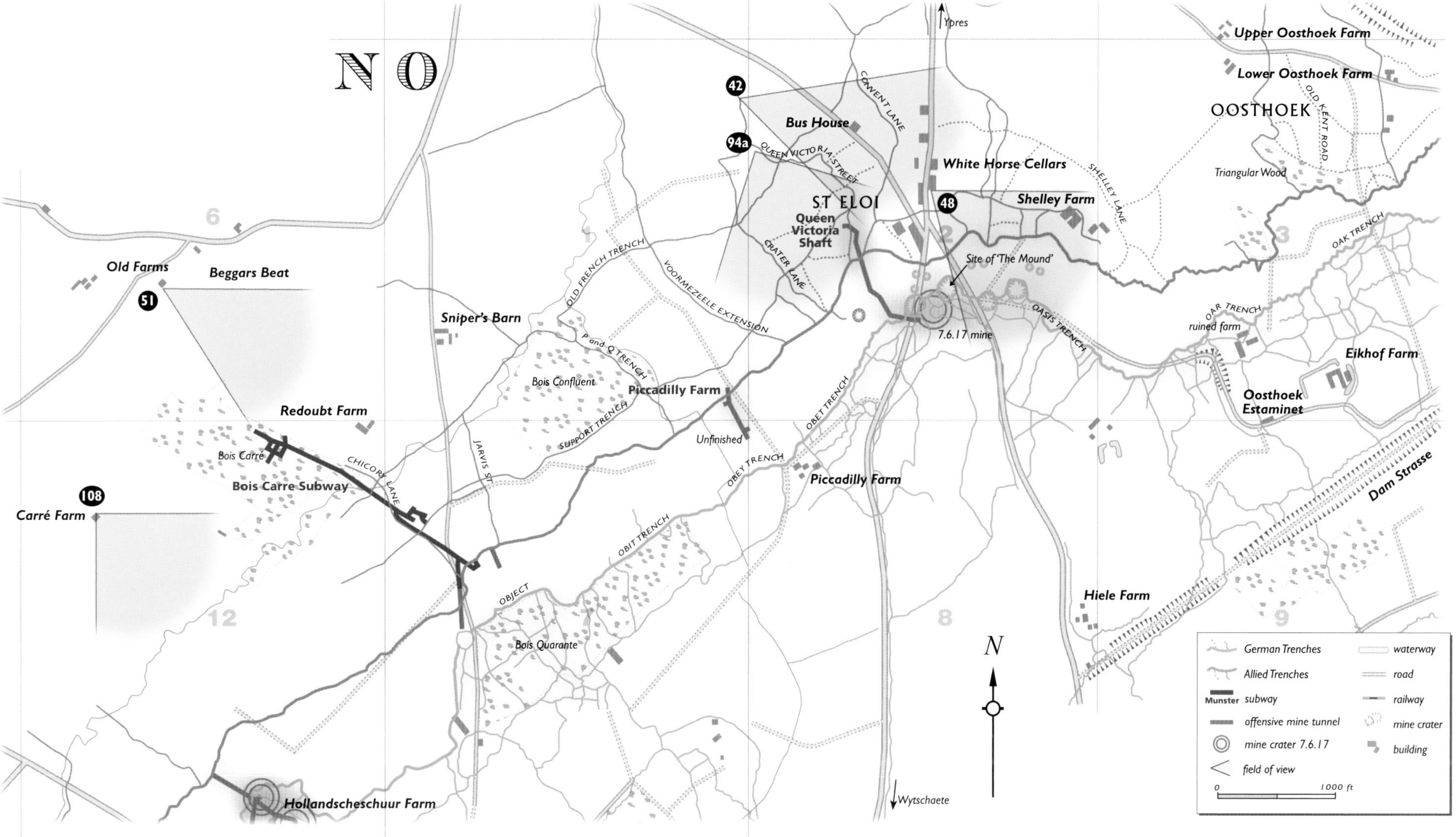
NO
Ypres
Upper Oosthoek Farm
Lower Oosthoek Farm
OOSTHOEK
OLD KENT ROAD
Triangular Wood
42
Bus House
CONVENT LANE
94a
QUEEN VICTORIA STREET
White Horse Cellars
SHELLEY LANE
48
Shelley Farm
ST ELOI
Queen Victoria Shaft
CRATER LANE
Site of 'The Mound'
7.6.17 mine
OASIS TRENCH
OAK TRENCH
OAR TRENCH
ruined farm
Eikhof Farm
Oosthoek Estaminet
Dam Strasse
6
Old Farms
Beggars Beat
51
Sniper's Barn
OLD FRENCH TRENCH
VOORMEZEELE EXTENSION
P and Q TRENCH
Bois Confluent
Piccadilly Farm
SUPPORT TRENCH
Redoubt Farm
Bois Carré
Bois Carre Subway
CHICORY LANE
JARVIS ST
Unfinished
OBET TRENCH
OBEY TRENCH
Piccadilly Farm
108
Carré Farm
OBIT TRENCH
OBJECT
12
Bois Quarante
8
Hiele Farm
9
N
Wytschaete
Hollandscheschuur Farm
German Trenches
Allied Trenches
Munster subway
offensive mine tunnel
mine crater 7.6.17
field of view
waterway
road
railway
mine crater
building
0
1000 ft

Bois Confluent
Wytschaete Church
Sniper's Barn
Grand Bois
Ruins of
Croonaert Chapel

one continuous nightmare of mud. Many of my heavily-laden bombers were engulfed in the trench, and had to be helped out. Words cannot describe the state of our new line, and rain was falling heavily to complete our discomfort. Practically the whole company front was under water, and the floating duckboards would fly up and hit the unwary one in the face when stood upon. In our company front there were three mine craters to hold. The North Staffords reported the Huns particularly hostile.

DIARY, CAPTAIN F. C. HITCHCOCK MC, THE LEINSTER REGIMENT

It was surface conditions such as this that made both trench life and shallow mining in the little St Eloi salient a most uncomfortable, unhealthy and arduous job. All the mine galleries trickled water through the roof and often flooded, unable to drain at more than a snail's pace thanks to the same running sand layer present at the Bluff and Hill 60. The Germans held the upper hand underground throughout 1915, with the British focused on defensive work for much of the time. Dozens of mines were blown, most of them hostile, and the mood amongst the infantry occupying the trenches just 50 to 100 m (54 to 110 yds) from the enemy was perpetually tense.

However, by trial, error and resolve, in April 1915 a section from 172 Tunnelling Company under the command of Lieutenant Horace Hickling managed to pierce the running sand layer and reach the dry clay at a depth of almost 12 m (40 ft) – and with a timber shaft. The achievement was not only admirable but momentous. Unknown to those concerned this single act sealed the fate of the German tunnelling effort in the Salient, for once Hickling's men had broken through other companies along the Messines Ridge were immediately ordered to follow suit. Whilst continuing to defend in the shallow galleries, Hickling and his OC, Major Clay Hepburn patiently planned and pursued a new deep offensive scheme, ultimately planting five mines in the clay close to the enemy front line. The deepest pair were 18 m (60 ft) beneath the trenches, a depth undreamed of by most tunnellers at that period. However, the key to the scheme at St Eloi (and indeed all others on the Western Front) was not that the mines had been planted, but that the delicate work had been completed without any sign of enemy suspicion or detection.

When the mines were blown on 27 March 1916 (their architects had both left the company by then), the resulting craters, German front line and the hated Mound became British property. In fact after centuries of standing sentinel on the ridge the Mound had ceased to exist to a topographical feature. It had been blown away. Panorama 94a shows the entire sector on 23 September 1916. Once more, it is noticeable that only a very limited area has been destroyed by mine, shot and shell. The photograph does not however, advertise the fact that the craters are now under German control. By the time night had fallen on 6 April the customary territorial status quo had been restored: despite a tenacious defence by troops of 2nd Canadian Division the enemy recovered all and even a little more than had been lost earlier. The craters are also notable as being the place where, between 27 and 29 March, Reverend Edward Mellish MC, a British Army chaplain, won a VC for repeatedly going out under fire to rescue over twenty wounded men, and where Captain William Congreve (mentioned in the Hooge section) was recommended for a VC for capturing almost 70 Germans in one of the craters. He received a DSO for this act, but would posthumously win a VC later in the year on the Somme. Congreve's father, Walter, was also a VC holder for

Top

Second Army Panorama 94, 23 September 1916. A view of the St Eloi craters after the Mound had ceased to exist as a topographical feature. The Germans are in sole possession of the March 1916 craters.

Above

Billy Congreve, recommended for a Victoria Cross after the actions around the St Eloi craters on 27 March 1916.

actions in the Boer War; this, the highest award for gallantry, has only been won by both father and son three times since its inception in 1856.

The date of 27 March 1916 was deeply etched into the worried brows of German mining engineers: on this day it was made crystal clear that although they had been operating under the impression of overwhelming underground superiority for so long – well over a year – in truth their British, Australian and Canadian counterparts were streets ahead at the tunnelling game; the fact had simply been kept quiet. A degree of panic set in at German *Pioniere* HQ, and although every effort was immediately made to counter the threat, not a single British deep gallery was knowingly located and destroyed by German *Mineures* by the time the underground conflict ended during the summer of 1917.

Canadian infantry also held the St Eloi trenches for a substantial period in 1916; chronicling the relief of the British here, writers record the destruction and squalour being so severe that the troops were unable to discern where the front line trenches were.

Like the rest of the Salient the lines at St Eloi remained immobile until the nineteen mines dug, planted

and protected over a period of almost two years were blown at 3.10 a.m. on the morning of 7 June 1917.

Two of the 27 March 1916 craters can still be visited, as can that of the giant 7 June 1917 mine, begun in early July 1916. Completed by Canadian tunnellers, it was the greatest explosive charge planted in the entire Messines scheme, employing almost 50 tonnes (50 tons) of ammonal. The mine chamber alone required almost two linear kilometres (5,800 ft) of timber in its construction.

Above and below right

An Honourable Artillery Company sniper in Sniper's Barn (see Panorama 51); and the view through a loophole towards his targets in Bois Quarante, a distance of around 400 m (437 yds).

Above right

Actions of the St Eloi Craters. Northumberland Fusiliers with their captured booty.

Messines Ridge

Moving south from St Eloi the front lines pass over into the Wytschaete–Messines area. This sector incorporates the full length of the ridge, traversing approximately 9 km (5.5 miles) of ground to Ploegsteert Wood in the south. The lines belly out westwards between the two ridge-top villages and on the map may appear to meander rather unnecessarily. However, the winding trace had been carefully considered and designed by German tacticians who simply selected the most advantageous contours for defence when the lines had first settled for the 1914/15 winter.

The entire ridge was seized from French, Indian and British forces during December 1914, and it remained in very firm enemy possession until the battle of 7 June 1917. There was another exchange of tenure in 1918 before the whole area was finally cleared of invading forces in September. Spectacular elevated views spanning all four years of conflict can be found in the panoramas taken from various positions on Kemmel Hill: these are Nos 62 (29 April 1915), 107 (24 March 1917), and *173* (15 October 1918). Kemmel was a magnificent vantage point from which the military, press and invited notables might watch barrages, raids, and even full-scale offensives in relative safety. It was here in a specially strengthened dugout that Sir Douglas Haig and his guests viewed the fireworks at the opening of the Battle of Messines.

The Messines Salient curved the opposite way to its northern neighbour, the combined pair describing an inverted S shape. The exaggerated concavity of the British positions guarding Ypres meant that British trenches could be bombarded frontally, laterally, and from the rear; although the Messines Salient was convex it did not invalidate the German advantage, simply because they held the higher ground everywhere along its length. The British held the hugely important Kemmel Hill, but in the place where it mattered most – trench level – they suffered from pitiable observational capacity.

Forced to establish early defences in unsuitable field positions during the winter of 1914, living conditions in British trenches in

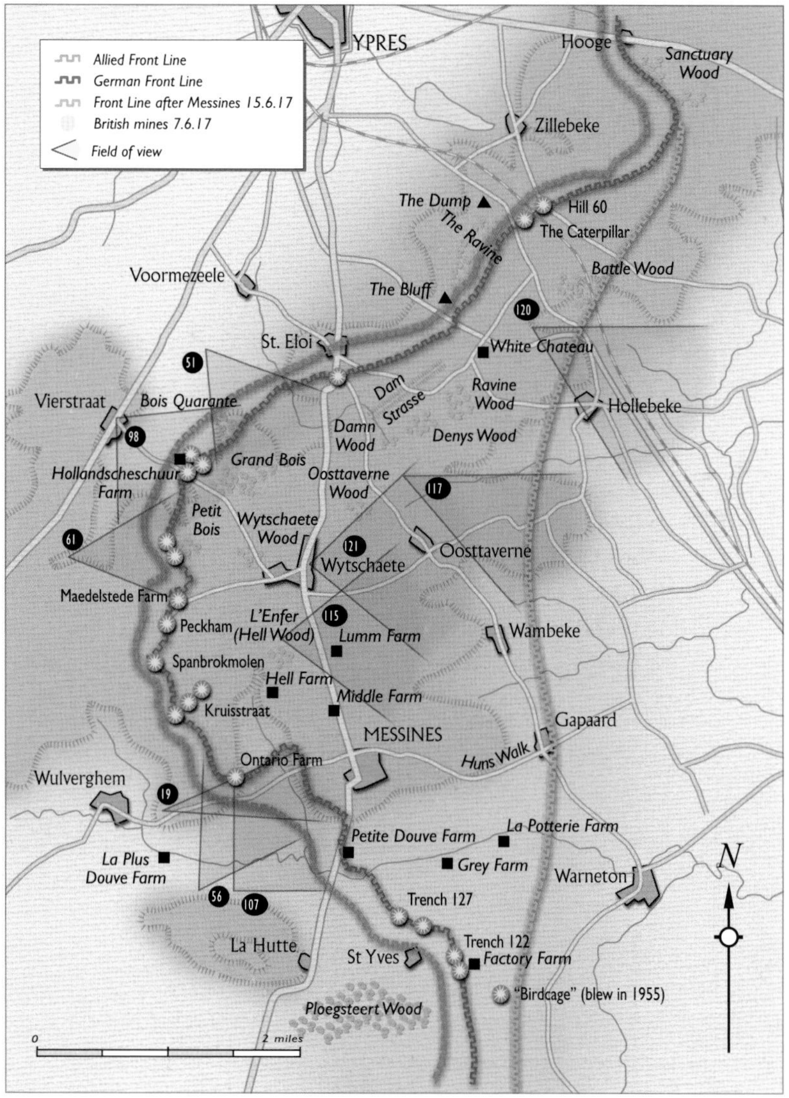

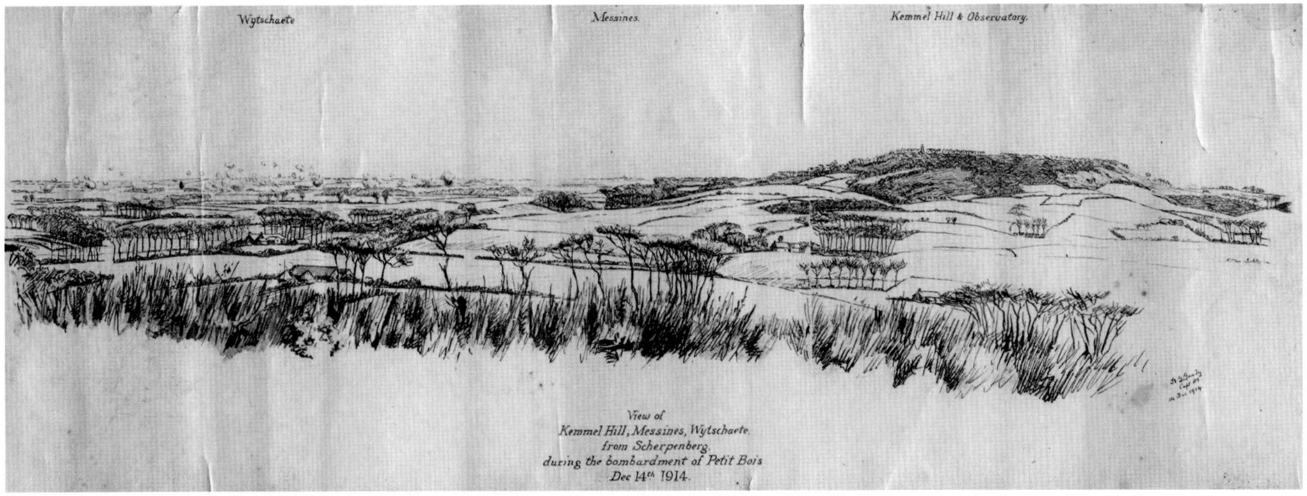

Above
A very early drawn panorama showing Kemmel Hill and the shelling of Petit Bois below the village of Wytschaete in mid-December 1914. The Messines Ridge was lost to the Germans at about this time, and not regained until June 1917.

front of the ridge were appalling. Where the lines occupied sloping ground at least a shallow trench could be dug and drained; in the valleys however, breastworks were mandatory. Even on the ridge itself the Germans had made certain that should the British be allowed to occupy any higher ground, it would be only be in places where there was a localized 'plateau'. The positions in front of Petit Bois below the village of Wytschaete for example, although well above the valley floor, became so waterlogged that during the 1914 winter men were chronicled to have paddled themselves around in wooden beer barrels cut in half!

The earliest panorama of the sector, and indeed in Belgian Flanders, is number 19, taken on 13 December 1914 at the beginning of the first long and uncomfortable winter of war. The camera is located near North Midland Farm, seen here through the trees below the church. Some early trench lines can be seen running across the upper slopes of the ridge below Messines village. These are German positions. The Allied lines cross the foreground before curving in front of the farm, whilst a communication trench runs along the ditch skirting the Messines–Wulverghem road to the right of the picture. The annotation makes it clear that the naming of features for trench mapping has begun, but several points are as yet only identified by grid reference. The attached map, a precursor to the standardized trench map, is a Belgian sheet overlaid with the British grid system. Note that unlike the photograph no places on the map are yet marked with English names. Eventually, even tiny and apparently mundane features would be christened by the troops. In the foreground lies one of many dumb victims of war.

It is profitable to compare this image with Panorama *28*, taken at the beginning of February 1915. Note the German front trench dug in on the upper slopes of the ridge, with a second line just below the crest. Due to their commanding positions Messines church and the Institution Royale (hospital) received a more severe battering than the remainder of the village. The guns of both sides share the responsibility for their destruction during the First Battle of Ypres. Although added damage is noticeable between the two dates, being more concerned with avoiding frostbite and trench foot, troops in this sector 'enjoyed' a period of relative calm at this time.

During the winter the consolidation and expansion of trench lines took place, with drainage being the greatest concern. By spring things were considerably better organized and the British trenches were now robustly garrisoned by drafts of Territorial troops. During Second Ypres the ridge did not form a part of the German offensive front and no movement took place south of Hill 60. In the subsequent two years however, the Germans converted the

Below
Panorama 62: a view from Kemmel on 29 April 1915, a week after the first gas attacks in the northern part of the Ypres Salient. Almost the entire span of the Messines Ridge is in view.

ridge into a veritable fortress: hundreds of concrete emplacements carpeted the slopes and lay secreted in woods, served by a magnificent network of deep and well-drained trenches, which in turn were attended by tramways, well-made roads and even aerial ropeways and monorails. And dotted in apposite locations throughout the sector were heavily fortified trench redoubts and farms.

The ridge is best known for the actions of June 1917: the Second Army's limited objective assault planned by its commander Sir Herbert Plumer. It had originally been Sir Douglas Haig's plan to oust the enemy from the heights during 1916, but several events conspired to force postponement. This was partly due to thorny negotiations over the Nivelle offensive, a huge Anglo-French scheme planned for 1917. Throughout 1916 these attack plans were in the process of gestation, with endless disagreements over who might do what and when. However, the most influential reason for delay was the massive German assault on Verdun in February 1916, an action which sucked in French reserves from every front. Added to their valuable and costly contribution to the Somme offensive, it left no leeway for an Anglo-French action in Flanders in 1916. A deferral of Haig's plans was unavoidable.

The delay turned out to be a godsend, however. More time for preparation meant better organization, better pre-battle training, more tank availability and a stronger artillery presence. Herbert Plumer was renowned as a meticulous planner – and he also knew that his offensive could not afford to fail. One of the main benefits of postponement fell to the sappers of the British, Canadian and Australian tunnelling companies who gained extra time to extend and multiply offensive deep mine schemes already in progress. Although nineteen mines were blown on 7 June 1917, the tunnellers had looked into the possibility of planting a staggering forty-nine individual charges, if time, the enemy, resources and geology allowed. Eventually, twenty-five were secreted beneath key enemy positions.

Similar geological conditions to those at Hill 60, the Bluff and St Eloi – the layer of running sand – also pertained along the slopes of the Messines Ridge. Apart from these formidable obstacles, the Germans, holding the higher contour as they universally did, consequently had to sink deeper shafts, and in the process often encountered a greater depth of running sand than the British.

Throughout 1916 and the first six months of 1917 British tunnelling activity was frenetic; as June 1917 approached their field engineer colleagues were employed on road building, tramway schemes, and the siting and construction of battery positions for the greatest number of guns ever assembled. The blowing of the mines was to be the signal to open fire. New communication trenches were also installed, and several deep underground 'subways' – literally tunnelled communications trenches – dug, plus dozens of deep dugouts to shelter and house troops and HQ staff.

Apart from the two mines at Hill 60 and the Caterpillar, and one vast charge at St Eloi, the other Messines mines were located beneath Hollandscheschuur

Above
The beautifully built and remarkably preserved incline to the Petit Bois mine system; and the interior of a deep tunnel system showing the intense blueness of the Ypresian clay.

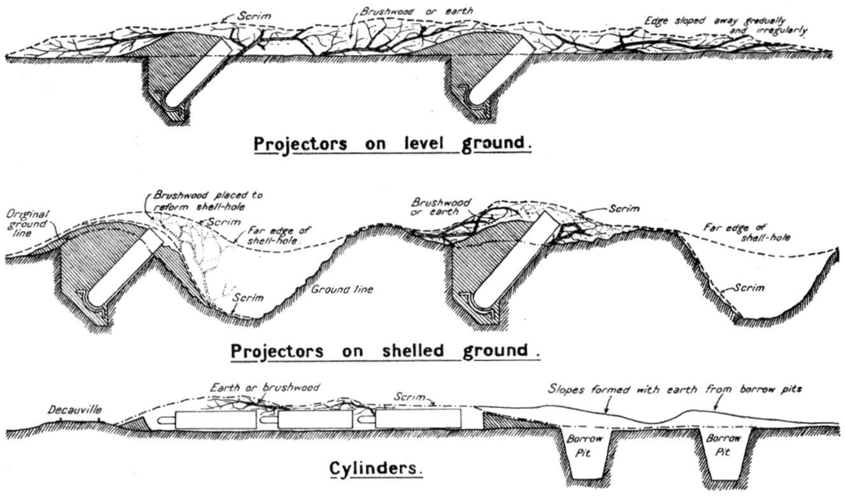

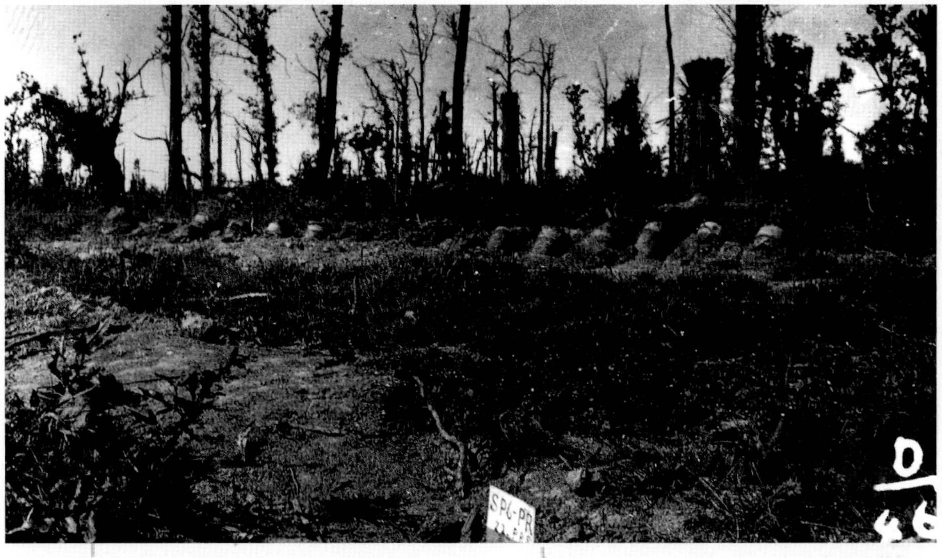

Above
Location of gas projectors in varying ground conditions.

Above right
Livens gas projectors in place ready for 7 June. The notice reveals that these are located near SP6 (Strongpoint 6).

Left
British front-line breastworks in the wet valleys below Messines in June 1917. Note the large, partially visible sign carrying the map reference of the position.

Farm (Nos *61*, *98* and *108*), where there were three, Petit Bois (*61*, *98* and *108*), where there were two, and additional ones each at Maedelstede Farm (61), Peckham and Spanbroekmolen. A leash of three was put in near Kruistraat Cabaret. Ontario Farm was undermined by one, and on the southern shoulder of the ridge below Messines village two had been driven from Trench 127, another pair from Trench 122 to the east, and a group of four at Le Pelerin immediately east of Ploegsteert Wood – the troublesome Birdcage (85). The charges totalled just under 454,000 kg (one million pounds) of explosive. The individual mine sites have all been identified in the relevant Wytschaete–Messines panoramas. One fully charged mine at Peckham was lost due to geological problems – the clay swelled and crushed the gallery timbers – and the approach tunnel and cables for a second mine (three were hoped for) at La Petite Douve Farm (78) were wrecked by a speculative German camouflet. Recovery attempts in both locations were pushed forward a top speed but ran out of time.

As zero day approached three Second Army Corps, X, IX and II Anzac, were fully trained and ready to assault the ridge. At the top of the sector the Welsh and West of England Divisions were allotted the task of overwhelming positions on the shoulder north of Wytschaete and advancing towards Oostaverne. The wide angled view in *106* covers this battlefront, whilst *115* shows the positions attained after the battle. In the centre the 16th (Irish) Division and the 36th (Ulster) Division were to assault side by side, taking Wytschaete village, its surrounding woods and much of the central crest. See *106* and also *121* for their first view beyond the ridge after its capture. At the southern end the New Zealand Division and 3rd Australian Division were charged with capturing the Messines village sector and making the right flank of the battlefront at Le Pelerin (85) secure. The elevated panoramas from Kemmel are particularly valuable for sub-dividing the various sectors attacked on the day: 107 shows all the 36 Division battlefront.

From Mount Sorrel to the Birdcage the total attack frontage was 16 km (10 miles). Plumer's stratagem required the capture of five consecutive objectives, marked on attack maps as red, blue, green, black, and black-dotted lines. The advance, coordinated with a carefully planned and practised creeping artillery barrage, was to pause three times to allow fresh waves of infantry to leap-frog through towards the final objective – the chord of the salient on the eastern slope of the ridge.

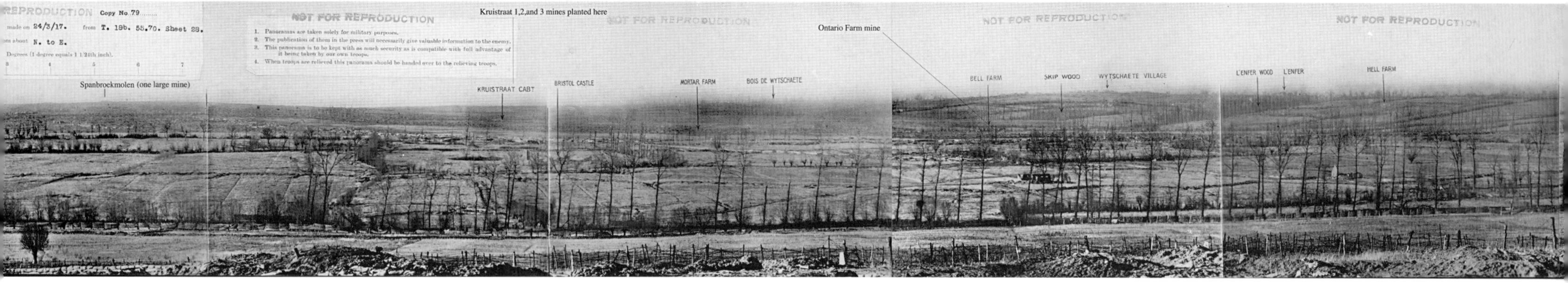

The final weeks were tense for the Second Army staff. Failure to gain control of the Messines Ridge would result in the next stage of Haig's grand plan – the advance through Passchendaele – being made impossible. Planning had been scrupulous, unhurried, and painstaking, and work in the tunnels (fighting obstinate geology more than Germans) was no less than astonishing. To assist the infantry seventy-two tanks were ready and eager to prove their worth, while 2,266 guns of all calibres patiently awaited the signal of the mines; they were to fire almost three million shells. None were more nervous than the tunnellers. Months and months had been spent, and many lives lost all for the promise of a single moment of glory. Although many of the great mines had been completed long before they were needed, one scheme at Factory Farm, was finished with just ten minutes to spare.

7.6.17

The night wore on with a miserable slowness but towards dawn the fire on both sides slackened and just before 3 a.m. we were ordered to leave the trench and lie out in the open. It was an impressive time – the gunfire ceased with the exception of an occasional shell here and there. A thick mist was over the land and we had to lie full length partly because of the shock that would result from the explosion of the mines and partly to prevent Fritz seeing us in the growing dawn. There was a strange groaning and rumbling from behind us and presently, looming out of the mist came a tank, moving straight towards us. We began to scramble out of its way but it turned off to the left and was soon buried again in the mist. Out of the silence came the song of blackbirds from a clump of battered trees a little way back, only to be rudely silenced at 3.10 a.m. by the simultaneous explosion of 19 mines. This will probably be accounted the greatest artificial explosion in recorded history. For several minutes the earth rocked to and fro, oscillating quite 12 inches. It was an experience which I shall remember very vividly for the rest of my life – all the phases of the preliminary bombardment, the calm silence that succeeded it suddenly broken by a most terrific uproar, the weird sights of moving men and things in the semi-darkness, the rolling clouds of smoke picked out every now and then with shooting tongues of flame, all formed a tremendously wonderful sight. It was stupendous beyond the imagination of even an Edgar Allan Poe. The blowing of the mines was the signal for all the guns on the front to open out. The noise rendered talking or shouting impossible. Every type of gun was in action, from immense howitzers to machine guns which were arrayed some little distance behind us and carried out a barrage all on their own. A few minutes later the 123 and 124 Brigades went over and we returned to the trench. As daylight increased I looked directly onto the line that was being battered and the sight was so awfully impressive that the real horror of it all was temporarily quite obliterated.

DIARY, SAPPER ALBERT MARTIN, 41 DIVISION SIGNALS

Wherever the mines had been planted Allied troops swept through enemy defences. The weather was warm and dry, suiting the tanks for a change, and casualties were mercifully but uncharacteristically slight. By nightfall every objective had been gained and consolidation was in full flow in preparation for the inevitable German counter-attacks. They came accordingly, and were everywhere repulsed. The ridge had fallen and episode two could proceed.

Top

Second Army Panorama 107, taken on 24 March 1917 in preparation for the June assault on Messines Ridge. With mine locations marked.

Above

The village of Messines under shellfire on 8 June 1917.

Right

Aerial view of the three giant craters around Hollandscheschuur Farm. All three still exist today.

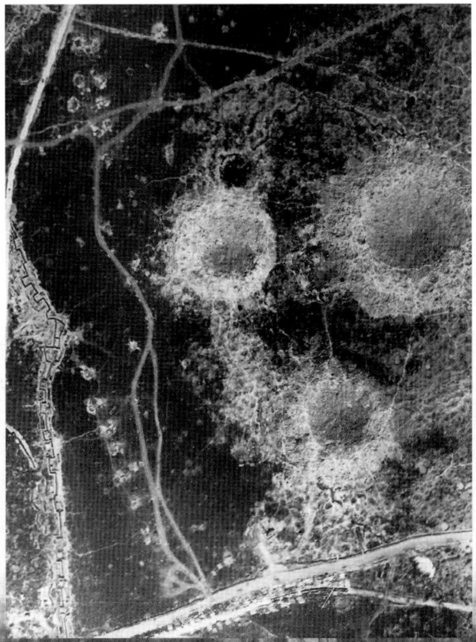

Right

Despite Plumer's success at Messines, it was Sir Hubert Gough – here shown in Messines village earlier in the war – who took charge of the next Salient offensive in July 1917.

Overleaf

Royal Engineers cleaning pillboxes and repairing captured trenches on the Messines Ridge immediately after capture. 8 June 1917.

The Salient's Southern Hinge

'Plugstreet', as Ploegsteert was soon christened by the British, lies at the foot of the south-west flank of the Messines Ridge, and forms the southernmost hinge of the Ypres Salient. Delimited by the River Douve in the north and the Warnave to the south, the latter sluggish waterway forming the Franco-Belgian border, the sector incorporated the villages of La Hutte (Panorama 22, below), St Yves, Le Pelerin and Le Gheer. The sector marks the important topographical dividing line between Belgian and French Flanders, a significant distinction, for the nature, quality, and indeed length of a soldier's life was greatly influenced by which side of the line he was called upon to serve.

31 October 1914

On going to the Cavalry Headquarters in search of news, I learnt that Messines had been taken during the night, and therefore advised (NB Staff Officers (!) "should rarely give orders") the subaltern to pack up everything and stand by to shift billets, and so out to work. There is a fairly steep hill just behind Kemmel village with a 'Belvidere Tower', something like the Duke of York's Column in W'loo Place, on top and we found time to visit it and had a lovely view of the daily battle about 2–3 miles away. The G [Germans] had taken Messines the night before – hence the panic – and our long guns were shelling the place to bits. Two gunners with telephones were on the Tower directing the fire of their batteries hidden in a hollow to our right, and very good shooting they made for the church soon caught fire depriving the G of a useful place to observe their artillery from. The only event of consequence was that we retook Messines that day and the G hurried up more reinforcements than we could and all sorts of stories were told the next morning. Artillery fire is lovely to watch – from behind – common shell or lyddite bursts when it hits and there is a huge cloud of dark smoke. Shrapnel bursts in pretty white puffs high up in the air and the effect of a round from a

Above
November 1914, First Battle of Messines: a British 18-pounder secreted in the garden of La Hutte Chateau.

Below
Second Army Panorama 22, 10 January 1915. An early example looking towards Messines village from La Hutte on the edge of Ploegsteert Wood. The sign reads, 'Footpath reserved for cyclists and pedestrians'.

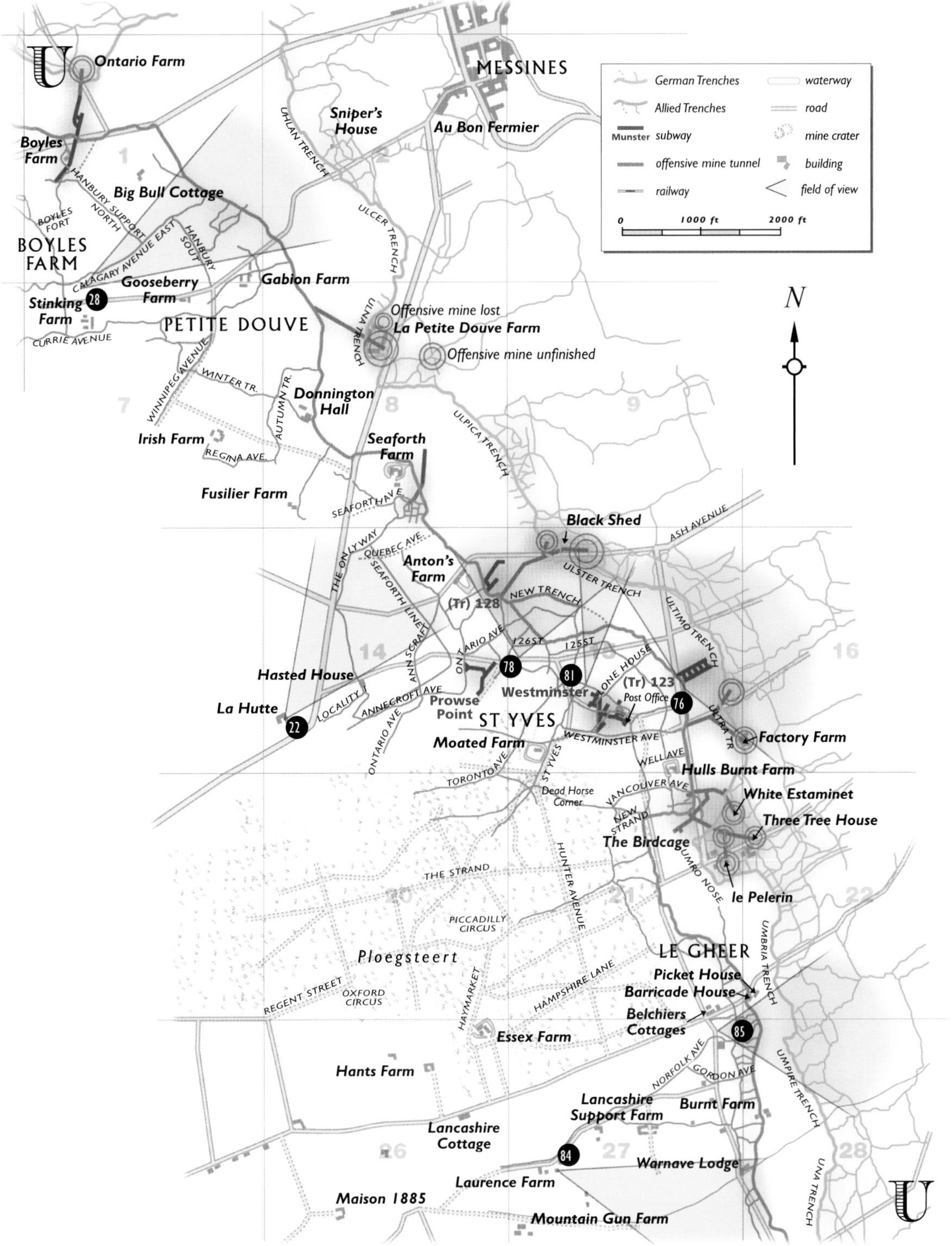

battery is six little white puffs which slowly melt away. As, so far, no shells had begun to reach near Kemmel we stayed the night there.

1 November 1914

We got out to work as usual after hearing of the loss of Messines once more.

Diary, Major S. H. Cowan RE, attached to Royal Engineers Staff at GHQ

The lines first began to form in the Plugstreet sector in mid-October 1914. On the day of Major Cowan's second diary entry, and despite the efforts of a costly London Scottish counter-attack, Messines and its ridge was to remain lost to the British for more than two and a half years.

In the autumn of 1914, French and British troops fought the invader for several weeks around Plugstreet, with the famous wood exchanging ownership several times. Although the Allies finally secured the lease, it was hardly a comfortable tenancy; the Germans, as in almost every other sector in Flanders, came to hold the topographic and tactical upper hand. A fascinating view from the La Hutte Chateau estate can be seen in Panorama 22; compare this landscape with that of September 1918 in number *173*.

After the loss of Messines and the close of the First Battle of Ypres the intensity of German attacks slowly diminished around Plugstreet. Although small by most standards, the final action of the year took place on 19 December. In an attempt to straighten out 'The Kink' (more frequently known as the Birdcage, see number 85), a small but troublesome loop in the line due east of the wood, a limited British enterprise was launched. The exercise, largely defeated by mud and British supportive artillery firing short, was fruitless and to many observers pointless. The Kink remained. It was not only the last offensive act of 1914 in the sector, but the last to take place at Plugstreet for several years. As pressure eased during the Michaelmas period the British started to put their primitive defences into some sort of order. It was not a simple matter: although coordinated offensives had dwindled away, harassing fire from snipers, mortars and artillery was commonplace.

On the 16th November [1914], Fishbourne and I started work on communications and a second line in Ploegsteert Wood – our movements through Ploegsteert village had to be timed exactly to avoid the monotonously regulated cross-roads strafe by the enemy. On this day we actually started making corduroy paths in Ploegsteert Wood and have always claimed that these were the absolute origin of the 'duck-walk' so universal later. Our first ones were made with stripped branches from the trees of the wood, but soon gave way to a better article made up in a saw-mill in Armentieres and brought out in stripped pontoon wagons. The second line consisted of a series of breastworks – digging was quite impossible; the water–level was already ground level. We also made a sketch map of the wood with local [British] names – and it was printed at General Headquarters and issued in the Brigade.

MAJOR B. K. YOUNG MC, 9 FIELD COMPANY RE

In the southern half of the sector around the village of Le Gheer and down to the River Warnave, the situation was less acute as the trenches on both sides of no man's land occupied very similar contours, and therefore faced similar problems with water and soils. It was in the Le Gheer sub-sector that Winston Churchill served as battalion commander to the 6th Royal Scots Fusiliers. Between February and May 1915, Churchill's advanced HQ lay just 300 m (328 yds) behind the front line at Laurence Farm. The sylvan Panorama *84* was photographed from this spot. Although the buildings no longer exist today, visitors can readily spot the old brick-built farm well, despite its being disguised beneath a modern concrete cupola. This would undoubtedly have been the source from which Churchill's servant drew water for cooking, for tea – and to add to the gin and whisky of the many high-ranking visitors received at the farm.

Throughout the first winter of war the RE and long-suffering infantry working parties struggled on the flat and low-lying ground to entrench, revet, drain and wire-in a set of practical defensive positions. January and February 1915 were exceptionally cold and wet, and while men struggled simply to keep warm and dry the defensive field-works continued. Buildings in no man's land were blown down to improve fields of fire, and many others behind the lines received similar treatment; a support line was installed, and later a substantial reserve position was developed behind (west of) Ploegsteert village. This latter was christened 'Torres Vedras' after the vast hilltop defences built by British military engineers in Portugal during the Peninsular War. In preparation for the likely renewal of German attacks, the following spring work also began on trench lines several kilometres to the rear running from the slopes of Kemmel Hill to Steenvoorde. All, however, were primitive by comparison to later fieldworks.

Winter conditions in the forward trenches were grim. Trench foot and frostbite were rife, and bronchial infections took a daily toll of men who spent much of their time on duty standing in what were little more than man-made ditches. Shelter from the elements was the ultimate consideration, but in a terrain where one was unable to delve underground, inadequate and insecure surface-built dugouts were obligatory. A direct hit from even the smallest shell was lethal. But there was no choice: the

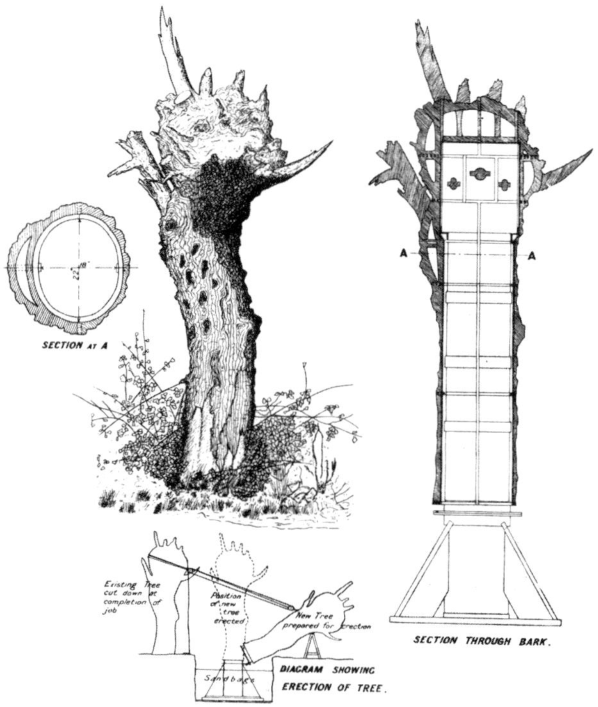

Above
Royal Engineer design and erection instructions for bogus trees; and a German photograph of a British observation tree captured during the Lys offensive of spring 1918.

Below
A Belgian baker delivering fresh bread to British troops in Ploegsteert Wood before Christmas 1914. Belgian children were also known to supply various items to troops, often coming into the front line itself.

Above
Bruce Bairnsfather in the village of St Yves on Christmas Day 1914.

Below
Bairnsfather's cottage in St Yves, in the cellar of which the first 'Fragment' was drawn on the walls.

Right
A typical Bairnsfather work. Many of his cartoons involved the hazards of observation.

maximum excavation depth before hitting water was less than half a metre.

Throughout the northern and central parts of the Plugstreet sector the British front line lay at the foot of a forward sloping hill. Although elevated positions to the rear provided unusually handy posts from which to observe the enemy trenches, a rare tactical benefit for the British, the slope created serious localized front-line problems. GHQ had already decreed that British forces were to remain in the positions occupied when the last action stalled. Although the landscape to the rear was better drained, allowing tactically superior and reasonable depth trenches to be installed, there were to be no exceptions. In the valley the British would stay. From the point of view of enemy observation, the Plugstreet and St Yves positions were doubly hazardous: not only were the front-line trenches overlooked from the Messines Ridge, but because of the sloping ground behind the British positions, communication routes were glaringly obvious to the enemy and simple to target with artillery. Here, as in so many other locations, GHQ's 'stay where you are' policy was absurd and irrational – and it would cost many lives.

By Christmas 1914 the task of linking up the 'Grouse Butts' and other forward posts around the St Yves salient had started in earnest. Substantial quantities of timber, sandbags and corrugated iron required for breastwork construction were now becoming easier to source, not least through the demolition of dozens of shell-damaged farms and houses close to the lines. Each night a fresh length of breastworks was added. By the end of March 1915 most gaps had been closed, both front and support lines were practically continuous, and a thin belt of barbed wire hung before the parapets along the full length of the sector. The final stretch of trench, a 250-m (273-yd) section, was completed by the RE during six hours of hard graft on the night of 22 April 1915; no doubt to the relief of the sappers concerned, it was noted at the time as one of the quietest nights of the war.

Ironically, although sniping and shelling were hardly infrequent (the forward edges of the wood quickly lost their verdant quality), after its bitter and bloody beginnings Plugstreet became one of the more tranquil sectors of the British Western Front, sliding into an environment of mild attrition. From spring 1915 trench raids were regular (when ground conditions suited), shelling, particularly of the many hamlets, farms and chateaux, was a convention, and sniping in particular became highly developed, ubiquitous and troublesome. The giant 160-degree Panorama *78* from (front line) Trench 123 illustrates the St Yves and Plugstreet defences in the summer of 1916.

Late December 1914 was an especially notable period at Plugstreet. Here, in the fields north and east of St Yves, the most northerly of several unofficial Christmas truces took place. One of most famous chroniclers of the event was Bruce Bairnsfather, the war's most celebrated and recognized 'officer cartoonist' as he became known in official circles. Then a lieutenant in the 1st Battalion Royal Warwickshire Regiment, Bairnsfather, the battalion's machine-gun officer, occupied a dugout in the cellar of the St Yves Post Office. Whilst there he enhanced the bare

"They've evidently seen me."

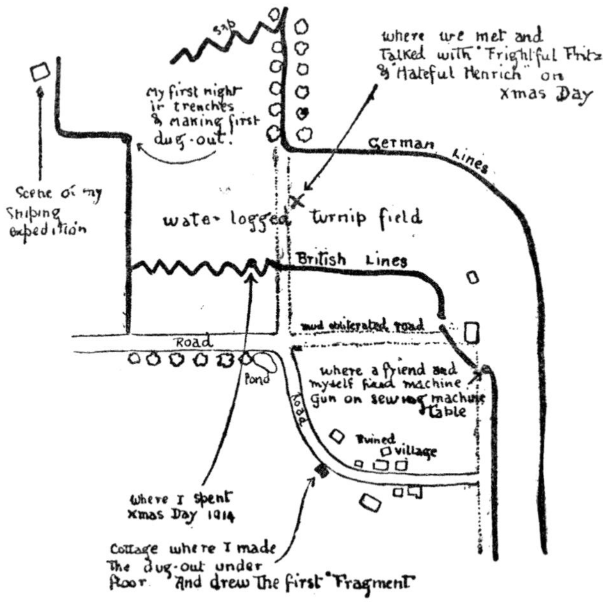

plaster walls with his own idiosyncratic sketches and cartoons. Ultimately, his greatest creation, 'Old Bill', a wise and phlegmatic soldier of the 'old sweat' variety, became known throughout Imperial forces on the Western Front. In 1915 many examples of his work could be encountered in several locations around Plugstreet. Fortunately for all of us, Bairnsfather was 'discovered' by a well-known British periodical.

This village [Ploegsteert] provided the scene for all Bruce Bairnsfather's original drawings for The Bystander. Perhaps some will remember "Old Bill" apprehensively approaching the village pump to get water, and the legend, "I know they'll 'ear the damn thing squeakin" – one of my jobs was to sandbag this pump and the approach to it. The originals of these sketches and many others were done in charcoal on dug-out and ruined house walls; more elaborate pictures were on the walls of the Brigade support "billet" at the Grand Munque Farm west of Ploegsteert Wood. Bairnsfather was Machine-Gun officer to the Warwicks, and consequently our paths at night in St Yves frequently crossed.

Lieutenant B. K. Young MC, 9 Field Company RE

Bairnsfather, who survived the war despite being wounded at Mousetrap Farm during the Second Battle of Ypres (see Left Sector panoramas) experienced the same truce on the same day as B. K. Young. As was reportedly the case in most instances, the first overtures for amity were made by the Germans. At St Yves it was the XIX Saxons who on

Above left
Panorama 81: a flower-filled no man's land at St Yves, photographed from Machine Gun House. It is marked on the plan below, drawn by Bruce Bairnsfather.

Left
Sketch drawn by Bruce Bairnsfather to show where his Christmas Truce took place. Panorama 81 is taken from the house opposite his 'cottage'.

Below left
A section of German trenches during excavation by Belgian archaeologists in 2004. The flower species which thrive in disturbed and neglected ground today gives us an idea of what many battlefields in the Salient may have looked like during the summer months of 1915 and 1916.

Above
Crater formed by one of the Messines mines of 7 June 1917. The state of the surrounding landscape indicates the weight of the artillery barrage which immediately followed the gigantic eruptions.

Above right
'The Path to Glory' – one of several routes of advance across the Douve Valley pegged out for 36th Division units in preparation for the June 1917 battle.

Christmas Eve first began by calling across a still and thankfully dry and frosty no man's land, then putting lighted candles and lanterns on the parapets. The following morning both sides left the safety of the lines to meet between the wire. The cessation of hostilities, although brief, allowed burial of the dead, and the troops enjoyed a rather different perspective of the battlefield to normal. For many it was the first glimpse of the 'Hun'; mementoes were exchanged, addresses too, and cultural swops made: cigarettes for cigars, and newspapers, badges and buttons. For one day at least, supplies could be brought up, fuel collected, defences improved and shelters built without worrying about snipers or shells. It was a release, albeit only temporary, from weeks of anxiety, and was greatly appreciated. It was, of course, not to last. Within days the following telegraphic order was issued from GHQ:

The Commander 2nd Army directs that informal understandings with the enemy are strictly forbidden to take place. He further directs that any officer or NCO found to be responsible for initiating any such understandings or for acquiescing in any such understanding proposed by the enemy will be brought before a Court Martial. This Order is to be at once communicated to the unit under your command.

3 January 1915
I'm afraid we hurt our Allies feelings a lot at Xmas time by informal meetings with the Enemy, and there are rumours of trouble in store for certain officers who allowed it. The following was told me as true:

A Bavarian regiment solemnly warned our folk not to trust the troops on their flank – adding they were 'D------ Prussians'. Also they said they themselves were to be relieved in a day or two by other Prussians and promised to throw out newspapers on the parapet so that our guns would know when to open fire, and get the range easier. Nice kind folk.
Major S. H. Cowan RE

The exact spot in front of St Yves where Bairnsfather's Christmas Truce took place is somewhat bizarrely illustrated in Panorama 81. Taken in August 1916 from Machine Gun House, the frozen 1914 battlefield is now a mass of wild flowers. No *76* also includes the area, in the region of no man's land beneath Messines village. The following two years were times of relative peace at Plugstreet. In October 1916 Canadian troops took over the sector for the first time, and later in June 1917, it was the turn of the II Anzac Corps.

Plugstreet's part in the Messines battle was no less critical than any other sector. RE tunnellers hoped to have at least ten huge mines lying in wait around the wood for the June offensive. The most northerly were at Petite Douve farm – a brace here at least, and perhaps a leash; a pair of charges called Trench 127 left and right were planted beneath a position known as Black Shed immediately north of St Yves (on the far side of the field where the Christmas truce had taken place), another two (Trench 122) under and near Factory Farm due east of the village, and four (but hopefully five) mines beneath the troublesome Birdcage at Le Pelerin (*85*).

The Petite Douve mine system was lost before the battle began. With one chamber fully charged and a second about to begin loading, a heavy speculative German camouflet crushed the gallery timbers and broke the detonator leads. An attempt to reach the mine via a fresh gallery driven from Seaforth Avenue was made but later abandoned when it was realized that time was too short. The 22,700 kg (50,000 lb) Petite Douve mine remains today, 25 m (82 ft) beneath the surface.

Trench 127's pair obliterated their targets according to plan, as did the Factory Farm mines, but those at the Birdcage – ultimately just the four – were, although completed, detonated and tamped, deliberately withheld. The mines lay beneath the extreme right flank of the battle scheme, and concern over potentially vigorous and coordinated opposition led GHQ to save the charges: they were only to be blown to disrupt heavy German counter-attacks.

The scale of the mine attack had greater consequences than anyone had imagined. Germans senses were numbed and morale fractured by the initial shock of the massive explosions, and as they were instantly followed by a concentrated and accurate creeping artillery barrage, and tank and air attacks, resistance on the ridge entirely collapsed in a matter of hours.

Being on the extreme southern edge of the battle zone the Plugstreet sector was not as greatly affected by the strike as its northern neighbours, where the advance was both swift and extensive. On 6 June, the day prior to the attack, the sector had also been engulfed by a prolonged hostile gas-shell attack, so the thousands of troops assembling for the assault in and around Plugstreet Wood and Hill 63 were neither in the best of condition nor humour.

The capture of the village of Messines was a part of the Anzac remit; it fell after determined opposition and house-to-house fighting. Between the village and St Yves eight tanks helped clear resistance and soon the whole of the southern shoulder of the ridge was in Allied hands. To the astonishment of British commanders the expected and feared German counter-attacks which had so often been successful in earlier battles, entirely failed to materialize. German troops seen massing near Warneton moved north to reinforce the Oostaverne Line east of the ridge, and no attack fell upon Plugstreet. On the evening of 7 June the new line ran from the Birdcage straight up the southern shoulder of the ridge. By the end of the battle two weeks later, it was still hinged at the Birdcage but had swung

Below
The comparatively bizarre landscape of battle near Hondeghem following the German Lys offensive of spring 1918. Panorama 160, 6 August 1918.

Above
Potatoes being grown close up to pre-prepared GHQ trench lines near Béthune.

slightly clockwise onto the upper eastern slopes of Messines Ridge. Calm then descended on Plugstreet once more. There had been no territorial rearrangement whatsoever in the southern sub-sector from Le Gheer to the River Warnave and therefore minimal effect upon everyday life.

Nine months later the final phase of conflict began at Plugstreet. By the beginning of April 1918 Germany had already regained all the 1916 battlefields on the Somme and a great deal more beyond towards Amiens. Seriously weakened, the British contracted their lines in the Ypres Salient, voluntarily giving up all the ground won at such appalling cost during the Third Battle of Ypres. They then waited for Ludendorff's second hammer blow to fall – in Flanders. On 9 April 1918 the weak Allied line near Neuve Chapelle, the site of the first British offensive of the war three years earlier, was broken. Extending the attack northwards German forces pushed and pushed again and again, forcing the line between Ypres and Neuve Chapelle further back, engulfing Armentières, and sweeping over the flanks of Kemmel Hill. By 12 April the advance was approaching the Forest of Nieppe. See Panoramas 90, *153* and 160. The areas immediately behind the old Salient were now great storehouses for materiel and hutted camps for troops. They had always been shelled and bombed and so were relatively familiar with hostile actions. Save for the passage of troops, those sectors behind Armentières however, had been entirely untouched by the war. Fighting here amongst the deep woods and dense crops was almost guerrilla style.

This was our first experience of a retreat, and I have never felt so humiliated in my life. The whole march back for no apparent reason was a very bad experience. All the way the road was lined with refugees – the usual group, an old man, a boy, two or three women, with a cart in front piled high with their household goods, a cow or two behind – dejection on their faces and all plodding stolidly along the endless pave of a French road on their hopeless journey leaving their homes and land behind. Also the loss of this country hurts, as it is so identified with England that one almost looks on it as English soil. Armentières, Laventie, Neuve Chapelle, and half a score more might be regarded as English, so well are they known to us.

I found a farm, and succeeded in getting the men and ourselves into it. In the kitchen I found a party of refugees, all women, dressed in black and very tearful, frightened and crowlike. I soothed them in execrable French, and obtained some coffee and eggs off them. In the barns there were stragglers from various units in pronounced states of fatigue and despondency, while some gunners were in another part,

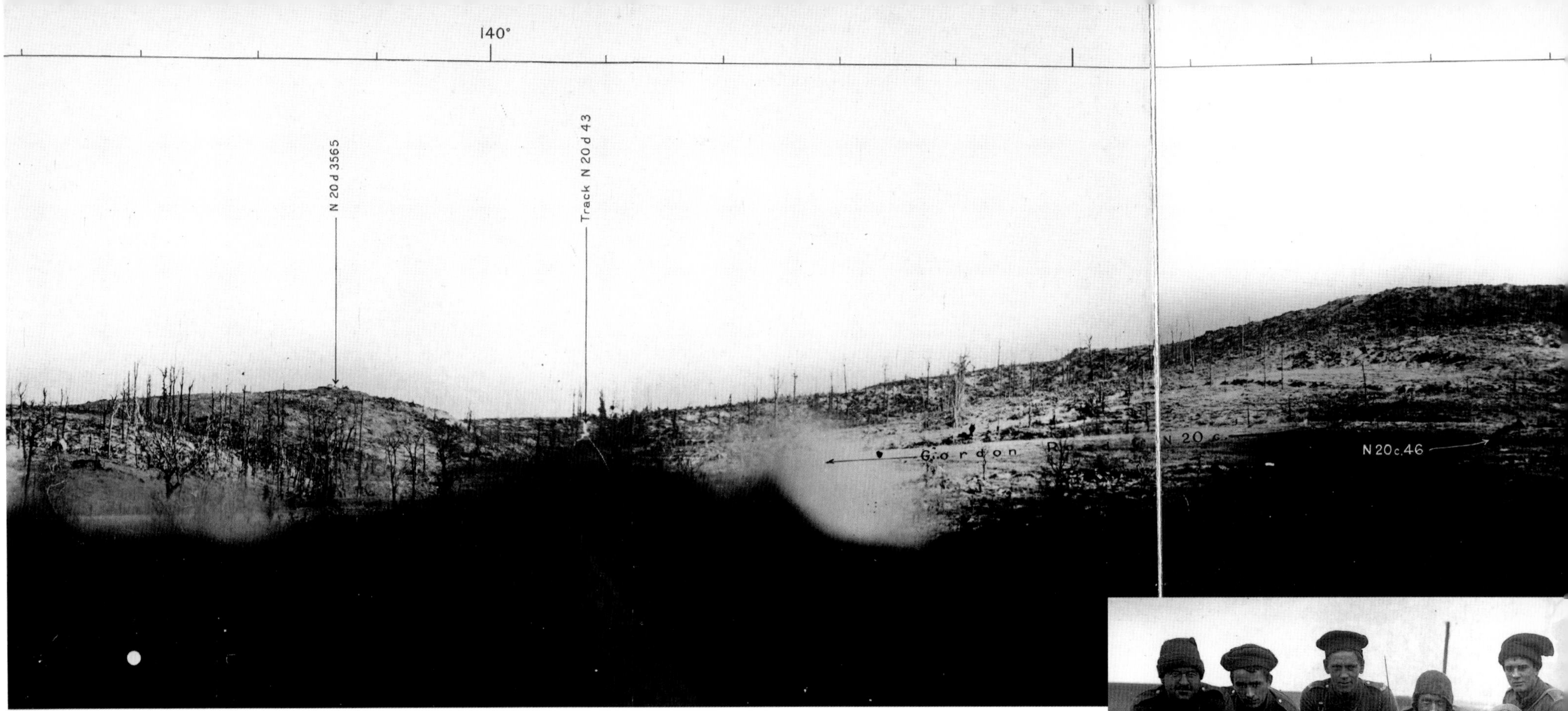

though to what guns they belonged I never found out. The straggler is a curious creature – he is firstly hopelessly lost, secondly he is always convinced that he is all that is left of his unit, and is generally full of totally inaccurate information – nevertheless he is generally filled with a perfectly honest desire to rejoin his unit – if only he can find it.

All day heavy guns were clattering back on their caterpillars. I was tired and the news or rather rumours from the south grew worse and worse till one was very near to despondency, watching, waiting, and knowing nothing. The flight of rumours was fascinating, Peronne, Lens, Ostend, Metz were all definitely stated to have fallen, and our anxiety for news was almost pathetic.

After breakfast General Williams rode up and gave us orders to garrison a portion of the reserve line by day and wire it by night. The orders were rather lurid, "To hold at all costs".

Diary, Lieutenant J R T Aldous MC 210 Field Company RE

After three and a half years of British and Dominion occupation Plugstreet was suddenly several kilometres behind enemy lines. Ypres still held out, but now the Germans, always close, were on the very doorstep. Bailleul fell and Meteren was threatened. However, as on the Somme, the Allies were always falling back into positions that had been carefully designed precisely for this very eventuality. A bow-string was being pulled back which would be later loosed with relentless energy. The furthest points reached in the Salient are illustrated in Panorama *165* taken near Locre, a village well 'behind' Ypres for the majority of the war, and 170, the position of maximum German advance beyond the once heavily afforested Kemmel Hill. In August 1918 the British forces in Artois and Picardy began to move forward once more. The Germans had no choice but to withdraw troops from elsewhere to support defences in the south, and pressure was thus released in the Ypres area. The Germans withdrew, first from the Salient, then from Kemmel. It was the 31st Division which in late September came again upon Plugstreet. It took three days to clear the wood for the last time.

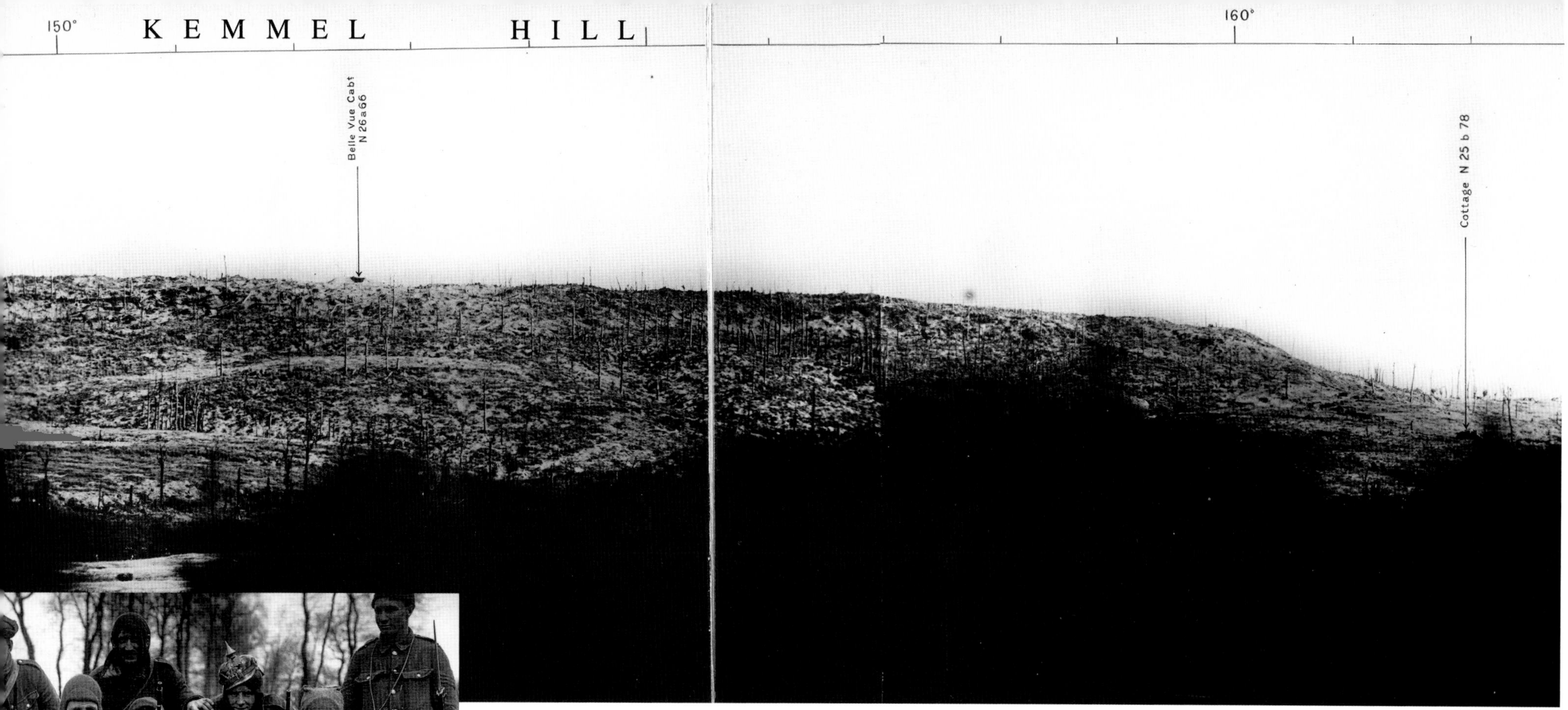

28.9.18 – 11.10.18 Ploegsteert Sector

Attack by 92nd and later all 3 Brigades. New line Lys (at Warneton) and Douve.

Constructed plank detours around the two craters on the 28th and 29th and being under direct observation came in for much shelling – in fact we were shelled off the X-roads 5 times the first day. On the road running east from La Hutte I found 4 planks lain across the road which, on investigation, were covering 4 Minnie shells with contact fuzes acting as a land mine – there were 14 shells in all. In fear and trembling Corporal Verity and I lifted the planks off the shells and we felt that Bosche might have arranged the fuze to fire when you pulled and not pushed, but nothing happened so we dug them up As all our RFA went over the road in a few hours time, it was a good thing we did so. Made another detour at Bakery Crossing `- there were 223 Sappers and Infantry lying dead in the crater and the 28 E Lancs were lying in profusion all along the main road: there were plenty of Bosche too and a lot of the men had Bosche revolvers. After that we tried to make a plank road 800 yards long at Ash Crater and started it in daylight and promptly got shelled off – after that we did it at night (2am – dawn) and finally got it finished about 3 days before I went on leave: just before I went we were standing to bridge the Lys for the infantry to attack over. I was glad to go.

DIARY, LIEUTENANT J.R.T. ALDOUS MC 210 FIELD COMPANY RE

Left

A raiding party of 1/8 King's Liverpools after a successful foray near Arras in 1916. In 1918 raiders and scouts often wore camouflage suits in the unsullied countryside.

Above

Panorama 170, 15 August 1918. The denuded rear slopes of Kemmel Hill during the German Lys offensive.

CHAPTER THREE:

THIRD YPRES

The troops of one division carried a devil-may-care attitude about them, while in others there would be a general atmosphere of – well, not undue optimism. And so the changes went on, as month followed month. There was to some extent a certain amount of monotony not in the life, but in the outlook. On one of my solitary trips to the trench I met an infantry officer. We stopped and had a chat. It was a late summer's morning and everything in nature looked supremely beautiful. The larks were singing overhead and for the time everything was peaceful. His conversation took a strange tone:

"I've been out here all my life and ..." He paused to think "No, that's not quite right, I mean I've been out here a long time. One's thoughts sometimes get confused." He looked over the trench with wistful eyes and turned round.

"Has it ever struck you that we are exiles?"

"No...not quite that."

"But we are. Think it out. It's 1916 now. I was here in fourteen. Only two years, but it seems a lifetime. It is a lifetime when you look at it from the proper angle – no one knows how long it will last."

"It can't last forever." I remarked.

"Of course not...but suppose it lasts another ten years and we're still living ... we shall be really old men – really old – physically and mentally worn out. Ancient relics of the past, and during that time we shall be exiles, exiles from our own homes."

"What about leave?"

"Leave? A few days, or at the most a week or two in a year. No, our real home is here, and as the years pass we shall know less and less about England – and CARE less, so that our own father and mother and sisters will become more and more unfamiliar, until we shall hardly know them. We shall shake hands when we meet, but our lives and their lives will have been lived so far apart that towards the end we shan't want to go home, and they won't want to see us. Yes, we are the real exiles."

LIEUTENANT F. G. HOWKINS, 253 TUNNELLING COMPANY RE, YPRES 1916

In the Salient, the feeling of inevitable interminability was widespread amongst British troops. Following the Second Battle of Ypres in 1915. The grim monotony of extension, repair and improvement became the norm. It was the hum-drum trench life of the infantryman: long periods of boredom punctuated by periods of short, sharp, terror in the form of shelling or raids.

Between the Second and Third Battles of Ypres,

Below
Two panoramas taken from Garden Villa near Wieltje. The upper example (Second Army No 7) is from June 1915, the lower (Fifth Army No 115) June 1917. They illustrate how little the landscape altered during the two years of stasis.

Pages 162–3
Devastation on the Gheluvelt Plateau during Third Ypres. Panorama 126.

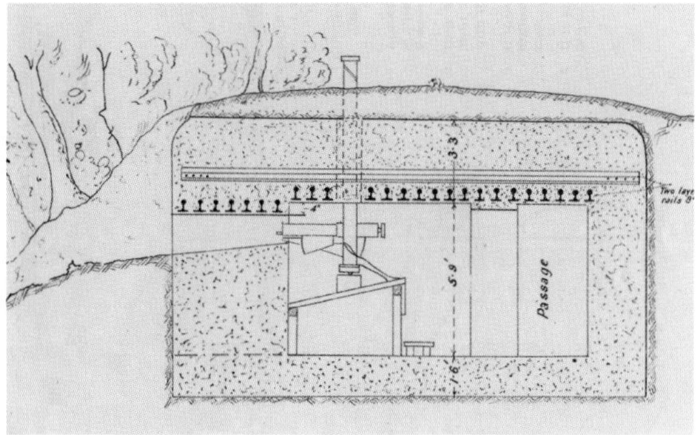

Above
German pillbox with integral machine gun, with a masking cover of earth and turf.

Above left
Belgian forced labour building German pillboxes and blockhouses on the Ypres front.

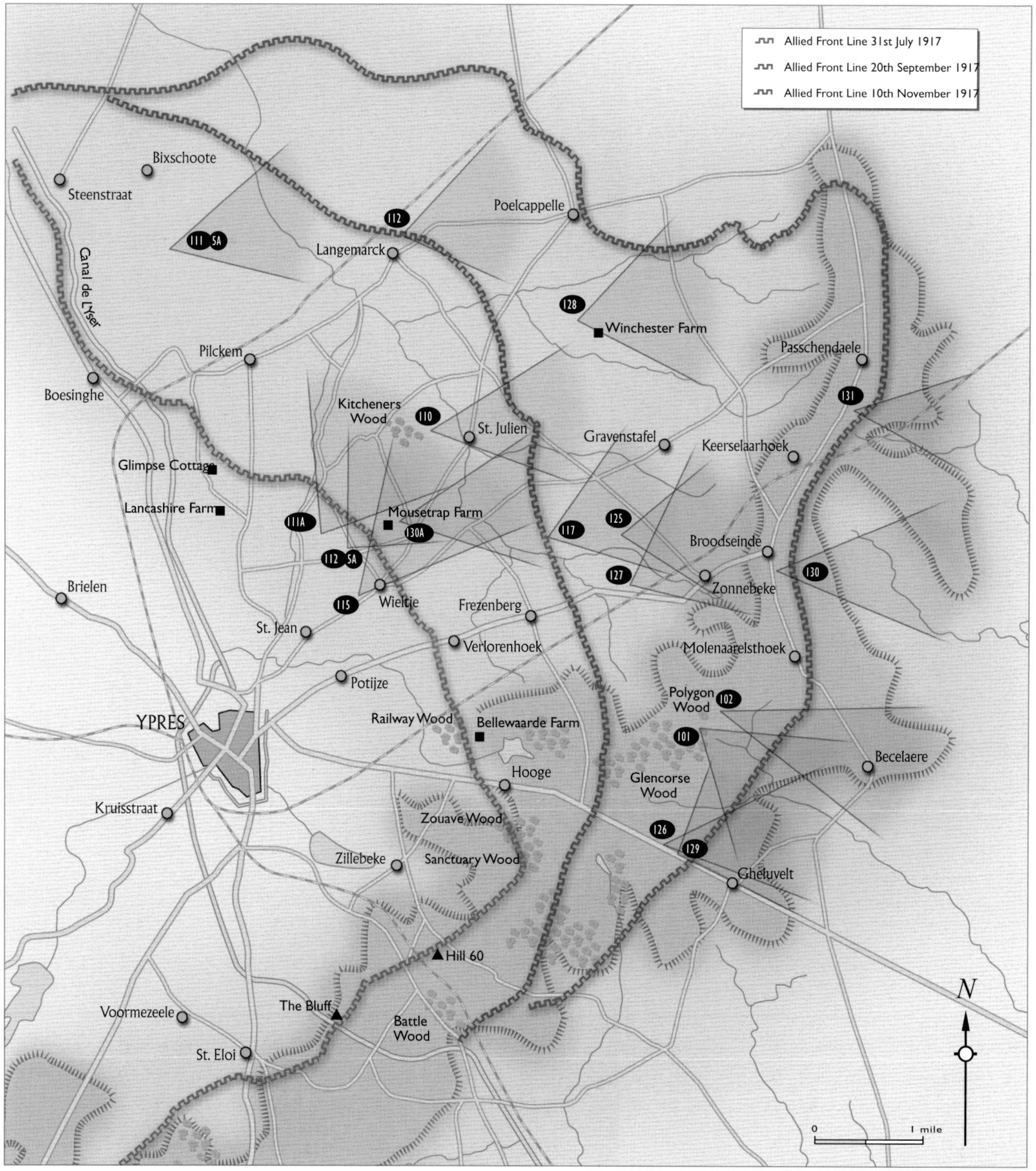

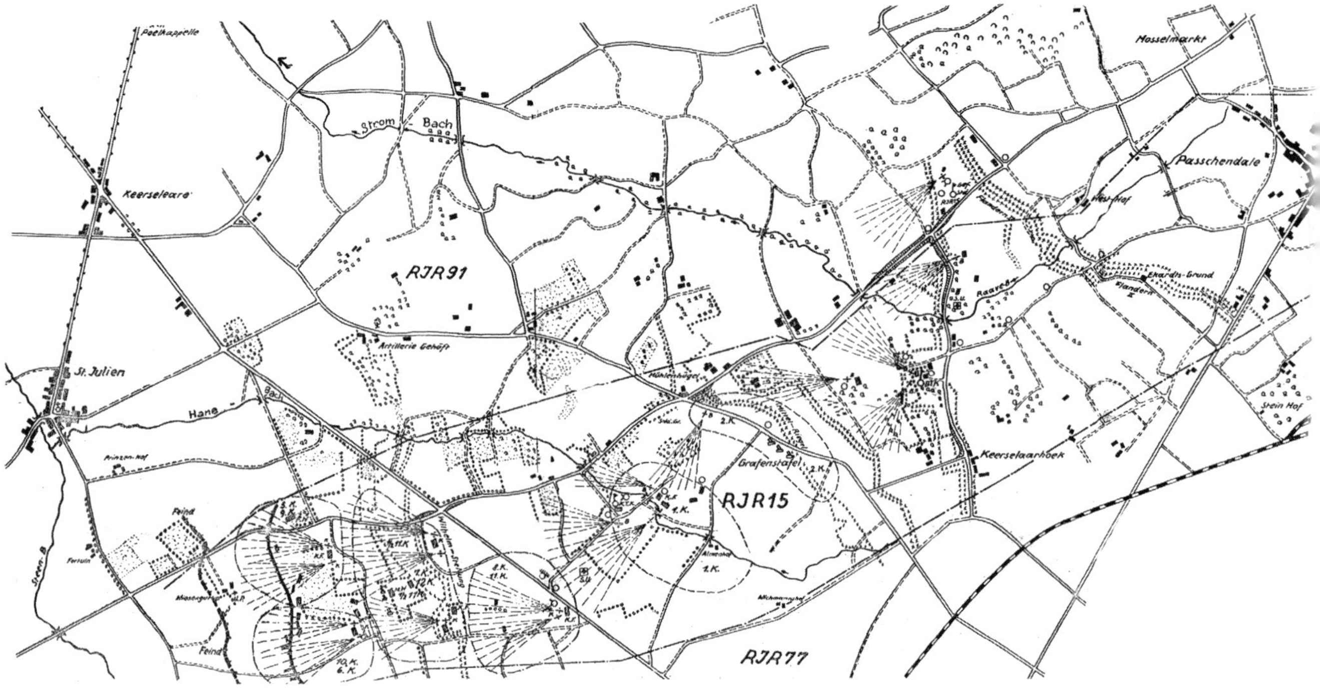

June 1915 to July 1917, a colossal amount of defensive fieldwork was undertaken by both sides throughout the Salient. The most profound and impressive scheme of all was the German 'Flandern Stellung', a complex defence-in-depth trench, redoubt and strongpoint system running from the borders of the Polder Plain through the Ypres and Messines Salients and beyond into French Flanders. At the heart of this fieldwork shield were thousands of steel-reinforced concrete blockhouses and pillboxes arranged and concealed in the most tactically auspicious topographical sites. The whole scheme created an area of connected, mutually supporting fortifications 9 km (5.5 miles) wide. It was designed to be unbreakable, and very nearly proved to be so.

The first test for the Flandern Stellung was at Messines in June 1917, but that assault, launched as it was by the monstrous power of mine warfare, was something unique, distinctive and limited. The greatest test came later – much too late for some, as the generals argued. On 31 July 1917, and for the subsequent three months, the northern extension of the Stellung in front of Ypres was tested by troops of almost a dozen nationalities on a front that focused on the dominating 'heights' of the Passchendaele Ridge system. For the troops facing the ridge it was to be one of the greatest ordeals of the war, and one of its most significant battles.

Before the storm

In the relatively subdued and militarily restrained period between Second and Third Ypres the hand of nature can be seen to have partially healed much of the battered landscape. Panoramas 111 and *112* – Fifth Army pre-battle reconnaissance photographs – illustrate this well. No 115, taken from Garden Villa on 3 June 1917 (compare also No 7 from the same location two years earlier) shows the zone from Mauser Ridge to Wieltje. The British front line can be picked out and traced running through the ruins of Crossroads Farm (see also No 4 from the farm itself in 1915): it had barely moved a metre between these two dates. Canadian Dugouts, gunpits pre-dating the Second Battle of Ypres, lie in no man's land, with just in front the freshly turned earth of the British jumping-off position: a simple trench forward of the front line specially installed for the attack of 31 July. 'Caliban Reserve' marks the second German line near the top of the ridge. The front-line trenches illustrated here are those from which the British troops climbed on the morning of 31 July 1917. The landscape may appear little changed in the two years, but this was not the case: the formidable multiple supporting lines of the Flandern Stellung lie in wait behind the foreground ridges.

Being the initial obstacle for the forthcoming battle, it was critical for the Allies to have some idea of how the enemy manned and protected his front line, and just before the offensive began in this sector the area around Morteldje and No Man's Cot was the scene of one of the war's more unusual 'tricks' – the 'Chinese attack'.

On July 28th, 1917, three days prior to the Fifth Army attack, a practice barrage was carried out along the whole Army front; some 300 figures were placed in position and worked for half an hour along the Corps front. The results obtained were that the enemy was discovered to be holding his front line, and five machine guns were located. On this

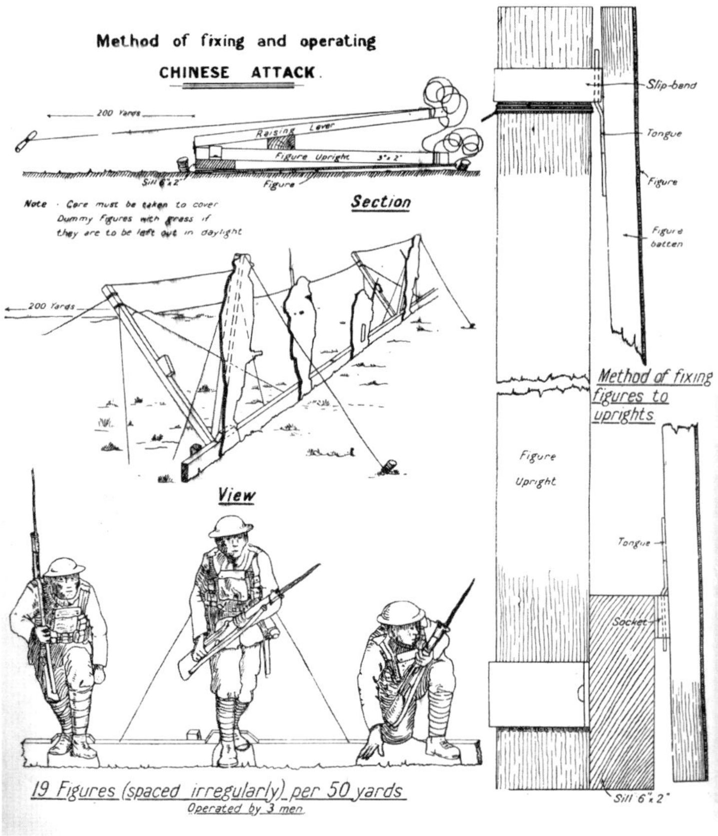

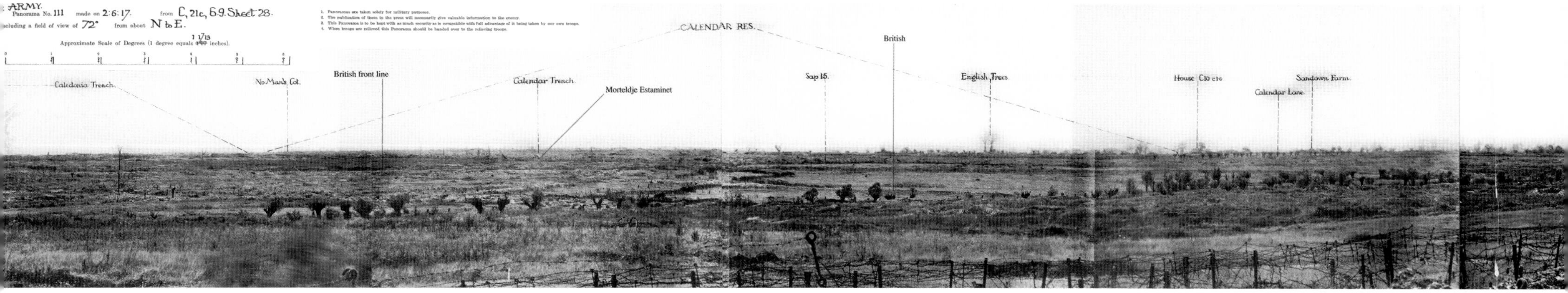
ARMY.
Panorama No. 111 made on 2:6:17. from C, 21c, 6.9. Sheet 28.
including a field of view of 72° from about N to E.
Approximate Scale of Degrees (1 degree equals 1 1/13 inches).
1. Panoramas are taken solely for military purposes.
2. The publication of them in the press will necessarily give valuable information to the enemy.
3. This Panorama is to be kept with as much security as is compatible with full advantage of it being taken by our own troops.
4. When troops are relieved this Panorama should be handed over to the relieving troops.
CALENDAR RES.
Caledonia Trench.
No Man's Cot.
British front line
Calendar Trench.
Morteldje Estaminet
Sap 15.
British
English Trees.
House C10 c16
Calendar Lane.
Sandown Farm.

Left

German plan showing the concentration of machine guns on RJR 15's narrow front. This concentration should be extrapolated across the entire battlefield.

Above

Panorama 111A of 2 June 1917 shows the Morteldje Estaminet area where a Chinese attack took place in preparation for Third Ypres.

Left

How a 'Chinese attack' was undertaken.

Below

A store of plywood troops ready for their bloodless forays.

occasion, after the barrage had ceased the figures were left standing to show the enemy that he had been fooled, with the idea that on the day of the real attack he would look twice before calling on his artillery to put down a barrage.

MISCELLANEOUS VOLUME, *History of the RE in the Great War*

Using smoke to cloak the true nature of the 'assault', at least three further Chinese attacks were set up during Third Ypres, but in these cases the object was to distract enemy attention and deflect flanking fire. All were profitable. The effort at Morteldje revealed that although the front line was lightly held, reserve and support positions higher upon the ridge were substantially more resistant. Panorama 111A shows the precise location.

The Germans were fully aware that the Messines endeavour had been a launch pad for greater things, and it was therefore natural to suppose that during two years of stasis on an extension of exactly the same battlefield (and with similar geology) the British must surely have also planted mines beneath their lines in front of Ypres. The devastating effect upon German morale of the 7 June blows had created a distinct paranoia, and in the weeks preceding 31 July their *Pioniere* blew many heavy camouflets in every known or suspected mining area in an effort to smash hostile British galleries, sever leads and flood systems. In the Boesinghe sector German airmen reported sighting British blue clay spoil, a sure sign of deep mining; it led to the evacuation of their front-line garrison to a reserve position almost a kilometre to the rear. The spoil was actually the product of tunnels being driven to hold nothing more hazardous than bridging materials for crossing the canal. In fact no mines whatsoever had been prepared for Third Ypres, the tunnellers had had insufficient resources to furnish anything beyond the huge scheme at Messines. With the absence of mines British infantry were therefore to rely predominantly upon artillery to prepare the ground for attack.

In advance of the Flandern Stellung lay the German outpost lines. These, it was felt, posed a lesser threat and could be neutralized by obliterating shellfire. It was concrete that most concerned Haig and his Staff. There were so many pillboxes and so many machine guns that unless they could be subdued by the artillery before and during attacks, a repeat of the first day of the Somme was feared. In addition, following the failure of the French Nivelle offensive in the spring the British were fully aware that the Germans had been able to substantially reinforce units in the Salient. The answer was to amplify artillery concentrations and barrages, even beyond the record numbers used at Messines. In the ten days before the battle 3,000 guns fired almost four and a half million shells at a cost of £22,000,000 – a price, incidentally, which could have bought 4,400 tanks.

It was high summer. The strike at Messines had taken place beneath warm sunshine, and Allied commanders rightly expected reasonable weather for stage two of their offensive. But Haig's decision, albeit under pressure from Sir Hubert Gough, commanding Fifth Army, and the French, to allow six weeks to shift the material axis of attack the few short kilometres northwards was to have serious consequences: they were six predominantly dry weeks. Neither Haig nor anyone else was to know that the summer was to be the wettest in living memory, but by waiting until 31 July a potential month of prime campaigning time had effectively been lost.

The battle opens

At 3.50 a.m. on Zero Day the opening attacks got underway. To the left of Boesinghe the French First Army Corps moved towards Houthulst Forest, with the Fifth Army and a Corps of Plumer's Second Army taking responsibility for the Pilkem, Frezenberg, Bellewaerde and Menin Road ridges: a total of twelve divisions. Despite Plumer's success at Messines, Haig had selected Gough, a cavalryman like himself and only forty-seven years old, to command the offensive because of his reputation as a 'thruster'. A rapid breakthrough was sought, and Plumer's patient 'bite and hold' tactics, although laudable and tested in action, were thought unlikely to secure the desired victory in the time allowed – before summer was out. The job of Plumer's Second Army therefore was to safeguard the right flank of the battlefront.

31 July 1917

Zero Day. Breakfast at 3a.m. Zero hour 3.50. It was dull but not raining and was really a pretty sight to watch our barrage in the dark. We moved forward to Lunaville Farm at 5.20 a.m. and reported to 1st Brigade. At 10 we saw the first batch of prisoners. At 10.30 we were ordered to move to Lapin Farm behind Abri Wood. We picked up our loads and set off. I waited for a few minutes as he [the enemy] was shelling the canal and then went forward again and without mishap arrived at Lapin Farm and got the men into Lapin Trench which was in a fair condition. Marris and I then reported to Brigade. The Brigadier was very cross with the 55th Company for not reporting sooner and also with 38th Divn. for not taking their ground. He explained the position: the 2nd Grenadier Guards had the Green dotted line on the left flank but not on the right because of the 38th, and here it curved back to the Green Line. He ordered me forward to Battalion HQ in Captain's Farm in the Green Line. We were off and on heavily shelled but no casualties except Corporal Shipley. We got the men in shell holes and bits of trenches and made them stand to. Several ran away; these, I and Sgt Clewer chased after, collected them up and got them safely into a trench. In about an hour's time things were again normal and, on collecting reports, we found we had 3 casualties to Sappers and 26 to carrying party and, as the position was uncertain, though apparently the attack had been squashed, the Col. ordered us home. We arrived at Lunaville Farm wet through at 2 a.m. (1 August).

LIEUTENANT HAROLD RIDSDALE, 76 FIELD COMPANY RE (WITH THE GUARDS DIVISION IN FRONT OF BOESINGHE)

At the end of the first day the British had advanced more than a kilometre in the northern sector before resistance checked the attacks and drove them back. Many units had reach their objectives and some indeed had gone beyond, but the advance was irregular and disjointed. In some places counter-attacks were fought off, in others the troops had moved forward so fast that they became isolated. On the whole, the day was a curate's egg.

However, it is the final line of Lieutenant Ridsdale's diary entry that encapsulates the defining feature of this opening period of fighting: rain. It would come to epitomize (erroneously) the entire Third Battle of Ypres. There had also been rain prior to 31 July, and although the British bombardments looked and sounded devastating, the soft ground served to severely diminish the destructive effect of high explosive shells. In such conditions it was no good a shell landing near a pillbox, a direct hit was required – and from a heavy calibre weapon – to have any chance of suppressing the defence. Although thousands of pillboxes dotted the landscape they were very small targets, and required immense shell concentrations to achieve success. Many surviving examples in the Salient today, all of which played a part in this battle, show remarkably little damage;

Left
Troops washing in a large shellhole which also forms the grave for at least seven soldiers. The central cross is marked with the name of a sapper of 475 Field Company RE, killed in action on 16 August 1917.

Above

The treacherous Zonnebeke marshes with the ruins of the church in a misty background. After September 1917 these marshes claimed many lives of men moving at night to and from the front lines on the Passchendaele Ridge.

Above right

Man's faithful partners in war. Shelling took a terrible toll of horses and mules throughout the war.

indeed some, such as those in the German cemetery at Langemarck, are entirely unscathed. Carefully built under camouflage, then concealed by earth and turf, a considerable number had also not been identified by aerial observation despite two years of survey; indistinguishable in the surroundings, the posts were often not spotted at all, and caused unsuspected havoc amongst advancing infantry. Once captured, however, they became a critical resource as no other form of shelter existed on the battlefield.

2 August

Raining hard again. The men went out to clean up some of the concrete MG emplacements of the Boche. We started on one in Hey Wood, a beauty, intact, concrete 6 feet thick, but in such a dirty state. We cleaned it up and built a sandbag parapet in front of the door as it faced the wrong way. Mason and I went reconnoitring for others. In the 'Blue Line' there were dozens, full of water and wreckage. Some were sound, one had been shifted bodily by one of our big shells. This trench was in an awful state; we saw several dead Germans and in one dugout 2 wounded Germans, of whom we told the RAMC, so that they might clear. We looked too at several of the farms; the concrete in these was completely wiped out. The heavy shelling on this part and the heavy rain made the ground awful, up to your waist in mud.

3 August

Finished the dugout at Hey Wood and made a reconnaissance of other concrete dugouts; nearly all were smashed. One we found full of German dead, dead for many days too. In another dugout, evidently an officers' mess, a shell had penetrated right through and killed the lot. There was a third instance of a dugout which evidently refused to surrender and, as the occupants came out, they were clubbed. There were 30 dead Huns outside this, all with their heads smashed in. As far as British dead, there were very few. I saw several Irish Guards and Grenadier Guards, one with his Bible in his hands.

4 August

The section was repairing the footbridges across the Canal, all of which had been smashed. We made 2 good ones and just at the end lost 2 men, Turner and Rossiter, Turner being seriously hit. The sun came out and it stopped raining, the first time for a week.

LIEUTENANT HAROLD RIDSDALE, 76 FIELD COMPANY RE

After three days of battle the attacks had still not secured the first objectives, but casualty lists had already reached 32,000. On the battlefield the combination of shelling and rain had produced almost impossible conditions for troops (and tanks) to negotiate after barely 24 hours of fighting. It required superhuman efforts not only to move artillery forward to assist the advance, but to relieve troops in forward positions. Medical personnel in particular were stretched from day one.

31 July 1917

The ground was heavy with the recent rain and it was stiff going especially as the men had had a stiff march the night before and heavily laden as they were. The Battalion moved up over the Steenbeek at 10 a.m. and I followed about 250 yards in the rear. I saw almost immediately that they were mostly all held up by machine-gun fire and that they were having casualties. It was clear that the stretcher-bearers would find it difficult or impossible to evacuate wounded, so I decided to push on and take my chance. My orderlies and I got by short rushes and taking shelter in shell holes, which were very plentiful. I was kept busy dressing wounded during the whole time. I was unable to evacuate stretcher cases as there were practically no stretcher-bearers left and only one stretcher. Besides, it was impossible to get a stretcher case back due to the machine-gun fire. I put the stretcher cases under the best cover available and I got any walking cases to try and get away when they felt able.

FOREST

HOUTHULST

Above
Fifth Army Panorama 110: the battlefield around Cannabis Trench near St Julien in August 1917.

Pages 170-71
Repairing landscape infrastructure and removing casualties from the field of battle during Third Ypres.

The Boche began to get round our right flank and casualties became more numerous about 4.30 p.m. I was loathe to leave but there was no way of getting the stretcher cases back. All my orderlies were wounded and I lost all my dressings. My Corporal of stretcher-bearers was wounded as also were most of the bearers. I had tried to get in touch with the OC Divisional Collecting Stations but the runner was wounded. I also got a stretcher-bearer who turned up to go back and get in touch. He took a written message asking for help about 3 a.m. of next day. I could not label the wounded as I had no tallies. About 8 a.m. August 1st six stretchers and 24 bearers turned up. They were only sufficient to evacuate the wounded in the Aid Post but not the wounded up front. There were no dressings sent. The going was very heavy and it was evident that even six bearers were too few as not only was the mud knee deep in places or deeper, and the ground so broken up by shellfire, but also the distance to the Collecting Station was too great.

The casualties of men are between 300-350 as far as I know. I myself received a bruise from an MG bullet at the side of the knee and another on the thigh from a piece of shell, but I am quite able to carry on. Three machine-gun bullets elected to pass through my clothing instead of myself for which I am duly thankful.

MAJOR JAMES ROGERS, RAMC, 4/5 HIGHLANDERS

The attacks continue

The attacks wallowed and stalled. A week was to pass before conditions improved sufficiently to press forward again. Haig, Gough and Plumer had long known that the most difficult nut to crack was going to be the Gheluvelt Plateau straddling the heights of the Menin Road beyond Hooge. The initial attack plan for the Pilckem, Langemarck and Frezenberg ridges had also included capture of the plateau, but on 31 July the British had come face to face with devastating German artillery fire and a well-constructed and heavily-manned defence. They were resolutely resisted, in many places thrown back, and eventually left clutching a gain of around 500 m (547 yds). Specialist German counter-attack troops, the Eingreif Divisions, had not even been required.

Panorama 110 from near Cannabis Support Trench in the St Julien area gives a good picture of the early Third Ypres landscape at this time, just as the weather began to improve. Engineers, Pioneers and Army Troops personnel have begun organizing the splintered battlefield for defence and communication. Duckboard tracks and plank roads are already laid and marked. The sign to the right of frame reads 'Springfield and Front Line [to left], and Crossroads Farm and Canal [right]'. It should be noted that there were two Springfields in the Salient; this one lies on the Zonnebeke–Langemarck road. Panorama 111, taken soon afterwards from Colonel's Farm (note signboard), a position just over a kilometre west of Langemarck and a little north of Harold Ridsdale's positions at Lapin Farm and Abri Wood. The dark mass of Houthulst Forest sits on the horizon. Note the mass of concrete emplacements spread across the entire landscape. Those captured were numbered (and also named) like the group in the foreground.

The photograph shows pillbox entrances to have been 'reversed' so as not to face the enemy: the RE created new

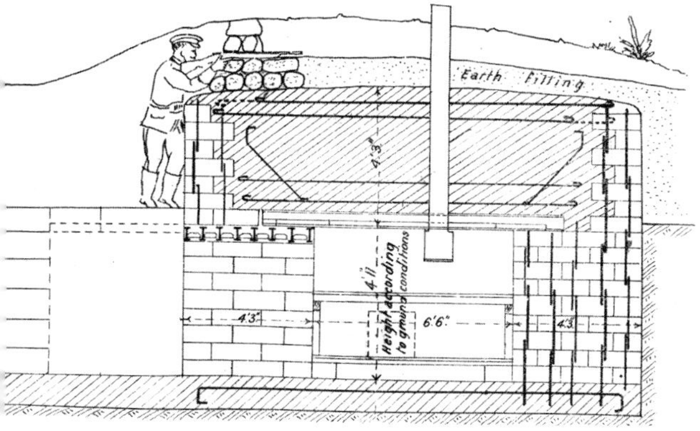

Above
Many pillboxes in the Salient were 'blind' – without loopholes – and were used for accommodation only. In the event of attack troops would man the firestep to the rear, as if in a trench.

Left
A carpenter puts the finishing touches to a grave marker.

Underneath
Panorama 111. Just behind the battle lines during Third Ypres before the rains came. Soldiers relax in a repaired landscape. Note the reversal of pillbox entrances and several rows of screens stretching across the entire battlefield.

doorways by drilling holes, packing them with explosives, and blowing apertures in what was once the front of the pillbox. Dense protective belts of barbed wire have also been reinstated. Note especially the ranks of screens stretching across almost the entire battlefield to obscure enemy views of British activity in the open. This was necessary only as long as the Germans still held the ridges and spurs; once driven from the higher ground their observational capabilities replicated those which the British had been forced to contend with since May 1915. A shirtless soldier can be seen 'chatting' (searching for lice) in the warm sunshine, whilst another group rest in the lee of a pillbox. The white pickets (painted on one side only) were critical to assist troops to find their way to forward zones at night. Dozens of notice boards are also visible carrying place-names, directions and map references.

The second attack on the Gheluvelt Plateau by II Corps on 10 August, was limited to the capture of the hamlet of Westhoek beyond the Bellewaerde Ridge, the meagre gain was again due to determined resistance, counter-attacks – and British artillery firing short. On 16 August fresh assaults upon Langemarck were brushed aside, and on the same day German Eingreif troops began to claw back ground lost on the plateau earlier in the battle. This was far from what Haig and his Staff had expected and hoped for. Time was critical and the moment for change had arrived. Gough's tactics were not working swiftly enough, so the next endeavour, known as the Battle of the Menin Road Ridge (20–25 September), was entrusted to the Second Army. Gough would remain on the Staff, but Sir Herbert Plumer was handed the reins.

Panorama *117* shows the view from the heights around Pommern Castle during the fourth week of August, towards the end of the period when the Fifth Army were pushing forward either side of Langemarck; No *119*, taken at almost the same time, has Canopus Trench in the immediate foreground. Poelcappelle is to the left, with the ruins of St Julien in centre frame, while Passchendaele Ridge lies in the distance on the right.

The actions of August 1917 brought the British to within striking distance of Zonnebeke, the village which lies at the heart of Third Ypres battlefields. Losses were now approaching 67,000, and the decision was whether to continue the fight or consolidate on the higher ground presently occupied and press attacks in other sectors, and indeed other theatres, such as Italy. Both the British Government and the Army agreed to push on in Flanders. The Menin Road Ridge, still practically undented, was target number one.

Gheluvelt and beyond

Whilst strategic discussions were underway in Whitehall, Plumer and his Staff had already appealed for and been granted a three week breathing space to plan an attack on the Gheluvelt Plateau. Preparations were carefully made, assaulting units assembled fresh, and reserve troops rested. The weather was also kind: at long last the skies cleared, and

188

very little rain fell throughout the battle period. Despite having an estimated forty per cent of their guns trained on the sector, the Germans were driven from it by Plumer's 'bite and hold' approach, a stratagem which sought strictly limited objectives, and asked no more from troops than they could reasonably be expected to achieve, an approach which also preserved energy to ward of counter-attack. In conjunction with this Anglo-Australian venture five divisions also advanced strongly on the left of the Ypres–Roulers railway towards Poelcappelle and Zonnebeke, across the ground shown in Panoramas *117* and *119*. Here at last was some truly encouraging progress for Haig, GHQ, the politicians, and the public. The breakthrough still appeared achievable if only a decent momentum could be built up. No 126 shows the desolation of the Gheluvelt Plateau after partial capture of the western end. The British front lines lie beyond the screens. Note that the ground is still dry.

Plumer's next assignment was the immediate acquisition of Polygon Wood (26 September to 3 October), Zonnebeke, and the high ground east and south-east of the now ruined village. Contrary to popular perception of Third Ypres, the weather had now entered a long spell of warm, rainless days and nights. So dry was it that transport created clouds of dust reminiscent of the Wild West. It was during this period that water supply caused many a headache.

Polygon was an Australian enterprise. Plumer's tactics were slightly complicated when on 25 September a weighty German counter-assault dented the Allied lines in the very sub-sector they were about to attack the following day. But he did not alter his plans: the attack went ahead and after a faltering start all objectives were taken, although at considerable cost. The view (taken later) from the top of the famous 'Butte' in Polygon Wood (where now stands the memorial to 5th Australian Division, the captors of the wood) can be seen in Panorama 101. Haig derived further encouragement from the victory and once more began to visualize cavalry surging over the Flanders ridges towards Roulers. The momentum he had prayed for was developing.

Two particular panoramas perfectly illustrate Plumer's approach at Polygon and Zonnebeke, Nos *120* and 125. When comparing the two, use Zonnebeke church (on the right of frame in both images) as the point of reference. Although all the Third Ypres panoramas are taken during the period of battle, No *120* conveys a particularly hazardous atmosphere. The foreground has been shelled and shelled again until not a blade of grass survives. A very recently fallen British soldier lies on the far right of frame. However, just beyond the narrow ribbon of territory currently occupying the attention of the artillery, relatively undamaged fields, hedgerows and houses can be seen. The photograph exemplifies the tactical concept: select a limited target, destroy it, capture, hold, consolidate and then repair it. No piece of ground was bombarded without reason. Again that the ground is still dry. Panorama 125 illustrates the immense amount of work undertaken from the moment this very same terrain had been secured. Until the Passchendaele Ridge was finally captured, all forward

Below

Canadian Pioneers taping out a route for a new duckboard track towards Passchendaele. In the latter stages of battle dozens of tracks – laid during the day as well as at night – snaked their way across the wilderness to the front line.

Above
Signposts and shelters on the ground around Zonnebeke in September 1917. From Panorama 125.

positions – the squalid mud pits of October and November in Frank Hurley and William Rider-Rider's tragically memorable images – could only be approached and vacated under cover of darkness, and on foot. There was no question of digging or blowing deep communication trenches as had been possible on the Somme. The Flanders geology and water table forbade it, so it was down to field companies, tunnellers, pioneers, Army Troops companies and infantry working parties to put in place and maintain a fresh infrastructure from the earliest possible moment. Throughout the Salient this entailed highly dangerous work, both day and night. A group of sappers can be seen putting the finishing touches to the junction of road and track just to the right of centre. The two main double-duckboards tracks through this sector were known as Jack and Jill.

The Germans still occupy the distant ridge at this time (the lens is deceiving – it is barely 3 km (2 miles) away), but plank roads, mule and duckboard tracks (fitted with special non-slip wire), and splinter-proof shelters now carpet the landscape. Pillboxes have been camouflaged, battlefield graves properly marked, and signage erected. The sign in the central section reads 'White pickets leading to Boethoek'. The track which it marks crosses the plank road (the main route between Zonnebeke and Langemarck) and heads on towards S'Gravenstafel, the exact area where Panorama 58 had been taken on 17 April 1915 (Chapter Two), nearly two and half years earlier. Nearer Zonnebeke, a party of sappers can be seen working on the duckboard/plank road connection of another track running parallel to the Boethoek route. Behind Zonnebeke church, and capped by a row of brooding blockhouses, sits Broodseinde Ridge.

Broodseinde Ridge

This was Plumer's next objective (Battle of Broodseinde Ridge, 4-8 October). It too was captured in ebullient if grisly style by Australian troops still smarting from heavy losses sustained in the battle for Polygon Wood. On the morning of 4 October the valley beneath the crest became a charnel house when a battalion of young and unblooded German troops were (accidentally) caught in the British pre-attack barrage when moving forward to counter-attack under cover of a dense mist. The survivors received no mercy from the advancing Australians. At the same time as the Broodseinde attack, a combined British/Anzac assault also made progress in the north at Houthulst, and centrally at Tyne Cot and S'Graventafel (see Nos 58 and *119*) across the unmarked fields in the Zonnebeke panorama, No *120*. It was an advance that brought the British to within stoning distance of Passchendaele church. The progress produced further delight at GHQ. Haig's cavalry were given orders to move forward and prepare for action.

From the tattered crest of Broodseinde, the first piece of ridge to be captured, an immense and wonderful vista of unblemished green fields, towns, villages and church spires emerged from the smoke of battle. The view with which the Australians were presented can be seen in No 130 (February 1918). The picture also includes an entrance

Below
Panorama 101 from the Butte in Polygon Wood. The extra height offered by the 'old rifle butt' gave the British a badly needed vantage point in the desolation of the Westhoek.

to one of several ridge-top dugouts which were installed during the winter months. This was where Haig wished to be. The enemy appeared on the point of collapse, and indeed were: Crown Prince Rupprecht was drawing up withdrawal plans. However, summer was already a memory, and October heralded what everyone dreaded most: the entrance of Germany's greatest ally, a change in the weather. During the weeks without rain tremendous progress had been made by the Allies; it may well have continued – but not in an engagement where such great concentrations of artillery were required. The rains began on 2 October, falling lightly until 7 October when they came down in torrents for two days.

We left Low Farm [Frezenberg], I think it was about 5 o'clock [8 October]. We had been there a few days sitting in shell holes under groundsheets. We were told to sit tight during the day, but were given jobs to do after dark – carrying parties mainly. There were plenty of pillboxes about for cover, but so many men had been brought up for the attack that it was officers only in there. You could peep out from under your groundsheet during the day and see parties of Pioneers doing roads and tracks in a sort of wilderness of rubbish and muck. A terrible sight. No one told us what we were to do or where we were going, just that we were attacking the next morning and would have a rest and a feed beforehand. The name Passchendaele meant nothing to us then.

That evening it was already raining and blowing before we set off, and there were I don't know how many men moving up this single duckboard track – the whole of our battalion anyway. It was alright at first, but as it got dark you had to make sure to keep close to the fellow in front so as to follow the track, because it didn't go in a straight line but meandered about round the lips of shell holes. They [the Germans] must have known what was on because the shells weren't long in coming when it was almost dark. After a while bunches of men got separated a bit, and people started falling off the boards and shouting. Now, we had been told that if anyone fell out or got into trouble we were not allowed to stop, because if one man stopped we all stopped and we'd never get to where we were going. You could hear those poor blokes calling out from the darkness. It was pitiful. I found out myself a few days later that once you were in those shell holes there was no way out without help: the mud was like wet soap, you see, like

Above
Panorama 130 taken from the crest of Broodseinde Ridge. For the first time in more than three years, the British were able to look down upon their enemy. Forward posts – which in 1918 replaced the continuous front line trench – were also connected by tunnels to the 'lee' side of the ridge.

Left
Australian troops sheltering in a deep dugout during the Third Battle of Ypres. As surface life became ever less tenable, so more and more dugouts were installed.

Below
Panorama 128, showing the left flank of the Third Ypres attack on 22 October. This is the ground near Poelcappelle. Little further progress was made from this position.

it had been in a basin of water for a week; terrible stuff. You couldn't get any purchase to climb out, and the shell holes were brimming with water. You just got more and more tired with struggling; then you got chilled. We knew the poor devils were going to die if they weren't got out. I tried to block my ears but it's not easy in the dark when you're carrying a rifle and pack and slipping all over the place trying to stay on eighteen inches of timber. Now, once the file broke up you were in a hell of a mess: sometimes you could see which way the track went by the Very lights or the flash of a shell, but most of the time we were like blind men: you had to slide one foot forward to see if the path was still there, bring the other up, and so on. So you can see that progress was slow.

We then met a party of pack mules coming down the track the other way. Oh, the language! The track was meant to be one-way. I think the poor things were shot by our officers just to get the path clear. We didn't know where we were going or how long we had to walk, we just kept going. Hour after hour. Then the duckboards ended and we came up on a road – the first bit of solid ground we'd stood on for hours. I was completely done up. We took shelter behind a big concrete pillbox [the left hand pillbox in Tyne Cot Cemetery] and I fell asleep on my rifle. It was light by then. I was so tired I didn't care if I lived or died; a bullet would have been welcome. I was woken up by an explosion or a gun firing close by or something. Well, we were hours late, there was no food, not even a drink. I found out later that we had been twelve hours or more on that march, but it didn't make any difference to the army. Mr Kay comes up and says "Come on lads, its our turn", and we just walked round the corner of the pillbox and up the hill into the battle. The Germans didn't have much to fear from me that morning. I never saw any of them, except dead ones, until dusk when they counter-attacked. We were in a cemetery on the edge of the railway cutting and I just emptied my rifle into a dark mass of men. It just seemed to break up and disappear. Then I crept into a pillbox and fell asleep – on the shoulder of a dead German officer, it turned out! We were relieved by the Australians the next day "You the LF's? Well piss off, we're here to relieve you." We needed no second bidding.

PRIVATE BERT FEARNS, 2/6 LANCASHIRE FUSILIERS

Bert Fearns had taken part in the initial attack of the Battle of Poelcappelle (9–12 October). It was the start of a month of true attrition. Plumer and Gough had told Haig that

although willing to persist if necessary, they would welcome an end to the offensive. Haig chose to persevere – not now with the hope of breakout – the primary objectives of the campaign had dissipated in the rain – but simply to annexe the final piece of high ground as a winter position. After a brief respite of a few dry days the first of three battles for Passchendaele was launched on 12 October. The wet weather was unrelenting. Although the engineers made wooden sledges to drag field artillery into position, without a road network the critical heavier guns could not be moved forward. Whilst entire field companies became engaged in extricating guns from the mire, almost 15,000 men were employed in the race to build and maintain forward roads. No tank could reach the front to assist in clearing the enemy from the ridge, and the weather spoiled any hope of adequate air support. The subsequent four weeks of fighting were more squalid than any other period of the war, and it is the images from this time which have come to exemplify the entire campaign.

12 October 1917

Owing to Joyce (my camera lumper) funking it, Wilkins and I set out in the car for Hellfire Corner (Menin Road 20 kilometres). Here we got on to the Zonnebeke railroad which has been shelled and blown to fragments during the past two years of straffing. It is now a raised bank of mud and bits of scrap iron rails. Already we are starting to rebuild it, and about 1,000 labourers were at work rail-laying. It will be of incalculable value to support the front lines and artillery, as the roads will be impassable during the winter. It's a bloody work, however, for it is being constantly shelled and numbers are daily being killed. It is littered with bodies both of our own men and Boche. Things were reasonably quiet till we got near to Zonnebeke – But the mud! trudge, trudge, sometimes to the knee in sucking, tenacious slime – a fair hell of a job under ordinary conditions, but with a heavy camera up and being shelled. I hardly thought "the game worth the candle". Nearing Zonnebeke we got into the Boche barrage, and as he was paying particular attention to the railway line (or rather what once was), it being the only possible means of communication with the front line about here: we had more than an exciting time. Shells lobbed all around and sent their splinters whizzing everywhere – God knows how anybody can escape them, and the spitting ping of machine gun bullets that played on certain points made one wish he was a microbe; under these conditions one feels himself so magnified that he feels every shell the Boche fires is directed for his especial benefit. This shelled embankment of mud was a terrible sight. Every 20 paces or less lay a body. Some frightfully mutilated, without legs, arms and heads, and half covered in mud and slime. I could not help thinking as Wilkins and I trudged along this inferno and soaked to the skin, talking and living beings, might not the next moment one of these things – Jee – it puts the wind up one at times.

We pushed on through the old Zonnebeke station (now absolutely swept away) up to Broodseinde and entered the railway cutting near the ridge crest. Shells began to fall just about a hundred paces ahead and their skyrocket-like whiz, without cessation passing too close overhead and bursting all around, induced us to retire. The light too,

Below
A tragic scene in the Ypres–Roulers railway cutting photographed by Frank Hurley on 12 October 1917. In a landscape which lacked any form of recognizable communication route, the line was an obvious feature underfoot, and became the salvation of many troops trying to find their way back to Ypres after night-time relief.

failed, and rain set in. We got no pictures but whips of fun. I felt great admiration for the stretcher bearers, who slowly plodded on with their burdens, trudging through mud and presenting a tempting target, for the enemy observation balloons had eyes on everything.

It was impossible to bring in many wounded under these conditions, and many poor devils must perish from exposure.

I noticed one awful sight: a party of ten or so, telephone men all blown to bits. Under a questionably sheltered bank lay a group of dead men. Sitting by them in little scooped out recesses sat a few living; but so emaciated by fatigue and shell shock that it was hard to differentiate. Still the whole way was just another of the many byways to hell one sees out here, and which are so strewn with ghastliness that the only comment is – "That poor beggar copped it thick", or else nothing at all.

CAPTAIN FRANK HURLEY, OFFICIAL PHOTOGRAPHER, AIF

Above

From Panorama 112 (undated, but during Third Ypres), taken in front of Langemarck village, showing British support positions screened by camouflage netting.

Hurley's description of railway repairs being made under shellfire demonstrates how serious the task of reinstating battlefield infrastructure was in the Salient. Panorama *112* taken from a position in front of Langemarck, shows the dire need for instant cover. It was achieved by the use of the ubiquitous elephant shelter which at least gave protection from shrapnel and most splinters – and rain. Dozens have been installed here. Duckboard tracks snake forward to the front lines, whilst to the left Houthulst Forest was a formidable target, full of concealed machine guns; although its edges were reached in 1917, it was not captured until 28 September 1918.

Right

Highlanders who fell in the attacks upon Zonnebeke, a village which, lying at the very heart of the battlefield, entirely ceased to exist.

Towards the end

As with the hidden warfare of military mining and the construction of dugouts, what one cannot see in these Third Ypres photographs is equally as astonishing as the symbolic landscape itself. Apart from the clearing of dozens of kilometres of beeks, ditches and other watercourses to ameliorate the waterlogged conditions, a massive communication system had to be installed throughout the newly captured territory. The task entailed digging narrow trenches to maximum possible depth, not for men but telephone wires. Engineer sections completed an average of 350 m (382 yds) of 1.5 m (5 ft) deep trench per night, installing clusters of cable as thick as a man's arm. The sappers would also lay down almost 480 km (300 miles) of trench tramway.

Panorama 128, taken from Winchester Farm on 22 October 1917 shows a group of battered pillboxes, possibly those used by Charles Carrington at the beginning of the month. Carrington's sojourn in the sector is described in his classic account 'Soldier From the Wars Returning'. He first writes, 'And ahead in the distance was the spire of Passchendaele church rising, not from the mud, but from green trees, an amenity it would not enjoy much longer.' The ridge can be seen here on a misty skyline.

My handful of men crossed the Stroombeek and skirmished up the other bank in the approved style to the pill-box called Winchester, where we met a platoon of the 6th on the flank of our objective. As we went forward we passed many dead and wounded men and noted grimly that the Germans far outnumbered the British. At Winchester, where shot and shell were flying briskly in several directions, I found the body of my friend Captain Powell of the 6th and the body of a German officer commanding that post. I took his automatic pistol which we thought a better weapon than our Webley revolvers.

No significant further progress was made from Winchester. From 26 October 1917, the final push to reach the high ground began. The Canadians were allotted the task of capturing Passchendaele; to their left elements of the Fifth Army attacked Westroosebeke (see No 128 again, and 130), whilst on the right X Corps looked again at the Gheluvelt Plateau with the object of capturing the village and Polderhoek Chateau. No 102, about 27 October 1917, shows a wrecked tank – this was the sole mechanised support for the attack on the chateau area. The attacks were designed to convince the Germans that an offensive on a wide front was still in progress; in fact Haig's true target was solely the high ground either side of Passchendaele. The appalling conditions defeated everyone but the Canadians, whose 1st and 2nd Divisions conquered the remains of the village on 6 November. A view of the devastation on the Gheluvelt plateau can be seen in No *129* taken close to Clapham junction near the Menin Road.

By 10 November, Haig knew he could achieve no more in Flanders. After three months of fighting British losses for the campaign now stood at almost a quarter of a million. The breakthrough attempt had failed, although pressure on the grateful French had been relieved. Now British troops and materiel could be provided to assist another ally, the Italians, under pressure following the hammer blow at Caporetto.

After capture and cleaning, the pillboxes on the lower ridge slopes were employed as dressing stations and shelters for wounded, as well as battalion and brigade HQs. Once the line had been carried to the crest and more splinter-proof and shell-proof dugout systems were becoming available, pillboxes were converted into stores for grenades and small arms and mortar ammunition. Many became cookhouses fitted with stoves, chimneys, shelving and cupboards: a bizarre evolution from horror to succour to nurture. The two famous blockhouses at the front of Tyne Cot cemetery (Irksome and The Barnacle) followed this sequence.

For the troops, the winter of 1917/18 was by far the most comfortable since the beginning of the war. Every kind of transport infrastructure was swiftly put in place, and a swathe of deep dugout schemes commenced. By March 1918 dozens of safe shelters were either finished or nearing completion. Several had been installed along the ridge crests, most with specially built OPs for artillery and survey – perfect locations for panoramic work. The most forward positions at this time were no longer trenches but outposts. Located on the forward slopes of the ridge and manned by four of five men, the posts would give early warning of attack and hold it up, allowing the garrison in traditional trench lines near the crest of the ridge to prepare a defence. Many posts were connected to the trench line by tunnel so that the troops could withdraw safely. It

Above
German 1916 panorama of Zonnebeke village. By November 1917 hardly a brick lay unbroken. Compare with Panorama 127.

Below left
Panorama 127. The Zonnebeke battlefield in the midst of conflict, with the church. September 1917.

Below
Panorama 102 showing the Polderhoek sector and the single tank which assisted the attack here in autumn 1917.

Overleaf
Canadian troops move through a shattered Ypres.

was another aspect of the evolution of tactics. Panorama 131 from Primus dugout just outside Passchendaele village, and 130 from its neighbour De Knoet on the Broodseinde ridge, illustrate the novelty of being able to look down upon German lines. The masking on 131 is due to its being photographed through a special aperture in an observation 'hood' at the top of a dugout shaft, the hole being deliberately cut to an irregular shape to disguise the position. The front lines were well-located, heavily defended, and well serviced and supplied, whilst the rear areas within the Salient now enjoyed the abnormal pleasure of being able to work entirely unobserved save by aircraft and balloons. They took full advantage, and the 'old' Salient was transformed.

The happy situation was not to last long, however; in April 1918 practically all the territory so hard-won during Third Ypres was voluntarily given up in defensive preparation for what was to be the final German attempt to take Ypres: the offensive of April 1918 – the Fourth Battle of Ypres.

Fourth Ypres, 1918

The German advance began on the Somme in March. It was expected, but because of a general dearth of manpower there was little to be done but defend. Whereas the German armies had been hugely bolstered in the West by the release of men from the now defunct Eastern Front, British and Dominion troops had been forced to transfer units to other theatres such as Italy, and from the Salient to bolster defences in front of St Quentin and Peronne. French troop numbers were also no longer growing; indeed they were not even stable but falling, whilst recruitment in Britain was able to supply less than 20 per cent of the numbers Haig required. The universal shortfall left the lines protecting Ypres seriously under-garrisoned. Withdrawal was unavoidable.

Panorama 131, taken close to Mousetrap Farm on 28 May 1918 reveals how in this sector the British were forced to pull back to the very lines which they had sought but failed to consolidate exactly three years earlier. A striking

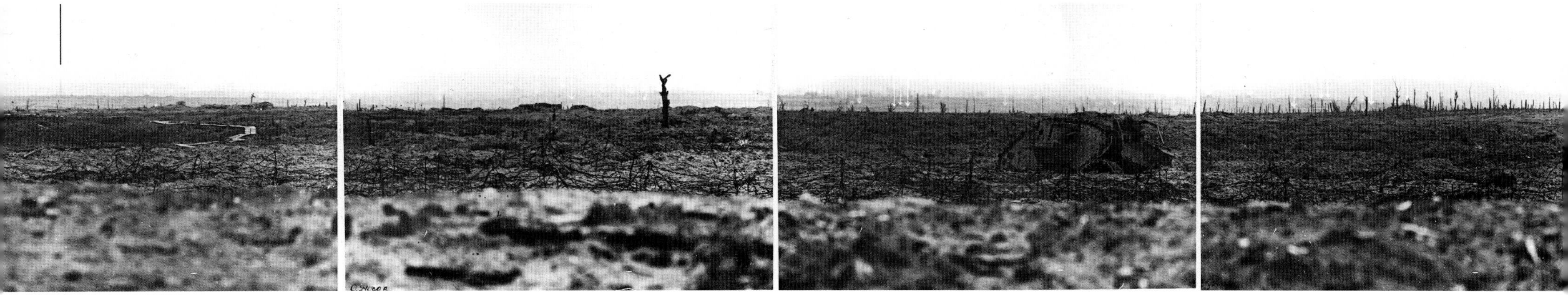

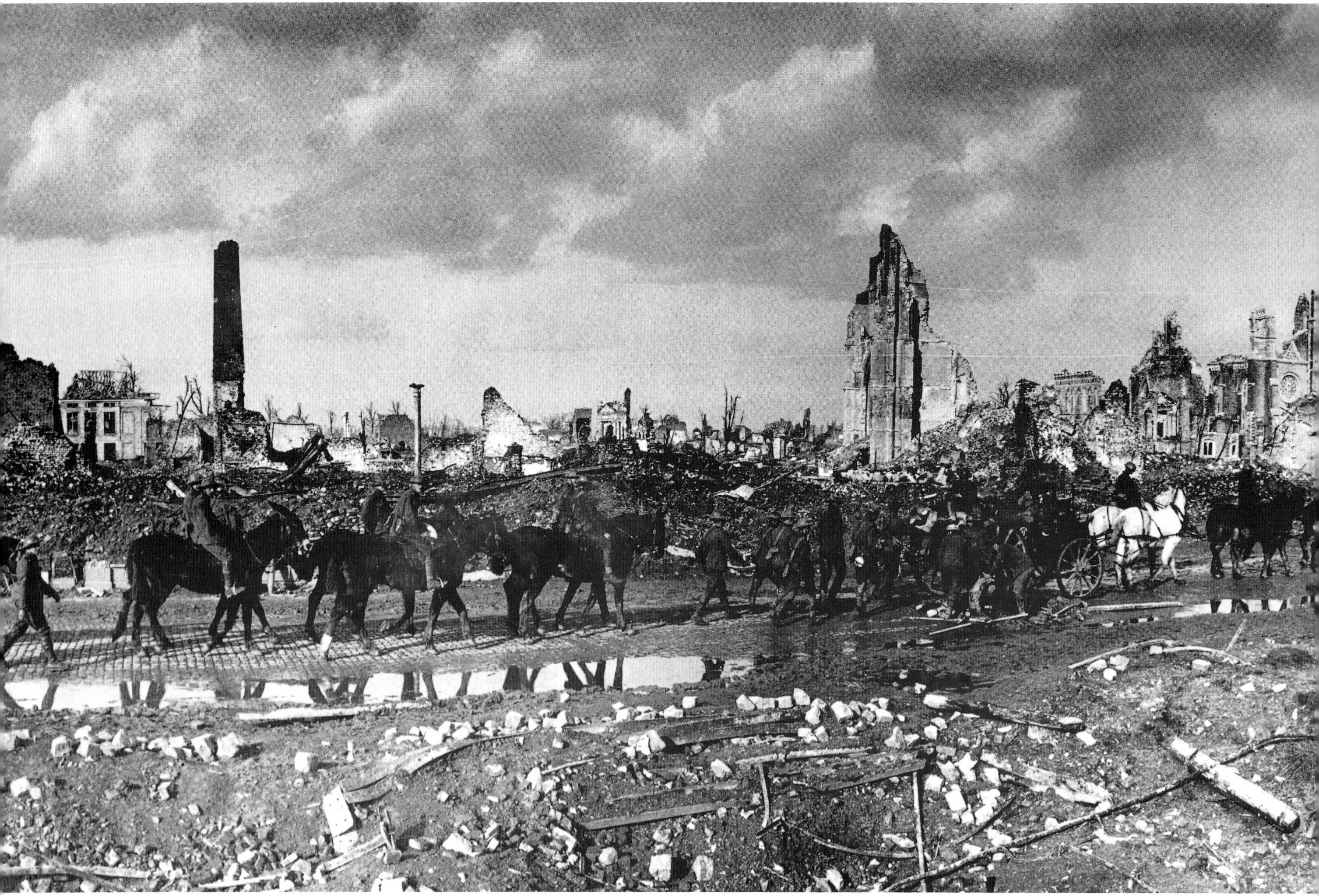

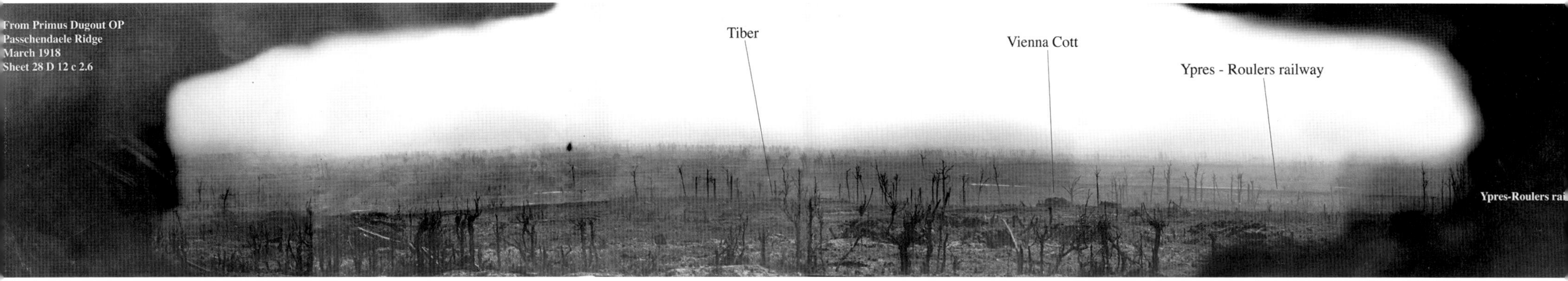

aspect of the picture is how nature has reclaimed the old battlefield. Although skeletal trees speckle the landscape, scrubby growth has replaced the bare earth of the previous autumn. Immediately behind the camera position lay an enormous area of railways, sidings, tramways, heavy artillery and RE dumps, surrounded by small clumps of hutted camps. A large and famous German concrete command post 'Cheddar Villa' is marked. Captured on 31 July 1917, this emplacement, now populated by cows, still exists and can be easily seen from the St Jean–St Julien road. It is especially well-known for the tragic events of 8 August 1917. The blockhouse was packed with wounded and resting men when a German shell entered the 'unreversed' doorway, killing many and grievously wounding others.

To the east of Mousetrap the German advance reached Hellfire Corner, whilst south of Ypres the British were pushed back to trench lines which bent round behind the town. Panorama 172 shows the village of Dickebusch on 8 August 1918. Between 1915 and April 1918 this sector was the site of great hutted and tented camps for troops on rest. At that time it lay almost 4 km (2.5 miles) behind the front lines; now it was the battlefront, with the German positions running through the village itself. The extent of their advance is indicated by the Messines Ridge lying far in the distance. The British positions – the GHQ lines built in 1915 and 1916 specifically for such an eventuality – held firm at this point. It was the furthest the Germans would advance at Ypres.

The next action in the sector involved a development that most thought never to see and many did not live to witness – the advance to victory. It was across these fields on 28 September 1918 that the Belgian Army strode, driving the enemy from the battlegrounds of First, Second, Third and Fourth Ypres. After four years, it took less than half a day to clear the whole of the Salient – only a little longer than the Germans required when they reappeared in 1940.

Above

Panorama 131, taken through a special observation slit, at the top of a shaft attached to Primus dugout on the Passchendaele Ridge. Within a few weeks of completion this position had been evacuated.

Below

Passchendaele reoccupied in 1918. German troops pass along what was once the main street.

Cottage H.28 a 24
Indus Farm H.28 a.20.
Panorama No. 172 made on 18.8.18 from H.27 b.70.70. SHEET 28
including a field of view of 65° from about S.E. to S.
(Approximate Scale of Degrees (1 degree equals 1·07 inches).
0 1 2 3 4 5 6
1. Panoramas are taken solely for military purposes.
2. The publication of them in the press will necessarily give valuable information to the enemy.
3. This Panorama is to be kept with as much security as is compatible with full advantage of it being taken by our own troops.
4. When troops are relieved this panorama should be handed over to the relieving troops.

Right

Searching for the bodies of missing soldiers after the war. Specialist teams quartered the ground of the entire Salient seeking clues to battlefield burials. An estimated third of a million men still lie undiscovered in the fields.

Below

Ypres, 1919. Hotel Ypriana: one of the first hotels to open up for business after the war. The initial trickle of pilgrims quickly swelled to a flood.

26.10.18

The journey was interesting in one way and that was we passed through all the battlefields of Ypres and Passchendaele: it was worse than I expected – for miles and miles the ground was just like Vimy or Messines ridges – all shell holes overlapping, with the exception that all the ground was thick oily mud and a good deal of it under water completely. There were an enormous number of German pill-boxes – especially on Passchendaele Ridge. There were no trees anywhere – just a few broken stumps to show where Polygon Wood had been and every trace of a house had disappeared. Ypres itself was of course completely ruined and not worth rebuilding I should think. The first inhabitable village we saw after passing Poperinghe was Dadizeele [see Panoramas 101 and 130].

Lieutenant J.R.T. Aldous MC, 210 Field Company RE

Below

18 August 1918. Panorama 172 marks the maximum extent of the German advance near Ypres during their great push in 1918. The Allied advance to victory began from these positions soon afterwards. Note heaps of British stores.

CHAPTER FOUR:

THE FORGOTTEN FRONT

ARMENTIÈRES TO GIVENCHY-LES-LA BASSÉE

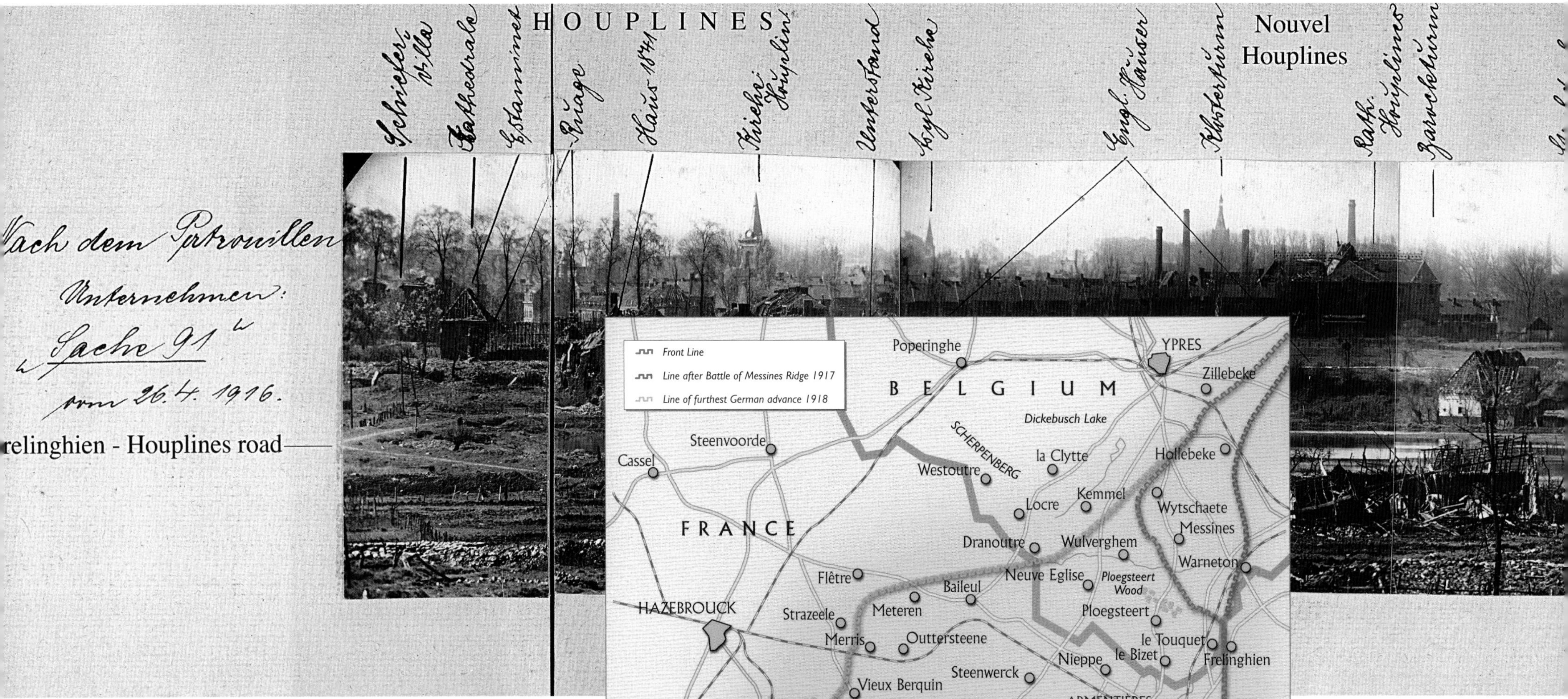

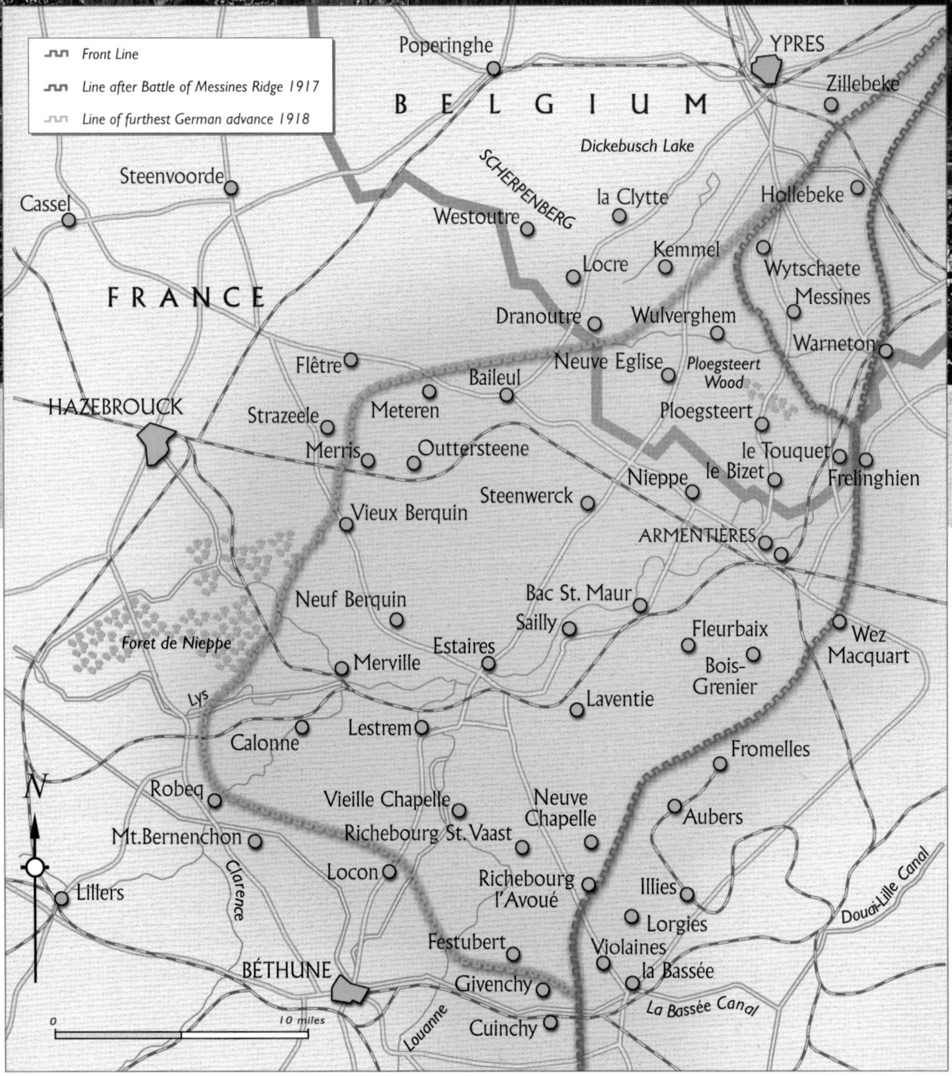

17 November 1915 – Aubers

I have learnt during the last few days that the most exaggerated stories of Flemish winter mud do not exceed the reality. The mud varies in consistency from the creamy variety of the adhesive kind which holds you fast like bird-lime and would suck off the long India-rubber hip boots with which the troops are now provided were they not strapped to the waistbelt, as they are. The country we have come to is flat, low-lying, and swampy. So sodden is the surface soil that trench-digging is out of the question, and the defences consist of lines of breastworks built up of sandbags.

Captain Rowland Feilding, 3rd Battalion, Coldstream Guards

Page 190–91
Panorama 121 from Chapigny Farm, showing the Aubers battlefield

Above
German Panorama G-12 looking from Frelinghien across the flooded River Lys, 26 April 1916.

Lying within the boundaries of ancient French Artois, the 'forgotten front' comprises the northern section of a wider battlefield zone covering the ground from the south edge of Ploegsteert Wood at the foot of the Messines Salient, skirting Armentières and following the Aubers Ridge to La Bassée a few kilometres north of Loos. To those who served there, these sectors were every bit as notorious as the battlefields of the Salient and the Somme, but today the flurry of encounters in 1915, the sole 1916 engagement in July at Fromelles, and the German advance of spring 1918 have largely faded from the collective memory in favour of the grand Somme and Passchendaele offensives. It is true that little of great strategic note was to happen until the German and Allied offensives of spring 1918, but despite its relative tranquillity, the forgotten front holds a unique appeal. The explanation lies in the seminal character of the 1915 battles, and the way the troops – of many 'remote' nations including West Indians, Australians, Canadians, South Africans and New Zealanders and Indians, plus the Portuguese, came to deal with the logistical problems posed by the distinctive nature of the battlefield terrain.

Armentières

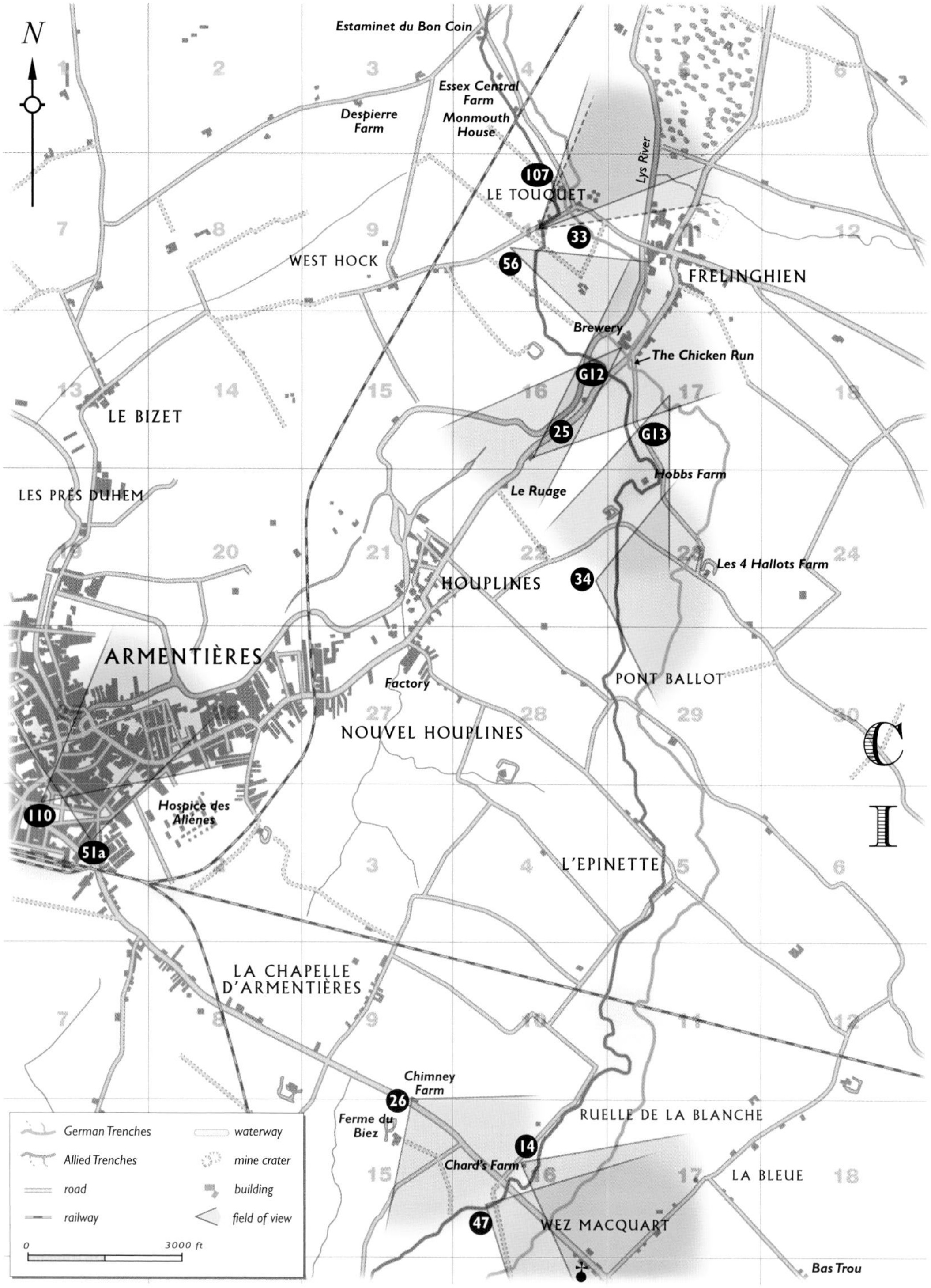

The light industrial town of Armentières, straddling the border of France and Belgium, was an important British focal point. It was first occupied on 17 October 1914 by General Pulteney's III Corps winning a race with an approaching a Bavarian division to it. This was the Battle of Armentières (13 October to 2 November 1914). Well served by good roads and railways, the town became an arterial hub for troops and supplies, housed infantry and artillery headquarters, and in its many terraced streets, provided ready-made billets for thousands of men.

Armentières was the regional depot for mountains of stores, and especially notable as one of several centres of manufacture and supply of the wide range of home-made trench warfare apparatus described in earlier chapters. Panorama *51A* from the tower of St Roch church in spring 1915, and No 110 (2 May 1917) from a factory chimney, present the British view of the entire Armentières sector over the rooftops the town. The German prospect of the sector and the River Lys can be seen in *G-12* (26 April 1916), with G-13 as its left hand continuation. See number 25 for the opposing British view on 29 January 1915.

Being barely 2 km (1.25 miles) from the front Armentières was a natural and undemanding target for German artillery, and was subjected to regular bruising between late autumn 1914 and spring 1918. Like a great many other towns and villages behind the lines, some local residents risked staying behind to benefit from the endless tide of troops which ebbed and flowed in search of a plate of egg and chips, a glass of thin beer or wine, or satisfaction of a more corporeal nature. The presence of local shopkeepers, labourers and merchants created a sense of

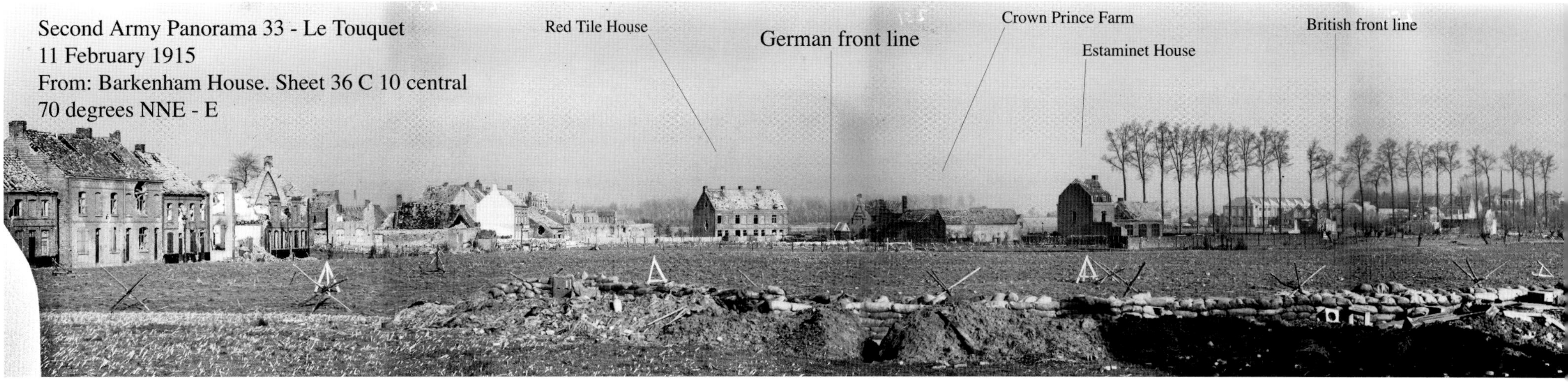

Above
The village of Le Touquet, from Barkenham House on 11 February 1915 (Panorama 33), and in May 2005. Remarkably little has altered here over the decades.

continuing commerce redolent of many small industrial towns in Britain, and 'fancy' unmilitary items, gifts, newspapers, and everyday comforts could be bought. Eventually, in early 1916 the persistency of the enemy guns persuaded the military authorities to evacuate the last of the civilians. When heavy shells pitched into the town red brick dust hung in the air, and as buildings caught fire streams of silver lead ran from the rooves of the ornate houses. Despite its dangers, many soldiers looked upon Armentières – and nearby Le Gheer, Le Touquet, Frelinghien, Houplines, Pont Ballot, L'Epinette, Wez Macquart, Rue du Bois and Bois Grenier – with affection, partly because, like Arras far to the south, they managed to retain a modest and somewhat peculiar degree of normality which transferred almost into the trenches themselves.

Le Gheer, being in Belgium, has been classified as a part of the Messines region, so the northernmost sub-sectors of the forgotten front are Le Touquet and Frelinghien, sitting respectively on the west and east banks of the Lys River. Two excellent Le Touquet panoramas show the village 'evolving' into a miniature attritional battleground. Number 33 taken in February 1915 shows a very simple single British trench line with the most meagre wire defences; number *107*, from December of that year offers us an entirely new impression. Once more the reason for the damage is the advent of underground warfare. In *107* – practically the same view as 33 – the houses have been torn apart by mines. The reason for its appearance is clear when one views the distance between the opposing lines. Had they been further apart, discouraging the tunnellers, damage would very probably have been minimal. Note also the Lys River in the background. No. 56 shows the view from Le Touquet across the river to Frelinghien, a town which was entirely in German hands (see also 25). As usual, the hotspots – even on the forgotten front – were the mining areas.

September 1915 – Bois Grenier

Everything was new to us as we tramped long through Grispot to the shattered village of Bois Grenier, where our advanced dressing station was concealed in the cellar of a brewery. Here we were lent a guide who led us along a road [see Panorama 11a] hidden from the Boche by canvas screens, to the entrance of a communication trench. This was followed on until we reach the trenches we were in search of. There was still none of that roar of cannon and rattle of machine-guns which we in our innocence had imagined went on more or less continually in trench warfare. In fact – again our blessed innocence – we had been just a trifle disappointed when, as we were stepping down into the communication trench and were feeling a trifle frightened and rather brave, a noisy little French newspaper-boy came running along the road bawling out "Dailimal paper," and took away a good deal of the glamour of our adventure.

PHILIP GOSSE

Delivery boys, even in the front-line trenches, were far from uncommon in certain sectors. In the Salient, cigarettes, sweets and other trifles were regularly delivered direct to the troops, whilst just behind the front lines fresh bread and buns were available from bakers' boys selling from dog-carts. Around Armentières life on the farms and in the villages just to the rear of the firing line continued relatively normally until the German advances of 1918. Panorama 27B shows the glorious rurality of the sector south of Bois Grenier. Note the man standing up, quite relaxed and secure behind his breastworks. This panorama gives us the first indication of the amount of material required in the construction of defence lines in this region. No 79 of the Aubers front exemplifies the narrow delineation between zones of war and zones of peace – the Battle of Fromelles had taken place only nine days before the latter photograph was taken, just around a kilometre in front of the camera location.

After an abnormally lengthy period in the Wez Macquart trenches south-east of Armentières, 2nd Lieutenant Robin Skeggs of B Company, 3rd Battalion, Rifle Brigade, of whom we have already heard, first came into the line here in October 1914. To a certain degree Skeggs protects his family from the grislier aspects of his existence, mainly sniping at this time, but his letters never-

Below

May 1916: a French couple living at Croix du Bac, less than 800 m (878 yds) from the front line trenches.

Bottom

A Second Army view (Panorama 110) over the roofs of Armentières.

Right
2nd Lieutenant Robin Skeggs outside 'Virtue Villa', his dugout in the trenches near Armentières.

Below
Skeggs' billet in Chapelle D'Armentières.

theless express the ambience and character of the war in the sector – and more. At this early stage, with lines expanding by the day, there was a continuing shortage of troops to man and maintain them. With relief systems not yet regularized into manageable periods, a unit would enter a sub-sector with little knowledge of how long they might be required to stay. After an inordinately lengthy period in the trenches Skeggs described his first taste of billets in the Armentières.

17 November [1914] – IN BILLETS!!!!!!

My dear father, As you see from my address we are at last in billets, and this is a great opportunity to write voluminous letters. The weather has been beastly, so when I heard we were for billets I decided to postpone my outburst of literary enthusiasm.

There is no great hurry for the thick socks. As things are just now I should need no more socks for a month anyway, but I would let you know progress and "degree of depreciation". You see we have done no marching at all since I got here, so one does not wear out many socks. The chief difficulty is the mud, which simply rots the socks, the feet, and everything it meets.

But to come to the present time. These billets!! I feel so overcome by the sense of comfort that I hardly realise the war is still on. You see the Battalion has been in trenches for a month. Today, by way of mild recreation, the Germans shelled our billets with Black Marias. I can assure you we had a very uncomfortable hour of it. By good fortune not one of our men was hit, but some civilians were wounded – most of them women. It makes one furious to see these poor creatures suffering so. What brought it on was one of our heavy howitzers had been shelling them all day very successfully, and this was retaliation. It was a sight after the shells began to drop thick around the houses – men women and children rushing down the street, the wounded leaning on the shoulders of their friends, transport drivers lashing their horses into a gallop to get away from the place, and everyone wondering where the next one was going to pitch.

This billet is an odd place. It is a shop. It contains enormous quantities of paint, crowds and piles of mattresses, boxes of female attire, a cellar of wine, and other things. The old gentleman who calls himself the proprietaire is a town councillor, keeps carrier pigeons, wears clogs and pince-nez, gets very excited and talks in a loud voice, and has many other vices and virtues. We have to climb right up to the top of his beastly old house to look at the pigeons and express our indescribable astonishment and admiration for their beauty and the skill with which he imprints his name on their wings. He is now nearly driving me frantic by turning the hands of the large kitchen clock so as to strike every hour of the day as he winds it up, shrieking to his

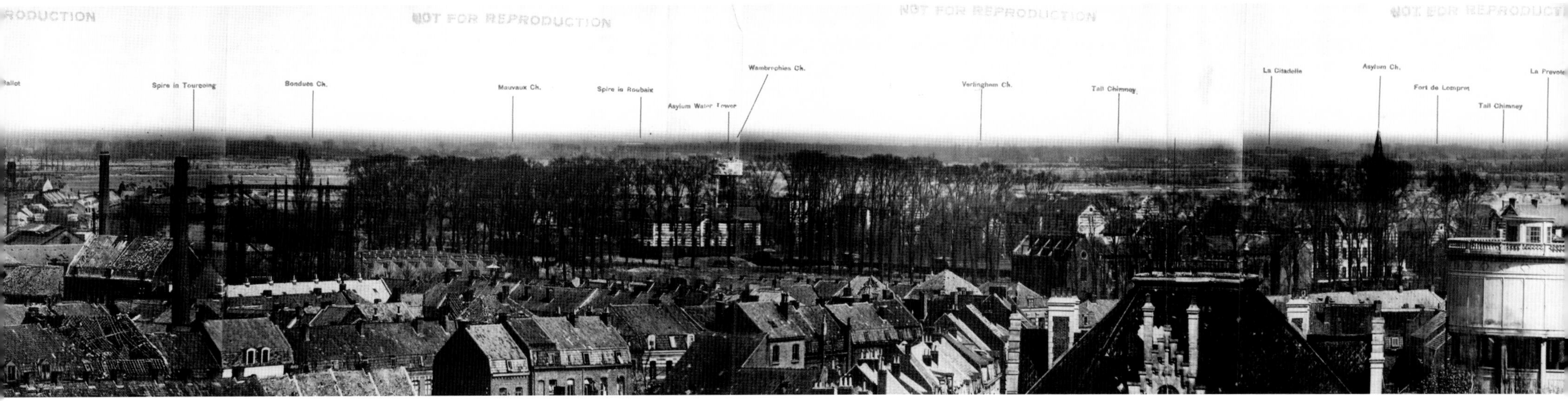

daughter the while about a hen which has or has not laid an egg, or something equally important.

There are five of us in this house. We feed uncommon well under the care of Tuck, the great one. He is the most celebrated servant in the Regiment. Last night for example he dined us on pea soup, roast chicken, cabbage, pommes sauté, rum omelette, a savoury, and wines. Not bad?

We expect to be in these billets for 2 or 3 days longer, perhaps even more, and then in the trenches again. There is some talk of our doing a week in trenches and 3 days billet alternately from now onwards – I don't know whether it will come off. Its just one of many rumours of course.

The sound of heavy shelling which we used to hear far away on our left has subsided now [the closing stages of the First Battle of Ypres], and things seem wonderfully peaceful all along the line here. Now, I must feed! Ever your loving son, Robin.

Skeggs' relief at being out of the line at last is palpable, and it was a feeling everyone who served in the sector at this time shared. The flat clay-based terrain meant that, as at Ypres, the rain took an age to soak away. The sodden ground, and the multitudes of unkempt streams and ditches, meant that water was never far away, creating, with the traffic of men, animals and machines, some of the worst conditions on the Western Front. To the troops, mud was by far the greatest enemy, and there is no diary, official account, memoir or poem relating to the sector which does not dwell upon its qualities. It created acute suffering and not just during winter months – the conditions were replicated whenever it rained.

2 January 1915

I don't want to stop until we have hammered them, but how I wish we could hurry the job up a bit. One regiment here still has an armistice with the people opposite. I was walking along the parapet this morning trying to devise some method of getting rid of some surplus water, when some fool of a gunner put a shell into the German trenches opposite. I thought sniping would probably start after that and jumped into the trench one time. It was only two feet deep in water, I'm glad to say; some are four feet.

Water is a great problem these days. It fills our trenches, it fills our boots, it fills our thoughts, it fills our days and our horizons. There is no room for anything else. I have given up drinking it and washing in it as a protest. The Hun is in the same fix. You can hear him baling all the time, and when we had the Xmas truce we saw him. The water runs from him to us, and we have dammed it up in between, which ought to make him sit up a bit.

DIARY, LIEUTENANT W. A. KERRICH, 55 FIELD COMPANY RE

Upon arrival in the Fleurbaix sector in the late autumn of 1914 Lieutenant Kerrich's section installed over one hundred dugouts, each housing two to four men – a welcome respite for those exposed day and night in the trenches. But after the first bout of winter rains only six remained serviceable, all others being under water. The trenches became so unbearable that digging down was no longer an option: building up became obligatory. Panorama 98 shows the scale, design complexity, and labour required in building breastworks. The structures required so much material that often only the parapet (the front wall) could at first be be built. It left a garrison protected from rifle fire and explosions to the front, but subject to splinters from shells landing to the rear.

The Christmas Truce, 1914

During the first winter the Armentières trenches were little more than ditches. The troops found themselves praying for lengthy periods of hard frost to stiffen the mud and freeze the water. The Christmas Truce of 1914 was one such period, and it was largely the appalling trench conditions which led to a considerably longer outbreak of harmony in the sub-sectors around Armentières than anywhere else on the Western Front.

My other job besides censoring letters is cleaning drains. If something is not done soon everybody in the trenches will be flooded out. We hope, however, to get a drainage system properly working soon, though it's a difficult job in a flat country with clay soil, where it rains every day. We had an Armistice on Xmas day and some of the officers went out and talked to the Germans half way between the two lines. They even drank good health to each other. Conversation was on strictly neutral subjects – the weather, the local beer, ski-ing in Switzerland and fem-

Above
Panorama 47 photographed from the trenches occupied by Robin Skeggs at the time he was in residence – 10 March 1915. The view of no man's land seen here is the exact spot where he experienced the 1914 Christmas Truce.

British borrow pit
German front line breastworks

Below
Skeggs' trench snapped from a sap in no man's land, illustrating the borrow-pit and the British breastwork parapet. This is the exact trench pictured above.

Right
Skeggs and his servant Rifleman John Bricknell, pictured on Christmas Eve 1914.

Left
Winter conditions in the Bois Grenier 'trenches'. A typical scene in French Flanders.

inine fashions. The Germans started it, being the first to come out of their trenches. Soon everyone was out, and all were talking and laughing and wishing one another Happy Christmas like lifelong friends. One officer swore he saw the head waiter of the Carlton among them. I don't think it very likely to happen again next Christmas. One day the Germans shouted "Heads down at one o'clock for your General is coming round." General Heyworth of the 20 Brigade is a very tall man with white hair and affects a big staff to walk with. The Germans got to know him well and used to shout out to our men, "Look out, here comes the General", when they saw him in the distance. Towards the end of the armistice you had to be careful because although the Germans in front might be friendly, you were liable to be potted at long range from an area where war had broken out again. Perhaps the most extraordinary fact of all was that there was never any artillery armistice at all. We discovered that they were as wet as we were. It was during this armistice too that we buried the dead between the two trenches.

DIARY, LIEUTENANT W. A. KERRICH, 55 FIELD COMPANY RE

Robin Skeggs' unit also participated fully in the truce, and Panorama 47 (10 March 1915) illustrates the very place he was serving when the photograph was taken; his letters and photographs relate directly to this image. The picture is taken from the British front line, at this time protected by no more than a few strands of wire suspended from rough pickets. On the far left of frame, evidence of a 'borrow-pit' can be seen, where extra earth has been excavated to fill sandbags for parapets. Strewn across the area immediately in front of the camera are hundreds of butter and jam, bully-beef and Maconachie tins, each an undeviating part of the soldier's staple diet in the trenches. The road crossing the image from left to right (follow the far telegraph poles) is that which is mentioned in Skeggs' letters; the village behind the high German breastworks on the far side of the field is Wez Macquart. Another view, Panorama 14, shows the same sub-sector in the early summer of 1915, and is taken from Chard's Farm, possibly named after Lieutenant John Chard VC RE, of Zulu War and Rourke's Drift fame.

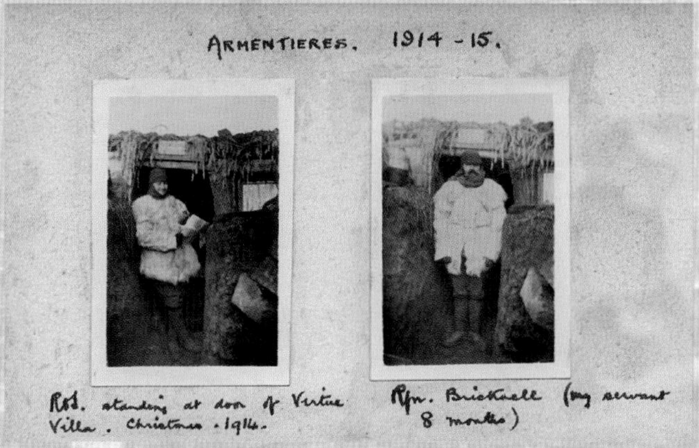
ARMENTIERES. 1914 - 15.
Rob. standing at door of Virtue Villa. Christmas. 1914.
Rfn. Bricknell (my servant 8 months)

26 December 1914 – Same old trenches

My dears, all the promised Christmas presents have duly arrived – and on Christmas day! By an odd chance and partly by good management they gave us two deliveries on Christmas Day. So the watch, pocket lamp, Christmas pudding, Vaseline, boxes of dates, cigarettes, Sphere – indeed everything – arrived just at the right moment. So you see you can rest happy that you provided us all with everything man could wish for the making of a merry Christmas – and we did really have a merry Christmas. I cannot thank you all – never adequately – for all these splendid gifts. The trouble and time and cost involved in finding, making and sending them must have been prodigious. You will be rejoiced to know that we had a complete and absolute truce for 24 hours on Christmas Day (really it lasted much longer), and about this truce I shall have much more to write.

The weather was ideal – a hard frost, and slight mist, but dry; and indeed the day could not have been better in any way. We had every bit as good a time in the trenches as anyone else – with huge yule log fires and so on. But this is only supposed to acknowledge the parcels, so I must not spoil a second letter by dabbling in the Christmas news. I repeat how much we have appreciated the countless good things you sent. Everything was just right – just what was wanted – and nothing superfluous – the plum puddings being simply superlative!

And now to the post office. With much love to all…Robin

The family were forced to wait a few days for Skeggs' literary appreciation of the remarkable events of Christmas Eve and the subsequent week.

31 December 1914 – Out of the same old trenches for a few hours

My dear father, Let me just repeat how very much I appreciated the Christmas parcels. They must have taken some buying and packing. I was very glad to get the new lamp. It is a great boon for getting about a wet trench at night. I now have three refills for it all told. The cardigan is magnificent, the slippers and so on are most acceptable. I have also had a most delightful selection of every conceivable kind of Christmas delicacies. I had two plum puddings (tophole), mincepies and tangerines (also tophole) raisins, three boxes of dates and lots of other things too many to enumerate. The whole show was an immense success – the mince pies even arrived unbroken! In the hurry I forgot to thank the maker for that parkin – it was the best parkin I had ever tasted – and so said all of us! Please send more, I prefer it to other cakes. The beautiful little watch is invaluable for people keep asking the time along the trench at night and one dare not strike a light sometimes.

I really must tell you something about our Christmas Day here. Every day up to Christmas Eve the sniping had been incessant, and very boring, and we had our daily dose of shelling – after meals, one or more. Then one morning a message was passed down the line "No one to fire – from Captain Pigot". I went down to C Company to find out why, and there I found half the company standing up with head and shoulders well above the parapet gazing at the Boche trenches. Apparently Pigot, after much difficulty and perseverance persuaded the Germans to cease fire with signalling to them with flags. He then proceeded to shout across at them and gradually a sort of understanding was arrived at. Whether it was largely his efforts or not – probably a divisional arrangement – I don't know, but anyway a written message came round the company on Christmas Eve to say that the captain desired that no firing should take place between midnight on the 24th/25th and midnight 25th/26th December. What actually happened was this: About 6 in the evening when everyone was feeling very contented after a large tea and because there was no rain, one suddenly realised that there was no sniping going on, and believe me not a shot was fired from that moment onwards. The next thing was the Boche began shouting across to us – they are about 250 yards from us – then our men found their voice and replied. There were several Germans who spoke English so we had salvoes of this kind: "Vee veesh you a merree Christmas – Vee vill play ze football wid you tomorrow" and so on. Our fellows making reply in suitable terms; "Garn, 'oo are yer gettin' at?" and the like. Then a pause. The next surprise was a whole bunch of lamps put up on top of the Germans trenches, until the whole line was lit up with scores of these things, making a weird display. Some of them performed a sort of Punch and Judy dance with them. These were left on until about nine or ten that night. And meanwhile they were singing carols and songs for all they were worth – quite decently too.

We were rather sceptical about all this and were very much on he alert for any unforeseen events – but the Boche were quite genuine and everything was perfectly quiet all night.

Next morning – Christmas morning – my servant woke me to announce that everyone was walking about all over place – he was quite indignant about it. The feeling gradually came over one that there real-

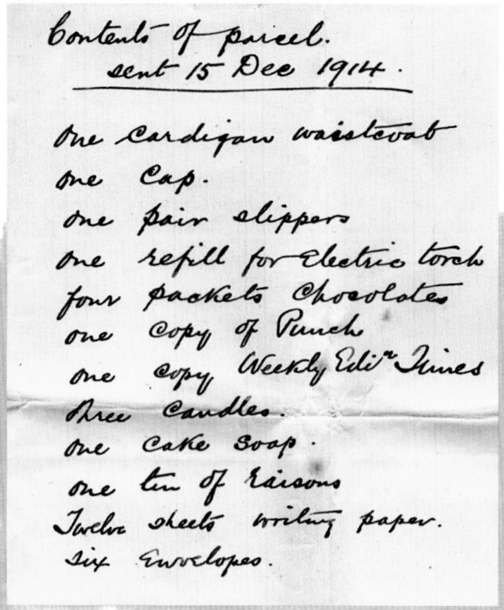
Contents of parcel.
sent 15 Dec 1914.

One Cardigan waistcoat
one Cap.
one pair slippers
one refill for Electric torch
four packets Chocolates
one Copy of Punch
one copy Weekly Edit^n Times
three Candles.
one Cake Soap.
one tin of Raisins
Twelve sheets writing paper.
six Envelopes.

Above
Contents of a pre-Christmas parcel sent to Robin Skeggs – including slippers!

Below
Weather for winter woollies at Wez Macquart. Men of Skeggs' B Company, 3rd Battalion, Rifle Brigade.

Above
An envelope signed for Robin Skeggs by a German soldier on Christmas Day 1914.

Below
Two rather fuzzy but unique views of the Christmas Truce at Wez Macquart. Skeggs was later furious with himself for not taking more care – and more photographs.

ly was a truce, and after several people had stood up on the parapet just to test matters, three of us officers walked over towards the Boche armed with nothing but papers, cigarettes and chocolate. They immediately came out and met us half way, and were quite affable. They said "Good morning, Sir" and so on, and after looking us up and down they began to get familiar. They signed postcards for us. We then said good day, and withdrew. This started the ball rolling and for the rest of the day there was a perpetual stream of men from the trenches to the halfway point. They shook hands, exchanged newspapers, they talked, exchanged cigarettes for cigars, they lit their smokes from the other fellows cigarette, and generally did everything you wouldn't expect them to do.

Both sides were very cheery, and although there were a few sour veteran old soldiers on each side who stood on the outside of the group and glared all the time, most people were perfectly friendly. It was a most extraordinary sight, I can assure you. There were over a hundred men from each side in the group once. There is a road which runs through our lines to the German lines (there is a village just behind their lines) and this was the common rendezvous. Some of their officers came over but were not much disposed to talk. They were very smartly turned out – and clean – but their men were filthy looking little devils. The senior officers mostly carried good bushy sandy beards and were "nice- and- pink- and- white". There were a few fine looking old soldiers among them – one old gentleman with a woman's fur toque round his neck – but the majority were fat sheep-headed little swine with the most diabolical Teuton expression imaginable. They nearly all came from Leipzig and belonged to the 107th Regiment. There were also gunners there – the 77th battery. They all belong to the 19th Saxon Corps. Such a large number of them wore those abominable German spectacles. They all wore the dull grey uniform with jack boots, but none of them wore their helmets, only the little round caps. They looked fat and well-cared for, the clothes in good condition. They had lots of store and good Christmas foods. Their marksmen wear a plaited cord hanging across their chest with a dummy bullet on the end of it. I got some German newspapers from one of them – they tell the most elongated lies imaginable.

They appear to be pretty well sick of the war for all that – but not in the least despondent. They often shout across to us "Are we downhearted? – NO!". A most uncommon good feeling was started between the opposing lines that Christmas day – so extraordinary has the understanding been that hardly a shot has been fired ever since – either way! People walk about on top, and the Germans get up on their parapets to dig, and alter their dugouts and so on – but we are very careful. One does not like to trust them too far. It has been a great blessing this lull, as it has enabled us to get stores of wood and other supplies from a farm nearby which would have been impracticable otherwise – and the supply of kindling wood is a difficult matter here. The men, on Christmas Day came back with a story that the Germans had said they would not fire until after New Years Day, if we would not – and by Jove it was true. It has been an extraordinary week – the big guns shelling away at one another far over our heads, day after day, but never a shot near our trenches. The understanding was only in the infantry. So we have really had a weeks armistice! I don't suppose much trouble will happen even after New Year's Day. On Christmas day the officers of "B" Company lunched together on turkey, plum pudding, and other dainties – so we deserve no sympathy. The weather was perfect – it froze the mud and we had a dry cheery day. We had sing-songs round huge log fires and thoroughly enjoyed ourselves. We had far more fun in the trenches than anybody anywhere else, I'm sure. I must tell you one of Tuck's little humourisms. He is a kind of Mrs Malaprop and continually says this kind of thing: "I see Fortune and Masons 'as sent us some Guillotine of chicken this week" and "We 'ave no salt-anna cake left". He will insist on calling a refuse pit a refuge pit and talks about the "consecrated" cocoa.

I am very sorry to say Sergeant Arnold was killed about a week ago. Shot clean through the head while directing fire from his trench. I was very grieved myself, for he was an awful good fellow. We had two sergeants in one platoon shot within 10 minutes that day – and yet we go for days without a man being hit.

About leave. I have long wondered whether to mention this to you. If I ever get any leave it won't be till about March, so I thought it better to say nothing about it. All the fellows go first who actually came out with the battalion, and only one at a time can go. The leave is for 10 days, of which two are spent in going and returning. I am about 6th or 7th down the list – so you see…? I say "if" I ever get any because if we start to advance, I don't see how we could go away on leave. And I suppose we must advance in a few weeks time – surely.

Now it is getting late and I must trek back to the trenches – about half an hours walk by the road – about an hour and a half and wet knees by the communication trench. We hope to have another pleasant day tomorrow – New Years Day. Every good wish to you all my dear folk, and to all old friends, for 1915.
Much love, ever your loving son…Robin.

Robin Skeggs' subsequent testimony offers us an outstanding portrait of the character and development of this unique sector before his departure for the Ypres Salient in June 1915. Having enjoyed a passive, festive and frosty end to 1914, the New Year brought not only the return of hostilities, but the inevitable nightmare of a thaw.

11 January 1915 – In Billets

My dear father, the address is "In Billets" – a very significant but deceptive address too, on this occasion. I will tell you why. We duly went into the trenches on the 9th, as I wrote you in my last letter. Trenches forsooth! We were warned before leaving billets that among these new trenches are some particularly bad. I and my platoon dropped in for one of the bad ones. We floundered about for an hour after leaving the road to get to our new trench – a distance of 400 yards from the road. I had to sit on top of a bank for 20 minutes hauling my men up, another man standing at the bottom shoving. Eventually we reached the "trench". The relieved officer indicated to me that that my trench was "there to there", and refused to show me round it – the customary courtesy. So I then proceeded to skirmish round to find out where the trench really was. I slipped down a ladder into water two feet deep, scrambled out on the opposite side into mud nine inches deep, crawled about for some minutes, and, finding nothing of interest, crawled back. I then tried wading along the trench, and got out of it when the water came up to my hips, to go back and fetch my platoon. We all waded through the water and eventually found the fire trench, which we proceeded to man – this was only one foot deep in water. We then set to work to dig ledges at the back of the trench to sit on, so that people's feet would be out of the water, at least. Of course, by this time we were all wet through, some only to the knee, some up to the armpits (one man fell into a trench where the water was five feet deep). So I ordered one man in three to run up and down all night (in turns) to keep their limbs warm. No one slept in that trench all night. We simply sat and shivered – try as you might, you could not keep your legs from rattling. With the arrival of daylight we simply had to sit still in the trench as the sniping was accurate.

The story ends by my telling you that we were relieved at 8 o'clock that night, and here we are in reserve billets dry again, but with men feeling very groggy. We are just going back to the trenches, but pray Heaven to a dry trench this time.

Still, we are cheery. Why not be? Its all in a days work. Expect to go into billets again very soon. Must be off now, much love to you all my dears…

The lines from which this letter was written can be seen in the finest view of all of Wez Macquart: Panorama 26 taken on 29 January 1915 from a mill building behind the line. The picture adequately conveys the desolate ambience that Skeggs describes. Chard's Farm is the tall farm building to the left of the road (No 14 is a later panorama taken from this spot). The roadside ditches are almost full of water, indicating the conditions troops had to contend with in the trenches. The solitary British line crosses the road just past the second bend; beyond lies no man's land and the barricades where the two sides met during the Christmas–New Year period. Note that there are as yet no communication trenches, just pathways to and from the line.

Above
Panorama 26: another view of the Wez Macquart sector from the chimney at Chimney Farm, 29 January 1915.

Below
Another Skeggs Truce picture showing the roadway pictured above and Skeggs' own photo – like the panorama, also from Chimney Farm.

Above
Spring 1915 – a scene in the front line breastworks at Wez Macquart snapped by Robin Skeggs.

Above
Skeggs' sketch illustrating his method of negotiating trenches and breastworks at night.

Right
Robin Skeggs' front line trench at Wez Macquart photographed by him during a particularly wet period in the 1914–15 winter.

The quiet sector

With the onset of spring and dryer weather the Armentières sector settled into a period of unusual and surprising peace. Apart from the odd belligerent but generally harmless 'demonstrations' where one side or the other sent over a few trench mortars and blasted away on the firestep for a while, the peace was broken only by snipers, the risk of which was heightened or lessened by the degree of caution exercised by the individual. The ambience and activities here stand out in stark contrast to what was simmering in the Ypres Salient at the same period, where the second battle was about to burst into life. Boredom and monotony was widespread. During the Battle of Neuve Chapelle (south of Armentières) in March 1915, Skeggs was so frustrated he bicycled down one evening to view the aftermath. As time passed, still with no sign of the kind of dashing action, he occupied his thoughts with designing improvements in and machinery for the trenches. His letters from this period include sketches of bulletproof shields, petrol-driven trench-digging machines, trench mortar designs, and several pleas for heavier guns (his father worked at Vickers in Sheffield, at that time producing artillery), all apparently required to be sent by post direct to the trenches. By the middle of April, however, the monotony was such that his thoughts were diverted by a fresh and yet more surprising activity.

16 April 1915 – Billets

My dear Father, Things are so quiet here we begin to wonder when they are going to declare war. Just opposite us they have hardly fired a shot at night during the last week, and it is frankly obvious from that, that they are up to some dirty work. Working on their wire or, I believe, digging a new trench just in front of the old breastworks. Anyway, they evidently are desirous of our keeping quiet, and they hope to do it by telepathy or suggestion.

The new notion of tinned fruit is a great success. Trotter happened to have some Devonshire cream the very day your fruit arrived, so we simply wallowed in loganberries and cream. I'm sure the blackberries or whatever they are will be equally good. Those and the soups do splendidly.

We are having very good weather. The fire trenches are bone dry – perfect – and flowers are coming up in the farms so we are transplanting them to the trenches! We have now several beautiful gardens along the trenches and just behind the breastworks. We plant turf and evergreens, apple trees, violas, daisies and all sorts. It would be a

strange subject for an artist. The sentry on duty midst lovely flowers, while the myriad 'jectiles swish around in showers!!

I am going to try to work on a pond and a fountain with gold-fish and a tennis lawn to fit round it. We have built a wonderful headquarters dugout village now. A sort of street paved with bricks, lined on either side by houses occupied by the O(fficer) C(ommanding) Company, the CSM, the signallers, the stretcher bearers, Tuck the cook, and the officer's mess – with gardens in between, along, and round about. We have a company notice board with a glass front, post boxes (pillar boxes) and goodness knows what else.

The next company to us have a bugle and a huge bell now. They blow mess calls and allsorts of things. It sounds so like barrack life now – it is almost like manoeuvres!

We have heard a lot about this battle for Hill 60 near Ypres, and this morning about 5 to 5.30 there was fearful bombardment somewhere miles to our left. I fear some poor devils were going through it. Probably Hill 60 again.

Will you send out my brown shoes – you know, the brogues. They will be excellent to wear during this hot weather, and I propose to get some shorts also – football breeks. These are for trench wear. I believe half the army will be asking for them soon.

I have been busy building myself a summer dugout. It is a light structure with a thick wooden roof lined with canvas. Bricknell and I made it entirely ourselves. The gardens cheer one greatly, and reduce the gloom of the bare mud. That is really why we worry about them. The fruit trees are just coming into bloom, and really the place is not looking so bad at all. I hardly ever thought Wez Macquart could look anything but depressing.

Hopwood has had a mess hut built, so we all mess together again, as we used to months ago – 5 of us. It is a delightful sunny little shed – like a tiny cricket pavilion, with 2 windows.

Best of wishes, dear man, and again many thanks for the ripping cap, Ever your loving son…

The day after this letter was written the Germans began using long range guns for the first time. The day after that tear gas shells were used for the first time at Hill 60. The contrast between the events unfolding in the Salient just a few miles to the north, and life on the Armentières front, is further defined in a subsequent letter Skeggs sent to his grandmother. She would have received this when the second battle was at its peak, with British newspapers concerned with poison gas attacks, lists of casualties, and the BEF everywhere falling back towards Ypres.

8 May 1915 – Trenches

My dear Granny, I'm writing this sitting in my garden at the back of my dugout. It is a lovely afternoon. The sun is going strong and there is just sufficient breeze to prevent it being too hot. We have laid a certain amount of turf already, and as I write there are three youngsters around me as busy as they know how. One has sloped off a bank to his satisfaction and is laying more turf along it. This is acting Corporal Hook of farming fame. Then Lilliot is preparing another piece of ground, while Reid, my horticultural expert, is planting violas, daisies and other things. He is bestowing such care on a little rose

Left

Sketch of shield requested by Skeggs. His father occupied a senior position at Vickers in Sheffield.

Above

Robin Skeggs' sketch of a front-line firebay at Wez Macquart complete with flowers, shrubs and fruit tree.

Below

First Army Panorama 27B shows a benign summer scene in the Bois Grenier sector, August 1915.

Above

A trench garden at Bois Grenier with proud horticulturalist.

Below

Robin Skeggs' sketch of his 'dugout village' at Wez Macquart and (inset) 'Something for the weekend?' The Queen's Regiment trenches at Fauquissart, April 1915.

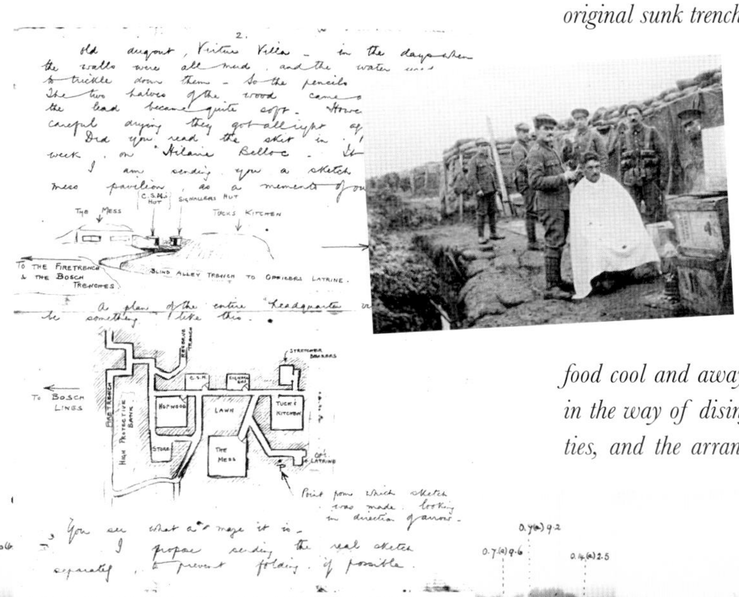

tree which he found this morning. It is being placed in a bed of its own and carefully tied up to a stick, while two shoots have been put in just alongside the dugout, and are to turn into crimson ramblers with a bit of luck. They thoroughly enjoy doing a bit of gardening "for the officer". I wish we could get some creepers – Canariensis or something that will climb and grow quick. You would like my garden seat because it is very sheltered from the wind in a snug little corner which gets the sun all day.

Now to answer Aunty's question: How can we make all these things in a trench? Well, they aren't in a trench really. It is a huge sunk area – all dug out for one purpose or another during these past seven months. Of course, you begin with a small trench, then when the wet weather came we had to raise the front parapet and fill in the trench partly, because of the floods. Thus we could crawl about behind under cover of the parapet. Gradually this bank has been raised, and earth has been dug away and dug away behind the trench until it is possible to walk about on a thing like a tennis court, all under cover of the parapet in front. So in these sunk areas we build all manner of things. I have just had father's very welcome letter and he too expresses surprise at our making gardens behind the trenches. Of course, there are now great lengths of breastworks along the line, mostly behind the original sunk trenches, and behind these raised breastworks, which are six or seven feet high, one can walk about across the field and so on, provided you don't go too far behind.

We are being extra careful now about sanitation you will be pleased to learn, simply on account of the approach of hot weather. I am going to the length of constructing well fitting wooden cupboards, which will be let into the ground on the north side of a bank to keep food cool and away from flies. All this in the trenches. Other things in the way of disinfectants and so on are provided in liberal quantities, and the arrangements for boiling all drinking water are being perfectly organised. These are all precautionary, preventive measures – not curative – you will understand. Aunt Ruby's parcel of respirators for the men has just come in. They are most excellent – much better than the ones issued to us a few days ago. I will send them round to the men shortly. We are particularly glad of them just now as we handed our others over to some people in the trenches. I understand the method of using the alkali. We have been most carefully instructed by the medical people exactly what to do. It has been dinned into the men many times this week. We now wear a special bag slung round our necks to carry the respirators in. They are never to be taken off whatever the man may be doing. We have tins containing water and a solution of soda every 2 or 3 yards along the trenches, and special big appliances for "gas fighting" have been issued. So really the war office have done quite well. Very many thanks to Aunt Ruby for making the respirators. They are just the thing. I think I have enough now. They may save us awful trouble. Well, very much love dear Granny, ever your loving Grandson…

The final flourish in Skeggs' section's desperate quest for adventure came just before the Rifle Brigade departed for Ypres warmer climes. This letter, however, was not written but received by Robin Skeggs. It came from his servant Rifleman John Bricknell, and was posted from St Thomas' Hospital, London.

Well now Sir I will just try and explain what we done on the fatal night. As you know me and Cpl Morris were working together, when we got to within a 100 yards of their trenches we advanced one at a time and I did not hear any think but Cpl Morris told me he heard someone talking on our left, and I told him it was one of those birds we generally heard at night, but we moved on again and got to their wire when we noticed some men moving on our right, and which I took to be a saphead, there seem to be a good few of them, at first I was for lying still, but eventually I took Morris's advice, then we decided

to retire, so I told Cpl Morris to get back about 15 yards while I covered him, then I got back, then he moved again, when I suddenly discovered some men on our left, they were very close and I let go at them, then I made a rush for it, but had only got a few yards when I was hit, it knocked me down, I could hear them moving in the grass, I also heard talking which sounded further away. I crawled for a little away, I fancied I heard footsteps very close to me so I got up and made a run for it, and I think I run for about 150 yards before I came across the connecting file who helped me back how I managed it I can't say. I was about knocked when I came across him.

I am sorry I failed in flying the flag on their trench I was most anxious to get it their. I think it was the grass that gave us away, it was very long in places, and I think their idea was to capture us, I am glad now I cheated them.

The Dr allows me up in a wheel chair since Wednesday morning, I can manage to walk about 20 yards with the aid of a stick, walls, beds etc, but I am doing fine, and shall soon be out with you again. Kindly remember me to the platoon.

Wishing you and all the boys the best of luck. Yours respectfully,
W. BRICKNELL

B. WHEN HE IS WARNED TO PARADE THE COMPANY FOR TRAINING.
THIS IS BRICKNELL WHEN HE HEARS THERE IS AN EXTRA RUM RATION TO BE ISSUED.

Bricknell and his pal Corporal Morris had made a wager with their 'orficer' that they could plant a Union Jack on the parapet of the German front line trench. 1916 continued in the same vein. Units had their meals in the open air, with officers sitting around tables with linen cloths. In the Laventie sector (christened The Nursery – see Panorama 79) the German line was known to be only intermittently occupied: a soldier known as 'The caretaker' marched along the trench twice a day firing his rifle from time to time. It is said that British troops would often visit the enemy lines before dawn and return at dusk, hoisting a green flag occasionally to signify 'all's well'.

The evolving trenches

Panorama *34* from Houplines, just north of Armentières, illustrates the next stage of the evolution of the Western Front and the trench lines that proliferated year-on-year. Although a few knife-rests are still visible, wire defences have now been substantially augmented by dense thickets of coiled and 'apron' entanglements. On the far right a large painted board indicates the point where trench numbers change, an intricate delineation system used throughout the Western Front. The photograph is taken in May 1915 from the British support position – a line which has been added during the winter months – and here shows half-trench, half breastworks, with earth banked up in front of the sandbag parapets for increased protection. The German breastworks lie on the far side of the grassy meadow – a distance of around 300 m (328 yds). The object marked as 'Alexandra Bridge' is a trench crossing; literally a bridge to

Above
Suppertime on the Forgotten Front. 1st Battalion Cameronian's HQ mess at Houplines, 18 November 1914.

Left
Skeggs' sketch and photograph of his servant, Rifleman John Bricknell, complete with lunch outside 'Virtue Villa'.

Above
A segment of Panorama 33 showing 'aeroplanes' in front of the trench.

Overleaf
Panorama 56: a view of Frelinghien across the River Lys from 'The Butcher's Shop' in Le Touquet. 15 April 1915.

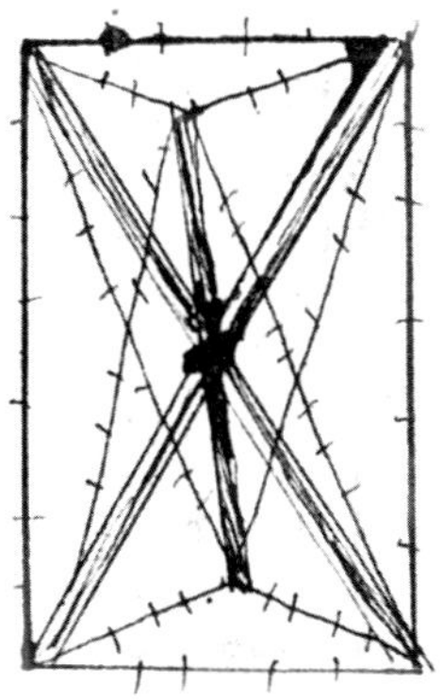

Below and right
An 'aeroplane' (right) and a 'knife-rest', two common forms of simple structures for suspending barbed wire.

allow easier access to and from no man's land.

Primitive early defences can also be seen in Panorama 33, of 'front line village' Le Touquet, also north east of Armentières. However, closer inspection of this picture from Barkenham House on 11 February 1915, reveals certain differences to those taken only a week or two earlier. In the British front line a sniper's loophole is evident, whilst on the far side of no man's land the Germans have driven their own loopholes through the high brick wall incorporated into their front line. That panoramic rarity, a soldier, is visible in the British trench in the form of supremely unconcerned-looking Tommy in standard issue soft cap – the 'gor-blimey' unbeloved of sergeant-majors in search of smartness. The camera angle makes him appear rather exposed to snipers. The wire beyond the parapet, although still somewhat spindly, is suspended from 'aeroplanes'.

Just before Christmas we ran a line of low wire entanglement in front of the high wire we had put out previously. It is not such a good obstacle but it does not get shot away so quickly as does the high wire. The 55th gave up trying to wire in front of the bad spot and adopted the system of throwing out 'aeroplanes'. Why so called, no one knows. They are of different kinds but the best one consists of three long sticks placed side by side, bound together at the middle, and then opened out. Barbed wire then joins up all the ends as shown in the sketch. They are simply thrown over the parapet. Afterwards, when the enemy has stopped shooting at them, one man may crawl out and tie them all together. This next type [the knife-rest] is more usual, but its not nearly so good because when the wire is shot away it's no obstacle, whereas the first type is still pretty difficult to get over as long as the sticks remain tied together.
Lieutenant W. A. Kerrich 55 Field Company RE

It seems peculiar to think of enemy troops deliberately shooting at barbed wire, but the activity is noted in many diaries and reports. The other common support, the 'knife-rest', was of little use as a deterrent without wire, and it was at this time that more effectively designed entanglements were being developed. Kerrich also emphasizes the importance of continually developing his defences during the winter months, and how when snow was on the ground the engineers worked wearing rectangles of white cloth, draping it over themselves like a tabard. In Panorama 56, showing Le Touquet's larger neighbour, Frelinghien, the trenches on both sides of no man's land are almost universally protected by knife-rests. On the right the River Lys is in spring (March) flood, and one can discern the point where the German lines 'hop across' the meandering waterway, becoming re-established on the far bank in front of Frelinghien. The British trenches followed suit just south of the town and these can be seen in Panoramas 25 and G-12.

Several mining schemes were commenced in the Armentières area, despite the presence of water-saturated running sands sitting upon impervious blue clay – just like the Salient. Panorama 33 was taken not far from the spot where British miners of the Northumberland Fusiliers secretly installed a pipe which siphoned river water from the Lys into German mine workings that had been accidentally encountered underground. The trick flooded them out and prevented work for a considerable period. These workings were shallow, and known as the Chicken Run. One of the British shafts is marked in *G-13*.

Aubers, Neuve Chapelle and Fromelles

South of the Armentières sector lies Aubers Ridge, a belt of country about 5 km (3 miles) deep and 15 km (9 miles) long. No extended periods of fighting devastated this ridge; but by directly shielding the important French town of Lille and German communications and supply hubs, it was always a potential setting for a major British offensive. The ridge itself, barely rising 15 m (50 ft) above the plain was hardly an outstanding topographical feature in peacetime; in war, however, it totally dominated the terrain to the north and west. It was to be the scene of several British struggles in 1915 – and the site of a tragic failure the following year.

For the first two years of war German defences along the slopes of Aubers Ridge were largely restricted to well-constructed and well-concealed trenches. The battles of 1915 and 1916 – Neuve Chapelle, Aubers, Festubert and Fromelles – encouraged greater investment in security, and in 1917 especially there was a substantial increase in the installation of reinforced concrete strongpoints. Like the trenches, pillboxes were organized in depth both in the front lines and the many villages dotted along the ridge crest, where almost every house concealed a camouflaged emplacement. German communication and access to the entire sector was excellent. Assisted in large part by forced local labour, careful advantage was taken of the proximity of Lille by improving roads, building light railways, and extending existing electric tram lines. The whole of the German forward area also benefited from Lille's mains electricity resource. Connecting most front line emplacements and dugouts to the power grid allowed powered pumping schemes to keep German trenches dry and comfortable. And even the concrete for pillbox construction was mixed electrically. The British enjoyed no such extravagances.

When the Allies finally overran the sector in 1918, the crest of the ridge was found to conceal huge numbers of observation posts, far more than had been suspected. Twelve were discovered in Aubers alone.

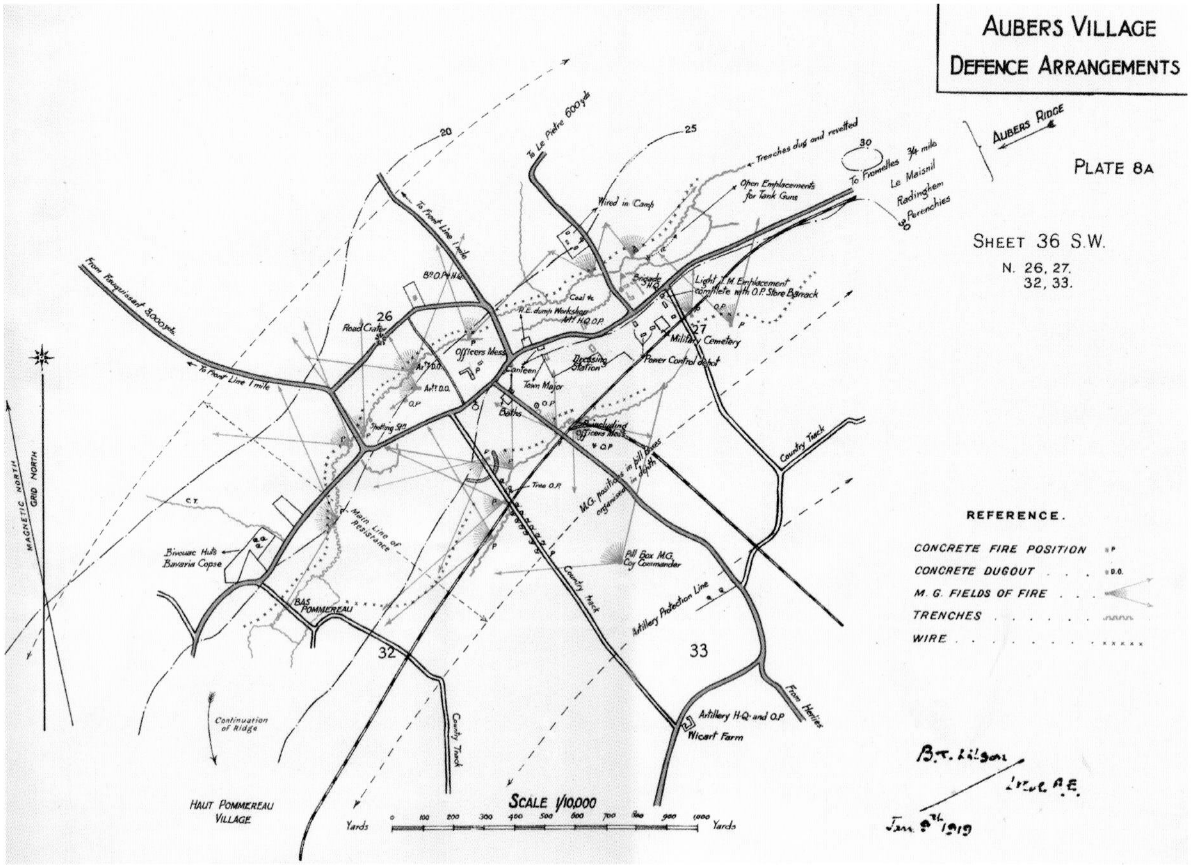

Above
A post-war survey of enemy defences at Aubers. The village was never captured by Allied attack, but was eventually evacuated by the Germans in autumn 1918.

Right
Typical German work on the Aubers Ridge: installing concrete strongpoints within buildings.

Background
A wooden trench tramway near Fromelles built by British engineers.

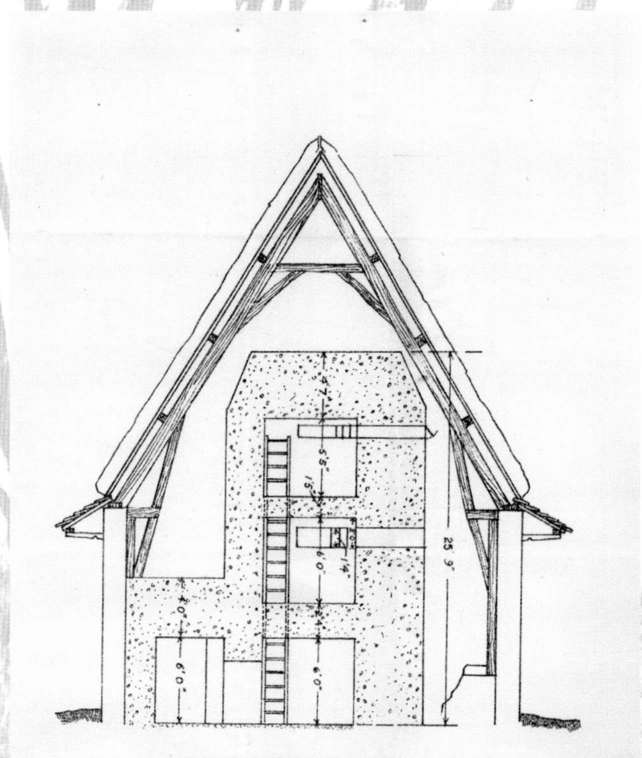

5 October 1918

Yesterday morning at 8.15, we resumed the advance through country devastated by the enemy, and by twelve (noon) had occupied a position just north of Le Maisnil (27), in front of Lille. It was an interesting march. The road has been very thoroughly mined [land mines, not tunnelled] by the Germans during their retirement, and great craters block the way at frequent intervals. We passed through the old German front and support lines. Never, in the course of the war, have I seen anything so elaborate. Whether they thought that some day we might make a frontal attack on Lille I do not know, but they have certainly put their best work into their defences here. There are hundreds of miles of barbed wire, and reinforced concrete so massive and so much of it that this portion of the line will remain a monument to the war for all time. All has, however, been blown up and abandoned, and the immensity of the destruction almost rivals that of the construction of this would-have-been impassable barrier – had the enemy chosen to defend it.

COLONEL ROWLAND FEILDING (EX-COLDSTREAM GUARDS)
1 CIVIL SERVICE RIFLES

The panoramas show most villages incorporating a brickworks, brewery, and a distillery, as well as the ubiquitous mills, all of which were substantial buildings, each requiring a chimney. Fitted with several stages of floors and ladders, these were used by observers, not least during the first major British offensive engagement of 1915.

Neuve Chapelle, 10-12 March 1915

The first set-piece confrontation by the BEF on the Western Front, Neuve Chapelle was a 'tuning-fork' battle, helping to set the tone for British offensives for the next three years. It was also a test: an opportunity to put an end to French taunts that because Britain had launched no offensives of her own, she was just an also-ran in a war in which most of the fighting and dying was being done by her allies. Sir John French, the BEF's Commander-in-Chief, made the decision to attack at Neuve Chapelle, whilst First Army commander General Sir Douglas Haig, later to succeed French as C-in-C, formulated the plan. The strike was to be carried out by IV Corps and the Indian Corps, with four divisions attacking on a front of around 3 km (2 miles). After capturing the salient with Neuve Chapelle village at its core, it was hoped that the Aubers Ridge might also fall; success might even present the opportunity of an advance upon Lille.

After careful reconnaissance (with aerial photography being used for the first time), artillery planning and swift and efficient troop concentration, the initial attack on 10 March 1915 was preceded at 7.30 a.m. by a bombardment of a little over half an hour by the greatest force of artillery the British could muster – over 340 mixed calibre guns. Haig's essential tactical requirement – surprise – was achieved, and in several places British and Indian troops overwhelmed elements of the single German Sixth Army division in residence. In under four hours Neuve Chapelle village was largely in Allied hands. It was a splendid start; soon afterwards a wedge a kilometre deep and more than three wide had been driven into the German lines.

13 March 1915

I'm mixed up in the business that is in the papers [Neuve Chapelle] but have done nothing exciting. It is most cheerful to think that we are going forward. We have taken a lot of prisoners. I don't know anything nicer than seeing a string of Bosches coming down the road – it makes you feel that you have done something. Everybody now is eagerly awaiting news of K[itchen-

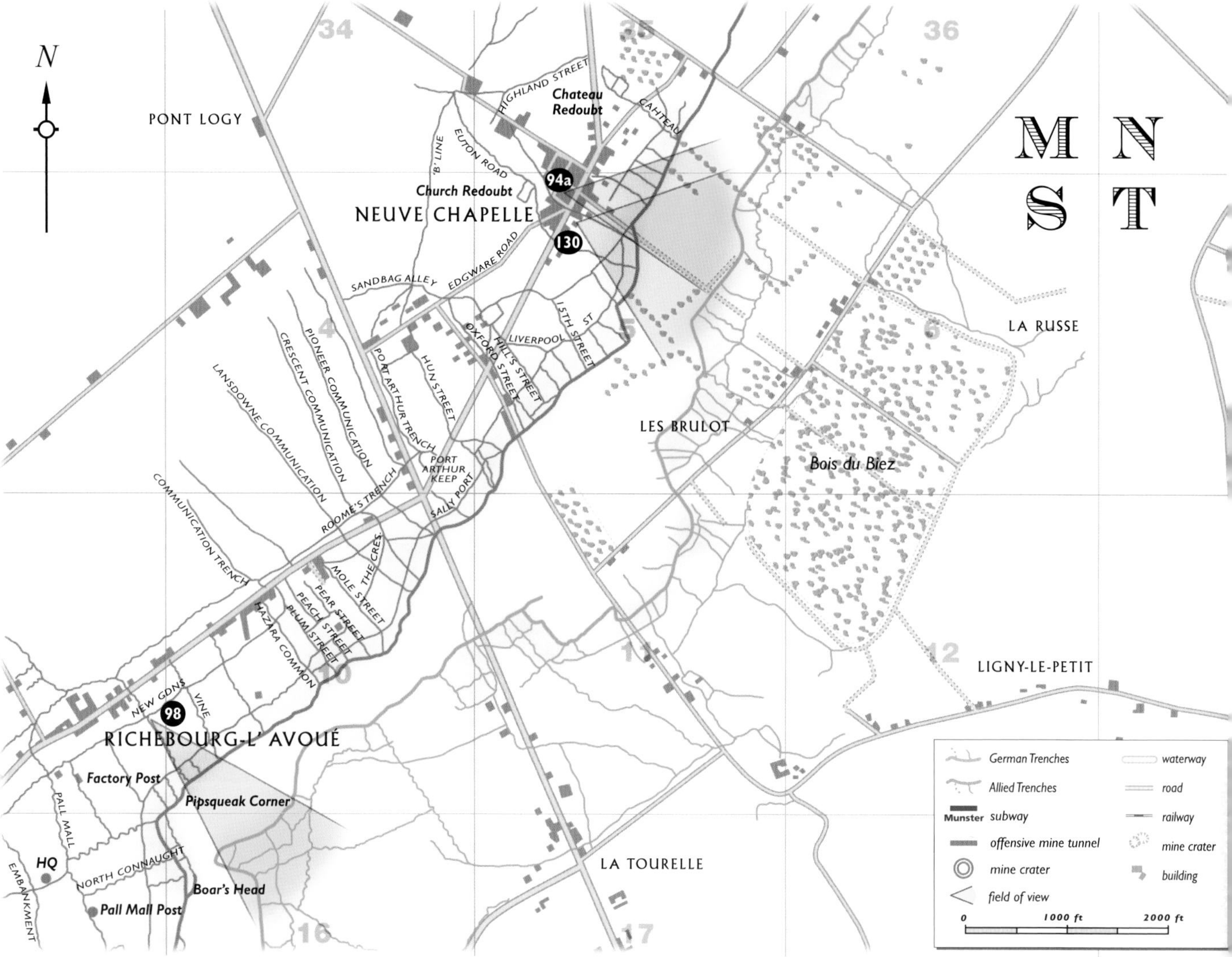

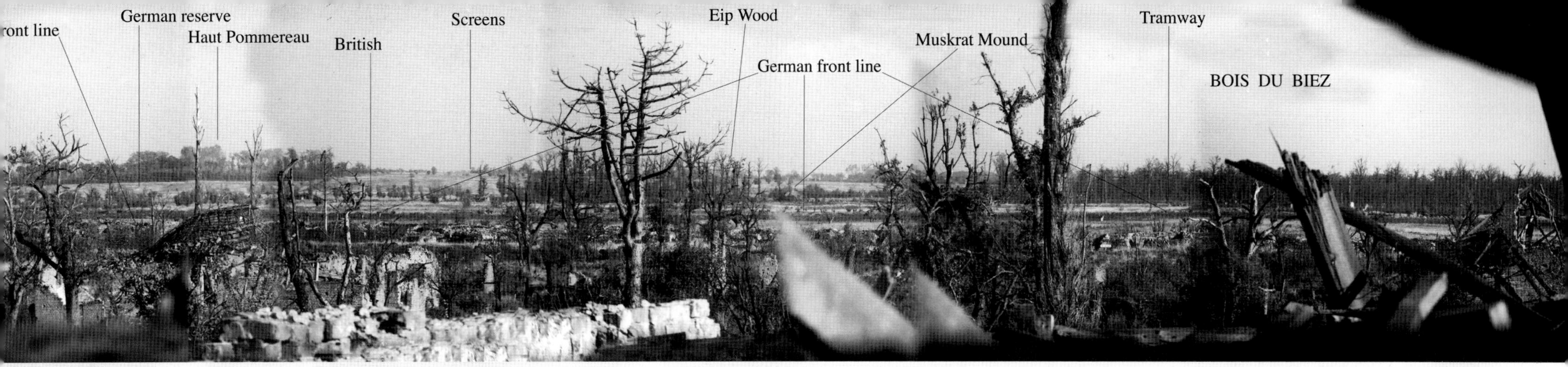

Above
Panorama 94, taken from positions in Neuve Chapelle on 21 October 1916. The village had been captured in March the previous year.

Below
British Cameron Highlander casualties close to the German parapet at Neuve Chapelle.

er]'s army. I suppose they must be coming as hostilities have recommenced. I believe the Germans were caught absolutely napping, and that we had hardly any casualties taking their front line of trenches. We attacked at least a month too soon for their programme.

16 March

We are pretty hard at it here. The German trenches that I have seen are not a patch on ours, so all these yarns about their being specially prepared are all rot, here anyway. We are on night work strengthening the new position we have taken and the dead lying around make it rather gruesome. There is no moon at present but the continuous stream of flares that the Germans send up to see if we are attacking makes an excellent light to work by. They are rather alarming at first until you learn that its absolutely impossible to shoot by light of a flare; all it can do is to let you know that the enemy is or is not attacking you. From the number of them that the Bosch is sending up I guess his nerves are badly on edge. I don't know what Bosch means, no one can tell me, but as it is a French term of contempt I expect it is something pretty bad.

DIARY, LIEUTENANT W. A. KERRICH, 55 FIELD COMPANY RE

Some began to think that a major breakthrough was imminent. Haig too had been optimistic, placing five divisions of cavalry behind the lines ready to exploit a breach. But then the edifice began to crumble. Although the new tactic of isolating an enemy position by laying down a curtain of fire to cut off both evacuation of forward troops and reinforcement from the rear was used very effectively (it was the first time the word 'barrage' was seen in a British report), the meticulous pre-battle planning and control dissipated soon after fighting had begun. Dispositions of attacking troops became unknown to Corps commanders, and officers in the thick of the action received fresh orders from their superiors only intermittently. Reports reaching HQ were faulty, leading to exhausted units being asked to push forward into areas thought to have been captured, but which were actually still strongly occupied by the enemy. The hiatus in communication became permanent, and the Battle of Neuve Chapelle dribbled to a halt, reverting to purely defensive consolidation in the lines which Lieutenant Kerrich's company were improving. The Germans hustled fresh troops into the sector, heavily shelled the captured positions, and on the second day launched a 16,000-man counter-attack against the Indian Brigade, an attack that was brilliantly and bravely fought off.

As soon as the battle was over engineers began to repair roads, close up window openings and doorways, and install loopholes. As the Germans plastered the village and its arteries with retaliatory shellfire, it was dangerous work. Panorama 94A shows an October 1916 view from 'Heath Robinson' observation post in Neuve Chapelle village. The panorama has been taken through a gap in the broken tiles of a roof. These positions would be held by the British until the German offensive of 1918. Panorama *130*, taken from a house on 'Edgware Road', immediately south of the village in August 1917, shows a summer view of the battlefield; the lines are still in exactly the same location as spring 1915, but have been greatly developed. Again, with a water level just over half a metre (1.5 ft) beneath the surface, breastworks are obligatory.

Although the village would stay in British hands, the Aubers Ridge, seen in the background of No *130*, still stared grimly down upon the troops. On 12 March Haig ordered another assault – without the benefit of artillery. The German wire remained uncut and defences undamaged, and this time the attack also lacked surprise. It is said that of those who went forward, none were to return. The next day, 13 March, with British and Indian troops around Neuve Chapelle hanging on to about 2 sq km (less than a sq mile) of newly captured territory, the offensive was finally called off. Casualties totalled around 11,000, with the Germans posting similar figures. Although the attack was more of a failure than a success, the British, in their inimitable way, took heart from the fact that an enemy position had at last been captured (as had 1,200 men), and if they had been the ones who gained ground, some form of defeat must have been inflicted. There was also the question of pride – the BEF had finally fought an independent action.

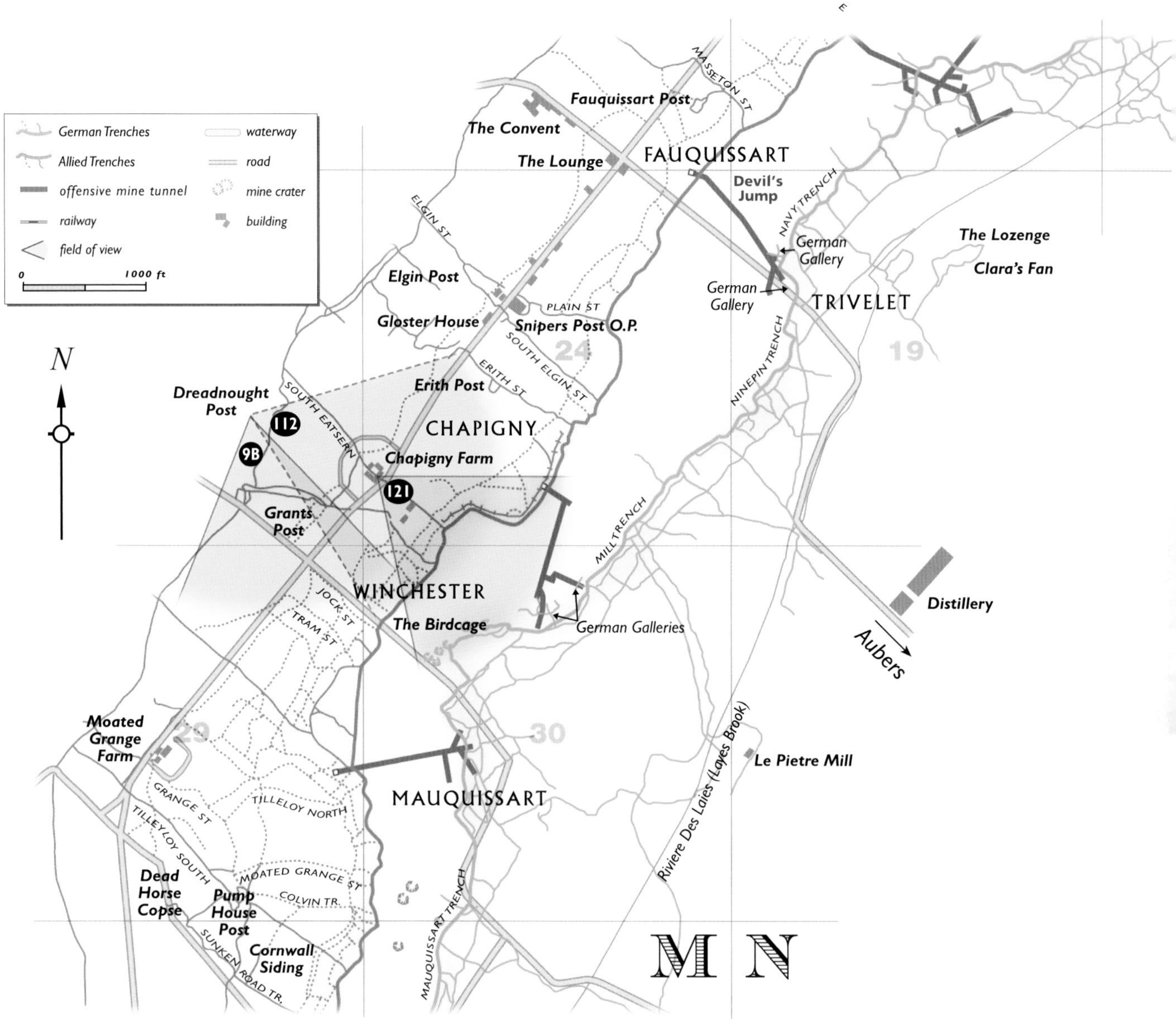

Battle of Aubers Ridge – 9 May to 19 June 1915

The next British attempt to storm the Aubers Ridge was a cooperative endeavour, and integral to a great French ambition. With the object of breaking through to threaten Douai and Cambrai and disrupt German lines of communication to other sectors, the French Tenth Army under General Foch would to attack the higher ground between Arras and Lens (including the Notre Dame de Lorette and Vimy Ridge system). Meanwhile the British First Army (I Corps, IV Corps and the Indian Corps) commanded by General Sir Douglas Haig, were to assault positions along the Aubers Ridge between Bois Grenier and Richebourg. See Panoramas 11A, 10 April 1915, for the northern limit of the battlefront, *9B* for the centre including the village of Aubers (compare also Nos *112A* and 121 with this panorama), and

First Army Panorama P 121
5 June 1917
From: Chapigny Farm
Sheet 36 M 24 c 1.4

Right
German searchlight sweeping no man's land at Houplines, seeking British patrols and wiring parties.

Below
A constant problem: RE signallers mending and laying multiple telephone cables to maintain permanent communication.

28 for Richebourg L'Avoue to the south of Neuve Chapelle, a frontage of about 15 km (9 miles).

Assisted by a five-day bombardment the French advanced quickly on day one, sweeping over German defences on the heights of Notre Dame de Lorette (see No *136* in the Chapter Five), into the valley beneath, and advanced well up the slopes of Vimy Ridge itself. But that was to be the extent of their success. To the left on the flat battlefields of Loos and Lens, and to the right at Arras, progress was grim: reserves failed to arrive on time and after three days the attacks faltered. There followed weeks of bitter, brawling and bloody trench to trench skirmishes, considered by many at the time as a wasteful perpetuation of the battle. It gained little for the French, whose losses totalled over 100,000 when fighting eventually terminated in June.

To the north, the British First Army was at a disadvantage from the start. The Second Battle of Ypres was still raging, soaking up troops and materiel, other essential resources had been siphoned off to support the Gallipoli campaign, and the entire BEF was suffering from shortages in every department. Nevertheless, preparations were comprehensive. Forward assembly positions were dug, plus new communication trenches; steps were cut in parapets for attacking troops, light bridges constructed for crossing ditches and streams, and portable artillery bridges fabricated to move field guns and other heavy materiel forward into newly captured ground. The northern hinge of the battlefield, the responsibility of IV Corps, can be seen in No 15, with the central sector incorporating Aubers village in No 86. Panorama 79 provides the wider vista of this battlefront from the British reserve lines. These three panoramas also cover the Battle of Fromelles front a year hence, described later.

Although GHQ had been determined to correct the mistakes made during the March assault at Neuve Chapelle (Nos 94, *99*, 121 and 130) ensuring that communication was improved, German wire cut, and defenders demoralized by a 'hurricane' bombardment, the 121 guns of the British artillery were only supplied with sufficient shells for a forty-minute barrage prior to the attack, the destructive and dispiriting effect of which was crucial to potential success. Many shells were also found to have been poorly manufactured, ending up as duds.

Despite the deployment of signalling aircraft, the battle was again characterized by confusion. The German defences were far stronger and better organized than anyone had imagined, and there was again a clash of order and counter-order, in this instance over the timing of an afternoon renewal of the assault (the support troops arrived long after earlier attacks had failed). Once more commanders in the line suffered from slow and poor communication with those directing the battle from the rear. The result for the first day: 11,500 casualties and tiny gains.

The territory assigned to the Indian Corps, once more around Neuve Chapelle where they had suffered so badly in March, can be seen in No *28* from Richebourg L'Avoue. The positions at the end of the battle are seen to be still occupied in No *130* taken on 17 August 1917. An excellent and surprising wide view of the rear areas of this complete sector can be seen in No 112 taken on 19 May 1915.

Below
First Army Panorama 121 from Chapigny Farm shows the Aubers battlefield in 1917, two years after the attack.

Festubert – May 1915

Haig's request to immediately renew the Aubers assault was overruled, but Joffre and Foch had no intention of allowing the British to rest, and encouraged an already willing Sir John French to attack again in a neighbouring sector. On the night of 15 May the second bout began, this time a little further south at Festubert, a battlefront which had been established during the first Battle of Givenchy between 18 and 22 December 1914 (see No 21).

With the benefit of a sixty-hour preliminary bombardment by 433 guns, the advance here was impressive, with British and Indian troops of the 2nd, 7th, and Meerut Divisions overrunning the German front lines and forcing the evacuation of several support positions. The attack was launched at 11.30 p.m., surprising the Germans; with later support from relieving 74th, 51st, and the Canadian Division (the latter having enjoyed a brief rest after their heroic defence of Ypres), an area of enemy territory almost a kilometre deep was captured. However, the gains grew more meagre with each successive day, and fighting was brought to an end beneath pouring rain on 27 May. The southern edge of the battlefield with its old and new lines is well illustrated in No 21 (12 July 1915), and in the left-hand half of No 74 taken from Givenchy village.

Casualties at Festubert reached a dreadful 17,000, a figure which dismayed commanders, troops, politicians and public alike, but it had been a striking effort from a tactical viewpoint. Many believed that the only reason for the cessation of fighting, and therefore the lack of greater success, was a shortage of shells to continue the bombardment of the enemy, softening them up in advance of successive waves of infantry. People of influence felt there was more than a little substance in this theory and tacticians began to muse upon devising the 'perfect' artillery fire plan for future offensives. It was here at Aubers that the original mould for Allied battle tactics on the Western Front was conceived: the accurate, prolonged and intense pre-battle bombardment was soon to be seen as the elemental ingredient for success.

It was also during the Aubers offensive that the uproar known as the 'shell scandal' emerged. On 14 May *The Times* reported that losses and failures were in large part due to a shortage of artillery shells. Public concern turned to outrage, and Asquith's Liberal government later fell. Most countries underwent their own versions of the shell scandal, but none had the same intensity nor created the same repercussions.

The territorial result of Aubers and Festubert for the British was the capture of around 13 sq km (5 sq miles) of ground, little of which was of useful strategic value. But there had been a sea change in tactical thinking: the British decided to prepare properly for a major breakthrough by taking a break from offensives here for the rest of 1915, increasing the ratio of heavy guns to field guns, and building up a substantial stockpile of ordnance (properly manufactured and reliable). They also started planning a

Above
First Army Panorama 21 showing part of the Festubert front after the battle on 12 July 1915. The ground is mainly flat, low-lying and wet, hence the name *Marais* – marsh.

Below
A signaller sheltering in the lee of captured German breastworks at Festubert.

colossal Anglo-French offensive for 1916. The days of narrow battlefronts were over; now GHQ was talking of attacks covering 30, 40 and 50 km (18, 24, 31 miles). In November 1915 winter again immobilized the front, and as in 1914 Christmas was a relatively peaceful period along the length of the line.

25th December 1915

X'mas Day. I have spent Yuletide in many climes and under various and diverse conditions but this X'mas, although uneventful, will always be, in many respects, unique. "Peace on Earth, Goodwill towards man". There is this year a bitter irony in the words. The conventional compliment "A Merry X'mas" springs to our lips from force of habit, but dies unuttered as we realise the cruel mockery of the words. "A Merry X'mas"? with half the peoples of the earth clawing and snarling at each others throats. 'A Merry X'mas"? when millions of aching hearts are suffering in silent bitterness and eyes long dry with lonely weeping are flooded anew before the vacant chair, as memories of him who sat and ate last X'mastide and is now no more, crowd through the mind. "A Merry X'mas"? with the gnawing fear, the aching suspense, the ever-present dread of bad news eating the joy out of so many hearts. No, there could not be for those at Home "A Merry X'mas".

But out here our lot is easier. The dear folks at home talk feelingly of "our poor soldiers', but it is they who really suffer most. Our danger is real enough but it is apparent, tangible. We realise it, we see it, and can grapple with it. We are spared the agony of uncertainty and dread which is the lot of our loved ones.

And so it was natural that we should seize the opportunity to make merry. For a little while we could forget the horror and the hideousness of war. Tomorrow we go out again to grapple with the task we have in hand, to do our work, quietly, cheerfully, without heroics or ostentation in the English way, but today at least we will revel, we will forget. Probably for these reasons X'mas in the firing line was in spite of everything, more cheerful and real than at home.

It may seem rather heartless, but personally I can truthfully say I never had a better time. The guns were very quiet which was something to be profoundly thankful for, as it enabled us forget the things we did not want to remember, at this season of Peace and Goodwill.

There is no better tonic for the appetite than active service and we did full justice to the ample fare. I regret to record that by the time we adjourned, just before midnight, several of my distinguished company were in that highly hilarious state of partial inebriation generally described as "tight". Probably many of the pure-puritan, sanctimonious church-going saints at Home would turn up their eyes like drinking hens in holy terror if they knew. But our consciences were clear. It was a little harmless revelry which allowed us to forget for a little while the hideous ghastliness of war, and we felt better for it.

Captain Matthew Roach MC, 180 and 173 Tunnelling Companies

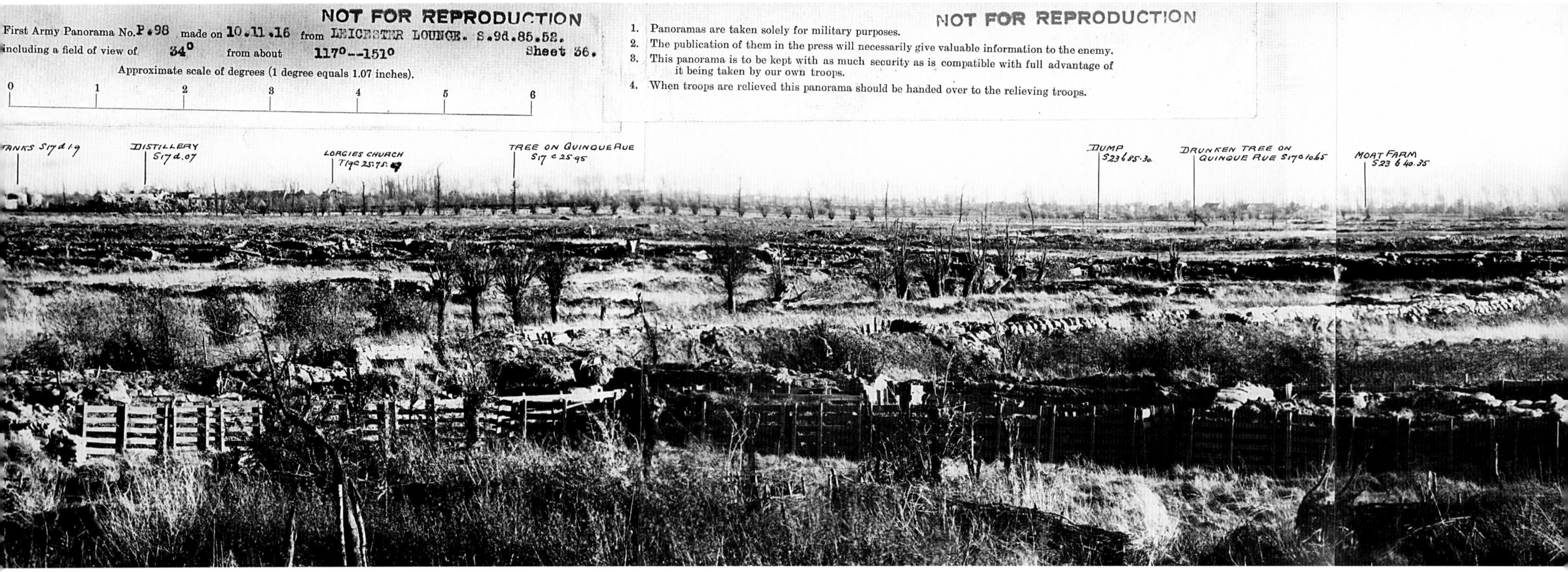

Development of fieldworks on the Forgotten Front. The top panorama (No 16) taken in May 1915 shows a single simple breastwork. By the end of the following year (No 98 – 10 November 1916) defence lines were multiple and formidable.

BRITISH LINE CROSSING DOTTED ROAD BETWEEN 15 & 12
GERMAN FRONT LINE BREASTWORK. NEAR LA QUINQUE RUE
NORTH BREASTWORK IN THE DISTANCE
N. END OF K5 WORK
K5
SOUTH BREASTWORK
NORTH BREASTWORK
NORTH BREASTWORK
SOUTH BREASTWORK

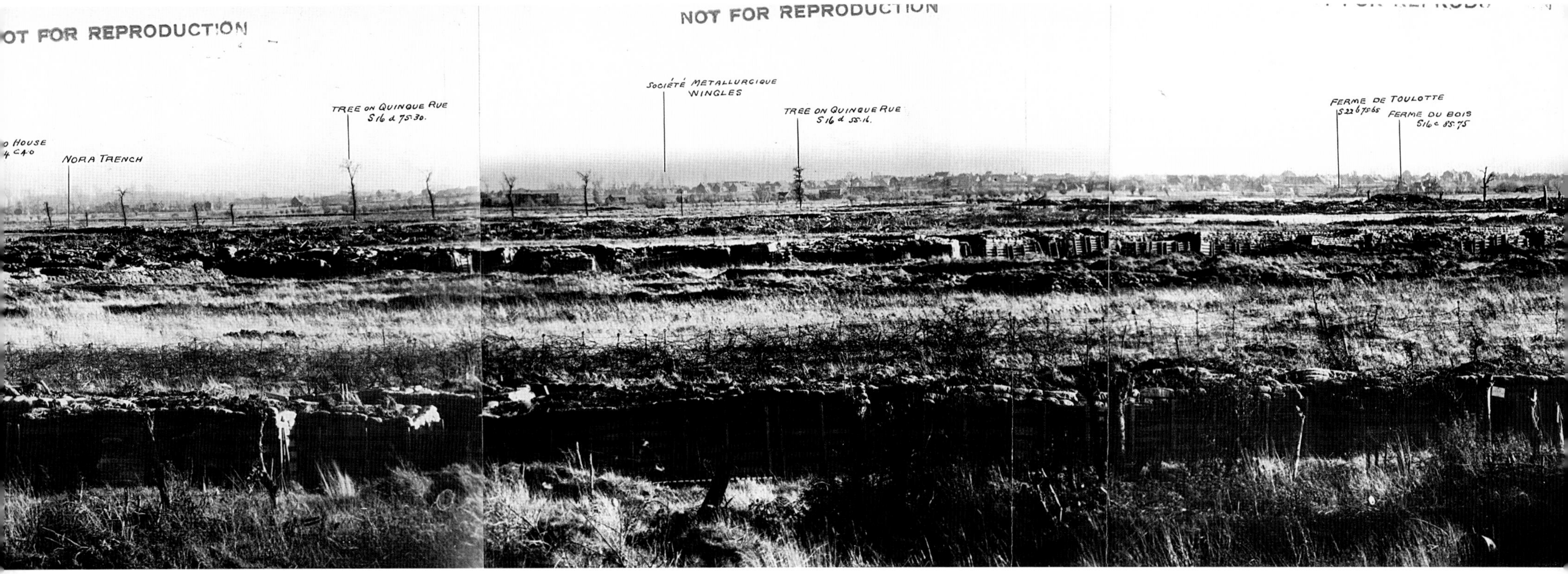
OT FOR REPRODUCTION
NOT FOR REPRODUCTION
NORA TRENCH
TREE ON QUINQUE RUE S16 d 75.30.
SOCIÉTÉ METALLURGIQUE WINGLES
TREE ON QUINQUE RUE S16 d 55.16.
FERME DE TOULOTTE S22 b 75.65
FERME DU BOIS S16 c 85.75

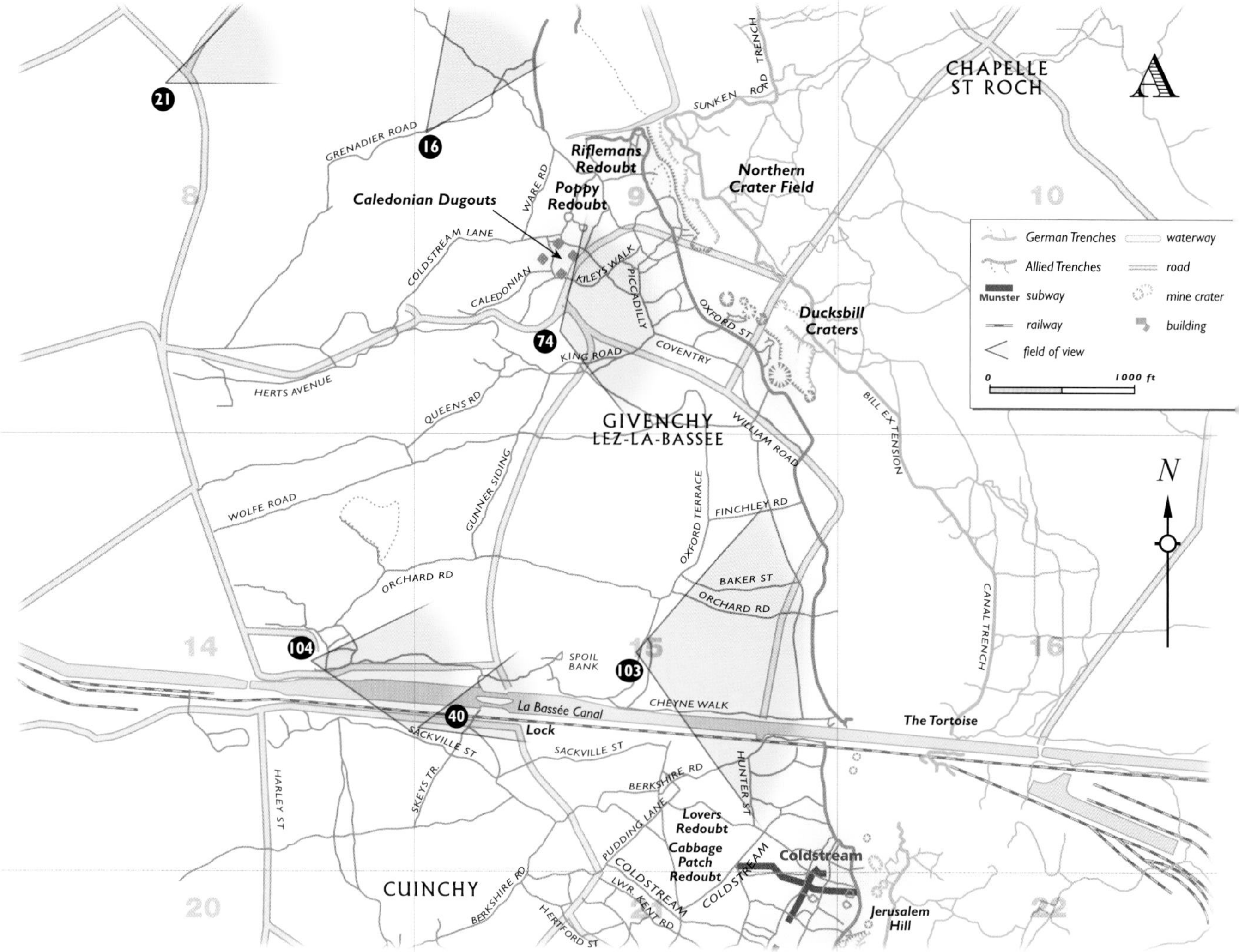

1916 brought with it many changes in the character of trench warfare. A comparison between Panoramas 16 (4 May 1915) *28* (19 August 1915) 98 (10 November 1916) and *99* (16 November 1916) clearly illustrates the evolution of defensive work in the Givenchy sector. From locations only a few hundred metres apart the panoramas illustrate the Boar's Head salient sector; Panoramas *97*, 98 and *99* show the British front and support positions to be heavily fortified and neatly and strongly constructed. Note especially the use of barbed-wire screw-pickets instead of the old wooden stake variety, and the depth and density of British entanglements compared to earlier pictures – ahead of both front and support breastworks. Such photographs give an idea of the amount of work required not only in building these lines but in supplying and maintaining them, especially in winter. The geology is still clay. So high was the water table that trenches were often no more than mere scrapes in the surface. The Festubert sub-sector was particularly bad with both the fire and communication trenches being no more than ditches to assist drainage. Massive breastwork structures were employed throughout the sector with duckboards often being suspended half a metre (1.5 ft) and more above the water to cope with sudden rises.

At least three large signboards marking spot map references are visible behind the front-line positions in Panoramas 98 and *99*. In the foreground of the latter a communication trench (Cockspur Street) is seen to have been revetted by woven wattle hurdles, a traditional and universal military engineer practice. This trench was viable only during dry periods. The shuttlecock fighting which took place here in 1914 and 1915 created a maze of

Above

Durham Light Infantry miners attached to 174 Tunnelling Company at work at a shaft-head near Houplines. The earth in the foreground is 'spoil' from the excavations.

Right and below

Sapper William Hackett VC, whose body and that of his colleague Thomas Collins still lie beneath the fields of Givenchy, within the field of view of Panorama 74 (below), taken on 14 May 1916.

used and disused trenches, those which intersected old enemy workings retaining the grim relics of conflict long after capture.

26 November 1915

After driving for about two miles along the road, we arrived at the little mining village of Givenchy round which some of the fiercest fighting of the campaign had taken place. But what had once been a village was now simply a grotesque collection of shot-riddled partly demolished walls. Every house was a shapeless ruin. The tide of battle had swayed uncertainly about this place for many months. The Canadians and the Manchesters had performed deathless feats of heroism in capturing the ridge behind which is our present position. Trenches and sandbag defence works can still be seen. On the outskirts of the village where the road turns sharply to the left is that blood-soaked spot which has, on many occasions, run red with the blood of heroes and which will be known as long as the British Army lasts as Windy Corner. The lorries were not allowed to proceed beyond this point and the remainder of the journey had to be done on foot. We were now quite close to the firing line and tired, dirty, mud-caked soldiers were straggling down, ration parties and light fatigues. The guns on both sides had now commenced paying the grim compliments which the irrepressible Tommy Atkins has facetiously termed the "morning hate". The uproar was deafening. The tearing crash of discharge followed by the duller boom of the bursting shell somewhere in the German lines over the ridge made a truly awful din. I tried to appear nonchalant and unconcerned but really I was tingling with excitement for here at last was war, real red war. We now left the road and turned into a deep communication trench which wound its sinuous way towards the firing line. Soon we arrived in the support trenches, the second line of defence. A little further on and we were in the firing line itself with nothing but a narrow shell-torn strip of about 60 yards separating us from the Boche trenches.

I spent the whole of the morning wandering about and endeavouring to get familiar with the twisting interwoven maze of trenches for which I, as mining officer, was to be largely responsible.

2ND LIEUTENANT MATTHEW ROACH,
180 TUNNELLING COMPANY RE

In 1915 the Givenchy sector was already famous for mining. Panorama 74 includes both the northern crater-field and those of the Duck's Bill – for which Matthew Roach was partly answerable. A glance at the offensive scheme map shows how mining commenced wherever the opposing lines approached to within a viable distance for tunnellers to reach the enemy trenches – in this sector up to 200 m (220 yds). The average width of no man's land was almost 500 m (547 yds) just north of the La Bassée canal, but narrowed substantially in front of Givenchy; mining here was therefore considered 'worthwhile'. Indeed it was in this sector that the first German mine attack had taken place just before Christmas 1914. The ground lost as a result of the blows can be seen in No 74 beyond the ruins of Givenchy church. This single act, which employed ten comparatively small charges beneath the trenches of the Indian Sirhind Brigade, kick-started an underground war which was to spread the entire length of the Western Front, culminating in Plumer's victory at Messines Ridge in June 1917. Also hidden within No 74 is the Shaftesbury mine shaft, at the

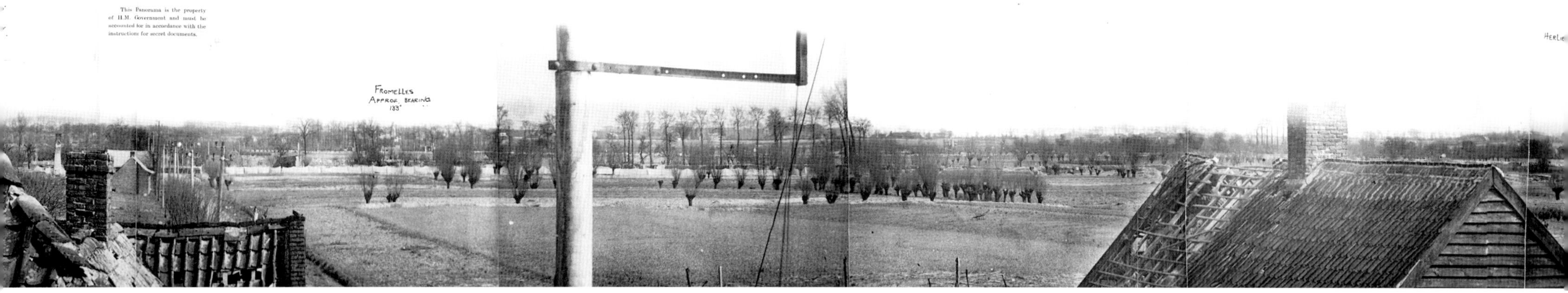

bottom of which still lie the bodies of Sapper William Hackett VC of 254 Tunnelling Company and Private Thomas Collins, an attached infantryman of the Welch Regiment. A month after this panorama was taken an enemy camouflet seriously damaged the new offensive gallery they were driving 12 m (40 ft) beneath no man's land. Five men were underground at the time, Hackett assist-edthree slightly injured colleagues to escape up the shaft, but was unable to move the seriously wounded Collins. As German mortars bombarded the site, the shaft grew ever weaker, and rescue teams were forced to withdraw. William Hackett could have escaped from the shaft, and was exhorted to do so, but deliberately chose to stay with Thomas Collins, telling the rescuers that a tunneller does not leave an injured comrade. Shaftesbury shaft later collapsed, and the bodies of both men were never recovered: an extraordinary story of premeditated courage, a courage which did not benefit from the heat-of-the-moment rush of adrenalin involved in acts of gallantry on the surface.

With the exception of mining, conditions here were similar to the rest of the front northwards to Armentières – beyond shelling there was little hostility. Because of this relative quiescence it was one of the sectors where newly arrived troops were deployed for induction into trench warfare.

[Winter 1916/17]

As first timers we were fortunate at not being thrown in at the deep end. There was little activity; the occasional German shell was viewed with interest – this interest tended to wane later on.

Spells of duty in the front line consisted of one hour on the firestep and two in the dugout. Here, if it was not too cold to sleep, we amused ourselves by putting food (if you could spare it) on the point of a bayonet and impaling rats. These were large well-fed creatures. Fires were not allowed, but Tommy cookers were sometimes issued – a miniature oilstove which lasted long enough to boil a Dixie of tea. On my first spell of duty the rum ration was brought round

Below
Observation position at Givenchy manned by troops of the 1/4 East Lancashire Regiment, 1916.

Above
Segment of an early panorama (14) of the Fromelles battlefield photographed from the railway station in April 1915, showing the ground over which Australian troops would advance in July 1916, and their target – Fromelles village.

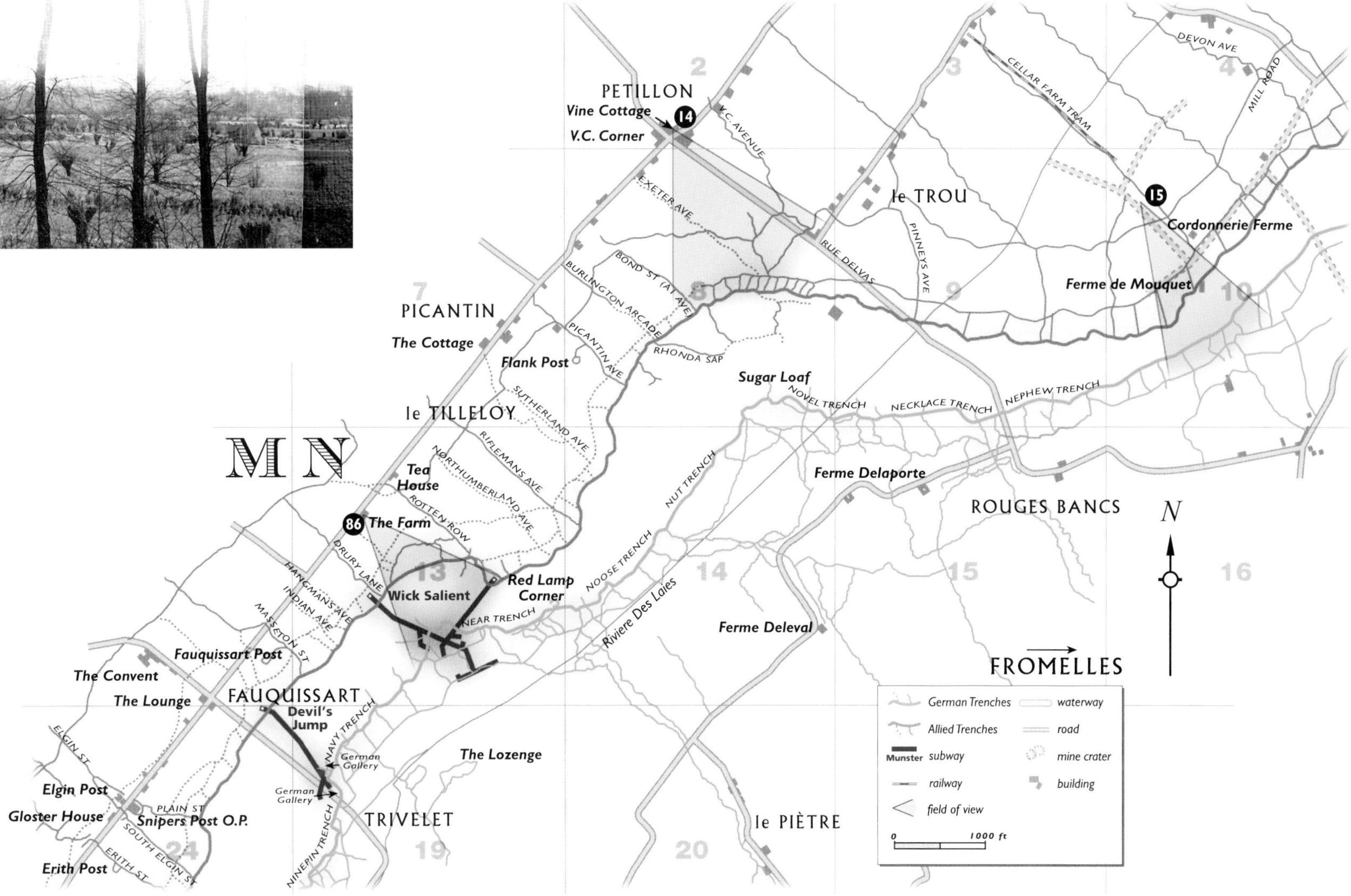

and liberal amount poured into my Dixie lid. This liquid was new to me, and having drunk it, far too quickly, the effect was magical. In No Man's Land tree trunks, broken off at a man's height, took on human form. If they were Germans, I was in no mood to challenge them. Alcohol can make you very benevolent (or quarrelsome!) The only excitement at night was watching Verey lights sent up by the Germans at regular intervals, and the rather more unpleasant habit of enemy machine gunners traversing in the hope of catching a wiring party or patrol. In the severe weather whale oil was issued to rub on our feet as a protection from frost bite – trench feet – and officers inspected to see this was done.

PRIVATE W. H. BASHFORD, BEDFORDSHIRE REGIMENT

Fromelles, 19–20 July 1916

By mid-1916 the German defences along the full length of the Western Front were already formidable. Like the great Stellung being extended and augmented in the Ypres Salient, the lines protecting Fromelles had also been bolstered since the British attack at Neuve Chapelle in the March of 1915. They would become far stronger yet. The enemy trenches were well placed, well camouflaged, well armed, and well endowed with concrete machine gun, artillery and trench mortar positions. Observation from atop the gentle ridge was deceptive – just a few metres made all the difference in the billiard table landscape. Here, the extra height was to prove critical; Panoramas 14 (from VC Corner) and 15 (from the Hornet's Nest OP) taken on the afternoon of 22 April 1915 give an excellent idea of the terrain of the forthcoming battleground from the British viewpoint. A wide view of the entire battlefield area can be seen in No 112.

The battle is often recalled solely as an Australian exploit, although during the battle of 19 and 20 July 1916 their 5th Division was accompanied by the British 61st Division. During the weeks prior to action, and 50 km (31 miles) to the south, the Somme offensive was already underway. Fighting was vigorous – and it was not going to plan. It was no coincidence that the Fromelles affair took place during the early stages of this battle. The first major Australian engagement on the Western Front, the venture was an integral component of the Somme. Although there was undoubtedly localized profit to be had in nipping off a bulge in the German lines known as the Sugarloaf Salient, the attack hoped to achieve a much wider strategic aim. If a substantial artillery bombardment could be laid down prior to the assault it was hoped the Germans might suspect it to be the overture to a bigger effort – another Allied

Above

Colonel Napier of the Royal Artillery examining maps at Cordonnerie Farm near Fromelles in preparation for the Battle of Aubers.

Above
First Army Panorama P86 taken on 22 August 1915 showing the southern part of the Fromelles battlefield, and the ground over which the British 61st Division attacked.

attack on the Aubers Ridge; if this ruse worked it would guarantee the re-routeing of substantial quantities of German support troops and materiel destined for defence and counter-attack on the Somme. Fromelles, therefore, was a diversion.

The battle plan formulated by General Haking, commander of XI Corps, and his staff, was unusual and ambitious. Over 300 guns of various calibres were to fire a three-day barrage. When the troops went over the top in the early evening the gunners would elevate their barrels to pummel the German support and reserve trenches. Like the battle strategy itself, this too was a ruse: the idea was that the defenders, naturally expecting an infantry assault when the barrage lifted, would rush from the cover of dugouts and pillboxes to man the front line, at which time the guns would be redirected to the originaltarget, catching them off guard and unprotected. If the sequence was repeated several times, it was hoped that the Germans would be sufficiently confused and fearful to remain under cover, allowing the infantry to advance relatively unmolested. To assist the assault a curious idea called 'pipe-pushing' had also been prepared by the 3rd Australian Tunnelling Company. It involved ramming explosive-charged pipes across no man's land at a depth of a metre or so using hydraulic jacks. When the moment of attack came they would be blown, thus creating an instant shallow communication trench part way to the enemy line.

Several hours before zero on 19 July (from their ridge-top OP's) the Germans spotted Australian and British troops concentrating for the attack, and laid down a prolonged bombardment which claimed many victims. Only three 'pipes' blew – the leads to the others were cut by shellfire. It was not an auspicious start, and the battle continued to be dogged by the same communication

Copy No. 9.
Panorama No. 79 made on 29-7-16 from O.P.M.4d 7.1 Sheet 36
93° from about N.E. to S.W.
Approximate Scale of Degrees (1 degree equals 1 1/13th inch).
1. Panoramas are taken solely for military purposes.
2. The publication of them in the press will necessarily give valuable information to the enemy.
3. This panorama is to be kept with as much security as is compatible with full advantage of it being taken by our own troops.
4. When troops are relieved this panorama should be handed over to the relieving troops.

problems experienced the previous year.

Above all, the German concrete emplacements were too numerous and too strong to be overly troubled by shelling, intense as it was. As the British and Australians crossed no man's land, machine guns and shrapnel cut a great many down. Part of the area so bravely attacked by the Australians in what they called 'the Fleurbaix stunt' can be seen in P15. The 61st Division made no gains on the day, although a request for a second assault at 9 p.m. was turned down. Their attacking front – after the battle – is that seen in P86. Two of the three Australian brigades, the 14th and the 8th, penetrated the enemy front and support lines and drove tenaciously on, searching for the next line of resistance. But as daylight began to fade they found themselves divided and isolated, with enemy troops infiltrating to their rear and fresh German reinforcements ahead. In the early hours of 20 July a retirement order was issued. Now almost surrounded, the men had to fight their way back over the same ground they had wrestled so hard to take. Losses totalled 7,000, of which 5,300 were Australians.

The Germans had guessed the attack was a feint, and the 12 hours of fighting brought no Allied territorial profit whatsoever. The only British gain was to deepen their reputation amongst the Australians for spinelessness in attack – an unwarranted hangover from Gallipoli. The battle had no effect on the Somme proceedings.

Panorama 86 (22 August 1916) shows the full vista of the Fromelles battleground. When this photograph was taken substantial numbers of fallen soldiers still lay in no man's land. It is said that the Germans later offered an unofficial truce to allow both sides to clear the battlefield of dead and wounded. The suggestion was rejected. Eventually, it was left to the Germans to remove the bodies of the fallen and bury them in unmarked mass graves behind the lines. The whereabouts of these graves is still being sought today.

Panorama 79 was taken from the Allied reserve positions less than ten days after the battle. It indicates the extreme concentration and narrowness of the area of battle and destruction. Although just a kilometre or two behind the lines, houses still stand and fields tilled and worked. The reserve trenches shielded by the British wire are practically invisible amongst the crops – precisely what the engineers sought to achieve. The camouflage made little difference in 1918 however, as German troops drove the British back from here beyond Estaires and Merville. Panoramas 90 taken from La Gorgue near Estaires, *153* (4 August 1918), 160 (6 August 1918) show the unusual nature of the battlefields of this penultimate period of war. The old front lines at Fromelles were retaken by the British on 4 September as the Advance to Victory gathered pace.

After the 1916 battle however, it was again in underground warfare where most of the action took place. At Epinette, Cordonnerie, the Birdcage (Mauquissait), the Wick Salient in front of Fromelles, and Givenchy in the south of the sector.

On rest – Béthune

Upon relief, most soldiers serving in the Fromelles, Festubert, Neuve Chapelle, and Givenchy trenches marched back a few kilometres to Béthune, a town similar in size to Armentières and Poperinghe, and used by the Army in the same way. Here, a man might stumble upon semblances of home comfort. A stay would often include a

Above
German officers in a comfortable deep dugout. The Germans were the first to go deep underground for shelter in certain geologically favourable areas.

Above
With food production a priority, just behind the British lines on the Aubers front agricultural life had to continue as normally as possible. This Second Army Panorama 79, was taken on 29 July 1916, just over a week after the Battle of Fromelles and its terrible losses.

Above
The shortage of horses for military use led to farmers utilizing whatever form of muscle-power was available. Here, a dog team harrows the soil.

de-lousing session where the uniform was 'cooked' to kill body lice and their eggs, an infestation which was practically universal. Although the cure was merely temporary, it offered at least a few itch-free days. Scabies too was a serious problem, and Béthune had its own specialist treatment rooms.

We all stripped off – the uniform went away to be boiled or steamed to kill the chat [louse] eggs – but we were told to hang on to our socks. There was a room with a row of barrels which were hinged at the side and with holes cut in the top. You opened them up like a door, and got inside. They put a towel round your neck to stop the vapour escaping, and then turned on what we later learned was sulphur. By God, it stung, especially where the skin was tender or raw from the scabies. Now, that's why we had been told to hang on to our socks – you only needed one actually – and this was used to put your privates in. I did as I was told – eventually! Well, you always have a clever bugger or two in every company, don't you, always one who knows better, and this fellow, he wouldn't do it, he didn't need to fuss about that. They tried to persuade him, but no, he wouldn't have it. Allright then, they said, he could do without, but don't say you haven't been warned. Now, it's not something that you'd normally do, put your privates in a sock, and my embarrassment was only covered up by watching the other lads … "juggling". It's not easy, I can tell you, gravity doesn't help. You can picture the scene – we all looked like stallions! Its not something I've ever been tempted to practice again, but it was worth the trouble then: by the time we came out of the barrels we may have looked like lobsters, but the fellow without a sock was howling for mercy.
PRIVATE BERT FEARNS, 2/6 LANCASHIRE FUSILIERS

After this kind of therapy, further 'treatment' equally unavailable in the trenches might be tempting.

Bethune proved an interesting town; one street displaying red lamps in the windows seemed very popular. As a country lad, a red lamp could mean a hole in the road, and you gave it a wide berth, but here they assured you a warm welcome. The old hands at the game must have been on intimate terms with the residents, as they entered without so much as a tap on the door. As these young ladies were not renowned for giving their services, one wondered how this luxury could be afforded on Army pay. Many of these men would have had wives or sweethearts, but with no more than a fifty-fifty chance of seeing them again, who could blame them for this indulgence?
PRIVATE W. H. BASHFORD, BEDFORDSHIRE REGIMENT

In spring 1918, at the moment of the great German attack of 9 April, Givenchy and all the sectors 16 km (10 mles) northwards were held by the Portuguese Corps. The timing of the attack seemed to have been carefully chosen, as it was launched just before they were due to be relieved by British troops, at about 4 a.m. A thick mist also assisted the Germans in overrunning the line which they had stared at for more than three years. The attack was halted after only small gains at Givenchy, and it was this sector which came to form the southernmost hinge of the German advance (Nos 103 and 104). Elsewhere, its speed and efficacy was staggering.

Those sectors south of the La Bassée Canal therefore remained static – for the moment. Panoramas 103 and 104 show how the geology and water table are beginning to change as the lines wind southwards through the Givenchy sector, with breastworks gradually tapering away into full-depth trenches. Once the La Bassée Canal had been vaulted, they display an entirely different character altogether.

CHAPTER FIVE:

COALFIELDS AND CRASSIERS

THE GOHELLE BATTLEFIELDS

As the boundary of the clay plain of Flanders and the chalk uplands of Artois, Vimy Ridge and its smaller cousin Notre Dame de Lorette created a formidable military barrier, a geological fracture destined to have a deep impact on the lives of soldiers struggling for topographical advantage.

This area of front had settled partly into place during October 1914 when, at the same time as the primary enemy thrusts at Ypres in Belgian Flanders, the Germans grasped both the above ridges and overran Loos and Lens. They were kept firmly out of Arras however, by French Alpine divisions, *Chasseurs*, *Zouaves*, *Génie* (engineers) and Senegalese troops. At the close of the defensive manoeuvres the town, like Ypres, was left at the centre of a salient. It was likewise subsequently pummelled by German artillery. In spring 1915 the sector was still defended entirely by the French, and the situation was still far from satisfactory. As the Germans held all the high ground north and south of Arras, General Ferdinand Foch, Commander of the French Army Group of the North, determined to launch an offensive to relieve the pressure on the town and drive the enemy from the surrounding ridges. The process had already begun at Notre Dame de Lorette to the north: in December 1914 and March and April 1915 the French had clawed back some of the ridge spurs, a move which created a reasonable launch pad for Foch's scheme, which he planned for May. The view towards Lens from the Notre Dame de Lorette positions can be seen in panoramas *136*, *84* and 85.

During the 1914/15 winter, however, the Germans had followed the same pattern of activity in the Arras and Vimy sector as elsewhere on the Western Front, entrenching, fortifying villages, creating interconnected communications, installing dugouts and strengthening cellars. Trench lines were also now fully continuous, making the enemy positions a formidably consolidated linear fortress. Foch's offensive, the Second Battle of Artois, raged from 9 May until 19 June 1915. The Germans were driven off Notre Dame and back (an average of just 3 km) (2 miles) but there was never a moment when the hoped-for breakthrough seemed even a remote possibility. Fighting predominantly in the low, marshy ground between the ridges, it was an engagement which became noted for the terrible suffering of troops in muddy conditions. In fact the Germans, defending the village of Souchez in the valley, had deliberately diverted watercourses to create a sort of

Pages 228–9
The Tower Bridge mine workings, Loos. This panorama, P96, was taken during the battle on 30 September 1915.

Right
French trenches on the Loos–Lens battlefields. When the British took over the sector many sights like this were encountered in the process of improving and extending the lines.

Below
First Army Panorama 84 photographed from Notre-Dame de Lorette Ridge on looks out over the battlefields towards Lens, a town which would eventually be reduced to rubble.

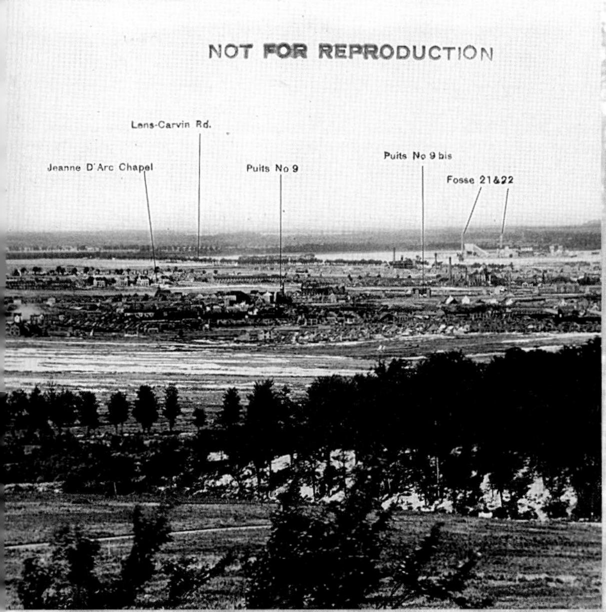

limited defensive inundation; a miniature version of the man-made sea on Belgian Polders. It was very effective.

Today, on the heights of Notre Dame de Lorette, the trenches have been preserved and can still be visited. They lie alongside an impressive monument, ossuary and vast cemetery. Desultory fighting mainly with grenades and small arms dribbled on after 19 June, but no more ground was gained, and the Germans still held the slopes of Vimy Ridge. For some reason the remains of many of the French soldiers who fell during this and the earlier battle were never cleared from the fields between the two ridges which enfold the village of Souchez. The area became known as the Valley of the Dead, a fact which is mentioned by many who served in the sector. See Panorama *136* for views of this battlefield.

On fine days I used to climb up the steep slope of the famous hill [Notre Dame de Lorette] and sit and gaze over the great battlefield spread out below or roam in search of birds. On bright days it was wonderful to be up there alone, but yet it just missed perfection. Although alone, one had all the time a sense of not being quite alone. This feeling may have been due to the knowledge that wherever you wandered a score of pairs of German eyes were watching you. Unaccompanied one was safe enough, but if half a dozen or more men were seen together they would soon have been shelled. Perhaps the sensation of being shadowed was due to the ghosts, the wandering spirits of the hundreds of French soldiers who had fallen there the previous year when they drove the Germans off the hill, and whose white bones and shreds of tunic still lay amongst the grass and wild flowers.

One day, while a small battle raged below, I sat with my back to it, and watched a tree pipit. It would rise up from a bush and fly at a steep angle until it was some thirty or forty feet above the ground when it would turn, head downwards, and glide swiftly towards the earth, with its wings held behind its back.

Lieutenant Philip Gosse, RAMC, 23rd Division

Despite the failure to break through, the enemy had at least been driven from one of the heights, a tremendously symbolic action for the French nation. But the 1915 fighting was far from over. Almost before the blood of these engagements had dried, the French – and British, who were in the process of taking over – were planning another huge foray.

The Battle of Loos, September–October 1915

Neither Field Marshal Sir John French nor General Sir Douglas Haig wanted the Loos attacks to take place. Neuve Chapelle, Second Ypres, Aubers and Festubert, all seriously costly battles, were still fresh in their memories, and the doomed Gallipoli campaign was diverting precious men and munitions from, as Haig and French saw it, their rightful place on the Western Front. However, pressure from the French based upon universal fears over a Russian collapse in the East, plus support for the scheme from Minister of War Lord Kitchener (who also rallied the support of the British Government) forced their hand.

French C-in-C General Joffre was never anything but categorical: in June 1915 he made known his desire for a decisive coalition resolution in the form of a set of multiple and devastating Allied attacks, followed by a general advance along the whole of the Western Front – before winter set in.

In tandem with an offensive (with thirty-five divisions) in the Champagne region, the French plan determined that eighteen of their Tenth Army divisions were to attack Vimy Ridge, whilst to the north twelve divisions of the British First Army (under Haig) would advance over the industrial Gohelle terrain either side of the small mining village of Loos. Discounting the non-combatant element, the formations totalled approximately 1,200,000 infantry, 60,000 cavalry, and 100,000 artillerymen.

The vast build-up to the Champagne offensive (known as the Third Battle of Artois) seemed to energize every rank of the French Army, not least because of the promise of 5,000-gun artillery support. Optimism was high, but sadly nothing was to change: the French fought themselves to exhaustion, losing 145,000 men in Champagne and a further 48,000 in Artois. Both plans failed in their ultimate strategic aims, but the Germans had at least been positively ousted from the Notre Dame Ridge and a vital French foothold was grasped close to the crest of Vimy Ridge (Panoramas *136* and 526 show these battlefields). It was a foothold which had exacted a terrible sacrifice, but one of which the French were justifiably proud. The battle may well have continued but for the shortage of ammunition and events at Gallipoli, Salonika and the Balkans.

The British battleground area lay between Givenchy just north of the La Bassée Canal, and the industrial town of Bully-Grenay in front of Lens; a frontage of around 10 km (6 miles). Haig expressed concern over the openness and flatness of the terrain (see Panoramas 52, 101, 108, 115 and 117), but above all it was the continuing lack of munitions which worried him most. The Minister responsible, David Lloyd George, and his French counterpart, agreed that it would not be until the following year that sufficient stocks could be built up to launch the kind of prolonged, intense and devastating barrage which Haig and C-in-C Sir John French desired. The two men were so uneasy that they suggested British attacks might take place against Aubers and Messines instead, but this idea was dismissed by the French. Furthermore, Kitchener and the British Cabinet strongly supported the Loos scheme. So Haig requested a full thirty-six infantry divisions to be sure of victory; he received nine. Even so there still existed an extraordinary imbalance between attack and defence: 11,000 Germans faced 75,000 British. Diversionary attacks were planned at Bellewaerde in the Ypres Salient (see Hooge sector), and at Le Piétre (Aubers) 16 km (10 miles) north of Loos (see Panorama 86, Fromelles sector). As for artillery support, forty-seven heavy guns and 894 field guns were to be made available. This was no mean arsenal, but the continuing shell shortage meant that an average of only one round per gun per eleven minutes could be fired. It was a pitiful way to launch a major offensive.

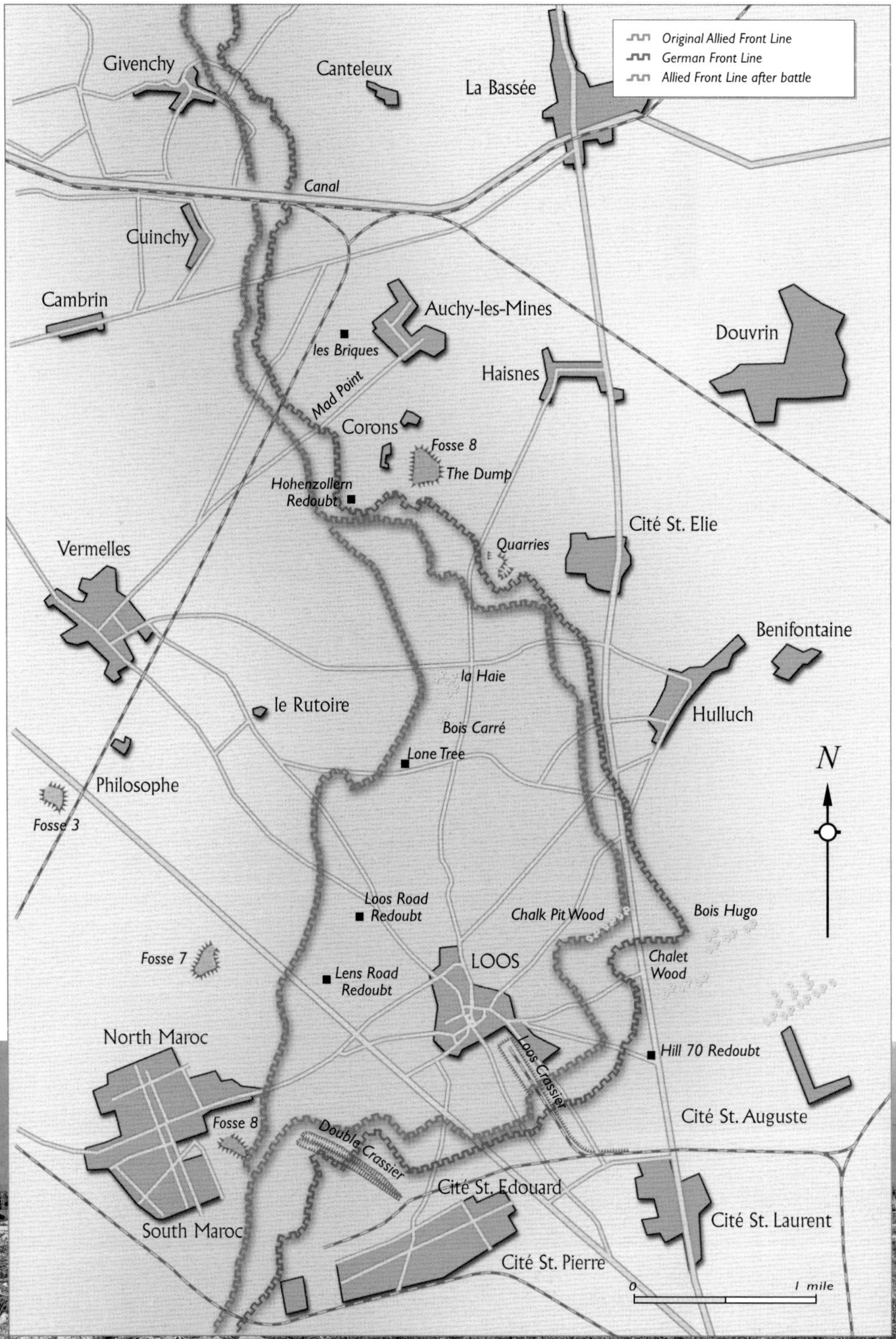

First Army Panorama P108
24 March 1917
From near : East Quarry Road
Sheet 36C G 12 c 75.70
85 degrees, 26 -111

Above
An improvised stretcher being brought through deep and secure German trenches in the Gohelle sector.

In Haig's view the only redeeming feature of the Loos battle plan, and one in which he was to grow ever more confident, was the recent availability of asphyxiating gas. Having seen the rent torn in the Allied lines at Ypres on 22 April by the first German gas attack, he envisaged the new weapon compensating for the lack of artillery. It was agreed that there was reason for a degree of optimism – but only if the attack was a surprise, the wind favourable, and sufficient gas cylinders brought forward. In preparation, therefore, 8,000 men transported 5,500 cylinders of chlorine gas into the front lines. It was almost exactly half the number requested, so 11,000 smoke candles, 25,000 phosphorus grenades, and 10,000 Stokes mortar smoke bombs were supplemented to at least create the appearance, if not the toxic effect, of the real thing.

Sappers of the newly formed Royal Engineer 'Special Companies' under the command of Major C. H. Foulkes RE (the initiator of panoramic military photography during the Boer War), tucked the unwieldy cylinders into specially made recesses beneath British parapets, running out hoses into no man's land just as the Germans had done at Ypres in April. Their field company colleagues installed 3,500 trench ladders and prepared 2,500 footbridges for crossing German lines. Then everyone prayed for a westerly breeze for Zero Day.

24 September

Nothing to do all day except packing our transport. We know for certain that attack is coming off next day for we are warned to be ready to move off at one hours notice. In the evening I go on guard with George and Camp. The Coy. is to move off at 10pm. We move off at ten and on the way to the trenches I notice thousands of troops moving up; everybody seems full of suppressed excitement. We (the sappers) go right up to the trenches, not front line but support trenches; transport remain in the rear. Bob, Camp and I still remain on guard and as we are out of rifle range we stand on parapet to watch. What a night, not a sound or a shot fired. Now and again a party of men looking very mysterious creep past us carrying ammunition, rations, etc.

Lance-Corporal G. J. Smith, 95 Field Company RE [7th Division]

After five days preliminary bombardment, at 5.50 a.m. on 25 September the gas valves were opened. The wind was not fully cooperative; across some fronts the release went well, in others it was less effective; at several places the chlorine gassed more British than Germans. After forty minutes the infantry swarmed forward.

25 September

Day of attack. I am on guard and about three in the morning the artillery bombardment started and now the Boches reply in earnest. The noise of firing guns and exploding shells becomes one continuous and deafening crash. About 4am Bob relieves me on guard and things are now getting very unhealthy. Large shells are dropping all around us. 5am the order is passed along to get something to eat. We have carried rations with us. The bombardment is still on and some ammunition carriers tell us that the infantry are going over about 7 o'clock. After breakfast we go to advance stores and draw barbed wire, pickets, guncotton and other material. So far we have been lucky and have not had a man hit. The gas is now going over. What a sight, huge clouds of gas and smoke go rolling over the German lines. The Boche replies with liquid fire shell.

7.30am. The infantry have gone over and we move down to our

Below
First Army Panorama 108 shows the flatness of the battleground and the importance of observation. Note the number of tall mine-head structures.

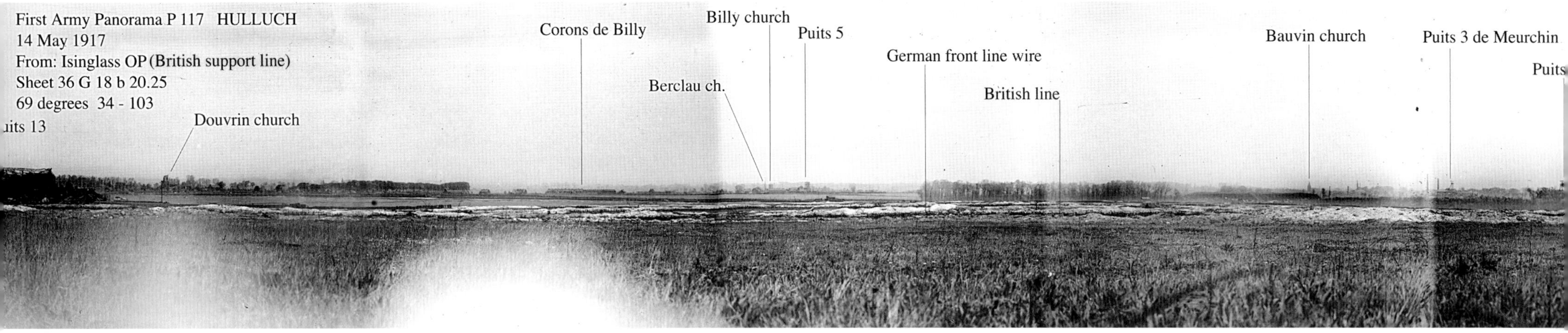

front line ready to follow them. We go over the top to front line and Gibson gets wounded. Things seem to have got very quiet all of a sudden; what is happening I wonder.

10am. At last we get the order to get ready for going over. Our officer says we are going nearly a mile past the German front line. Bob is near me, he smiles and says "Now we are for it."

11am. Well, here we are, what's left of us, about a mile past the Boche's front line, cross roads in front of Hulluch, and the getting here. At 10.15 we got the order to get on top and a few of us scrambled out of the trench on to Hulluch road and moved forward. Now we see the battle in full swing, some wounded tell us that five lines of trenches have been taken. To our right I notice some guns moving for-

Above
First Army Panorama 117 shows the open aspect of the Hulluch sector. Ultimately, the forward trenches were approached solely by subway. Mine craters define the position of no man's land.

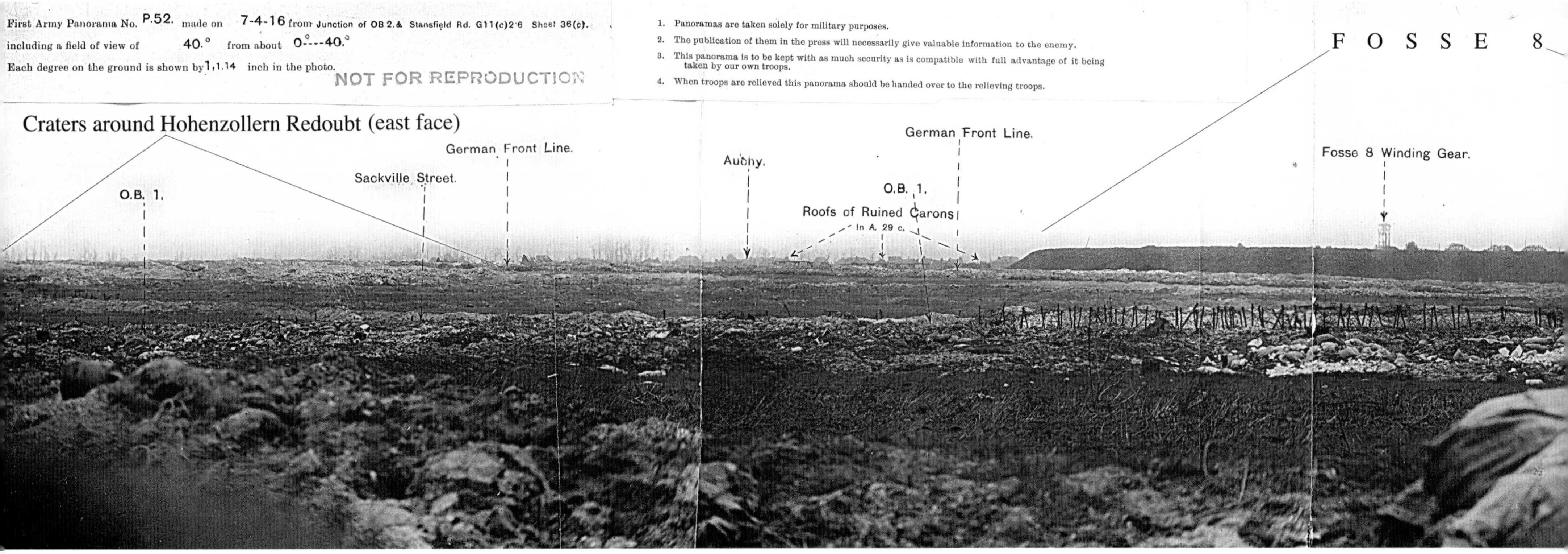

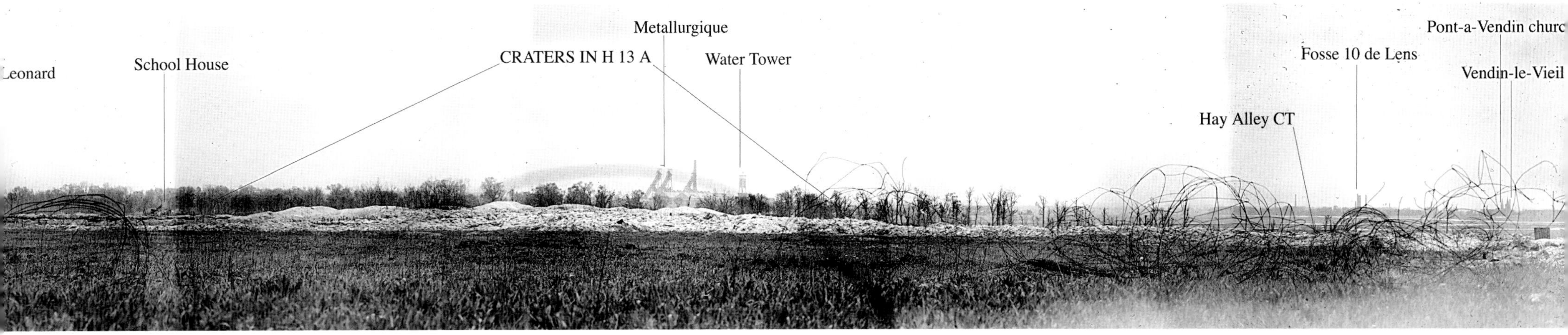

Below

First Army Panorama 52: the southern face of the Hohenzollern Redoubt, with Fosse 8, the slag heap also known as The Dump, dominating the sector. It lies immediately behind the German lines.

ward. Did not have much time for looking round tho', for as soon as everyone was out of the trench our officer takes the lead and away we go down Hulluch road. We got past the German front line and then we saw and got the full horrors of war. The attack was still in progress on our right and we see our men leaping from the ground and rushing forward. What a sight, dozens of men falling and we do not escape, for we suddenly come under heavy machine gun fire; Bob George was running beside me, and he suddenly goes over with a long drawn sigh. A Jock near me mutters 'killed', but somehow I did not realise that my best chum had gone under. We wavered and the officer shouts come on men, come on for your own lives and on we go. There are dead and dying all over the place. When we got to the cross roads

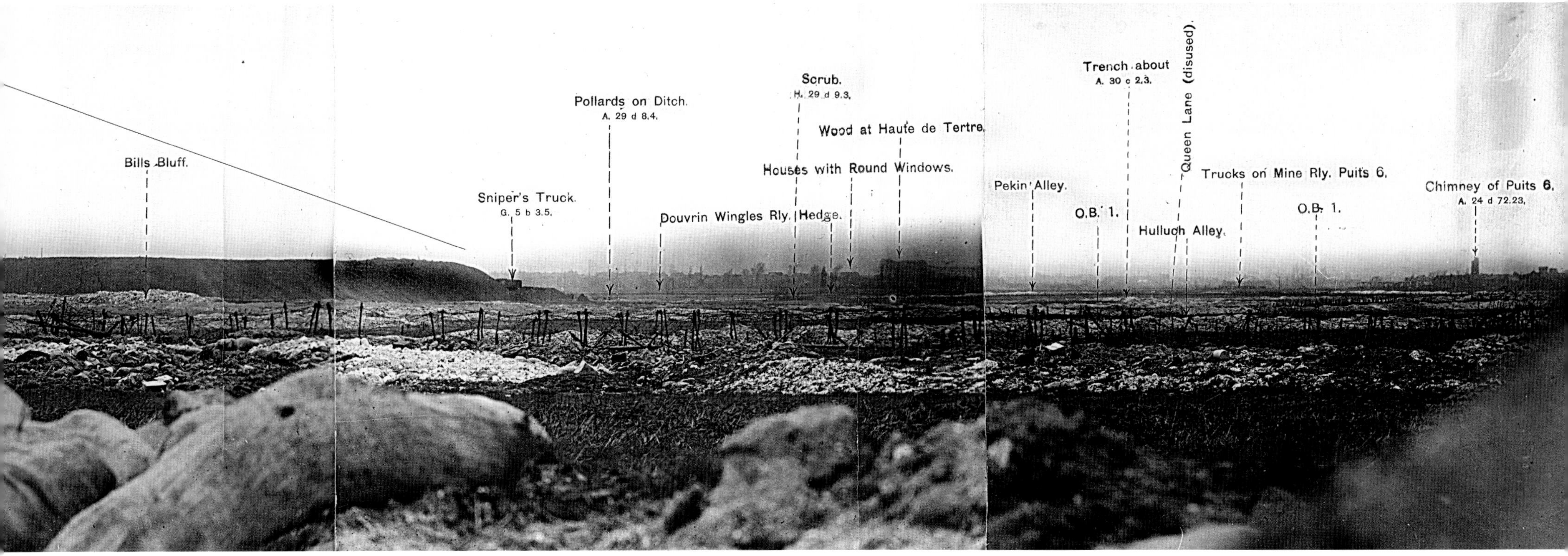

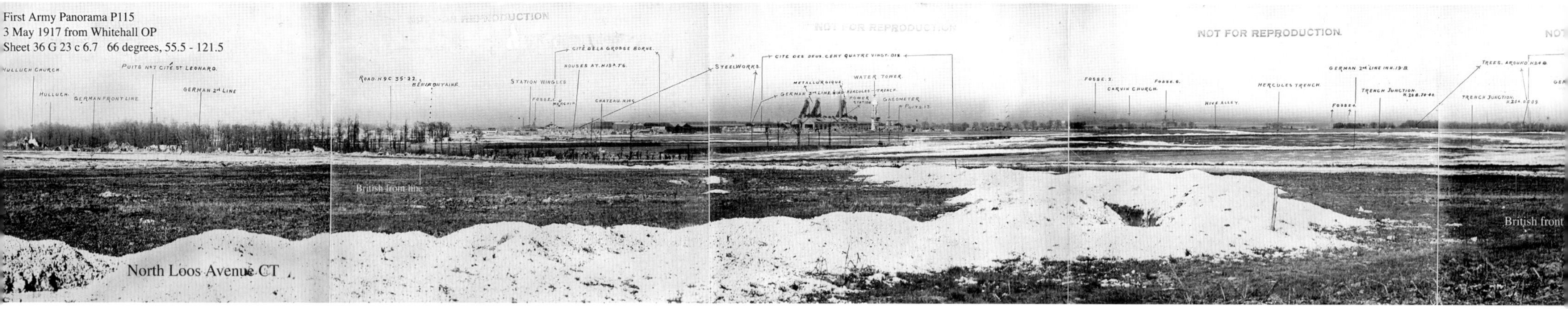

the officer rallied what there was left of us and told us to take cover. About twenty of us have found cover in a half dug trench, and sniper has picked off two men already; wonder if I shall survive the day; it is awful but I do not feel afraid, the excitement is too strong. We start digging trench deeper. Time 11.15.

27 September relating to the 25th

After digging trench deeper we hunt round and find our packs which we had thrown off, also materials which we carried. Oh the agony of those packs, not much trouble to find one tho', there are hundreds to be had. Several lines of reserves have passed over us during the day. About 5pm some of us went back for some wire and pickets. We pass several of our own company lying dead. I find Bob just where he had fallen. Poor Bob, how sick I felt, but I could do nothing so had to leave him. We carried back some more wire and as it is now getting dark we went forward to where the infantry were digging in. Everything is very quiet now, and we get two rows of wire out without any trouble and go back to the old German support line. Here we are told to make ourselves as comfortable as possible. We were hardly settled down before we got the order to stand to. The Germans are making a strong counter-attack and to make things worse it has started raining. I shall never forget that night. The rain was coming down in torrents, our fellows are retiring and we expect the Boche on us any minute. I feel wretched and tired and have no food since breakfast this morning. Hundreds of our fellows are retiring down Hulluch. Our C.O. tries to stop them, he does to a great extent and I hear him tell another officer that his men are going to hang on to the last. The C.O. shouts for a cyclist and as I am nearest I tell him I am one. He gives me a message for the Hants. Fortress Coy., who are at Vermelles, asking them for reinforcements. I drag one of our cycles out of a hole and start off on my journey. It was impossible to ride tho. It is pitch dark and raining, there are dead and dying all over the road. The dying and wounded are crying and shouting for stretcher-bearers. There are smashed limbers, reinforcements trying to get up, some guns trying to get into new positions and some retiring. Shells are screaming and bursting all around and everything is confusion. My cycle is soon smashed by a gun and I save myself by jumping into a trench, ugh, onto some poor wounded Jock. He groaned and asked for water. I have none. I tell him I will send some stretcher-bearers to him and continue my journey, find the Hants. Coy., deliver the message, and act as guide for them back to where our boys are. We have some narrow escapes going back, several of the Hants. being hit, six being killed outright with one shell. The boys are still standing to when I get back but the danger is over and our infantry are driving the Germans back again. It is now Sunday morning. About day-break several of us with some infantry are told off to reverse the fire-step of a German trench.

LANCE-CORPORAL G. J. SMITH, 95 FIELD COMPANY RE

Above
Naval gun night-firing. Heavy guns were more widely available for the Loos offensive than other 1915 battles.

In places, especially in the central and southern sectors, Haig effected the surprise he had hoped for, and the First Army experienced another successful opening sequence of attacks, capturing the German front line, occupying Loos

Above
The geology of the Gohelle sector allowed deep entrenchments. This panorama, First Army 115, shows North Loos Communication Trench cutting across the vast expanse of open, flat, coverless battlefield.

itself, and entering the terraced streets of the *cités* clustered around the pitheads. For a while it seemed that the British would reach the strongly wired German second position before it could be reinforced by support troops, but disorganization and loss of direction led to confusion, and the fleeting opportunities which separate success from failure were lost. The momentum of the advance was severely truncated by Sir John French's decision to withhold fresh troops until nightfall rather than continue the tide of advance created by the initial dawn attacks. In any case, reserves had also been held so far to the rear they were unable to intervene at the decisive moments. Haig, and others, later came to believe firmly that this was the key to the breakdown. The following day the Germans had sufficiently regrouped and recovered to launch powerful counter attacks, driving the British back and recapturing more than half of the ground lost. Haig was allowed another crack on 13 October, which was very firmly repelled. The Battle of Loos was over. It had come close to success; a few parties of British troops had penetrated the entire German defence line, but too many had been cut down in the initial stages of battle. As for the enemy, they had been sufficiently alarmed as to begin preparations for the evacuation of GHQ in Douai.

Loos was the fourth failure of 1915 for the British, and this time losses reached almost 48,000 men; at Vimy the French figure was almost identical. In the wider Artois offensive the total was 143,567. Sir John French was recalled for home service, his place soon to be taken by Haig. It had been the first time the BEF had experienced the efficacy of the new German tactic of defence in depth, whereby several sets of prepared defence lines were always available for troops to fall back upon when driven out of forward positions. Within a year, on every sector of the Western Front, both sides were employing the same policy.

During the summer and autumn of 1915 the British gradually relieved the French in every sector from La Bassée to the River Somme. No more major attacks took place in the Gohelle, Vimy and Arras sectors until the offensives of spring 1917. During the intervening summer months the plains in front of Loos and Lens turned green and red with lush grasses and an abundance of poppies. However, many sub-sectors did not follow the same pattern as their northern 'forgotten front' neighbours and fall into dormancy: to keep up the morale of the troops, raiding – including many daylight forays – was common, and military mining became continuous and widespread

Right
A private road in Lens: reserved solely for the use of German boots from late 1914 until autumn 1917 when Canadian troops captured this part of the town.

Cuinchy and Cambrin

Situated immediately south of the La Bassée Canal, the Cuinchy sector covers a frontage of about 800 m (875 yds). Named after a small village just behind the British lines, it was an unique battlefront due to the presence of the notorious brickstacks, huge rectangular stockpiles, about thirty in all, of tens of thousands of carefully placed bricks, the product of the area's clay geology. Although only divided from the Givenchy and Festubert sectors by the canal, Cuinchy had a reputation as a 'lively' area both above and below ground. It was also the northern limit of the industrial battlegrounds of Gohelle which incorporated both Loos and the major industrial town of Lens. Panoramas *40*, 103 and 104 offer superb elevated views of the Givenchy and Brickstack front from both sides of the canal, and show the latter's highly unusual character. A view from the village of Cuinchy itself can be seen in No *60*.

Following the model common to Flanders (Cuinchy is just beyond the southern boundary of French Flanders) the advantage of elevation rested marginally with the Germans. On the British side the ground nearest the canal (on both banks) sat on a rise, and excavations here could be deep and thereforekept relatively dry; those farther to the south were lower, and although being less well drained and requiring pumping schemes and careful maintenance, were infinitely more comfortable than positions just a kilometre or two north of the canal beyond Givenchy. The Cuinchy trenches bisected the Brickstacks, most of which sat within German lines, with others lying inside British territory. Hostile stacks were allocated a letter, whilst 'friendly' ones were numbered. Being on average around

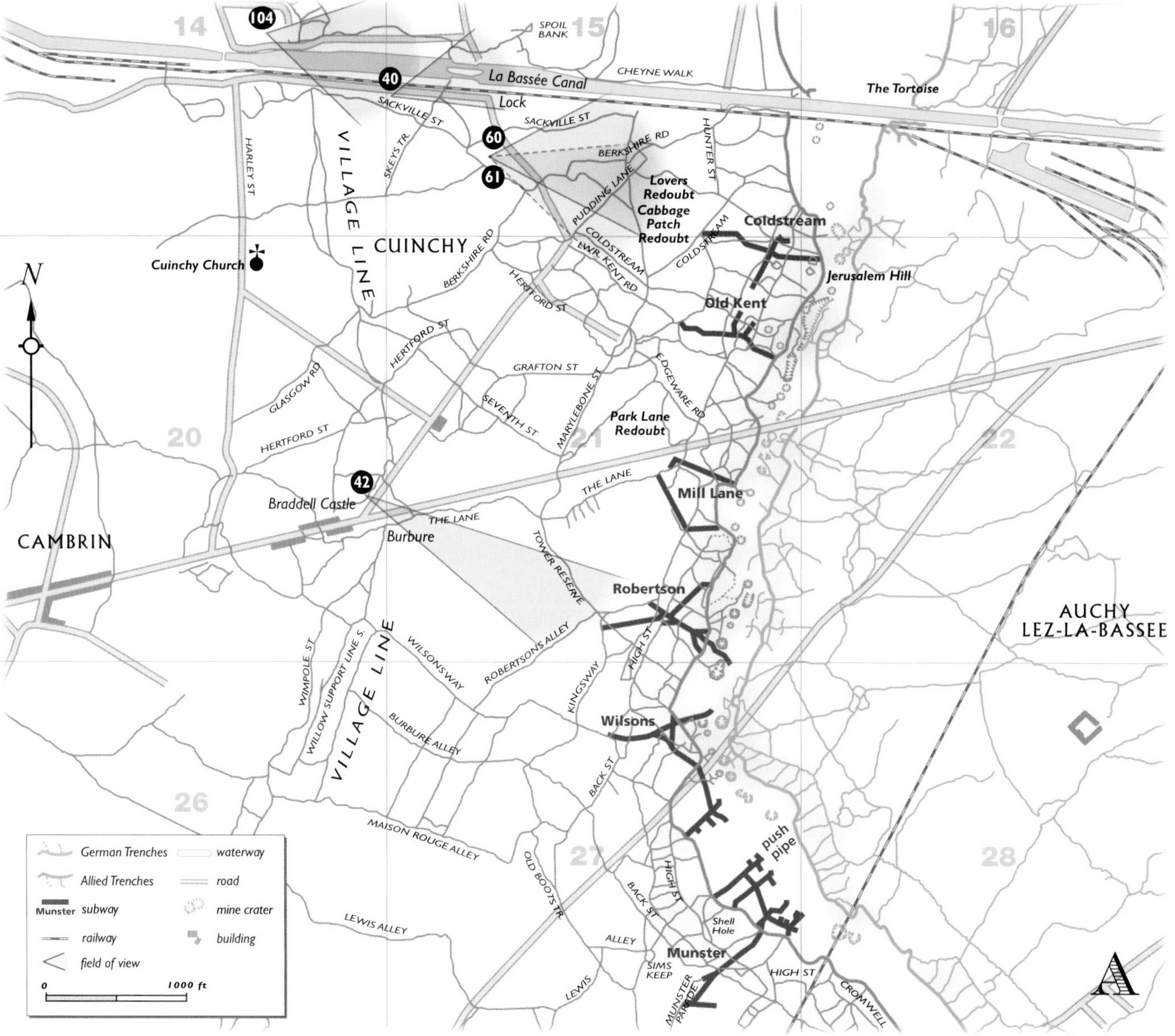

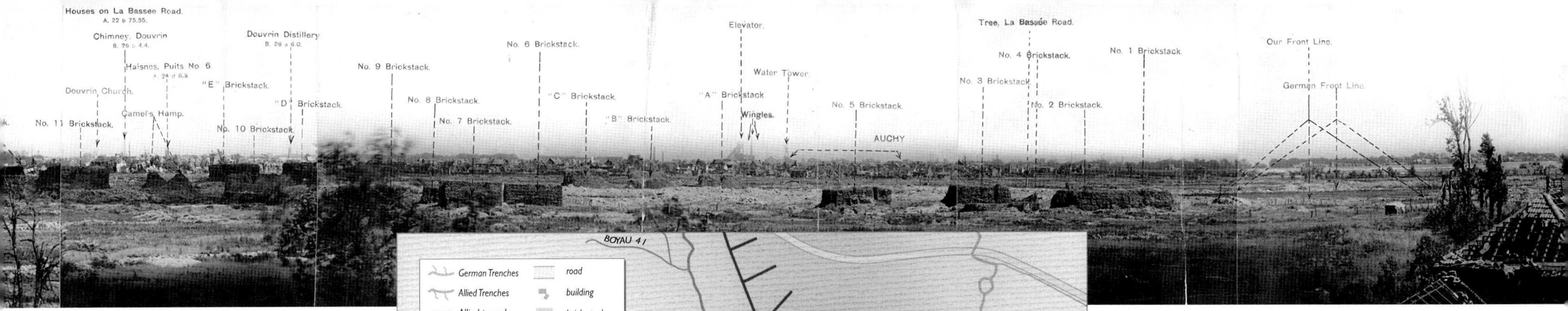

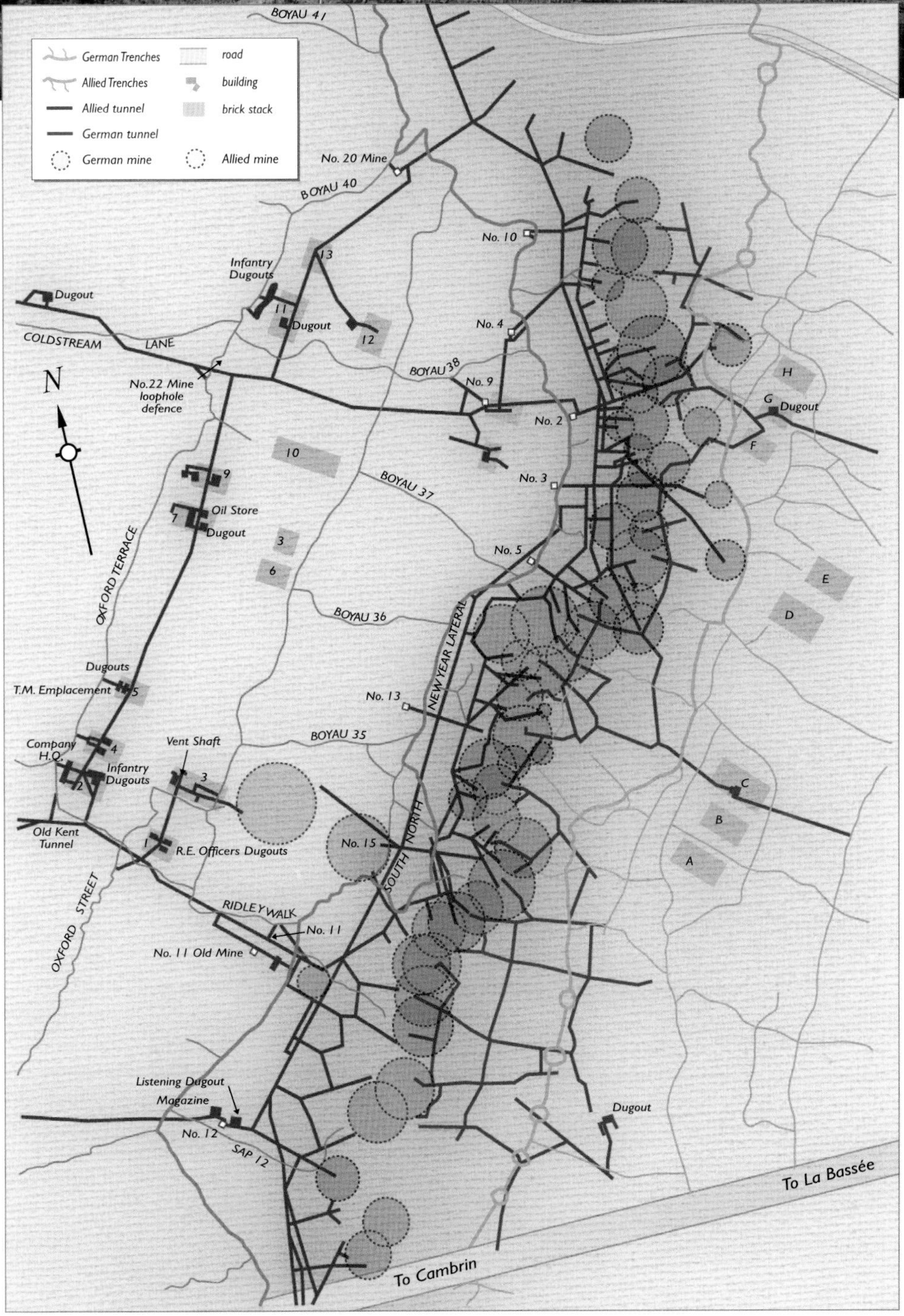

Above

First Army Panorama 61 offers an excellent view of the Cuinchy Brickstacks in April 1916: this was a bizarre and unique sub-sector with an atmosphere unlike any other part of the Western Front.

10 sq m (12 sq yds) and a full 5 m (16 ft) in height, they were universally employed for observation, sniping and even machine-gunning from camouflaged positions *within* the stacks. However, as natural targets for artillery and especially trench mortars, they were unhealthy places from which to ply any of these trades. Panorama A (undated, but spring 1915) more than adequately portrays the leaden atmosphere of the sector. Note the narrowness of no man's land and how itis almost entirely composed of mine craters.

The incessant attention of snipers, gunners and mortar teams made life at Cuinchy more taxing than in many other sectors of the region. Some very heavy fighting took place in January 1915, but once the lines had stabilized it was military mining which most concerned front line residents here.

August 24th 1915

The battalion went into the line at Cuinchy at 3pm in relief of the 1st Berks. Life in the trenches on the La Bassée front was quite different from what it had been at Bois Grenier and Laventie. The sense of war was always present. The visible difference was the slightly elevated site on a ridge. Deep trenches could be dug because there was natural drainage in its medium loam or clay, sand and chalk. In the absence of rock it was easy to mine and counter-mine. Mining was the primary activity, and the only novelty in trench warfare the Battalion found in its new area. Where a mine was sunk the infantry in garrison had to find a carrying-

fatigue for the spoil sent up by the miners. The tactical advantages of a mine successfully blown caused daily activity in sapping and wiring; and small arms, bomb, trench mortar and artillery covered or hindered the work. The knowledge that dirty work was going on underground gave a new meaning to sounds. The tread of an unseen man pacing up and down for warmth on the bricked or duck-boarded trench, the tap of a foot beating time to a tune running in someone's head, the drip of water, any repeated sound of that sort, was apt to be hair-raising – especially in the small hours when vitality is low and we are alive to fancy's prompting – until familiarity with a mined area bred disregard.
THE WAR THE INFANTRY KNEW, CAPTAIN J.C. DUNN

No mans land at Cuinchy varied in breadth from 80 to 275 m (85 to 300 yds), with the narrowest portion lying at the centre of the sector. By mid-1916 the whole area had become a mass of overlapping mine craters, so numerous that in many places their raised 'lips' often completely obscured the opposing trenches. Beneath and inside each stack British engineers and German *Pionieres* carved out the most secure of dugouts, and these were connected not only to neighbouring stacks, mine galleries and mine rescue stations, but eventually to the deep communication subways.

In the same way that towns were dangerous places to be caught under shellfire on account of flying brick and stone fragments, so this too could be an unhealthy spot. With bricks literally lying everywhere, a shell explosion was sure to disperse various sized lumps of rubble in every direction and over long distances. The arrival of the steel helmet was therefore particularly welcome at Cuinchy. The British received the first batches of the Brodie pattern – introduced because of the serious and increasing incidence of head wounds – on 20 October 1915, but the

Above
Undated (c.1915) Panorama A taken from a dangerous spot either on top of or within a brickstack. Mine craters are visible in the narrow band of no man's land. The big central crater has probably been blown to destroy a wide area of underground battlefield, and everything within its 'sphere of destruction'. A British soldier's head (with soft cap) is just visible within the curving trench in front of the crater.

Left
German *Pionieres* in their dugouts near Cuinchy. Note the untimbered rear wall – the chalk geology is largely self-supporting.

Above
Narrow French trenches near Loos, widened and remodelled by the British when they took over the sector.

Below
Lieutenant Robert Graves, who served in the Cuinchy sector with the Royal Welch Fusiliers in the summer of 1915.

helmets were in such short supply that only those serving in the front lines received 'a tin-lid'. It was here and in the trenches of neighbouring Cambrin that the writer and poet Robert Graves served during the late spring and summer of 1915. In *Goodbye To All That* his descriptions of both sectors offer a subtle flavour of everyday life in the line, and on rest in Béthune and its neighbouring villages. Edmund Blunden, who also served both here and on the Givenchy front, gives marvellous descriptions of both sectors in *Undertones of War*.

Although mining was equally prevalent in adjacent Cambrin, this sector possessed an entirely different 'feel' to Cuinchy. Here, the trenches were deep and narrow, much dryer, but difficult to negotiate at the best of times on account of their limited width – a legacy of early French occupation. Each spring the two sectors were noted for the rather peculiar phenomenon of plagues of frogs and mice – possibly due to the countless dark and damp crevices provided by the brickfields. During the summer months dense vegetation sprouted from parapet and parados, 'roofing in' trenches with a verdant canopy. In the space of a few hundred metres, therefore, the nature of the trench environment altered immeasurably simply by reason of the geology: at Cambrin the clay beds of Flanders taper away, to be replaced by the free-draining, predominantly chalk-based subsoils of Artois. From this point southwards quarry symbols are suddenly conspicuous upon trench maps, and in towns and villages older buildings feature a larger percentage of natural stone in their construction. The nature of smaller settlements also alters: the randomly spaced agriculture-based cottage settlements built over centuries are replaced by the terraced and paved industrial streets of the *Corons*.

Due to the incessant daily damage by German trench mortars interrupting essential supply, approaches to the front line were by subway – underground communication trenches, courtesy of 251 Tunnelling Company RE – and in these too one may see how the alteration in geology affected tactics: in the clays to the north of the canal there are no subways; the dry chalk from this point southwards encouraged their ubiquitous use.

At around 150 m (165 yds), no man's land at Cambrin had a similar average width to Cuinchy. It too was pitted by mine craters, the most famous of which were the two greatest, aptly named Etna and Vesuvius. Another small brickfield was present, but the sector was more notable for other aspects: it was the beginning of the Lens coalfield area, and in being adjoined to Cuinchy, was also part of the northernmost flank of the Loos offensive of 25 September 1915. In preparing for this battle, the two sectors received a substantial proportion of the 5,500 gas cylinders brought forward for Britain's first major foray into chemical warfare. It was here too that the chlorine curled back onto troops assembled for the assault. The consequences were tragic, resulting in only a very limited advance being made on the northern flank. Worried RE Special Brigade officers responsible for the discharge had warned of the risks only to be told that the agreed release programme must be adhered to. A major part of the problem lay in the fact that during this early period personal gas protection was still primitive, consisting of the 'goggle-eyed bugger with a tit', a flannel bag impregnated with gas neutralizing phenol-hexanate, with mica eye-pieces and a rubber outlet valve. The device, known as a PH helmet, was deployed by pulling it down like a paper bag to cover the entire head, tucking the open end into the tunic collar to form a doubtful seal. The moment this was done, however, the eyepieces steamed up, severely impairing vision; in addition, the positioning of the valve also meant it was impossible to effectively aim a rifle. On the day of battle most men kept their gas-helmets rolled up on top of the head like a cap, but the gas arrived so unexpectedly and in such concentration that for many it was too late to don them effectively.

The Germans had been prepared for the attack in any case. In the same way that the Somme battle was launched the following summer, two mines at Cuinchy intended to assist the 2nd Division attack were blown before zero – *ten minutes* before – alerting the enemy and allowing them to prepare defences. Three more mines were blown immediately before the assault, but their effect and damage was inconsequential as the Germans had already vacated several parts of the front line in favour of using support trenches as the main line of defence. Having clambered across the crater field at great cost, the British captured empty trenches: it was the only gain on the northern flank.

Before and after Loos, the major offensive activities in both sectors were sniping and mining, although there were one or two notable and fascinating exceptions:

6 Octber 1916

Well, this morning I started off a bit later than usual and met a Trench Mortar officer friend of mine. "Coming to watch?" he said. "Watch what?" "Don't you know we are having a daylight raid?" he whispered. He told me the time and ten minutes later I was in a sniper's post with a clear view and cheek by jowl with a Padre captain, the first clergyman I had seen with a steel helmet on. Two minutes before time I ducked my head when our guns and Trench Mortars started. They put on as pretty a barrage as one could wish and then the Padre shouted "There they are!" and twenty of our fellows headed by an officer were over the parapet and streamed across no man's land like a pack of hounds. The Padre and I stood up forgetting all about Boche bullets. One of the most thrilling moments I've ever experienced, and I've come to the conclusion that in a charge the excitement of battle will carry you a long way. At that moment I would have given anything to have been in that rush. You could see the bayonets gleam in the sun which first came out at that moment. Then you could see them jump and disappear. All the time our guns were going and the Boche support line was just a cloud of dust which drifted back towards us. And then suddenly out of the cloud our men came streaming at a dog trot with the officer in the rear. The Padre counted them, "All safe, thank God." Then one fell forward on his face, but he had only stumbled and was up again and twenty seconds later they were all safe. I met them as they came out of the communication trench, panting after their run. Some had bayonets and others revolvers and bombs. They were in shirt sleeves open at the neck and looked fit and happy, but were all disappointed at not getting a prisoner, which meant six days leave. They found the trench deserted but bombed some dugouts, they told me gleefully. It is considered an absolute insult to Boche so I'm told, for a party of men in broad daylight to raid a trench and return unscathed, and has hardly ever been attempted before. He is evidently a bit peeved as he has been strafing us ever since.

SECOND LIEUTENANT H. L. MORTON DSO, 255 TUNNELLING COMPANY RE

The prevalence of mining led to numerous similar small-scale forays into enemy territory, with a mix of infantry and sappers seeking out enemy shafts and dugouts to molest with mobile charges. Despite the absolute necessity to counter an enemy underground assault, and despite a year of underground warfare in the sector, Morton, in common with every other tunnelling company, had difficulties persuading senior infantry and artillery colleagues of the need for mining – until they had been woken to the threat by a German blow. Although unseen, a colossal amount of work was required to install, extend and maintain mine systems. In October 1916 255 TC's new shaft was subjected to perpetual strafing by heavy German trench mortars know as 'rum jars'.

9 October 1916

Later on in the day he started to search for our new shaft and came very close indeed. I was standing at the top when the whistles went with the fatigue party. We all looked up but could see nothing. Then sh-shoo-sh, and we crouched. An awful bang on the parapet. I laughed outright with relief. The man next to me got a lump of earth on top of his tin hat. After this we retired underground for half an hour. I hear Shepherd was driven underground yesterday by continual strafing from rum jars. He got so angry that he finally went around to the Artillery officers dug-out and asked them why they did not put the Boche guns out of action. He told them he had seen the flash and knew exactly where the gun emplacement was. They hummed and haaed and finally he volunteered to bring his miners up and attack the gun with lumps of chalk, which would be more effective than artillery. He then left.

SECOND LIEUTENANT H. L. MORTON DSO

Morton notes in the same letter that one in five rum jars was a dud. This excerpt is meant to be as informative as it is mildly amusing: the final line confirms that the geological transformation from clay to chalk takes place here; it affected a huge change in the nature of trench life, trench construction, personal security and military tactics from this point southwards. Cambrin, therefore, is the beginning of what is called the 'transition belt'.

Above

Snipers – an ever present risk at Cuinchy and Cambrin. This is a British team working on the canal embankment.

Right

A bleak German view of one of the Hohenzollern craters. Note that much of the upturned ground is clearly chalk, but some patches of surface loam are also visible.

Below

Another advantage of deep trenches: captured design for a German trench latrine.

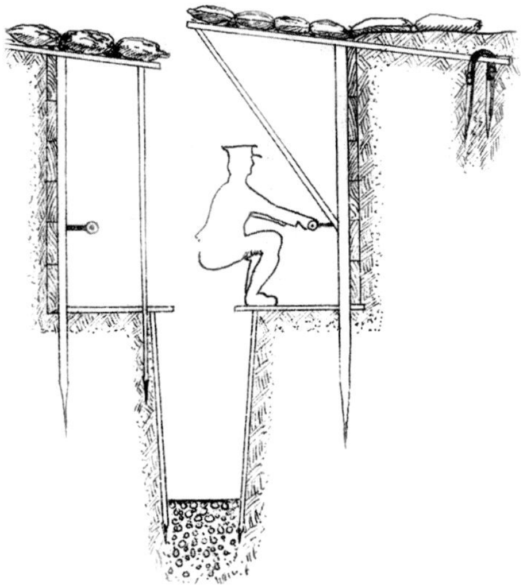

Hohenzollern, the Quarries and Hulluch

The adjoining sub-sector to the south was certainly no stranger to violence and bloodshed. The Hohenzollern Redoubt, a diminutive salient bulging out towards the British lines, (dubbed according to Kaiser Wilhelm's monarchical name), was a veritable hell-hole, developing a reputation similar to Hill 60, Hooge and the Bluff at Ypres. The Germans were renowned for incorporating every useful contour into their tactical scheme, either by advance or retirement, and in the practically flat Gohelle landscape the fancifully named Mont d'Auchy into which the redoubt was burrowed was just a few meagre metres higher than the surrounding countryside. But it was a critical feature – and one which would be retained at great cost.

The redoubt, which can be partly viewed in Panoramas 42 and 52, covered a tiny area on contemporary

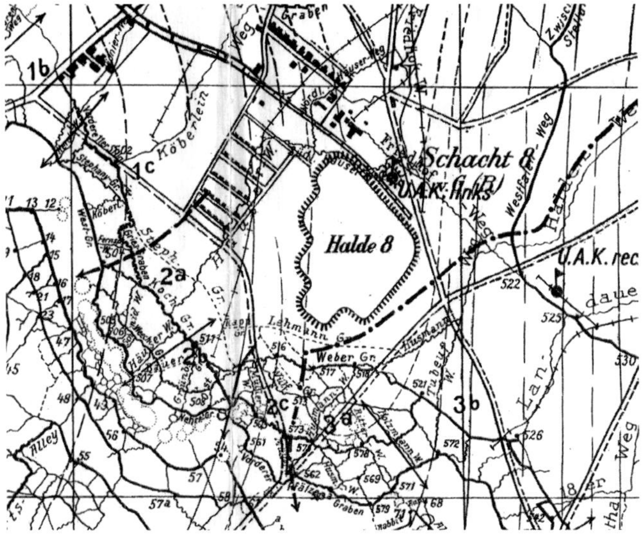

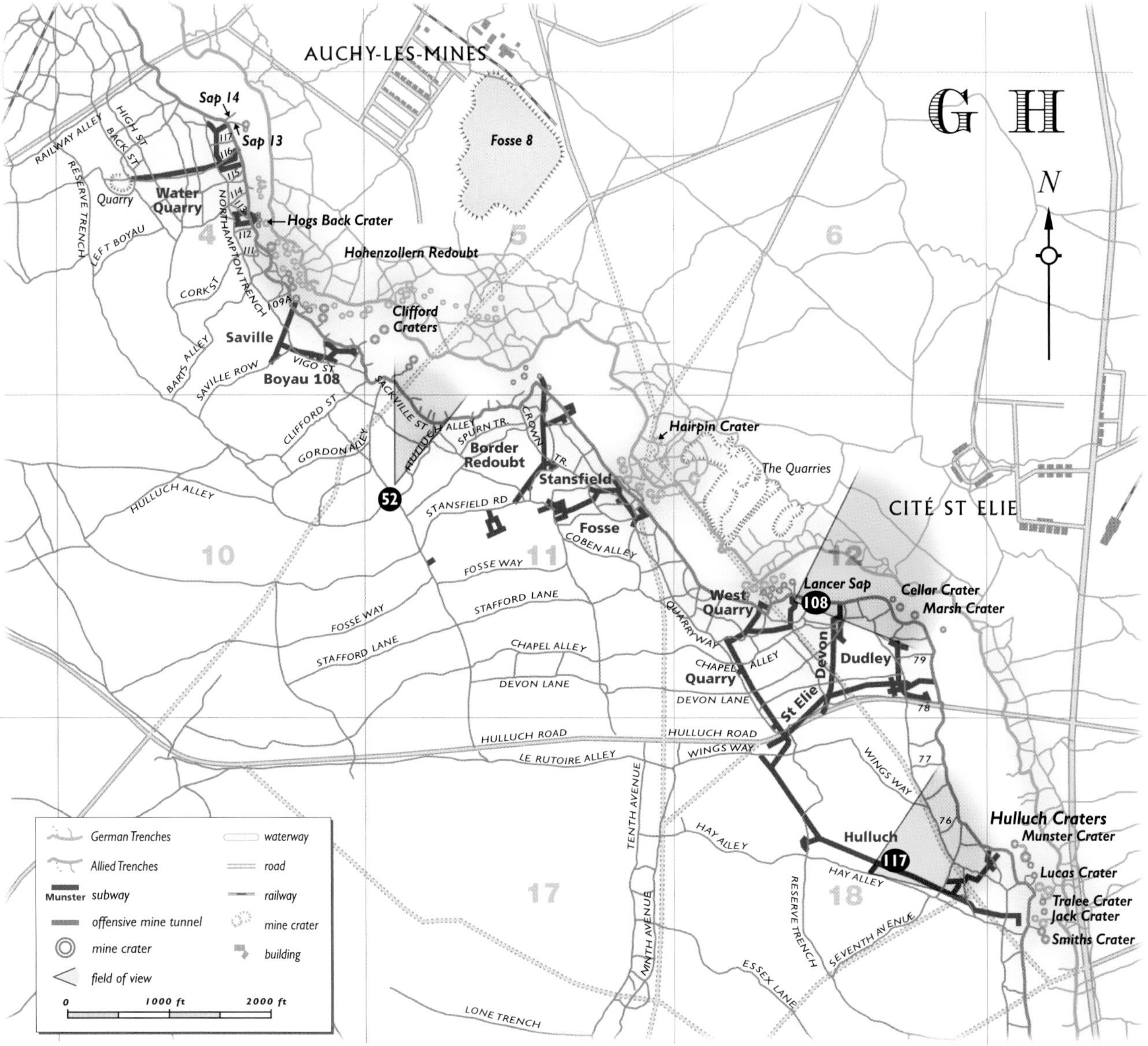

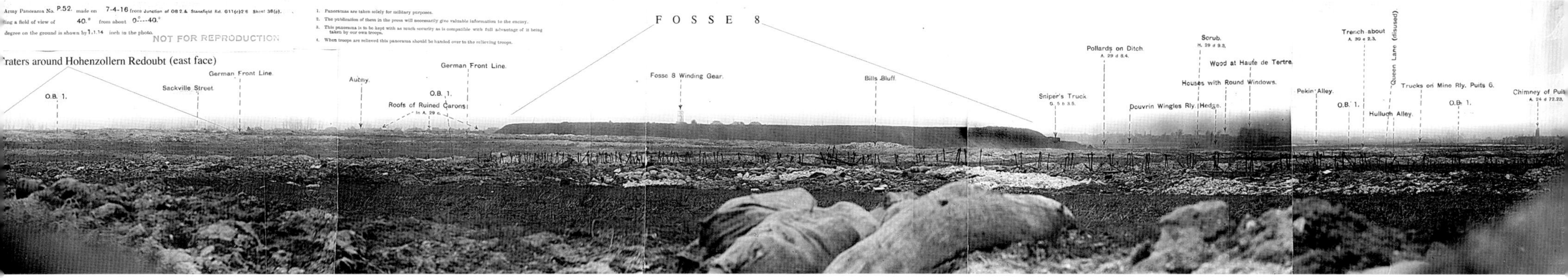

Above
Segment of Panorama 52 showing the Fosse 8 slag heap known as The Dump, April 1916. The fighting at this time was mainly underground.

Opposite
German trench map segment of the Hohenzollern Redoubt area.

trench maps, and although captured in its entirety by the 9th (Scottish) Division with the help of gas and Russian saps (shallow tunnels crossing beneath no man's land) on 25 September 1915 at the beginning of the Battle of Loos, the position was soon lost to a series of typically venomous German counter-attacks. By 3 October the British were left clinging grimly onto its nose. For a short time the front line trench was *shared* by both sides, the troops being separated by rude sandbag blocks, but when the line settled and consolidated, no man's land grew to be a narrow crescent-shaped strip of shattered ground strewn with the remains of those who had fought for possession of the Redoubt. Engineers on both sides took full advantage of the nearness of the enemy, digging tunnels at several depths and blowing dozens of mines. For two years fighting both above and below ground was equally bitter, the slenderness of no man's land and the crater field especially encouraging the use of short-range weaponry such as grenades, rifle grenades and mortars.

19 October 1915

This shambles (you can call it nothing else) is about 200 yards in front of our old fire-trench. The part of it which we hold and the communication trench leading to it have been so shelled that, at the time we took them over, they were no longer trenches but ditches, very wide and shallow, with frequent upheavals in the floor, indicating the positions of dead men, now wholly or partly covered with earth splashed over them by the bursting shells and the passage of troops. It would, I suppose, be an exaggeration to say that the parapets of this place are built up with dead bodies, but it is true to say they are dovetailed with them, and everywhere arms and legs and heads protrude. The artillery certainly did its work well here. The surface of the ground over a large area has been reduced to a shapeless jumble of earth mounds and shell-holes. The formidable wire entanglements have gone. On all sides lie the dead. It is a war picture of the most frightful description; and the fact that the dead are, practically speaking, all our dead, arouses in me a wild craving for revenge. Where are the enemy's dead? We hear much of them but do not see them.

DIARY, LIEUTENANT ROWLAND FEILDING, COLDSTREAM GUARDS

Much of the subsequent fighting at Hohenzollern was simply to claim ownership of holes in the ground – the craters and their raised lips – and success was calculated according to how many one held. As in the Ypres Salient crater-fighting here was no less feared by the infantry, simply because of the appalling casualty rates associated with this specialized combat: the Germans excelled but, as elsewhere, the benefits of occupation seldom repaid the terrible sacrifice of capture. During the Loos fighting consolidation of mere square metres of gained ground was carried on day and night, and even a short tour of duty at Hohenzollern could reduce a battalion's strength by half.

15 October 1915

Had to dig 2 saps for bombing out of Sap L. Sap L connects our firing line with west face of Hohenzollern Redoubt which we now hold. Went up Sap L by daylight to fix work and a gas shell landed quite close which made me feel quite bad. The sap was about 2 feet deep and therefore rather risky going up it. Saps dug were to be 18 feet long and 4 feet wide, and 4 foot 6 inches deep and connected by communication trenches. I was greatly hindered by relieving parties and shell fire.

16 October
Bad headache from gas shell. In evening had to wire from 50 yards our side Big Willie (leading from west face of the Redoubt to German lines) to our fire trench. This entanglement ran down the side of Sap K, a sap parallel to Sap L. I had charge of French wire, divided men into parties of three every 20 yards. These men went out 40 yards from sap at 11.20pm and we worked homewards but, as Corporal Cooper made a curve, we gradually got further out till we were 100 yards out. Lt. Baile looked after the barbed wire and at 12.15 he had just left me to go back to sap when he was shot through the heart. I assisted to carry him back to the sap but he was dead. On reaching sap I learned that 2 Lt. Baker was wounded in the leg and had been removed.

17 October
12.30am Ramsden sent for me and we did not finish the wiring, about 40 yards remain to be done. We slept and talked till 5 when a bomb attack was started up Big Willie and the forward two trenches leading to the west face of the Redoubt. We were in readiness to block the trenches but were not required. We stayed on till 4.30pm during which time we ere heavily shelled and all entanglements destroyed.

20 October
Working on revetting in Hohenzollern Redoubt. We were making a traverse of sandbags where one of our dead lay; stench was abominable and we were revetting from this traverse to a T sap. This west face is very badly knocked about and dead bodies are lying everywhere, increasing the difficulty as earth is very scarce as you keep on uncovering these bodies. In the afternoon I arranged in company with Scots Guards to start a point d'appui at the T in Sap K now called Savile Row. We wired from the T to our fire trench last Saturday. The left branch of T is a new Sap to West Face of Redoubt and the right is a new trench to sap further east. A double MG emplacement was started to enfilade the right branch and Big Willie, and to enfilade the left branch and fire across to Point 60. It was also arranged to continue the right branch back 18 feet so as to form a bombing sap in case Germans come down the left branch from H Redoubt.

21 October
Went round to look at MG emplacement with OC. Anxious enquiries were also made as to result of the bomb attack in the Left Hand end of Hohenzollern Redoubt as I was present when CO Irish Guards planned the attack, giving him a bit of technical information. In evening paraded with Penfold to work on West Face.

22 October
On West Face of Hohenzollern Redoubt. We had to sap 18 yards from the West Face to a new trench which had been dug from an old German sap coming out of the middle of the West Face towards the left hand end of the Redoubt. This was completed in 12 hours, then I laid out this trench for traverse for a fire trench. MG emplacement was also continued in Savile Row. I noticed a dead Captain 20 yards in front of the MG emplacement. During the sapping 3 dead bodies were unearthed. One a Prussian officer 6' 6" high; from him we got 2 maps, 2 postcards and 1 diary, which were left at Headquarters. The sap started out of the new piece of trench gained in bomb attack on 21 inst. Many trophies are to be found in the way of German helmets, picks, shovels, rifles etc., and entrenching tools. Some of the sights of the dead bodies are most revolting.

DIARY, LIEUTENANT HAROLD RIDSDALE, 76 FIELD COMPANY RE [HAROLD RIDSDALE'S COUSIN WAS LATER KILLED AT HOHENZOLLERN]

On 13 October 1915, during the week following the end of Loos, two brigades of 47th (Midland) Division were charged with recapturing the Redoubt. Gas was again employed, but in meagre quantities. The artillery failed to cut the protective wire and the result of the Midlanders' efforts was a loss of over 3,500 men. Although very high-ranking officers were killed and several VCs won during the struggle for possession of the Hohenzollern, one of the most famous names to fight there was the brother of the future Queen Elizabeth, the Queen Mother, Captain Fergus Bowes-Lyon of 8th Black Watch, who on 27 September led 100 of his men forward to help ward off a German counter-attack. Whilst fighting in the east face (see Panorama 52) he was killed by a shell burst. His body was never recovered.

Behind Hohenzollern lay the small village of Auchy-les-Mines. This too was a critical topographical point as it

Above
The Hohenzollern Redoubt under shellfire and cloud gas attack on 13 October 1915. The white cloud in the centre is smoke, which was released to confuse the Germans.

Below
The poet Charles Sorley was killed here in 1915.

Overleaf
Segment of First Army Panorama P108, 24 March 1917, showing the mine crater field in front of St Elie.

Below
Hulluch craters – aerial view. The British trenches are in the bottom left corner of the frame. Mine craters entirely fill no man's land, whilst the German positions occupy the rest of the photograph.

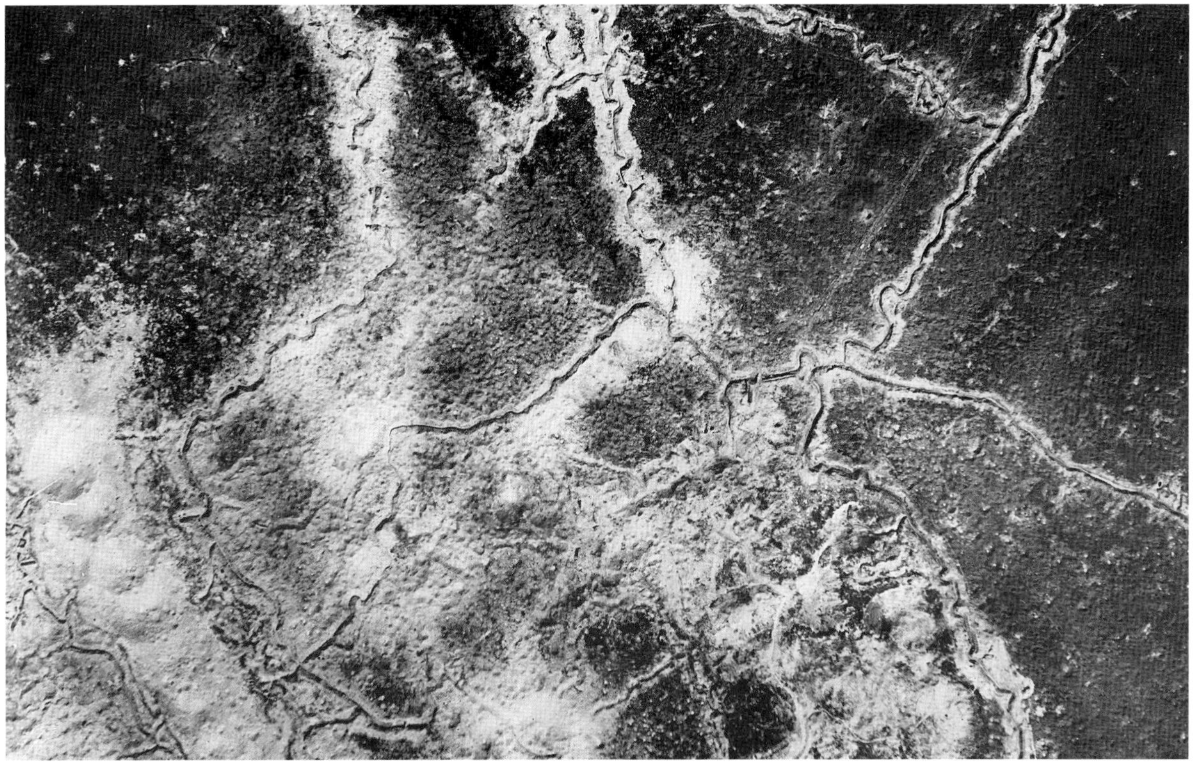

was adjacent to one of the northernmost pits of the Loos and Lens coal mining area. From here to Vimy Ridge the most important features in the landscape now become twofold: the *Crassiers*, the great slag heaps which dominate the battlefield, and the towering ironwork winding gear at the coal-mine shaft heads. For obvious reasons, all were of the highest military value. Panorama 52 (7 April 1916) of the Hohenzollern sector shows Fosse 8 (today replaced with a rubbish dump) glowering over the British lines, and the terraced *Corons* of Auchy; in the foreground lie the craters along the southern face of the redoubt. This desolate piece of ground is the route which the two 47th (Midland) Division brigades followed during their 13 October attack.

Panorama 108 shows the observational value of the *puits* in the flat Gohelle landscape, and also Sellar and Marsh craters, the results of tunnelling activities in front of Cité St Elie, a part of the Hulluch system entrusted to 253 Tunnelling Company. The front line (and tunnels) in this sub-sector were served by Quarry, Devon, Dudley and St Elie subways, all of which lie beneath the trenches shown here. It was also the scene of an attack by 2nd Worcesters. At 1 p.m. on 27 September 1915 all four companies of the battalion moved forward in waves, directed by the commander of the 7th Division, Major-General T. Capper, and their own Major P. Wainman. The Worcesters got no closer than 200 m (220 yds) from the enemy before they were forced to go to ground in primitive trenches already occupied by the dead and wounded of earlier attacks. The entire garrison, including the injured, were evacuated under cover of darkness throughout the night. The following day, over 300 casualties were listed for the battalion, and both the officers named above had been killed. Gun Trench, also marked on this panorama, was the site where poet Lieutenant William Noel Hodgson of *Before Action* fame (written shortly before the Battle of the Somme), won his Military Cross. On 13 October 1915, another celebrated poet, Charles Hamilton Sorley of 7th Battalion, the Royal Sussex Regiment, was killed by a sniper in an attack on the Hairpin Trench; the location is obscured by the tangle of barbed wire to the left of frame.

Panoramas 115 and P97 especially illustrate the effect the change in geology has had upon the physical nature of the battlefield and entrenchments compared to those north of the La Bassée Canal. Without the need for breastworks considerably fewer sandbags and a fraction of the timber were needed for revetment, and trenches could be dug to a full 2 m (6 ft) in the free-draining chalk. The harder geology also meant that the proportion of picks to shovels was greater than that required for clay! However, chalk was a noisier medium to excavate, especially where bands of tough flints, a common feature in chalk, were present, and this created problems for working parties on both sides: the noise of steel tools ringing on the hard stones travelled sharply across a dark and quiet no man's land – to the welcoming ears of vigilant enemy machine-gunners. The nature of the underground war was also fundamentally altered by the change in geology. In clay and sand one could work almost silently, but in chalk there was no way to achieve this except by a painstakingly slow and careful 'nibbling', a method which was so slow as to be

almost entirely unacceptable. The same sound heard through 20 m (65 ft) of clay might be heard at 100 m (330 ft) in chalk. Clay-kicking was of course impossible: with the pick being the compulsory digging method neither side held the upper hand. However, it required a skilled eye to make good headway in the tough ground; experienced men, usually from coal mines in the UK, who were accustomed to identifying the geological weak points – fissures and cracks – could achieve twice the driving rate of less skilled colleagues. The ubiquity of chalk geology in the Artois and Picardy uplands, meant that this situation prevailed throughout the rest of the British-held front. The visible product of tunnelling – craters – are marked on all the maps of the sector. They were widespread. The fine operational details for every one of these remarkable and chilling tunnelling schemes can be found at the National Archives at Kew, and the Royal Engineers Museum and Library near Chatham.

Immediately adjacent to Hohenzollern lay the Quarries and Hulluch (pronounced Ooloo). Panoramas 117 and 115, both of May 1917, are taken from positions some 200 m (220 yds) inside the 25 September 1915 German front lines – the extent of the eventual British gain in this area after the battle. On the extreme right of Panorama 117, Hay (Haaie) Alley communication trench can be seen; beneath it lies the Hulluch Subway, which served both the front line and the mines associated with the craters pictured.

Panorama 101, which appears to be broken but in fact was taken in three pieces to protect the photographer (wisely sheltering behind the brickwork), shows the view from the east side of Loos after the Guards Division had fought their way through the village to occupy these trenches. Although the frame is disjointed and some features are duplicated close to the edges of the central breaks, the panorama is valuable in illustrating not only the post-battle 1915 landscape, but also the northern part of the Hill 70 territory attacked by the Canadians on 15 August 1917 as a ruse to draw German attention away from Third Ypres (a wider view of the entire Hill 70 battlefield can be seen in Panorama 125). During and after this successful Canadian engagement the industrial area was mangled by the artillery of both sides until France's one-time premier coal-mining region presented a deplorable and saddening spectacle.

To Lens, Thelus, Vert Tilleul, Vimy to Lens. Even worse damage than in Albert and Bapaume. (Albert, pre-war 7,500 inhabitants, Bapaume 5–6,000, Lens 35,000) What remains? A few pillars sticking out of a pile of debris indicating the site of the church. Number 13 of the Lens mines, the Fosse St Elie, was activated shortly before the war; the Germans blew up the whole installation; the extraction machinery was broken up and destroyed, the boilers shattered . . . a titanic pile of twisted iron and tangled beams; boilers punctured with machine gun fire, shafts inundated. This is premeditated, deliberate ruin. A desolate landscape, flooded, inhabited by dead trees, ruined houses, villages destroyed, towns wiped out.

Above
A German soldier buried by the effect of heavy mortar fire during the fighting for Hill 70 in 1917.

Below
Panorama 101: the Hill 70 sub-sector photographed in November 1915 after the Battle of Loos, but almost two years before it would fall into Canadian hands.

Above
A segment of Panorama 137 showing the terrible destruction in and around the industrial town of Lens in September 1917.

Inset
15 January 1919: an engineer officer ponders the task of rebuilding the coalfields. RE officers assisted the French for many years after the Armistice.

Clearing up alone will take years, thousands of hectares are riddled with trenches, and there are thousands more to sift through, thousands of kilometres of barbed wire, and there are still thousands of kilometres more. The fields are being cleared of munitions, and the quantity of shells on and under the ground can be counted in hundreds of thousands, in millions. Temporary shelters have been sent, but there are few to be seen. Some fields are under cultivation, but how many remain barren!

Yet there are some people living in these whited sepulchres of villages and towns. They find shelter in cellars, making rough rooms, and stove-pipes can be seen sticking out of the ground; no water, no light, no drainage. . . the wretchedness of our refugees continues, like that of our liberated peoples, the folk who have been repatriated.

UNION DES COMITES DES REFUGIES DES DEPARTMENTS ENVAHIES, 1919

The kind of sight which greeted the French Refugee Committee can be seen in Panorama 137 taken from the Bois de Riaumont near Lievin in September 1917, and looking beyond Lens over the eastward extension of the coalfields behind Vimy Ridge towards Douai. Because the entire region close to the front lines was so heavily industrialized, many find such scenes more shocking than those of the agricultural regions of the Somme and Ypres. All this appalling devastation was caused in less than three months in 1917.

The Dumps and Crassiers

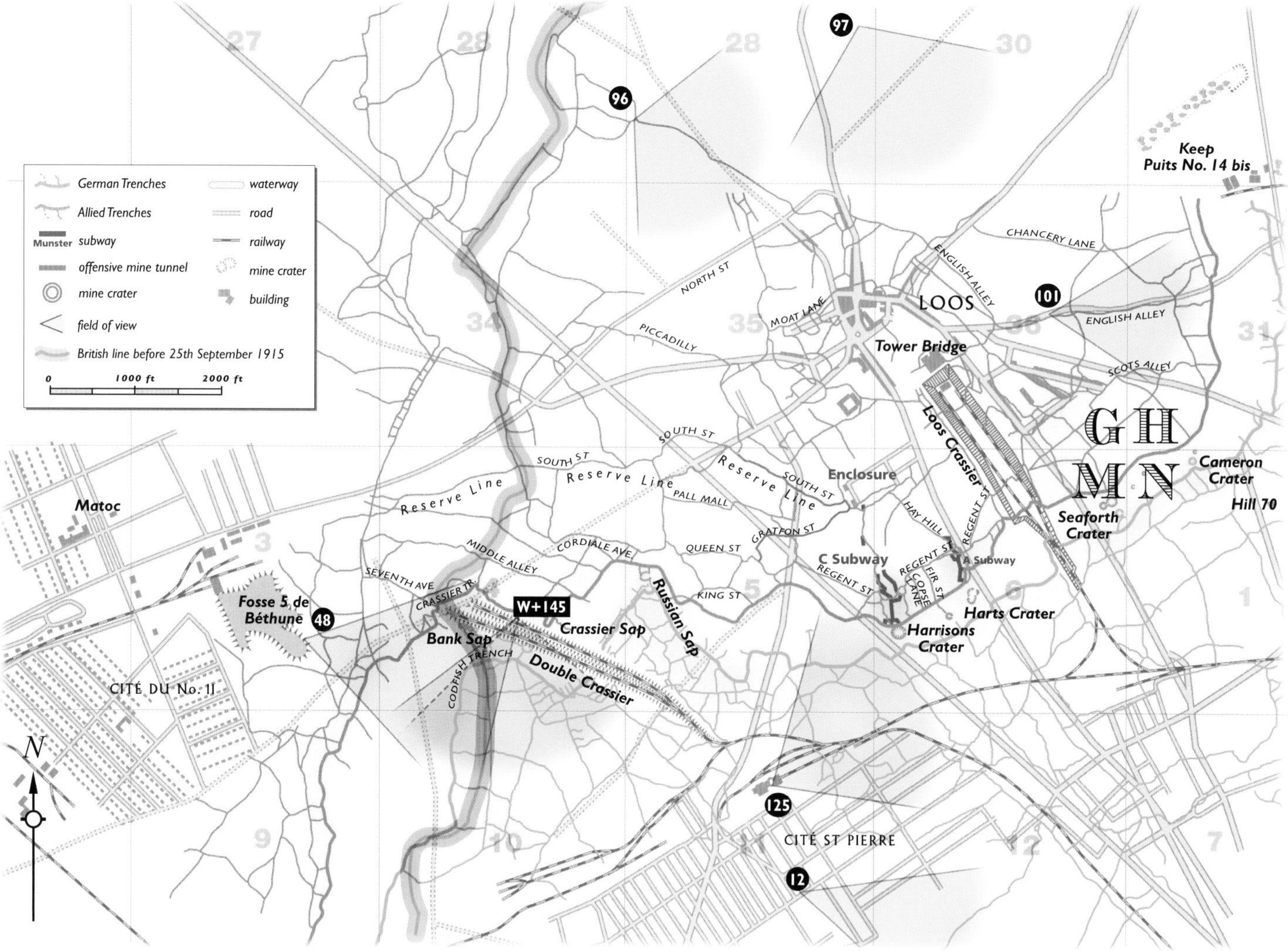

The most recognizable and famous features on the Gohelle battlefields, the dumps and *crassiers* of coal waste, were critical points for observation, and therefore fiercely attacked, mainly with artillery. Eyewitnesses report high explosive shells bursting upon the heaps of inky-black waste creating a fountain of earth resembling a volcanic eruption – see No 120 for the results. None of the original wartime features of this kind still exist, but the huge conical *Terrils* which dominate the Loos landscape today (and also existed elsewhere in the sector during the war – see No 137) sit on the site of the most renowned example, the Double Crassier. This was a multiple affair: a pair of 15 m (50 ft) high parallel linear slag heaps formed by the gradual tipping of waste from an ever-extending light railway – a typical feature in

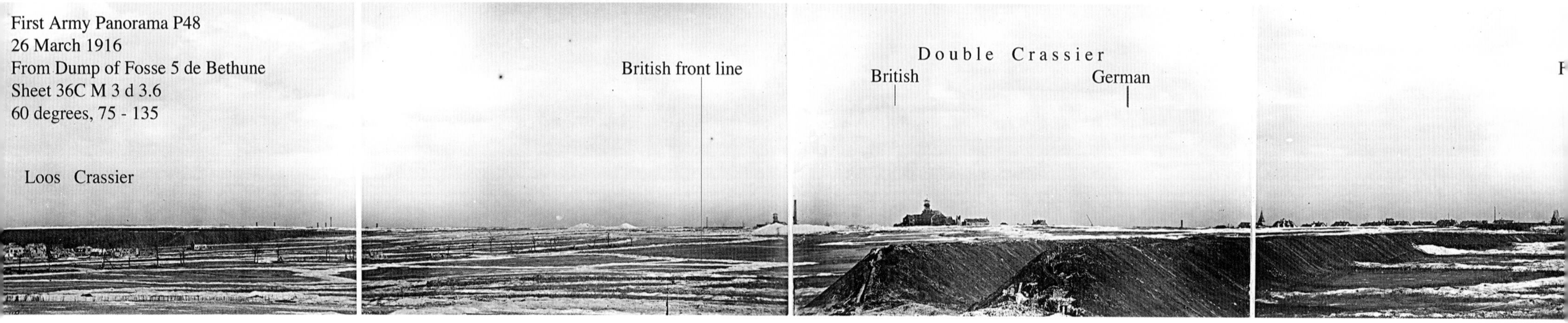

Above
The imposing and rather elegant mine winding-gear which was dubbed Tower Bridge sits astride the head of the Loos Crassier. Panorama 96, 30 September 1915.

mining areas the world over. Panorama 48 illustrates the origin of the *double* nomenclature, and also shows another heap to the north-east: the Loos Crassier, with at its northern end the winding gear known as Tower Bridge, a structure used very effectively by the Germans for observation until almost entirely destroyed by British guns. See Panoramas 96 and *97* for two spectacular views, and also the ground over which the 21st Division attacked on the first day of Loos, just a few days beforehand. Lieutenant Rowland Feilding of the Coldstream Guards inspected the ground pictured soon after the pictures were taken.

2 October 1915

Hopwood and I crossed our old front line and Noman's Land – here about 500 yards wide – past the Lone Tree to the German trenches. The ground was strewn with our dead, and in all directions were wounded men crawling on their hands and knees. It was piteous, and it is a dreadful thought that there are occasions when one must resist the entreaties of men in such condition, and leave them to get in as best they can, or lie out in the cold and wet, without food, and under fire, as they often have to do for days and nights together. We had some timbers thrown over a trench as a bridge for some of them who said they had been trying all day to find a way across; but we had our own work to do, and we also had to get back and report to the battalion, so we could not do much; – indeed, it would have been a never-ending job had we attempted it.

The German trenches, which for so many weeks we have looked at only from the other side of Noman's Land, were very like our own. The barbed-wire entanglements in front of them were, however, far more formidable than ours. These formed a regular maze, and how

Below
The 'football pitch' between the two *crassiers* in Panorama 48. Compare this view with No 125 (5 July 1917) on the next two pages.

our men got past them is a mystery. The ground was littered with German rifles, and bayonets, and bombs, and equipment of every sort. The air still reeked of gas, which clung to the ground and made our eyes smart; and every now and then a shell came crashing over from the other side, or a flight of machine-gun bullets made us bob. The battalion arrived about nine o'clock, and we spent the night – till 3am – lying in the open. We them marched to the German trenches, which we manned.

LIEUTENANT ROWLAND FIELDING, *War Letters to a Wife*

Panorama 115 is photographed not far from the 'Lone Tree' mentioned above. The tree was a solitary flowering cherry situated (before the battle) in no man's land, and very often mentioned by chroniclers of Loos. Another feature is Chalk Pit Wood, the place where Rudyard Kipling's son, Lieutenant John Kipling of the Irish Guards, was reputedly last seen before being posted as missing on 27 September 1915. He and his unit attacked across these fields. Rowland Feilding watched this very attack – his own battalion were in support, and followed the Irish into the wood and quarry.

After the Battle of Loos the *crassiers* pictured in Panoramas 96 and *97* were still held by the Germans, and as soon as the line settled into stasis tunnellers got to work not only undermining them but also installing infantry subways to facilitate invisible and safe troop movement to and from the front lines: the panoramas have already shown the depth and narrowness of communication trenches here; it only took one unit to go 'down' an 'up' trench, and traffic chaos ensued. Deep subway schemes were undertaken right along the La Bassée–Lens front, and indeed at Vimy and Arras too. They were a truly 'Commonwealth' effort, dug by Australians, Canadians, New Zealanders and British tunnellers, as well as Pioneer and Army Troops companies. The systems, which often included every 'comfort' including electric lighting and ventilation, plus piped water, helped to save thousands of lives as well as ease the traffic problem. The whole sector was also honeycombed with hundreds of deep dugouts, many of which are connected to the subway schemes; so many dugouts of all sizes were installed on both sides that it is not yet even possible to produce an accurate total number.

Panorama 48 (26 March 1916) is taken from an important British observation post atop the 14 m (46 ft) high Fosse 5 de Béthune (Panorama *84*). The ground between the two *crassiers* (Loos on the left, Double Crassier to the right), visible on both panoramas, is famous for the action of the 18th London Irish Rifles (47th Division). As the gas and smoke clouds dissipated after the opening swirl of battle on 25 September 1915, the battalion went into action across these fields kicking a football ahead of them. The Irishmen overwhelmed the enemy trenches, surged through Loos village and drove on to Hill 70 (see Panoramas 96, 101 and 125), before being driven back to within a few hundred metres of their original starting point.

A wide view of this area showing all the *crassiers*, *puits*, *sièges* and *fosses* on the southern battlefield to the northern

Above

The wide field of view of Panorama 125 (5 July 1917), showing Hill 70 in the middle.

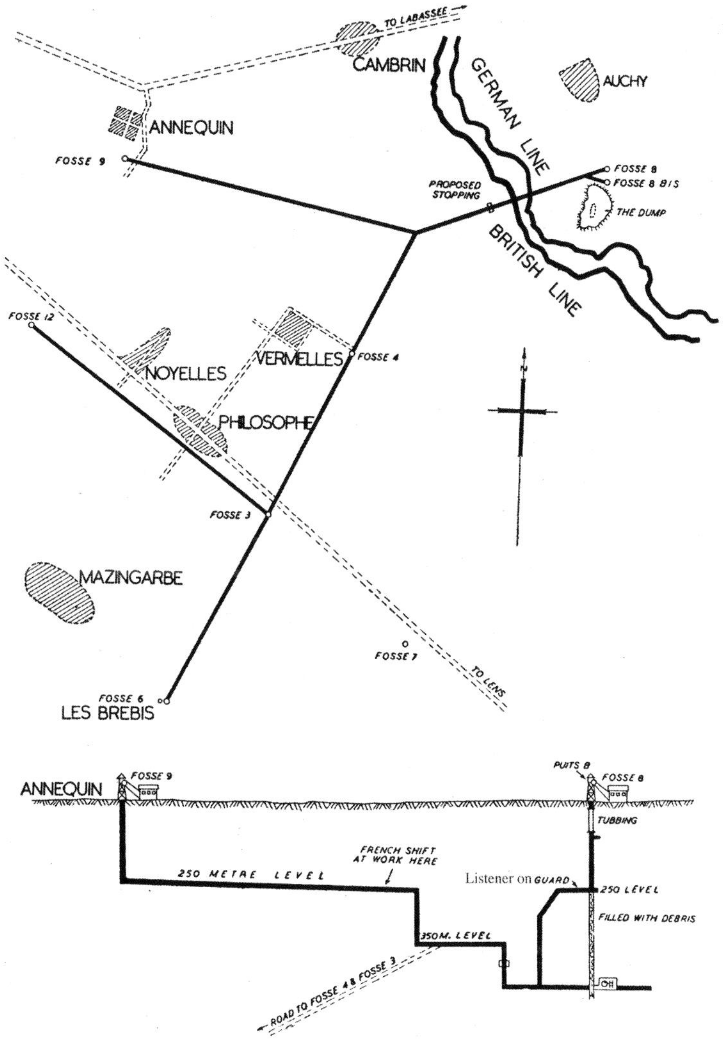

Above

Whizz-Bang Corner became a famous trench tramway crossing in Liévin after the town's eventual capture in 1917. The Canadian Corps are in control here.

Right

Plan and section of parts of the civilian coal mines where the bizarre action of September 1917 took place almost 500 m (1,600 ft) underground in the Fosse 8 mines.

flank of Vimy Ridge where the next sector transition begins, can be seen in Panorama *84* (13 August 1916) taken from Laurel OP on the slopes of Notre Dame de Lorette.

The coal mines and ancillary workings served as safe storehouses for trench equipment, weapons and ordnance, with the many caverns and cellars dug beneath the towns and villages providing sheltered and adequate accommodation for troops alongside the dugout schemes. So numerous were the choices of artillery targets in this industrial landscape, that many civilians calculated that the risk of remaining behind to earn money by working for the British was worthwhile. The presence of mining and heavy engineering guaranteed a more than tolerable road, rail and tram network on both sides of the line. For a while, even in the forward areas, the mines continued to be worked for their precious fuel resources. Furthermore, as more refined metals such as brass, bronze and lead became more difficult to source thanks to the British naval blockade, everything of value was stripped out and sent to Germany to be converted into military hardware. Public buildings and churches received similar treatment.

The coalfield was large, complex, well developed and highly productive. Several new mines had only just gone into service prior to the outbreak of war, but several of the older workings were already connected underground. A curious example of the military consequences of this entirely normal peacetime operation involved the German-held Fosse 8 (Panorama 42 and 52). The workings at the bottom of the mineshaft were also connected underground

to Fosses 3, 4, 6, 9 and 12, all of which lay behind *British* lines. It was thought at the time that spies passed to and fro between the two lines via these routes. French mine officials were naturally fearful of irreparable explosive damage being done which would lead to the flooding of the mines (to reach the mineral deposits at depth the shafts descended through around 150 m (490 ft) of waterlogged ground beneath the chalk), so it was decided to build concrete barricades in the 'roads', the name given to galleries in coal mines, and to place twelve armed (military) miners and listeners – at a depth of 240 m (790 ft) underground! This was done. In order to block British entry to Fosse 8 the Germans dropped railway trucks, animal and human carcases, and other debris down the shaft, filling it entirely and shattering the winding gear and ladderways. On 26 September, in an unique episode on the Western Front, the Germans discharged quantities of chloro-picrine down the Fosse 8 shafts, knowing that the natural drafts would take the gas down to the lower level, and disperse it throughout the system. All the 170 Tunnelling Company men on duty underground at the time died, despite a typically courageous, selfless and determined attempt by rescuers to save them. Latterly, several mine shafts and surface works were wantonly blown up by the Germans. Steel-tubbed civilian shafts were universally employed here, the same method as the British military tunnellers used in the clays of Flanders. Readers can imagine the effort and cost required to reconstitute breached shafts of up to 300 m (985 ft) deep.

Slag

The Double Crassier was one of the most bizarre slices of the Western Front after Loos in September 1915, as each side claimed ownership of one limb of the *crassier*. Views from the British-held portion (see diagram and map) can be seen in No 145 (5 August 1916) and Panorama *W*. Their tunnellers grabbed the initiative here, and managed to plant seven mines of between 1,000 and 4,000 lbs before the Germans were fully organized for underground work; these were blown on 7 March 1916. The craters, although rather awkward to see as the ground was entirely made up of uniformly coloured mine waste, are pictured in Panorama 48: careful scrutiny reveals disruption of the flat *crassier* top (*W* and 145 show the views through some of the gaps in the ridge of the German *crassier* caused by the blows). they can also be discerned in No 48, where the white streaks extending to the right from the *crassier* base reveal the entrances to German countermines. In such a terrain the chalk spoil was impossible to camouflage. Tunnelling in this 'semi-organic' material was made yet more difficult and uncomfortable than usual because of what the REs called 'heating', a natural condition replicating the process which takes place in a compost heap. It made the galleries stifling places in which to work. This same panorama also illustrates the two opposing communication trenches mounting the end of each *crassier*.

To its the south lay the major conurbation of Lens and its surrounding *cités*. This was the quintessential industrial battlefield, and the panoramas may well surprise readers as much as they did the author. Lens had been under German control since October 1914. Strongly fortified, it lay on the extreme southern edge of the Loos battlefield in 1915, and saw little action during the fighting. The town did not fall in the Allied attack of August 1917, and only gave up outlying defences the following month when the Canadians annexed 2 km (1 mile) of line at Hill 70. Panorama 12 shows the lines of summer 1916 running

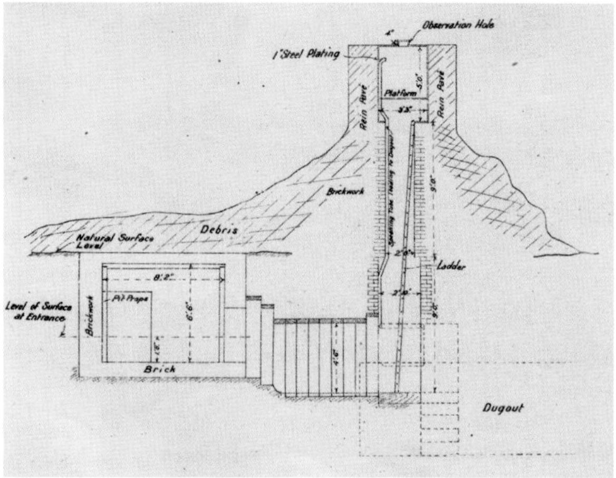

Above

R.E plan of brick-built pavé-reinforced observation dugout sited within a slag heap.

Below

First Army Panorama 48 reveals the importance and value of the slag heaps in the Gohelle landscape. This image is taken from Fosse 5 on 26 March 1916. The Double Crassier is shared.

Above

The view from the crest of the British arm of the Double Crassier on 5 August 1916 showing the damage caused to the German arm caused by the March mines.

Right

Royal Engineer plan of the Double Crassier mines, blown by 173 Tunnelling Company on 7 March 1916.

Underneath

First Army Panorama 120: a view of the Calonne sector of the Lens battlefield from Fosse 5.

across a mixture of railway embankments, terraced streets, canals and rivers, and open fields, all within the same sub-sector. The Douai plain can be seen in the far distance. Panorama 120, taken at nearby Calonne in the early spring, is one of the most remarkable images of the collection and offers a fine 'feel' of the battlefields of this region, in particular giving an excellent impression of the destructive power of the guns. The picture shows the British trenches cutting across the railway embankment, to the left of which can be seen heaps of white chalk; this is the spoil from Marble Arch subway, the entrance of which the troops entered here, safe in the lee of the slope. The subway extends under the railway, beneath the tip of the *crassier* to the right (serving Fosse 5 de Liévin which is just behind the camera), and has three exits emerging into the front line trenches beyond (out of view). On the extreme right the swelling foothills of Vimy Ridge are visible, marking the transition from the plains of Gohelle to the Artois plateau and the Arras sector. Number *146* (5 August 1916) details the exact geological linking point ans shows the other Givenchy at the southern extremity of the sector – Givenchy-en-Gohelle.

Military mining schemes on levels from 5 to 40 m (16 to 130 ft) deep were universally present around Lens as they were in the more northern sector, and it was this rather than surface warfare which occupied the opposing forces throughout 1916. In April 1917, however, Lens fell under siege and throughout the rest of the year fighting was of an unique house-to-house, street-to-street nature. Huge numbers of properties on its western outskirts were destroyed by the Germans to obtain clear fields of fire, and the combination of deliberate destruction and persistent siege-like shellfire reduced the town to rubble.

The German withdrawal to the Hindenburg Line in mid-March 1917 did not affect the situation at Lens as it

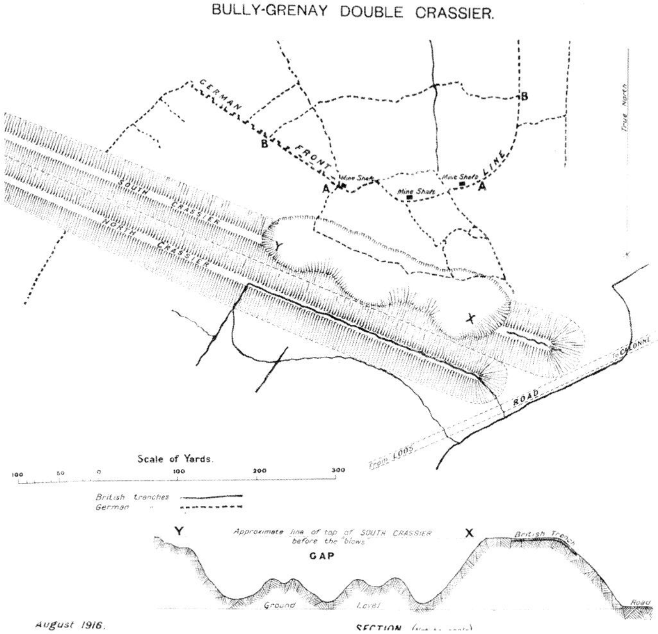

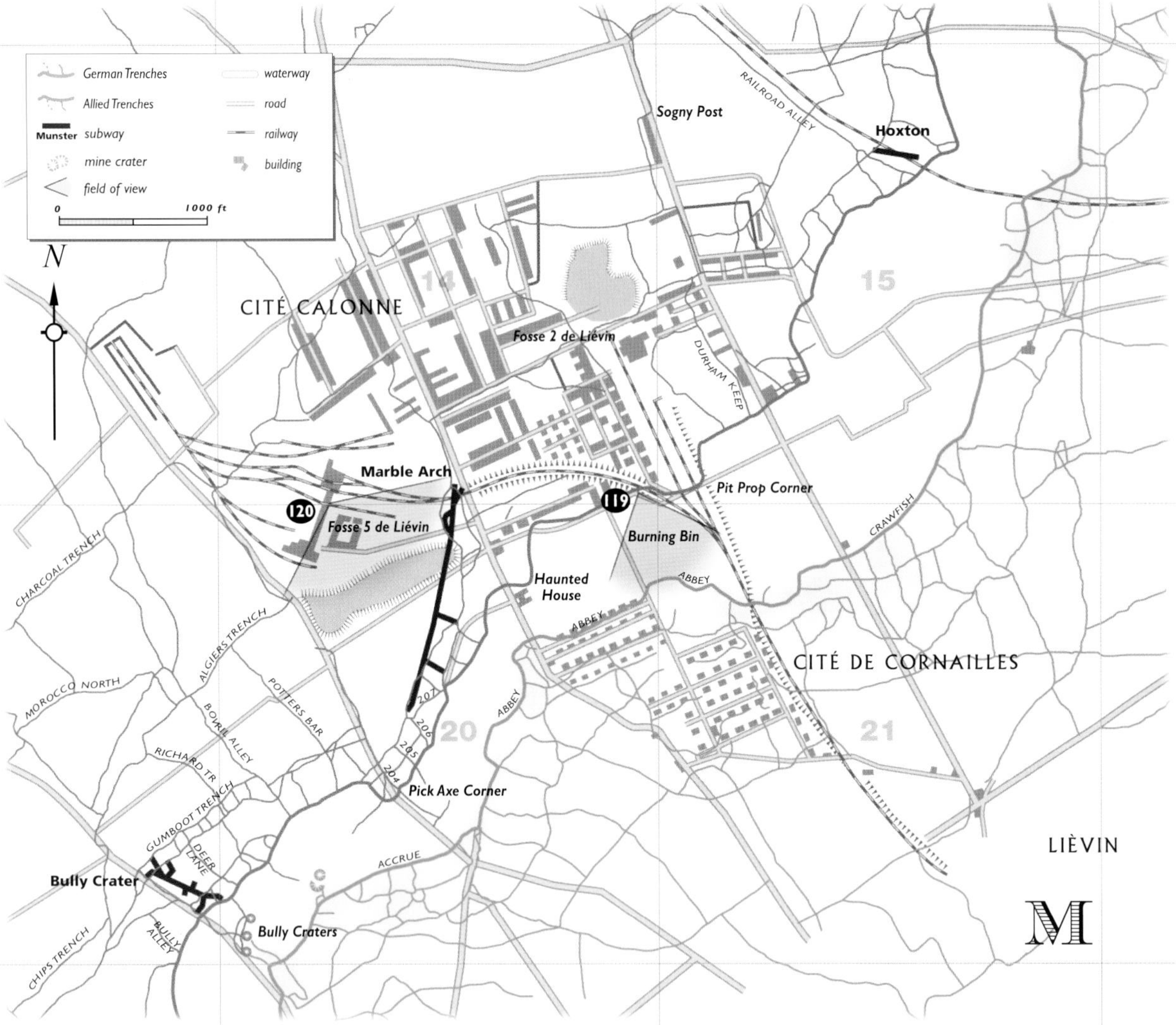

lay outside the northern boundary of the area of evacuation. But the defences had been bolstered in a similar way to the 140 km (90 miles) of massive Siegfried Stellung field fortifications now running behind Vimy and in front of Cambrai and St Quentin (see 565 in Vimy/Arras chapter); indeed, this was a continuation of the powerful German reserve line, the Wotan Stellung, east of Lens. The wooded hills over which it ran sheltered swarms of machine guns, whilst behind lay massed batteries of guns which delayed the British advance and further pulverized the town and its *Cités*. No progress beyond this line was made until spring 1918 when the sector became relatively quiet. It was only when the Allies advanced to the north astride the Lys and south at Cambrai, that the German garrison defending Lens was forced to evacuate, leaving behind a trail of devastation which took decades to repair.

The panoramas taken from Notre Dame de Lorette and Givenchy-en-Gohelle (Nos *84*, 85, *136*) should be regarded as applicable to actions in both the Gohelle, Vimy and Arras sectors, and viewed as a part of the following chapter.

Below

The town of Lens in July 1916, before its total destruction the following year. First Army Panorama 12.

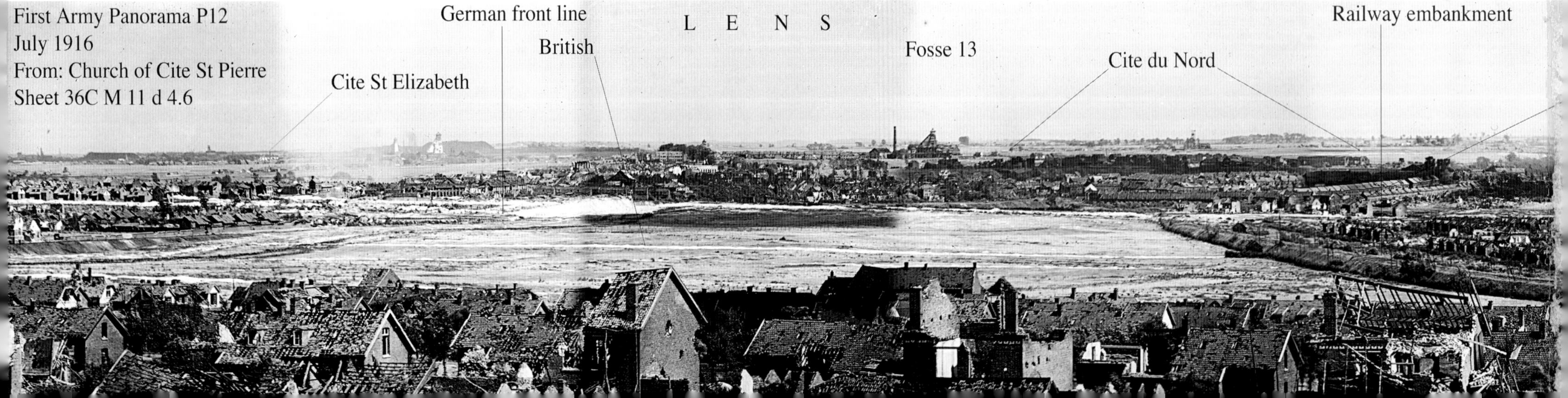

Above
January 1919. Two of the earliest civilians to return to Lens sift the wreckage for unbroken and repairable furniture.

CHAPTER SIX:

VIMY RIDGE AND ARRAS

Both the Arras and Vimy sectors were taken over by British forces in March 1916, relieving the French Tenth Army which had struggled so relentlessly throughout 1915. This portion of the Western Front had formed in October 1914 in a similar way to the Ypres Salient. Arras, an equally handsome medieval trading centre, was 'visited' by the Germans in September who likewise left after a couple of days to dig in on the ridges to the north and east. As trench warfare was established the town became the object of intense German artillery interest; it too was to form the hub of a salient, although one by no means as accentuated as that of Ypres.

Following the three unrewarding French attempts to break the German line via the Vimy Ridge route in 1915 (the three battles of Artois), the sector drifted towards relative tranquillity in the same way as many other erstwhile boisterous areas both to the north in French and Belgian Flanders, and south in the Somme region. As soon as the Tommies arrived, however, the atmosphere heated up, largely as a result of deliberate British belligerence in the form of raids, bombardments and general harassment: it was said at the time that this was a desire to make an impression on the French as much as the Germans. No significant attacks had

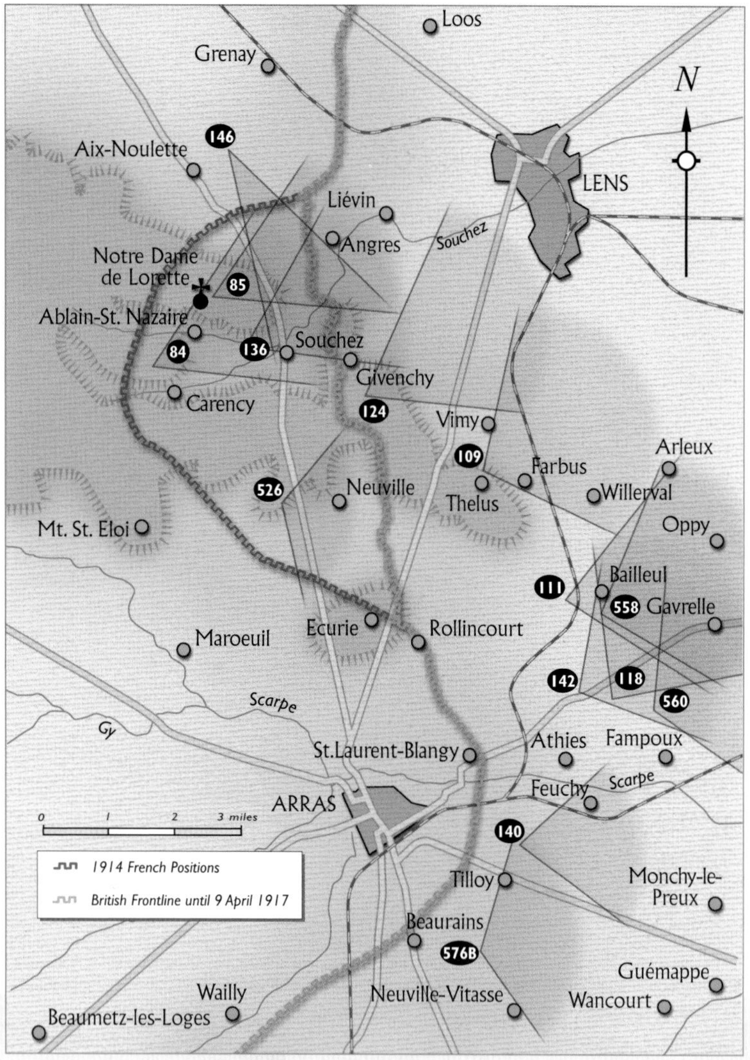

Above

RE survey officers are shown around French trenches on Notre Dame de Lorette Ridge in advance of British occupation.

Pages 264–65

Segment of First Army Panorama 535, July 1916. The view over the rooftops of Arras towards the village of Beaurains.

Below
15 March 1915. Nervous looking troops in front-line French positions on the Notre Dame de Lorette Ridge. Views are extensive – but perhaps it was thought too risky to show one's head on the Ides of March.

Bottom
Part of the 126-degree prospect from *Les Ouvrages Blancs* in May 1916. The full field of view of Panorama 526 extends from the Vimy Ridge craters to Beaurains south-east of Arras.

taken place in the sector since October 1915, but plans were in hand to change all that.

The territory commences near the foot of the northern slope of Vimy Ridge and curves gently around Arras, crossing the Scarpe River north-east of the town, then heading south-east towards Beaurains. Readers will note that panorama provenances shift from First to Third Army on Vimy Ridge itself, conforming with the change in military boundary. The designated battleground can be seen in Panorama 526 from Ouvrages Blancs, a position captured by Pétain's XXXIII Corps on 9 May 1915 during the Second Battle of Artois. Broadmarsh Crater, to the left of frame, still exists today on the crest of the ridge not far from the vast Canadian Memorial, which would also appear on this photograph had it existed at the time. At the other end of the image lies a distant Beaurains. Almost the complete Arras and Vimy battlefront is shown: Panorama *146*, from Maison Gaba, completes the picture, presenting the northernmost sector at Givenchy on the northern shoulder of Vimy Ridge, and the parcel of flat ground around the southern Lens pitheads which was also incorporated into the battle plan. At the same time this panorama shows the precise and highly important area of geological transition from the Gohelle plain to chalk plateau.

Hill 145 was the highest point of Vimy Ridge, and it was just here that the Canadian Memorial was erected after the war. The landscape is today much more heavily wooded. The mine craters marked towards the right of frame lie between the two front lines. Panorama 535 gives a general elevated eastward view from a factory chimney in Arras. Taken in July 1916 the picture shows much of the ground attacked by the Third Army in April the following year. A brace of soldiers can be seen in the otherwise deserted streets; about 1,000 civilians still lived in the town, but it was only after dark that Arras came alive. Two other panoramas from high points, Nos 505 and *507*, give us detail of the battlefront and the state of the town in spring 1916, with No 505 especially offering an understanding of the relative positions of several of the eastern hotspots: Roeux, Monchy, Feuchy, Point du Jour and Tilloy.

Once more, the British 1917 attacks here were a part of a wider strategy – the Nivelle Offensive. In mid-December 1916, General Robert Nivelle had succeeded Joseph Joffre as French commander-in-chief. Joffre, resigning on Boxing Day, was appointed technical adviser to the French Government, a post which carried no power of military command at all. He had planned to continue the attritional struggle of 1916 on the Somme well into 1917, further wearing down a substantially weakened German

defence, but Nivelle, arriving as the heroic defender of Fort Douaumont at symbolic Verdun, had other ideas. Upon taking up the C-in-C post he instantly unveiled a new plan, which was subsequently agreed with Sir Douglas Haig and British Prime Minister Lloyd George.

There had for some time been Anglo-French 'discussion' over who should assume supreme command of the Allied forces. After some deliberations regarding which man – Haig or Nivelle – was to control future united enterprises, an uneasy agreement was reached. Nominally, Nivelle achieved his aim to be Allied C-in-C, although in practice the prevailing unwritten rules continued to operate, with the British retaining total control over the actions their forces would undertake. In reality the only genuine difference was that a closer liaison between Haig and Nivelle would apply. Furthermore, although Nivelle was indeed to take overall command of the upcoming offensive, his powers would only last until the endeavour was concluded. In this way a knotty period of argument and debate, which could have led to very serious complications, was resolved. Nivelle's fresh plans, slightly adjusted, were agreed: the French would launch another massive attack on the Aisne, whilst the British were to burst out from Arras on a 39-km (24-mile) front between Vimy and Beaurains, partly with the now habitual aim of drawing German reserves away from the French venture, but also to threaten Douai and Cambrai.

As a result of losses sustained at Verdun in the spring of 1916, on the Somme through the summer and autumn of that year, and recently at the hands of the British Fifth Army on the River Ancre, in February 1917 the German High Command determined to make a strategic withdrawal to the pre-prepared fortress of the Siegfried Stellung, known to the Allies as the Hindenburg Line. Unlike the rest of the Western Front this line did not follow any marked features, but ran fairly straight across the contours, whether ridges or valleys. The existing Quéant–Drocourt line behind Lens attached itself to the powerful Wotan position east of Arras, and this connected first to the Alberich subsector and thence to the Siegfried section which ran on passing to the north of St Quentin. As Alberich formed the hinge of the retirement, so it would lend its name to the

operation. The move was skilfully and successfully completed in mid-March 1917 with the Germans relinquishing territory averaging 32 km (20 miles) in depth. Although troubling Nivelle little in the south it affected certain parts of the prospective Arras battleground, creating a need for a British readjustment south-east of the town. By the eastward fluctuation of the line near Beaurains the battlefront was shortened by several kilometres.

Although the Operation Alberich evacuation itself presented few concerns to British planners, following up into the region vacated by the Germans certainly did: the troops discovered a barren wasteland. Lethal booby traps of all kinds were discovered everywhere, whilst nothing of practical use had been left intact: roads and railways were destroyed, water supplies contaminated and anything resembling a billet razed to the ground. The engineers, already hard pressed making arrangements for Flanders later in the year, were required to rebuild some form of basic infrastructure before any offensive action could take place. Fortunately, in the territory selected for attacks the affected area was not great, the problem being most serious in the Fourth Army area south of Arras, which of course was not included in the offensive scheme. However, there was the perennial question of improving and maintaining existing roads, a problem which reared its head before all offensives. The pounding of tens of thousands of mechanized vehicles and heavy guns on surfaces designed

Above left
French women making camouflage netting under RE supervision.

Above
A Royal Garrison Artillery 9.2-inch howitzer ready for action. Artillery preparations for Vimy and Arras were comprehensive.

Opposite
A post-war photo of the entrance to Coburg Subway, one of the many subterranean arteries feeding the front lines along the Vimy Ridge.

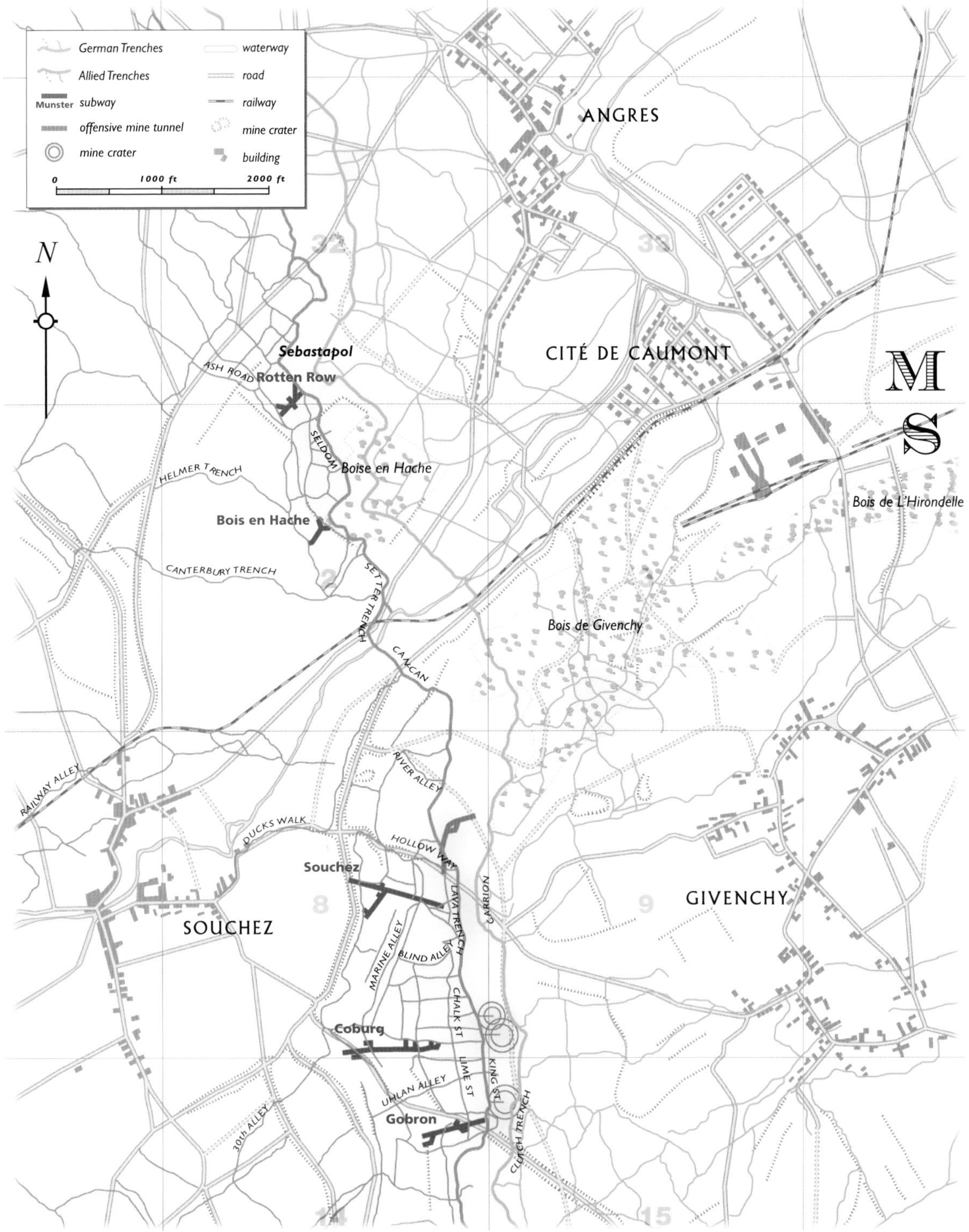

to carry light horse-drawn traffic, combined poorly with unseasonably late wintry conditions: many routes were torn to shreds. Twelve major arteries were therefore selected and urgently attended to. Apart from highway reconstitution and reinforcement, bridges were strengthened and dumps established along the entire battlefront to hoard stone and timber for road use in the narrow forward area which was likely to be destroyed by shellfire.

In the north at Vimy, the Canadian Corps had largely relieved British units the previous autumn, and their continuation of preparations on and beneath the front had been substantial. The extraordinary nature of the positions the Canadians inherited can be seen in Panorama 511 taken from The Pulpit near Neuville St Vaast. The camera location is close to 'Sheba's Breasts' in No 526. The map for this sector shows that long before battle commenced approaches to the line were already entirely by subway.

The date of the attack remained a military secret, but early rumour fixed it as April 15th. As the subways neared completion, electric lights were installed and protected with expanded metal screening. Blueprints were placed at each entrance showing a plan of the subway including entrances, exits, battalion headquarters, dressing stations, cookhouses etc, etc. The infantry issued detailed instructions for policing each subway and we realized we were approaching the climax of our work. Finally, the date of the attack was set as April 9th and by that time we had removed a prodigious amount of chalk. Taking into consideration the increased area of the dugouts, we estimated that in all we had driven the equivalent of approximately 12,000 feet of subway.

Major F. J. Mulqueen, 182 Tunnelling Company RE

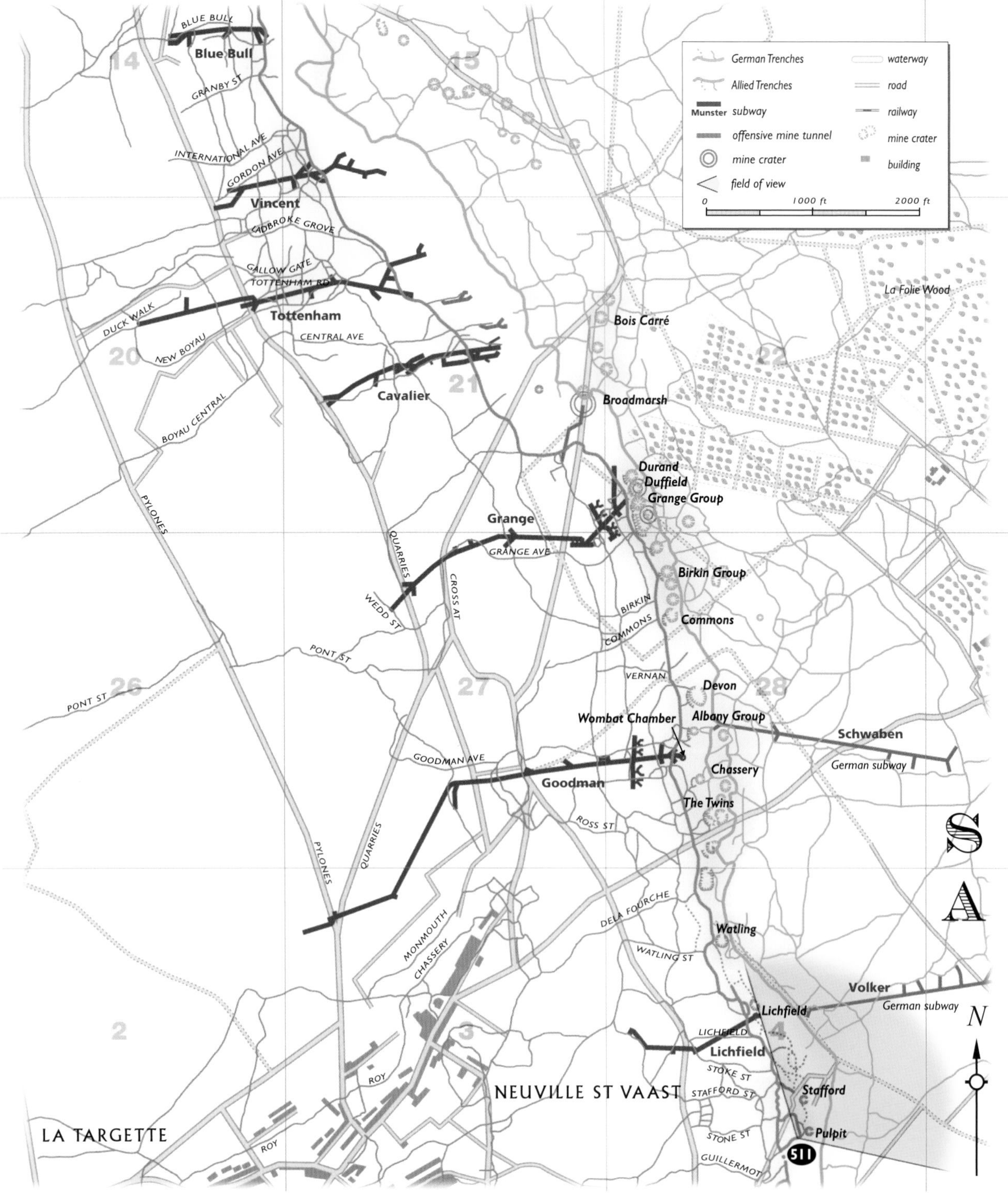

Above

British shells exploding in German wire on Vimy Ridge.

Below

One of the infantry subways on the Vimy Ridge.

Above
This segment of Third Army Panorama 511 from The Pulpit shows the extraordinary proximity of opposing lines in certain parts of the Vimy sector. 2 April, 1916.

Below
An intrepid explorer in an offensive mine gallery beneath the ridge. Compare the dimensions of this tunnel with the subways.

By this time, just as they had done in the Ypres and Messines Salients, French, British and latterly Canadian tunnellers had also achieved total domination over the German *Pioniere* in offensive and defensive mining. In Arras itself, there had been similarly outstanding subterranean endeavours: the New Zealand tunnelling company completed a vast system of underground communication that connected the town centre with the main sewer system, which in turn linked via subway with the forward trenches in the more exposed south-east sector. In reaching the lines these subways had joined a series of chains of ancient individual *boves*, cathedral-like underground quarries from which the stone to build Arras had been procured centuries before. Here, over 13,000 men enjoyed safe accommodation, running water, electricity and a fine system of supply via tramways which extended right back through the sewers into Arras itself.

On arrival at Arras [8 December] it was found that the work to be done was to assist the 64 Field Company RE in digging deep and large dug-outs for the purpose of accommodating troops for a huge offensive a few months hence. The work on the dug-outs entailed continuous work in 8-hour shifts, as the ground was for the most part chalk, the work was rather hard. Three sappers worked on each dug-out during the shifts with six or eight infantry as working party to carry the chalk spoil away in sand-bags as the sapper dug it. Most of the dug-outs were to be reached by a staircase about 30 feet deep, which was to lead to a big chamber capable of accommodating from 50 to 300. Nearly twenty of these dug-outs were in progress in different parts of this section, and in addition a New Zealand Company of mining Engineers were engaged in exploiting huge natural caves, etc. [The boves].

When the sections were taken up the line the next day they had a good view of the whole town. Only troops on duty were allowed in the street during daylight, and then the steel helmet and gas helmet had to be always carried with them. To get to the position where the work was to be done meant marching through the main street, where a scene of desolation presented itself. Shops stood on both sides of the street, and very few had missed the effects of enemy shells. Huge holes were to be seen in either the roof or walls of most shops, whilst some had been knocked out of all recognition.

Barbed wire entanglements and other obstacles had been built at intervals in preparation for any enemy attack. The railway station was a pitiable sight. Thousands of panes of glass were smashed, large pieces of masonry had been knocked off by shell fire, whilst inside was a picture of indescribable confusion, chairs, desks, cupboards, long grass and water all adding to the poignant scene. To loiter in the square was to court disaster, as the enemy had a clear view down one of the straight main roads.

Running parallel with the main road leading to the trenches, a communication trench had been dug between the road and the houses on the side of the road. In some cases the journey continued through shattered factory buildings where the walls were sufficiently high to cover all signs of movement of troops, and trenches were not required. Other parts went through gardens enclosed by high shrubbery, whilst another part actually meant going through the ruins of a house. Where any rooms existed in these houses, troops were billeted, and it was no uncommon thing to go down the communication trench and hear a piano being played by a British Tommy billeted in the house.
UNIT HISTORY, 203 FIELD COMPANY RE

With the subways in place surface movement became almost entirely unnecessary, and forming up before and during battle was almost a formality. The *boves* and subways lie beneath the surface seen in Panoramas 505, *507* and 535. They may seem like ideal cover, but the reality was somewhat different.

22 April 1917

Having got the horses tied up to the wagons, the drivers were led down a dark, narrow stairway beneath a ruined house, into caves where they were to sleep. The caves of Arras are said to be mediaeval catacombs, extending for many miles through the chalky soil. This part of them consisted of high vaulted caves [the boves], the walls dripping and running with damp. The floor was crowded with close-packed infantry, lying chock-a-block, while no words can describe the foul sweaty smell and decaying, suffocating heat. Putting it as best as I could to the vote of the men, crowding and peering behind me, their rifles and kits on their backs, I found that opinion seemed to favour a return to fresh air. Fortunately the weather had turned warmer and they bivouacked in the field with the horses.

2nd Lieutenant J. Glubb, 7 Field Company RE

'Normal' sapper pre-battle provisions also had to be attended to: protected ammunition dumps and bomb stores, trench ladders and bridges, duplication of communication trenches for designated 'up' and 'down' activity, water supply depots and stores, and preparations to extend tramways the moment territory was captured.

However, the Germans too had been far from idle, and bolstered their *defences* at least to the same degree as the British had examined their offence. Counter-attack tactics, already a forte, were revised and practised, and support and reserve positions upgraded towards the high standards of the Hindenburg Line trenches and barbed wire. They also employed equally impressive underground accommodation, communication and storage schemes. The defences facing the British and Canadians were no less than formidable: the words 'enemy breakthrough' did not appear in the German lexicon.

The First and Third British Armies prepared for the offensive, a total of fourteen divisions. The territory from Lens to Neuville St Vaast (Panoramas *146* and 526) was to be the responsibility of General Sir Henry

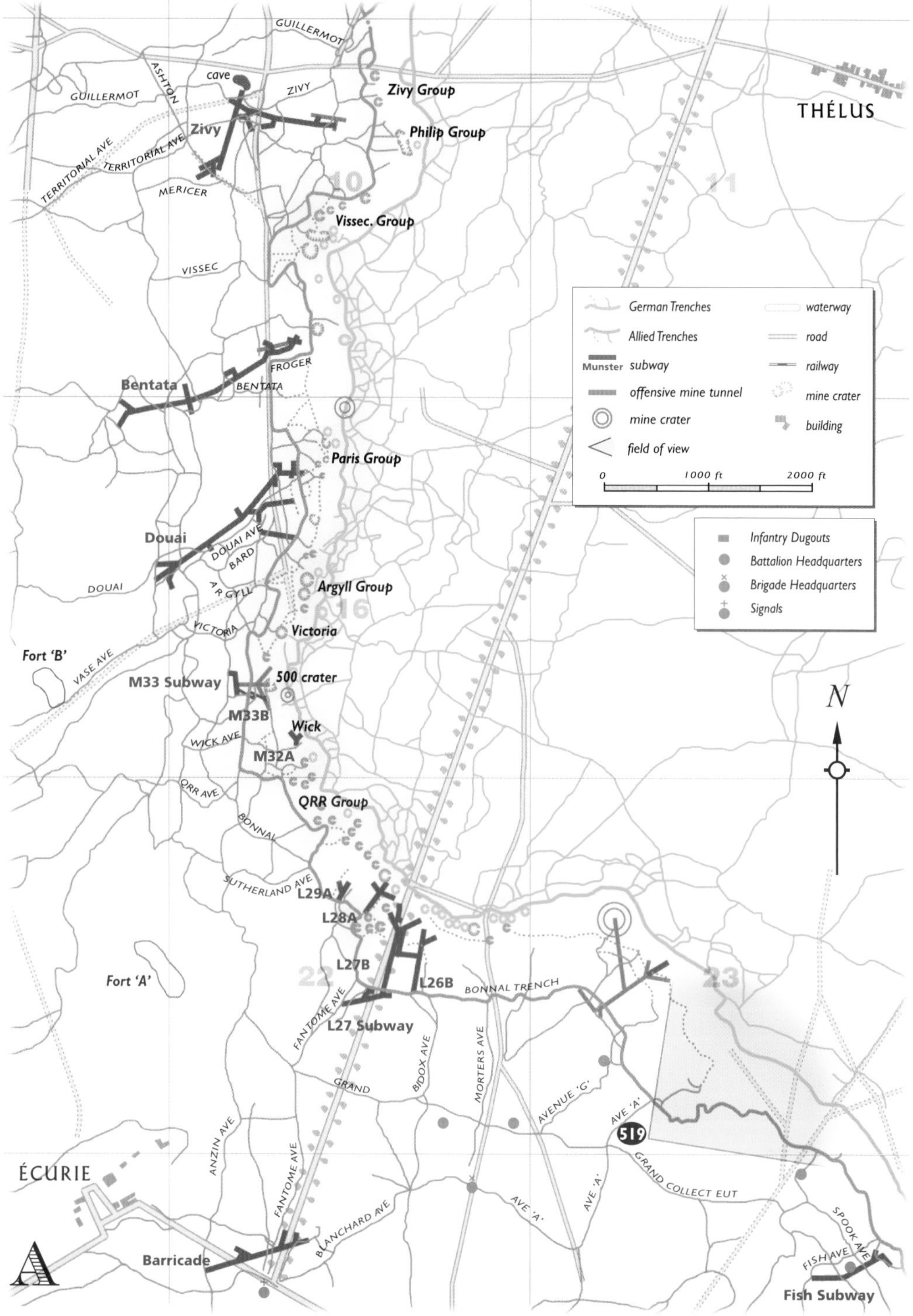

Left
Third Army Panorama 505. Another view over the Arras rooftops in May 1916. The town was to suffer much more damage during the next twelve months.

Right
The extraordinary range of the Arras caves and subways, also showing locations of the 'town panoramas'.

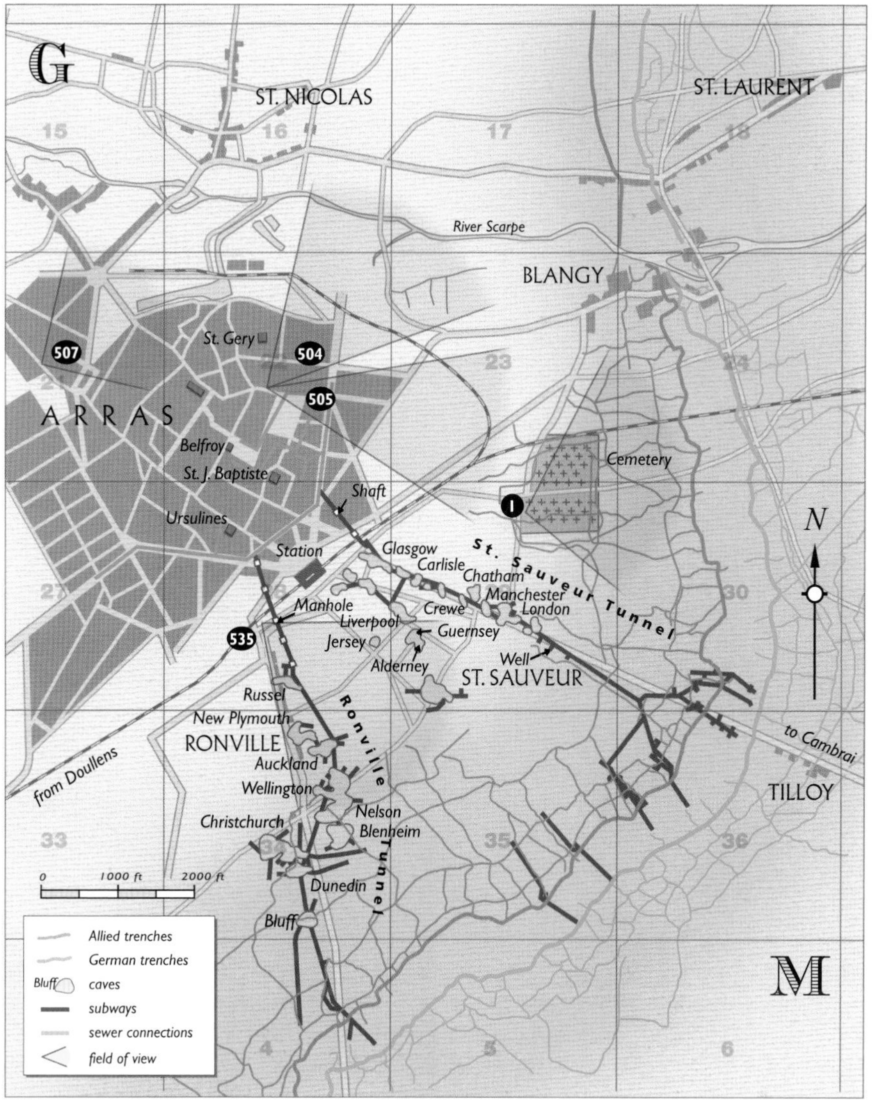

Below
Canadian troops relax in a corner of one of the Arras *boves*.

Horne's First Army, which comprised three divisions of the Canadian Corps plus the British 24th Division and 13th Brigade. Once the ridge had fallen, the Douai railway hub was Horne's target, but this would entail breaking the immensely powerful Quéant–Drocourt Wotan line. Known to the British as The Switch, this great field fortification running behind Lens, in front of Douai and southwards to Alberich, formed the northerly extension of the Hindenburg defences.

The Third Army under the command of Sir Edmund Allenby adopted the larger share of the battleground, encompassing the ground astride the River Scarpe, across the gently rolling ridges east of Arras, to Croisilles, the village which formed the northern hinge of the Hindenburg Line after the March 'adjustment'. Allenby's target was Cambrai. Forty tanks were made available. Much to the disgust of tank commanders – after their experiences on the Somme they had requested a mass attack – it was decided to deploy the machines piecemeal, with 8, 16 and 16 tanks allocated respectively for each of the Third Army's three corps. None were allotted for the more precipitous ground at Vimy. As for air support, with a total of almost 360 machines, aircraft were more numerous than ever. Unfortunately they faced Baron Manfred von Richthofen and his 'flying circus', and would come out a poor second best.

A five-day preliminary bombardment by 2,800 guns, almost 1,000 of which were heavy, signified that surprise was not intended: GHQ felt that the tactical lessons learned during the long Somme offensive (staged advances rather than a great push, assisted by creeping barrages), combined with improvements in training, and with considerably greater tank and aircraft support, the prospects for success were fair to good.

Zero Day was eventually set as 9 April 1917, Easter Monday. In order to quieten hostile artillery, German batteries were effectively targeted with gas shells less than half an hour before zero. Having approached the line in complete security via the many subway systems, the infantry went over the top at 5.30 a.m. in cold, grey, sleety conditions, advancing behind a crisply delivered creeping barrage.

Left
Canadian troops sweeping over the crest of Vimy Ridge.

Below
Canadians advancing over no man's land with tank support on the southern shoulder of the ridge.

In fact, the Germans were taken by surprise. Certainly, they had expected an attack – but two to three weeks later than it was actually delivered. Consequently, specialist counter-attack troops were still in reserve many kilometres behind the line, and extra artillery support had not been brought forward. Most important of all, hostile counter-battery fire had been curbed by British guns, which meant that the all-important creeping barrage could be maintained at the high concentration envisaged in the plans, and infantry molestation kept to a minimum.

Day One was a great success: the Canadians and British captured the entire Vimy Ridge and swept on to its eastern slopes. Their first view of the plain of Douai from the newly won ridge can be seen in Panorama 109; the picture was taken within 24 hours of capture on 10 April from a position in Thélus Trench just behind Count's Wood. It shows the landscape to be snow dusted, an important factor in the opening phase of fighting. Note the German light railway crossing the picture, bridging the German communication trench where the photographer is ensconced.

Further gains were made in subsequent days, but at greater cost and far less swiftly than the advance of day one. In Panorama 109 the trenches of the Quéant – Drocourt line are visible on the plain below the ridge, and it was these positions which first held up and then finally halted the general advance beyond Vimy. The situation on 22 April can be seen in Panorama *111*, with the village of Bailleul in the foreground. After the opening period of battle the territory between Bailleul and Fampoux on the Scarpe was practically devoid of German troops. The Dominion forces could have meandered through almost

First Army Panorama No. P. 109 made on 10-4-17, from Thélus Hill, A.6.a.9.8, Sheet 51b, including a field of view of 103° from about 12°–115°.
Approximate scale of degrees (1 degree = 1.07").
0 1 2 3 4 5 6

Right
A tentative first look from the freshly captured positions on the ridge. The prospect was a revelation to most.

Overleaf
Muscle-power and firepower. Manhandling howitzers into position further down the line near Arras, 1917.

Below
The view from Thélus Hill across the Douai plain. First Army Panorama 109, 10 April 1917.

unscathed, but were unaware of the circumstances. During the night the gap was plugged by several battalions of young German troops. Panorama *519* shows the ground around Thélus which the 1st Canadian Division needed first to secure to reach Bailleul. Note the depth of the enemy defences in this, the Zwischen Stellung sub-sector of the enemy line. Oppy Wood, village and the surrounding territory which next had to be negotiated for any further advance can be seen in Panorama *118*, and also No 558, which illustrates the plain beyond Vimy from Arleux to the ill-famed Roeux Chemical Works, and ahead as far as Douai itself – the First Army's ultimate goal. The picture also possibly includes a British victim of the Red Baron's 'Circus'.

It was a good day on the crest therefore, but the advance had not been as dramatic on the ridge's northern shoulder (Panorama *146*); here, the important Pimple had been snatched but Givenchy itself was to hold out for the next two weeks. The task of capturing Gavrelle, seen in Panorama *118* under artillery and probably mortar bombardment on 23 April, was handed to the 63rd (Royal Naval) Division. Present at this attack, and leading the second wave as commander of the Hood Battalion, was Arthur Asquith, son of the late Prime Minister, brother to Raymond who had died the previous year on the Somme, and friend of poet Rupert Brooke who had served in the same battalion before his death. Having made his way into the pulverized village Asquith noted (at the time) that the

battle was a difficult close-quarters affair, with skirmishing through the streets and from house to house, especially with grenades. As soon as the village fell the inevitable enemy counter-attack was launched, an attack that was crushed by British shrapnel and machine-gun fire. The Hood Battalion's final objective was a section of trenches around the 'Windmill Maze' just beyond the village, but despite costly attempts no further progress was made. On 28 April the same division advanced from Gavrelle, and again made no gains. On the same day, however, a Brigade of 2nd Division troops managed to penetrate Oppy Wood, but were too weak to establish a firm position and were driven out. By the end of the battle the British had annexed the section of the Quéant – Drocourt Line

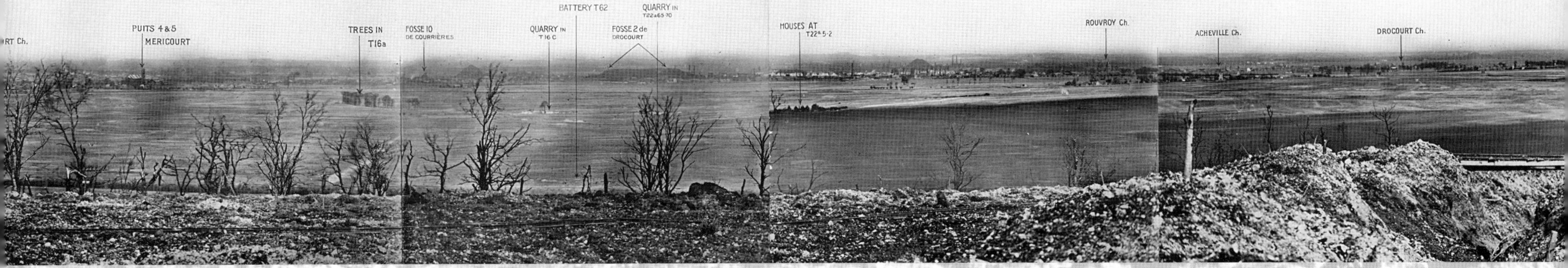

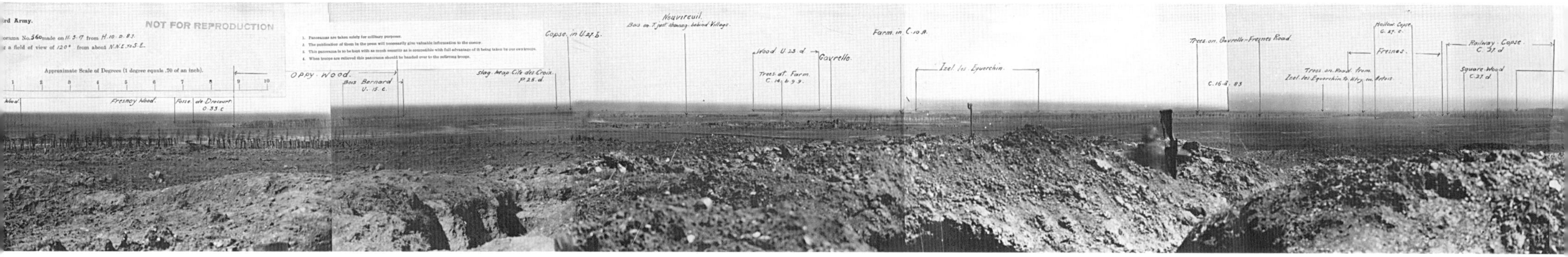

Above
Third Army Panorama 560, 11 May 1917. The advance is well underway, with Roeux and several other targets under fire in preparation for infantry assault.

beyond Gavrelle seen in the panorama; it was a line that remained fixed until the Advance to Victory the following year. These panoramas therefore show the entire territory over which the battle was fought in the Vimy sector. Panorama 558, taken almost two weeks later, shows the bombardment to have moved beyond the villages at the foot of the ridge towards the Quéant–Drocourt positions.

Moving down the line, Panorama *504* shows the ground south of Gavrelle over which the British 9th Division attacked on zero day, driving left to right across the hillside beyond Blangy. By the evening they had advanced beyond the field of view of this panorama to overlook Roeux in the Scarpe valley. That prospect can be seen in Panorama 560. It is a commanding position, and clearly one which the watching Tommy in the picture enjoyed. Roeux, however, with its light industry, tunnel system and fierce defences including the infamous Chemical Works, was to be one of the toughest nuts to crack. In the middle of April a three-day assault on the village failed, and it was following this action that Haig ordered a pause in the programme. There was no question of a complete cessation to the battle because Nivelle still required cooperation, so Roeux was sure to be assaulted again. The moment the newly captured ground in this sub-sector had been consolidated the engineers moved in to clear the Scarpe of obstacles to allow transport of ordnance forward and wounded rearward by barge, a means of travel which avoided the uncomfortable jerking and shaking when carrying stretchers through trenches and subways.

On the near bank of the river the 12th and 15th Divisions moved across the ground seen in the extraordinary Panorama 140, reaching the crest of Observatory

Below left
Winklepicking. Searching German dugouts for wounded and enemy soldiers lying low.

Below
Segment of a panorama looking across Arras Cemetery. The communication trench weaves between the tombs before passing through a breach in the cemetery wall.

Right

Cavalry muster for the attack on Monchy.

Below

Following up. Field guns passing through Arras Cemetery on 12 April 1917.

Ridge and looking steeply down into Battery Valley – note the German ordnance storage emplacements and gunners' shelters. The guns are out of sight beneath the slope of the hill in the foreground. The next target in this sector was Monchy-le-Preux. Haig and Allenby had brought up the cavalry ready to exploit any swift forward movement, and this hilltop village and the ridges beyond were key potential candidates for mounted operations. But the late wintry weather was against them, and the attack, planned for the evening of Zero Day, was postponed. However, Allenby was to waste little time whilst the Germans were weakened, and at 5 a.m. on 10 April his troops advanced beneath a fall of late spring snow. Three brigades of the 37th Division, supported left and right by the 15th and 3rd divisions respectively, moved towards the village. They were accompanied by six tanks. Thanks to the myriad flares sent up by understandably nervous German observers the British were spotted and fired upon by every available gun. The tanks drove into and past the village, although one suffered, like the infantry, at the hands of British shells falling short – their artillery had not been informed of revisions to the original plans and were unprepared. Still the troops managed to reach Monchy, and street fighting – a new experience for almost everyone in the division – broke out.

Now it was the turn of the cavalry. Having waited patiently behind Orange Hill (see Panorama 140), at 8.30 a.m. the 10th Hussars and Essex Yeomanry careered into battle – the first time in over two years that mounted troops had been used in their rightful role. A third mounted unit,

the Northamptonshire Yeomanry, spotted the charge and followed on at speed, clearing the open ground and galloping into the village. They too were spotted. The Germans did precisely what the British would have done and dropped a box barrage on Monchy – a manoeuvre which encircled a restricted position with exploding shells, preventing access and egress. The luckier cavalrymen near the edge of the village evacuated as fast as their mounts could take them. Inside, dismounted and horseless troopers joined the infantry, first to shelter from flying shrapnel, splinters and masonry, then in consolidating the positions. After a short respite another yet heavier box barrage claimed the lives of almost every remaining horse – and many men. Eyewitness accounts of this action are as harrowing as any of the entire war. The troops hung on, however, and by the evening of 11 April Monchy was firmly British property, remaining so until spring 1918 when the line was pulled back towards Arras. It was captured by Canadian troops for the final time (again using tanks) in August 1918. A splendid view of the ground in front of the village on 6 May 1917 appears in Panorama *556*, still with one of the April tank casualties squatting forlornly on the battlefield.

Following the victory at Monchy attention was refocused upon Roeux and Wancourt (the latter village is not well covered in the panorama collection). Like Arras and almost every other settlement on the chalk plateau south of Vimy, mediaeval boves existed beneath Roeux, providing shell-proof cover for the defenders. With only limited British artillery cover available after the opening few days of battle, several costly assaults were needed before Roeux was to fall. Allenby's plan for the renewal of attacks after Haig's requested hiatus involved a 51st Highland Division all-Scottish exhibition. On 21 April the line had been carried forward to the edge of the village on both sides of the railway. The Scots made spasmodic penetrations into the German lines on the first day, but control in the semi-

Above

The village of Monchy after the battle.

Left

The result of a single shell falling amongst cavalry.

Above
Third Army Panorama 140, April 1917. Observatory Ridge: where the cavalry gathered for the attack on Monchy.

Right
Typical map of underground caves (in this case from the Somme). Every town, village and hamlet in the chalk regions was undermined – and fortified – in this way.

industrial battlefield, watched from afar by commanders receiving little information from the smoke-shrouded valley below (whose own runners were unable to get through), was minimal: success or failure was purely down to the actions of the individuals. By the 23rd most units had lost commanding officers, some being entirely without any commander above the rank of sergeant, and the situation was as chaotic and unclear as ever. Unknown to the attackers, it was the interconnected series of boves beneath the village which were the root of their problems, the tunnels allowing German troops apparently driven from one place to reappear in another. For those who knew of them, the

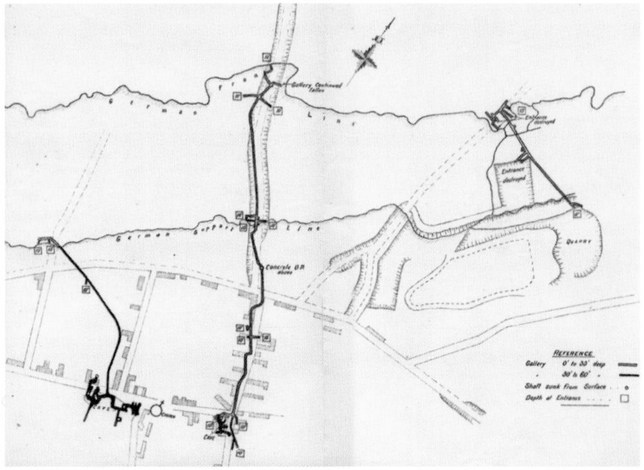

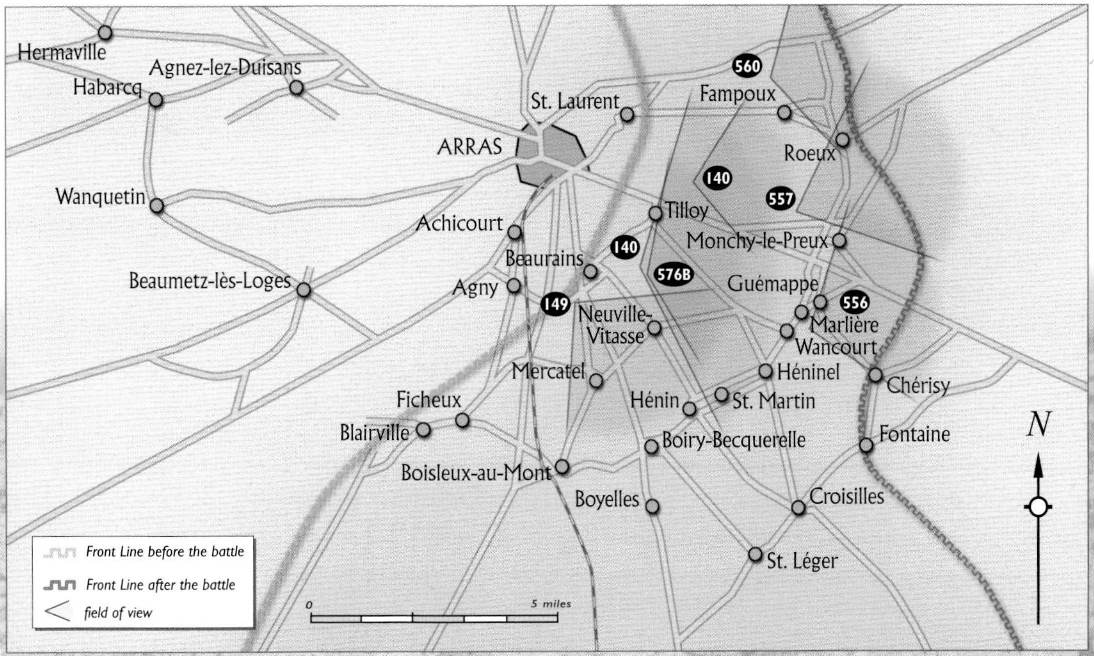

caverns also presented instant shelter from shelling; when the Germans' own artillery bombarded the village, their men simply slipped below ground.

Five tanks supported the Scots, and were instrumental in the division achieving a tenuous but temporary hold on Roeux. If more had been available perhaps the outcome might have been permanent, but during the evening of the 23rd they were driven back to the original start line on the outskirts of the village. The following day 2,000 gaps had appeared in the division's ranks. For the three-day period of fighting in all of the Arras sub-sectors casualty figures approached 10,000.

Haig and his Staff met their Allied counterparts to discuss the Anglo-French situation. Although Nivelle was determined to carry on, his attacks on the Chemin des Dames had been crippled, with tactics and losses that were causing serious alarm, even amongst the unswervingly

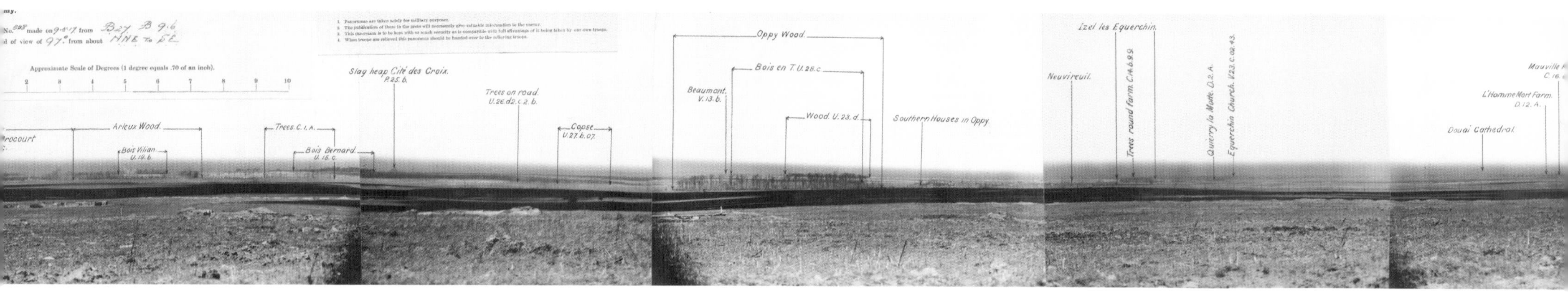

loyal ranks of the French Army. Haig was quietly informed that the Paris government was about to remove Nivelle, possibly in favour of General Philippe Pétain – and in the middle of an offensive. This was to become the French Army's 'mutiny' period, when some units refused to go into the line and others refused to fight. It was too much for the government to bear: both Nivelle and his great offensive were doomed. On 15 May he shambled out of office, and Pétain strode in. By this time mutinous behaviour had become widespread, but by a mixture of tact, care and tough discipline against certain of the ringleaders, Pétain managed to rejuvenate the spirit of the French Army.

Whilst vacillations and recriminations were in full swing, the British and Dominion forces at Arras had to make decisions regarding continuity of their offensive. Whilst Haig listened, considered and deliberated in Paris, Horne and Allenby were being persuaded to press on by General Launcelot Kiggell, Haig's chief-of-staff. Consequently, Roeux was again attacked on 28 April; it was a more catastrophic assault than ever. On the same day Asquith's Royal Naval Division men moved forward from Gavrelle, also for no reward whatsoever; one brigade darted in and were forced out of Oppy Wood, and the only success was that of the Canadians on the left at Arleux (Panoramas 109 and 558). Casualties rose.

Haig returned to Arras in the certain knowledge that Nivelle and his offensive were living on borrowed time. His decision had been made: the Arras offensive was to be curtailed, mainly to profit summer plans for Messines and

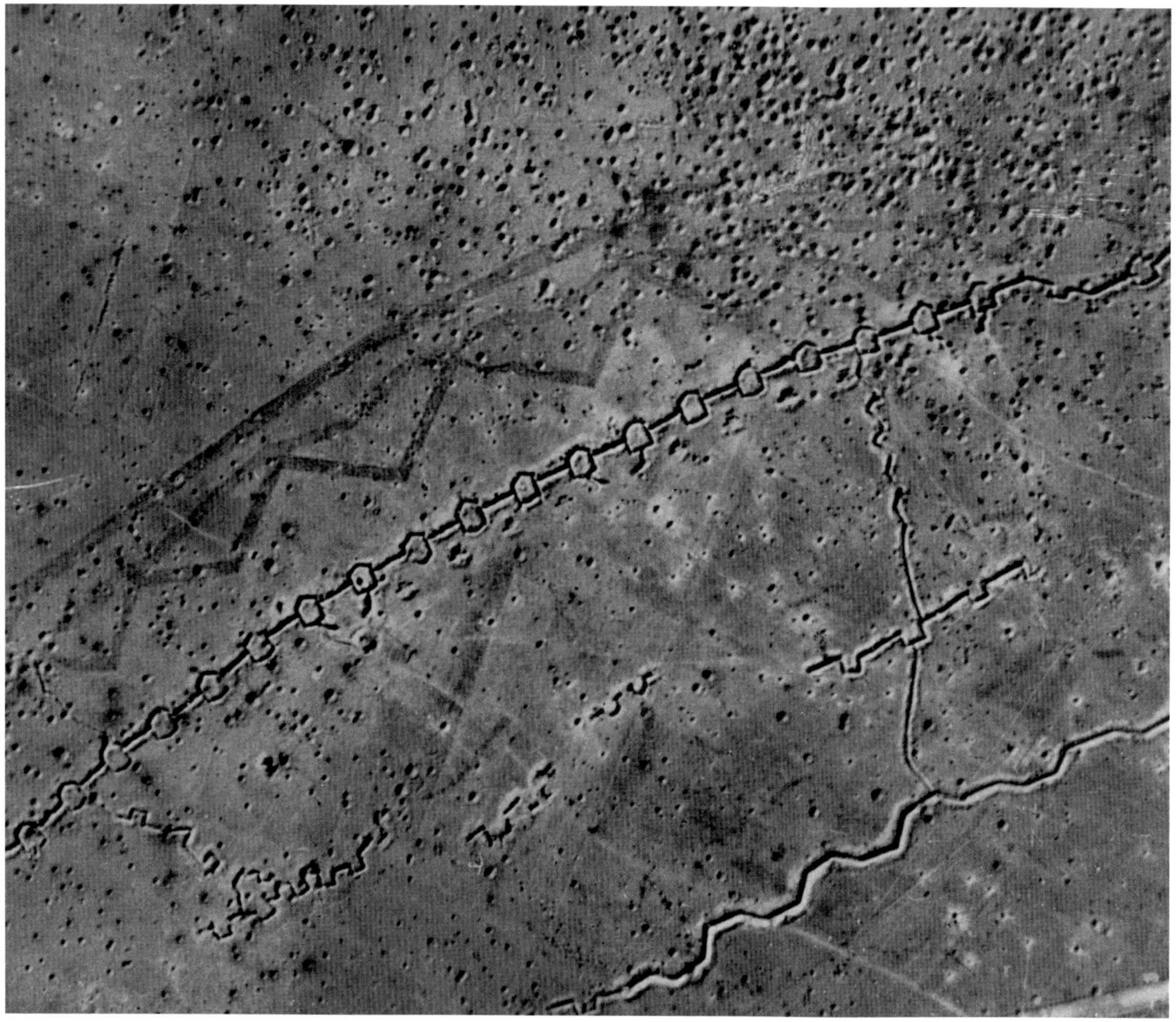

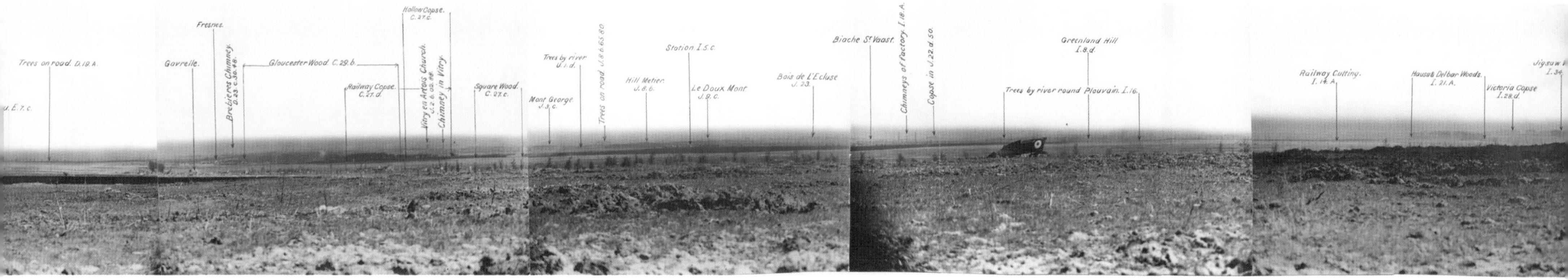

Above

Panorama 558. A Third Army example taken during the Battle of Arras. Shells are bursting in and around the ruins of Arleux. Roeux lies in the valley over the ridge to the right of frame.

Left

Aerial view of the German second-line defences at Oppy. Each 'lozenge' along the trench line contains a machine gun team which fired over the heads of troops in the lower-contour front line. Note the dense belts of protective wire.

Right

The splendid medieval gables of Arras in ruins. Although rebuilt in the same way as Ypres, 'new and old' properties in the town are easily discerned today.

Ypres, and on the Belgian coast. However, operation orders had already been drawn up for further assaults east of Arras, and Haig allowed them go ahead, just to add a final couple of weeks support to the drawing down of the French offensive. His aspirations no longer included a breakthrough towards Douai or Cambrai, but simply the attainment of respectable defensive positions. This time the First and Third Armies would be joined by I Anzac Corps, part of General Sir Hubert Gough's Fifth Army.

On 3 May, in an atmosphere of intense apprehension, battle was joined. There had been disagreement over zero hour, disagreement over mechanized support (the Australians chose not to use any because of potential complications in barrage plans when both infantry and tanks attacked together), and disagreement over the suitability and experience of certain units designated for the assault. The actions of the Third and First Armies were soon over. By the use of gas and crushing artillery fire the Germans brought all attacks to a standstill within 24 hours. The Third Army gain was half a kilometre near Monchy; the First Army captured just over a kilometre of ground and the village of Fresnoy.

In the shape of the 2nd Australian and 62nd (British) Divisions, the Fifth Army meanwhile threw themselves upon the ruins of the Bullecourt sub-sector – at night. The attack achieved a scanty foothold, but unlike their First and Third Army neighbours, it was not all over for the Australians. With the help of 5th Australian and 7th Division colleagues they fought on for another fortnight, slowly widening the line of resistance and tightening the grip on sectors around the now utterly pulverized remains of the village. Having fought off the most powerful of several counter-attacks, on 15 May the fighting began to draw to a close. The last action took place on 17 May when the 58th Division finally nailed Bullecourt village. German communiqués said their troops had voluntarily evacuated the village, but 7,481 Australian casualties told the true story. Unfortunately, no panoramas of this sector are available at present.

Almost inevitably one of the last acts would take place at Roeux. The village, its chemical factory and the tunnels finally fell to the 4th Division on 11 May. In Panorama *557* (7 May) the area can be seen under shellfire. After the victory at Roeux, however, there were further engagements, and indeed further minor successes, but all were launched simply to deceive the Germans into believing that the Arras affair was not yet over. It was.

Left
Disruption of movement. A massive crater in the centre of Athies, blown by the Germans during their withdrawal to the Hindenburg Line.

Now it was Flanders that filled Haig's waking and sleeping moments, and this time he was in sole control. The French agreed to take over a section of Fourth Army battlefront to release more British troops for the Flanders escapades, planning for which was almost round the clock. This was just as well for Haig, for Arras was an episode he would prefer to forget. There had certainly been a gain of ground along the entire battlefront, but the actions had conferred no strategic benefits whatsoever. His forces had suffered just over 4,000 casualties per day over the two-month period of action, with a very similar number recorded for German losses: this was attrition in its true sense, and it set many a heart against any future compliance with French requests for supportive engagements.

Action at Arras continued: trenches were lost and won back again, and the Germans ceaselessly bombarded the British until the Third Ypres offensive severely curbed ordnance supplies to all other fronts. Within weeks, under the irresistible hand of nature, the battlefield was changing its character again.

Three months before, during the Arras battle, these downs had been a vast brown desert of contiguous water-soaked shellholes. Now the whole hillside was covered with long weeds, almost breast-high, clothing the whole area in rank green. I should not have believed that nature could have worked so fast. I particularly remember the ground east and south of Wancourt, covered with great splodges of red poppies and blue cornflowers, the most deep, brilliant patches of flowers I have seen for years.
2ND LIEUTENANT J. GLUBB, 7 FIELD COMPANY RE

Right
August 1918. Waste not … An erstwhile communication trench on the Vimy Ridge – now the perfect milieu for celery.

PUISIEUX CHURCH
L. 20. b. 7·6.
BIEFVILLERS CHURCH
H. 10. a 9·2

CHAPTER SEVEN:

THE SOMME

31 December 1915

The last day of the old year. What, I wonder, will 1916 mean to the world? Will it mean the end of Armageddon? Will the destiny of England and the world be decided ere its course is run? Will this great year be the turning point in human history? In the brief span of time between tomorrow and another year tremendous issues will be decided, thousands of millions of treasure will have been spent on the savage art of killing, millions of lives will be wasted, the blood of legions of the finest products of human evolution will dye the protesting earth.

And to what end? If this is the war that will end war, it will perhaps be justified. If this is the raging, purging fire that will leave the world cleansed and purified, with loftier ideals, with more of brotherhood, more of human sympathy, more of charity, then it will not have been futile. But I am pessimistic. War has never hitherto proved a panacea for the evils that afflict and retard man's moral progress. Rather it seems to me it is, in its very nature, opposed to all that is highest and best. It is not to the nobler passions that it appeals, but to the baser. All that is lowest and most primitive in the human heart is fostered and encouraged by war. The morality won in the years of peace is largely overcome by those lower instincts against which we have fought. Savagery, cruelty, greed, lust, the craving for power, the breaking and binding of the weak and helpless, the apotheosis of Might, the exaltation of the animal, the repression of the spiritual. These are the effects of war as I see it every day. There are those who tell that we will be miraculously improved. I do not believe it. Progress only comes by evolution. War is revolution. War is Hell.

LIEUTENANT MATTHEW ROACH MC RE – KILLED IN ACTION, 2 JULY 1916

Planning the push

Soon after Christmas 1915 Haig and Joffre began to plan the Allied summer offensive for the forthcoming year. Once more it was to be a two-pronged Anglo-French affair, and once more disagreement ensued. Whilst Haig favoured a thrust in Flanders without any preliminary softening up attacks, Joffre preferred a move astride the River Somme preceded by months of aggravating minor actions. The inevitable compromise resulted: Haig gave way on location – it would be the Somme – but prevailed with his chosen timing of July 1916.

The French contribution was to be constrained by one of the bloodiest offensives in military history. On 21 February 1916 German forces launched a massive and prolonged assault upon the symbolic French fortress of Verdun. The stratagem was intended to frustrate any Allied offensive planned for later in the year, and win time for Germany to crush Russia once and for all. Verdun and its protective salient of trenches were to be systematically

Above
One of the earliest panoramas of the Somme battlefield. This segment of Third Army Panorama 3, of 4 August 1915, shows the area today occupied by the Newfoundland Memorial Park at Beaumont Hamel.

Pages 286–87
Flowers on the Somme. The Serre battlefield in 1916. Panorama 521.

Below
Trench work still to be done! Christmas Day 1915 in the Hebuterne Trenches.

Above
A French shrine in the Hebuterne trenches, discovered by Royal Berkshire troops on taking over in July 1915.

bludgeoned for five months. The positions held, but the fighting drained the life-blood from the French Army – and slashed a serious rent in the fabric of Haig and Joffre's offensive plan for the summer. As French agonies multiplied in the south it became clear that the Somme assaults would be doubly necessary, not only to try to force the elusive breakthrough, but also relieve pressure upon Verdun. The December plans were therefore radically altered: of the forty divisions originally earmarked by Joffre for the offensive, only eight could now be spared, and as a result the projected 97-km (60-mile) attacking front astride the River Somme withered to 40 km (25 miles).

27 July 1916

This is a lovely part of France: no hedges at all, except round grass fields, odd to relate, and the whole country laid out in little patterns of growing crops: some green, some yellow, and some red with poppies. Woods are mostly very square and distinct and dense: it reminds me of the picture in Alice in Wonderland looking down on the chess-board country. It is all rolling country, like the Downs of England, only all cultivated. The women do all the work: marvellous how they do. I have been picking some lovely wild flowers here. The corn is a perfect blaze of colour. It is quite fair country for riding, and in the intervals of work I go out with my batman and explore the country. Usually there is just enough room between two crops for a horse to get through: you strike bits of grass and clover to canter over, and always the most gorgeous views. In the evenings, as we are training and not fighting, we knock off. The officers rig up a badminton court with two poles and a bit of string and play. The men go for walks, or sit about the orchards and write and croon sentimental songs. In evenings here it is the most peaceful scene in the world, though all the while we hear a distant rumble: the never ceasing guns about ———. I am in no danger now, but shall soon be far worse in the soup than anyone since Loos. But I shall have the pleasant feeling – I hope – of hitting the Boche really hard.

2ND LIEUTENANT J. T. GODFREY, 103 FIELD COMPANY RE

The Somme battlefront had formed in the autumn of 1914 during the 'Race to the Sea' period. At that time, however, it was only French faces that a German soldier gazing across no man's land would see: British Third Army troops took over all the territory from Arras to the River Somme during the 1915 summer. The first panoramas taken in July and August of that year show pastures practically unmarked by shelling, with leafy and shady woods and copses, and buildings of all kinds still standing, even close to the front lines. Panorama 3 is the earliest example featured here.

It was here in Picardy that the greatest contrast with the waterlogged swamps of Flanders was evident. Field positions too were remarkable: the British held at least an equal proportion of the upper contours, so topographical advantage was localized and largely balanced between the two sides. Courtesy of the chalk geology almost every trench on the Somme could be made to be deep, supremely protective and comfortable. True, both sets of trench systems were already intensely developed according to the defence-in-depth template struck by the Germans during 1915, but a live and let live philosophy had long prevailed on the Picardy downlands. Until late June 1916 the battleground was a land of wild flowers and skylarks; there were patrols, but most energy was spent in improving fieldworks and maintaining 'healthy' trenches. Trench garrisons were minimal, and the sector was so calm that the British Third Army became known as the 'Deathless Army'.

The days slowly pass away. A few rare shells disturb the mustard and darnel blossoming along the parapet. The men rest during the afternoon. At stand-to, this summer evening almost conjures one to believe that war is a pleasant state. The sun has gone behind the ridge; but the sky is still flushed from his passage. Across the valley, the air is turning pearly grey, with here and there brown smudges where Fritz cooks his evening meal, Adinfer Wood has lost its sinister air and wild life must be waking among the trees to business no more cruel than our own. A lark bids a reluctant farewell to the day and drops down among the tussocks on the ridge. Faintly from far away comes the hum of an aeroplane. Now that pastoral music, the rumble of wheels, begins over the countryside, both east and west, the rumble of ration limbers, English and German, creeping steadily towards the line. The air holds the sound, magnifies and disperses it, making of it a homely background, in front of which some familiar tune whistled by the man in the next bay as he rubs an oily rag over his rifle brings a fleeting nostalgia for an English lawn, shadowed by a walnut tree, dew, and a lamp behind a window pane. In the distance a single gun, half afraid of the quiet, speaks once, and for a few seconds tears the evening into clanging echoes. The first flare rises from the trenches, curves and sinks, a brilliant lily.

GUY CHAPMAN, *A Passionate Prodigality*

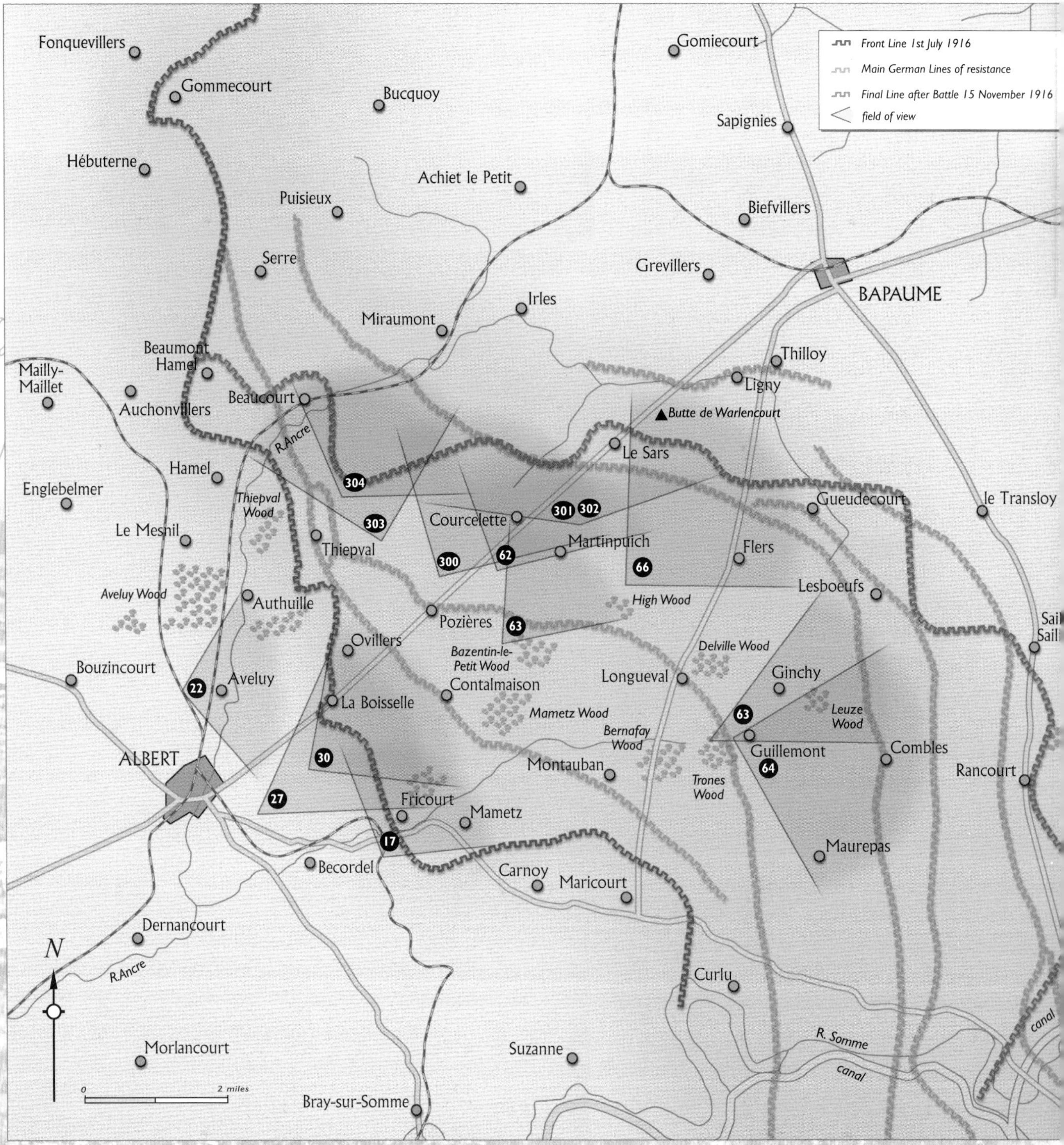

Above
Peaceful moments like these were commonplace for many months after taking over the Somme sector. A card game in a British officers' dugout near Fonquevillers in August 1915.

Below
Australian troops in their billet – a requisitioned barn.

Above right
Mud on the Somme roads. Specially designed horse-drawn toboggans were manufactured to transport both wounded and supplies.

Overture to action

The coming battle demanded the most intensive preparations of the war to date. They were nothing less than a marvel of logistics. Apart from the great deluge of guns, ordnance, machinery and other materiel, sleeping arrangements for the seemingly boundless influx of troops were critical and RE companies vied with each other as to how many sets of wired bunks they could churn out each day. Hundreds of barns in rear areas were cleared and fitted out. Every house, cottage, school and public building was commandeered, and even churches did not escape the billeting officer's gimlet eye. Troglodyte accommodation was also available: most towns and villages on the Somme had been built in the same way as Arras, from stone quarried underground.At Fonquevillers in December 1915 the sappers had utilized the ancient *boves* beneath the cemetery.

The Sappers had been building a big kitchen range containing two ovens and two stoves from derelict houses, at the foot of a shaft, which would serve as a chimney. Two days earlier a Minnie had landed in the graveyard about ten feet away from the shaft, and must have loosened the earth around it. The heavy rain further loosened it with the result that on the afternoon of Christmas Day the shaft timbering collapsed and fell with about 50 tons of earth on top of our kitchen range below. Our first intimation at the billet came from an excited and breathless sapper who blurted out that tons of earth, and corpses and coffins were lying around. This proved to be somewhat exaggerated. We found, on investigation, a strange medley of earth, chalk, corpses, broken bits of coffins and tombstones piled on top of our kitchen range after a 40-foot drop. There was a lady with long flaxen hair, and one poor gentleman, who has been turned out of his coffin, lies with his skull just visible under the earth, and the broken coffin a few feet away. It seems rather a shame to have a fall like that after a period that might be anything up to 200 years peaceful rest.
LIEUTENANT H. F. EBERLE, 2 FIELD COMPANY RE, *My Sapper Venture*

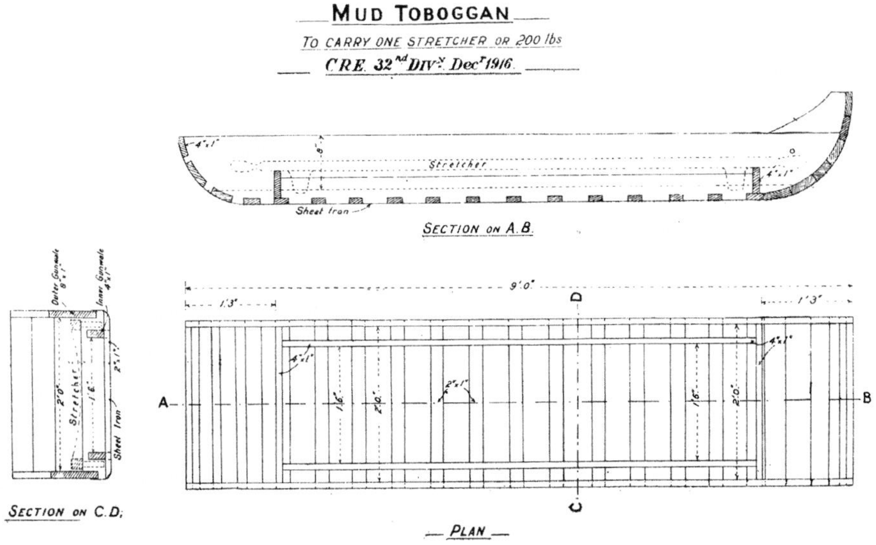

Fortunately, when preparations were in full flow in spring 1916 the Nissen hut made its first appearance, and clusters of camps sprang up around towns, villages and hamlets. The reason for locating here rather than in more accessible open countryside was simple: water supply. The Somme is an area where water is readily available – if one can reach the great depth at which it resides. Villages had built-in water sources in the form of wells, although most needed augmenting with deep boreholes to cope with the hugely increased military population. This aspect of 'supply' was as important than any other, as an army can neither fight nor be provided for (by horse, mule and machine) without water. Army Troops companies therefore rigged up new pumping stations, four-inch mains, pipeline spurs, reservoirs, horse-troughs and stand pipes along the entire length of the battlefront, with piped supplies reaching almost into the front lines themselves.

Finding the French trenches well positioned but often narrow, badly revetted and universally insanitary, immediate reconstruction and modification work was initiated by sappers and pioneers across the entire network. Mud was found to be severe and problematic during wet times, it especially built up on boots in a way that the Flanders variety did not. But at least the land tended to

Poplar E.23c.30.90
M.G E23B.70.05.

dry infinitely more quickly when the rain ceased. Drainage and drying however, tended to slow as a garrison increased in size. This was a result of 'puddling'. In the same way that canals had been made waterproof for centuries, the involuntary coating of the floor and lower sides of trenches with impervious clayey mud, carried upon the boots of tens of thousands of men, caused problems even after light showers, literally creating miniature canals by holding water in place. Reorganization of drainage systems again purloined a great deal of the sappers' time and effort.

As the 1916 winter turned to spring, front-line trench and wire defences were heavily strengthened, principally to deter or forestall any attempt on the part of the Germans to scupper the coming offensive by launching an attack themselves. Only a few deep dugouts were installed, for they would surely soon be redundant once the battle was under way. Plenty of shallow but adequate 'tunnelled' cover was available in the slopes of the hills and banks of sunken roads. Those shelters considered less safe but necessary were strengthened with burster (an upper layer of material which force a shell to explode before delving deeper into the earth) and deflection (to deflect the course of a shell as it pierces the surface) courses in brick, steel and sandbags – and, of course, timber. The felling of trees was always a sore point for French authorities on the Somme. The local agricultural communities were aware that wood was going to be in great demand for reconstruction and fuel following the war, and wished to hang on to whatever decent stocks they could. The British required huge quantities for pickets to augment the flimsy French wire entanglements (see right section of Panorama 18, 22 September 1915), to revet the expanding trench network (especially new assembly positions and communication routes), roads, and also for dugout, tunnel and Russian sap support. However, as early as August 1915 local woodland owners had already forced the RE to cease felling. Subsequently, timber was supplied from other areas of France, and from Britain, her dominions, the Baltic and America.

30 July 1915

On our first day we felled about 60 trees. They are previously marked for us as being suitable for sizes required, and in an orderly progression through the wood. There are two good Somerset lads with experience of tree-felling in my section. They know that the first essential is to keep the blades of the felling axes very, very sharp. Our daily quota of trees felled has been rising rapidly, as the other sappers have learned the knack of felling with speed and safety. When the trees are cut down the stouter branches are cut up into lengths, suitable for high and low entanglements, others for revetting posts and brushwood hurdles.

22 August 1915

Alas! The axe has fallen, this time not on the trees, but on us. The French owners or authorities have decided that no more felling of trees could be allowed. On Friday evening I received a copy of a Signals message from Corps HQ to the CRE. It stated that permission for cutting was being withdrawn by the French, with the added advice from Corps 'pending actual receipt of cancellation, cut all you can.' Underneath this our Adjutant wrote 'Fell like blazes.' The result was that yesterday we concentrated on felling and cut down 346 minimum 8-inch diameter trees, and sent away 33 full wagon-loads. It has seemed in some respects rather a shame to have cut down so many fine trees. It is, however, part of the price of war, and we shall never know how many lives they may save, in the protective use to which they are being put.

LIEUTENANT H. F. EBERLE, 2 FIELD COMPANY RE, *My Sapper Venture*

Above
A British 15-inch howitzer in action. The greatest concentration of heavy guns to date was brought up for the Somme.

In addition to communication and jumping-off trenches, multitudes of assembly positions were dug, covered and camouflaged, largely by infantry. Battery positions with gunners' shelters for hundreds of artillery pieces of all sizes were also required, with nearby tramways and light railways for shell supply, plus magazines both near the guns for ordnance and in forward positions for small arms ammunition, grenades and mortars. Finally, the great stockpiles of stores and materiel necessary to supply a 'big push' were brought forward and deposited at RE dumps, ready for the forward surge in July. Close to the lines at intervals of around 650 m (711 yds) sheltered

Junction of Trenches
E 18c. 97.95.
Quarry E 18 c. 75.50.
Quesnoy Farm
E. 14 A. 25.50

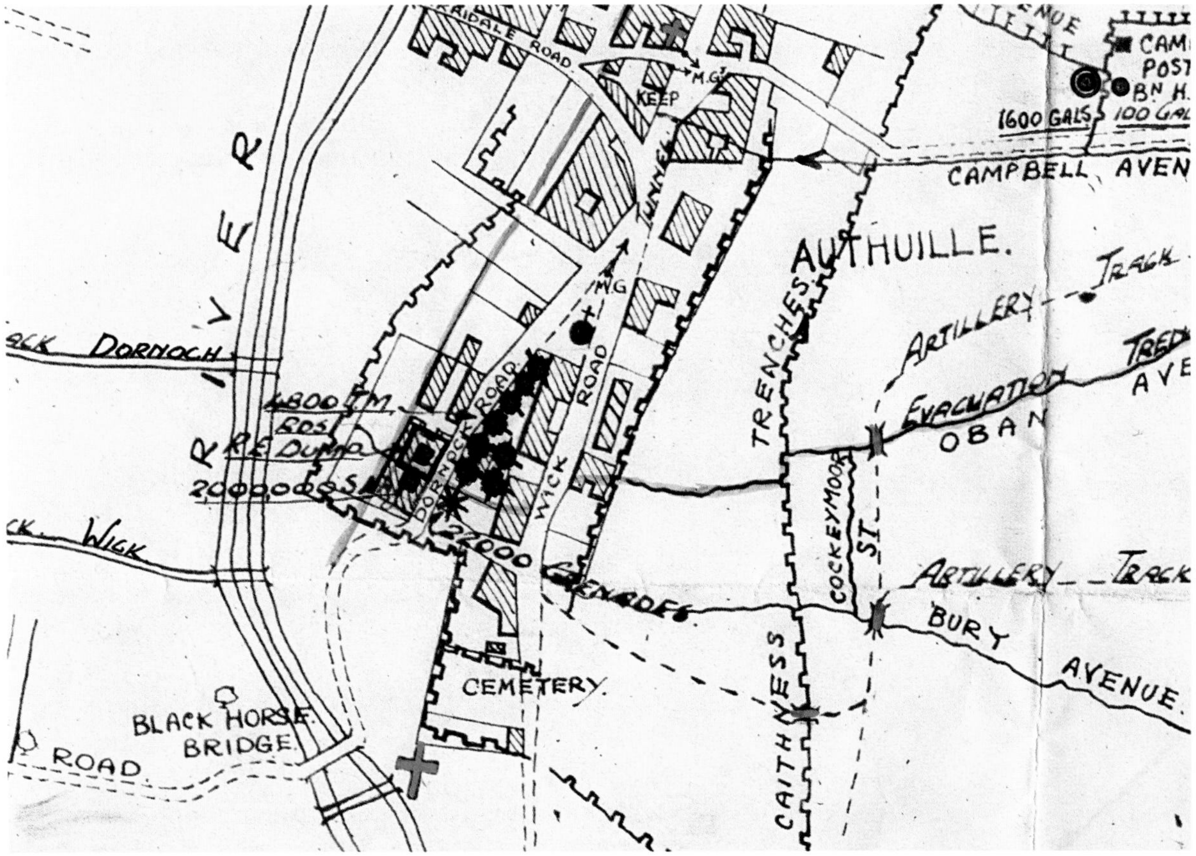

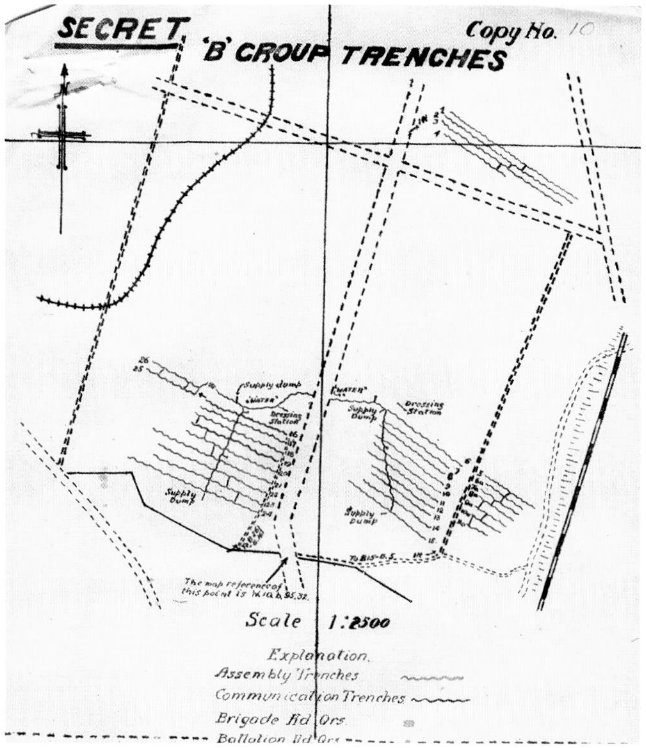

Above right
Detail of 8th Division CRE map showing a small arms, bomb and mortar cache just behind the front lines at Authuille.

Right
One of several sets of assembly trenches in Aveluy Wood. The plans allowed two linear feet (60 cm) of trench space per man.

Underneath
Third Army Panorama 518, taken just four weeks before the battle began, reveals how the British were fully aware of the potential weaponry in the German lines. It shows Gommecourt, where no gains were made at all throughout the battle.

ordnance caches each contained a standard 4,800 trench mortar bombs, 22,000 grenades and no less than 2,000,000 rounds of small arms ammunition. Tens of thousands of pack-horse and field artillery bridges were manufactured: a glance at any pre-battle panorama or aerial photograph shows how many trenches would need to be crossed in the event of penetration into enemy territory. The German workings were not only abundant but deep, often wide, and covered the entire landscape as far as the eye could see: without bridges, no water, food, tools, wire, timber, ammunition or supportive light guns could be brought forward.

As for the troops, much of the battle was to be fought by a 'civilian army', the product of the vast initial wave of volunteers, not only from Britain but across the Empire, now trained and keen for action.

The plan

The British Fourth Army was to spearhead the offensive. The Third Army shifted northwards again, leaving behind just one attacking corps on the extreme left of the battlefront opposite Gommecourt. Sir Douglas Haig and the General Staff expected nothing less than a total breakthrough, and issued orders for the cavalry to muster in the lee of woods and hills. The attacks were to be direct, frontal and piercing. When the three lines of German positions had been broken, all on elevated ground, the rest of the northern garrison of the Third Army would finish the job, rolling down the line southwards from Arras.

With little attempt to disguise their intentions – because the battle was to be founded upon artillery firepower it was impossible to do so anyway – the British amassed an attacking force of 400,000 troops, including three mounted divisions. Their actions were to be launched by an overture by 455 heavy guns, the greatest concentration of Allied firepower of the war at that time.

La Brayelle Farm
E.23 D. 90.20.
Strong Poi
E. 29 A. 20
Top of "Little Z"
E.23 c. 47.10.
Bottom of Little "Z"
E.23c 40.20.
M.G E.23c.75.25.
Trench Junction
E.23c. 77.30

M.G E.23c.50.80.
Essarts Willage
Bottom of the "Z"
E 23 c. 60.70
Top of the "Z"
E.23 D. 28.50.
Trench Junction
E.23 c. 55.35.
Strong Point.

The abundant field artillery was allotted the critical task of wire-cutting. First would come a grand and extended pre-battle bombardment, and then a series of barrages would lift to preordained positions in the German support, reserve and switch lines as the attacks went in. The infantry were to employ the wave system for the advance. The day of the protective creeping barrage, used extensively in 1917 operations, had not yet fully dawned, and the security of attacking troops was down to the efficacy of artillery in cutting wire and destroying enemy positions before an advance, and keeping hostile heads low during battle. As predominantly New Army men – Kitchener volunteers with between five and twelve months training – the fighting divisions may have lacked battle experience (some had never been in the line at all), but they were keen and anxious to achieve. Some but not all divisions had been sprinkled with 'stiffeners' in the form of regular experienced battalions.

On the first day of battle Haig expected to bite off around two miles of enemy territory along the entire front, a move which would so weaken the enemy that a break-through could be vigorously exploited by his beloved cavalry. In this way almost two years of stasis was to be decisively banished, and a war of movement reintroduced. Being reconnaissance photographs, the majority of the panoramas inevitably show the lines held and attacked on 1 July 1916. There are several spectacular images captured later in the battle, but it should be made clear that the concentration on the now hugely symbolic opening phase is not the author's choice!

Responsibility for the northernmost sector, Gommecourt, was entrusted to three divisions of General Edmund Allenby's Third Army. These positions can be seen in Panorama *525* (20 May 1916), and in 518 and 529, both taken on 1 June, exactly a month before the infantry battle began. The main burden of attack, encompassing all the ground south of Gommecourt to Maricourt, close to the wide marshy valley of the River Somme itself, fell upon the shoulders of fifteen divisions of Henry Rawlinson's Fourth Army. On their small sector north of the river and in the battleground to the south the French eventually managed to deploy just five divisions. With reserves, the total Allied fighting force numbered three-quarters of a million men dispersed within some twenty-seven divisions; they faced a German Second Army with less than sixteen.

Opening of battle

The first salvos howled from the British guns at dawn on 24 June 1916, and the bombardment was to build in intensity to the very moment of attack at 7.30 a.m. on the first of July. Three million shells were to obliterate wire and pulverize German forward defences (and defenders) to a point where resistance would be negligible. To further enhance the prospect of victory several heavy mines had been planted, Russian saps dug well out under no man's land, and gas shells fired by the tens of thousands. With British air superiority in the sector already absolute, Douglas Haig's military barometer appeared set fair for success.

On the opening day the French opted to attack two hours later than the British – and without a preliminary bombardment. Excellent progress was made owing largely to the surprise of the unsignalled assault and the concentrated array of heavy guns which thundered into life as soon as the troops left the trenches. Once the battle was under way they continued to enjoy overwhelming artillery superiority, and carried almost all initial objectives. For Britain, the first day was the most disastrous in her long and distinguished military history, with no breakthrough, and no momentum to carry secondary attacks forward. Pre-battle planning had been patchy. Gas was to be employed, and plenty of cylinders had been supplied, but they had been used several days in advance of 1 July. Nine mines varying from 2,000 to 60,000 lbs had been laid beneath enemy strongpoints, each designed both to signal and assist the moment of assault, plus a host of other smaller 'shock' charges. After interminable but inconclusive discussion the largest mines were blown at various times up to ten minutes before zero, lessening the desired effect and giving the Germans the clearest indication that an infantry attack could be expected at any moment. In an interesting comparison with the hugely successful Messines

Above
A British gas attack in progress near Fricourt in the days leading up to 1 July.

Below
Sergeant of the Royal Engineer Special Companies inspecting gas cylinders installed in a sheltered position ready for a release.

Right
British tunneller of 252 Company RE working in the chamber of the Hawthorn Ridge mine.

mines of 7 June 1917, German commanders here on the Somme habitually evacuated areas suspected of being undermined. It was a strategy which was to be strongly and repeatedly advocated by Otto Fusslein, commander of the German *Mineure* in Flanders the following year, but in vain: the advice was ignored by his superiors, with disastrous results. To the surprise and dismay of British tunnelling commanders on the Somme, German diaries captured after 1 July showed that many apparently successful and damaging earlier British blows had 'lifted' nothing more than empty trenches.

Although mines had been used many times already since early 1915, their employment had always been 'casual'; the Somme was the first time a comprehensive British underground scheme had been deliberately planned to assist an infantry attack. But it was not the only work the tunnellers undertook. One of the most significant misunderstandings/oversights/errors of 1 July is often ignored: the squandering of many shallow tunnels – 'Russian saps' – covertly installed at considerable cost in lives by Royal Engineer tunnelling and field companies during the months before battle.

The tunnellers had recognised that the fight would once more be a question of time against distance. Due to the great width of no man's land in many sub-sectors of the battlefield some of the saps were almost a quarter of a mile long. The accompanying sub-sector maps illustrate their positions, and the scale of the wasted potential: many had been driven to within *27 m (30 yds)* of the German wire. At the forward end of some the RE had advocated the use of small mines, partly as a destructive shock tactic to throw defenders into confusion, and partly to open up the tunnel for close-range action against German front-line defenders, and then later for essential communications. The tunnellers had advocated the use of small but heavily 'overcharged' mines – explosions which were not only sufficiently powerful to blow open the sap-heads, but also lift a large amount of earth into the air: enough to create a 'crater lip' over 2 m ($6^{1}/_{2}$ ft) high. The idea was to provide instant cover from enemy machine guns – frontally, and most especially laterally from enfilading positions along the German front line. Some sap-heads were to be used as multiple machine-gun, trench-mortar and even flame-thrower positions, the weapons playing upon the enemy parapets and deterring defensive action in intermediate and support lines. Others were earmarked for troops: having opened the ends up during the night whilst the artillery kept the enemy firmly under cover, streams of infantry could emerge at the very instant the bombardment lifted and bolt the short distance into the German lines before the enemy could emerge from their dugouts and man defences. The RE later suggested that 'a few dozen men loosed from each sap-head at the same moment would have seized the trenches before they were occupied – mere dozens where thousands failed.'

But general pre-battle planning, organization and communication in respect of the saps' use had been less than imaginative: so confident were the divisional commanders in the efficacy of the artillery that firstly they eschewed the use of several suggested and easily achievable additional mine schemes, then failed to adequately organise machine-gun and trench-mortar teams. Finally, the secrecy of the project (highly necessary as the Germans could and did destroy some of the saps with surface charges planted at night) meant that most of the infantry who could have benefited on 1 July were informed of the existence of saps on their sub-sector either too late or not at all. The tunnels had been specifically constructed to drastically curtail the width of no man's land – and consequently the time it took to traverse the killing zone; as so many were improperly employed, or indeed entirely unused, the majority of the British infantry fell long before they even reached the points from which they might have attacked – the sap-heads. Having opened them in readiness, the tunnellers who had toiled for so long in preparation could do nothing but look back at the carnage. Almost 60,000 men were killed, wounded or missing on the first day alone. On 4 July 1916 Major R. S. G. Stokes, the Assistant Inspector of Mines who had partly overseen the Russian sap scheme, wrote the following post-mortem in his official diary:

The British assault commenced at 7.30 am and the impression gained by Donald [Captain A. W. Donald, section commander in charge of 252 Tunnelling Company saps garrisoned with Stokes mortar teams] was the marvellous boldness and unwavering onrush of the men. But the enemy machine-guns were so ready and active, that all were swept down. Donald's opinion, from his personal observations, is that under the circumstances machine guns in these forward posts would have been more effective than S. Guns. From where he was, he could have swept the parapet.

Broadly, in the 4th and 31st Divisions area nine galleries were carried close to the enemy lines north of the Hawthorne Redoubt [Panoramas 3, 4, 59 and 60], and except for firing a certain number of Stokes Gun rounds were not utilised in the attack. Cat and Beet galleries in 4th Division sector opened out very close to enemy lines. Donald states that men opening out were bombed from the enemy trenches. Instead of having blown a charge to destroy the trench and dugouts, we had men digging near the enemy parapet. The comparatively long distances between lines in this sector led to the failure of the infantry attack. But this long distance was also the RE opportunity, owing to the surprise that was possible in carrying out gallery schemes. Under the methods followed, too much thought seems to have been given to facilities after the occupation of enemy lines, and too little to the means of getting infantry across 200 yards of good field of fire for machine guns. The failure to utilize the northern saps for blowing destructive and demoralizing charges at the moment of attack appears to have been an error.

The amount of work done by the 252 Co. since they started this scheme about April 20th, ten weeks before attack, has been very great, and so far as actual working results are concerned no estimates could have reckoned on further progress from this one company. The Coy. is rather depressed now owing to the uselessness of its 10,000 feet of galleries in assisting the attack, and will naturally work now with poorer spirit.

The lack of knowledge of the tunnels added immeasurably to the misery of that first day: some saps were accidentally discovered by the infantry, but many lay unused.

Ancillary reasons for failure were also plain. Geology played a critical role. The deeper one delves into the earth, the more influence geology exerts. The fact that the Germans had enjoyed a long period of relative inaction prior to facing an offensive on this front, allowed them to utilise the hospitable chalk geology to their own strategic ends. During the bombardment leading up to 1 July their troops sheltered in extensive deep dugout systems, workings which had long been installed within the defence-in-depth organization along the full length of their battlefront. Within this arrangement the *boves* of every village and hamlet had also been incorporated as built-in refuges for reserve troops. On the surface each village was wired in, fortified and connected to its neighbour by trenches. With defence-in-depth covering all the ground from the front lines to Bapaume, the entire Somme battlefield was a fortress some 16 kilometres deep. When the barrage lifted on 1 July the German defenders emerged with undamaged machine guns into battered but still serviceable trenches – and wreaked havoc from the parapets. As line upon line of heavily-laden British soldiers began the long slow traverse of no man's land, flares signalled the German artillery to open fire, and shrapnel, one of the most devastating weapons against men in the open, united with the bullet to complete a day of tragedy.

Ironically, the British were aware of the tactics the Germans were likely to employ, not only because prisoners had reported the existence of deep shelters, but because precisely the same sequence had been witnessed a year before. In a letter written on 21 June 1915 General Henry Rawlinson himself had placed the 'chief cause of failure' of the Aubers attacks upon the dugouts and cellars into

Above
Entrance to the Hawthorn Ridge mine. The pipe on the right is part of the ventilation system. The position has been made deliberately unobtrusive to avoid aerial observation and the unwelcome attention of German mortars.

which 'the garrison withdrew during the bombardment so that when the moment came for the assault they were able to rush out and line their trenches without having suffered to any serious extent from the hellish bombardment we had given them.' Both he, Haig and the rest of the planners were fully conscious of the existence of German underground shelters on the Somme front.

For the first week of battle British attacks were repeatedly forced back to their starting points or pinned down in shell holes, sunken roads and the natural folds of no man's land. It was to be 11 July before most of the German front line had fallen – and the struggle was only just beginning. By the 18th the Germans had reinforced, doubling the original number of troops in the sector, and transferring fresh artillery firepower from Verdun. Pressure upon the beleaguered town was thus lifted, indeed, the French were presently able to mount counter-attacks of their own in that sector. But the agonies were simply being transferred from Frenchman to Briton. Every advance on the Somme became slender and terribly costly, gains minimal and often temporary, and captured ground, rather than being firmly secured and exploited, had to be grimly clung onto. Operations by both day and night returned meagre profits, either due to a lack of support, or dogged German defence. The month of August saw little change in British fortunes, but in early September spirits were raised: the battlefront was suddenly to expand as the French Tenth Army launched a second major and wider assault south of the River Somme.

Their attack spurred the British to move against Flers (with tanks being used for the first time), against Morval, and once more against the hated Thiepval Ridge. Success continued to be meagre, yet amongst these bloody actions a definite creeping forward movement was discerned by Haig and his staff. The offensive now entered a period of genuine attrition, and would continue. Operations in October followed a similar pattern: obliterate and occupy, obliterate and occupy, metre by metre. By the end of the month a distinct salient had been formed, its apex following the trace of the ancient Roman road running north-eastwards from Albert towards Bapaume. By now the British and Dominion forces' casualty list was colossal, Kitchener's volunteer army had been effectively decimated (the casualties were almost exactly one man in ten), and a deep disillusionment was setting in both at the front and at home, where whole communities were traumatized by the losses. Haig, implored by Joffre to persevere to allow the French to pursue their now new offensive objectives at Verdun, determined to continue the advance as long as the weather allowed. The 'penetration' continued, but it was so slow that even in the midst of battle the Germans were comfortably able to construct new trench lines to fall back upon if necessary. Eventually, the Allied advance slowed to such an extent that the advantage passed to the enemy.

On a sleet-laden 18 November, after the battles of the Ancre and Beamont Hamel had secured a few more square kilometres of ravaged ground, the offensive drew to a close. Maximum penetration into enemy territory had been almost 12 km ($7\frac{1}{2}$ miles), but in most sectors the figure was pitifully reduced. The strategic gain was nil. Combined Allied and German losses lay close to 1,120,000 men killed, wounded and missing. Unlike Haig's next foray at Ypres in Belgian Flanders, a battleground which had caused the downfall of almost every attacking army since pre-Roman times, there had been nothing wrong with the Somme as an arena for battle; the problem lay in entrenched thinking just as much as entrenched Germans. The one single devastating lesson was that without being able to follow a precise and controlled creeping barrage which could lead an attack until *all* the trenches in a system had been overrun – an entirely impossible phenomenon as guns could not be brought forward and laid speedily enough to achieve it – the infantry could never be expected to attack with success. Indeed, the battle only suggested that the enemy could perhaps defend forever if needs be. And this would remain the case until a man could be made bulletproof and guns fully mobile. A new way of attacking and a new way of thinking was required. The Cambrai campaigns of 1917 and 1918 would begin to initiate just such a revolution – the tank revolution.

Gommecourt

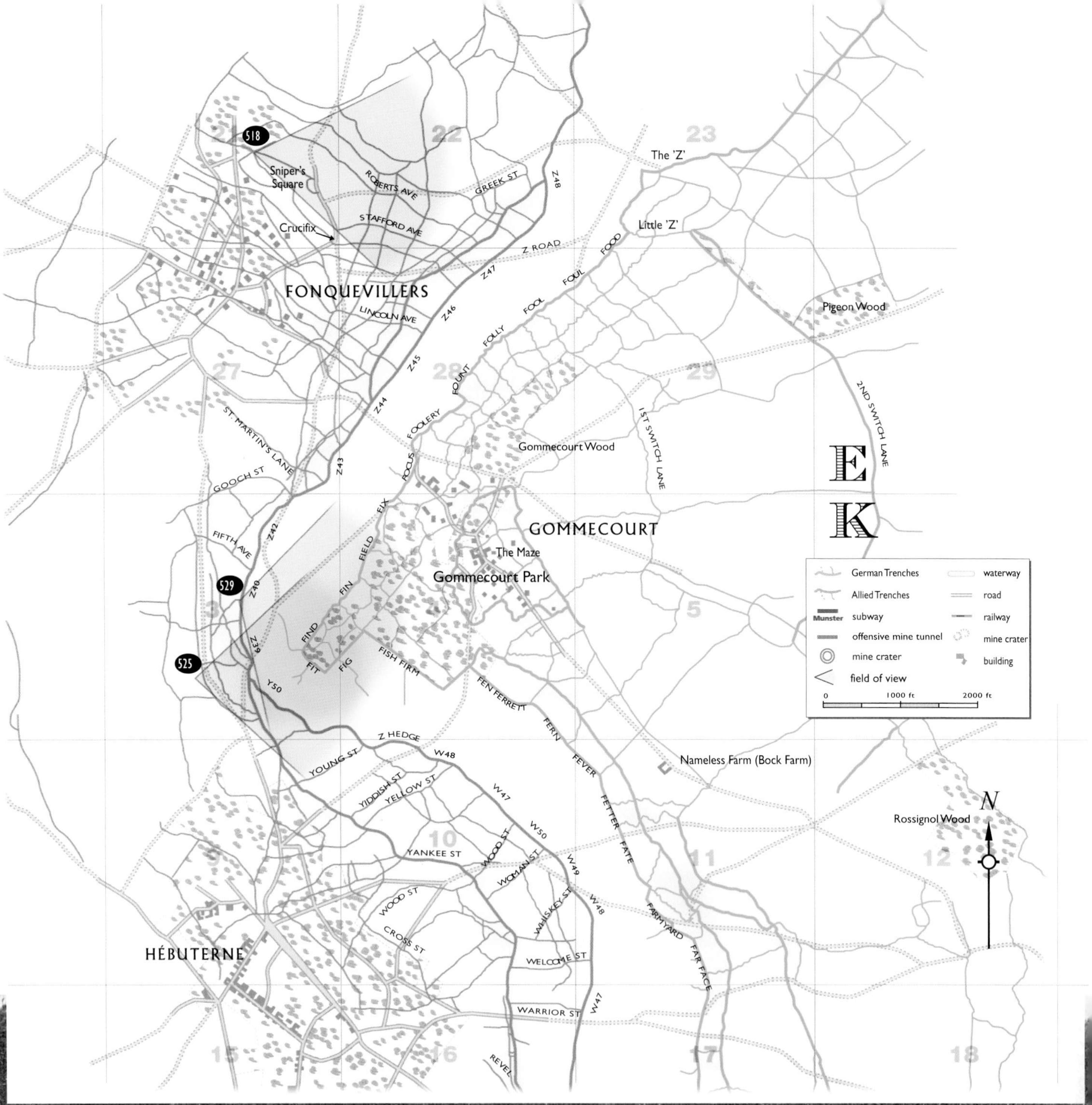

On the northernmost point of the battlefront before the village of Fonquevillers, the 46th and 56th Divisions of VII Corps were given the unenviable task of creating a diversion for more pungent events at neighbouring Serre and Beaumont Hamel by respectively attacking the north and south of the Gommecourt salient, and cutting off the village. The job was unenviable because the sector was immensely strongly defended and wired in. Panorama 529, which shows the area attacked by the 56th to the right of frame and the 46th Division to the left, illustrates the density of the enemy entanglements. On 1 July the wire stopped the northern attack in its tracks. It was uncut. With men struggling to make forward progress, German machine guns and artillery shredded the assault. Panorama 518 (1 June 1916) reveals that the British were fully aware of the precise location of several machine-gun positions and strong points in this sub-sector – they are clearly marked

Right
Beaumont Hamel. Troops receiving instructions on the eve of battle.

on the image. On the southern face of the Gommecourt salient the initial thrust overran the enemy front line but became isolated by a heavy hostile barrage. Running low on bombs and ammunition, and with support troops being cut down the moment they set foot upon no man's land, the remnants of the successful first wave fell back, first to the German front line, and then the trenches from which they had moved off at 7.20 a.m. that morning. Losses within the entire sector were appalling: almost 7,000 casualties from just two divisions. And no gain. Field positions here did not alter for the rest of the battle; indeed, British troops were only to set foot in Gommecourt Wood, Park and village when the Germans withdrew to the Hindenburg positions in February the following year.

Moving south, and still on 1 July, Panorama *525* (20 May 1916) links Gommecourt with its neighbouring Serre sector. The London Scottish (part of 56th Division) attacked Rossignol Wood but were driven back by field artillery firing through the gap between Rossignol and Gommecourt woods, plus enfilade machine-gun and rifle fire from positions beyond the point in the picture where Gommecourt Wood tapers towards no man's land.

Panoramas *61* (4th Army, 17 May 1916) and 521 (Third Army, 6 May 1916) encompass the entire Serre battlefield and beyond. The two images share separate provenances as at this time the area formed the Army boundary. On Day One of the battle the sector achieved a terrible notoriety for the heartbreaking demise of the 'Pals' battalions, units composed of comrades from the industrial towns of Yorkshire, Lancashire and Durham who had joined up together and stayed together in uniform. Many were also related. As part of the 31st Division, their attacks entirely failed, mainly due to British artillery being unable to dispose of the machine-gun threat: German teams had sheltered in plentiful deep dugouts and *boves* during the week-long bombardment. Panorama 521 shows the clear German fields of fire from the environs of Serre. Many of the men who rose to attack from this very camera position would not even reach their own front line, which is clearly marked. Panorama *61* situates Serre and other villages and features within the wider battlefront. The sub-sector map shows several Russian saps crossing beneath no man's land: these were especially dug for 1 July but lay unused. After the failed attacks at the beginning of the battle, a plan to employ the saps properly was drawn up for renewed action

Below
Gommecourt Wood remained unconquered throughout the Somme fighting. Photographed from the British front line, Third Army Panorama 529 clearly shows no man's land, which just 4 weeks later claimed so many lives.

in October, but it was to be November before the next assault on Serre took place. Reserve Army (formed on 23 May 1916 and later renamed Fifth Army) Panorama *303* taken on 7 October 1916 shows the nature of this locale after three months of fighting. The original 1 July lines have moved forward to reach the camera location, but Serre, Puisieux, Gommecourt and Rossignol Wood are still firmly in German hands. On 13 November elements of the 3rd and 31st Divisions were charged with the capture of Serre. By this time ground conditions had seriously deteriorated. The clay-laden surface *loess* had turned many parts of the battle-area into shallow seas of sloppy sludge; roads required constant draining and scraping, and every hollow inevitably filled with deep, sucking mud. Even getting out of a trench over the slimy parapets was a challenge. Two of the RE tunnels (see map: Mark and John galleries were now high and wide enough to transport field artillery) were actually used by British machine-gun teams in the attack, but were of little assistance: surface conditions resembled those more often associated with the 1917 Flanders offensives, and partly because of this the assault was again a costly failure. Like Gommecourt, Serre village was never captured, and only occupied in February 1917 after the German retirement.

Panorama *303* also marks the scene of heavy fighting by Canadian troops in the three days after the 7 October. In the struggle to take Regina Trench a most unusual Victoria Cross was won by Piper J. C. Richardson, 16th Battalion, 1st Canadian Division, who begged for (and obtained) permission to pipe his unit over the top. The battalion was held up by wire (marked on the panorama), and whilst they struggled to cut a route through, sustaining serious casualties in the process, Richardson piped, pacing the edge of the entanglements. The Canadians drew fresh impetus from his skirling notes and took the enemy trench.

Above

Third Army Panorama 521: the Serre battlefield as seen on 5 May 1916. The British forward positions run through John, Luke and Mark Copses. These were the lines from which the Pals battalions attacked on 1 July and suffered so badly.

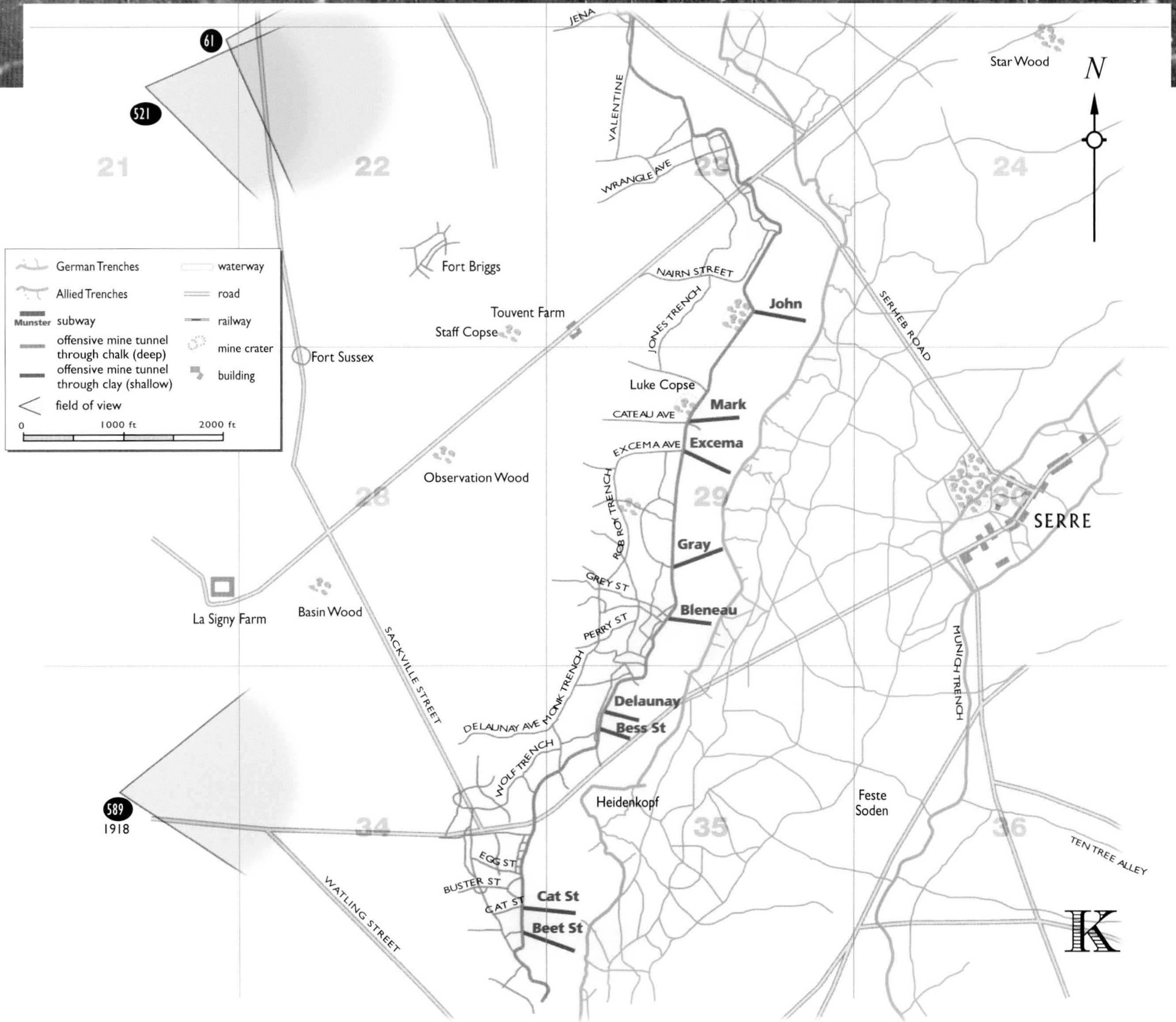

Right

The Serre map shows the unused Russian saps dug for 1 July. Note how close they were taken to the German line.

Below

British troops occupying a position close to Regina Trench in September 1916.

Richardson was then detailed to assist in evacuating wounded and escorting prisoners from the field, which he did, leaving his pipes behind. On his way back over no man's land he thought better of the decision and rushed back to pick them up. He was never to return and is today buried not far from Regina Trench in Adanac Cemetery in Miraumont. The panorama raises the question as to whether commanders knew of the wire guarding the trench, as it is indicated on the picture with a question mark. See also the surprising Panorama 304 taken more than a week later from Stuff Redoubt (16 October 1916) which shows the same battlefield where the above actions took place, but presents an entirely different impression and ambience, simply because of improved weather conditions and wider angle of view. The seemingly ubiquitous poet Edmund Blunden set up bombing blocks in Stuff Trench, a continuation of Regina Trench, on 23 October, just as the Redoubt was finally falling.

Left
Edmund Blunden, who saw action in several sectors during the war, served on the Somme in October 1916.

It was Geoffrey Salter speaking out firmly in the darkness. Stuff Trench – this was Stuff Trench; three feet deep, corpses underfoot, corpses on the parapet, while shell after shell slipped in crescendo, wailing into the vibrating ground, that his brother had been killed, and he had buried him; Doogan had been wounded, gone downstairs into one of the dug-out shafts after hours of sweat, and a shell had come downstairs to finish him; "and," says he, "you can get a marvellous view of Grandcourt from this trench. We've been looking at it all day. Where's these men? Let me put 'em into the posts. No, you wait a bit, I'll see to it. That the sergeant-major?"

Moving along as he spoke with quick emotion and new power (for hitherto his force of character had not appeared in the less exacting sort of war), he began to order the newcomers into sentry-groups; and stooping down to find what it was snuffing at my boots I found it was a dog. He was seemingly trying to keep me from treading on a body. I caught sight of him by someone's torch or flare; he was black and white; and I spoke to him, and at the end of a few moments he allowed me to carry him off.

EDMUND BLUNDEN (11TH ROYAL SUSSEX), *Undertones of War*

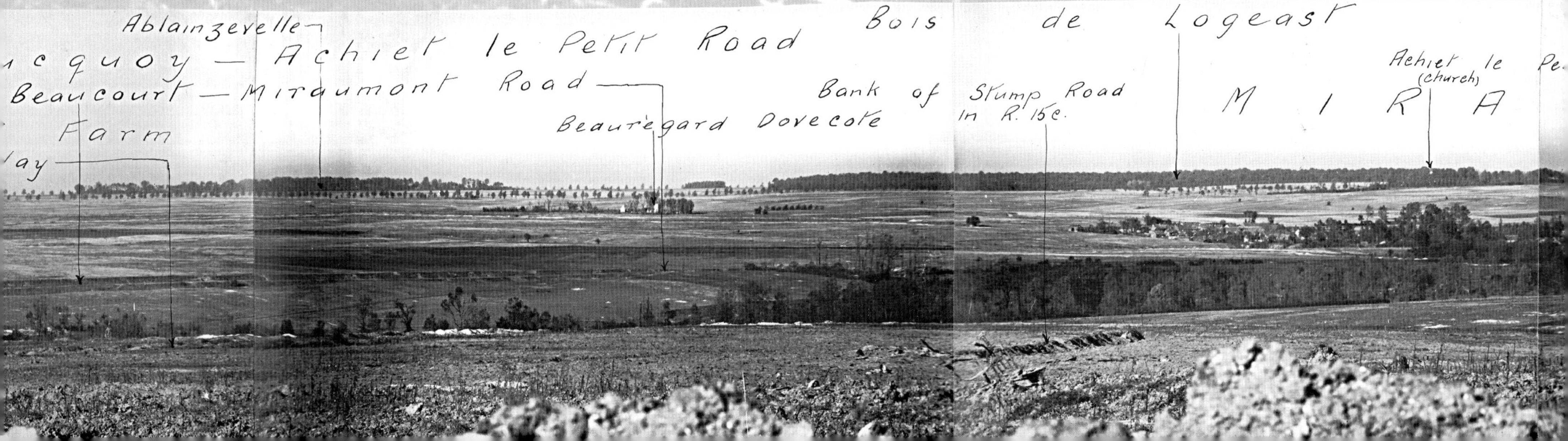

Below

Reserve Army Panorama 304. A panoramic surprise. This photograph, taken from near Stuff Redoubt, is dated 16 October 1916. The battle has been raging for over fourteen weeks, yet farms, fields and villages just beyond the fighting zone lie almost undamaged.

Redan Ridge and Beaumont Hamel

This officer came back, and then went away. He did this about four times at about twenty-minute intervals. He kept on looking at his watch. The last time he appeared he said "Come on, lads. Time we went." They had a scaling ladder in this bay: that was a wooden ladder with about four rungs. The officer went first, then the other two chaps, and then me. Of course I had those ruddy ammo boxes and my rifle, so didn't go over the top with dash as you might say – more of a humping and a scrambling really. No yelling 'Charge' or anything like that. I kept my eye on the officer just ahead. He turned to wave us fellers on and then down he went – just as though he was bloody pole-axed. I just kept moving, I wasn't really thinking straight. My job was to keep pace with the gun team. 'Don't lose me,' the Number One had said. So I kept on. And there was blokes laying everywhere. I couldn't see nothing what happened to the left of me because I had my ammunition boxes on that shoulder, but where the first waves had been – to my right – there was bodies everywhere and the troops trying to advance had to jump over them. I was running past one fellow – he had a big wound in his leg – and he shouted 'Best of luck to you, mate!' Luck I was certainly going to need, judging by what was going on. The machine-gun bullets was like hailstorm. I could see near four hundred yards ahead and to my right, I reckon, and there wasn't a man upright in the middle of No Man's Land. And yet those poor old Newfoundlanders went straight on. You had to admire them. But thinking about it later, I could weep.

CHARLIE 'GINGER' BYRNE, MACHINE GUN CORPS, *I Survived, Didn't I?*

Part of the Beaumont Hamel sector was bought by public subscription (mainly through the efforts of the women of Newfoundland) after the war, and is still preserved today as the tremendously poignant Newfoundland Memorial Park. The 1 July attack in this sector was launched by the springing of the famous Hawthorn Ridge mine, a 40,000 lb charge which, had it not been blown ten minutes before the infantry went over, could well have achieved a success (albeit localized) similar to the Messines mines of June 1917. As a direct result of the early firing the crater was not captured, although the near lip was occupied for a few hours. It ultimately only served to improve German positions on the ridge. Panorama 4, taken from the British front line on Hawthorn Ridge itself on 5 August 1915, shows the northern half of the sector. To the left of frame the Redan Ridge was a site of concentrated underground warfare: white crater lips are visible on the skyline. At this time they are mainly the product of previous French underground work, but mining was continued by British tunnellers right up to the middle of 1916; evidence can be seen in Panorama *60* taken just weeks before battle began in 1916. On 1 July the ridge was the objective of the 4th Division, who lined up for the attack with two battalions of the 48th (South Midlands) Division on their left.

Left
A nervous-looking Major R.D. Perceval-Maxwell of 13th Royal Irish Rifles in the Hawthorn Ridge mine.

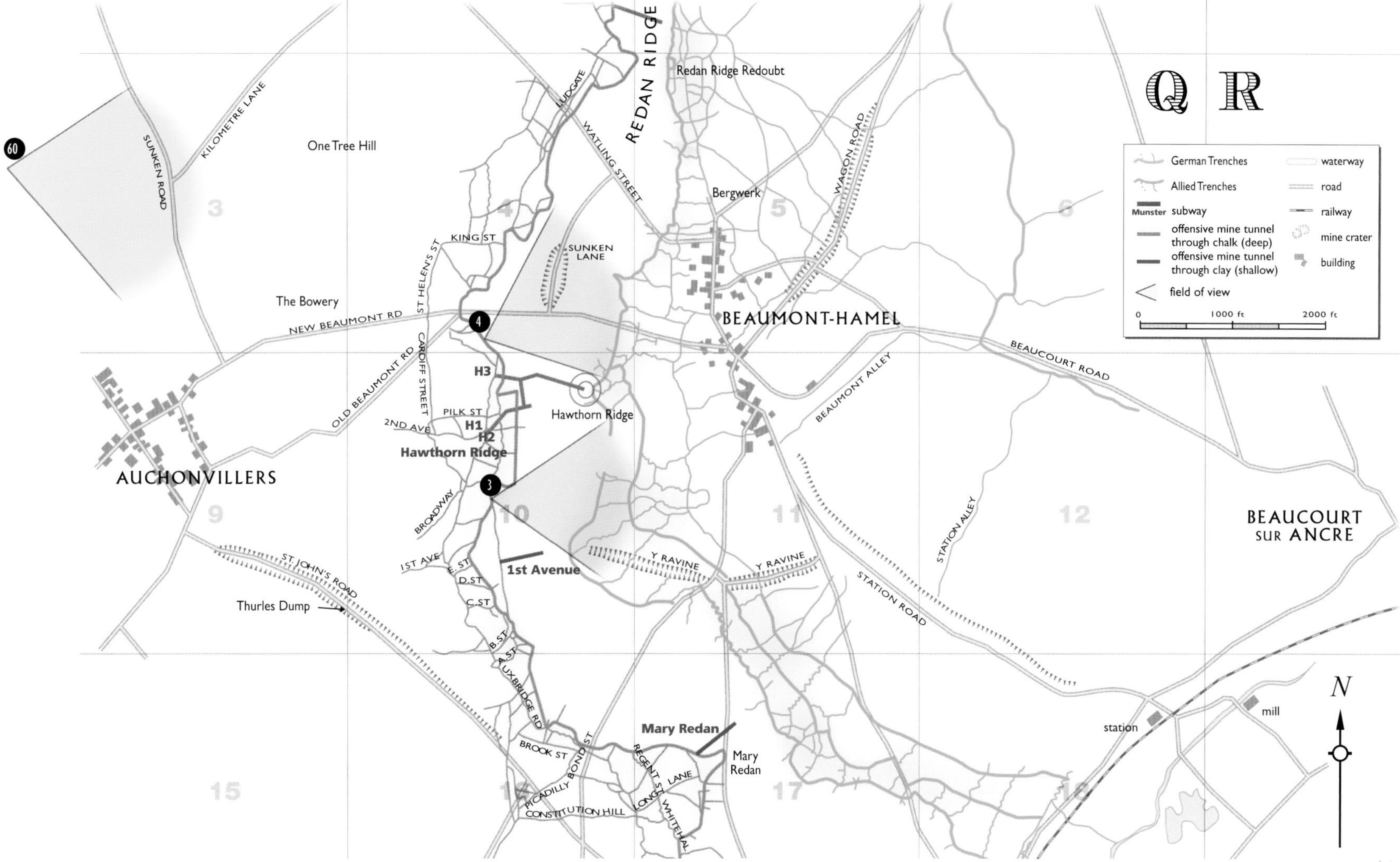

Right

Troops of the 16th (Public Schools) Battalion, Middlesex Regiment prepare for battle on the morning on 1 July. Their position here, part of a large linear dugout system known as 'White City', can be seen in Panorama *60*.

The German lines here and in front of neighbouring Beaumont Hamel village were ideally situated on forward slopes and ridge tops, and all were peppered with deep dugouts. As usual, the village had its system of ancient *boves*, each interconnected to tunnel and subway schemes, all of which afforded excellent cover. The capture of this sub-sector was the task of the 29th Division, who were also required to assault the lower, backward sloping ground in front of Y Ravine (the site of the present Newfoundland Park) immediately to the south – this area is covered in Panorama *60* (17 May 1916). The advance along the valley sides, which dropped down to the wide belt of marshes bordering the River Ancre and beyond towards Thiepval,

was a 36th (Ulster) Division undertaking. A view of the entire sweep of ground from the Redan to Thiepval can be seen in Panoramas *2* and 59. Although separated by ten months these two pictures give a fascinating indication of the pre-battle character of the region. With each image covering almost the identical field of view, two things stand out: the almost entire lack of damage to the landscape – even in Panorama 59 which was taken just five weeks before the great offensive began – and the vast increase in entrenchment and defensive wire work carried out between 1915 and 1916. The minimal evidence of shellfire is particularly striking: in Panorama *2* Thiepval village is recognizable as such, and the chateau (Grand Sapin), although battered, still stands. Both were later wiped from the face of the battlefield; the latter was never rebuilt. In Panorama 59 even the spire of Hamel church still reaches elegantly through the treetops. The most telling feature in this panorama, however, protects the German front and support line trenches – deep and dense masses of barbed wire. The same substantial approach was applied to every enemy trench throughout the entire Somme sector. The picture gives an excellent illustration of the kind of defences which faced the British troops on 1 July 1916. It also illustrates exactly what defence-in-depth means: multiple,

Above
Third Army Panorama 4, dated 5 August 1915, shows the scene of the abortive Lancashire Fusilier attack of 1 July. The men mustered in the sunken lane then advanced up the hill towards the village. The view is little changed today.

mutually-supporting trenches connected by switch lines as far as the eye can see. Each successive parallel line of trenches seen here do not denote front, support and reserve lines – these key 'main' positions were separated by one or two kilometres (see map); the majority of those pictured behind the forward German positions in Panoramas *2* and 59 are *intermediate* defence lines.

The parent body for the 4th and 29th Divisions at Beaumont Hamel was VIII Corps. Over the ground illustrated in Panoramas 3, 4 and *60*, on 1 July they were to suffer the worst casualty figures on the entire Somme battlefront. Within twenty-four hours more than 13,000 losses were sustained. The reasons for failure were twofold – the ubiquitous underground dugouts – and wire. Although taken in August 1915, the density of the latter can clearly be seen in Panorama 3; by the summer of the following year it was yet more daunting. Behind the German front line is a 10-m (33-ft) deep valley – from which treetops can be seen protruding in the panorama. This is Y Ravine, one of many similar dried-up river beds in the region – relics of the immediate post ice-age era. Apart from safely housing gun batteries, all ravines formed major German arterial routes which were almost impossible for British artillery to draw a bead upon. Y-Ravine was connected to a series of further sheltered sunken ways to the north, east and south, each of which provided excellent cover for every troop movement, transport and batteries of guns. Tunnels were driven into its flanks, linking with several forward positions including machine-gun posts (one is marked in the panorama), and serving deep and substantial dugouts, many with beds, mirrors, dining areas etc.

At 7.30 a.m. on 1 July the 4th Division on the Redan Ridge were charged with taking Pendant Copse (see Panorama *303*), a strong point protected by another powerful position known as the Quadrilateral (the 'Heidenkopf' to the Germans), deliberately positioned to present an authoritative field of defensive fire. The troops managed to overrun four lines of enemy trenches, and small groups even penetrated the copse, a terrific achievement, but the disastrous events unfolding to fellow battalions on their right made the new positions untenable. Having tried to consolidate, a retirement order came through at about 1.30 p.m., and the troops withdrew. Inevitable German counter-attacks and heavy shrapnel barrages cut down supporting units, and by the evening the few survivors were back where they had started.

Since dawn the German front line had been hardly visible due to dust clouds from the British barrage, so those units attacking the Redan Ridge (see Panoramas 5 and *60*) left the trenches full of confidence. However, on emerging over the parapet they immediately came under heavy fire from left and right as well as the ridge itself. With numbers quickly dwindling in crossing no man's land, the survivors found the wire largely uncut, and dropped into the long grass in search of invisibility. Elements of supporting units reached the enemy trenches, but having negotiated a storm of bullets and shrapnel were too weak to hold.

At Beaumont Hamel village the story was the same. The barrage and the big mine had been heartening and confidence-inducing to the Lancashire troops. Their assembly position for the attack – the famous 'sunken lane' – can be seen in Panoramas 4 and *60*. The narrowness of no man's land between the opposing lines is particularly evident in the former. This little cutting (later incorporated into the front line as Hunters Lane) – was forward of the British front line, but being sheltered from enemy gaze and bullets was chosen as the jumping-off point. However, the ground separating Briton from German was by no means level, there was first the bank of the sunken lane to scale, another embankment halfway across, and then an uphill struggle to the wire. The men were cut down as they emerged from the lane: the mine, fired ten minutes before their attack, had given the Germans all the warning they needed; and the guns were waiting on the parapets.

Miraculously, I breathlessly reached the sunken road, practically leaping the last yard or two and diving into its shelter. Picking myself up and looking round, my God, what a sight! The whole of the road was strewn with dead and dying men. Some were talking deliriously, others calling for help and asking for water…once more we sprang into that fusillade of bullets. In a few moments I must have been alone and quickly decided to drop into a shell-hole. I felt almost certain that most

of the men had been killed or wounded. Anyhow, I could look back over no man's land towards our own trenches. Hundreds of dead lay about and wounded men were trying to crawl back to safety; their heart-rending cries for help could be heard above the noise of rifle fire and bursting shells. As I lay there watching their painful efforts to get back to our line I noticed these poor fellows suddenly try to rise on their feet and then fall in a heap and lie very still. Shells whistled over my head and dropped amongst the poor fellows, blowing dead men into the air and putting others out of their misery. As I gazed on this awful scene and realised my own terrible danger I asked God to help me…Over to the right I could see where our neighbouring battalion, the Royal Fusiliers, had gone over the top. Suddenly I noticed a few of them running for their lives back to their front line. This made me think that Fritz was counter-attacking and I fully expected to hear him coming at the double for my shell-hole. Sudden fear must have spurred me to action, for in a flash I sprang from my shell-hole and dashed madly for the sunken road, flinging myself into it as Fritz's bullets whistled all about me, and almost jumping on to two of our men who were busy making a firing step in the side of the road.
GEORGE ASHURST, 1ST BATTALION LANCASHIRE FUSILIERS, *My Bit, A Lancashire Fusilier at War*

Next to the Lancashires, the 16th (Public Schools Battalion, Middlesex Regiment) attacked Beaumont village. Moving over ground to the left of the mine crater they made no headway and were forced to retire. Many of the wounded crawled back into the sunken lane. Up on Hawthorn Ridge itself the Royal Fusiliers, supported by the Royal Dublin Fusiliers, were charged with carrying the village. They suffered in the same way as their Middlesex neighbours, and the scale of loss led to a calling off of the planned Dublins' attack.

The taking of Y Ravine and the village of Beaucourt beyond belonged to the South Wales Borderers, a battalion of the Border Regiment, and the King's Own Scottish Borderers. When their attack failed in the same way as others – in the face of uncut wire and machine guns – the 1st Battalion of the Newfoundland Regiment went forward alongside Worcestershire, Essex and Hampshire troops, attacking down the slope seen in Panoramas 3 and *60*. Sadly, as had so often been the case in earlier battles, coordination between British artillery and infantry failed: the barrage which had been planned to protect the attacking units advanced far too fast to be of assistance, moving well beyond German lines which housed hundreds of spitting guns. The attack was utterly disastrous, with the Newfoundlander battalion alone suffering over 600 casualties. The few survivors stayed alive thanks to slight topographical folds in the ridge creating 'dead ground', shielding those who could reach it. There was no gain either on the right where a second Fusilier battalion, the 1st Inniskillings, lost more than 550 men. Other units in supporting roles shared the same fate, and there was no success in any part of the sector.

Subsequent days were spent bringing in the wounded, and an unofficial truce was arranged to perform this most necessary of tasks. Plans for further attacks on the positions astride Beaumont Hamel were drawn up and postponed several times, and it was not until 13 November that the next major foray was launched. By this time the Germans, not without reason, regarded the positions as almost impregnable – which was their precise aspiration when planning and utilizing the topographical and geological advantages of the landscape. The Redan was

Above
The Hawthorn Ridge mine goes up ten minutes before the attack.

Above left
1 July, Beaumont Hamel. A wounded man is assisted across a sunken road.

Above right
Men of the 16th (Public Schools) Battalion, Middlesex Regiment retire across the Hawthorn Ridge in the face of an impenetrable storm of gunfire. The mine crater is just out of frame to the left, with British trenches visible to the top of the picture.

Right
An officer (believed to be the commanding officer, Colonel Hamilton-Hall) can be seen leading men to the safety of dead ground with his stick.

assaulted in mid October, and the Quadrilateral taken on the 15th (see No 304), but moves against the Beaumont Hamel sector continued to be unsuccessful. However, at the very tail end of the Somme offensive the 51st (Highland) Division devised alternative tactics for their endeavour: on 13 November there were to be no general frontal attacks; after another mine blow beneath the southern shoulder of the 1 July crater (the original tunnel was reopened and reused) the troops were to assault almost the identical positions as on the fateful day in July. All the signs were adverse on the 13th: the weather was bad, the ground sodden and visibility poor. Fortunately, the latter was to confuse and disjoint the German defensive artillery, and the Scotsmen delivered all that had been asked of them: the ridges, ravines and village of Beaumont Hamel were at last in British hands.

The Ancre to Leipzig

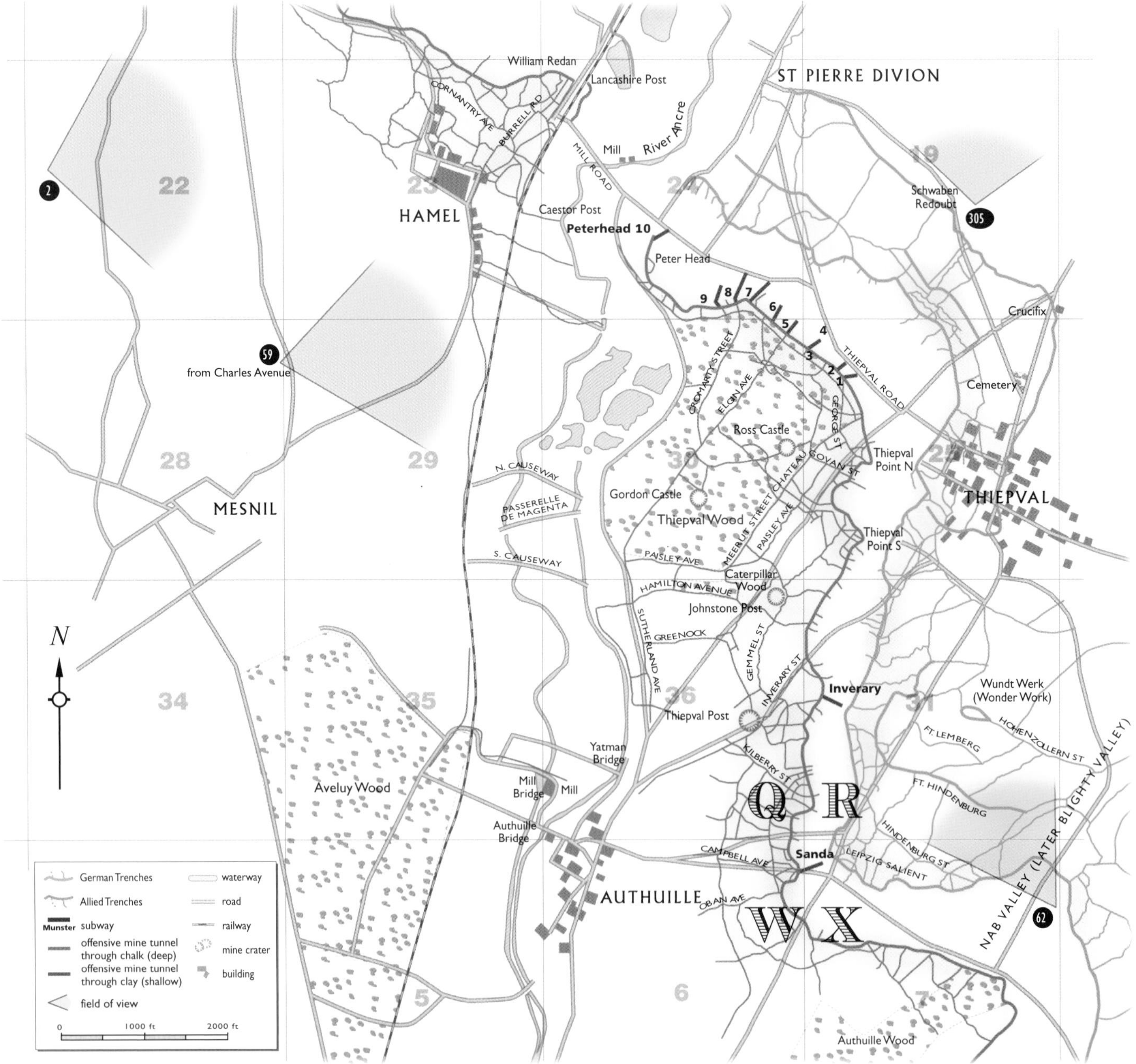

As the site of the greatest memorial to the missing on the Western Front, the little hamlet of Thiepval is today probably the most visited sub-sector of the Somme. To either side of the village, itself a bastion during the war, lie the Schwaben and Leipzig redoubts, both ridge-top fortresses. Little has changed here in the intervening decades since 1918; indeed, fewer people live in Thiepval now than in 1914, and it is a place where the visitor can readily appreciate the colossal task that British troops faced when they left the safety of their trenches on 1 July 1916.

The whole area fell under the control of X Corps. The ground to the north of the village – the responsibility of the 36th (Ulster) Division, facing their very first battle – is covered in Panoramas *2* and 59, both of which offer a magnificent and, with hindsight, somewhat distressing prospect of the battlefields of the first few days of fighting, and indeed long afterwards. For similar wide views to the south – the Leipzig Salient – see Panorama *22* (9 October 1915), this was 31st Division territory during the opening sequence, with the 49th (West Riding) Division in reserve.

As the panoramas show, the whole of the plateau incorporating Schwaben, Thiepval and Leipzig was one huge towering stronghold. German troops serving here enjoyed the customary comprehensive underground protection and communication, whilst on the surface the panoramas reveal skilfully sited trenches, and the outstanding

Above
Elgin Avenue in Thiepval Wood, taken before the battle on 1 July 1916. This was one of the major communication routes from the rear of the wood to the front line (see map).

Right
A British front line trench in Thiepval Wood, taken on 1 July by Major R.D. Perceval-Maxwell, second-in-command of 13th Royal Irish Rifles, 36th Division.

Below
Panorama 59: the Fourth Army view of the Theipval Wood and Schwaben Redoubt area from Charles Avenue on 16 May 1916 – just six weeks before the battle.

fields of fire they commanded. The curving shape of the German lines meant that converging enfilade fire was a serious concern for troops advancing anywhere within most of the concave central section, and British GHQ were fully aware that without thorough wire-cutting and bludgeoning of enemy positions by artillery prior to an infantry assault, prospects would be grim. The village and redoubts therefore received a systematic and prolonged hammering, and the wire was cut … but of course there were still the dugouts. The map shows several Russian Saps in place before 1 July, most of which were ready to become twin Stokes mortar emplacements as soon as the heads were opened up, but few of which were utilised.

The 36th Division's objective for day one was the capture of not only the Schwaben Redoubt but also positions along the Ancre Valley, including Beaucourt-sur-Ancre and, on the plateau south of the river, Stuff Redoubt, another powerful strong point over a kilometre inside German territory. No mines had been laid to 'assist' the troops in this sector, so success or failure depended upon the dash of the infantry and how well the artillery had prepared the way.

When the whistles blew the tremendous initial surge by the Ulster troops from their positions in Thiepval Wood surprised the German defence. Assisted by a smoke screen the momentum carried them over the front line and into the Redoubt proper. On the right however, the attack upon Thiepval village was summarily brushed aside by the Germans; from here the resulting enfilade fire upon successive waves of Irish troops was heavy – as were casualties. The first flurry of attacks left a part of the

Schwaben in British hands, but the fields on either side of Mill Road were strewn with many dead and wounded. Because the defence of Thiepval had been so complete and withering, no progress could be made with the original plan – to get behind the village via positions secured within the Schwaben Redoubt – but a small party of Ulstermen forayed out eastwards across the plateau towards the German second line, reaching Stuff Redoubt before one of their own artillery barrages fell upon the position, forcing withdrawal. The view from this redoubt just before it was finally and fully captured in October can be seen in Panorama 304 (16 October 1916). Without support and in peril of counter-attack the party had no choice but to withdraw to the Schwaben. At noon no other troops had yet appeared on either flank: to the north at Gommecourt, Serre and Beaumont Hamel, no gains had

been made; apart from a tiny pocket of success on the Leipzig Spur, progress had been either nil or negligible all the way down the line down to La Boisselle, 3 km (1.86 miles) to the south. By now the Schwaben Redoubt was being pummelled by enemy guns of all kinds, and had become a death trap. By mid-afternoon the Ulstermen's ammunition was running perilously low, and the men were exhausted. Reserve troops of the 49th West Riding Division attempted to reach and support the Ulsters but were cut down by machine guns from Thiepval village the moment they left the shelter of Thiepval Wood. Repeated attempts by this division during the forthcoming weeks also failed. No man's land, seen as an empty stage in Panoramas *2* and 59, and devoid of cover save the low banks of the road, was veneered with dead and wounded. Mill Road especially was swamped by men seeking any kind of shelter. The Schwaben Redoubt was evacuated during the night. The cost to the 36th Ulster Division was almost 5,000.

The position was not assaulted again until 26 September, when the 18th (Eastern) and 39th Divisions finally took the entire ridge. During four days of fighting every attacking unit again suffered serious casualties. The Redoubt fell on the second day; the view from its north face (taken on Christmas Eve, 1916) can be seen in Panorama *305*. The picture illustrates the intensity of the prolonged fighting for this tortured fragment of Picardy. Although little more than a kilometre from the British lines of 1 July, Beaucourt Mill, seen here on the extreme left of frame, marks the limit of the 36th Division's advance along the Ancre River valley on 1 July, yet the mill was only decisively captured (by the 63rd Naval Division) on 14 November.

On the first day of battle the centre of the sector incorporating Thiepval village held out without any undue anxiety on the part of the Germans, partly because of the habitual communication breakdown between British gunners and infantry. Receiving reports that troops had already entered the village early on the morning of 1 July, the gunners quite rightly desisted from shelling it. But there had been no such infiltration and the German defenders made the most of the lack of attention, cutting down troops to right and left as well as the British frontal attack. Immediately south of Thiepval lay another bastion: the Leipzig Spur. There were two major points of resistance to overcome here: the Wonderwork Redoubt high up on the flank of the ridge just south of the village, and the Leipzig

Above
The present view from Charles Avenue. The great Memorial to the Missing has replaced Thiepval Chateau, and the Ulster Tower has sprung up; otherwise the landscape is much as it was before the battle.

Right
An unprepossessing but unique photograph taken by Major Perceval-Maxwell in the German trenches of Schwaben Redoubt on 1 July. The positions were only held for a matter of hours on the first day of battle, and were not fully captured until October.

Salient, the great jutting, square jaw thrusting towards Authuille and the Ancre valley, with at its heart another strong point, the Leipzig Redoubt.

As at Schwaben, the British had excellent views of the Spur from high ground to the west, but it told them little of the security that lay deep beneath the enemy trenches. Approaches were enfiladed not only from Thiepval but also another spur to the south, that at Ovillers-la-Boisselle. With Mouquet Farm as their objective, at 7.30 a.m. on 1 July, 32nd Division troops were already lying in no man's land waiting for the barrage to cease. The moment the shelling shifted rearwards they rushed the German front line. The guns had done good work on the wire, and with the attack pouncing so swiftly several forward positions of the Leipzig Salient quickly fell to the 17th Highland Light Infantry.

Again, it did not take long for the enemy to reorganize, and British supporting units did not fare well: now fully aware of the situation every German machine gun came into action. Once more, shelter on the open glacis was almost non-existent; the troops appearing from the shelter of Authuille Wood trudged up the slope of no man's land into a whirlwind of crossfire from Ovillers and Thiepval, with the 11th Borders (the Lonsdale Battalion) suffering particularly heavily. Panorama 62 (22 August 1916) is taken from the original German front line on the Ovillers Spur, one of the positions which was able to shower this attack with lead before the troops reached their own front line. The ground pictured is exactly that attacked by the Lonsdales.

The wood ran to a point and ended on our front line. We had barely gone another five yards when it seemed to rain bullets, it was hell let loose. The Corporal dropped, shot through the hand. I made one dive for a shell hole for cover. A few more men dropped beside me; we stayed there for a moment, we had only got to our feet when those cursed machine-guns opened out worse than ever. I had nearly got clear but rolled back again, how I missed being hit was a miracle as bullets were hitting every foot of ground and sending up spurts of dirt round my head. The rest were not so lucky, everyone but two of us were out of action. BB was lying dead at the back of the hole and two wounded men beside him, the rest on top. I knew I couldn't stay there and

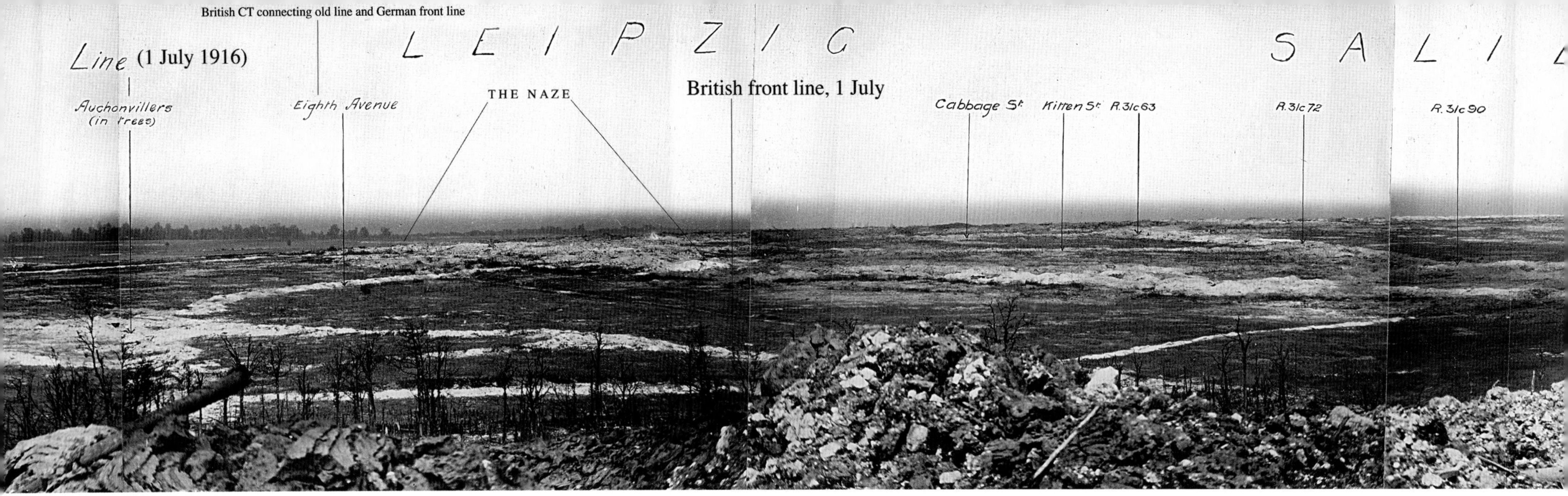

Above

Segment of Reserve Army Panorama 62 taken from positions north of Ovillers captured on 1 July. The fortress village of Thiepval appears ready for capture, but it refused to fall for several more weeks.

Background

Wiltshire Regiment troops advancing at Thiepval on 7 August.

told the other chap I was going to make a dash for it. I got to my knees, raised my head above the hole and looked round. When I thought it safe I scrambled to my feet and ran like a hare for our front line. This I jumped and fell sprawling amongst the barbed wire.

ANONYMOUS LONSDALE SOLDIER, *The Lonsdale Battalion*

Looking across Nab Valley (later Blighty Valley), the dreadful vulnerability of the assaulting troops is made apparent. The siting of the British line prior to 1 July seems almost ridiculous: from this angle it appears that the Germans could observe every movement within the trenches. Thiepval and its protective woodland has been razed to the ground.

Parts of the Leipzig Redoubt were seized and held on 1 July and in subsequent days a succession of units nibbled away at positions across the rest of the Spur, bit by bit, fighting off counter-attacks, bombers, gas and even liquid fire. The day before Panorama 62 was taken, the RE successfully employed a push-pipe to blow a communication trench across no man's land, an action that assisted the 1st Wilthires to bomb their way into the possession of a further tranche of German front and support line. The British were then able to use their secured gains here as a launch pad for Phase Two of the battle in this sector. But the cost of this meagre success was astronomical: on 1 July 9,000 casualties were listed for X Corps alone, (more than half of them were Ulstermen). Again, it was to be September before the positions fell entirely into British hands.

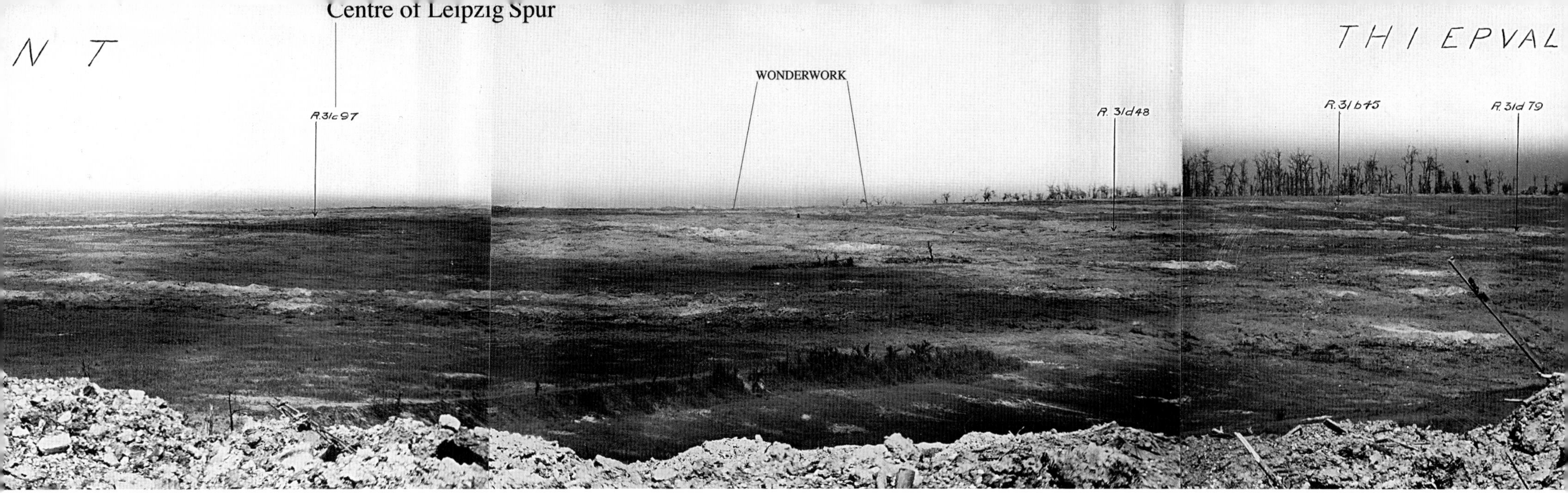

Right
Two British observers scrutinize the German lines at Thiepval.

Far right
Fighting carried on close to Thiepval for several months after the Somme battle closed. These are the weary faces of Manchester Regiment men after their successful advance in the Ancre Valley in January 1917.

Across the Roman Road

Moving south from Thiepval Ridge, the tactical nature of the topography alters once more. The contours are largely shared by both sides, but the strong points are still strictly on the German side: the villages of Ovillers-la-Boisselle and La Boiselle. Panorama 12 (24 August 1915) gives a superb view of the situation in the sector, and marks several of the most important features, including the target for Day One – the high ground either side of Pozières church. The two villages are separated by the ancient arrow-straight route built by the Romans connecting Albert and Bapaume. At the time Panorama 12 was taken La Boisselle was already a mangled ruin, mainly due to the village being effectively shared by both French and German troops until summer 1915. It was the usual story: close proximity of trenches led to the outbreak and proliferation of mine warfare, which was fiercely continued by the RE in the form of 179 Tunnelling Company when the British took over the sector. Ovillers, by contrast, appears relatively undamaged –there was no mining. Note how both villages dominate no man's land. A wider orientating view which relates these villages with Thiepval and many other features within the complex Somme landscape of battle can be found in Panorama *22* (9 October 1915). For further help with orientation see Panorama *13* (24 August 1915) and also No *27* (26 October 1915) taken from the rear area south-west of Fricourt near a British heavy artillery battery; the left section (of both panoramas) shows Ovillers and La Boisselle villages, and on the far ridge Pozières Mill, part of the target for 1 July. Note also the heavily whitened patches in places along the front lines: these are signs of mine warfare upheavals – craters.

Responsibility for the Ovillers operation was handed to the 8th Division. No man's land in this sector varied in width from almost 750 to around 200 m (820 to 220 yds). As with all attacks of the 'wave' variety it was clearly important that units move forward in unison, avoid collisions with those ahead and behind, and resist 'bunching', whilst at the same time staying in contact with other troops on each flank. The Division's 70th Brigade, on the left, moved against the Ovillers Spur (see Panorama 62, taken from the German front line which this unit attacked and entered),

Below

An aerial view of the Y Sap area, showing the results of mine warfare at La Boisselle. The Albert–Bapaume road passes through the middle of frame, with Y Sap to its left and La Boisselle village to the right.

Bottom

The Ovillers and La Boisselle battlefield as seen on 24 August 1915 in Third Army Panorama 12. Y Sap stands out.

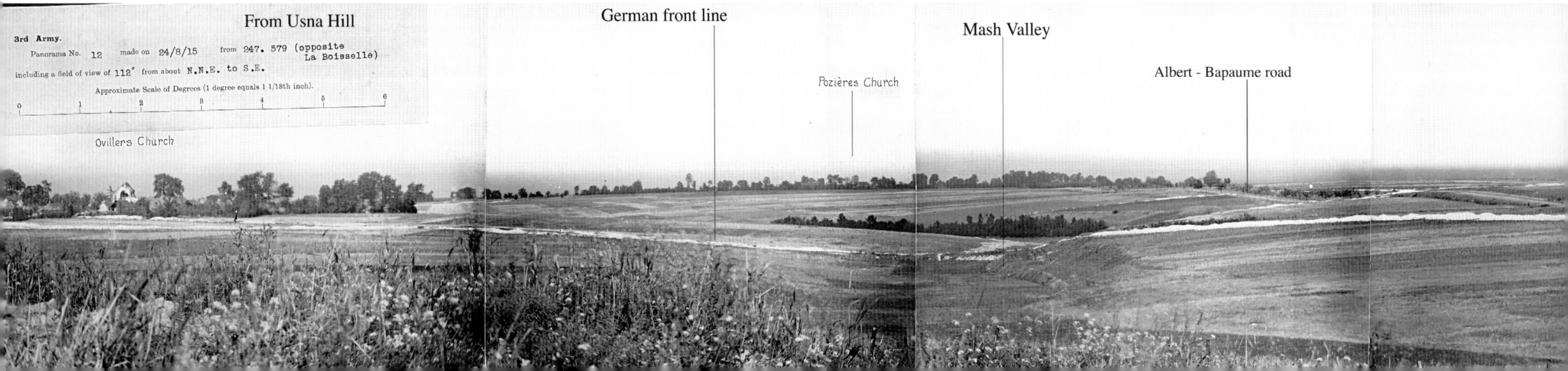

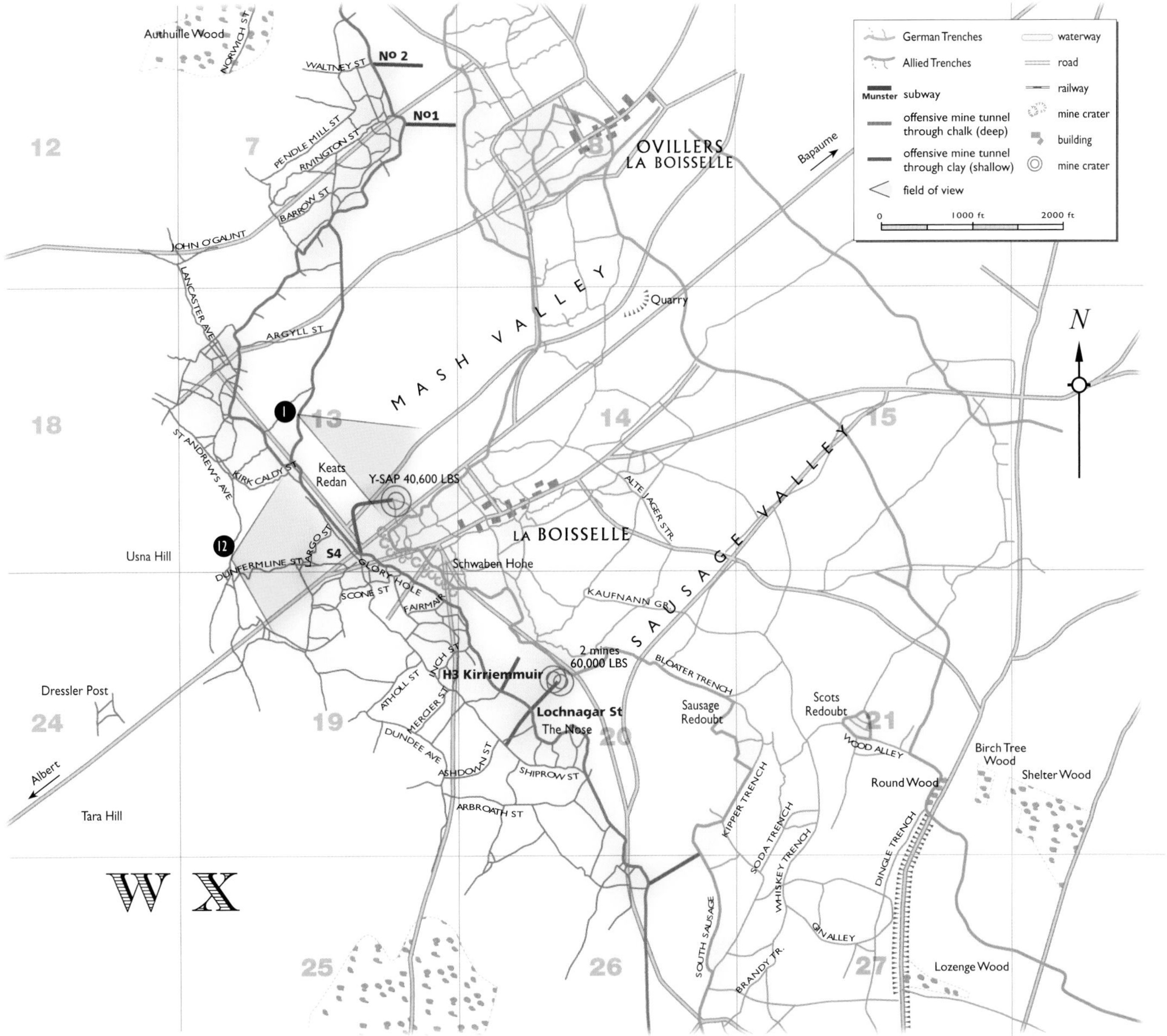

whilst the other two brigades, the 25th and 23rd, assaulted the village and a long and wide depression running parallel with the road called Mash Valley. The worst ground to negotiate lay here, in front of the village and immediately north of the Albert–Bapaume road, but close up against La Boisselle. As Panorama 12 amply illustrates, the terrain across the entire sector again lacks any form of cover, leaving troops horribly exposed. All three brigades lost heavily, although elements of the 70th drove through the enemy front line and beyond before being brought to a halt. The 23rd Brigade advanced up Mash Valley. The blowing of a 40,000 lb mine beneath Y Sap (very clearly visible in Panorama 12) just two minutes before zero assisted their attack by destroying resident nests of machine guns. In crossing no man's land, however – very wide at this point – the British were severely punished; around seventy men reached the enemy trenches and remained for a few hours before being bombed out. The 25th Brigade were practically annihilated, with less than a dozen men reaching the German wire. Subsequent supporting waves fared even worse. After the initial surprise, the perfectly sited German guns had the range, and knew from whence the British would appear. The grim evidence for this can be seen in a 'panorama' taken on 3 July (by an official rather than a panoramic

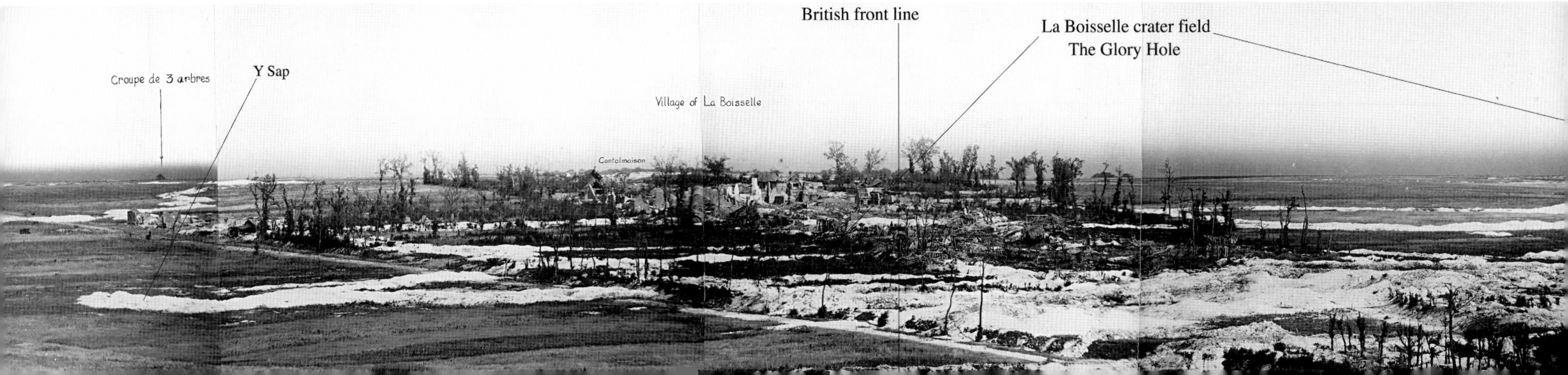

photographer, see pages 324–25) from a similar but more forward position to Panorama 12. Y Sap crater, the biggest single-charge mine until the vast charges employed at Messines, is impressive on the right, but as one pans left into Mash Valley the sight becomes tragic. The ground is carpeted with the bodies of British soldiers. Several men also lie dead in the grass in the foreground – behind the British front line. These are support troops, cut down before they reached their jumping off point, an incident which was all too common in almost every sector.

At the moment of firing Y Sap I think we just synchronised watches and when it came to the time we just pooped the handle down. J C Allan was with me in the dugout. Directly the handle went down he nipped out to the top to make sure it had gone off. There wasn't much of a kick, and I said "Cor, strike me pink," or something worse, "it hasn't gone off." He was up on the top and said, "Cor, strike me! Hasn't it! Come up and have a look." This dugout was in the communication trench, so we were back about 30 or 40 yards. When I went out there was still a helluva lot of smoke about – a wonderful sight. After this affair I saw the infantry attack. It was a terrible sight. They were just lying out there in the open like stooks of corn, in extended order. The infantry went over unopposed to begin with. Then they got held up on both flanks, uncut wire, same old story. Finally it was frightful slaughter – wicked, the cream of England went west. At the time there was nothing much to see except smoke and dust, but afterwards when they kept attacking, attacking, attacking, it was frightful.
Captain Hugh Kerr, 179 Tunnelling Company RE

Towards 7.45 the West Yorkshires began moving forward down the gentle slope into the furnace. Apparently they advanced across the open – I saw those near me climb out of their trench. The enemy's machine guns, some 1,400 yards from my position, now swept the crest like a hurricane and with such accuracy that many of the poor fellows were shot at once. This battalion had 280 casualties in traversing the 600 yards to our front line. For the past hour, or thereabouts, groups of wounded had been dribbling back along Hodder Street, among them latterly, several who were unhurt, or only slightly so, but who had given way to terror…No man's land was strewn with prone forms; up against the hostile wire they showed thickly, the regimental helmet badge being easily recognised on some. Not all of these were casualties, however; among them were men driven out of the German trenches and taking what cover they could in shell holes amid the long grass decked with sunlit scarlet poppies on our side of the enemy's wire entanglements. These men remained still as the dead to avoid drawing fire till darkness should screen their escape; others would make a dash singly or crawl patiently towards our trenches, sniped at all the way…
Diary of Major (later Brigadier-General) James Jack, *General Jack's Diary*

In the La Boisselle attack south of the road, another heavy mine (Lochnagar, 60,000 lbs, but in two separate charges and chambers) created a little more confusion than its Y Sap sister, but the result of assaults against the village and positions around Sausage Valley were equally disastrous. Panorama *30* covers this precise battlefront most of the features which played a part in the attacks of 1 July and subsequent days are illustrated and annotated. Attacking in four waves, the thrust was carried forward by the entire infantry establishment of 34th Division. If a panorama like the Ovillers example had been taken here, the scene would have been identical. British artillery had crushed the village prior to the battle, but the defensive garrison, either secure underground or safe in intermediate trench dugouts, was intact. Ten minutes after the whistles blew, over three-quarters of the initial wave of British troops had become casualties, the massed ranks of slowly advancing men presenting straightforward targets. Unlike other sectors, some of the Russian saps installed here were actually put to practical use, but not surprisingly quickly filled with wounded. They were found to be too constricted to allow a swift flow – indeed any flow – of men.

Kerriemuir, for a total length of 410 feet, the last 150 feet of this tunnel was excavated with the bayonet only, for silent work, the whole tunnel being in chalk. Enemy patrols were constantly heard passing over the top at night. The tunnel had 12 – 14 feet of cover, chalk, with a few feet of clay on top. Size of tunnel here was 5' 6" x 3' 6"x 2' 6". This tunnel at the end was stepped up to within 2' of the surface at a point 120 feet from the enemy line, and was holed up to the surface on the night Y-Z Kerriemuir was immediately used as a communication, I myself saw with what eagerness, by parties carrying

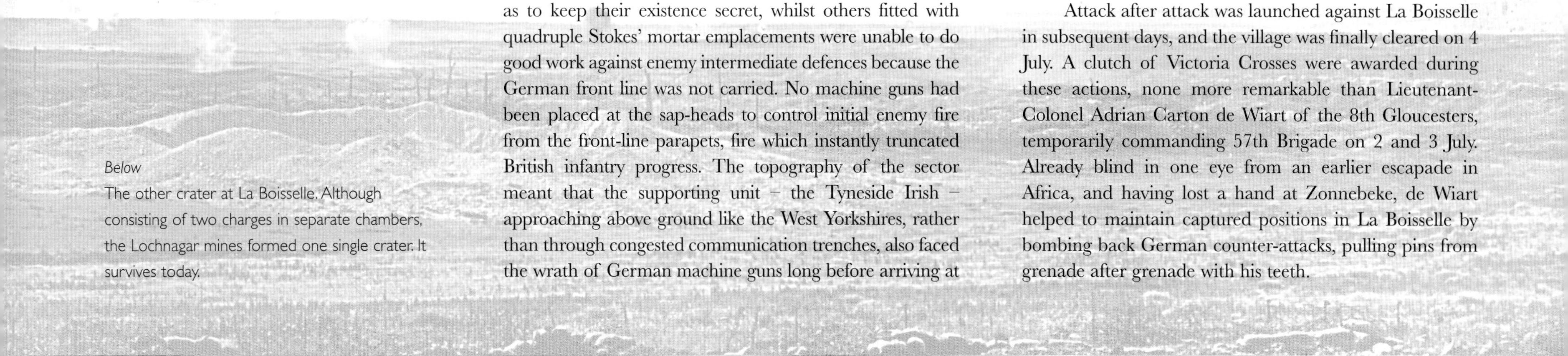

Left
The view from the Albert-Bapaume road looking down over the captured German front line running from La Boisselle to Ovillers. September 1916.

Below
The other crater at La Boisselle. Although consisting of two charges in separate chambers, the Lochnagar mines formed one single crater. It survives today.

bombs and other supplies up, and by wounded coming down, Consequently it was immediately blocked… Wounded men will always seek the nearest shelter, and consequently every such tunnel must permit of travel both ways.
Report to CRE III Corps by Major H. W. Hance, OC, 179 Co. RE 27.7.1916

As it became increasingly evident that the attack was not going well, certain saps were not immediately opened up, so as to keep their existence secret, whilst others fitted with quadruple Stokes' mortar emplacements were unable to do good work against enemy intermediate defences because the German front line was not carried. No machine guns had been placed at the sap-heads to control initial enemy fire from the front-line parapets, fire which instantly truncated British infantry progress. The topography of the sector meant that the supporting unit – the Tyneside Irish – approaching above ground like the West Yorkshires, rather than through congested communication trenches, also faced the wrath of German machine guns long before arriving at their jumping-off point: to reach the front line the Irishmen first had to cross more than a kilometre of open ground – the terrain pictured in Panoramas 12 and *30*. Just a handful were to set foot upon no man's land. Small parties of Scottish troops managed to seize small sections of the initial front-line targets and move on beyond, some to Birch Tree Wood on the ridge top overlooking Contalmaison (see Panorama *30*) where they consolidated, linking with other troops moving forward north of Fricourt.

Attack after attack was launched against La Boisselle in subsequent days, and the village was finally cleared on 4 July. A clutch of Victoria Crosses were awarded during these actions, none more remarkable than Lieutenant-Colonel Adrian Carton de Wiart of the 8th Gloucesters, temporarily commanding 57th Brigade on 2 and 3 July. Already blind in one eye from an earlier escapade in Africa, and having lost a hand at Zonnebeke, de Wiart helped to maintain captured positions in La Boisselle by bombing back German counter-attacks, pulling pins from grenade after grenade with his teeth.

Mash Valley on 3 July 1916 and in May 2005, with the village of La Boisselle beyond. In the archive panorama, Y Sap crater lies to the right of frame. To its left no man's land can be seen to be covered with the bodies of British soldiers from the actions of the previous two days fighting. Casualties can also be seen in the immediate foreground, behind the British front line trench. British shells are bursting on the German support lines beyond La Boisselle. In the same way as this comparison, many other sectors of the Somme battlefields have altered little over the decades.

Above

1 July 1916. The Tyneside Irish advance towards La Boisselle.

Fricourt and Mametz

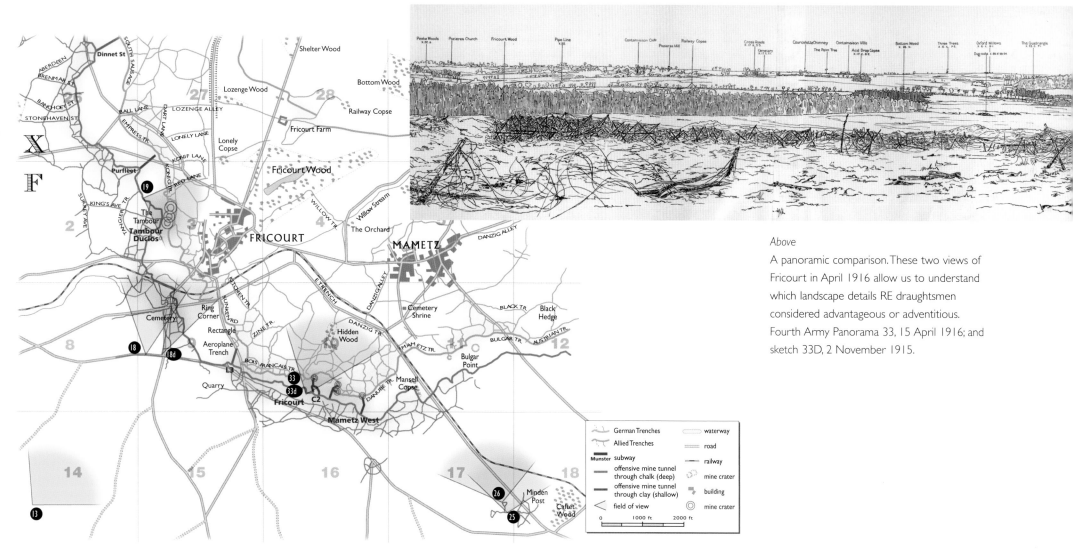

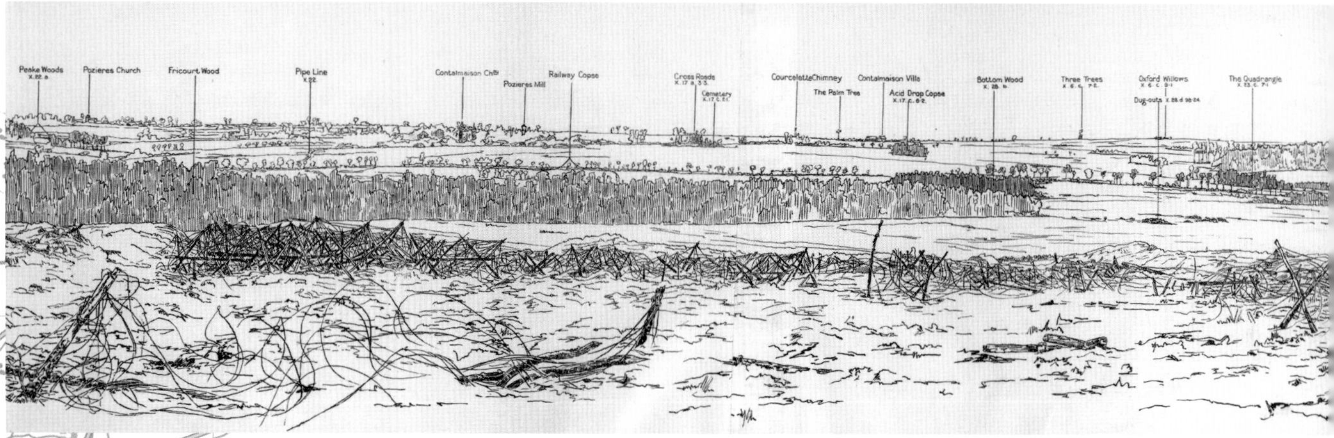

Above

A panoramic comparison. These two views of Fricourt in April 1916 allow us to understand which landscape details RE draughtsmen considered advantageous or adventitious. Fourth Army Panorama 33, 15 April 1916; and sketch 33D, 2 November 1915.

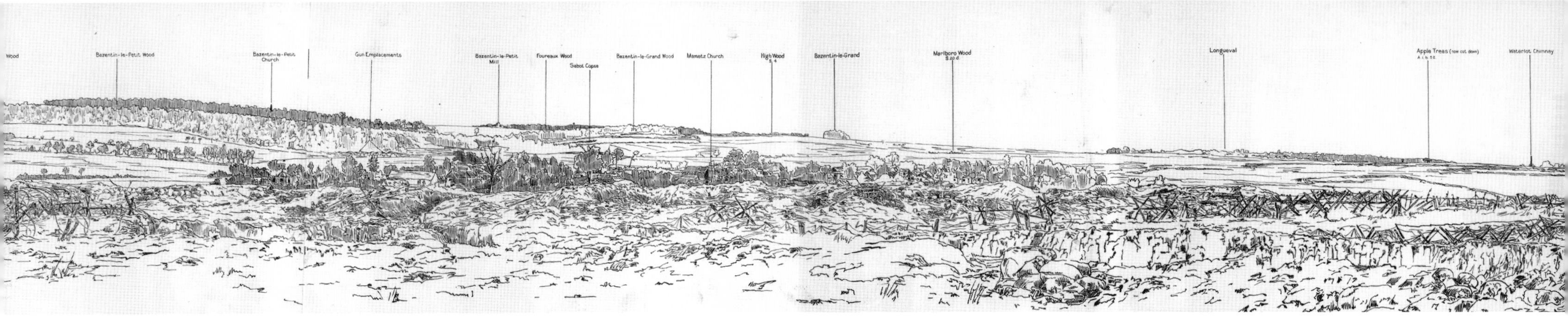

4 July 1916

After exploring these remains of the German trenches we went on to Mametz village where living man was represented by the Salvage folk and a few infantry making their way up to the new front line. Scarcely a wall stands, and of the trees nothing remains but mangled twisted stumps. The ruins present an appalling and most gruesome picture of the havoc of war, seen fresh, which no pen or picture can describe. You must see it, and smell it, and hear the sounds, to understand. It brings a sort of sickening feeling to me even now, though I consider myself hardened to such sights. To give an idea of the long period of time through which the line at this point has remained stationary, I may say that in No Man's Land I saw two skeletons, one in German uniform, the other in the long since discarded red infantry breeches of the French.

ROWLAND FEILDING, *War Letters to a Wife*

The efforts of the 21st and 7th Divisions (XV Corps) in this sector were considerably more fruitful than their northern neighbours astride the Roman Road. Their 'patch' was the ground between Birch Tree Wood and Carnoy. It was the penultimate British sector in the southern Somme theatre, with as the initial targets the fortified villages of Fricourt and Mametz. It is often stated that Fricourt was entirely destroyed during 1915, but Panorama 33 (15 April 1916) dispels the myth. Panorama 25 (22 October 1915) offers an informative view of the neighbouring Mametz area. Both show how the British occupied respectable field positions in the sector; Fricourt appears to be especially at their mercy in No 18 (22 September 1915), which in 18D also has a corresponding drawn panorama. On the extreme left a sub-sector called The Tambour (The Drum) is marked on the ridge; another view southwards over Fricourt from a

position very near The Tambour can be seen in No 19 (22 September 1915). This was also an area where in 1914 the lines had settled close enough for mining to be later initiated, and for 1 July 1916 three charges of 25,000, 15,000, and 9,000 lbs had been planted by 178 Tunnelling Company RE, as well as five smaller mines of between 500 and 200 lbs. The three Russian saps in the sector – Dinnet Street, Balmoral Street and Purfleet – were those planned to conceal flame-throwers. In the event only Dinnet Street was actually employed as the enemy line opposite the other two was not captured. An alternative drawn view, 33D, also exists for Panorama 33, made from the identical location as the photograph by an RE draughtsman. The sketch was prepared on 2 November 1915, some six months before the photograph, but the landscape appears to have altered little. In Panorama 18 – Aeroplane Trench, so named because of its shape – was another area where the opposing lines were close; just to the right of the picture in a sub-sector named *Bois Francais*, mining was also under way. In preparation for 1 July, 1,500 troops were accommodated in specially enlarged galleries near the British front line here, and five mines were planted beneath the German trenches, the two largest being those at Casino Point (Carnoy sector) and Bulgar Point, which employed charges of 2,000 and 5,000 lbs respectively (see map). The other three were smaller affairs planted at the ends of Russian saps close up against the German lines. Two saps with twin machine-gun emplacements had also been driven forward towards Aeroplane Trench, but in the same way as so many other examples, they were to lie unused: the machine-gun officer who was to command the guns on 1 July was absent on the day, and when tracked down his sergeant said he had received no orders at all.

Below
The 7th Division's attack on the Fricourt–Mametz valley, 1 July 1916. A heavy shrapnel shell is bursting over the advancing troops.

Above
Third Army Panorama 19: the view over Fricourt from the Tambour trenches on 22 September 1915.

Below
Third Army Panorama 18: the prospect from the south side of Fricourt taken on the same day as No 19. The true size of the village is made clear. To the right, the Aeroplane Trench is marked.

The first wave of the 21st Division attack north of Fricourt initially gained ground with relatively small losses, but after the shock of the barrage and the Tambour mines had worn off, the Germans soon appeared from their subterranean lairs to open severe machine-gun fire on each successive supporting wave. The advances of battalion after battalion hoping to threaten and unsettle the Fricourt garrison by a northerly outflanking manoeuvre were held up in this way. Despite serious casualties, by mid-morning elements of several units had struck beyond the enemy front and support lines, crossed the sunken road marked in Panorama 18 as Road X 21 d 4.4 and taken up positions on the ridge crest in and around Lozenge Wood and Round Wood. Panorama *17* marks every important feature on this part of the battlefield, but compare also Nos 18 and *26*. The troops held off an enemy counter-attack, and the order to consolidate came through in the late afternoon. By the end of the day the line was firmly held; importantly, it protruded behind Fricourt to the north.

Because of the known strength of its defences, no frontal attack was planned for Fricourt on 1 July. To the south the 7th Division tried to follow the same strategy as the northern attack, and drive left of neighbouring Mametz before curving towards Fricourt Wood behind the village. They too met with devastating defensive fire from strong points in both villages, Mametz cemetery and the surrounding woods. Although a few men managed to reach the village, the 20th Manchesters and especially the 7th Green Howards suffered terrible losses as soon as they set foot upon the open glacis before the village. Eyewitnesses speak of the dead lying in lines, in the same wave formation that they attacked.

One of the most poignant and tragic events in this sector involves the 9th Battalion of the Devonshire Regiment. Panoramas 19, 25 and *26* all show a small wood known as Mansel Copse. It was from here that the Devons were ordered to advance on the morning of 1 July. Some time before the attack, one their officers, Captain Duncan Martin, had scrutinized the operation orders, considered his positions and those of the enemy, and come to the conclusion that unless the British artillery annihilated certain dangerous features, he and his men were unlikely even to survive the first few moments of the assault. Whilst on leave before the battle Martin built a small model in plasticine to illustrate his prediction that a machine-gun post situated in Mametz cemetery would, unless neutralized, cause havoc with both his and any preceding or ensuing units. The orders remained in place. As Martin led the Devons from Mansel Copse and across the open ground towards Mametz both he and many others were cut down by the very gun he had warned of. Its precise location and open field of fire is made exceptionally clear in Panorama 25, as is Mansel Copse itself, and the fields where the Devons

fell. A fellow officer in Martin's battalion, Captain William Noel Hodgson MC (see Chapter Five) also died in the attack. Only a few days earlier Hodgson had written his celebrated poem 'Before Action', an affecting work which suggests he may well have known of and shared Martin's fears.

> I, that on my familiar hill
> saw with uncomprehending eyes
> A hundred of Thy sunsets spill
> Their fresh and sanguine sacrifice,
> 'Ere the sun swings his noonday sword
> must say good-bye to all of this:
> By all delights that I shall miss,
> Help me to die, O Lord

Both officers and the 170 men who fell alongside them are buried in one of the front-line trenches used on 1 July. Today it is the shady and poignant Mansel Copse Cemetery. The prominent authors Siegfried Sassoon, Robert Graves and Bernard Adams, all officers in the Royal Welch Fusiliers, served in this area, as did the Welsh poet David Jones. Sassoon watched the 1 July attacks, and passed over the captured ground after the sector had fallen into British hands.

As we went up the lane toward Mametz I felt that I was leaving all my previous war experience behind me. For the first time I was among the debris of an attack. After going a very short distance we made the first of many halts, and I saw, arranged by the roadside, about fifty of the British dead. Many of them were Gordon Highlanders. There were Devons and South Staffordshires among them, but they were beyond regimental rivalry now – their fingers mingled in blood-stained bunches, as though acknowledging the companionship of death. There was much battle-gear lying about and some dead horses. There were rags and shreds of clothing, boots riddled and torn, and when we came to the old German front line, a sour pervasive stench which differed from anything my nostrils had known before.
SIEGFRIED SASSOON, *Memoirs of an Infantry Officer*

Despite its reputation as a stronghold, the Devonshires' target, Mametz, was the first village on the battlefront to be captured on 1 July. This attack, combined with the successful northern incursion, left Fricourt outflanked on both sides and in danger of enclosure, a situation that encouraged the Germans to quietly evacuate under cover of darkness. In the middle of the night a patrol of the 8th Staffords moved gingerly into the village to assess enemy strength. Most of the German troops had already moved out, but over one hundred were apprehended before they

Above
Third Army Panorama 25 showing the scene of the Devonshires' ill-fated attack from Mansel Copse. The German machine gun which did such terrible damage on the morning of 1 July was secreted in Mametz Cemetery.

Below
A comfortable German dugout beneath Fricourt converted into a RE Signal Exchange. September 1916.

Above

Siegfried Sassoon, who watched the attacks on Fricourt and Mametz, was awarded a Military Cross for a later action not far from these villages.

could withdraw. Fricourt was in British hands by noon on 2 July. A new defensive line was wired in during the afternoon linking the two villages with Round Wood, Lozenge Wood and a much smaller copse (two trees only) on the ridge known as The Poodles. Although the divisions which captured the sector sustained over 8,500 casualties, their gritty work was received with elation at GHQ. The fight for control of the sizeable and to the north-east formed the next supremely attritional stage of the offensive.

Those days on the Somme were not in favour of bird watching. For one thing there were practically no birds in the battle area, and for the other there were more urgent matters to occupy one's time and attention.

But even at shattered Fricourt there was something pleasing. In the vault of what had once been a house a pair of swallows had their nest, and all day long kept flying in and out through a dark opening in the ground. They must have built their nest, laid their eggs, and hatched their young during an almost continual hail of shot and shell. I wondered if in happier pre-war summers this same pair of swallows nested under the eaves of the house which once stood there, and if, when it was destroyed, the homing instinct had been so strong that in spite of every inducement to go elsewhere they had nested in the cellar of their old dwelling.

PHILIP GOSSE, *Memoirs of a Camp Follower*

Above

Fallen German troops in a front line trench, Mametz 1916.

Carnoy and Montauban

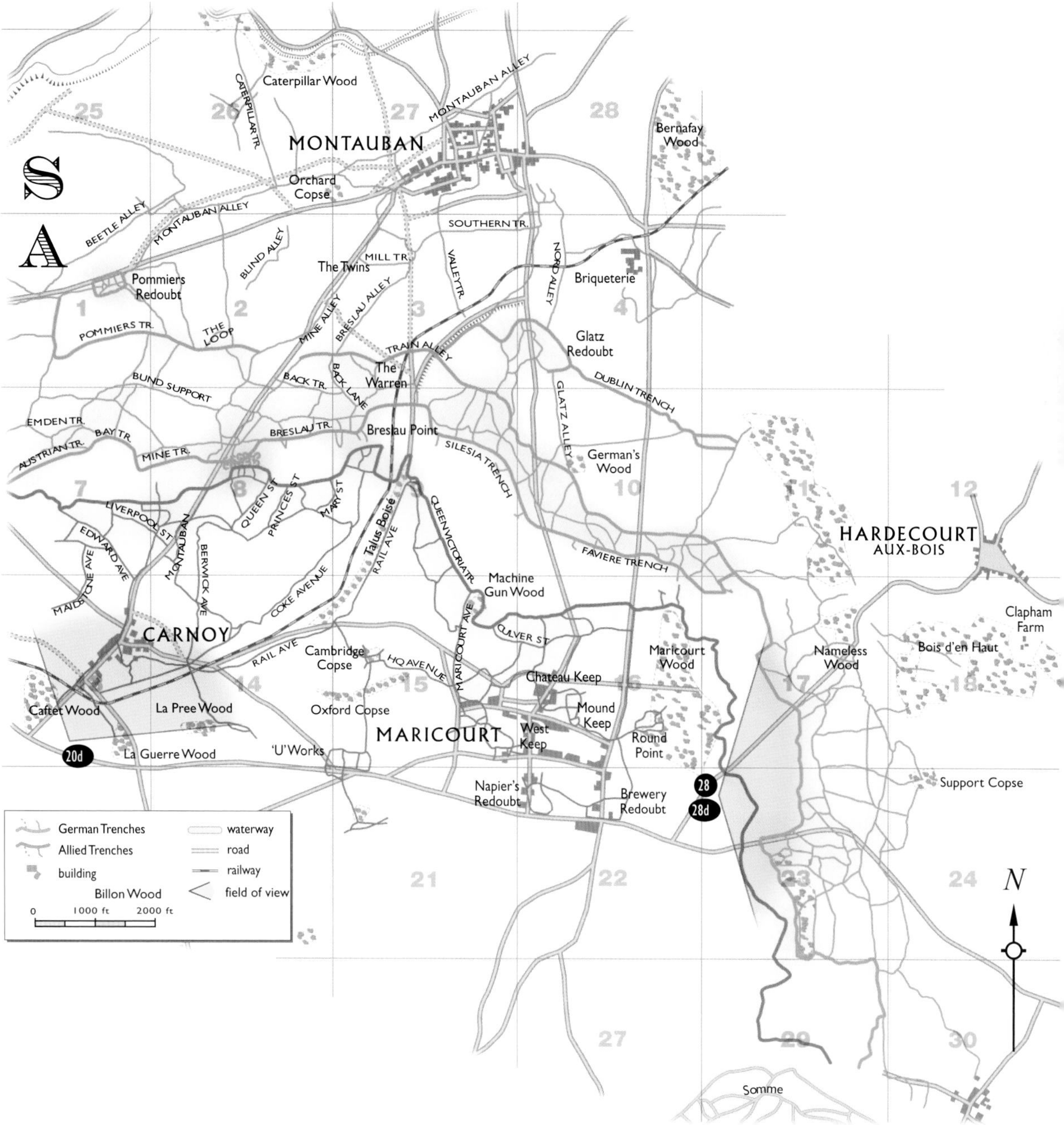

As the pre-1 July line skirted Mametz, it took a sharp turn eastwards, passing in front of Carnoy and heading across towards Maricourt, before switching southwards once more to the banks of the Somme River. Maricourt was the extreme right flank of the British line; all the territory beyond this point southwards became French responsibility. The advance from here was to be in an east-north-easterly direction taking in the great woods, Trônes, Bernafay, Mametz and Delville. Panorama 28 (26 October 1915) encompasses practically all this flanking territory and some of the more famous woods, whilst No *30* offers a northern aspect, at the same time illustrating the relatively small distances between apparently distant points. La Boisselle and Montauban for example: as the crow flies, they are not as isolated as one might think, but a trip from one to the other via the trenches is considerably more lengthy. See also two further drawn examples of this sector in Nos 20D and 28D. Montauban and the influential woods beyond also appear in Nos 33 and 33D.

The two divisions which made up XIII Corps, the 18th (Eastern) and 30th, were assisted on 1 July by an impressive array of French heavy

Above
Official Canadian cinematographers set up their camera to film part of the battle for Courcellette.

guns which augmented their own artillery to deliver the total annihilation of German strong points and wire defences. Montauban was razed, and even deep dugouts crushed under the storm of high explosive. The differences did not end there: tactics not employed in any of the northern sub-sectors had also been developed by the XIII Corps staff: a protective creeping barrage was used for the first time, and dugouts, cellars and *boves* were 'mopped-up' by dedicated teams, precluding the chance of advancing troops being attacked from the rear after a position had ostensibly been overrun – an all too common occurrence elsewhere. The only fly in the ointment on Day One was that the 5,000 lbs Casino Point mine was blown a little later than planned, simply as a result of poorly synchronized timepieces. Despite seeing numbers of infantry already advancing across no man's land the tunnelling officer nevertheless decided to blow; the mine did its work well, quelling potential enemy resistance, but also causing several British casualties in the fallout.

The Russian saps were also used to their proper purpose, and in addition several push-pipe schemes were initiated, this time successfully, the blows producing linear craters up to 50 m (55 yds) long, over 2 m ($6^{1}/_{2}$ ft) deep and 4 m (13 ft) wide – perfect instant communication trenches. Due to the hard ground in this area, and the noise created by tunnelling activity, the miners were forced to drill holes in the working face and fill them with vinegar, thus softening the chalk and making work less audible to hostile ears.

On 1 July all objectives were attained by both the British and French. The Montauban brickworks, a powerful strong point marked in several panoramas, were captured by the 20th King's Liverpool Regiment. One of four Pals battalions in the 30th Division, it was sister to the 17th, which on 1 July 1916 was the southernmost British unit, not only on the Somme battleground but the entire Western Front. The advance took the British to the crest of Montauban ridge, from where they were able to consider the next series of targets. By this time the battle had been reported as a victory at home; for the first time a full-length film had been made, to be shown in cinemas and village halls across the country. It became an instant success. The *Battle of the Somme* achieved huge critical and public acclaim, and two further productions were completed before the 'big battle' format was dropped. Even the troops themselves were treated to a performance.

September 5, 1916

To-night I have been with others to see and exhibition of the "Somme film", which was shown upon a screen, erected in a muddy field under the open sky. Presumably by way of contrast Charlie Chaplin was also to have appeared, and I confess it was chiefly him I went to see. However, I came too late, and saw only the more harrowing part of the entertainment. This battle film is really a most wonderful and most realistic production, but of necessity be wanting in that the battle is fought in silence, and, moreover, that the most unpleasant part – the machine-gun and rifle fire – is entirely eliminated. Of the actual "frightfulness" of

Below
Another comparison of panoramas, each with a huge field of view – 147 degrees. Panoramas 28 (26 October 1915) and 28D (28 December 1915). The photographed example reaches to Curlu, beyond the right flank of British responsibility on the Somme.

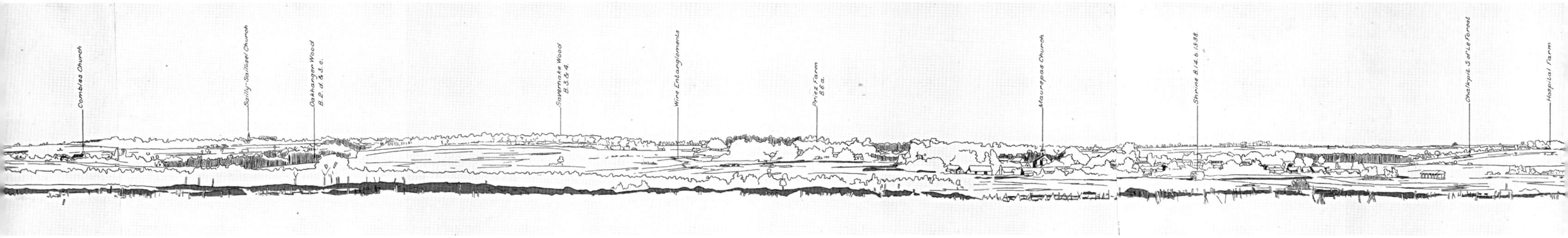

war all that one sees is the bursting shells; and perhaps it is as well. I have said that the battle is fought in silence; but no, on this occasion the roar of the real battle was loudly audible in the distance.

I must say that at first the wisdom of showing such a film to soldiers on the brink of a battle in which they are to play the part of attackers struck me as questionable. However, on my way home, my mind was set at rest upon this point by two recruits who were walking behind me

Said one, "As to reality, now you knows what you've got to fice. If it was left to the imagination you might think all sorts of b—— —- silly things."

I wonder where his imagination would have led him had he not seen the Cinema. Would it, do you think, have gone beyond the reality? Hell itself could hardly do so. I think sometimes that people who have not seen must find it difficult to comprehend how undisturbed life in the trenches can be on occasion: equally how terrible can be the battle.

ROWLAND FEILDING, *War Letters to Wife*

Into and out of the woods

As a result of an almost universal lack of gains in the northern and central sectors of the battlefield, and the surprising success in the south – well over a kilometre on a front of more than five – the period following the opening phase was spent considering how not to repeat the same mistakes again. In the meantime attacks were sustained, and continued to be costly. The Germans made every attempt to snatch back their few losses, but also concentrated upon reinforcing defences in preparation for future British assaults. General Sir Hubert Gough's Reserve Army entered the fight at the end of the second week of July and began planning actions north of the Albert–Bapaume Road, but Sir Douglas Haig, Sir Henry Rawlinson and their staffs looked to the right flank, where the enemy appeared a little demoralized, for the next assault. On 14 July, after a three-day shelling of the 'softening-up' variety, a five-minute hurricane bombardment heralded a crack-of-dawn attack from positions along the length of the Montauban Ridge, and behind the shield of a creeping barrage. It was possession of the woods which the British sought – the casualties sustained in attacks over open ground were too costly. In this impending stage of conflict they had no thought of a major breakthrough, but rather a gradual wearing down of the German forces, a blotting of resources, with perhaps the chance of serious penetration once the very necessary reorganization had taken place – 'In another six weeks the enemy should be hard put to find men,' said Haig. His cavalry were still waiting.

The 14 July attacks were a success, delivering another leap forward to take the main German second line, including Trônes Wood and the two villages of Bazentin. But Longueval village, Delville Wood and High Wood, each on the perimeter of the advance, held out. The struggles for control of these major woods were long and bloody, and in an earlier era would probably have ranked as major battles in themselves. Unfortunately very few panoramas of the woods exist, although ongoing identification work on many outstanding unannotated examples may yield more in the future. A fragment of a High Wood panorama can be seen in HW1. It was two months before

Right
RE survey of captured German dugouts near Mametz Wood. The existence of many systems like this throughout the battlefield were the single major reason for slow allied progress and debilitating casualty figures.

Below right
All the comforts of home: a German officer's dugout chamber, complete with electric light and whitewashed walls.

Below
A fragment – Panorama HW1 – showing one of the most costly pieces of ground on the Somme battlefield – High Wood.

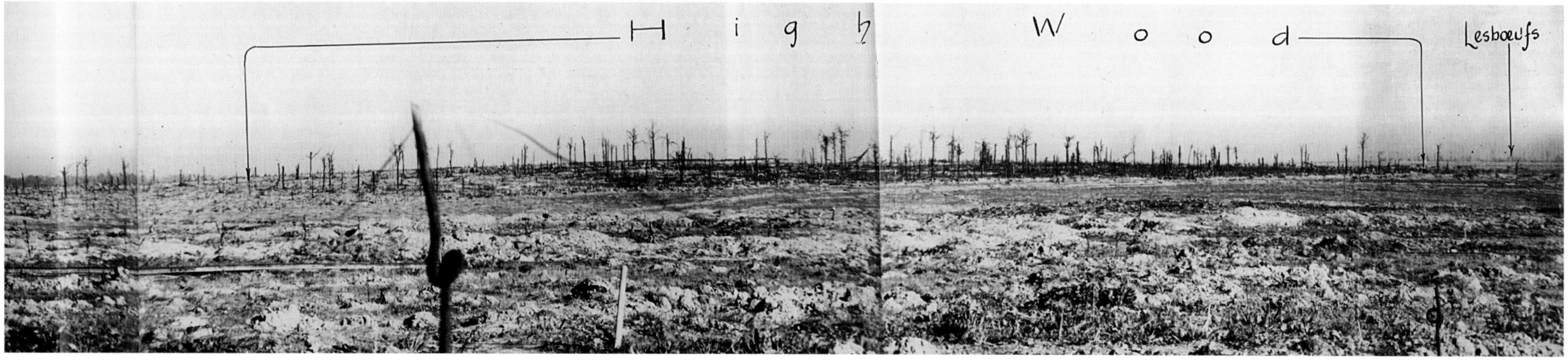

GERMAN TUNNELLED DUGOUTS.

— MAMETZ. —

(Dimensions in Metres)

From plan captured 10.7.16

Order of Work

1. Tunnel.
2. Engine Room.
3. Well.
4. Shelters. N6. N7. N8. N9.
5. Kitchen.
6. Passage to Kitchen.
7. Officers Shelter.

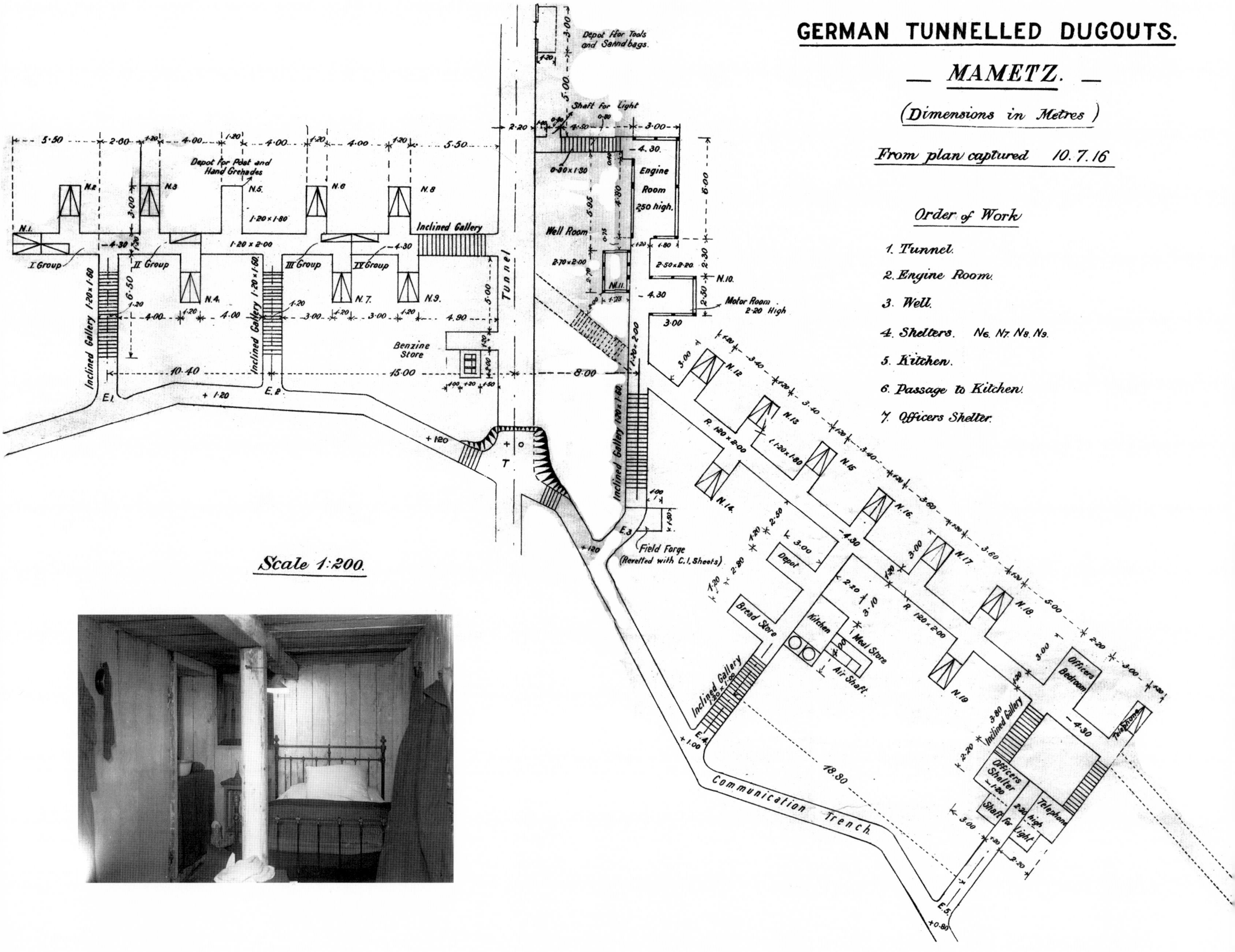

Scale 1:200.

this expanse of splintered stumps was clawed into British possession. The full panorama probably includes the location where Robert Graves was wounded in mid-July. Attacked on 15th, Delville Wood became a graveyard for the South African Brigade; almost three-quarters of their 3,000-strong force failed to answer the roll-call after three days of fighting. This kind of slow destruction and erosion was to characterize the rest of the battle. The elevated views of Panoramas 33 and especially 28 show the prospect faced by the British as they entered this unceasingly attritional phase. Callous as the strategy appears to be today, it was quite quickly effective: German assaults on Verdun were called off on 11 July, and the transfer of troops northward to the Somme began.

Ovillers, such a maelstrom on 1 July and in each subsequent attempt, fell at last on the 15th, and towards the end of the month the 1st Australian Division (part of the Reserve Army) advanced further up the Albert–Bapaume road to assault Pozières village and mill. To the north, they also attacked the fiercely defended Mouquet Farm; 23,000 casualties and six weeks later Pozières had fallen, but the farm was still German property. Panoramas *22* and *30* reveal an apparently derisory distance separating Ovillers from Pozières, and illustrates the intolerably (for the Australians) slow progress made, whilst No *62* (4A), taken on 1 August from the Australian front line during the fighting, offers us a flavour of the landscape in the midst of battle. By the end of August the positions – now handed over to Canadian troops – were at the point of a distinct salient. The Thiepval Ridge positions and Mouquet Farm, are well 'behind' this point on the front, but *still* under German control. As the Reserve Army nibbled away north and east of Pozières, German defences on Thiepval Ridge became ever more vulnerable; once the bastion of Mouquet Farm had been breached by the 11th Division on 26 September, Thiepval soon fell (on the 28th). Remarkably, parts of the Schwaben Redoubt held out until 14 October.

As a part of the costly assaults upon the High Wood–Longueval ridge, August also saw repeated fierce attacks in the Guillemont and Ginchy area, on the right flank of the battlefield. Fighting began here on 14 July and continued until 14 September; by now the Somme ribbon of destruction was beginning to widen and intensify.

On 31 August my lot were working on a trench just to east of the road to Flers, north of Bernafay Wood. There was a fair amount of shelling going on, and I had just left one little party with orders to spread out a bit more. Then I heard a new noise, as if many of the shells arriving were dud (you developed a very sharp ear for such noises or changes in noise – and realised that this must be the new gas-shells, of which we had had some warning: so I ordered gas-masks, which were still the wet-flannel type with a mouth-piece. I was going to the rest of them to see that they had put on their gas-masks when I heard a heavy thud that meant a shell in the trench. The men were very jittery, as the very word gas frightens them badly: but I knew this was much more serious, as a couple of them were screaming. I dived back to see what had happened: when I got round the corner five

Above
Temporary grave markers of the many Australian troops who fell at Pozières in 1916, photographed a year later.

Below
The village of Courcellette in a segment of Reserve Army Panorama 300 taken on 21 September 1916. The lack of damage to features beyond the immediate battle zone is again striking.

yards back, there were five of my chaps at the bottom of the trench, all burnt black, and the trench sides too: and two of them were alive and screaming, with great chunks of flesh torn from them. It was essential to do something to relieve their pain, and I simply could not see to do the job in a gas-mask, so I ripped it off and got down to making a splint out of a rifle and some puttees, putting on first field dressings and so on: these were almost a bad joke, as one man had lost the whole of his calf muscles, and I could see the other's heart. Eventually I got them to the 1st aid post, and am glad to think it was not a wasted effort, as I heard later that they had survived. But by then both my breathing and my heart were pretty funny. But never let it be said that my troubles were even a quarter of those of the infantry; in that war by comparison I regard all infantry – the PBI or poor bloody infantry as they were soon called – as heroes of inconceivable gallantry and endurance.

2ND LIEUTENANT J. T. GODFREY, 103 FIELD COMPANY RE

Below

The monsters move up, 15 September 1916. Four Mark I tanks refuel on their way into battle for the first time.

Panoramas *63* and *64* illustrate the landscape change – very close to where the above incident took place. It was also within these panoramas just a few days earlier that Captain Noel Chavasse 10th King's Liverpool – the Liverpool Scottish) won the first of his two Victoria Crosses, assisting wounded on the battlefield after one of a sequence of failed attacks on Guillemont. Another casualty in this area was Lieutenant Raymond Asquith, 3rd Grenadier Guards, son of the erstwhile British Prime Minister. On 15 September he suffered a bullet wound to the chest and died soon afterwards. Asquith is buried in Guillemont Road Cemetery, later established close to the spot from where Panorama *63* was taken. The village fell to a brigade of the 16th Irish Division on 3 September, six days before Tom Kettle, a well-known literary and political Irish figure, disappeared. His body was never recovered. On the same day, and probably within the scope of these same panoramas, Major Cedric Dickens of 13th Londons died during an advance upon Leuze (Lousy) Wood. His grandfather was the novelist Charles Dickens.

Ginchy, to the left of Panorama 63 (4A), also fell to the 16th Irish on 9 September, on almost the same date that the village had been lost to the Germans two years earlier.

14 September

We marched up with the sappers to some dugouts behind Mametz Wood, so as to be handy for the show, which is to take place tomorrow. We took section wagons with us but most of the mounted section waited at Bécourt. Zero hour is 6.20 a.m. tomorrow. This afternoon was to me one of the rare occasions when the war has been dramatic and exciting. I was quite thrilled watching the long streams of troops and wagons pouring up the Mametz road. Then, all of a sudden, I heard a strange noise, accompanied by shouts and cheers, and saw the most extraordinary-looking vehicles approaching, with men sitting on them cheering. They were a kind of armoured car on caterpillars and each towed a sort of perambulator behind it. They are said to be the new assault wagons, called tanks. I don't know if the Germans knew about them, but the secret has been very well-kept on our side. None of us had any idea of their existence.

LIEUTENANT J. GLUBB, 7 FIELD COMPANY RE

It was from Ginchy that tanks made their very first appearance in battle. At 5.15 a.m. on 15 September 1916 (the day High Wood fell) male tank D1 left its starting point in the ruins of the village. Captain H. W. Mortimore and his crew piloted the lone tank across the battlefield; two designated sister-machines had failed to make it, with one ditched and the other broken down. Three-quarters of an hour later thirteen more fuming monsters grumbled out towards Flers (see right-hand of Panorama *F1*). Panoramas *62* and *63*(*R*) show the ground over which on the same day Canadian troops were supported by the northern group of three further tanks in their triumphant

attack on Courcelette, also seen in the foreground of Panorama 301/302 (5 October 1916).

This latter magnificent giant example of the panoramic photographer's art takes us all the way to the final line and final target for the British and Dominion forces on the Somme battlefield. As the Albert–Bapaume road sweeps away over the ridges and into the distance, a small ancient tumulus is visible to the right – this is the Butte de Warlencourt, where the fighting at last ceased on November 1916. It appears much whiter and more conspicuous – as so many narratives remark – in Panorama *F1* (22 September 1916), but both examples show that the battlefields at this time are far from the tortured expanse of wasteland which are so often described. Pys Church appears unmarked, and the Albert-Bapaume road retains its lining if trees. Even the telegraph poles and cables survive. However, there was still another months of fighting left, and conditions would severely deteriorate. Attacks upon the Butte from these positions claimed many a life before the battle was brought to an end. It is recorded that a few men of the Durham Light Infantry were spotted on its slopes on 5 November. These were troops of a three-battalion DLI advance which found themselves in a morass of mud in the fields in front of the hill, where they were shot down. It was the most costly day in the unit's history. The Butte stayed in enemy hands over Christmas and New Year 1916, but was voluntarily given up as German forces drew back to the Hindenburg Line in February.

Epilogue on the Somme

Discussions over whether the Somme was worthwhile have lingered since the offensive was only a few weeks old. There is no doubt that the British learned many a tactical lesson by the sobering experiences they had undergone, and that these were put into practice later in the battle and especially during the offensives of 1917 and 1918. Present-day appreciations suggest that there was some damaging indecision as to which strategy – bite-and-hold or grand thrusting breakthrough – should be utilized at the beginning of the battle. From mid-September a much more concrete and decisive approach is discernible, and victories are more complete, swift (given the increasingly dreadful conditions) and tenable. That Haig's much-maligned attritional approach worked was thanks in large part to the Germans, whose commanders chose to defend their territory 'to the last man', with obstinate and unrelenting counter-attacks. The resulting reconsideration of German tactical thinking was manifested in the Hindenburg Line defences, begun in the autumn of 1916. There is no doubt that the British attacks severely damaged both the numerical establishment and morale of the German Army, and of course drove them from the important crests north of the Somme, but it seems more than unlikely that had the offensive been continued a breakthrough would have been achieved. The battle had to be fought because the war had to be won, but it may well have been mud – Napoleon's "fifth element" – which thwarted a complete Allied victory in 1916.

The lessons learned during 142 gruelling days of combat were visibly applied later by the addition of Lewis gun and mobile Stokes mortar teams to infantry battalions, giving them more firepower to overcome individual strong points; in the continued the development of flash-spotting and sound-ranging the artillery greatly enhanced counter-battery fire; new shells were also developed, and creeping

Above

Segment of the huge Reserve Army Panorama 301-302. This remarkable example shows the area where much fighting took place during the final month. Note the condition of the Butte de Warlencourt (right of frame), which remained in German possession. Even at this late stage of the battle, the telegraph poles along the Albert-Bapaume road still stand! A surprising image.

Below

Mud – the essence of the latter days of the Somme offensive. A mule carries a heap of trench waders to the line. Straps (which attach the boot tops to the belt) trail through the mud.

Below
To the last man. A young German machine-gunner who remained with his weapon to the last. This picture was taken the next time the Allies advanced across the Somme battlefields – 19 September 1918.

Right
May your God go with you: a Christ figure being salvaged from a Calvary near the Butte de Warlencourt.

barrages became the norm. Training regimes for assaults were intensified and prolonged, and underground offensive schemes received wholehearted backing from GHQ, Better communication was universal.

The evolution may have been slow and bloody, but lessons were learned: it was simply a painfully gradual process – as it always had been throughout military history. In 1918 the Somme battlefields were fought over twice more by British and Dominion forces, once in retreat in March 1918, and a second time later that year as a part of the final Advance to Victory. Only one panorama has been selected for these 1918 actions, number *589* (29 May 1918). The camera position is not far distant from that of Panorama *60* taken almost exactly two years earlier – from just behind the lines attacked on 1 July 1916. The 1918 landscape is almost entirely devoid of trees, houses and any indication as to previous or present human occupation, yet it seethes with life. Tens of thousands of men live amongst the wasteland. It should not be thought, however, that the emptiness is simply down to the devastating power of the guns: this image was captured eighteen months after the 1916 battle, and following the bitter 1917/1918 winter; a period when salvage teams had cleared the battlefield of all useful and repairable military materiel, and when every scrap of timber was gathered either to develop and restore new forward positions, dugouts, roads, or, more importantly to the infantryman, for fuel.

Starlings were always the first civilians to re-occupy shattered strips of Picardy won back by our advancing troops. Whatever they found to attract them I do not know. Had they been carrion feeders it would have been explained, for there were feasts spread out for vultures. But starlings prefer a diet of fruit and insects. Of the first there was of course none, of insects there were flies in plenty as well as crawling ones, which thrived and multiplied on the clothing of living man. As for animals these seemed to have all disappeared, even if trapping had been practicable. Nothing could live in that horrible poison-drenched shell-ploughed waste but man, and his chances of survival were slender. Even the obsequious trench rat had disappeared. But I did get one addition to my collection in the battle area, which turned out to be a specimen of the very rare subterranean vole, Pitymys subterraneus, which burrows to a depth of four and five feet in the earth. It was picked up dead in a trench at Contalmaison by a soldier who gave it to me.

PHILIP GOSSE, *Memoirs of a Camp Follower* (WHILST SERVING AS A MEDICAL OFFICER, CAPTAIN P. H. G. GOSSE WAS ALSO COLLECTING SMALL MAMMAL SPECIMENS FOR THE BRITISH MUSEUM)

CHAPTER EIGHT:

ARMOUR AND ARMISTICE

CAMBRAI AND 1918

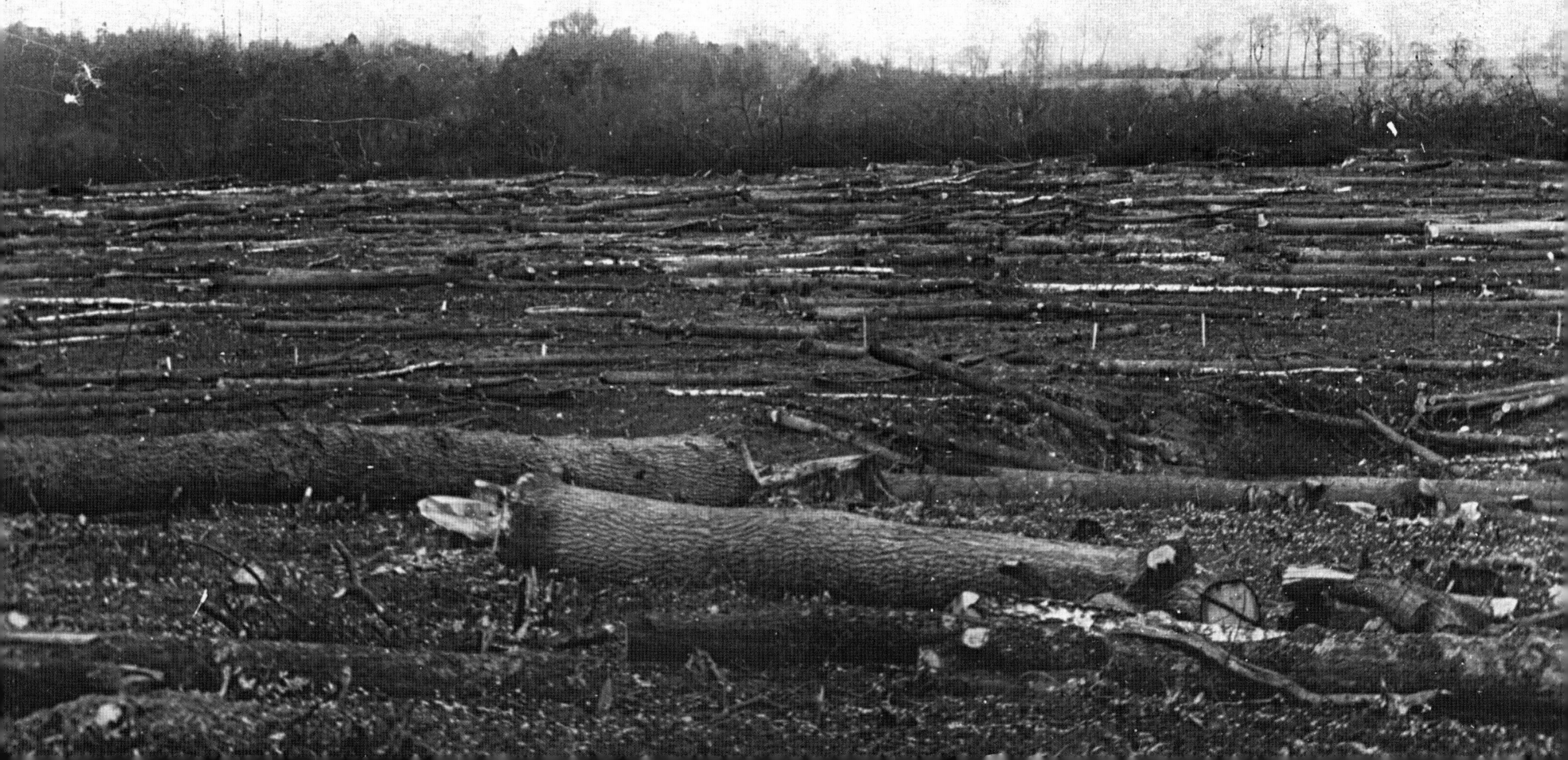

Cambrai

Pages 340–41
Panorama 307: trees felled near Havrincourt Chateau to impede Britsih movement.

Below left
An oblique aerial photograph showing the robust defences of the Hindenburg system.

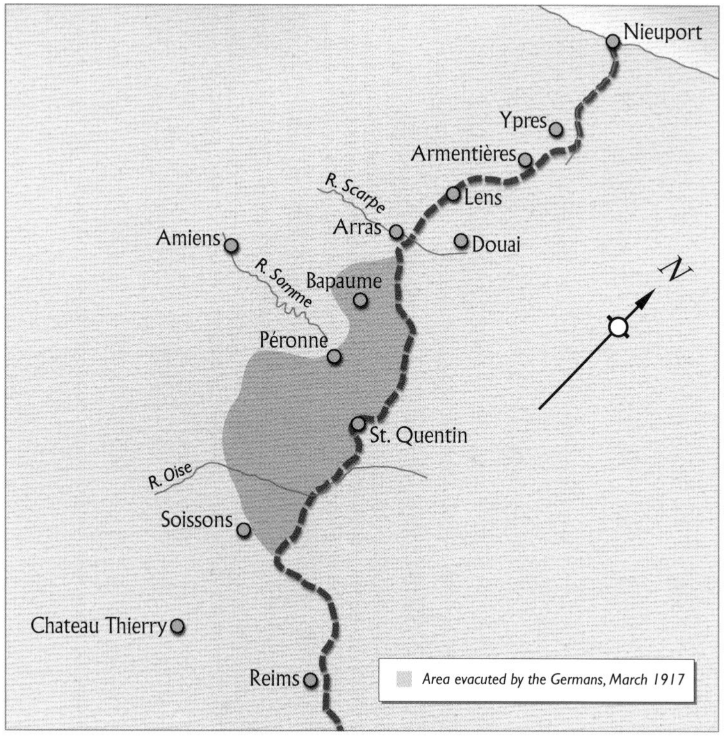

As the first period [of the war] may be denoted as the reign of the bullet and the second the reign of the shell, the third was the reign of the anti-bullet. We introduced the tank, and though, until the Battle of Cambrai was fought, on November 20 1917, our GHQ in France showed a tactical ineptitude in the use of this weapon that was amazing, ultimately it beat their ignorance and stupidity and won through.
MAJOR-GENERAL J. F. C. FULLER

The battle for Cambrai of November 1917 was most notable for the first enthusiastic use of the tank as an offensive weapon. Although they had been tried in small numbers in several actions during and since the Somme battles the previous year, few commanders were willing to envisage what might be achieved if an assault was planned around them rather than acting as just ancillary assistants to the infantry – and especially if deployed in generous numbers. It has been suggested that due to deeply entrenched old-fashioned thinking at GHQ the new weapon might have created fears that it would usurp the importance of both the infantry and the force dearest to their hearts, the cavalry. The initial attitude was epitomized by Lord Kitchener who, somewhat surprisingly for a Royal Engineer, regarded tanks as 'a pretty mechanical toy but with very limited military value'.

As in so many other aspects of the Great War, with hindsight it seems astonishing that Tank Corps personnel were almost alone in sensing the potential of the new technology, and this appears all the more extraordinary when one considers that in 1916 and 1917 the Germans had no such machines of their own, and few robust dedicated anti-tank measures.

The Tank Corps had begun its gestation in May 1916 as a retrained and re-organized Heavy Section of the Machine Gun Corps. Four of the first six companies arrived in France in August 1916 with seven machines each: three male, three female and one spare. The 27-ton monsters were literally land-based Dreadnoughts. Although slow and unreliable at first, they were entirely bullet-proof, could carry guns of several varieties, shield

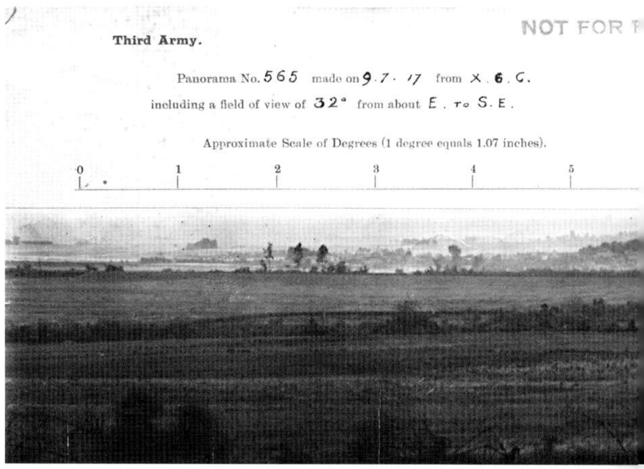
Third Army.
Panorama No. 565 made on 9.7.17 from X.6.C.
including a field of view of 32° from about E. to S.E.
Approximate Scale of Degrees (1 degree equals 1.07 inches).
0 1 2 3 4 5

Above
Another new weapon introduced in 1917. The instantaneous fuse allowed a shell to burst at the very moment of impact, spraying shrapnel, splinters and other fragments in large quantities, at low-level, and over long distances.

infantry, crush or drag away barbed-wire entanglements, transport ammunition, and, in utilizing caterpillar tracks instead of wheels, traverse almost any terrain, including trenches. And they instilled terror. With the tank alone, the restoration of mobility became more than just a dream – but only if substantial numbers were used.

What was seen at first was the same blinkered thinking that characterized the first two years of the war. Tanks were tried on battlefields which thanks to the attentions of the artillery had become morasses. They impressed but failed to excel in early actions at Flers, the Ancre, Arras and Bullecourt; even the apparently enlightened first mass deployment at Cambrai in November 1917 could not be attributed to a general faith in the machinery and personnel. Haig himself was certainly not without enthusiasm for tanks, but as plans for Cambrai were being proposed and developed by the Corps themselves during the summer of 1917, the Field Marshal was still optimistic for a breakthrough in the traditional artillery/infantry/cavalry fashion in front of Ypres in Belgian Flanders.

The two most voluble proponents of large-scale tank warfare were Brigadier-General Hugh Elles, commander of the newly-formed Corps, and his thrusting second-in-command and Chief Staff Officer at Tank Corps HQ, Lieutenant-Colonel J. F. C. Fuller. In mid-June 1917 Fuller had written a memo about the use of tanks and the best sectors – those between Cambrai and St Quentin – to deploy them. On 3 August he met Elles for discussions and the next day at Montreuil both men presented to Haig himself a more comprehensive version of the memo. On the 5th the plan was put to Third Army HQ, requesting appraisal of their idea to employ a massed tank attack within an innovative and carefully structured artillery, infantry, cavalry and aerial offensive, and most importantly *on terrain which suited the weapon*.

During 1917 the battle lines across the plains of Picardy had remained virtually static. As the Third Battle of Ypres slithered towards its frightful inconclusivity, Haig gave way to some of Elles' and Fuller's wishes. Casualties in Flanders echoed the terrible lists posted in British cities, towns and villages during the Somme and Arras, and the mood amongst the troops, fighting in the most squalid conditions of the war to date, had become sombre. Although their reaction was profound, it did not manifest itself in mutiny as in the French Army, but the feeling that GHQ was letting the ordinary foot soldier down was more than strong, and it was growing. There appeared to be no leading of men in Flanders, and many were beginning to believe that each successive offensive was directed by staff officers situated further and further behind the action. In late August 1917, with his Passchendaele plans and hopes falling apart at the seams, Haig felt the need to salvage something in the eyes of his troops, the British Government, and the British public – and it may as well be something adventurous and dramatic. In mid-October 1917 he sanctioned the Cambrai plan first put to him on 16 September.

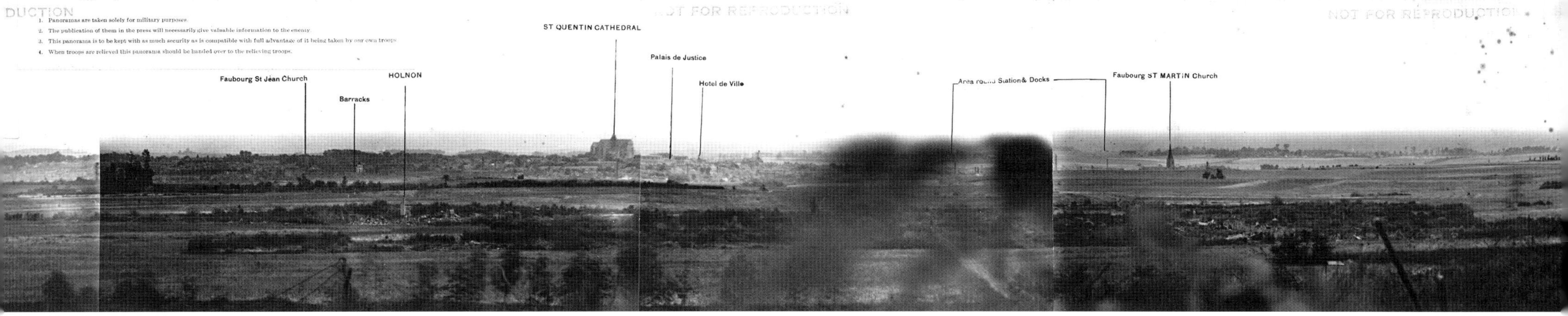

DUCTION
1. Panoramas are taken solely for military purposes.
2. The publication of them in the press will necessarily give valuable information to the enemy.
3. This panorama is to be kept with as much security as is compatible with full advantage of it being taken by our own troops.
4. When troops are relieved this panorama should be handed over to the relieving troops.
ST QUENTIN CATHEDRAL
Palais de Justice
Faubourg St Jean Church
HOLNON
Barracks
Hotel de Ville
Station& Docks
Faubourg ST MARTIN Church
NOT FOR REPRODUCTION

Below
St Quentin, the city at the centre of the Hindenburg Line positions to which German forces withdrew in February 1917. Third Army Panorama 565, 9 July 1917.

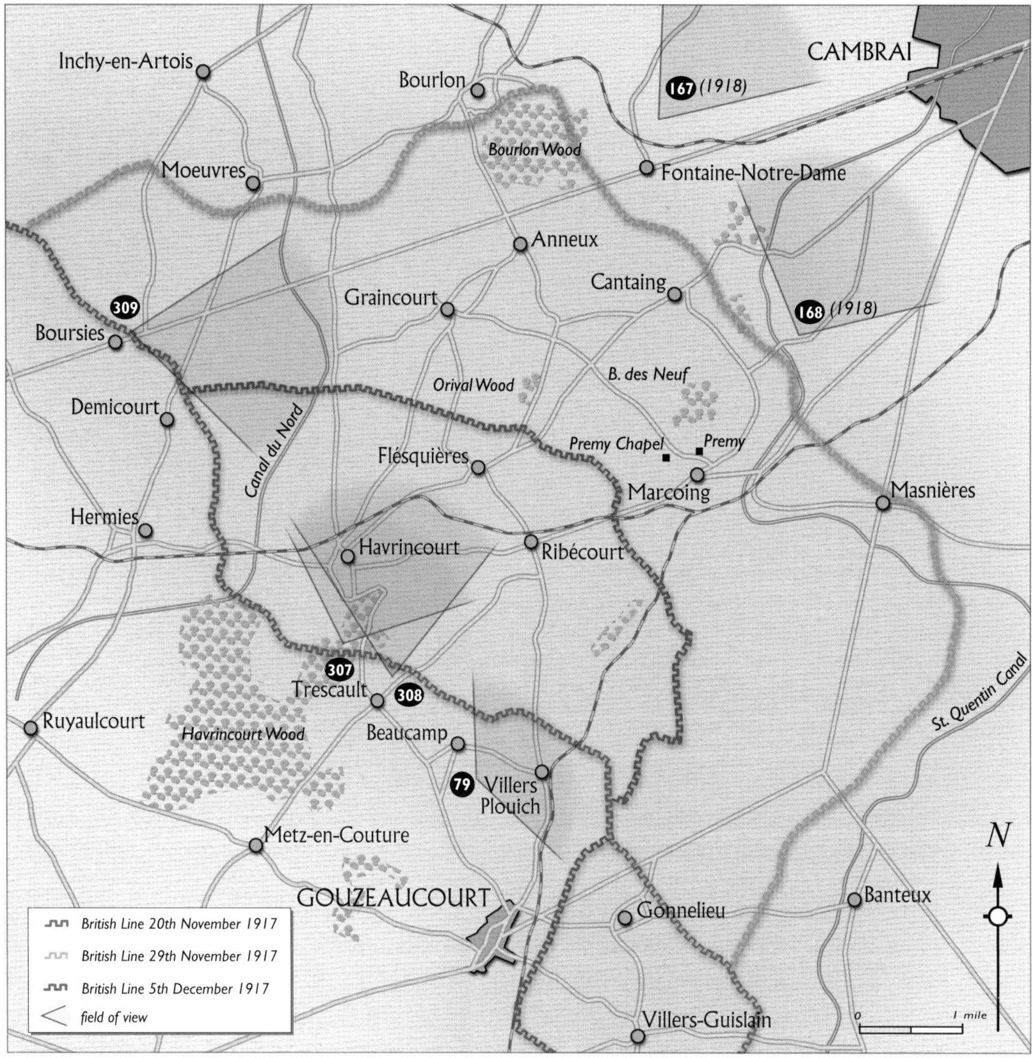

The battleground selected for the final Allied offensive of the year was the open and almost unscathed Artois downland south-east of Arras, which was garrisoned by General Sir Julian Byng's Third Army. As a soldier whose thinking was remarkably unfossilized given some of the company he kept, Byng was in many ways an atypical commander, and he wholeheartedly supported Elles and Fuller's plans. The British lines had moved forward into positions facing the Hindenburg Line during the spring of 1917, crossing the devastated area evacuated by the Germans during their February retirement. This sequence of panoramas are all taken from these lines. The southernmost extension of the British-held area of retirement is marked by Panorama 565 (9 July 1917) of the St Quentin sector.

Above
The attacking front for November 1917. Fifth Army Panorama 308 was taken in April 1917, a few weeks before plans for a tank assault began to be formulated.

Right
A tank going through its paces at Wailly in October 1917.

Far left
Hindenburg Line wire.

Tactics at Cambrai were to differ radically from all those which had gone before; the dawdling and detrimental barrages of the Somme and Ypres were things of the past; here, there was to be no preparatory artillery action at all. With the terrain undamaged the great machines were to advance across no man's land as a wall of steel – a bulletproof cavalry charge that could also crush the massive Hindenburg Line wire entanglements. Negotiating the formidably deep and wide German trenches was to be achieved by 2-ton tightly-bound fascines of brushwood carried on the roof of each tank which would be dropped into the trench to act as a 'bridge'; the subsequent wave of machines would in turn deploy their fascines in the next line, and in this way the entire defence-in-depth system could be vaulted and the clear ground beyond exploited.

The 'non bullet-proof' contingent, consisting of eleven divisions of infantry and five of cavalry, would follow behind the tanks, 'mopping-up' defences before bursting out into open country themselves. In their original plans Elles and Fuller had worked on a rapidly moving creeping barrage to pilot a limited attack followed by a swift withdrawal – in effect a heavy mechanized trench raid – but Byng favoured a much more ambitious assault with a much more ambitious goal – no less than a full breakthrough. It troubled the tank men.

Artillery was to be restricted to quick-firing field pieces only, which in the first instance would pinpoint not trenches but selected points of resistance, positions which for the first time had been registered by survey triangulation

– plotting and ranging targets using maps alone. Every battery received pre-ordained targets across the whole battle area which meant that guns could be brought into position and ranged at the last minute, avoiding the disclosure of intention associated with the range-finding of normal pre-battle concentrations. The critical difference was that the guns would only open fire when the attack started – and not a moment before. Surprise was the goal. As the attack progressed light guns could also be brought forward over unbroken ground in tandem with the advance to pressurize pinpointed positions farther to the enemy rear.

The all-important aspect of geology was to play a key

role once more. Whereas in Flanders such an attack would have been out of the question at this time of year owing to waterlogged ground, here on the unsullied free-draining chalk uplands and without an all-obliterating barrage, the objective could well be achievable – as long as the gods were kind enough not to open the heavens at the most inconvenient moment. Tanks had failed for this very reason in July and August at Ypres, although there were a couple of brilliant, though small, successes, one of which secured a posthumous Victoria Cross for Captain Clement Robertson, the first for the Corps. It was a risk Haig and Byng had to take. The timing – November – combined with the scale, made Elles and Fuller nervous, but desperate for an opportunity to prove the worth of their new Corps, the long-awaited chance was grasped with resolve.

The chosen sector of gently rolling downland was situated between two important waterways, the Canal du Nord and the St Quentin Canal, on a front of 10 km (6 miles). Panorama 308 (28 April 1917) covers a large part of the prospective battlefront and illustrates the unblemished nature of the landscape. The target was not actually Cambrai, but the commanding heights of the ridge capped by Bourlon Wood, a position which dominated the Agache valley through which snaked the Canal du Nord, and the Scheldt river and canal. In the panorama the Hindenburg Line is well camouflaged and hidden; there are a few shellholes, but nothing sufficient to trouble tanks. The only major visible eruption lies in the road from Hermies to Havrincourt – a large mine crater, one of many hundreds blown to slow hostile advances. Ahead of Byng's men lay a section of the Hindenburg Line believed to be lightly defended. The plan was to penetrate the three massively entrenched defensive lines, and sweep on to the summit of the ridges capped by Bourlon Wood, Havrincourt and Flésquières, all pictured in the panorama. If this high ground could be consolidated a descent upon Cambrai was feasible. As soon as the lines were broken the cavalry would be sent in to cross the St Quentin Canal, encircle the town and strike out beyond. Panorama *79* (Third Army) is a later shot taken on 6 May 1917 from the extreme southern edge of the battlefront. The sector's proximity to Cambrai is highlighted here – the town is just 12 km ($7^1/_2$ miles) from the camera.

Above
A tank climbs the bank of a sunken road before passing through a group of captured German guns *en route* for Bourlon Wood. Graincourt, 23 November 1917.

Planning for the tank attack was emphatic: the entire machine establishment of the Tank Corps was made available, with 476 machines being brought forward under tight security. It was, however, highly secret. Having brought the tanks by rail – thirty-six trains transporting twelve tanks each – the massive machines had to be unloaded, moved, hidden and prepared, much of the work being carried out beneath the cloak of darkness. On the misty morning of 20 November 378 fighting tanks were ready for action; the remainder were to be employed in supply and communication, with a number being especially fitted with grappling hooks to tear great holes in the wire defences allowing passage of horse, mule, man and gun. The initial stage of the battle was so successful few at GHQ could believe what they saw in reports. In half a day a 9.5-km (6-mile) wedge was driven into the German Second Army; at Ypres the same gains had taken more than three months to achieve at the cost of 250,000 casualties.

After the plan had been revamped by Haig and Byng, Elles and Fuller put much thought into tank tactics and deployment. Their counsel was to hold back sufficient reserve machines to exploit success should it come, because even if the enemy failed to knock the machines out by gun-

Right
German dead in a trench at Flésquières, 23 November 1917.

fire, mechanical breakdown and ditching was sure to substantially deplete numbers in the main strike force. But Byng would have none of it – all must go over together, and at 6.10 a.m. on 20 November 1917 – led by Elles himself – they emerged *en masse* from the morning mists and smoke cover. Despite heavy showers (throughout the battle period) the free-draining geology preserved good travelling conditions, and the monsters immediately wreaked havoc – without the customary pre-attack bombardment, surprise was complete. With the weather kind enough and no bombardment there were few shell holes, no mud, just 'good going'. Guns and machine guns by the score were captured; with German troops demoralized – terrorized even – by the sight and sound of hundreds of tanks, resistance was weak; consequently Allied losses were almost unnaturally meagre.

As we moved forward the ground sloped slightly down; in the distance, nearly a mile ahead, I could see several tanks rolling forward steadily. There did not appear to be any organised defence against them. Some changed direction to meet isolated spots of resistance, mostly from machine-guns. One or two had come to a stand-still, probably with engine trouble as they did not appear to be damaged by enemy action. From the general situation it seemed to me that the German infantry had either fled at the apparition of the tanks or had pulled out deliberately, leaving their machine guns to do what they could. On the whole I saw very few Jerries about, dead or alive. The fact that the German High Command had been given fourteen months' warning of the advent of tanks would surely inspire careful planning to ease the blow when a big tank assault appeared imminent. Is it possible that over 400 tanks could assemble near our front line, without Jerry knowing anything about it?
George Coppard, *With a Machine Gun to Cambrai*

But almost 180 tanks were lost on the first day – sixteen to a lone German field gun manned a by a single gunner– and without reserves it was once more down to the infantry – breasts against bullets – to push the advantage home. By the early afternoon of Day One the initial dash and

Right
German prisoners awaiting transport to the cages.

spontaneity had already disappeared from the battlefield, the cavalry, yet again farcically slow in moving forward, were only just crossing no man's land, and the same problem which had been faced over two and half years earlier during the breakthrough at Neuve Chapelle was beginning to rear its head again – coordination and communication was falling apart.

Whilst the German Second Army commander General Georg von der Marwitz was holding his head in despair and preparing for withdrawal, the attack was beginning to crumble. Within a few days Crown Prince Rupprecht of Bavaria, Commander of the Northern Armies had spotted the weakness and brought up reserves from French Flanders and the Aisne sector. On 30 November crushing counter-attacks by experienced German infantry in conjunction with extensive and prolonged mustard gas bombardments began to drive the British back. In a repeat of Somme-style fighting the heaviest casualties were sustained in skirmishes for villages and woods such as Havrincourt, Bourlon, Anneux, Moeuvres and Flésquières. At Havrincourt sixty tanks were allocated to the 49th (West Riding) Division. Their target was the ground seen in Panorama 308 which offers a closer view of the village and the obstacles placed in their way by the Germans. Havrincourt Wood has been felled a) to create clear fields of fire, and b) to lay down obstacles for tanks and troops; note how the trees have all been felled with trunks perpendicular to the line of attack. Whereas troops were forced to step over the trees, it was stumps which troubled tanks most; unless they were correctly negotiated the machines could end up 'balanced', pivoted between the tracks, and without traction. One tank, G12, was torn open in this way, and two others also came to grief on stumps. Nineteen came out of the scrap at the end of the day. Havrincourt fell, but was regained later. Flésquières, in the centre of the battleground, remained in German possession throughout the first day but was evacuated during the night.

Fighting at Bourlon was especially bitter. Without occupying the ridge it would be impossible to hold any of the gains made. For five days attack and counter-attack followed one on another, but neither side prevailed. A two-day hiatus followed, during which the British prepared another powerful assault with tank support. The density of the woodland can be seen in Panorama 309 (29 April 1917) taken from Hermies. This was a 40th Division target and the troops had never worked with tanks before. Sixteen machines attacked the wood frontally, whilst others skirted the flanks. It was taken on 23 November at grave cost. Extra infantry divisions were drawn from rest areas to pursue the advantage, with two arriving from Flanders on the 21st, and seven others en route from various sectors. Progress continued to be slow, exacting a heavy price in lives. Despite the reintroduction of every available tank – just over sixty machines – after thirteen days of battle the Germans had mustered a massive counter-attack

Below

The tank that tried to cross the Canal du Nord: 'Flying FoxII'.

FIFTH ARMY.
Panorama No. 309 made on 29-4-17 from North of Hermies (about J 18 d 0 0) including a field of view of 75° from about North by East to East South East.
Approximate Scale of Degrees (1 Degree equals ·9 inches).
1. Panoramas are taken solely for military purposes.
2. The publication of them in the press will necessarily give valuable information to the enemy.
3. This Panorama is to be kept with as much security as is compatible with full advantage of it being taken by our own troops.
4. When troops are relieved this Panorama should be handed over to the relieving troops.
Beetroot Factory in J.18.d.
Bourlon Wood
GRAINCOURT
Fontaine Notre-Dame
Spires of Cambrai (barely visit
St Gery
Cathedral

force and driven the British back. Cavalry were again held up by machine-guns (often a single gun) and had been unable to cross the Canal du Nord; this was partly the fault of a tank which attempted to use one of the precious bridges and caused it to collapse.The awful price paid to claim the Passchendaele Ridge was still fresh in Haig's memory – he dare not enter into another bloody extended bout of attrition. In addition it appeared that substantial British assistance might be required on the Italian front. Haig ordered withdrawal. The fighting came to an end on 7 December.

Haig blamed Byng for failure; Byng blamed poorly trained troops. An 'independent' enquiry found no fault in the doings of any officer above the rank of Brigadier, so several middle-ranking scapegoat commanders lost their jobs. But there was a bitter recognition at GHQ of what had gone wrong, and a silent acceptance that at Cambrai the greatest opportunities of the war had been missed. The tanks had entirely proved their worth, and it was suspected by all, not least the furious Elles and Fuller, that a supply of fresh reserve machines and swift exploitation by cavalry would have assured a fabulous victory. Although few believed that a breakthrough could have been decently exploited due to the dearth of available reserves, the shattering of the 'impregnable' Hindenburg Line with such ease came as a revelation to all. The Tank Corps gained another VC. Sadly, it was again a posthumous award, to Captain R. W. L. Wain.

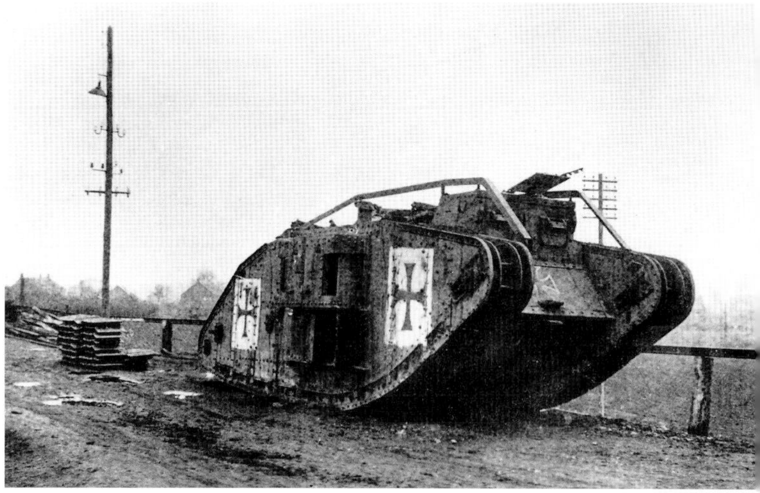

Right
A captured British machine in its new livery.

The battle led to a sea change in attitude: it was no longer imprudent to place generous confidence in tanks. The infantry were loath to go into action without them, and a massive scheme to immediately expand the Corps was put in place. The Germans certainly saw their worth, salvaging many from the battlefield for use against the Allies the following year. In September 1918, on the same battlefield, 478 of the next generation of much faster and more manoeuvrable Mark Vs would sweep through the enemy defences. As Allied commanders were shaken from their mental lairs by the tank's performance at Cambrai, so the face of battle changed for ever. This and future wars would never be the same again.

Below
The northern section of the November battlefront, with the dark mass of Bourlon Wood on the far ridge. Fifth Army Panorama 309.

1918

23.3.18

The latest news is that the Bosche penetrated into our battle area all along the front and the 5th Army have given way, and he is 5 miles into their area. The remnants of the 59 and 34 Division and all MG's were attacked by 8 Divisions in dense masses: they fired every round of am[munition] they had into the Bosche but had not enough to kill them all: these tactics of using vast masses of men and ignoring the initial cost seems to be most successful as the Bosche have advanced as far in 4 days as it took us in 8 months of hard fighting in '16 on the Somme. It is a lovely day and the Germans ought to do wonders in such ideal weather for an offensive. All the regiments have their bands playing round us, and it is very difficult to realise that 4 miles away things are practically unthinkably terrible. The shelling has slacked off very much today – the Bosche is obviously moving up his guns fast, preparatory to another attack tomorrow morning. Our orders are to dig in the early hours of tomorrow morning, so we ought to be able to see life, or rather death. The band of the 4th Grenadiers has just started up "H M S Pinafore", no shelling is going on and everything is peaceful: but I can just imagine the Germans straining every nerve to bring up their guns for tomorrow morning – flogging their mules up the slopes of the next ridge but one, and driving their caterpillar tractors at twice their possible speed.

Telephone message received 24.3.18. Wire from YCA begins. According to information received from 6 Corps at least two cases have been reported in which a man dressed as a Brigadier has given orders for guns and troops to clear out as quickly as possible when there has been no reason for this. This is probably an enemy agent and all units are warned to be on their guard against this. He should be caught if possible. Also reported that Germans are sending men dressed as British officers or civilians to create panic in villages by giving orders such as everyone to clear out at once.

Lieutenant J. R. T. Aldous MC, 210 Field Company RE

In March 1918 German forces broke through across the Somme battlefield, with the 'Michael' offensive inflicting a massive defeat upon the British. In just two weeks their advance covered some 70 km (43 miles); the fact that it ground to a halt was not down to British and Dominion troops forcibly quelling attacks, but simply a question of the Germans oustripping lines of supply in a battlefield salient which lacked road, and therefore transport, capacity. The identical sequence of events was repeated in May at Chateau Thierry with the 'Blücher' and 'Gneisenau' offensives: this time the advance – again into a salient – was almost 50 km (31 miles) in four days, and the French were as comprehensively thrashed as the British. However, retreating forces always enjoy the advantage of falling back upon stores, guns, ordnance, food, reserve troops, depots, and are naturally minded to counter-attack whenever possible. The

Above
A heartbreaking case of *déjà vu* – British dead on the Somme battlefield in 1918.

Left
The first British prisoners captured during the German offensive of spring 1918 are marched through a village near St Quentin.

Above
Panorama 167 of the Cambrai battlefield in September 1918, shortly before the town was liberated.

Below
A British runner wounded during the German offensive is treated by officers of the 1st Battalion, Middlesex Regiment.

final German effort to secure Amiens took place on 4 and 5 April, and this was checked and driven back by Australian supporting troops brought down especially from the Second Army in Flanders. If the Germans, now unable to keep up the offensive pressure on the Somme, chose to remain in both this newly-created salient, and the one facing the French in the south, it would be tantamount to strategic suicide. But choose they did. There are few panoramas for this period, and those that do exist are of relatively poor quality. The best, No 163, shows British positions before St Quentin; these are the lines occupied by British troops immediately before the German attack of 21 March 1918.

The Battle of the Lys

It was mainly against the Forgotten Front that the Germans made their greatest gains during the series of 1918 battles. Between Arras and La Bassée the attack was a half-hearted affair, and despite being numerically far superior the Germans were easily beaten off, but from 7 April in the 'Georgette' offensive they began to push the Allies back from Neuve Chapelle, Laventie and Bois Grenier – places where the lines for so many years had remained not only static but placid. The retreat reached Nieppe and Merville, and receded almost to Hazebrouck. Now the war took on a more guerrilla-type nature. After years of knowing precisely where one's enemy was, open warfare came as a shock to many and led to confusion and chaos. Calculating where the majority of the available enemy forces were stationed, Haig gave Plumer permission to withdraw from the Passchendaele Ridge system if necessary – a move which must have caused men who had served in the Salient during the offensive of the previous year agonies of sadness and disappointment. On 10 April, preceded by the now routine heavy bombardments of high-explosive and mustard gas, the battle extended northwards into Belgian Flanders. The following day Sir Douglas Haig's now famous message to the troops concluded with:

There is no other course open to us but to fight it out. Every position must be held to the last man. There must be no retirement. With our backs to the wall and believing in the justice of our cause each one must fight on to the end. The safety of our homes and the freedom of mankind alike depend upon the conduct of each one of us at this critical moment.

To many of the rank and file troops, these words were probably the first instance of 'direct' contact with their Commander-in-Chief. Although most narratives describe the news – serious as it clearly was – being treated in the same way as always, with droll disdain, it is surprising how often one comes across a copy of Haig's special 'Order of the Day' carefully saved amongst the papers of men who were serving at that time. The effect of these words upon the troops must have been considerable.

By 16 April the Messines and Passchendaele ridges were both back in enemy hands, and the profile of the Salient tightened like a noose upon Ypres. For the first time German boots stood upon Hellfire Corner. The lines were being pushed ever further into areas which had never been touched by the war, country which was richly agricultural and still fully populated by the local civilians. Evacuations lik those seen in 1914, and the entire ambience began to replicate the uncertainty of the early days of conflict.

All the way up the road and in fact all over the countryside, houses and whole villages were on fire, lighting up the whole district. One most pathetic side of the war which was very much in evidence during that march up to the line was the dreadful fate which the livestock on the farms had to suffer: when the owners of these farms cleared out they were in such a hurry that they left all their livestock tied up in the barns with the result that many were killed by shell fire, many were burnt in the farms, and those which escaped starved to death in their sheds. On our way up the air was full of the cries of those miserable animals and the smell of burnt flesh was easily recognisable in some of the roads as we passed along. Wherever possible our men freed the beasts, but of course that night we had no time for any such pastimes. Fleets – if one may use the word – fleets of wheelbarrows were proceeding down the road carrying stretcher cases as the supply of stretchers was of course totally inadequate for the tremendous number of stretcher cases. During the march we passed the usual collection of debris – an overturned General Omnibus at the corner, an aeroplane (British) crashed just beside the road etc., and close to the line, a cow ran full tilt into us.

LIEUTENANT J. R. T. ALDOUS MC, 210 FIELD COMPANY RE

Just after the middle of April the assault was held up in front of Hazebrouck by British and French units. Hostile attention was then diverted to the Flanders hills – Kemmel, Scherpenberg, Mont Rouge and Mont Noir. The Germans flung in an assault against the north of Ypres, at Merckem. It too was resisted. Another against the Belgians followed the same pattern. A final flurry of attacks were launched on 25 April, with Bailleul and Poperinghe as the targets. With unprepared French troops receiving no warning of potential attack, Kemmel Hill fell (see Panorama 170), but, disconcerted by their sudden leap forward, German troops halted in fear of counter-attacks. Renewing the fight the following day the advance crept forward to the outskirts of Locre (Panorama *165*), where it was just held in check by the French. Now, the positions prepared during the winter of 1914/15 were put into service. On 27 and 28 April whilst the Germans paused to catch their breath, the Allies consolidated and prepared for what was to be the final hostile assault. In the event only tiny gains were made on either flank of the battlefield. At 10 p.m. on 29 April, in conference with his army commanders, Ludendorff agreed that the battle could not be won, and the offensive was terminated the following day. By the end of April

Left
The final call to arms. The defence of Hinges Ridge: a 51st Division soldier with an aged ally. Locon, 10 April 1918.

therefore, the entire northern offensive had been halted.

The final German design to break through in Flanders was launched with a 'diversionary' offensive against the French in the *Chemin des Dames* sector on the Aisne. This began successfully on 27 May as offensive 'Goertz' and ended in failure as 'Gneisenau' on 14 June. Ludendorff's idea had been to draw British forces south to support the French, then attack again in Flanders in the 'Hagen' offensive. Whilst everyone wondered what the enemy would do next a steady period of consolidation and reinforcement took place. In Flanders, stasis of a very different kind returned. As the corn and wheat, already long sown, had grown into the impenetrable walls of vegetation (which often still block battlefield vistas to this day), it became more and more difficult to know where one's enemy was. This uncharacteristic terrain can be seen in Panorama 90, but especially in Panorama 160 which shows deliberate diagonal tracks through cornfields taking the place of excavations. No trenches whatsoever can be discerned, although they certainly existed.

12.7.18

An interesting show took place at 10 a.m. yesterday morning resulting in the capture of 3 Bosche officers and 139 men. An Australian officer and Serjt went wandering through the corn in camouflage suits to see what there was to see and they met 2 fat Bosche asleep in a post: they went back with them and brought out the platoon and then the company commander brought out the whole company. The company on the flank got to hear of this and went over the top too. Result: Australian line advanced 800 yards to just behind Celery Copse, 3 officers and 139 men prisoners. One platoon of the first company to go over was left behind to liaise with 11 EY [East Yorkshires] and to form a flank. (The attack must have been rather a surprise for the German Battalion commander: hardly a shot was fired till the end. The OC Battalion must have been gaily sending up runners with "Nobby" messages etc., and have gradually grown suspicious when none came back. Finally someone would come up and tell him that two of his companies had suddenly and silently vanished away and that the Australians were now sitting in the support line. I bet that CO is now en route for Berlin.)

Now look at the British method. OC Platoon on flank asks OC Company for instructions, who asks Battalion, who ask Brigade, who ask Division, who ask Corps – none of the units being willing to take the responsibility of an advance thereby imperilling the Australian flank and letting a glorious opportunity slide. The Company commander of course received no instructions and did not move. Nothing happened. Now today we learn a proper organised show is to be made tomorrow morning, barrage and everything: the Bosche is of course ready by now and expecting it. RE assistance was asked for and OC went round to Brigade to ask for instructions and there learnt that 11 E. Yorks went over on their own this morning and took the objective. (Tern Farm) without orders, and so the attack tomorrow morning is off.

Below
First Army Panorama 90, taken in the summer of 1916, illustrates the unusual nature of the battleground during the German Lys offensive in 1918.

Why couldn't they have done this yesterday? Instead of letting the matter get into the hands of the staff who took two days to give an answer.
Lieutenant J. R. T. Aldous MC, 210 Field Company RE

This is an example of one of the many minor actions which took place during the summer of 1918. Another panorama illustrates the landscape of a second, this one carried out by the Australians at Villers-Brettoneux. It is unfortunately a little unedifying (the photographer appears to be working at great risk) as the opposing lines are not just indistinct but entirely invisible; however the picture is included both to mark the action of 4 July as a rehearsal (with tanks) of the kind of fighting which would shortly take place during the Advance to Victory, and also to contrast the difference in landscape between the northern and southern battlegrounds.

Enter the Doughboys

Having declared war in April 1917, the Americans, commanded by General John J. Pershing had a million men in France by July 1918 (almost twice that number were in Europe when the war ended). Their arrival had to no small degree prompted the series of massive German spring offensives, but although several 'doughboy' detachments fought defensive actions alongside the French on the Aisne in May and the Marne in June, the AEF (American Expeditionary Force) was not to act as an offensive unit until the St Mihiel attacks in September. Although a limited success, the venture was considered commendable for troops inexperienced in trench warfare, and silenced many of Pershing's numerous critics in France and the USA. A further operation, the Meuse-Argonne offensive, launched in late September 1918 in the forests east of Verdun, was their last major engagement on the Western Front. In these few months the American casualty list reached an astonishing 264,000 men. The most important British action of the late-summer period took place at La Becque, near Vieux Berquin, several kilometres to the rear of the old lines at Neuve Chapelle.

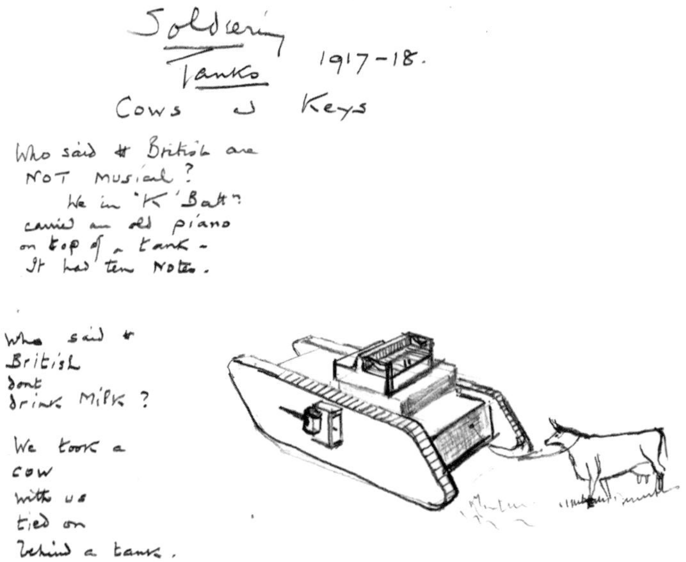

15.9.18

Rode over to Vieux Berquin with Wakeford in the afternoon. Revisited Verte Rue and the field where K must have been killed. Although it is so far from the line, everything is just as it was on June 28th – German equipment, arms etc. still lying strewn about in the same places. We rode up to the factory and looked over the bridge which W crawled out to from the front posts and blew up one night – a dead Bosche was floating in the Becque there just where the bridge had been. We looked at our old billets at Le Paradis which we occupied on April 13th – they had been in no man's land for some time and then in our lines and had not improved with time: the old 4th Guards Brigade HQ was on the ground and the 40th Div. Omnibus (General) still lying at Le Paradis as it was lying when we came up on April 13th. My wire was still up at Verte Rue but very badly blown about by shells. It's extraordinary what memories that field brought back – I could see Callender and myself cowering in that shell slit (half full of water) and the large shell hole nearby in which 3 or 4 wounded men – badly wounded and covered with blood – were lying heaped on top of each other and writhing and groaning in their pain. It seemed almost desecration to see lorries and ASC driving along these roads, and I know I could never bear to see trippers over the ground where men went through such inconceivable agonies: fancy 'Arry and 'Arriete after the war flirting and eating winkles on the ground where the Guards Brigade were cut up – where each man died fighting although surrounded and dead tired: where De Longueville fought and although surrounded could only say "Surrounded? All the better – we can kill all the more of them –

Page 354–55
British troops falling back during the Lys offensive take advantage of nature's bounty whilst they can. Marquois, April 1918.

Left
Having been wounded in 1916, Lieutenant Robin Skeggs transferred from the Rifle Brigade to the Tank Corps, where he rose to the rank of major. His sketch shows how he and his men went into battle at Canrai in 1918! Sadly, his letters from this period have not survived.

anyway, they're all old men." And then hundreds of those bastardly strikers swarming over the ground, sucking orange peel and frolicking light-heartedly over the graves of men who died that these shirkers might live in peace and quietude at home in England.
LIEUTENANT J. R. T. ALDOUS MC, 210 FIELD COMPANY RE

In August 1918 the Allies launched the first major counter-attacks, the British thrusting forward in front of Amiens with a mountain of provisions and an efficient road and railway system behind, and a landscape little battered because of the very pace of the rout during March and April before them. The advance was no less stupendous than that of the Germans' earlier endeavour, and it nearly withered in the same way. But the counter-thrust on the Somme was an attack which so heartened the Allies and so weakened the Germans it began an offensive domino effect which spread along the length of the front, in Picardy, Artois and Flanders. At the beginning of September the original 1914–18 lines were regained, and the tide swept on.

19/9/18
I am writing this epistle in a gas-mask – do not be alarmed: it is only practice. The latest order is that we have to wear them half an hour a day to get accustomed to them. It is really very funny, as it is a Divisional order: so precisely at the hour of 11, the whole of your little world becomes mute, with goggle eyes and somewhat stertorous breathing: and not a sound is heard in the land for half an hour. The war is going exceedingly well, and with any luck the show may be over next year. It rather depends upon the psychology of the Hun proletariat. If they really get wind of all our successes, and realise its all up, it is quite possible they will try to take it out on the party responsible – viz the Prussian grandees. I expect to see the whole affair go on for a bit more yet, and then crack suddenly and gloriously.
2nd Lieutenant J. T. Godfrey, 103 Field Company RE

The Hindenburg Line was cracked on 29 September; Passchendaele fell to the Belgians the next day. Kemmel was also retaken – see Panorama *173* for the view which greeted the British. On 9 October the Canadians entered Cambrai (see Nos 167 and 168 taken in September 1918 on the eve of the attacks and also all other Cambrai panoramas as the

Above and right
Return to open warfare. Australian troops near the old Hindenburg Line firing at German soldiers avoiding an artillery barrage. 18 September 1918.

1918 battles were fought over the same ground as the previous year), and a few days later Lille, Menin and Tourcoing were liberated. At the beginning of November Valenciennes was once more delivered into French hands. There was talk of an armistice, but the whole war had been characterized by such things (some units kept rumour books), and despite the obvious and ongoing success no one was prepared to entertain the thought of an end to proceedings until it happened. Just three days before 11 November, hearsay grew more concrete. Once confirmed, the build-up to potential peace naturally led to horrible last-minute fears on the part of the long-suffering troops.

7 November 1918
The attack is apparently coming off on the morning of the 11th and Hewson told me that he was moving up on the 8th to relieve the 94th who are holding just at present. The attack is being carried out on a two battalion front, ourselves working with the right battalion and having about 1000 yards of flooded marshes to cross. C Coy. Koylis are working with us and carry the bridge up to the site whereupon we put it across.

8 November 1918
4 Section moved off early in the morning. Belile going on ahead to fix the billets: the last runner reports that no billets have been found, so I

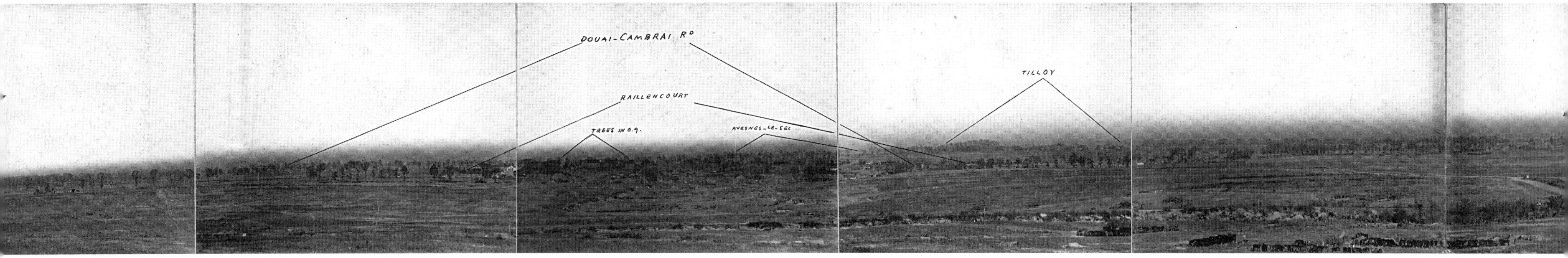

sincerely hope Foch will have concluded his armistice before we move up tomorrow. I really think hostilities should cease within the next day or two and I only hope the armistice is ratified before the 92 Brigade attack on Monday morning – I almost think if I was a private in the 92nd Bde and was told to attack at a time like this I'd see the authorities somewhere before I obeyed the order. There are more shops in Courtrai than I thought and I spent quite a pleasant morning having my hair cut and drinking chocolate in a café. If it weren't for the shortage of whisky I should be feeling quite happy today – I hope historians will record this fact in their histories "the latter part of the war was marked by a very serious shortage of whisky which did more to lower the morale of officers than any operation conducted by the enemy."

9 November 1918

On the night of 8th we all made agreement with the Major, that if any news of the armistice came through he would send Armitage round to our billets at once to let us know: when, therefore A came round and woke me up at 3.30 a.m., I got all ready to rejoice but was speedily undeceived as an order had come through that the Bosche were retiring on our front and that we had to move up at once to S …

10 November 1918

Went out with Verity again, this time on a horse, though, to road-reconnoitre into Renaix. Renaix is quite a large town and presented a scene of indescribable enthusiasm – all the inhabitants were in the streets and every house was beflagged and large flags were hung across the streets from house to house. At one house at which we stopped to water our horses, they presented us with Grand Marnier ad lib, and a bit further down the road I was forcibly dragged into a back room full of people who all stood up on my entry – a fiddler and pianist then materialised and they played God Save the King seven times over, myself feeling almost embarrassed during the proceeding. After that we drank together, clinked glasses etc., shouted Vive La Belgique for some time: after that the whole assembly began talking to me at once in rapid French – I managed to interpret one story mainly because it was shouted in my ear by a hefty looking man who showed signs of embracing me at intervals – he apparently had been told by a German officer to accompany him when the Germans evacuated the town and had shot the German officer through the head, of which rather brave act he was inordinately proud. Finally got away and rode back meeting the Company on the move to Billets at Orroir.

11 November 1918

Marched from Orroir into Renaix (or Ronse as it is in Flemish). On the way Stuffy Lambert passed us in his car and shouted that the armistice had been signed and was coming into force at 11 a.m. – the men gave a cheer and then commenced singing: it is the first time I have ever heard them sing and they kept it up all the way. We are billeted in very nice houses near the railway station and the owners simply tumble over themselves to do anything for us. In my room is a large bouquet with "Welcome to our liberators" written on it. Apparently our Div. HQ knew on the night of the 10th that the Armistice would be or was signed, and knowing this the 92nd Brigade was ordered to attack this morning and take the west bank of the Denore before 11 a.m. – in my opinion the man who was responsible for this order is nothing better than a murderer and deserves to be hung. Luckily Bosche had evacuated the ground and so an attack was unnecessary.

LIEUTENANT J. R. T. ALDOUS MC, 210 FIELD COMPANY RE

Below

It was a thankfully brief introduction to war for these young German soldiers captured during the Allies' Advance to Victory in late 1918.

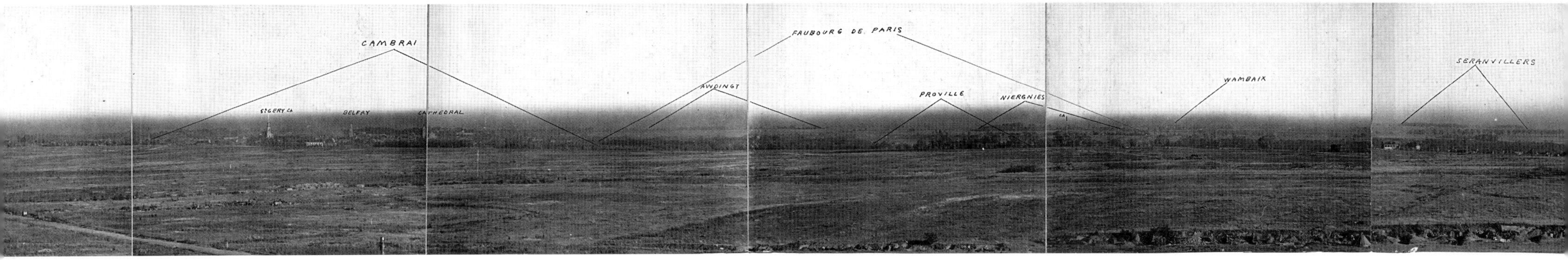

Above

Segment of Panorama 168 from September 1918 showing a view of Cambrai during the Allies' advance to victory. The city is about to be liberated.

Right

British cinematographer filming what is purported to be the last shot of the war.

Epilogue

Based upon such an extensive area, this book is necessarily generalized. It has not been easy to avoid inserting swathes of personal accounts to illustrate events in individual sub-sectors within each sector, but enthusiasm has been forcibly repressed by having to produce a book which readers could at least lift.

Whilst the panoramas at last show us the authentic character of the many varying environments of the British Western Front, it is nevertheless true, and always shall be, that the most important component of the entire body of First World War research is the testimony of the participants themselves. Many archives illustrate the extraordinary quantity of materiel demanded by the conflict; wars, however, are not fought by things but people, each an individual, each a separate battle unit, and each with his or her own history, thoughts, fears and well of deeper feelings. In 1914 lives were transformed from normal to entirely abnormal; many voluntarily glided into an alien world where all of society's recognized reference points and values were absent: an all-male world, a world where money became practically unimportant, and a world where life itself proved daily to be horribly fragile, and all too often absurdly cheap. Thousands never physically recovered from the experience, and many more suffered psychologically, spiritually and emotionally for the rest of their lives. The features which constantly reappear are courage – not the heroic variety – but courage in simply 'sticking it'; and two other critical ingredients, humour and comradeship. I hope that a sense of each has seeped into the pages of this book. If not, the panoramas might remain as depopulated as they so often appear.

The families who waited daily for news were entirely unable to comprehend the landscape, sights, sounds and smells of the battlefields, painted in words by their menfolk during and after the war, and the Western Front is certainly not a world that I, nor anyone else who did not take part can ever hope to properly appreciate. However, with the panoramas we can at least now understand what that alien world looked like, and place our own personal perceptions, received wisdom and knowledge within it.

Anyway, the bally war is over, which is a great thing. It is a joy so great that nobody yet realises what it means. I am certain I cannot realise what peace is. To think that I shall not have to toddle up among the 'obus'es and mitrailleuses again, and never hear another shell burst. It is simply unimaginable. Everyone here took it very quietly. There was a little cheering when the news came round at about midday on the eleventh: and that was all. As a matter of fact I had a most strenuous bridge repair that day, and didn't finish until 1 a.m. the next morning: so it didn't make any difference, and hasn't yet – outwardly. The only difference is that feeling of oppression at the back of one's brain is slowly lifting. Can you send me a good German grammar and phrase book: I might as well learn their miserable language!

2nd Lieutenant J. T. Godfrey, 103 Field Company RE

Left
To the victor the spoils. A proud young man from Cambrai with an impressive souvenir – a German anti-tank rifle.

Southampton –
First glimpse of "Blighty"
1919.

Timeline

Timeline of key events of the First World War. Entries in *italic* refer to theatres other than the Western Front.

1914

28 June: Archduke Ferdinand, heir to Austro-Hungarian throne, is assassinated in Sarajevo, Bosnia, by Gavril Princip.

28 July: Austria-Hungary declares war on Serbia.

29 July: Russia partly mobilizes in support of the Serbs.

1 August: Germany (an ally of Austria-Hungary) declares war on Russia. France mobilizes in support of Russia.

3 August: Germany declares war on France.

4 August: Germany invades neutral Belgium. Britain (a guarantor of that neutrality) declares war on Germany.

7 August: First units of the British Expeditionary Force (BEF) arrive in France.

10 August–1 September: Austrians invade Russian Poland.

15 August: Russia invades East Prussia

19 August: USA declares its neutrality. *Russia invades Eastern Galicia.*

23–24 August: Battle of Mons. Retreat of the BEF.

23–31 August: Germans rout Russian forces in Battle of Tannenberg.

5–15 September: Germans repeat Tannenberg victory at First Battle of Masurian Lakes.

6–10 September: First Battle of the Marne. German progress in France arrested. War of movement slows.

9–14 September: German troops in France forced to fall back to the River Aisne.

12 September–22 November: The First Battle of the Aisne followed by the Race to the Sea, mutual northward outflanking attempts by both sides. This period sees the beginning of trench warfare.

26 September: Indian Corps land at Marseilles for service on Western Front.

4 October: Austro-Hungarian counter-offensive in Galicia.

14 October: Canadian units arrive in Britain.

19 October–22 November: First Battle of Ypres. Trench systems begun in earnest.

2 November: Russia declares war on Turkey.

5 November:France and Britain declare war on Turkey.

21 December: First German air raid on British mainland.

1915

31 January: First deployment of poison gas by German forces near the Polish town of Bolimow.

4–22 February: Second Battle of Masurian Lakes confers no strategic gains to either Germans or Russians.

18 February: Germany launches unrestricted submarine warfare on shipping heading towards British waters, attacking military and merchant vessels of all nationalities.

10–13 March: Battle of Neuve Chapelle delivers a tiny gain for BEF.

18 March: British and French ships bombard Turkish targets in the Dardanelles hoping to make Turkey yield, but make little impression. Formulation of invasion plans begins.

22 April–25 May: Second Battle of Ypres. First use of poison gas on Western Front at Ypres. Canadian troops now in action alongside the BEF.

25 April: In the Dardenelles, Allied seaborne assault on Gallipoli peninsula begins.

1–5 May: Germans drive Russians back at the Battle of Gorlicz-Tarnow.

7 May: British passenger liner Lusitania *is torpedoed and sunk by a U-boat. In the face of international outrage Germans insist the ship was carrying war materiel.*

9 May: Battle of Aubers Ridge. Beginning of a sequence of combined Allied offensives on Western Front.

15–25 May: Battle of Festubert. Small British gains.

9 May–18 June: Second Battle of Artois (French) around Arras, Vimy and Souchez. A failure.

23 May: *Italy joins the Entente Allies. Advances across its northeastern border against Austria.*

29 June–7 July: Italian forces attack Austrians in the first of ten battles of the Isonzo. Little progress is made.

13–15 July: Massive German offensive begins in the East; the aim is to totally destroy Russian Army, then concentrate on the Western Front.

22 July: A great defensive retreat is ordered by Russian commanders. Poland evacuated.

25 September–15 October: Third Battle of Artois includes British autumn offensive at the Battle of Loos. Minimal gains on all fronts, but Germans are driven off Notre Dame de Lorette ridge north of Arras.

30 November: Serbia falls to German, Austro-Hungarian and Bulgarian forces.

19 December: Sir Douglas Haig appointed commander-in-chief of British Forces, replacing Sir John French.

1916

24 January: Conscription begins in Britain.

21 February–18 December: Battle of Verdun (French). German attempt to 'bleed the French white', according to plans laid down on 20 December 1915.

14 May–3 June: Austrians attack Italian forces in the Trentino Offensive, but fail to make serious headway.

31 May: In the North Sea, the Battle of Jutland sees the only major contest between British and German battle fleets. The fight ends with honours roughly even and no true victor.

4 June–17 October: The Russian Brusilov Offensive mutilates the Austrian Army but German reinforcements help stop the retreat at the Carpathian Mountains.

5 June: Lord Kitchener, British Secretary of State for War, dies at sea after his ship hits a mine.

1 July–19 November: Battle of the Somme. Anglo-French offensive astride the River Somme. Small but costly gains.

27 August: Romania declares war on Austria-Hungary.

2 September: Combined German, Turkish and Bulgarian force invades Romania.

8 September: Hindenburg and Ludendorff change German tactics: defence-in-depth established along the entire line.

15 September: First use of tanks in war, by British at Flers on the Somme.

23 September: German forces begin construction of the Hindenburg Line.

6 December: Bucharest occupied by German-led forces, which capture large stocks of grain and oil.

7 December: Lloyd George replaces Asquith as British Prime Minister.

21 December: French commander-in-chief Joseph Joffre is sacked, to be replaced by the ambitious and confident Robert Nivelle.

1917

3 February: United States cuts diplomatic relations with Germany.

6 February–16 March: Operation Alberich – a 40-km (24-mile) withdrawal of German forces to Hindenburg Line system leaving 'scorched earth' in the evacuated territory.

24 February: Britain shows US Government a German communication with Mexico that proposes an alliance to attack the USA.

11 March: Attacking the Turks in Mesopotamia, British forces advancing from Basra take Baghdad.

12 March: Revolution consumes Russia, harming Entente *prospects in the West.*

15 March: Abdication of Tsar Nicholas of Russia, but new regime keeps Russia in the war.

26 March-October 31: Advancing out of Sinai from Suez, British, aided by Arab irregulars under Lawrence, push Turks into Palestine, taking Gaza.

6 April: USA declares war on Germany.

9 April–4 May: Battles of Vimy Ridge and Arras – British and Canadian supporting assaults to assist the French Nivelle Offensive. Vimy Ridge falls to Canadians, but Arras proves to be the most costly battle of the war for British and Dominion forces.

16 April–20 April: French Nivelle Offensive. Its complete failure leads to a shattering of morale, and mutiny in French Army.

17 April–10 June: Period when French troops say they will defend but not attack.

15 May: Robert Nivelle sacked as French commander-in-chief, to be replaced by Petain, who quickly announces a tactical change onto the defensive.

7-14 June: Hugely successful limited British assault against the Messines Ridge in Flanders, launched as a prequel to Third Ypres.

28 June: First American troops disembark onto French soil.

29 June–18 July: Russian Kerensky Offensive. Highly promising attack that begins well, but ends in a 240-km (149-mile) withdrawal.

31 July–18 November: Third Battle of Ypres, culminating from 12 October in the two Battles of Passchendaele.

1–5 September: On the Baltic German forces capture Riga.

24 October–26 December: Austro-German offensive at Caporetto take them firmly into Italian territory.

7 November: Bolsheviks seize power in Russia and declare desire for peace.

20 November–3 December: Battle of Cambrai, where massed tank attacks deliver early promise, but initial breakthrough remains unsupported and ultimately fails.

1 December: First meeting of Allied War Council including British, French, Italian and US ministers for war.

9 December: Capture of Jerusalem by British. Turkish forces retreat north towards Damascus.

15 December: Germany and Russia agree an armistice at Brest-Litovsk.

1918

3 March: Germany and Russia sign Treaty of Brest-Litovsk, allowing German Eastern Front forces to transfer to the Western Front.

21 March–5 April: The German 'Kaiserschlacht' Offensive pushes the British back 64 km (39 miles) from the Hindenburg Line across the old Somme battlefields, but runs out of momentum and support.

9–29 April: Battle of the Lys sees German forces drive forward in Flanders with variable success.

27 May–6 June: The Germans embark upon an offensive which becomes known as the Third Battle of the Aisne, again pushing the French back to the Marne as in 1914. Again, momentum is lost.

28 May: American troops go on the offensive for first time, at Cantigny.

15 July: Second Battle of the Marne sees a limited and insufficient German success against the French in a final push for victory.

22 July: Germans pull back once more to Hindenburg Line.

8 August: The 'black day' of the German Army. Canadians, Australians and massed tanks crush German defences to reach the Hindenburg Line.

12–16 September: First independent attacks by US Army.

26 September: Huge Allied assault bursts through Hindenburg Line.

28 September: Ludendorff and Hindenburg recommend peace talks – armistice suggested.

1-30 October: British forces take Damascus and Beirut. Turkey signs armistice.

3 November: Austria, having declared independence from Germany, agrees armistice terms with the Allies.

9 November: Kaiser Wilhelm II of Germany abdicates.

11 November: The Armistice is signed.

BIBLIOGRAPHY

REC: Extracts from the Proceedings of the Royal Engineer Committee
REJ: Royal Engineers Journal
REL: Royal Engineers Library
REM: Royal Engineers Museum
IWM: Imperial War Museum
NA: National Archives (Formerly Public Record Office)

Select Bibliography

Anon., (1871-1925), *Extracts from the Proceedings of the Royal Engineer Committee*, School of Military Engineering, Chatham
Anon., *The Pilgrims Guide to the Ypres Salient*, Herbert Reach, London, 1920
Anon., *Manual of Map Reading and Field Sketching*, HMSO, London, 1921
Anon., *Supply of Engineer Stores and Equipment, The Work of the Royal Engineers in the European War, 1914-1919*, RE Institute, Chatham, 1922
Anon., *Report on the Survey of the Western Front 1914-1918, Appendix VIII*, HMSO, London, 1924
Anon., *The Wipers Times*, Eveleigh, Nash & Grayson, London, 1930
Anon., *History of the Corps of Royal Engineers, Volume V*, Institution of Royal Engineers, Chatham, 1952
Adams, Bernard, *Nothing of Importance*, Strong Oak Press and Tom Donovan, 1988
Ashworth, Tony, *Trench Warfare 1914-1918*, Macmillan, London, 1980
Bardgett, Colin, *The Lonsdale Battalion 1914-1918*, GC Book Publishers Ltd, Wigtown, 1993
Bairnsfather, Bruce, *Bullets and Billets*, Herbert Jenkins, London, 1916
Barton, P., Doyle, P. and Vandewalle, J., *Beneath Flanders Fields, The Tunneller's War 1914-1918*, Spellmount, Staplehurst, 2004
Behrent, Arthur, *As from Kemmel Hill*, Eyre & Spottiswood, London, 1963
Blunden, Edmund, *Undertones of War*, Cobden-Sanderson, London, 1930
Brice, Beatrice, *The Battle Book of Ypres*, John Murray, London, 1927
Brown, Malcolm, *Tommy Goes to War*, Dent, London, 1980
Brown, Malcolm, *The Imperial War Museum Book of the Western Front*, Sidgwick & Jackson, London, 1993
Brown, Malcolm, *The Imperial War Museum Book of 1918*, Pan, London, 1993
Brown, Malcolm, *The Imperial War Museum Book of the Somme*, Pan, London, 1997
Brown, Malcolm and Seaton, Shirley, *The Christmas Truce*, Leo Cooper, London, 1984
Bulletin Belges des Sciences Militaires Tome II, *Les Operations de l'Armee Belge*, Bruxelles, 1928
Byrne, Charles 'Ginger', *I Survived, Didn't I?*, Leo Cooper, London, 1993
Carmichael, Jane, *First World War Photographers*, Routledge, London, 1989
Carrington, Charles, *Soldier from the Wars Returning*, Hutchinson, London, 1965
Channing, N. & Dunn, M., *British Camera Makers – An A–Z Guide to Companies and Products*, Parkland Designs, London, 1996
Chapman, Guy, *A Passionate Prodigality*, Ivor Nicholson and Watson, 1933
Chapman, Guy, *Vain Glory*, Cassell, London, 1937
Charlton, Peter, *Pozieres, 1916*, Leo Cooper, London, 1986
Chasseaud, Peter, *Topography of Armageddon, A British Trench Map Atlas of the Western Front*, Mapbooks, Lewes, 1991
Chasseaud, Peter, *Artillery's Astrologers, A History of British Survey and Mapping on the Western Front 1914-1918*, Mapbooks, Lewes, 1999
Clayton, Ann, *Chavasse, Double VC*, Leo Cooper, London, 1992
Close, Colonel Sir Charles, and Winterbotham, Colonel H. [Eds.], *Text Book of Topographical and Geographical Surveying*, HMSO, London, 1925
Congreve, Billy, *Armageddon Road: a VCs Diary 1914-16*, London, 1982
Coombs, Rose, *Before Endeavours Fade, A Guide to the Battlefields of the First World War*, Battle of Britain Prints International, London, 1983
Cooper, Bryan, *The Ironclads of Cambrai*, Souvenir Press, London, 1967
Coppard, George, *With a Machine Gun to Cambrai*, HMSO, London, 1988
Crawford O. G. S., *Said and Done: The Autobiography of an Archaeologist*, Weidenfeld & Nicolson, London, 1955
Doyle, Peter, *Geology of the Western Front, 1914-1918*, Geologists' Association, London, 1998
Dunn, J. C., *The War the Infantry Knew 1914-1919*, Jane's, London, 1987
Eberle, V. F., *My Sapper Venture*, Pitman, London, 1973
Edmonds, Charles, *A Subaltern's War*, Peter Davies, London, 1929
Edmonds, Brigadier-General Sir James, (1923-25) *History of the Great War Military Operations, France & Belgium, 1914*, Macmillan, London
Edmonds, Brigadier-General Sir James, *History of the Great War Military Operations, France & Belgium, 1915*, HMSO, London, 1932
Edmonds, Brigadier-General Sir James, *History of the Great War Military Operations, France & Belgium, 1916*, HMSO, London
Edmonds, Brigadier-General Sir James, *History of the Great War Military Operations, France & Belgium, 1917*, HMSO, London
Edmonds, Brigadier-General Sir James, *History of the Great War Military Operations, France & Belgium, 1918*, HMSO, London
Farrar-Hockley, Anthony, *Death of an Army*, Batsford, London, 1967
Falls, Cyril, *The First World War*, Longman, London, 1960
Feilding, Roland, *War Letters to a Wife, France and Flanders, 1915-1919*, Medici, London, 1929
Flemer, J.A, *An Elementary Treatise on Photographic Methods and Instruments*, Chapman and Hall, London, 1906
Fletcher, David, *Landships – British Tanks in the First World War*, HMSO, London, 1984
Frizot, Michel, *The New History of Photography*, Konemann, Koln, 1998
Fuller, Colonel J. F. C., *On Future Warfare*, Sifton Praed & Co., London, 1928
Fuller, Major-General J. F. C., *The Army in My Time*, Rich & Cowan, London, 1935
Gardner, R. B., *The Big Push*, Cassell, London, 1961
Gibbs, W. C., *A Record of the 203 Field Company (Cambs.) Royal Engineers 1915–1919*, Heffer & Sons, Cambridge, 1921
Giles, John, *Flanders, Then and Now*, After the Battle, 1987

Giles, John, *The Somme, Then and Now*, After the Battle, 1986
Girardet, Jean-Marie, Jacques, Alain, and Duclos, Jean-Luc Letho, *Somewhere on the Western Front, Arras, 1914-1918*, Documents d'Archéologie du XXe siècle, No. 8, Arras, 2003
Gladden, Norman, *Ypres 1917. A Personal Account*, William Kimber, London, 1967
Gleichen, Lord Edward, *Chronology of the Great War, 1914-1918*, Greenhill, London, 2000
Gliddon, Gerald, *The Battle of the Somme, A Topographical History*, Sutton, Stroud, 1998
Gosse, Philip, *Memoirs of a Camp Follower*, Longmans, London, 1934
Grant Grieve, W. and Newman, Bernard, *Tunnellers*, Herbert Jenkins, London, 1936
Graves, Robert, *Goodbye To All That*, Penguin, London, 1977
Gray, Randal, *Chronicle of the First World War*, Facts on File, Oxford, 1990
Griffith, Paddy, *Battle Tactics of the Western Front*, Yale University Press, New Haven and London, 1994
Harrison, G. H. (Ed.), *Index to Extracts from the Royal Engineer Committee Proceedings 1871–1927*, School of Military Engineering, Chatham, 1905
Harrison, Major G. H., *Index to Extracts from the Proceedings of the Royal Engineer Committee*, School of Military Engineering, Chatham, 1925
Haythornthwaite, Philip J., *The Colonial Wars Source Book*, Caxton Editions, London, 2000
Hitchcock, Captain F. C., *Stand-To, A Diary of the Trenches 1915 – 1918*, Naval and Military Press, ND
Holmes, Richard, *Tommy: The British Soldier on the Western Front, 1914-1918*, HarperCollins. London, 2004
Holt, Major and Mrs, *Major and Mrs Holt's Battlefield Guide to the Somme*, Leo Cooper, 1996
Holt, Major and Mrs, *Major and Mrs Holt's Battlefield Guide to the Ypres Salient*, Leo Cooper
Horne, Alistair, *Death of a Generation*, Macdonald, London, 1970
Hyde, R., *Panoramania – The Art and Entertainment of the 'All-Embracing View*, Trefoil Publications, London, 1988
Johnson, Douglas Wilson, *Battlefields of the World War, Western and Southern Fronts, A Study in Military Geology*, Oxford University Press, American Branch, New York, 1921
Johnson, J. H., *Stalemate! The Great Trench Warfare Battles 1915 – 1917*, Arms and Armour Press, London, 1995
Lewinski, J., *The Camera at War*, W.H. Allen and Co., London, 1978
Liddle, Peter (ed.), *Passchendaele in Perspective, The Third Battle of Ypres*, Leo Cooper, London, 1997
Macdonald, Lyn, *1914*, Penguin, 1987
Macdonald, Lyn, *They Called it Passchendaele*, Penguin, London, 1978
Macdonald, Lyn, *Somme*, Penguin, London, 1993
Macdonald, Lyn, 1915, *The Death of Innocence*, Headline, London, 1993
Mark VII, *A Subaltern on the Somme in 1916*, Dent, London, 1927
Masefield, John, *The Old Front Line*, Heineman, London, 1917
Marix-Evans, Martin, *Over the Top, Great Battles of the First World War*, Arcturus, London, 2002
MacGill, Patrick, *The Big Push, An Episode of the Great War*, Herbert Jenkins, London, 1916
Macksey, Kenneth, *Vimy Ridge 1914-18*, Pan/Ballantine, London, 1972
McCarthy, Chris, *The Somme, The Day by Day Account*, Arms and Armour Press, 1995
McCarthy, Chris, *Passchendaele, The Day by Day Account*, Arms and Armour Press, London, 1995
McKee, Alexander, *Vimy Ridge*, Pan Books, London, 1968
McNicholl, Major-General R. R., *The Royal Australian Engineers, 1902 – 1919*, Corps Committee of the Royal Australian Engineers, Canberra, 1979
Michelin & Co., *Les Batailles de la Somme*, Michelin, Paris, 1920
Michelin & Co., *Arras et les Batailles d'Artois*, Michelin, Paris, 1920
Michelin & Co., *Les Batailles de Picardie*, Michelin, Paris, 1920
Michelin & Co., *Ypres et les Batailles d'Ypres*, Michelin, Paris, 1921
Middlebrook, Martin, *The First Day on the Somme*, Allen lane, London, 1971
Middlebrook, Martin and Mary, *The Somme Battlefields, A Comprehensive Guide from Crécy to the Two World Wars*, Viking Books, 1991
Mitchell, F., *Tank Warfare, The Story of the Tanks in the Great War*, Thomas Nelson, London, 1933
Moorhouse, Brendon, *Forged by Fire*, Spellmount, Staplehurst, 2003
Nicholls, Jonathan, *Cheerful Sacrifice, The Battle of Arras 1917*, Leo Cooper, London, 1990
Norman, Terry, *The Hell They Called High Wood*, William Kimber, London, 1984
Oettermann, Stephan, *The Panorama, History of a Mass Medium*, Zone Books, New York, 1997
Oldham, Peter, *The Hindenburg Line*, Leo Cooper, London, 1997
Orr, Philip, *The Road to the Somme*, Blackstaff Press, Belfast, 1987
Pasley, Lieutenant-Colonel, C. W., *Course of Military Instruction*, John Murray, London, 1817
Passingham, Ian, *Pillars of Fire*, Sutton, Stroud, 1998
Pitt, Barrie, *1918, The Last Act*, Macmillan, London, 1962
Porter, Major-General W., *History of the Corps of Royal Engineers, Volume I*, Institution of Royal Engineers, Chatham, 1951
Porter, Major-General W., *History of the Corps of Royal Engineers, Volume II*, Institution of Royal Engineers, Chatham, 1951
Prior, Robin and Wilson, Trevor, *Passchendaele, the Untold Story*, Yale University Press, London, 1996
Proceedings of the Royal Engineer Committee 1914-1918, *Extracts*, School of Military Engineering, Chatham, various years
Pulteney, Lt. General Sir William, and Brice, Beatrice, *The Immortal Salient*, John Murray, London, 1925
Reed, H., *Photography Applied to Surveying*, John Wiley and Sons, New York, 1888
Reed, Paul, *Walking the Salient*, Leo Cooper, Barnsley, 2001
Reed, Paul, *Walking the Somme*, Leo Cooper, London, 1997
Richards, Frank, *Old Soldiers Never Die*, Private publication, London, 1933
Sheffield, Gary, *The Somme*, Cassell, London, 2003
Smithers, A. J., *Honourable Conquests – An Account of the Enduring Work of the Royal Engineers throughout the Empire*, Leo Cooper, London, 1991
Spagnoly and Smith, *A Walk Round Plugstreet*, Leo Cooper, London, 1997
Steel, Nigel and Hart, Peter, *Passchendaele, The Sacrificial Ground*, Cassell, London, 2000
Terraine, John (ed.), *General Jack's Diary*, Cassell, London, 2000
Terraine, John, *White Heat, The New Warfare 1914-1918*, Guild Publishing, 1982
Thys, Robert, *Nieuport 1914-1918*, Constable, London, 1922
Wade, Aubrey, *The War of the Guns*. Batsford, London, 1936
Warner, Philip, *The Battle of Loos*, William Kimber, London, 1976
Warner, Philip, *Passchendaele*, Sidgwick & Jackson, London, 1987
Watson, Colonel Sir Charles, *History of the Corps of Royal Engineers, Volume III*, Institution of Royal Engineers, Chatham, 1951
Winter, Denis, *Death's Men*, Penguin, London, 1979
Wolf, Leon, *In Flanders Fields*, Longmans, London, 1959

Journal papers

Baker-Brown, Brigadier-General W. (1951), History of the Corps of Royal Engineers, Volume IV, Institution of Royal Engineers, Chatham

Barton, P. & Doyle, P. (in prep.), Over the Parapet. Panoramic Photographs of the Great War

Donnelly, Captain A. (1861), Photography and its Application to Military Purposes, Journal of the Royal United Service Institution, 5 (16), 2–18

Foulkes, Major-General C.H. (1957), The Photo-reconnaissance Section RE, Royal Engineers Journal, 71, 281–288.

Fuller, Colonel JFC (1925), The Principles of Defensive Warfare, Royal Engineers Journal

Ironside, Major-General Sir Edmund (1927), Fortification in War, Royal Engineers Journal

King, C.J.S. (1935), Engineer Intelligence from Photographs, Royal Engineers Journal, 208–213

Stotherd R.H. (1867), Description of an Application of Photography to Surveying Purposes called 'La Planchette Photographique' in the Paris Exhibition of 1867, Paper VI, 128–130

Manuals

Manual of Field Works, 1925, HMSO, London

British Trench Warfare 1917–1918, A Reference Manual, IWM/Battery Press

Trench Fortifications 1914–1918, A Reference Manual, IWM/Battery Press

Field Fortification: Notes for Labour Battalions (author J. E. Edmonds), HMSO, 1915

Notes on the Interpretation of Air Photographs, The War Office, 1924

Work of the RE in the European War 1914–1919, Institution of Royal Engineers, Chatham, 1926:

Geological Work on the Western Front

Military Mining

Miscellaneous

Supply of Engineer Stores and Equipment

Work under the Director of Works (France)

Experimental Section

Water Supply

Diaries and Memoirs

Bashford, W. H., *A War Remembered*, (Unpublished memoir) REL

Bond, Major R. L., *The 23rd (Field) Company RE in the Great War 1914-1918*, REJ, 1929

Godfrey, J. T. G., Diary and Memoir, REM

Mulqueen

Ridsdale, Lieutenant Harold, RE, 76 Field Company

Roach, Matthew, Diary, REL, 9403.16

Smith, Lance-Corporal G. J., RE, 95 Field Company

Papers

Anon., *Memorandum on Advanced Water Supplies*, Third Army, March 1917

Botte, Capitaine R., *The Evolution of Field Fortification during the late War,* Revue Militaire, June 1921

Dobbie, Colonel W. G. S., *The Operations of the 1st Division on the Belgian Coast in 1917,* REJ, June 1924

Dunlop, Captain D., *Defence against Gas,* REJ, June 1930

Everett, Major M., *Sapper Officers in War,* REJ, March 1931

Fuller, Colonel J. F. C., *The Introduction of Mechanical Warfare on Land and Its Possibilities in the Near Future,* REJ, November 1920

Fuller, Colonel J. F. C., *The Principles of Defensive Warfare,* REJ, June 1925

Fuller, Brigadier J. F. C., *The Problem of the Last 800 Yards,* REJ, June 1930

Guggisberg, Major F. G., *Suggestions for carrying out Field Company Schemes,* REJ, October 1915

Hertzberg, Major H. F. H., *The Reorganization of the Engineering Troops of a Canadian Division – Great War 1914-1918,* REJ, December 1924

Holbrook, Major A. W., *Engineers or Pioneers?* REJ, September 1931

Ironside, Major-General Sir Edmund, *Fortification in War,* REJ, March 1928

Normand, Colonel J., *The Evolution of the French Defensive Doctrine,* REJ, December 1921

Perrott, W. G., *Drainage of a Section of the Trench Area: France, 1915-16,* REJ, December 1933

Pressey, Major H. A. S., *Notes on Trench War,* REJ, June 1919

Tatham, Captain H., *Tunnelling in the Sand Dunes of the Belgian Coast,* REJ, December 1923

Wood, Major W. L., *Earthworks,* REJ, June 1930

C de L G., *Concealment in Field Works,* REJ, October 1918

Wilson, Lieutenant-Colonel B. T., *Studies of German Defences near Lille,* Royal Engineers, Chatham, 1919

FURTHER READING

Prologue

The opening campaigns of the First World War and the development of the Western Front are dealt with in many works (e.g. Falls 1960; Gray 1990; Brown 1993), and in detail in the British Official Histories, written by Sir James Edmonds during 1923-48. Other books providing detail and colour, particularly of the development of key areas, include: Bulletin Belges des Sciences Militaires (1928) for operations on the Coast; Anon. (1920) and Brice (1925) for the Salient; Middlebrook and Middlebrook (1994) for the Somme; and the various Michelin guides produced after the war (Michelin 1920-21). The geography and geology of the Western battlefields is discussed by Johnson (1921), Chasseaud (1991, 1999) and Doyle (1998).

The peculiarities of trench warfare and its operation, so clearly illustrated in the panoramas, are the subject of many works. Manuals and treatises written by contemporaries are particularly useful, and include: Anon. (1871-1925), Anon. (1922), Anon. (1924), Harrison (1905, 1925), Proceedings of the Royal Engineer Committee (1914-18), Fuller (1925) and Ironside (1927). More recent works on trench fortification include: Brown (1993), Brice (1999) and Griffith (2004). Ashworth (1980), Winter (1978), Terraine (1982), Brown (1980, 1993), Ashworth (2000) and Holmes (2004) describe in some detail the aspects of life of the soldier 'in the trenches'. The peculiarities of trench combat, tactics and strategy are discussed in excellent detail by Griffith (1996, 2004); for the underground war, see Barrie (2001) and Barton et al. (2004).

The history of the camera at war is discussed in Lewinski (1978) and Frizot (1998). Interesting insights into the development of thought on the subject are provided by Donnelly (1861) and Foulkes (1957), and of the role of the Royal Engineers in the new science by Royal Engineers (1854), Porter (1951a, b) and Watson (1951), and, in general, by Smithers (1991). Jane

Carmichael's (1989) book reviews the role and activities of private and official photographers and cinematographers in the First World War.

The development of the panorama format is described by Hyde (1988), and its use in the First World War, by Barton and Doyle (in prep.). The application of panoramic photographs and sketches in reconnaissance during the First World War has not been the subject of much recent work, but is reviewed in various contemporary texts and manuals, for example: Anon. (1921), Close and Winterbotham (1925); and among older treatises, such as those of Stotherd (1867), Reed (1888) and Flemer (1906). Descriptions of the cameras available are given by Channing and Dunn (1996). Reviews of survey by the Royal Engineers on the Western Front are given by: Anon. (1924), Anon. (1952), King (1935) and Chasseaud (1999). Interesting insights are provided by the work of participants, such as Crawford (1955) and Foulkes (1957).

Chapter One

Adequate accounts of the opening campaigns on the Flemish Coast are given in the Bulletin Belges des Sciences Militaires (1928), and in one-volume histories, such as that of Falls (1960). A detailed account of the town of Nieuport during the First World War is given in Thys (1922). Edmonds' Official History for 1914 provides much information on the opening campaigns.

Chapter Two

The Development of the Ypres Salient is dealt with in the relevant volumes of the Official History, as well as one-volume accounts of the war (e.g. Falls 1960). Chasseaud (1991) provides an invaluable atlas of the trench maps of the lines that composed the arc of the Salient. Contemporary or near contemporary guides to Ypres give much detail, including Anon. (1920), Michelin (1920) and Brice (1925). Farrar-Hockley (1967) is an interesting account of the First Battle of Ypres, with Macdonald (1993) providing information on the development of the Salient in 1915.

The facsimile editions of 'The Wipers Times' gives a flavour of contemporary 'Eepree' (Anon. 1930), while Congreve (1982) provides an important account of activities from one who was there. The 'mining sector' is discussed in detail by Barton et al. (2004). The Battle of Messines Ridge is described in detail by Passingham (1998) and Barton et al. (2004).

Chapter Three

The Third Battle of Ypres has attracted a large body of literature, both from participants, and from historians. The Official History remains a primary source, but other important accounts, with widely differing interpretations of the battle, include: Wolfe (1969), Warner (1987), Macdonald (1992), McCarthy (1995), Prior and Wilson (1996), Liddle (1997) and Steel and Hart (2000). Edmonds (1929), Wade (1936), Behrent (1963) and Gladden (1967) provide very useful published accounts from participants.

Chapter Four

This sector is largely neglected in contemporary literature, although the Official History provides a valuable reference source. Other information is given in Macdonald (1915), amongst other popular accounts. Important, and rightly celebrated, accounts by participants include those of Blunden (1930), Graves (1930), Sassoon (1930) and Dunn (2001). The Christmas truce of 1914 is described in excellent detail by Brown and Seaton (1984), as well as by Bruce Bairnsfather (1916), who was a participant.

Chapter Five

Despite its importance the Battle of Loos, like the other 'forgotten' sectors of the Western Front, has received scant attention. Apart from the detail given in the Official History, the only other accounts include those of Warner (1976) and Macdonald (1993). Important contemporary accounts by participants include those of MacGill (1916), Feilding (1929) and Graves (1930).

Chapter Six

Besides the relevant volumes of the Official History, the Arras and Vimy sectors have been examined in the books by Macksey (1976), Nicholls (1990), McKee (1966) and Girardet et al. (2003). The immediate post-war guide published by the Michelin Company (Michelin 1920) provides useful information.

Chapter Seven

Like Third Ypres, the Somme has received much attention, from the end of the 1916 battle through to the present day. Masefield (1917) gives an important pen-picture of the battlefield at the close of the 1916 campaigns. Detailed descriptions of the front and battlefields are given by Gliddon (1994), and Middlebrook and Middlebrook (1994), and in the immediate post-war guide by the Michelin Company (Michelin 1920). The day-by-day progress of the 1916 battles has been plotted by McCarthy (1995). The conduct of the 1916 battles are discussed, with varying degrees of criticism, in the following: Gardner (1961), Middlebrook (1978), Norman (1984), Charlton (1986), Macdonald (1993), Brown (1996) and Sheffield (2003). Accounts by participants include: Mark VII (1927), Edmonds (1929), Feilding (1929), Dunn (2001), Sassoon (1932), Carrington (1965) and Terraine [ed.] (2000). For strategy and tactics see Griffith (1994).

Chapter Eight

Cambrai has received some attention from analysts of tank warfare, with an early account being that of Mitchell (1933). Cooper (1967) remains an important study, as does Moorhouse (2003). Coppard (1988) is an excellent account by a participant. Fine detail of the tanks' contribution at Cambrai in 1917 can be found in Gibot and Gorczynski (1999). The actions of 1918 are examined in the Official History, Brown (1998) and Pitt (1962).

ACKNOWLEDGMENTS

My thanks must first go to Professor Peter Doyle, who was to have co-authored this book but due to unavoidable professional commitments was sadly unable to devote the considerable time to the project that I know he had wished. His contributions to the panorama selection, planning of the book's structure and initial first tranche of writing were invaluable in forging a framework for later drafts.

Apart from the photographers themselves, the greatest credit is due to those who have conserved the panoramas for over eighty years. The fact that the pictures survive at all as a collection, and are preserved in a condition to allow digitization is entirely due to the diligence of the staff of the Imperial War Museum down the decades since 1918. To try to lighten the very heavy digitization load for the museum's darkroom staff and meet publication deadlines, some images which appear on the CD-Roms were sourced and scanned from my own panorama assortment, other archives and several private individuals; all, however, exist in the IWM collection. My thanks therefore go to the Royal Engineers Museum and Library who offered a considerable number, and to Jon Bell, Dr Peter Chasseaud, Nick Cornwall, Peter Fielding, Graham Hall, John Maw, Stephen Spaven and Johan Vandewalle. I apologise to those who so kindly offered their images, but discovered there was no space left for inclusion.

At the Imperial War Museum:
My thanks to Bridget Kinally, once Keeper of Photographs at the IWM and now Head of Visual Resources at the Wellcome Library, whose enthusiasm kick-started the project in 1997; to Jane Carmichael (former Director of Collections at the IWM and now occupying that position with the National Museums of Scotland) for clearing copyright and reproduction routes; to Hilary Roberts, who uncovered and delivered the photographs from several points of storage at IWM Duxford, and has consistently offered invaluable professional advice and assistance throughout the project as well as clearing a desk in her office for me to catalogue the collection. Thanks also to David Parry for his warm welcomes, countless answers to queries, and patient searches, and to his curatorial colleagues Ian Carter, Emma Crocker, John Delaney (now at Duxford) and Alan Wakefield. In the bowels of All Saints, where the complex and time-consuming copying work took place, I am more than grateful to Jeremy Richards, Manager of the Photographic Unit (I still prefer the ominous Head of Dark Rooms), who, under huge pressure, shuttled so many deadlines to complete the digitization; to David Wood (now with the National Gallery) whose many early scanning and digitizing tests proved so inspiring; Glyn Biesty, the Archive Co-ordinator, for co-ordinating, John Hunnex for the negative selection, and Matthew Gonzalez for carrying out the bulk of the digitization. And to Rose Gerrard for endlessly (and generally fruitlessly) searching IWM central files for information about the origins and history of the collection and its photographers.

To Nigel Steel, Head of Research and Information, for encouragement, advice and the extraordinary encyclopaedic knowledge which he is always so willing to share, and his colleague Terry Charman for courageously reading a seriously uncorrected proof. And finally to Peter Hart for his infectious – and quite unavoidable – enthusiasm.

At the Royal Engineers, Chatham:
In the magnificent RE Museum, the very building where so many Sapper photographers carried out their training, my gratitude goes to curator Rebecca Cheney for opening every possible door to facilitate research, and granting permission to use quotes, panoramas and photographs, and to her staff Craig Bowen and Beverley Williams for supplying a stream of documents, copies, e-mails and scans. In the treasure trove of the RE Library, curator Maggie Lindsay Roxburgh came up with so much of the historical background data, revealed astounding unique photographic material which I never could have imagined existed at all, and arranged permissions for copying and reproduction. Thanks too to her staff Karen Harvey and Roni Schnable.

To John Slater and Roger Crosby of Slater Crosby in the Chatham Dockyard for assisting so efficiently and swiftly with the stitching of digitized images; to Bill Smuts for his excellent maps – a tough assignment; and to the book's designer Les Dominey and his wife Jane for their hospitality.

I am very grateful to Marc Dewilde, Mathieu de Meyer and Pedro Pype of the Belgian Institute of Archaeology for allowing us to follow every inch of their superlative and standard-setting Crossroads Farm excavations, and for granting permission to use images from the digs.

On the technical side my gratitude goes to CD designer Paul Peppiate of VTR North in Leeds, who has been unceasingly supportive throughout the many years of the project's gestation, to Nick Andrews the macromedia coder, and especially to Matthew Robson of Liquid Studios, whose onerous task it was to develop the CD-Roms. Once or twice I very nearly believed I understood what he was talking about. Once, I think. But perhaps not.

My thanks also go to Professor Richard Holmes for his foreword, to Laurence Martin for permission to quote from his grandfather Albert's diaries, to Colonel James Aldous OBE for the words of his father, J.R.T. Aldous, to PFD on behalf of the Estate of Mrs Claire Blunden for permission to reproduce the extract from *Undertones of War* by Edmund Blunden, and to Spellmount Publishers for the extracts from *War Letters to A Wife* by Rowland Feilding; to Richard Van Emden and Jeremy Banning for the marvellous friendship, advice and support which helped me so much, especially in the latter few months of work; to the Clinch family of Syndale Farm, Ospringe; to Bex and Tom; and finally to Pete Duncan of Constable & Robinson for saddle-soaping the commissioning editor's whip before wielding it – frequently.

PICTURE CREDITS

THE PANORAMAS
All the panoramas listed below copyright © **Imperial War Museum**. Army provenance numbers are not included in this list.

Note that some panoramas cover extensive swathes of territory spanning more than one sector: in these cases the panorama number is repeated under each relevant sector. An asterisk * indicates a panorama taken from a location in the rear of the front line area, not appearing on the mapping. Panoramas appearing only on CDROM are indicated in *italic* in the main text.

Chapter One: The War Begins – Early Battles and the Belgian Coast/CDROM 1

(see page 66: Aisne Valley general map)
2 Aisne Valley 15 September 1914: on CDROM only
15 Aisne Valley 23 September 1914: pages 64-5
A2D Aisne Valley (drawn) 21 September 1914: page 67
A1D Aisne Valley (drawn) 29 September 1914: on CDROM only

(see page 75: Belgian Coast general map)
3 Nieuport (gunpits)*: pages 80-81
32 Nieuport-Bains, 10 February 1915: on CDROM only
38A Nieuport, 18 February 1915: pages 68-9
39 Nieuport-Bains, 18 February 1915: page 69
63 Nieuport, 20 May 1915: pages 74-5
72 Nieuport, 5 June 1915: pages 70-71, 72-3
87 Nieuport-Bains, 22 July 1917: pages 78-9
94 Nieuport, 22 September 1917: pages 76-7
538 Nieuport, June 1917 NOM: page 80
G1 From Lombartzyde, 1916: pages 60-61, 78

Chapter Two: The Salient – First and Second Ypres, and Messines Ridge/CDROM 1

(see page 86: Ypres Salient and Messines Ridge general map)
62 From Kemmel, 29 April 1915: pages 144-5
106 From Kemmel, 24 March 1917: on CDROM only
153 Bailleul area, 4 August 1918: on CDROM only
160 Hondeghem area, 6 August 1918: pages 158-9
165 Locre area, 10 August 1918: on CDROM only
170 Rear of Kemmel Hill, 15 August 1918: pages 160-61
172 Dickebusch area, 18 August 1918: pages 188-9
173 From Kemmel, 15 September 1918: on CDROM only
G-11 From Zandvoorde, 1916: on CDROM only

(see page 92: Pilckem sector map)
4 Crossroads Farm, La Brique, June 1915: page 100
7 Garden Villa, Wieltje, 10 July 1915: pages 98-9, 164-5
8 Turco - Hampshire Farms, Pilckem, 13 July 1915: pages 94-5
10 South Zwaanhof to Glimpse Cottage, Canal Bank, 29 July 1915: pages 92-3
58 From Gravenstafel, 17 April 1915: page 90
96 Lancashire to Hampshire Farms, 9 November 1916: on CDROM only
102A From Hasler House, St Jean, 1 March 1917: pages 104-5
G-2 From Passchendaele Brewery (left half), April 1915: pages 82, 84-5, 91
G-3 From Passchendaele Brewery (right half), April 1915: on CDROM only

(see page 106: Frezenberg sector map)
6 From The Pagoda, Potizje 10 November 1915: pages 106-7
7 Garden Villa, Wieltje, 10 July 1915: pages 98-9, 164-5
37 Hussar and Dragoon Farms, 11 November 1915: on CDROM only
38 Hussar Farm, 11 November 1915: on CDROM only
101 From Potizje Chateau, 27 January 1917: pages 104-5
102A From Hasler House, St Jean, 1 March 1917: pages 104-5
G-4 Frezenberg, undated*: on CDROM only

(see page 108: Hooge, Railway Wood and Sanctuary Wood sector map)
1 From Railway Wood, June 1915: pages 108-9
2 From Y-Wood, 2 July 1915: pages 114-5
3 Railway Wood, 2 July 1915: on CDROM only
5 Hooge and Menin Road, 6 July 1915: pages 112-3
44 From Sanctuary Wood, Spring 1915*: page 118
70 From Hellfire Corner, 1 June 1915: pages 110-11
85 Bellewaerde Farm area, 10 September 1915: pages 116-7
87 Bellewaerde Farm area, 11 September 1915: pages 114-5
88 Railway Wood and Bellewaerde Ridge, 11 September 1915: on CDROM only
101 From Potizje Chateau, 27 January 1917: pages 104-5
G-5 From Hooge (left half), June 1916: on CDROM only
G-6 From Hooge (right half), June 1916: on CDROM only
G-7 From the Kurpromenade, November 1916: on CDROM only
G-8 Zouave Wood, undated: pages 118-9

(see page 119: Observatory Ridge sector map)
68 From Observatory Ridge to Hill 60, May 1915: pages 124-5
82 Armagh Wood to Hill 60, 14 August 1915: on CDROM only

(see page 125: Hill 60 sector map)
55 Hill 60 from The Dump, 10 April 1915: pages 126-7
55A Hill 60 from The Dump, 10 April 1915: on CDROM only
G-9 From N.E. of Hill 60, July 1915: pages 122-3
G-10 From Hill 60, July 1915: on CDROM only

(see page 133: Bluff sector map)
41 From The Bluff, 23 February 1915: pages 138-9
48 From White Horse Cellars (St Eloi), 11 March 1915: on CDROM only
67 From International Trench, 26 May 1915: on CDROM only
69 White Chateau and Canal, 26 May 1915: page 132
114 From Beef Street, 25 January 1917: pages 136-7
128 From The Bluff Craters, Spring 1917: pages 134-5

(see page 141: St Eloi sector map)
42 St Eloi Village, February 1915: on CDROM only
48 St Eloi (White Horse Cellars), 11 March 1915: on CDROM only
94A St Eloi craters, 23 September 1916: pages 142-3
108 St Eloi to Wytschaete, 10 April 1917: on CDROM only

(see page 144: Messines Ridge general map)
19 Messines Village, 13 December 1914: pages 86-7
51 From Voormezeele to Wytschaete, 20 March 1915: pages 140-41
61 Wytschaete Village area, 18 April 1915: on CDROM only
56 South end of Messines Ridge from Fletcher's Field, April 1915: on CDROM only
98 Messines Ridge from Vierstraat, 17 November 1916: on CDROM only
107 Spanbroekmolen to Messines, 24 March 1917: pages 148-9
115 From Oostaverne, 14 June 1917: on CDROM only
117 From Goudezeune Farm, 7 July 1917: on CDROM only
120 From Hollebeke, 17 July 1917: on CDROM only
121 From Wytschaete Mill, 17 July 1917: on CDROM only

(see page 153: Messines Ridge South, St Yves and Ploegsteert sector map)
22 From La Hutte Chateau, 10 January 1915: page 152
28 Messines Village, 3 February 1915: on CDROM only
76 From St Yves, 19 July 1916: on CDROM only
78 From St Yves, 24 July 1916: on CDROM only
81 From St Yves, 2 August 1916: page 156
84 From Laurence Farm, Le Gheer 8 August 1916: on CDROM only
85 The Birdcage, Le Gheer 8 August 1916: on CDROM only

Chapter Three: Third Ypres/CDROM 1

(see page 165: Third Ypres general map)
58 From Gravenstafel, 17 April 1915: page 90
101 From Polygon Butte, undated: pages 178-9
102 Polderhoek area, undated: page 185
110 Cannabis Trench, St Julien, undated: pages 172-3
111 (5 Army) From Colonel's Farm, Pilckem, undated: pages 173-6
111A Morteldje Estaminet area, 2 June 1917: page 167
112 (5 Army) Pilckem Ridge area, 2 June 1917: on CDROM only
112 Houthulst Forest to Passchendaele, undated: page 183
115 From Wieltje, 3 June 1917: page 164
117 Pommern Castle towards Passchendaele Ridge, undated: on CDROM only
125 The Zonnebeke battlefield, undated: page 179
126 The Gheluvelt Plateau, undated: pages 162-3
127 Zonnebeke battlefield after capture, undated: page 184
128 From Winchester Farm, 22 October 1917: pages 180-81
129 From Clapham Junction, October 1917: on CDROM only
130 From Broodseinde Ridge, early 1918: pages 180-81
130 1918 Battlefield from near Cheddar Villa, 28 May 1918: on CDROM only
131 From Primus Dugout, Passchendaele ridge, early 1918: page 188
G-2 From Passchendaele Brewery (left section), April 1915: pages 82, 84-5, 91

G-3 From Passchendaele Brewery (right section), April 1915: on CDROM only

Chapter Four: The Forgotten Front – Armentières to Givenchy-les-La Bassée/CDROM 1

(see page 194: Armentières sector map)
11A From Bois Grenier, 10 April 1915*: on CDROM only
14 Wez Macquart from Chard's Farm, May 1915: on CDROM only
25 Frelinghien from Houplines, 29 January 1915: on CDROM only
26 Wez Macquart from Chimney Farm, 29 January 1915: pages 202-3
33 Le Touquet, 11 February 1915: pages 195, 207
34 From Houplines, June 1915: on CDROM only
47 Wez Macquart from BFL, 10 March 1915: pages 198-9
51A From Armentières rooftops, March 1915: on CDROM only
56 Frelinghien from Le Touquet, 15 March 1915: pages 208-9
90 Estaires (rear area), summer 1916: pages 352-3
107 Le Touquet village, 28 December 1915: on CDROM only
110 From Armentières rooftops, 2 May 1917: pages 196-7
153 Bailleul (1918 actions), 4 August 1918*: on CDROM only
G-12 From Frelinghien towards Houplines and Armentières, 26 April 1916: pages 192-3
G-13 From Frelinghien: Chicken Run mines, 28 April 1916: on CDROM only

(see page 212: Neuve Chapelle sector map)
94A Neuve Chapelle, 21 October 1916: pages 212-3
98 Neuve Chapelle from La Quinque Rue, 10 November 1916: pages 218-9
130 Neuve Chapelle, 17 August 1917: on CDROM only

(see page 214: Aubers sector map)
9B Aubers Birdcage, 9 April 1915: on CDROM only
27 Birdcage (rear area), 28 August 1915: pages 204-5
112A Aubers, 26 April 1917: on CDROM only
121 Aubers, 5 June 1917: pages 190-91, 214-5

(see page 216: Festubert sector map)
28 Richebourg L'Avoué, 19 September 1915: on CDROM only
97 Festubert from White Hart, 9 November 1916: on CDROM only
98 La Quinque Rue from Leicester Lounge, 10 November 1916: pages 218-9
99 Boar's Head Salient, 16 November 1916: on CDROM only

(see page 220: Givenchy sector map)
16 La Quinque Rue, 4 May 1915: pages 218-9
21 Givenchy, 12 July 1915: pages 216-7
40 From the La Bassée Canal bank (south), 9 February 1915: on CDROM only
74 From Givenchy village, 14 May 1916: pages 220-21
103 From the Spoil Bank, 1 March 1917: on CDROM only
104 From the Pont Fixe Distillery, 4 March 1917: on CDROM only

(see page 223: Fromelles sector map)
14 Fromelles from railway station, 22 April 1915: pages 222-3
15 Fromelles, 22 April 1915: on CDROM only
79 Fromelles reserve lines, 29 July 1916: pages 226-7
86 Fromelles from Rue Tilleloy, 22 August 1916: pages 224-5
112 Fromelles (rear area), 19 May 1917: on CDROM only

Chapter Five: Coalfields and Crassiers – The Gohelle Battlefields/CDROM 2

(see page 238: Cuinchy-Cambrin sector map)
40 From the La Bassée canal bank, 9 February 1915: on CDROM only
42 From Braddell Castle, Cambrin, 17 June 1916: on CDROM only
60 From Hun Vue in Cuinchy village, 24 April 1916: on CDROM only
61 The Brickstacks from Cuinchy, 23 April 1916: pages 238-9
A Close up panorama of Cuinchy craters, undated: page 240

(see page 244: Hohenzollern–Hulluch sector map)
52 Hohenzollern and Fosse 8, 7 April 1916: pages 234-5, 245
108 Cité St Elie, 24 March 1917: pages 232-3, 248-9eeeeEE
115 Hulluch to the Chalk Pit, 3 May 1917*: pages 236-7
117 Hulluch craters, 14 May 1917: pages 234-5

(see page 252: Loos and Lens sector map)
12 From Cité St Pierre church, July 1916: pages 262-3
48 From the Double Crassier, 26 March 1916: pages 252-3, 256
96 Tower Bridge area, Loos, 30 September 1915: pages 228-9, 253
97 Loos and Tower Bridge, 30 September 1915: on CDROM only
101 Hill 70 15 November 1915: pages 250-1
125 Loos and Hill 70 from Fosse 11, 5 July 1917: pages 254-5
137 Lens to Avion, September 1917*: page 251
145 From the Double Crassier, 5 August 1916: page 261
Panorama W from the Double Crassier, undated: on CDROM only

(see page 262: Calonne sector map)
119 Cité des Cornailles from Pit Prop Corner, Liévin, 1916: on CDROM only
120 Lens to Vimy Ridge, 1916: pages 2-3, 257-60

Chapter Six: Vimy Ridge and Arras/CDROM 2

(see page 266: Vimy–Arras general map)
84 Hulluch to Vimy Ridge from Notre-Dame de Lorette, 13 August 1916: on CDROM only
85 From Notre-Dame de Lorette, 26 June 1917: page 230
109 The Douai Plain from Thélus Hill, 10 April 1917: pages 274-5
111 Fresnoy to Biache St Vaast, 22 April 1917: on CDROM only
118 Oppy to Fresnes (Gavrelle under shellfire), April 1917: on CDROM only
124 Fosse 14 to Douai from Hill 145, 22 April 1917: on CDROM only
136 Vimy Ridge from Notre-Dame de Lorette, 12 October 1917: on CDROM only
142 Bailleul to Gavrelle, April 1917: on CDROM only
146 Givenchy (en Gohelle) to Vimy Ridge north, 5 August 1916: on CDROM only
526 Vimy Ridge to Beaurains, 21 May 1916: pages 266-7
558 Oppy to Roeux, 9 May 1917: pages 282-3

(see page 270: Vimy Ridge Central sector map)
511 From The Pulpit, Neuville St Vaast, 2 April 1916: page 271

(see page 272: Vimy Ridge South sector map)
519 The Thélus battlefield, 24 April 1917: on CDROM only

(see page 273: Arras Town sector map)
1 From Arras Cemetery, undated: pages 6, 278-9
504 From Arras rooftops looking north-east to east, 26 March 1916: on CDROM only
505 From Arras rooftops looking east to south, 1 May 1916: page 272
507 From Arras rooftops looking north to east, 29 March 1916: on CDROM only
535 From Arras rooftops looking east to south, July 1916: pages 264-5

(see page 281: Arras battlefield map)
140 Battery Valley, April 1917: pages 280-81
149 Telegraph Hill to Mercatel from Beaurains, April 1917: on CDROM only
556 Monchy-Le-Preux area, 6 May 1917: on CDROM only
557 Roeux battlefield, 7 May 1917: on CDROM only
560 Arleux to Roeux, 11 May 1917: page 278
576B Tilloy-Les-Mofflaines to Wancourt from Beaurains, undated: on CDROM only
595 Adinfer Wood sector, 5 June 1918*: on CDROM only

Chapter Seven: The Somme/CDROM 2

(see page 290: Somme general map)
17 La Boisselle to Fricourt from reserve lines, 19 September 1915: on CDROM only
22 Thiepval to Méaulte from west of Aveluy, 9 October 1915: on CDROM only
27 La Bisselle to Delville Wood from reserve lines, 26 October 1915: on CDROM only
30 Ovillers to Montauban from Arbre Tréfle, 27 October 1915: on CDROM only
62 Martinpuich village, 1 August 1916: on CDROM only
63 Ginchy and Guillemont, 15 August 1916: on CDROM only
63 (Reserve Army) Courcellette to Martinpuich, 11 September 1916: on CDROM only
64 Guillemont, 15 August 1916: on CDROM only
66 (fragment) Warlencourt to Flers, 22 September 1916: on CDROM only
300 Courcellette, 21 September 1916: pages 336-7
301-302 Courcellette to Guedecourt, 5 October 1916: pages 338-9
303 Serre to Miraumont from near Thiepval, 7 October 1916: on CDROM only
304 From Stuff Redoubt, 16 October 1916: pages 306-7
HW1 High Wood panorama, undated: page 334

(see page 302: Gommecourt sector map)
518 The Gommecourt 'Z's', 1 June 1916: pages 293-6
525 Gommecourt Wood and Park, 20 May 1916: on CDROM only
529 Gommecourt village to Serre, 1 June 1916: pages 302-3

(see page 305: Serre sector map)
61 The Serre battlefield from Bucquoy to Observation Wood, 17 May 1916: on CDROM only
521 The Serre battlefield from The Palace, Hebuterne, 6 May 1916: pages 286-7, 304-5
589 Serre to Thiepval, 29 May 1918: on CDROM only

(see page 309: Beaumont-Hamel sector map)
3 Y-Ravine area, 4 August 1915: pages 288-9
4 Beaumont-Hamel and the Sunken Lane from Hawthorn Ridge, 5 August 1915: pages 310-11
60 The Redan Ridge and Beaumont-Hamel from north of Auchonvillers, 17 May 1916: on CDROM only

(see page 314: Thiepval sector map)
2 Achiet to Thiepval from support lines near Hamel, 28 July 1915: on CDROM only
59 Beaumont-Hamel to Thiepval from Charles Avenue, 16 May 1916: page 315
62 The Leipzig Salient and Thiepval, 22 August 1916: pages 318-9
305 From the north face of the Schwaben Redoubt, 24 December 1916: on CDROM only

(see page 321: La Boisselle sector map)
1 Mash Valley, 3 July 1916: pages 324-5
12 La Boisselle and Ovillers, 24 August 1915: pages 320-1

(see page 326: Fricourt and Mametz sector map)
13 Becourt: Montauban from The Pavilion, 24 August 1915: on CDROM only
18 Fricourt village from opposite The Aeroplane Trench, 22 September 1915: pages 328-9
18D Drawn panorama Fricourt village, September 1916: on CDROM only
19 From the Tambour towards Fricourt and Mametz, 22 September 1915: pages 328-9
25 Fricourt, Mametz, Mansel Copse, 22 October 1915: pages 330-1
26 Mansel Copse to Montauban, 22 October 1915: on CDROM only
33 Fricourt area from the front lines to the south-east, 15 April 1916: pages 326-7
33D Drawn panorama of Fricourt area from the south-east, 2 November 1915: pages 326-7

(see page 332: Southern Somme sector map)
20D Drawn panorama from Contalmaison to Leuze Wood, undated: on CDROM only
28 Montauban to Curlu from trench facing Montauban Brickyard, 26 October 1915: pages 332-3
28D Drawn version of panorama 28, Montauban to Curlu, 28 December 1915: pages 332-3

Chapter Eight: Armour and Armistice – Cambrai and 1918/ CDROM 2

(see page 344: Cambrai general map)
79 Bourlon Wood to Gonnelieu, 6 May 1917: on CDROM only
148 Villers Bretonneux area, 10 June 1918*: on CDROM only
167 Approaches to Cambrai city, September 1918: page 351
168 Sancourt to Seranvillers, Cambrai area, September 1918: pages 360-1
307 Havrincourt Park, 28 April 1917: pages 340-41
308 Havrincourt to Flésquières, 28 April 1917: pages 344-5
309 Bourlon Wood to Havrincourt, 29 April 1917: pages 348-9
565 St Quentin sector, 9 July 1917*: pages 342-3

SUPPLEMENTARY IMAGES

Courtesy of Barbara Woodward: 128 top. **Courtesy of J.L. Gloriant**: 244. **Courtesy of Mrs Patience Hilton**: 140 top. **Courtesy of the Cassels Family**: 112 left. **Hertfordshire Archives and Local Studies**: 109 bottom right. **Imperial War Museum**: 5 (Q56731), 12–13 (CO3393), 14–15 (CO2192), 18–19, 21 (Q96060), 22 (Q57170), 23 (Q57319), 26 (Q50467), 27 (CO149), 29 (Q5788), 30 (Q50726), 33 top (Q582), 33 bottom (Q10283), 35 top (Q49221), 36 bottom left (Q4600), 36 bottom far left (Q4853), 37 top (Q663), 37 bottom (HU87956), 39 bottom left (Q51574), 39 bottom right (Q8447), 40 top (Q87301), 40 bottom (E[Aus]1120), 41 bottom left (Q8452), 42 top (E[Aus]4632), 43 top right (Q95957), 43 bottom left (Q43470), 44 top (Q600), 44 bottom left (Q55536), 44 bottom right (Q56988), 45 bottom (Q95960), 51 top left (Q31117), 54 bottom (Q3205), 56, 57 bottom (E[Aus]1278), 58 top (CO2246), 58 bottom (E[Aus]1220), 59 (Q777), 62 (Q 10896), 63 top (Q49220), 63 bottom (Q60708), 65 top (Q57222), 66, 69 middle (Q57068), 70 bottom (Q57068.), 71 bottom (Q49170), 77 right (Q2877), 79 bottom, 80 middle, 81 middle (E[Aus] 4631), 84 top (Q55578(8)), 87 top (Q60737), 88 bottom (Q49355), 91 bottom left (Q55560), 91 bottom right (Q10965), 92 bottom (Q56927), 94 bottom (Q3963), 96 top (Q51650), 96 bottom (Q585), 97 bottom (Q668), 101 right, 107 top right (Q6422), 110 bottom, 112 top (Q49751), 114 top (Q55578), 117, 120 (HU72879), 121 (HU72880), 122 top (Q55578[57]), 125 top (Q44168), 127 bottom (Q45382), 132 top (Q56706), 136 bottom, 143 middle left (HU77886), 143 middle right (Q492), 143 bottom (HU77888), 146 bottom (HU87967), 147 top right (HU87962), 148 bottom (Q2295), 149 middle right (Q60693), 150–51 (Q2323), 152 top (Q56163), 154 bottom (Q56167), 157 left (Q23523), 157 right (HU87961), 158 top (Q9781), 160 bottom (Q510), 167 bottom (Q95959), 168 middle (Q11562), 168–9, 169 right (Q5773), 170–71 (CO2192), 171 bottom (Q5885), 178 right (CO2253), 180 middle (E[Aus]1129), 182, 183 bottom (Q11657), 186–7 (CO3881), 189 middle (Q100427), 189 right (Q100914), 196 top (Q634), 198 bottom (Q51568), 205 top (Q57072), 205 middle right (Q56173), 206 top (Q51528), 211 background (Q51626), 215 top (Q51551), 213 bottom (Q49213), 215 middle (Q10714), 217 bottom (Q90277), 221 top left (Q87300), 222 bottom (Q6474), 224 bottom (Q56180), 226 bottom (Q107717), 227 bottom (Q542), 231 top (Q49243), 236 bottom (CO1323), 237 bottom (Q11789), 241 top (Q49282), 246 top right (Q29002), 250 top (CO2030), 251 top inset (Q9956.), 255 middle left (CO3876), 263 top (Q9963), 267 top (Q49240), 268 top right, 268 middle (Q7091), 270 middle, 274 middle (CO1575), 274 top (CO1159), 275 top (CO1351), 276–7 (CO2979), 278 bottom left (Q7012), 279 top (Q3218), 279 middle (Q6456), 280 middle (Q2377), 280 bottom (Q3879), 284, 283 bottom, 285 (Q9782), 288 bottom (Q90927), 289 bottom (Q56803), 291 top left (Q90921), 291 bottom (E[Aus]2168), 292 (Q4196), 298 top (Q55066), 299 (HU87951), 300–1 top (HU87931), 303 top (Q734), 304 bottom (Q1441), 306 top (Q101795), 308 top (HU87950), 309 (Q796), 312 top right (Q754), 312 top left (Q752), 313 (Q750), 315 top left (HU87947), 315 top right (HU87949), 317 bottom (HU87939), 318–9 background (Q1142), 319 middle (Q1069), 319 right (Q1794), 322 top (Q4123), 323 bottom (Q3999), 324 top (Q67–69), 325 inset (Q54), 328 middle (Q89), 330 bottom (Q1396), 331 bottom right (Q4218), 331 bottom left (Q101780), 333 top (CO820), 335 bottom (Q1384), 336 top (E[Aus]998), 337 top (Q5576), 338 bottom (Q1565), 339 bottom left (E[Aus]3351), 339 bottom right (Q3874), 343 top (E[Aus]2106), 344 bottom (CO3392), 345 bottom (Q6424), 347 top (Q6315), 346 top (Q6337), 347 bottom (CO2984), 348 top (Q56826), 349 top (Q56823), 350 bottom left (Q51460), 350 right (Q23683), 351 bottom (Q6542), 352 top (Q6502), 354–5 (Q6527), 357 (E[Aus]3260), 358–9 (CO3393), 360 bottom (Q85285), 361 bottom (Q3353), 362 (Q7103). **Johan Vandewalle Archive**: 38, 42 bottom, 51 top right, 51 bottom, 53 top right, 77 middle, 85 top, 89 right, 90 top, 107 top left, 110 right, 111 middle, 116 top, 116 middle, 118 middle, 129, 146 top middle, 146 top right, 154 top right, 164 top, 188 middle, 233 top, 240 bottom. **National Museums and Galleries of Wales**: 241 bottom. **National Portrait Gallery**: 109 bottom left. **Parapet Archive Trust**: 20, 31, 32, 45 top, 54 top, 57 top, 98 bottom, 99 bottom, 100 bottom, 101 left, 102 top, 102 bottom, 103 top left, 103 top right, 103 bottom left, 103 bottom middle, 103 bottom right, 104 right, 113 top, 113 middle, 124 top, 137 bottom, 195 bottom, 197 left, 197 top right, 199 bottom left, 199 bottom right, 200 top, 200 bottom, 201 top, 201 bottom, 202 middle, 202 bottom, 203 middle left, 203 bottom left, 203 bottom, 204 top left, 204 top right, 205 middle left, 206 bottom, 242 top, 243, 271 bottom, 310 bottom, 316–7 top, 324 bottom, 356 bottom. **Royal Engineers Library**: 25, 28, 34, 35 bottom, 36 top, 39 top, 41 top, 41 bottom right, 43 top left, 43 bottom right, 46, 47 top, 47 bottom, 48 top left, 48 top right, 48 bottom, 49 top left, 49 top right, 49 bottom left, 49 bottom right, 50, 53 top left, 55 top, 55 bottom left, 55 bottom right, 68 bottom left, 69 right, 71 middle, 75 top, 76 middle, 76 bottom, 78 middle, 81 bottom, 88 top, 89 left, 97 top, 104 middle, 135, 147 top left, 154 top middle, 155 bottom left, 165 top, 166 top, 166 bottom, 177 bottom, 210, 211 middle, 242 bottom, 247, 255 middle, 256 top, 261 bottom, 266 top, 270 bottom, 273 bottom, 269, 281 right, 282 bottom, 291 top right, 287 top left, 287 top right, 298 bottom, 320 top, 335, 342 bottom left, 363. **Royal Engineers Museum**: 52, 145 top, 149 middle left, 207 bottom, 221 top right.

INDEX

Page numbers in *italics* refer to illustrations.

Abney, Lieutenant (later Captain Sir) William 47
Adams, Bernard 330
Advance to Victory 188, *188-189*, 226, 339, 356, *360*
Aeroplane Trench 328, *328-329*
Aisne, Battle of the 21, 53, 62-67, *64-65*, *66*, *67*, 74
Alberich 268
Albert *290*
Albert-Bapaume Road 320-323, *320*, *322*, 336, 338, *338-339*
Aldous, Lieutenant J. R. T., MC 159-160, 161, 189, 350, 352, 353, 356-357, 360
Allan, J. C. 322
Allenby, Sir Edmund 273, 279, 280, 282
American Civil War 47
American Expeditionary Force 356
Ancre, Battle of the 301, 343
Ancre Valley 56, 315, *319*
Annequin *255*
Antwerp 23, 67, 68
Arleux *282-283*
Armentières 87, 159, *192-193*, 193-207, *194*, *196-197*, 197-198
Armistice 360, 362
Arnold, Sergeant 201
Arras 30-31, *55*, 195, 215, 230, 266-269, *269*, *270*, 271-275, *272-273*, *276-277*, 278-283, *281*, *283*, 285, 343
  Cemetery *6*, *278-279*
artillerymen, Australian 58, *58*
Artois, First Battle of 29-30, *30-31*
Artois, Second and Third Battles of 230-231, 267
Ashurst, George 312
Asquith, Arthur 275
Asquith, Lieutenant Raymond 275, 337
Athies *284*
Aubers 192, 196, *210*, 216, 232, 300-301
Aubers Ridge 29, 87, 193, 210-211, *211*, 213-214
  Battle of 37, 214-215, *214-215*, 216
Auchy-les-Mines 29, 246-247
Australian troops *33*, *40*, *42*, *57*, 58, *58*, *180*, *291*, 356, *356-357*
Authuille *297*
Aveluy Wood *297*

Bailleul 33, 160, 274, 275, 352
Bairnsfather, Lieutenant Bruce 155-156, *155*, *156*
Balaklava Harbour *47*
balloons, observation *44*, *57*
Bapaume 56, *290*
Barker, Robert 52
Bashford, Private W. H. 222-223, 227
Battle of the Somme 333-334
Bayeux Tapestry 52
BBC television 32-33
Beaucourt Mill 316
Beaumont Hamel 301, *303*, 308-313, *309*, *310-311*, *312*, 315-316
  Newfoundland Memorial Park *288-289*, 308, 309
'Before Action' 247, 330
Belgian Army 68, *68*, 70, *70*, 74, 75, 78, 94, 188
Belgian civilians *62*, *154*, *164*, *352*
Belgian Government 84
Belgium 21
Bellewaerde 232
  Farm 111, *111*, 112, 116
  Ridge 108, 109, 110, *112-113*, 168
Béthune 226-227, 241
Birdcage, The ('The Kink') 153, 158
Bixschoote 90, 91
'Blucher' offensive 350
Bluff, The (Palingbeek) 88, 96, 122, *131*, 132-139, *133*, *134-135*, *136-137*, *138-139*
Blunden, Edmund 104, 241, 306, *306*
Boer War 23, 25, 34, 48-49
Boesinghe 97, *156*, *167*
Bois Grenier *40*, 195, 196, *198*, *204-205*, 351
Bois Quarante *143*
Bond, Major 44
Boundary Commissions 48
Bourlon Wood 346, 348, *348-349*
Bowes-Lyon, Captain Fergus 246
Brady, Matthew 47
Brandon, Ensign 46
Bricknell, Rifleman John *199*, 205-206, *206*
Brickstacks 30, 238-239, *238-239*, *240*
Brisco, Captain 134. 135
British Army 46-49 *see also* Royal Engineers, Corps of
  Army Printing and Stationery Service 57
  General Headquarters (GHQ) 21, 25, 26, 106, 114, 155, 158, 215, 217, 273, 315, 331, 339, 342, 343, 346
  Light Dragoons, 4th 46
  School of Military Engineering 47
British battlegrounds 30-31
British Expeditionary Force 21, 62, 64, 67, 84, 215, 237
  armies *31*
    First 95, 214, 215, 231, 236, 272-273, 275, 283
    Second 78, 146, 147, 148, 168, 177
    Third 267, 272, 273, 283, 289, 290, 297, 298, 344
    Fourth 268, 297, 298
    Fifth (formerly Reserve) *31*, 168, 177, 183, 268, 283, 304, 334
    New 298, 301
  Australian Tunnelling companies 77-78, *79*, *128*, 225
  brigades
    9th 110
    11th 96
    13th 273
    23rd and 25th 321
    57th 323
    70th 320-321
    76th 134
    92nd 360
    Australian 8th and 14th 226
    Canadian 3rd 94
    Cavalry, 5th 64
    Guards 66
    Indian Sirhind 221
    Infantry, 21st, HQ *63*
    Northumberland, 149th 95
    Rifle, 3rd *31*, 50, 98-106, *98*, *103*, 115-117, 196-198, 199, 200-201, *200*, 202, 203-206
    Rifle, 8th 115
    Rifle, 76th 112
    South African 336
  Camouflage Company 45
  corps
    I 85, 90, 214
    II 62, 177
    III 193
    IV 212, 214, 215
    VII 302
    VIII 311
    IX 147
    X 147, 183, 314, 318
    XI 225
    XIII 332-333
    XV 327
    Anzac 147, 157, 283
    Canadian *255*, 269, 273
    Indian 212, 213, 214, 215
    King's Royal Rifle, 7th 115
    Machine Gun 308
    Royal Engineers *see* Royal Engineers, Corps of
    Tank 342-343, 346, 349
  divisions
    1st 78, 79
    2nd 216, 275
    3rd 279, 304
    4th 283, 308, 311
    5th 123
    6th 113, 115
    7th 85, 90, 216, 233-236, 283, 327, *328*, 329
    8th *297*, 320
    9th (Scottish) 244-245, 278
    11th 336
    12th 278
    15th 278, 279
    16th (Irish) 147
    18th (Eastern) 316, 332-333
    21st 253, 327, 329
    24th 273
    28th 132-133
    29th 309
    30th 332-333
    31st 160, 303, 314
    32nd 78, 317
    34th 322, 349
    36th (Ulster) 147, *157*, 310, 314, 315, *315*, 316
    37th 279
    39th 316
    40th 348
    41st 138
    46th 302
    47th (Midland) 148, 246, 247
    48th (South Midlands) 308
    49th (West Riding) 314, 316, 348
    51st (Highland) 280-281, 313, *352*
    56th 302
    58th 283
    59th 349
    61st 224, 226
    62nd 283
    63rd (Royal Naval) 275, 282, 316
    66th 78
    Australian 147, 178, 179, 224, 283, 336
    Canadian 142, 184, 216, 275, 304, 306
    Guards 168, 250
    Indian 87, 95, 216
    Irish, 16th 337
    London, 47th 138, 139
    New Zealand 147
    Welsh 147
    West of England 147
  Honourable Artillery Company *88*, *120-121*, *143*
  Middlesex (Public Schools) Battalion, 16th *309*, 312, *313*
  'Pals' battalions 303, *304-305*, 333
  Pioneer Battalion 37
  regiments
    Argyll and Sutherland Highlanders *32*
    Bedfordshire 222-223, 227
    Black Watch, 8th 246
    Border 312, 317, *317-318*
    Buffs (Royal East Kent) 94
    Cameron Highlanders *32*, *213*
    Cameronians, 1st *206*
    Civil Service Rifles, 1: 211
    Coldstream Guards 192, 245, 253-254
    Devonshire 109-110, 329-330, *330-331*
    Dragoon Guards, 4th 62, 65
    Dublin Fusiliers 312
    Durham Light Infantry *221*, 338

East Lancashire 161, 222
Essex Yeomanry 279
Green Howards, 7th 329
Grenadiers, 4th 350
Hampshire *132*
Highland Light Infantry, 17th 317
Highlanders, 4/5: 169, 172, *183*
Hussars, 10th 279
Inniskillings, 1st 312
Irish Guards 254
King's Liverpool *160-161*, 333
King's Own Royal Lancaster *5*
King's Own Scottish Borderers 312
Lancashire Fusiliers 180-181, 227, *310-311*, 312
Lancers, 9th 62-64, 65, 66, 67
Leinster 140, 142
Lincoln 111
Liverpool Scottish 111, *112*
London, 1/13th 337
London Irish Rifles, 1/18th 254
London Scottish *87*, 153, 303
Manchester 221, *319*, 329
Middlesex, 1st *351*
Monmouthshire 123
Newfoundland, 1st 312
Northants Yeomanry 110, 279-280
Northumberland Fusiliers 110-111, *143*, 207
Princess Patricia's Canadian Light Infantry 109
Royal Artillery *224*
Royal Fusiliers 110-111, 312
Royal Garrison Artillery *268*
Royal Irish Rifles, 13th *315*
Royal Scots Fusiliers 110-111, 154
Royal Sussex 104, 306
Royal Warwickshire, 1st 155-156
Royal Welch Fusiliers *241*, 330
Scots Guards *22*, *64-65*
South Lancashire *20*, 136-137
South Wales Borderers 312
Staffordshire, 8th 330
Sussex, 7th 247
Tyneside Irish 323, *325*
West Yorkshire 109-110, 322, 323
Wiltshire, 1st 318, *318-9*
Worcester 110, 247
Special Works Park 45
British troops *63*, *112*, *351*
Broadmarsh Crater 267
Broodseinde Ridge 28, *90*, 179-183, *180-181*, *184*, 185
Brooke, Rupert 275
Brussels 68, 84
Bull Farm 112
Bullecourt 283, 343
Bully-Grenay 232
burials, battlefield *189*
Burland, Private Richard *48*
Butte de Warlencourt 338, *338-339*
Byng, General Sir Julian 344, 345, 346, 349
Byrne, Charlie 'Ginger' 308

Calonne *2-3*, *257-260*, *262*
Cambrai *12-13*, 273, 301, 357, *358-359*, *360-361*, *362*
Battles of 31, 342-351, *344-345*, *348-349*, *350-351*, *356*
Cambrin 241-242
camouflage, art of *44*, 45, *45*, *268*
Canadian Memorial 267
Canadian troops *12-13*, *27*, 58, *58*, 117, 132, *178*, 221, 250, *273*, *274*, 280
Canal de Furnes 70
Canal du Nord 346, 348, *349*
Cannabis Support Trench 172, *172-177*
Capper, Major-General T. 247
Carey, Lieutenant G. V. 115
Carnac battery 79, *80-81*
Carnoy 332-334, *332-333*, 336-339
carpenter, British *172*
Carrington, Charles 183
Casino Point mine 328, 333
Cassels, Lieutenant G. R. 112-113, *112*, 114, 116, 127
casualties *94*, *116*, *213*, *347*, *350*
Caterpillar, The 29, 122-124, *124-125*, 126-129, *126-127*, *130*, *131*
cavalry, Allied *63*, *279*, *280* *see also* horses
Chalk Pit Wood 254
Champagne offensive 231
Chapman, Guy 58-59, *59*, 290
Chard, Lieutenant John, VC RE 199
Chard's Farm 199, 202
Chateau Wood 58, *58*, 116
Chatham, Fort Pitt Hospital *48*
Chatham, Royal Engineers HQ, Museum and Library 47-48, *49*, *52-53*, 250
Chavasse, Noel Godfrey, VC and Bar MC 95, 111, 337
'Cheddar Villa' emplacement 188
Chemin des Dames 281, 353
Chimney Farm *202-203*
China (Opium) War, Third *48*
China Wall communication trench *104-105*, 119
'Chinese attack' 166-167, *166*, *167*
Chinese Labour Corps *39*
Christmas Truce, 1914: 155, 157, 198-201, *198-199*, *201*, 202
Churchill, Winston 154
cinematographers, Allied *333*, *361*
coal mines 29, 255-256, *255* *see also* slag heaps
Coburg Subway *269*
Cody, Colonel William *48*
Cogge (lock-keeper) 70
Collins, Private Thomas 221-222, *221*
Comines 67
Commonwealth troops 193 *see also* Australian troops; Canadian troops
communication cable, British *38*
communication centre, German artillery *110*
Congreve, Walter, VC 143
Congreve, Captain (later Major) William, VC DSO 111-112, 113, 142-143, *142*
Connery, Private John *48*
Coppard, George 347
Cordonnerie Farm *224*
Cotton, Private 67
Courcellette *333*, *336-337*, 338
Cousins, Private 64
Coutele 22
Cowan, Major S. H. 24, 126, 140, 152-153, 157
Crawford, Lieutenant O. G. S. 55-56, *55*
Crimean War 46-47, *46*, *47*, *48*, 53
Croix du Bac *196*
Crossroads Farm 99, *99*, *100*, *102*, *103*, 104, 166
Cuinchy 30, 128-129, 238-241, *238-239*, *240* *see also* Brickstacks
Curlu *332-333*

Dagnell (41st Division Signals) 138
Daily Mail 49, 50
Daily Mirror 50
Daily Sketch 50
Dammstrasse 132, 138
Dawson, Ensign 46
De Lisle, General 62, 63, 65, 67
De Vinck family 108
de Wiart, Lieutenant-Colonel Adrian Carton, VC 323
Delville Wood 334, 336
Dickens, Major Cedric 337
Dinnet Street 328
Dixmude 28, 75, 87
dogs *91*, *227*
Dohl, *Pioniere* *137*
Domesday Book 48
Donald, Captain A. W. 300
Doogan (11th Royal Sussex) 306
Douai plain *274-275*, 275
Double Crassier 252-253, *252-253*, 256, *256-261*
Dump, The (Fosse 8 slag heap) *234-5*, *244-245*, 247
Dunn, Captain J. C. 239-240

Eberle, Lieutenant H. F. 291, 292
Edmonds, Brigadier-General R. E. 33
Eikhof Farm 132, 133
Elles, Brigadier-General Hugh 343, 345, 346, 347, 349
engineers *68*, 70, 78, 132
England, National Records 48 *see also* Kew, National Archives
equipment 39
barbed wire and supports *41*, 206, 207, *207*
cameras 48, 49, 55, *55*, 57
camouflage netting *268* *see also* camouflage, art of
charges, *camouflet* 43
'Chinese attack' 166-167, *166*, *167*
corpse, fake, for observation *45*
duckboards 39, *39*, *102*
dugout frames *39*, *97*
fascines, brushwood 345
gas alarm, improvised *92*
gas attack wind vanes *96*, 98
gas masks *96*
gas projectors *147*
grafting tool 114
helmets 240-241
map, trench *57*
mud toboggans *291*
Nissen hut 291
observation tower, telescopic *49*
observation tree 45, *154*
periscopes, trench *5*, *43*, *54*, *132*
pontoons *78*
pump, Bethune-pattern trench *35*
sandbags 37
shield, bulletproof 203, *204*
spades 34
targets, papier-mache head *43*, 45
telephone cables *38*, *215*
telescopes 44
wire entanglements *41*

Fearns, Private Bert 180-181, 227
Feilding, Captain (later Colonel) Rowland 192, 211, 245, 253-254, 327, 333-334
Fenton, Roger 46, 51
Festubert 216-217, *216-217*, 220-223
Fitzgerald (4th Dragoons) 65
'Flandern Stellung' trench 166
Flanders and the coast, landscape of battle 27-29
Flanders Plain 28, 33, *36*, 74, 86, 353
Flers 301, 337, 343
Flesquières 346, *347*, 349
Fleurbaix sector *44*, 198
flooding *see* inundations
Foch, General (later Marshal) Ferdinand 81, 214, 216, 230
Fonquevillers 291, *291*, 302
food production *33*, *158-159*, *226-227*, *284*, *354-355*
Ford, Lance Corporal 49, *49*
fortifications, European 22-23
Forward Cottage *100*, *101*, *102*
Fosse 5 de Béthune mine 254, *256*
Fosse 8 mine *234-5*, 255-256 *see also* Dump, The
Foulkes, Lieutenant (later Major-General) C. H., RE 49, *49*, 233
Foye *33*
Frelinghien *192-193*, 195, 207
French, Field-Marshal Sir John 21, 90, 91, 95, 96, 212, 216, 231, 232, 237
French Army 230, 281-282, 288-289, 343
XXXIII Corps 267
Algerian Division, 45th 94
Algerian troops (Turco's) 67, 93
Cavalry Corps 90
First Army Corps 168
High Command 96
Tenth Army 214, 215, 231, 266, 301
Territorial Division, 87th 94

French civilians *23*, *26*, *32*, *62*, *196*, *263*, *268*, *352*, *362*
French Refugee Committee (Union des Comites des Refugies des Departments Envahies) 250-251
French shrine *289*
Fresnoy 283
Frezenberg Ridge 28, 96, 97, *104-105*, *106*, 168
Fricourt *326-327*, 327-331, *328-329*
Fricourt-Mametz valley *328*
Fromelles 30, 193, *211*, 215, *222-223*, 224-226, *224-225*, *226-227*
Frontiers, Battle of the 62
Fuller, Lieutenant-Colonel (later Major-General) J. F. C. 34, 342, 343, 345, 346, 349
Fusslein, Otto 299
Fyfe, Private F. A. *112*

Gallipoli 231
Gandy, Captain J. G. *67*
Gardner, Alexander 47
Gardner, Private 65
gas, asphyxiating 25, 80, 88, 91-94, *91*, 95, 96, *96*, 98, 126, 233, 241, *298*, 336-337
Gavrelle 275
Geerearts, Henri 69, *69*
General Jack's Diary 322
geology of the battlefields 27-31, 128, *128*, 129, 247
'Georgette' offensive 351
German Army
  I Corps *21*
  Army, First 62, 64
  Army, Second 298, 346
  Army, Fourth 74
  Army, Sixth 212
  Eingreif Divisions 172, 177
  General Staff 20, 23
  High Command 268, 347
  Pioniere *91*, 115, *137*, 167, *240*
  Pioniere-Mineure 113, 134, 143
  Saxon Corps, 19th 157, 201
  Uhlan cavalry 84
German troops *107*, *111*, *124*, *125*, *250*, *331*, *339*
Gheluvelt *64-65*, 87, 183-184
Gheluvelt Plateau *162-3*, 172, 177, 178-179, 183, 184
Ginchy 336, 337
Givenchy 37, 216, *218-219*, 220, *220*, 221, *221-222*, 227, 238, *269*, 275
Glubb, 2nd Lieutenant J. 272, 285, 337
'Gneisenau' offensive 350, 353
Godfrey, 2nd Lieutenant J. T. 289, 336-337, 357, 362
'Goertz' offensive 353
Gohelle sector *236-237*, 237, 238, 244, 247, 252
Gommecourt 297, *293-296*, 298, 302-304, *305*, 306, *306-307*, 315-316
  Wood *2-3*, *302-303*, 303
Goodbye To All That 241
Gosse, Lieutenant (later Captain) Philip H. G., RAMC 196, 231, 331, 339
Gough, General Sir Hubert *149*, 167, 168, 172, 177, 181-182
Graves, Lieutenant Robert 241, *241*, 330, 336
Grenfell, Captain Francis Octavius, VC 63
Grenfell, Captain Julian, DSO 109, *109*, *110-111*
Guillemont 336, 337

Hackett, Sapper William, VC 221-222, *221*
'Hagen' offensive 353
Haig, General (later Field-Marshal) Sir Douglas 78, 90, 91, 144, 146, 148, 212, 214, 351
  Cambrai 343-344, 346, 349
  coalfields and *crassiers* 231, 232, 233, 236, 237
  Somme 288, 289, 297, 298, 301, 334, 338
  Third Ypres 167, 168, 172, 177, 178, 180, 182, 184
  Vimy Ridge and Arras 268, 278, 281, 282, 283, 285
Haking, General 225
Halifax, Nova Scotia, Citadel *50*
Halkett, Major 46
Hamilton-Hall, Colonel *313*
Hammond, Lance-Corporal John 46-47
Hance, Major H. W. 322-323
Hasler House observation post *104-105*
Havrincourt *340-1*, 346, 348
Hawthorn Ridge and mine *299*, *300-301*, 308, *308*, 312, *312*, *313*
Hazebrouck 352
health of soldiers 40, *40*, 226-227
Hebuterne Trenches *288*, *289*
Hellfire Corner 188, 351
Hepburn, Major Clay 142
Herenthage Chateau 119
Heyworth, General 199
Hickling, Lieutenant Horace 142
High Command Redoubt *94-95*
High Wood 334, *334*
Hill 60 (Zwarteleen) 88, 96, 98, *107*, 108, 122-124, *122-123*, *124-125*, 126-129, *126-127*, *129*, *130*, *131*, 203
Hill 70: 250, *250-251*, 254, *254-5*, 256
Hindenburg Line 268, 272, 273, 338, *342*, 344, 345, 346, 349, *356-357*, 357
Hinges Ridge *352*
History of the RE in the Great War 166-167
Hitchcock, Captain F. C., MC 140, 142
Hodgson, Lieutenant (later Captain) William Noel, MC 247, 329-330
Hohenzollern Redoubt *234-5*, *243*, 244-247, *244*, *246*, 250
Hollandscheschuur Farm 146-147, *149*
Hondeghem *158-159*
Hooge and mine 87, 88, 108-119, *112-113*, *114-115*, *117*
  Chateau 108, 110, *110*, 112
Horne, General Sir Henry 272-273, 282
horses *169 see also* cavalry, Allied
Houplines 195, 206, *206*, *215*
Houthulst Forest 90, 183
Howkins, Lieutenant F. G. 45, 164
Hulluch 29, 234, 235, *234-5*, 236, *244*, 247, *247*, 250
Hunter-Cowan, Major S. 112
Hurley, Frank 58, *58*, 179, 182-183, *182*

I Survived, Didn't I? 308
Illustrated War News 50
Imperial War Museum 59
'Into Battle' 109
inundations *68*, 69-70, *70-71*, 71, *72-73*, 74-78, 81

Jack, Major (later Brigadier-General) James 322
Joffre, General Joseph 66, 95, 216, 231, 267, 288, 289, 301
'John McCrae' dressing station 97
Jones, David 330

Kaaie Salient 97
Kaiserschlacht offensive 81
Kay, Mr (2/6 Lancashire Fusiliers) 181
Kemmel Hill 28, 144, *144-145*, 147, 159, 160, *160-1*, 352, 357
Kerr, Captain Hugh 322
Kerrich, Lieutenant W. A. 198-199, 207, 212-213
Kerriemuir tunnel 322-323
Kettle, Tom 337
Kew, National Archives 250 *see also* England, National Archives
Kiggell, General Launcelot 282
Kipling, Lieutenant John 254
Kitchener, Lord 231, 342
Kitchener's Wood 94, 95
Kluck, von 62, 64

La Bassée 84, 87, 193, 239-240
La Bassée Canal 227
La Becque 356-357
La Boisselle 58-59, *59*, 316, 320, *320-321*, 321, 322, 323, *324-325*, 332
La Brique *31*, 98-106, *98-99*
La Hutte Chateau *152*, 153
La Petit Douve Farm 147
Lancashire Farm 93
land drainage 35-36, *35*, 292
Langemarck 87, 90, 91, 169, 172, 177, 183, *183*
Langlois, Colonel Charles 53
Laventie 206, 351
Le Cateau 62, 63
Le Gheer 154, 195
Le Piétre 232
Le Touquet 195-196, *195*, 207, *208-209*
Leipzig Redoubt and Salient 314, 316-317, 318
Lens 29, 30, 67, 230, *230-231*, 250, *251*, 256, 261, 262, *262-263*
Liège 23, 84
Liévin *255*
Lille 64, 210, 357
Lloyd George, David 232, 268
Lochnagar crater 322, *322-323*
Locre 352
Lombartzyde-Bains *71*
London Stereoscopic Company 49
Lonsdale Battalion, The 317-318
Loos 29, 30, *30*, 117, 230, *231*, 236-237, 252, *252*, 253
  Battle of 42, 231-237, *232-233*, *234-235*, *236-237*, 241, 245, 250, *250-251*
Lucas-Tooth, Captain D. K. 63, 65
Ludendorff, General Erich 159, 352, 353
Lys, Battle of the *158-159*, 351-353, *352-353*, *354-355*, 356-357, 360
Lys, River 68-69, *192-193*, 207, *208-209*

Macdonald, Lyn 33
machine-gunners 58, *58*, *107*, *339*
Mametz *326*, 327-331, *335*
  Cemetery 329, *330-331*
Mansel Copse 329, 330, *330-331*
Manual of Field Works *34*
Marden, 2nd Lieutenant B. G. 'Biffko' 62-64, 65, 66, 67
Maricourt 332
Marne, Battle of the 62-65
Martin, Captain Duncan 329
Martin, Sapper Albert 138, 148
Marwitz, General Georg von der 348
Mash Valley 321, 322, *324-325*
Maubege 23
Mauser Ridge *94-95*, 95, 97
Méhedin, Léon 53
Mellish, Reverend Edward, VC MC 142
Memoirs of a Camp Follower 331, 339
Memoirs of an Infantry Officer 330
Memorial to the Missing *316-317*
Menin 85, 357
Menin Road 84, *84*, 87, 97, 108, 109, 110, *110-111*, *118-119*, 119
  Ridge 28, 168, 177
Merckem 352
Messines *86-87*, 96, *148*, *149*, 152, *152*, *157*, 158, 166, 167
  Battle of *29*, *37*, 42, 138, 144, 152, *152*
Messines Ridge 28, 78, *86-87*, 87, 123-124, 129, 142, 144-148, *144-145*, *148-149*, 159, 188, 221, 351
Messines Salient 144, 193
Meuse-Argonne offensive 356
'Michael' offensive 350
Military Cross *103*
Military Engineering, Part II, Attack and Defence of Fortresses, 1910 25
mining 42-43, *42*, 113-114, *113*, 117, 122, 127-128, *131*, 132, 134, 136, 142, 146-147, *271 see also* tunnelling
Ministry of Information shop *51*
Moeteldje Estaminet 167, *167*
Monchy-le-Preux 267, 279-280, *279*, *280*, *281*

Mons Canal 62
Mont d'Auchy 244-245
Montauban 332-334, *332-333*, 336-339
Morris, Corporal 203-204
Mortimore, Captain H. W. 337
Morton, 2nd Lieutenant H. L., DSO 242
'Mound of Death' 28, 29, 122, 140, *140*, 142
Mount Sorrel *118*, 129
Mouquet Farm 336
Mousetrap Farm 94, 96, 156, 185
Mousetrap Ridge 97
mules *169*, *338*
Mulqueen, Major F. J. 269
My Bit, A Lancashire Fusilier at War 312
My Sapper Venture 291, 292

Namur 23
Napier, Colonel *224*
Neuve Chapelle 159, 212, *212-213*, 215, 351
  Battle of 37, 203, 212-214
Newfoundland Memorial Park, Beaumont Hamel *288-289*, 308, 309
Nicholas, Lieutenant Tressilian C. 56
Nicklin, Richard 46-47
Nieuport 68, *68-69*, 69, 70, 75, *75*, 76, *76-77*, 78, 80-81, *81*
Nieuport-Bains (now Nieuwpoort-Bad) 27, 77, *79*
  Barrel Post *77*
  Casino and seashore *76*
  station *69*, *77*, *78*
Nieuport-Dixmude railway 69-70, *72-73*, *74-75*
Nivelle, General Robert 267-268, 281, 282
Nivelle Offensive 146, 167, 267, 268
no man's land 41-42
Noordvaart Canal 70
Norton-Griffiths, John, MP 114
Notre Dame de Lorette 214, 215, 230, *230-231*, 231, 255, 262, *266*, *267*
Nuyten, Lieutenant-Colonel 69-70
observation 43-45, *43*, *44*, *48*, *49*, *54*, *57*, *71*, *104*, *154*, *222*
Observatory Ridge 88, 108, 117, 119, *119*, *124-125*, 126, 278-279, *280-281*
officers *122*, *128*, *132*, *226*, *266*, *351*
Ontario Farm 147
Oosthoek Ridge 132, 138, 139
Operation Alberich 268
Operation Dynamo 27
Opium War, Second *48*
Oppy Wood 275, 282, *283*
Ostend 67, 68
O'Sullivan, Timothy 47
Ouvrages Blancs *266-267*, 267
Ovillers-la-Boisselle 317, 320, *320-321*, 321, 336

Pagoda, The *106-107*
Palingbeek *see* Bluff, The
panoramas 52-59
panoramic perspective, and perceptions of terrain 57-59
Passchendaele 27, *82*, *84-85*, 85, 91, 117-118, 181, *188*, 357
Passchendaele Ridge 28-29, 87, 90, *90*, 91, 122, 128, 166, 177, *184*, *188*, 349, 351
Passionate Prodigality, A 58-59, *59*, 290
'Path of Glory' *157*
Peckham 147
Pendant Copse 311
Pendered, Corporal John 46-47
Pennycuick, Lieutenant J. A. C., DSO 124, 127

Perceval-Maxwell, Colonel R. D. *308*, *315*, *317*
Perry, Corporal 64
Pershing, General John J. 356
Pétain, General Philippe 282
Petit Bois 145, *146*, 147
Petite Douve Farm 157, 158
Phillip Augustus, King of France 33
photograph, first forensic *49*
photographers, engineer 47-49, *47*
photographers at the front, and panoramas 55-56
photographic tradition and the British Army 46-49
photographing in the First World War 49-51 *see also* panoramas
photographs, Daguerrotype 52
photography, aerial *25*, *50*, 53-54, *53*, *88*, *89*, *101*, *117*, *136*, *247*, *282*
Picardy 29-30, *30-31*, 290, 343
Pigot, Captain 200
Pilckem Ridge 28, 87, 90, *94-95*, 95, 97, 168
Pioneers, Canadian *178*
Ploegsteert ('Plugstreet') 152, *153*, 154-161
  Wood *152*, 154, *154*, 158, 160, 193
Plumer, General Sir Herbert 78, 95-96, 146, 147, 168, 172, 177, 178, 181-182, 351
Poelcapelle 177, 180-181, *180-181*
Polder Plain 27-29, *28-29*, 69, 70, 71
Polderhoek sector *185*
Polygon Wood *85*, 88, 178, *178-179*, 179
Pommern Castle 177
Poperinghe *32*, 67, 105, 352
Portuguese Corps 193, 227
Potijze Chateau 97
Powell, Captain 183
Pozières 336, *336*
press photographs/photographers 50
prisoners of war 80, *80*, *347*, *350*, *360*
propaganda, German postcard 51, *51*

Quadrilateral 311, 313
Quarries, The *244*, 250
Quéant-Drocourt line 273, *274-275*, 275, 278

'Race to the Sea, The' 67, 68-71, 74-81, 289
Railway Wood *108-109*, *117*
Ramscapelle *70*, 74, *74-75*
rat hunt *107*
Rawlinson, General Henry 300-301, 334
Redan Ridge 308-313, *309*
Regina Trench 304, *305*, 306
Reid (3rd Rifle Brigade) 204-205
Renaix 360
Richardson, Piper J. C., VC 304, 306
Richthofen, Baron Manfred von 273, 275
Rider-Rider, William 58, *58*, 179
Ridsdale, Lieutenant Harold 106-107, 168, 169, 245-246
Rifle Farm 110, *110-111*
Rip Van Winkle 46, *47*
Roach, Lieutenant (later Captain) Matthew, MC RE 20, 217, 221, 288
Robertson, Captain Clement, VC 346
Robertson, James 46, *46*
Robertson, Lieutenant-General W. R. 100
Roeux 267, 278, *278*, 280-281, 282, 283
  Chemical Works 275, 278, 283
Rogers, Major James, RAMC 169, 172
Roisel 63
Romans 33
Ross and Co. 55, *55*
Roulers 85
Royal Engineers, Corps of *26*, 33, 34, 35, 36, 46, *47*, 75, 96, *149*, 291, 299, 318
  carpenter *172*
  Chatham HQ, Museum and Library 47-48, *49*, *52-53*, 250
  'factories' 39, *39*
  field companies
    2: 291, 292
    7: 272, 285, 337
    9: 154, 156
    23: 44
    55: 198-199, 207, 212-213
    59: 62, 124
    64: 271
    76: 106-107, 168, 169, 245-246
    95: 233-236
    103: 289, 336-337, 357, 362
    203: 271
    210: 159-160, 189, 350, 352, 353, 356-357, 360
    475: *168*
  Field Survey Companies 44, 56-57
  Grave *116-117*
  Lowland Field Company, 409: 79
  photographers 47-49, *47*
  Printing Company 55
  sergeant *298*
  Signal Exchange *330*
  'Special Companies' 233, *298*
  survey officers *266*
  'telephotographic unit' 49, *49*
  tunnelling companies
    170: 256
    172: 134, 142
    173: 217, *261*
    174: *221*
    175: 24, 112-113, *112*, 126-127, 140
    178: 328
    179: 320, 322-323
    180: 217, 221
    182: 269
    184: 20
    250: 134-136
    251: 241
    252: 242, *299*, 300, *308*
    253: 164, 247
    255: 242
Royal Engineers Journal 50
Rupprecht, Crown Prince of Bavaria 180, 348

St Elie 247, *248-249*
St Eloi *45*, 88, 96, 122, 129, 139, 140, *140-141*, 142-143, *142-143*
St Julien 95
St Mihiel 356
St Quentin *342-343*, 351
St Yves 155-156, *155*, *156*, 157
Salter, Geoffrey 306
Sanctuary Wood 88, *88*, 108, 110, *112-113*, 116, *118-119*, 119
Sassoon, Siegfried, MC 330, *331*
Savy 63
Scarpe valley 278
Schaw, Colonel Henry 47
Schlieffen, Count Alfred von 20, 21
Schlieffen Plan 20, 23, 62, 64, 65, 84

Schwaben Redoubt 314, 315, *315*, 316, *317*, 336
Scotland, National Records 48
Sebastopol, Redan *46*
'Sebastopol, The Taking of' 53
sergeant, Royal Engineers *298*
Serre 303, 304, *304-305*, 315-316
Shaftesbury mine shaft 221-222
Shepherd (255 Tunnelling Company, RE) 242

shop, Ministry of Information *51*
siege warfare 21-23
Siegfried-Stellung fortress 268
signaller, British *216*
Skeggs, 2nd Lieutenant (later Major) Robin Oliver, MC *31*, 50, *356*
'Forgotten Front' 196-198, *197*, *198-199*, 199, 200-202, *200*, *201*, *202*, 203-205, *203*, *204*, *205*, *206*
Ypres, First and Second 98-106, *98*, *100*, *101*, *102*, *103*, *104*, *113*, 115-117
skirmishing *66*
slag heaps (*crassiers*) 247, 252-261, *254-255*, *257-260*, 262
see also coal mines
Smith, Lance-Corporal G. J. 233-236
Smith-Dorrien, Sir Horace 62, 95
snipers 43-44, *44*, 56, *120-121*, *143*, *242*
'Soldier From the Wars Returning' 183
Solomon, Solomon J. 45
Somme offensive 27, 31, 84, 224, 273, *288-289*, *290*, *293-296*, *350*
see also Beaumont Hamel; Gommecourt; Redan Ridge
planning the push 288-290
overture to action 291-297
the plan 297, 298
overture and opening 298-301
epilogue 338-339
Somme region, landscape of battle 29-30, *30-31*, *36*
Sorley, Charles Hamilton *246*, 247
Souchez 230, 231, *269*
'stand-down' and 'stand-to' 40, *40*
Stokes, Major R. S. G. 300
Stuff Redoubt 315
Stuff Trench 306
Switch, The 273
Talbot, Gilbert and Neville 105
Tambour, The (The Drum) 327, 329
tanks 24-25, 273, 279, 281, 301, 337-338, 342-343, 345, *345*, 346-348, *346*
'Flying Fox II' *349*
male tank D1 337
Mark I *337*
Mark V 349
Tatham, Captain H. 134-136
terrain, perceptions of, and panoramic perspective 57-59
They Called it Passchendaele 33
Thiepval 310, 314, *314*, 315, 316, *316-317*, 318, *318-319*, 336
Ridge 301, 336
Wood *314*, 315, *315*, *319*
Thys, Captain Robert 70
Tibet *47*
Times, The 67, 109, 216
Toc H 105
Tourcoing 357
Tower Bridge 253, *253*, *254*
trench warfare 32-33
birth of 21-23
development of 26-28
trenches *see also* land drainage
'borrow-pits' 35, *35*, *199*
breastworks 34-35, *146*, *199*, *216*
in chalk geology *30*
communication *37*, *104-105*, 119
construction methods 37-38, *37*
digging 34, *34*, 36-37
dugouts *36*, *42*, *226*, *278*, *291*, *330*, *335*
French *231*, *241*
German *89*, *232-233*
hygiene in 38
identity of 38
infantry subway *270*
latrines 38, *242*
life in 38-41 *see also* Skeggs, 2nd Lieutenant Robin Oliver, MC
pillboxes *165*, 168-169, 172-177, *177*
revetment, corrugated iron *103*
saps/sapping 42
'saps, Russian' 299-300, 303-304, 315, 322, 328, 333
and terrain 33-35
tramway, wooden *211*
Tuck (3rd Rifle Brigade) 198, 201
tunnellers 77-78, *79*, 80-81, *81*, 146, 271, 299-300, *299*, *308*
tunnelling 42-43, *42*, 113-114, *113*, 117, *118*, 119, 127-129, *131*, 132, 134, 136, 142, 247, 250, 254
see also mining
Turco Farm *94-95*, 96
Turner, Brigadier-General R. E. W. 94
Tyne Cot cemetery 181, 184

Ulster Tower *316-317*
underground warfare *see* mining; tunnelling
Undertones of War 241, 306

Valenciennes 357
Valley of the Dead 231
Vauban 22
vehicles *33*, *45* *see also* tanks
Verdun 23, 31, 146, 268, 288-289, 301, 336
Vermelles 29
Villers-Brettoneux 356
Vimy Ridge 29, 30-31, 214, 215, 231-232, 237, 266-269, *269*, *270*, 271-275, *271*, *272*, *274*, *275*, *276-277*, 278-283, 285, *285*

Wain, Captain R. W. L. 349
Wainman, Major P. 247
Walker, Major (later Brigadier-General) G., DSO 62
Wallworth, Private Wilf *20*, 136-137
Wancourt 280
War Budget 50
War Illustrated 50
War Letters to a Wife 327, 333-334
War Office 46, 50, 51, 114
War The Infantry Knew, The 240
water supplies *36*
weapons 22 *see also* tanks
anti-tank rifle, German *362*
field guns *152*, *279*
flamethrowers *114*, 115
grenades 233, 297
howitzers *268*, *292*
Lewis gun 338
mortars, trench *101*, 233, 297, 338
naval guns *69*, 79, *236*
rifles 43, *120-121*
shells, instantaneous fused *343*
Western Front, formation of 20-21, *24*
Westhoek 177
Wez Macquart *54*, 98, 102-103, 195, 196, *198-199*, 199, *200*, *201*, 202, *202-203*, *204*
White Chateau 97, 132, *132*, 137, 138, 139
Wieltje 95, 106, 107
Wilbraham, Captain Bernard, RE 57
Wilhelm II, Kaiser 68, 84, 244
Winchester Farm 183
Wingles 29
Wipers Times, The 37
With a Machine Gun to Cambrai 347
Wood, Major W. L. 34
Woodroffe, 2nd Lieutenant Sidney Clayton, VC 115
Wotan Stellung position 262, 268
Wytschaete 96, 147
Wytschaete-Messines Ridge 87, 88

Y Ravine 309, 311, 312
Y-Sap *320-321*, 321, 322, *324-325*
Young, Lieutenant (later Major) B. K. 154, 156
Young, Private William *48*
Ypres *23*, 28, 67, *82*, 85-86, 87, 107, 126, 160, *188-189*
Hotel Ypriana *189*
Ypres, First Battle of 23, 84-87, 90-91, 145
Ypres, Second Battle of *51*, 86, 87-88, *90*, 91-97, *92-93*, 145, 156, 215
after battle 88-90, 98-107
Ypres, Third Battle of *14-15*, *40*, 45, 59, 117, 159, 164, *165*, *166*, *173-176*, 285, 343
and the dunes 78-81, *80*
before the storm 166-167
battle opens 168-169, *170-171*
attacks continue 172-177, 178-179
Broodseinde Ridge 28, *90*, 179-183, *180-181*, *184*, 185
towards the end 183-185
Ypres, Fourth Battle of 185, *186-187*, 188-189
Ypres Clay 28
Ypres-Comines Canal 122, 132, *132*
Ypres-Comines railway line 122, 126, *127*, *129*
Ypres-Roulers railway 90, 96, 107, *108-109*, 109, *110-111*, 178, *182*
Ypres Salient 30, *31*, 58, 78, *86-87*, 87, 88, *89*, 90, 96, 97, 128, 159, 160, 203
Yser, River 68, 69, *69*, 74, 76, 77, 78, *79*, 80, 87

Zeebrugge 68
Zillebeke 126
Zonnebeke *168-169*, 177, 178, 179, *179*, 182, *183*, *184*, *185*
Zwarteleen 126 *see also* Hill 60